PENGUIN REFERENCE

THE PENGUIN DICTIONARY OF AMERICAN ENGLISH USAGE AND STYLE

Paul W. Lovinger was a staff reporter and columnist for newspapers for two decades. His freelance writings include *The Marijuana Question* (with Helen C. Jones), a widely acclaimed study of the drug as viewed by scientists and users. He also writes songs, both music and lyrics (specializing in children's and novelty). He lives in San Francisco.

THE PENGUIN DICTIONARY OF
AMERICAN ENGLISH USAGE AND STYLE

A Readable Reference Book,
Illuminating Thousands of Traps
That Snare Writers and Speakers

PAUL W. LOVINGER

PENGUIN REFERENCE

PENGUIN REFERENCE
Published by the Penguin Group
Penguin Putnam Inc., 375 Hudson Street,
New York, New York 10014, U.S.A.
Penguin Books Ltd, 80 Strand,
London WC2R 0RL, England
Penguin Books Australia Ltd, Ringwood,
Victoria, Australia
Penguin Books Canada Ltd, 10 Alcorn Avenue,
Toronto, Ontario, Canada M4V 3B2
Penguin Books (N.Z.) Ltd, 182–190 Wairau Road,
Auckland 10, New Zealand

Penguin Books Ltd, Registered Offices:
Harmondsworth, Middlesex, England

First published in the United States of America by Penguin Reference,
a member of Penguin Putnam Inc., 2000
This paperback edition published in 2001

1 3 5 7 9 10 8 6 4 2

Copyright © Paul W. Lovinger, 2000
All rights reserved

LIBRARY OF CONGRESS HAS CATALOGED
THE HARDCOVER EDITION AS FOLLOWS:
Lovinger, Paul W.
The Penguin dictionary of American English usage and style : a readable
reference book, illuminating thousands of traps that snare writers
and speakers / by Paul W. Lovinger.
p.   cm.
ISBN 0-670-89166-5 (hc.)
ISBN 0 14 20. 0046 9 (pbk.)
1. English language—Usage—Dictionaries.
2. English language—Style—Dictionaries.   I. Title.
PE1464 .L68 2000
428'.003—dc21   99-053704

Printed in the United States of America
Set in Sabon
Designed by Joseph Rutt

CONTENTS

INTRODUCTION

Watching Our Words

Aim; Form

The volume in your hands is meant to be both useful and enjoyable, a readable dictionary for all who are interested in our language.

In A-to-Z form, it is mainly a guide to good usage of English, the American variety, contrasted with some 2,000 quoted examples of misusage and questionable usage. It does the job of "illuminating many traps and pitfalls in English usage" (as my editor puts it). I have sought to provide clear explanations in plain language. This book is designed for general readers as well as those who work with words.

The examples were drawn from the popular press, broadcasting, books, and a variety of other sources, mostly in the latter eighties and the nineties. Each entry devoted to a specific word or phrase contains one or more of those quotations. The troublesome forms are contrasted with the proper forms (which are emphasized by *italics*) and definitions are given.

Entries on general topics are presented too; they deal with matters of grammar, punctuation, style, and so on. A list of them, with further description of the two types of entry, appears under "General Topics," following this introduction.

With few exceptions, the examples have determined the choices of word entries. Thus the book in part amounts to an informal survey of contemporary problems in English usage.

Both perennial problems and new ones come up. Of the misuses discouraged by earlier books on English usage, some persist; others have not turned up, but, as though to take their place, new offenses against the language have emerged.

Here are some hints for finding your way around the volume:

- Main entries, headed in **boldface**, are arranged alphabetically, letter by letter.
- Many entries are divided into sections, which are numbered and titled. The sections of an entry are arranged alphabetically, and their titles are listed at the beginning, after the main title. Some sections contain subsections, distinguished by letters and titles.
- There are numerous cross-references, some standing alone and others within entries. For instance, in the C's under **Comma** it says *See* **Punctuation,** *3,* referring the reader to the entry. Many entries refer to related entries. Alphabetical order is used in listing any series of cross-references and various other series.

Viewpoint

This work could be viewed as an antidote to laissez-faire lexicography and anything-goes grammar. The doctrine that whatever emerges from people's lips is the language and that many verbal wrongs make a right is not advocated here. Nor is the cliché of English as "a living language" dragged in to justify bad English.

On the contrary, I do not hesitate to distinguish between right and wrong usage when the difference is clear. My inclination is to question deviant forms, challenge innovations to prove themselves, and resist senseless fads. (See also the final section of this introduction.) I thereby risk being labeled a "purist" by some critics—as though impurity were desirable.

Perhaps in a long-range, philosophical sense there is no verbal right and wrong. But that view does not help you and me in choosing our words and putting together our sentences clearly and properly according to the educated norms of society. Those holding the permissive views follow most of the norms themselves. They do not say or write, "Them guys hasn't came," or "I ain't did nothin nohow," although some people are apt to do so. For the most part, the laws of grammar have not been repealed.

Not that one should be pedantic either. The book does not flatly condemn split infinitives, prepositions at the end of sentences, conjunctions at the beginning, sentence fragments, or phrases like "It's me." But it does value precision over fashion, logic over illogic, and grammatical correctness over "political correctness." (In my view, those who mutilate our language for political motives do wrong.)

At times the difference between correct and incorrect usage is hazy. English has an abundance of words,* more than any other language, and multiple ways to express almost any idea. Our language is so complex that nobody ever learns it all and that even its leading authorities occasionally stumble. They disagree and one finds fault with another. Their differences concern both specific points and standards of strictness or looseness in the use of words and grammar.

Some loose uses of words or phrases and some slang that may pass harmlessly in informal conversation are inappropriate when transferred to serious writing or even serious speech. This book will help the reader to make sound choices.

Examples

Samples of sentences that clearly fall into the *wrong* category follow. The first few are (alternately) by professionals of broadcasting and journalism. A correction follows each quotation. (Each comes up in the main text.)

"There were roofs completely tore up." *Torn* up.

"I like to serve it with croutons . . . that is flavored with olive oil." *Are* flavored.

"Police said ——— and ——— built the bombs theirselves." *Themselves.*

"It would be more racism showing it's ugly head again." *Its.*

"There is a way to empower your

---

*The Oxford English Dictionary, seeking to record all English words, says it covers more than 500,000 words and phrases in its twenty volumes. The Guinness Book of World Records places the count at more than 600,000 words plus 400,000 technical terms, a total exceeding a million. It numbers the Shakespearean vocabulary at 33,000 words and expresses doubt that any person uses more than 60,000.

children and make them far more better . . . students." Delete "more."

"Women have smaller brains then men." *Than.*

"The . . . campaign has got to break into the double digits to be respectful." *Respectable.*

(Headline:) "Be Happy She Prys." *Pries.*

Additional slip-ups, by people in other fields, include these:

(Advertising:) "I always wanted to loose weight." *Lose.*

(Book publishing:) "Allow someone else to proofread [edit?] it . . . who will not be affraid to be biased in their opinion." *Afraid* to be *unbiased* in *his* opinion.

(Diplomacy:) "It is quite clear that the crisis has reached a critical point." Better: the *dispute* or the *situation.*

(Education:) "Me and my kids live in a dormitory." *I* and.

(Law:) "No one is free to flaunt the tax laws." *Flout.*

(Medicine:) "We're obligated to do that biopsy irregardless of the physical findings." *Regardless.*

(Psychology:) "Their child don't look so good." *Doesn't* look.

The book debunks some widespread misbeliefs. If we do not fully understand the meanings of certain words or if we accept some clichés on their faces, we may believe that fury rages in the "eye" of a storm; a "fraction" is a small part; the character "Frankenstein" was a monster; to "impeach" an official is to oust him from office; a jury can find a defendant "innocent"; pencils contain the metal "lead"; a "misdemeanor" is not a crime; prostitution is the "oldest profession"; an exception "proves" a rule; the Constitution guarantees "the pursuit of happiness"; and so on.

The criticism of any extract does not negate the overall merit of the work that is quoted.*

Clarity

Clarity is a leading theme of this book. More than 100 entries deal with the problem of *ambiguity* (noun): the state of being *ambiguous* (adjective), able to be interpreted in two or more different ways. Consider this sentence: "When P—— was hired by H——, he had a criminal record." Which one is "he"? (That example is from **Pronouns, 1.** Consult also the cross-reference **Ambiguity** and the next section of this introduction, *Wounded Words.* General examples of fuzzy prose appear in **Verbosity** and other entries.)

Clear expression requires clear think-

---

*Of 2,000-odd examples of misusage or questionable usage, almost half originated with newspapers, news agencies, or magazines; about a fifth each with broadcasters and books; and a tenth with people in many other fields or miscellaneous sources, described in the text. A few appeared in other reference works.

The single most frequent source of examples was *The New York Times* (usually the national edition), which occasionally is quoted here approvingly too. Newspapers distributed in the San Francisco Bay area and TV and radio broadcasts heard there were significant sources. Dozens of other newspapers, from most regions of the country, yielded examples too. So did 120 books, mostly nonfiction. Some correct or incorrect examples, not counted above, were composed where fitting.

The sources of the quotations are not usually identified by name. Space did not permit the publication of a list of such sources (although it had been contemplated). But a variety of reference works consulted as sources of information are listed in the back of the book.

ing. It helps also to be versed in the distinctions among words and in the elements of grammar, including tense, number, mood, parts of speech, sentence structure, and punctuation. Even so, clarity may not survive hastiness, inability to express ideas simply, intentional hedging, lack of facts, language that is too pompous or too slangy, obscurity of ideas or terms, overloading of sentences, overlooking of double meanings, stinginess in using words or punctuation, too little thought, or too much abstraction and generality without concrete examples.

Then, too, muddiness and confusion can overcome our best efforts. Writers on the English language often compare it with other languages and glory in its complexity, variety, and subtlety. Yet the language is so complex, with varieties of expression so vast, subtleties so fine, and such a proliferation of word meanings, that it can trap any of us at some time or other. Unqualified praise helps no one. Let us be aware of the difficulties and try to overcome them.

Greater efforts to write and speak clearly, accurately, and sensibly would mean more understanding, something that society needs.

Wounded Words

One of the problems is that English is being deprived of the benefit of many distinctive words as looser meanings develop. The addition of the new meanings renders some of the words ambiguous. I call them wounded words.

Examples of those words and their strict meanings follow; loose meanings are in parentheses. Which meaning a writer or speaker has intended is not always plain from the context.

A *fabulous* story is one that is characteristic of a fable (or a good story). An *impact* is a violent contact (or an effect). A *legendary* figure is mythical (or famous). One who is *masterful* is dictatorial (or skillful). To *scan* a document is to examine it carefully and systematically (or quickly and superficially). If a scene is a *shambles,* it shows evidence of bloodshed (or disorder). If an incident *transpired* this year, this year is when it became known (or happened). When an *ultimatum* is given, a threat of war is issued (or a demand is made). That which is *viable* is able to live (or feasible).*

Many loose or questionable uses are widespread. Does that mean we have to follow suit? Of course not.

Save the Language

New words continually appear. Those that fill needs are generally desirable. What ought to be questioned or resisted are the watering-down of distinctive words that we already have, the creation of ambiguity and fuzziness, the breakdown of grace and grammar, and irrational verbal fads.

Change characterizes the history of English; but whereas innovations in the main language used to be tested slowly by time, and street slang usually stayed there, they are now both thrust upon the public almost instantly by the media of mass communication.

---

*Among words in similar condition are these: *accost, alibi, anticipate, bemuse, brandish, brutalize, burgeon, careen, classic, cohort, compendium, connive, cool, culminate, decimate, desecrate, destiny, dilemma, disaster, effete, eke, endemic, enormity, erstwhile, exotic, fantastic, formidable, fortuitous, fraction, gay, idyllic, incredible, increment, internecine, jurist, literal, livid, marginal, mean (noun), minimize, neat, obscene, outrageous, paranoid, pristine, quite, sure, travesty, unique, utilize, verbal, virtual, vital, weird, wherefore, willy-nilly.* The words emphasized in this section have separate entries.

Our language is an invaluable resource, as much a part of our heritage as forests, wildlife, and waters. Yet where are movements for verbal conservation? Who campaigns to save endangered words? When do we ever see demonstrations against linguistic pollution?

To support the cause of good English, you and I need not join a group, attend rallies, or give money. We can contribute every day by knowing the language, shunning the fads, and watching our words.

P.W.L.
San Francisco

GENERAL TOPICS

Here is a list of the titles, or headings, of this book's main *topic entries*—that is, entries that deal with general topics.

They are distinguished from *word entries*—which discuss how to use the particular words in their titles. (Those entries are not listed.)*

Following this list comes a list of cross-reference titles on general topics.

Abbreviation
Active voice and passive voice
Adjectives and adverbs
Anachronism
BACK(-) prefix and pairs
Backward writing
BI- and SEMI- prefixes
Capitalization
CIRCUM- prefix
Clause
Cliché clash
Clichés
Collective nouns
Comparative and superlative degrees
Comparison
Complement
Confusing pairs
Contractions
Crimes (various felonies)
Dehumanization
Division of words
Double meaning
Double negative

Double possessive
Ellipsis
Expletives
FACT- words
Gerund
Guilt and innocence
Hawaii
Homophones
I and i
Infinitive
Iran
Italic(s)
-IZE ending
Joining of words
Metaphoric contradiction
Modifiers
Modifying
Mood
NANO- prefix
Nouns
Number (grammatical)
Numbers
Paragraph

---

*The titles in the two categories differ in their use of capital or lower-case letters:

- The title of a *topic entry*, such as **Punctuation** or **Verbs,** is printed in lower-case letters, except for an initial capital. (Prefixes and suffixes, in capitals, are a further exception.)
- The title of a *word entry*, such as **AFFECT and EFFECT** or **COMPRISE,** is printed in capital letters, except for any incidental word, like **and.**

(In a word entry, the lower-case **and** indicates a contrast between the main words. A comma—as in **BEMUSE, BEMUSED**—separates forms or words in the same category.)

The following list presents cross-reference titles on general topics. They are found in their alphabetical places in the text. (Cross-reference titles on specific words are not listed. Additional cross-references, untitled, may be found within many entries.)

THE PENGUIN DICTIONARY OF
AMERICAN ENGLISH USAGE AND STYLE

A

A and AN. The choice of using *a* or *an* before a word depends on the sound of the word. Use *a* if the next word begins with a consonant: *a* daisy, *a* good egg. Use *an* if the next word begins with a vowel: *an* ape, *an* easy victory.

The wrong choice showed up in three newspapers. A federal official was quoted (or misquoted) as saying, "We are concerned any time there is a allegation of serious wrongdoing. . . ." In another news story, an investor "filed a $800 million lawsuit." In a column, a presidential candidate drove "a M-1 tank."

Corrections: It is "*an* allegation," because *allegation* begins with a vowel sound. It is "*an* $800 million lawsuit," because *eight* begins with a vowel sound. (The number phrase would be pronounced as *eight-hundred-million-dollar*.) And it is "*an* M-1 tank": Although *m* normally is a consonant, the letter as such is pronounced *em*.

A precedes the sound of the *y* consonant, even if the initial letter is usually a vowel: *a* European, *a* ewe, *a* uniform. The use of *an* before such a word is not standard.

An precedes a word starting with a silent *h*: *an* hour, *an* honorable man. Using *an* before a pronounced *h*, in a word whose *h* was once silent, like *historic* or *humble*, is an uncommon practice in the U.S.A. but more common in Britain. It is observed by a few American writers and speakers, such as an anchor woman who said, "NASA today called off an historic space mission."

The foregoing rules assume that one needs *a* or *an* (indefinite article) and not *the* (definite article). *A* or *an* goes before a word or phrase denoting a person or thing (noun) but not a specific one. The person or thing is usually singular but sometimes plural: *a* few good men, *a* great many people.

A or *an* is properly omitted from some common constructions. One variety contains *no* followed by an adjective: "no better time" / "no more beneficial discovery" / "no such animal." Another contains *kind, sort, type, species,* or the like: "that kind of gem" / "this sort of thing" / "some type of evergreen."

Meaning can hinge on the presence or absence of *a* or *an*. "A novelist and poet spoke" suggests one person. For two persons, an extra *a* is necessary: "A novelist and *a* poet spoke" (although "*both* spoke" makes it clearer). "The zoo will acquire an apteryx, or kiwi"—two alternative names for the same creature. But "The zoo will acquire a koala or *a* wombat"—one or the other.

In writing certain phrases that contain *a*, particularly *a lot* and *a hold*, some people erroneously affix the *a* to the noun. *A while* may be properly written as one word sometimes, but not always. *See* **A WHILE and AWHILE; HOLD; LOT.**

See also **THE.**

Abbreviation. *1. Code letters. 2. Three forms.*

1. Code letters

A newspaper article uses the initials "APS" eleven times but never says what they stand for. In the same issue, another article mentions "WIPP" twice without explaining it. Another newspaper mentions "North Carolina A&T State University" three times in an article, never informing the readers (mostly non-Carolinians) what "A&T" stands for.

A piece by a news agency cites a "DOE study done by Aerospace Corp. of Los Angeles." The context indicates that the research did not involve female deer. But the uninitiated reader has no way to relate those three letters to "Energy Department," which is mentioned several paragraphs before and after "DOE."

Unless initials are as widely known as U.S., C.O.D., M.D., and the letters of the broadcasting networks, the full name or phrase should be used at first. If the initials will be used thereafter, the full name may be linked to them in this way: "Albuquerque Public Schools (APS)" or "Department of Energy (DOE)."

Often initials are unnecessary. In subsequent references it may be clearer to refer, for example, to *the schools* or *the department*. Better yet, repeat the full name, if it is not too long.

Even when initials are explained at the start, they can challenge one's memory if there are too many of them. A book on international law contains statements like this: ". . . The remaining 40 NNNS parties to the NPT had still not . . . [concluded] a safeguards agreement with the IAEA." One chapter uses such forms some 300 times. A reader needing a reminder has to go back and hunt for it.

In telling of the bags O. J. Simpson took to "LAX," was a television reporter lax in assuming that everyone knew the airline industry's code for the Los Angeles airport? San Francisco newscasters continually spell out "SFO," never identifying it as their airport's code. It has at least eighteen other meanings.

One of those newscasters said on the radio, "There will be no water rationing this year for East Bay MUD [pronounced "mud"] customers." Some listeners may have heard of the East Bay Municipal Utility District. Others may wonder who would want to buy mud.

2. Three forms

Technically, three main condensed forms may be distinguished, though all three are often lumped under the word *abbreviation.*

An *abbreviation,* strictly speaking, is a short version of a word or phrase in writing, such as *Rep.* for *Representative* and *etc.* for *et cetera.*

An *acronym* is pronounced like a word; it is formed from initials or parts of a name or phrase. Examples are *AIDS* from *acquired immune deficiency syndrome* and *LORAN* from *long-range* (aid to navigation).

An *initialism* is composed of initials that are spelled out in pronunciation, letter by letter, such as *FBI* for *Federal Bureau of Investigation* and *cc* for *cubic centimeter(s).*

See also **Punctuation,** 8; *and* **Titles,** 2.

ABDOMEN. *See* **STOMACH.**

ABIDE and ABIDE BY. To *abide* something usually means to endure it, to tolerate it. "Can you abide such hot weather?" It can also mean to await it.

A columnist thinks that the press has treated a certain local politician too kindly. The politician "has succeeded in making himself the personification of the city." An attack on him therefore becomes an attack on the city "and no one can abide by that." It should be "and no one can abide that." Omit "by."

To *abide by* something is to comply with it, conform to it. "I abide by the law." / "I'm a law-abiding citizen."

The past tense and past participle of *abide* is *abode* or *abided*.

ABOUT TO. *See* NOT ABOUT TO.

Absolute constructions. *See* Modifiers, 1D.

Abstract noun. *See* Nouns, 1.

ACCEPT confused with EXCEPT. *See* EXCEPT and EXCEPTING; Homophones.

ACCORDING TO. *According to* is a common phrase that is used in sentences like these: "A promising discovery in the fight against flat feet was made this week, according to a local professor." / "According to the sect, the world will come to an end next Thursday."

It tells us that the statement is made on the authority of the one quoted. It implies that the writer does not vouch for the veracity or sense of the statement or may even question it. Thus it should be used with caution.

News people sometimes append "according to" to what should be matters of objective fact. For example:

According to the administration, Contra aid will run out September 30.

Will it or won't it? If the writer has any doubt, he should find out for himself.

Some statements are too obvious to need *any* attribution, let alone the "according to" form. This item is no scoop:

Many Jewish students at SF State will not be attending class today due to Rosh Hashana, the Jewish New Year, according to A—— S——, Di-

rector of Programs of the Northern California Hillel Council. [*See also* DUE TO.]

Is the reporter so afraid of sticking her neck out that she requires the weight of authority behind an announcement of a holiday?

ACCOST. To *accost* is to approach and speak to someone first. A panhandler and a person seeking directions *accost* people on the street. Some have the mistaken idea that it means to assault or attack.

A news report on national television said that several friends were "accosted by a white mob." Probably *attacked* should have been used instead of "accosted."

A city official, speaking about assaults on parking officers, referred to "their chances of being accosted." He meant *assaulted*.

Accuracy and inaccuracy. *See* Numbers, 5; Quotation problems, 1; Reversal of meaning.

Accusative case. *See* Pronouns, 10 A.

ACCUSED, ALLEGED, REPORTED, SUSPECTED. 1. *Accused in the news media*. 2. *Two adverbs*.

1. Accused in the news media

"An accused mass murderer finally gets his day in court," it was announced on local television. This would have been a better way to phrase it: "A man accused of mass murder finally. . . ." What the newscaster essentially called him was a mass murderer who had been accused.

Such misuse of the participle *accused* has become fairly common among news people. They assume that it protects them from any libel suit. When they describe someone as an "accused thief," for example, they mean he is not definitely a thief, just one who has been accused of being a thief. But to call someone an "accused thief" is still calling him a thief. "Accused" modifies "thief"; it does not mollify it. Similarly an "accused doctor" or "accused lawyer" is a doctor or lawyer who has been accused.

The misuse of *alleged,* as a synonym for "accused" in its objectionable sense, has long been established among journalists. An example: "Dazed and bleeding from a vicious assault . . . Laurie M—— pleaded with alleged attacker David A—— to take her to a hospital. . . ." *Alleged* normally means declared as such without proof. But the sentence essentially says the accused man committed the crime; "alleged" scarcely mitigates the nastiness joined to his name. A fairer phrasing would be: ". . . Laurie . . . pleaded with her attacker—alleged to be David . . . —to take. . . ."

Suspected is apt to be treated in the manner of the other two questionable words. The comments about *accused* hold for *suspected.* A "suspected assailant" is an assailant who is suspected, according to the literal meaning of the words. In stating that "serious damage has been done to national security by convicted or suspected spies," two newspaper by-liners show that they regard "suspected spies" the same as convicted spies. (*See* **Guilt and innocence,** *3.*)

The word *reported* often is used in a similar grammatical way. Although usually applied to incidents, rather than people, its presence can raise questions. For instance, when a news story mentions a "reported crime," is it referring to a crime that has been reported to the police, or is it just using "reported" in its vague, journalistic sense, as a supposed hedge against legal action, or as if to say: "We're not sure that it happened, but we were told that it did"?

Writers and editors should be aware that none of the four words in question will protect them against suit. It is not enough to say "There really was an accusation"—or "allegation" or "report" or "suspicion"—if its substance was false or erroneous. As a rule of thumb, avoid charged prose if there is no charged defendant.

2. *Two adverbs*

Allegedly and *reportedly* (a later arrival) occupy the domain of the news media, and there they should be confined. They are used in this way: "The accused man allegedly [or "reportedly"] struck the victim." In grammatical terms, the selected adverb modifies the verb, *struck.* Someone ought to explain in what manner the accused person struck the other when he "allegedly" struck him or "reportedly" struck him.

During our Persian Gulf war, a banner in an American newspaper cried: "Hussein reportedly asks for asylum in Algeria" (referring to President Hussein of Iraq). The "report" came from a French newspaper, which cited no source. No more was heard of it. We need not ponder the unimaginable act of "reportedly asking"; a larger question is involved: When an editor finds a story so shaky that he must qualify its headline with "reportedly," should he not think twice before running it at all?

ACRONYM. *See* **Abbreviation.**

ACROPHOBIA. *See* **HOMOPHOBIA.**

"ACROSS FROM." These two sentences, which appeared in newspapers in Texas and New York, raise questions: "The farm is across from the plant." / ". . . This man's brother was across from the President's house with a gun. . . ." Across what? The tracks? The street? The park? Use of the slang term "across from" requires that the topographical entity in the way be obvious.

Active voice and passive voice.

An announcer broadcast the following sentence, and in a sense he spoke with two voices.

If you're in the market for high-quality furniture, this sale should not be missed.

Notice how weak the sentence gets after the comma. It starts out in the *active voice* and finishes in the *passive voice*. It would have more punch if it followed through actively: ". . . don't miss this sale" or "you should not miss this sale." The inconsistency as much as the relative weakness of the *passive voice* impaired the announcement.

Voice is the form of a verb that indicates whether the subject of a sentence *performs* the action or *receives* the action. The two sentences that follow express the same thought in two ways.

- "Matilda found a chinchilla" is in the *active voice*. The subject (Matilda) *performed* the action.
- "A chinchilla was found by Matilda" is in the *passive voice*. The subject (a chinchilla) *received* the action.

The *active voice* is more direct and usually more forceful than the *passive*. Nevertheless, the *passive* has a place. You may want to emphasize the doing and play down the doer. The identity of the doer may be obvious, unknown, insignificant, or indefinite: "Letterpress printing is not used much now." / "Flags are being lowered to half-mast." / "The package was delivered yesterday." / "It just isn't done."

A book on world history says, "The Neolithic stage in culture is characterized by the following important innovations:" Five numbered paragraphs follow. Such a format lends itself to the passive.

Too much *passive* can get dull. Scientists load their writing with it. If you read research papers, you can get the idea that scientists never *do* anything. Somehow everything *is done,* as though by magic. Take the following description of an experiment, from a biology annual (emphasis added).

Stock suspension of normal erythrocytes *were* prepared from freshly heparinized rat blood. . . . The plasma and buffy coat *were* removed, and the cells *were* washed. . . . The supernatant of the first washing *was* discarded, and the cells *were* resuspended and diluted. . . . NACl dissolved in 10 ml sodium buffer, at the appropriate Ph, *was* chosen for the preparation of the hypotonic solutions. . . . The required standard 50% hemolysis *was* reached by adjustment of the NACl concentration.

The combining of voices can produce a sentence that is not just weak but also ungrammatical. It happens when a verb in the *active* part does not agree with anything in the *passive* part. Such a sentence appears in the foreword of a generally admirable dictionary. The sentence preceding it says the editors do not give merely the essence of a definition.

Instead, the reader is given the necessary additional connotative information, even if it means devoting a good deal of space to doing so. . . .

The sentence is *passive* up to the second comma; thereafter it is *active*. That fact alone does not spoil it. The trouble is that the words "doing so" do not refer to anything. If, for instance, the sentence began (in an *active voice*) "Instead, *we insist on giving the reader* the necessary . . . ," *doing so* would fit. Another way to correct the sentence is to make the second part ". . . even if it *requires* a good deal of space."

Double passives can be awkward. This is acceptable (though not an illustration of energetic reporting): "The suspect was said to be wanted in three states." This, however, is too clumsy for publication: "The peak was again attempted to be climbed." Better: "Another attempt was made to climb the peak." A passive *believed, reported, said,* or *thought* will tolerably combine with another passive. Many others will not: *attempted, begun, forgotten, proposed, sought,* and so on.

AD and ADD.   *See* **Homophones.**

ADAPT and ADOPT.   To *adapt* something is to adjust or change it so as to make it suitable for one's purpose. Hollywood writers often *adapt* novels to the screen.

To *adopt* something is to accept or take it as one's own—unchanged—as one would *adopt* a child.

An anchor man who referred to "the platform that the Democrats adapted in Atlanta" chose the wrong word. It should have been *adopted.*

By the way, *adopted* children have *adoptive* parents.

Adjectives and adverbs.   *1. In general. 2. Placement.*

1. In general

An adjective describes someone or something. (In terms of grammar, it modifies a noun or pronoun.) Examples of adjectives are *green, wet,* and *European.*

An adverb describes an action, or it further describes a description. (It modifies a verb, an adjective, or another adverb.) Examples of adverbs are *thinly, probably,* and *increasingly.*

It seems as though every piece of writing about improving one's English has to contain some mistake. (The book you are now reading is probably no exception.) So a newspaper article on legal English indirectly quotes a judge "who advises lawyers to write like good newspaper reporters: simple and straightforward." And ungrammatically?

You may write a *simple* piece or write a piece that is *simple*—this word is an adjective only. But you write *simply*—this word is an adverb only.

Unlike *simple* and *simply, straightforward* may be used either as an adjective or as an adverb.

Among other words that serve both as adjectives and as adverbs are *down, far, fast, first, little, much, same, straight, very,* and *well.* They have one form only. (They are sometimes called *flat adverbs.*) The following are more examples of words that double as adjectives; used as an adverb, each has an alternative form ending in *-ly,* the form of most adverbs: *bright, cheap, loud, quick, sharp, slow, strong, sure,* and *tight.* Some writers consider the *-ly* form—*brightly, cheaply,* etc.—more formal or fancy.

In some cases, adding *-ly* changes the meaning. Each of these is a combined adjective and adverb: *hard, high, late.* And each has an *-ly* form with a different meaning: *hardly, highly, lately.*

Hyphens should never be attached to adverbs ending in *-ly:* "a *strongly* worded letter" / "the *rapidly* moving train." (Some adjectives end in *-ly* and are subject to hyphenating when attached to participles. *See* **Punctuation,** 4D.)

Sometimes an adjective is erroneously used for an adverb and vice versa. An attorney general said, "We take it very serious"—instead of *seriously,* the adverb. A psychologist said, "You've done all of those things that sound wonderfully"—instead of *wonderful,* the adjective. (*Sound* is a linking verb. *See* **Verbs,** *1F.*)

Descriptive terms ought to be stinted, used only when needed to paint a picture. Some writers and speakers shovel them out when the unadorned facts would suffice. In prose characteristic of supermarket tabloids, a reporter said on a television network, "Amazing new research has led to an astonishing discovery" (about the migration of brain cells). *See also* **CELEBRATED; GRISLY** (etc.); **Synonymic silliness.**

Adjectives or adverbs come up in hundreds of word entries and such topic entries as **Comparative and superlative degrees; Comparison; Double negative; Joining of words; Modifiers; Modifying; Nouns; Participle; Possessive problems; Series errors; Tautology; Verbs.**

2. *Placement*

An adjective may go just before the noun it modifies, as in "A *yellow* bird appeared" (an *attributive adjective*); or it may follow a linking verb, as in "The bird was *yellow*" (a *predicate adjective*).

Contrary to the syntax of many languages, in English we would not be likely to speak of "a bird yellow." Normally an adjective does not immediately follow the noun it modifies. Exceptions are found in poetry, for instance: "thy spirit . . . With its life intense and mild. . . ." *See also* "**PROOF POSITIVE.**"

Where to put adverbs often perplexes people. Typically an adverb goes just before a simple verb: "They *often* bring flowers." It may go at the beginning of a sentence or clause or at the end, particularly if it gets emphasis: "*Unfortunately* she failed." / "The river is rising *rapidly.*"

The placement of an adverb can drastically affect the meaning of a sentence, such as this one: "A plan for reducing the work force *slowly* has been prepared." The sentence is ambiguous. Does it refer to "A plan for *slowly* reducing the work force" or does it mean that the plan "has *slowly* been prepared"?

If an auxiliary is helping the verb, it is perfectly proper for the adverb to go between them: "We will *soon* know the results." / "His support would *quickly* vanish." Some writers have the mistaken notion that an adverb cannot split a verb phrase, such as *will know* or *would vanish*. That notion seems to stem from the concern about split infinitives.

A news story said "her family's home badly was damaged." The sentence structure has a Germanic flavor. Telling the story orally, the writer would probably say "her family's home *was badly* damaged."

Similarly, a news story in another paper said "the stadium measure heavily was favored." Better: "the stadium measure *was heavily* favored."

An author wrote, "I have no great objection to . . . its [Cockney] being denied officially the status of a dialect." Better: "being *officially denied.* . . ."

If a verb has more than one auxiliary, it gets complicated. The adverb normally goes after either the first or second auxiliary, depending on what it is supposed to modify.

- "You will *always* be welcome in our house." Here the adverb applies to the whole compound, *will be welcome,* and follows the first auxiliary, *will.*
- "He will be *sharply* reprimanded." Here the adverb specially applies to the main verb, *reprimanded,* and goes right before it.

When in doubt, one can play by ear. If it sounds right, it is likely to be right.

An adverb made up of a number of words often follows a verb phrase. "I have said it *again and again.*"

When it comes at the beginning, an adverb can modify an entire sentence or clause. "*Usually* she arrives early and bakes the bread." *Usually* applies to both *arrives* and *bakes.* It is a mistake to overlook the effect of the adverb on the second verb, in this manner: "*Skillfully* he concluded the difficult operation but collapsed from exhaustion." Make it "He *skillfully* concluded" to avoid saying, literally, that he skillfully collapsed.

As a rule, an adverb should not separate a verb from its object. "Liza solved quickly the puzzle" should be "Liza *quickly solved* the puzzle."

See also **Infinitive**, 4; **Verbs**, 4.

ADMISSION. 1. *Acknowledgment.* 2. *ADMISSION and ADMITTANCE.*

1. *Acknowledgment*

When it does not have anything to do with entry, *admission* is acknowledgment that a statement is true, a statement that reflects more or less unfavorably on the one making the acknowledgment.

Admission can range in seriousness from a trivial concession for the sake of argument to a confession of a crime. It can be used in a general sense ("Taking the Fifth Amendment is not admission of guilt") or specifically, applying to something acknowledged ("His admission that he took an illegal drug did not prevent his election").

Your acknowledgment of a fact that does not reflect upon you, except perhaps favorably, is not an *admission*. The word does not fit this sentence, from an article by a news service:

> A new 13-city survey finds Philadelphia diners, by their own admissions, to be the most generous tippers of the lot. . . .

The finding may be based on their own accounts, figures, numbers, reports, responses, statements, statistics, or words. But it is not based on their own "admissions," because being a generous tipper is not usually considered something to be ashamed of, at least in American society.

2. *ADMISSION and ADMITTANCE*

Now for the kind of *admission* that does have to do with entry: it is the act or fact of being allowed to enter, the right to enter, or, loosely, a charge for entering.

In the sense of entry, *admittance* is similar. It too means the act or fact of being allowed to enter or the right to enter. However, *admittance* usually is limited to literal entry into a specific place. ("A locked gate prevented our admittance to the garden." / "Admittance to the kitchen is restricted to employees.")

Admission often has the added implication of a privileged entry, as into a group, a profession, or a place of entertainment. ("Your admission to the society has been approved." / "What is the cost of admission to the show?") Moreover, *admission* may be used figuratively. ("The judge permitted the admission of her testimony.")

For both nouns, the usual adjective is *admissible,* meaning able to be accepted or admitted. ("Hearsay generally is not admissible evidence." / "Only those with tickets are admissible.") *Admittable* is rare.

See also **ADMIT**.

ADMIT. 1. *"ADMIT TO."* 2. *Handled without care.*

1. *"ADMIT TO"*

A main headline in a California newspaper identifies a politician who "Quits Senate, Admits to Corruption." And an Oregon newspaper reports on a broker in trouble: ". . . he denied today ever admitting to the $18,619 in missing funds."

Admit, when used in the sense of acknowledge or confess, should not be followed by "to." English idiom allows *admits wrongdoing* or *admitting a mistake* but not "admits to" or "admitting to" an action. (Just omitting the "to" will not rescue the second sample. He denied admitting, not "the $18,619," but the *disappearance* of it. Or he denied admitting *that* $18,619 *was missing*.)

Admit to is proper when the meaning is to permit one to enter a group or profession: "She was admitted to the club" or "The state admits to the bar only those who pass the examination." *Admit to* is correct also in the sense of permitting physical entrance: "The gate admits to the house." / "The guards will not admit to the plant anyone lacking proper identification."

2. *Handled without care*

One of the meanings of *admit* is to confess wrongdoing. The word is so commonly used in that sense that it must be handled with care when a more neutral use is intended. *Admit* (as a transitive verb) can mean also to concede the truth of a trivial allegation or to acknowledge a shortcoming that is quite innocent: "I admit I've been slow to answer my mail lately, but I've been busy."

The word tempts headline writers by its brevity and can mislead them and their readers. A headline read, "Montoya Admits Forgeries." It seemed to say a U.S. senator had confessed crimes, but the text said something much different: While acknowledging that a campaign finance report of his filed in New Mexico bore false signatures of two campaign officers, he said he was shocked to learn of it. A safer headline—perhaps "Forgeries 'Shock' Montoya"—would have avoided the incriminating juxtaposition.

See also ADMISSION; CONFESS.

ADMITTANCE. *See* ADMISSION, 2.

ADOPT and ADAPT; ADOPTED and ADOPTIVE. *See* ADAPT and ADOPT.

"ADULT." *See* EXOTIC.

Adverbs. *See* Adjectives and adverbs.

ADVERSE and AVERSE. *See* Confusing Pairs.

ADVICE and ADVISE. *Advice* is the noun, meaning an opinion on what to do about a problem. "I'm going to the lawyer for advice." *Advise* is the verb, meaning to recommend or to give advice. "The lawyer will advise me."

All that is common knowledge, is it not? Maybe not. A sign in a window offers "TAROT CARD READINGS BY MISS GLORIA" and "ADVISE ON ALL PROBLEMS." (One problem is her name. A sign on a wall calls her "*Mrs. Gloria*.")

Some authorities object to the use of *advise* to mean inform, notify, say, state, or tell. It is common in business— "Please advise which model is desired"—and can suggest business jargon when used elsewhere.

One who advises is either an *adviser* or an *advisor*. The press customarily insists on the *e* spelling. The *o* spelling is in line with the adjective *advisory*, which is spelled only that way.

ADVOCATE. The verb *advocate* means to recommend or promote (a cause). It is a transitive verb only. That is, it must transmit its action to an object. You *advocate* something.

It was misused in these press quotations: "Herlihy . . . has been advocating for the name change. . . ." / "The new organization . . . is advocating for a one-year moratorium. . . ." Omit each "for." The man "has been advocating the name change." The group "is advocating a one-year moratorium."

If "advocating" were changed, say, to *arguing, pleading, pressing,* or *pushing,* both quoted sentences could accept *for*. All four verbs are intransitive (not needing an object) as well as transitive. One can also *argue* an issue, *plead* a case, *press* charges, or *push* a broom.

A policeman used *advocate* unidiomatically in another way: "They advocated other people to violate the law." He may have been thinking of another word: "They *encouraged* other people to violate the law."

An *advocate* (noun) is one who promotes a cause or who pleads someone's cause, perhaps as an attorney. "The senator is an advocate of lower taxes." / "She acted as his advocate at the hearing."

As a verb, *advocate* is pronounced AD-vuh-kate. As a noun, it may be pronounced the same way, but more often it is pronounced AD-vuh-kit.

AFFECT and EFFECT. *1. AFFECT: the more common verb. 2. EFFECT: the noun to remember.*

1. AFFECT: the more common verb

To *affect* is to influence or make a change in (something). A newspaper article used the wrong verb:

> It [the Senate] is also a position of power, an opportunity to effect one's world.

A senator can *affect* the world, not "effect" it.

Similarly, "effecting" should be *affecting* in this sentence, from an editorial in another paper:

> Until these cases are resolved, suspicion will hang over the White House like a noxious plume, effecting everything that goes on beneath. [Watch out for noxious feathers!]

Another meaning of the a verb is to feign or give the appearance of (something). For example: "Actors ably affect accents."

To *effect* is to bring about, carry out, or accomplish (something). Example of the e verb: "Each executive effected economies." It is used much less often than the other verb.

Instead of "affect," this headline

should have used *effect:* "How to affect a peaceful overthrow."

2. EFFECT: the noun to remember

As nouns, the two words are easier to choose between. You will probably want to use *effect,* the result of a cause.

Affect refers to emotion or feeling. Only psychologists seem to have affection for *affect.* It is pronounced with emphasis on the first syllable, unlike the other noun and the two verbs.

In both of these press examples, "affect" should be *effect:*

> Texaco Inc. has announced a deal that seems certain to set off a major debate in the United States about its affect on energy security. . . .

> The Justices Are People[;]
> Climate of Their Era May Have an
> Affect

Another newspaper got both the noun and the verb wrong in the same article:

> . . . It's not clear what affect the nominations will have on the polls. . . . "The PRI has tried to effect social policy by driving away poor families. . . ."

Change "affect" to *effect* and change "effect" to *affect. See also* **IMPACT.**

AFTER. *After* (preposition) is sometimes replaced by *subsequent to,* a correct but pretentious synonym. "Subsequent to dinner" is no improvement over "after dinner." The modest *after* is a useful word on all levels of English, though sometimes overused.

After (conjunction) is a well-worn tool of the press, used to string episodes together in reverse chronological order. As shown by the newspaper excerpt below, the word is not limited to one use per sentence. A state supreme court affirmed a robber's conviction, finding that a revolver taken from his car without a search warrant was valid evidence.

> C—— is serving a five-year sentence after pleading no contest to the charge that he robbed a gas station mini-market in Long Beach, after brandishing a revolver. [*See* **BRANDISH.**]

The sentence is overstuffed with ideas and its double *after* runs the sequence of events backward. Better: "C—— had used the revolver to rob a gas station mini-market in Long Beach. Charged with the robbery, he pleaded no contest and received a five-year sentence, which he now serves."

Some authorities prefer *after* to *following* (as a preposition): "He spoke after [not "following"] dinner." One grammarian accepts that use of *following* only when the two events are related by more than time: "Following the riot in Union Square yesterday, six men will appear in Circuit Court today."

See also **CONDITION,** 1.

AGGRAVATE. To *aggravate* is to make an undesirable condition worse; for instance, "A chill aggravates the flu." An *aggravation* is (1) a worsening of that condition, or (2) the thing that makes it worse. A trouble or burden, not a person, is *aggravated*.

The extracts, from three metropolitan newspapers, illustrate none of those meanings, only the loose use of the words to signify annoy(ance), vex-(ation), stir(ring) up, or the like. Such use is common in colloquial speech and casual writing; it is out of place in more formal media.

> The measures apparently were calibrated to be harsh enough to undercut pressure from Congress for additional sanctions but not so harsh as to aggravate Beijing into a deep breach in the Chinese-American relationship. . . .

> The gas men returned in the nick of time, but the aggravation led the Brooklyn woman to ponder the fragile dependency of modern life.

> Usually when world leaders make state visits, the local population is uninterested at best, or perhaps slightly aggravated by the inconveniences, such as rerouted traffic and disrupted schedules at the airport.

The first could have used *provoke;* the second, *annoyance, irritation,* or *vexation;* the third, *annoyed, irritated,* or *vexed.*

AGORAPHOBIA. *See* **HOMOPHOBIA.**

Agreement in number. *See* **Number (grammatical).**

AHEAD (time). *See* **FORWARD** and **BACK (time).**

A HOLD. *See* **HOLD.**

"-A" instead of HAVE. *See* **HAVE, HAS, HAD,** 2.

"A" instead of personal pronoun. *See* **Pronouns,** 2 A.

"AIN'T." It is hard to imagine a syndicated writer who does not know that "ain't" is widely impugned as illiterate, so let us assume that this one used it deliberately:

> And Giuliani got to run in a year when everybody knows that whatever it is that's just around the corner ain't prosperity.

Why "ain't"? Was it humor of some kind or verbal slumming? *Is not* or *isn't* or *is no* would have fit the sentence and spared the writer the appearance of ignorance.

The same questions may be addressed to the scientific author who titled a chapter "Black Holes Ain't So Black." His reason for avoiding the proper *Are Not* or *Aren't* is equally obscure.

The American Heritage Dictionary has called the word "beyond rehabilitation." Only 1 to 6 percent of its usage panel (105–166 members) has approved of its serious use in writing; 16 to 19 percent, in speech.

Merriam-Webster has viewed it differently: The word is "used orally in most parts of the U.S. by many cultivated speakers. . . ." That comment in *Webster's Third New International Dictionary* provoked ridicule; one wag wondered "where Webster cultivated those speakers."

"Ain't" is common in the most casual of colloquial speech as a substitute for *am not, are not, is not, have not* and *has not*. It may be suitable for writing when the writer is quoting someone or simulating spoken slang. It appears in many songs, like "It Ain't Necessarily So."

"Say it ain't so" (plus a name) has become a cliché. Its legendary origin in a boy's challenge to an arrested baseball player is well known. So when a newspaper corrected the expression in a headline—"Say it isn't so, Joe" (about a football star's lawsuit against another newspaper)—it looked wrong.

See also "AREN'T I?"

ALIBI. *Alibi* is a legal term. It is a defense in which a defendant contends or tries to prove that he was somewhere else than at the scene of a crime when it was committed. In Latin, the word's source, *alibi* means *elsewhere*. An *alibi* may be truthful or not, as any other type of defense may be.

Unfortunately, that noun has come to be used conversationally to signify an excuse for a misdeed, often an excuse that rouses suspicion or is downright spurious. Outside of the legal community, the popular misuse casts a shadow on the legitimate use of the word.

An associate of a peace foundation recommended that Washington outline criteria for Russian admission to the International Monetary Fund to "offer the Government some alibi for unpopular austerity measures." Change "alibi" to *excuse* or *justification*.

ALIVE. *See* LIVE, *1*.

ALLEGED, ALLEGEDLY. *See* ACCUSED, ALLEGED (etc.).

ALL NEW. The bombardment for generations by "new" products, "new" services, and "new" entertainment may have desensitized the public to novelty. Now many advertisers and TV networks seem to feel that anything new has to be announced as "*all* new" just to get anyone's attention.

So on four networks we hear these announcements: "the all-new Mazda truck" / "an all-new 'Simpsons' " / "the all-new Mitsubishi Galant" / "Herbie's back with an all-new adventure." The items are not brand-new in all respects. Each is just a *new model* or *new episode*, but evidently the writers of the commercials do not consider that new enough.

ALLOT. *See* LOT.

ALL READY. *See* ALL TOGETHER and ALTOGETHER (etc.).

ALL RIGHT. Many people seem unaware that *all right* is composed of two simple words, *all* and *right*. The phrase is frequently misspelled, sometimes as "allright" but usually in this manner:

"Henry took a turn for the worse alright."

Putting it in a quotation (that one was in a medical book for the layman) does not absolve a writer. And the fact that some permissive dictionaries condone the misspelling is no excuse as long as it is widely viewed as a sign of ignorance.

All was not right with Henry. The intended meaning there was *certainly*. That is the meaning in the odd sentence below (another quotation, this one in a leading newspaper).

"Virginia has made history, alright, all right, but race is still very much something that has to be contended with."

Perhaps an editor inserted the right version but forgot to delete the wrong one.

In addition to that meaning and the literal meaning of *entirely right*, *all right* embraces a variety of other, more or less informal meanings: *adequate, agreeable, correct, good, O.K., permissible, safe, satisfactory, uninjured, well, yes*. It is both an adjective and an adverb.

It should be placed after the word it modifies. "This restaurant is all right." Placed before the noun—"This is an all-right restaurant"—it becomes slang.

"Alright" may have been hatched by analogy with *already*. But "alright" and *all right* have the same meanings and the same pronunciations; the two syllables get about equal stress. *Already* and *all ready*, however, have different meanings and different pronunciations. *Already* stresses the first syllable, whereas *all ready* gives the first and second syllables even stress. *See also* ALL TOGETHER and ALTOGETHER, -READY, -MOST.

ALL THAT. *See* Anachronism, 4; THAT, ALL THAT.

ALL-TIME RECORD. *See* RECORD.

ALL TOGETHER and ALTO-GETHER, -READY, -MOST. An author erroneously wrote that people "came altogether" instead of "came *all together*."

All together (adjective phrase) means in a group: "At last our family is *all together*." *Altogether* (adverb) means entirely, all told, or on the whole: "The rumor is altogether false." / "Altogether 107 were present." / "How was the show altogether?"

Similarly *all ready*, meaning completely prepared ("The group is all ready to go"), differs from *already*, meaning by this or that time ("but the plane has already taken off").

An editor dictated a letter that should have said, "Your comments are all most heartening." Instead of *all most*, his secretary typed "almost," suggesting that the addressee's comments were not quite heartening.

See also ALL RIGHT.

ALLUDE and ELUDE. *See* Confusing pairs.

ALONG WITH. *See* WITH, 2.

ALREADY. *See* ALL TOGETHER and ALTOGETHER (etc.).

"ALRIGHT." *See* ALL RIGHT.

ALSO. 1. *Adverb, not conjunction.* 2. *Placement.* 3. *Synonyms.* 4. *Wrong use.*

1. Adverb, not conjunction

Also, an adverb, should not be forced to do the work of a conjunction, or connector—at least in writing. That is the consensus of grammatical authorities. For instance: "He carries nickels, dimes, and quarters, also half-dollars." Tacking on an afterthought to a written sentence in that manner is considered juvenile. Afterthoughts in impromptu speech cannot be helped.

Some of those authorities object to starting a sentence with *also*: "I was running to escape the rain. Also I didn't want to be late for work." Better: "I was running to escape the rain and also to get to work on time." The "also" could even be omitted.

To start a sentence with *also* is a journalistic peculiarity. This is typical: "Also named were. . . ." A more idiomatic start might be: "*Others* named were. . . ."

2. Placement

The placement of *also*, like that of some other adverbs, can substantially affect the meaning of a sentence. These two sample sentences are the same except for the location of *also:*

- "He was *also* charged with theft." (It was one of multiple charges against him.)
- "He *also* was charged with theft." (He as well as another person was charged with that offense.)

The misguided belief that compound verbs may not be split sometimes leads a writer or editor to choose the second form when the first is right. A news agency reported a prison sentence for a man paid to influence an attorney general. The next paragraph:

E. Robert ———, a legal consultant for Wedtech, also was fined $250,000 for misrepresenting the funds he received from the company.

Inasmuch as no one else was fined $250,000, make it "was also fined . . ."

A quotation from a magazine illustrates the opposite error:

The new Central Park Zoo will also have an underwater window to see their polar bears.

Also would have been in the right place if the magazine's previous sentence had described other features planned for the new zoo. Actually that sentence describes an underwater window to see polar bears at a zoo in another city. "The

new Central Park Zoo *also* will have" one. (The sample has another fault: "their" should be *its. See* **Pronouns,** *2B.*)

See also **Adjectives and adverbs,** 2.

3. Synonyms

Too, likewise, in addition, and *besides* are synonyms for *also* and can be more precise at times. But use one at a time.

Warning of the danger of winds' knocking over trees, a city park official said redundantly, "Nature's pretty but it's also dangerous too." The sentence can take either *also* or *too* but not both.

4. Wrong use

A different misuse of *also,* as well as other faults, is illustrated by this passage (dispatched by a news agency two years before the collapse of the U.S.S.R.):

The chairman of the House Armed Services Committee says Soviet President Mikhail S. Gorbachev appears to be carrying out his pledge to make sizeable cuts in Soviet Forces in Eastern Europe.

But Rep. Les. Aspin, D-Wis., added that Soviet forces have also increased artillery strength in Eastern Europe.

If the first of the two sentences told of, say, increased infantry strength, "also increased" would pass muster. As it stands, only artillery is increased, so "also" makes no sense.

By "also," the writer may have meant *at the same time.* That is not what *also* means. *See 3.*

The passage illustrates another journalistic peculiarity: The first sentence mentions "The chairman" and the second sentence mentions "Aspin," but nothing ties the two together. Either the first sentence should have named him ("*Rep. Les Aspin . . . ,* the chairman of the House Armed Services Committee, says . . .") or the second sentence should have mentioned his rank ("But Rep. Les

Aspin . . . , *the chairman, adds . . . "*—present tense, as in the first sentence). A similar illustration is the news dispatch in 2.

See also NOT ONLY, a phrase often accompanied by *but also.*

ALTAR and ALTER. *See* Homophones.

ALTERNATE and ALTERNATIVE. *See* Confusing pairs.

ALTOGETHER. *See* ALL TOGETHER and ALTOGETHER (etc.).

A.M. *See* A.M., P.M., NOON, MIDNIGHT.

Ambiguity. *See* Adjectives and adverbs, 2; ANOTHER; APPARENT, APPARENTLY; AS, *1, 4, 5;* AS and LIKE, *1;* BECAUSE, *1;* BETWEEN, *3;* BI- and SEMI- prefixes; BILLION; DATA; Double meaning; Double negative, 2; Double possessive; Ellipsis; FARTHER and FURTHER; FORWARD and BACK (time); FORMER; FREE, 2; GAS, *1;* GO OFF and GO ON; GREAT; HAVE, HAS, HAD, *1;* Infinitive, *4;* Introduction (to the book), *Clarity (ambiguity* defined), *Wounded Words* (65 words listed, representing entries); LATTER, *1* (end); LET, LET'S, *1;* LIKE, *1;* Modifiers, *3B;* NEAR MISS; NOT; Nouns, *4;* Numbers, *1, 10;* Participle; Prepositions, 2, *5;* Pronouns, *1;* Punctuation, 3, *12;* Reversal of meaning; Run-on sentence; SPEAK TO, TALK TO; Synonymic silliness, 2; THAT, 2; THAT, ALL THAT; THAT and WHICH, *1, 2;* THE, *1, 2;* THIS, 2; TO, 2; TOO, *1;* UNLIKE, *1;* WHICH, *1;* WHO, *1.*

AMBIGUOUS and AMBIVALENT. *See* Confusing pairs.

AMERICAN INDIAN. *See* RACE and NATIONALITY.

AM NOT. *See* "AREN'T I?"

AMONG. *See* BETWEEN, *1.*

AMOUNT and NUMBER. A computer book says, in explaining a desktop publishing program, "The total amount of hyphens appearing in one paragraph can also be determined."

"Amount" should be *number.* The following colloquy helps to explain the use of the two words.

"How much are lemons?"

"A dollar a pound." (The amount of money.)

"How many are in a pound?"

"Four or five." (The number of items.)

"How much fruit will I need for half a gallon of lemonade?"

"About a pound." (The amount of fruit.)

Use *amount* when you are interested in "how much"—how much money, fruit, labor, or anything else. It pertains to a singular noun.

Use *number* when you are interested in "how many"—how many lemons, people, hyphens, or other items. It pertains to a plural noun.

A.M., P.M., NOON, MIDNIGHT. "The shoot-out took place right after 2 A.M. this morning," a newscaster announced redundantly.

In his sentence, "A.M." and "morning" meant the same thing: the period from immediately after midnight to immediately before noon. He could have said "right after 2 A.M. today" or "right after 2 o'clock this morning."

A.M. stands for the Latin phrase *ante meridiem,* meaning before noon. An English adjective with the same meaning is *antemeridian.*

P.M. stands for the Latin phrase *post meridiem,* meaning the same as the English adjective *postmeridian:* after noon. It represents the period from immediately after noon to immediately before midnight.

In referring to the stroke of 12, you can say 12 *noon* or 12 *midnight,* or just *noon* or *midnight.* To avoid confusion, do not abbreviate. Sometimes "12 M." (meridian) is used for noon and "12 P.M." for midnight. But the "M." can be misinterpreted as an abbreviation of "midnight" and people may not know what to make of the "P.M."

Midnight ends a day. So "midnight Wednesday" is the end of Wednesday, not the beginning of Thursday.

A.M. and P.M. are spelled also with lower-case letters (a.m., p.m. or *a.m., p.m.*) or small capitals (A.M., P.M.).

AN. *See* A and AN.

Anachronism. *1. Historical revision. 2. Illogical captions. 3. Retroactive retitling. 4. Untrue dialogue.*

1. Historical revision

In 1867 Secretary of State William H. Seward signed a treaty "to purchase Alaska from the Soviet Union"—at least that is what the hostess on a national radio show said (111 years later). Various commentators have called Seward ahead of his time; he would have had to be fifty years ahead to deal with the Soviet Union, which came into existence in 1917. The treaty was with *Russia.*

That is an example of an *anachronism,* a verbal or graphic misplacement in time, a chronological error. *Chronology* shares with *anachronism* the root *khronos,* Greek for *time.* (*Ana-* means *backward.*) Sometimes *anachronism* is used erroneously in place of *anomaly* or *contradiction,* but time is the key.

We are concerned here mainly with the distortion of history by the intrusion of things that came later, particularly names, terms, and expressions. *Anachronisms* are inevitable in fiction representing the future: 1984 turned out

differently from 1984 (a fact that does not detract from the eminence of Orwell's book).

An almanac *anachronistically* stated that the Internal Revenue Service (IRS) was "founded in 1862." It was so named in 1953 as a new identity for the Bureau of Internal Revenue. A television interviewee said Al Capone, the gangster, was arrested for "IRS violations." Make it *tax* violations. Capone died in 1947.

This statement was made in a TV documentary about the search for the missing link by archaeologists in Africa:

Tools were first recognized by Louis Leakey, when he came to this remote corner of Tanzania in 1931.

Leakey went to *Tanganyika.* Tanzania was formed in 1964 (from the union of Tanganyika and Zanzibar).

2. Illogical captions

Captions of photographs published in the popular press are apt to juxtapose past and present illogically, as this caption in a Sunday paper does:

UNDER THE GAZE of a mannequin Saturday, Steve C—— . . . tries salmon sausage . . . at the Pittsburg Seafood Festival, which continues today.

"Saturday," yesterday, he "tries" it? "Tries" should be *tried.* The writer has forced upon the present tense the impossible task of representing the past as well as the present (the festival "continues today"). Having set an action in the past, a sentence cannot bring in the present tense to represent that action.

To write that "strawberries await buyers Thursday at Whole Foods market . . ." would normally imply that buyers could expect them next Thursday. But the quotation is the caption of a picture taken yesterday, Thursday, and published today, Friday. It should have (1) left out the day, or (2) said "strawberries *awaited* buyers Thursday . . . ," or (3) said "strawberries *are pictured* [or "*are shown*"] *awaiting* buyers Thursday. . . ." Then the present tense would not be forced into a role it could not fulfill.

See also **Tense** for discussion of the proper and improper mixing of time elements.

3. *Retroactive retitling*
This sentence was attributed to a news service:

> Time magazine reported Sunday that independent counsel Donald Smaltz is investigating a charge made by a former pilot for Tyson Foods that he helped convey cash payments from the company to President Clinton while Clinton was governor of Arkansas.

Impossible. No "payments from the company to President Clinton" could have been made while he was governor of Arkansas. He held those offices at two different times. Change "President" to *Bill.* Anyone who does not know that Bill Clinton was elected president would not be likely to read the story. One could speak also of *now President Clinton,* although such use of *now,* as an adjective, is uncommon. (The allegation has not been proved. The statement involves several layers of hearsay.) *See also* **FORMER.**

4. *Untrue dialogue*
In portrayals of historical eras on television, the dialogue is liable to contain expressions that did not come into vogue until later. Sometimes loose grammar of the future is thrust into characters' mouths.

By a decade or two, three series portraying the past anticipated such contemporary expressions as "That's for sure" / "Give me a break" / "I don't believe this" / "I love it!" / "We're [or "I'm"] out of here" / "all that" ("She wasn't here all that long. . . . I didn't think it was all that serious").

AND. *1. Excess. 2. Lack.*

1. *Excess*
Among pedagogic rules that went too far was the one that forbade anyone to start a sentence with *And.* Few if any pupils thought to say, "But the Bible does it."

An occasional use of *And* to begin a sentence can be beneficial: It can associate that sentence with a related one when putting them together in one sentence would be unwieldy.

There is less justification for starting a paragraph with *And.* The purpose of a new paragraph is to separate its idea from what preceded. But on rare occasions such use of *And* may be warranted as a stylistic device.

Some journalists seem to be reacting vigorously to that pedantic shall-not by going to the other extreme:

> And the trend toward greater specialization . . . also adds to costs.
>
> And Dr. Sidney Wolfe says costs rise because patients do not have to worry about the bills—the government and insurance companies do it for them.
>
> And Wolfe cautions that with more doctors now owning a share in new testing equipment, there is an increasing incentive for them to order extra tests.
>
> And the number of physicians clearly is growing.

All of the four quoted sentences—three of which start paragraphs—come from one newspaper story. One in every seven sentences begins with "And."

2. Lack

And (a conjunction: it connects words, phrases, etc.) can mean *also, in addition, plus, together with,* and *as a result*. Sometimes *and* is incorrectly replaced by "but" or "plus." *See* BUT, *1;* PLUS.

Having more than one *and* in a series, or enumeration, is not wrong and may be necessary. An irrational avoidance of *and* results in a common mistake. *See* **Series errors.**

AND THAT, AND WHICH, AND WHO. *See* THAT, *3;* WHICH, *3;* WHO, *2.*

ANECDOTE and ANTIDOTE.
An *anecdote* is a short, often amusing, account of an incident. An *antidote* is a medicinal substance that counteracts a poison. (Both words are Greek in origin. The first is from *anekdotos,* unpublished, from *an-,* not; *ek-,* out; and *dotos,* given. The second is from *antidotos,* antidote, from *anti-,* against, and the same *dotos.*)

Occasionally the two words are mixed up. This dialogue was said to have taken place in a university class:

> [Instructor:] If a person gets poisoned, what do you do?
> [Coed:] Give him an anecdote.

Laughter may be a good medicine, but you can carry it too far.

ANNIVERSARY. One television
newscaster said of Romania, "This weekend is the six-month anniversary of the revolution." Another said the Czechs "were marking the one-month anniversary of the bloody police crackdown." From a book: "As the unprecedented prior restraint reached its two-week anniversary. . . ."

They all spoke nonsense. *Anniversary* stems from the Latin *anniversarius,* which means returning yearly. The prefix, *anni-,* originated in *annus,* year, out of which developed the English words *annual* and *annuity.* The suffix, *-versary,* came from the Latin *vertere,* to turn.

So an *anniversary* is the yearly return of the date of an event, or an observance or celebration of the event on that date in a later year. "Today is the *tenth anniversary* of" an event is enough. "Ten-year anniversary," as some are saying, is redundant.

A lesser period than a year may be commemorated in other ways: "It is six months since . . ." or "one month since . . ." or "As two weeks passed since the unprecedented prior restraint was imposed. . . ."

If enough people deem it important to commemorate an event of a recent month, possibly a new word would be useful. I nominate *lunaversary.* It allows us to say, "Today is the first [or sixth] lunaversary of" the given event. The prefix is from *luna,* Latin for moon. Two-week commemorations are not common.

ANOTHER. *Another* (adjective and
pronoun) is paradoxical, at times emphasizing similarity, at other times emphasizing difference. It can mean (1) one more of the same kind ("I'll have another portion") or (2) one that is different ("They speak another language"). Sometimes it can suggest (3) resemblance ("This city is becoming another Manhattan") or (4) variations on a theme ("We've had one problem after another").

Although a flexible word, it is not a general substitute for *additional, more,* or *others.* Some question its use with unequal numbers. It is correct to say, "We're giving a $100 bonus to Betty and another $100 to Charlie." *Another* emphasizes the likeness. What is questionable is a use like this: "The Yanks scored four runs in the first inning and another

three runs in the second." The "another" serves no function there but
would be useful if the Yanks scored "another *four.*" Make it "and three runs in
the second" or, for emphasis, "and three
more runs in the second."

"Another" does serve to prevent ambiguity in this sentence: "Five people
were treated at the hospital and another
three were admitted"; but a better phrasing is "and three *others* were admitted."

This sentence, from a book about the
English language, has more than one defect:

> The number of words in use with full
> entries in the *OED* is 171,476, plus
> another 47,156 which are obsolete.

Omit "another"; the second number
does not match the first. Nor does the
second category match the first: The
47,156 words are not part of "The number of words in use." This is a possible
revision (with the appropriate parallels
and pronouns): "The number of words
with full entries in the *OED* is 218,632,
comprising 171,476 words that are in
use plus 47,156 words that are obsolete."

A related problem concerns *other.*
"Of eleven men questioned, five were
charged with gambling and the other six
were cleared." The first set does not have
six, so it is not technically right to speak
of "the other six." *The six others* would
be proper. Better yet, just delete "the
other."

See also **NOTHER.**

ANTE- and ANTI- prefixes. *See*
Homophones.

Antecedent. *See* **Pronouns,** *1;* **THIS,**
2; **WHICH,** *1;* **WHO,** *3.*

ANTICIPATE. The Latin verb *antici-
pare* means to take action beforehand.
That is the primary meaning of its English offspring *anticipate* (verb, transi-

tive). It is to act in advance of an event,
either to forestall it or to meet it with the
appropriate preparation. "He is a great
chess player and anticipates his opponent's moves long in advance." / "They
anticipated the crash by selling most of
their stocks."

Usually, however, it serves merely as a
fancy, four-syllable synonym for *expect.*
"We anticipate visiting our in-laws this
holiday." So common has that use been,
it may not be easy to tell if someone is
using the word loosely or strictly.

> U.S. Attorney William ——— said
> here last night he anticipates dropping
> the local case and deferring the prose-
> cution to San Diego.

Does it simply mean he *expects* to do
those things? Or does it mean that he is
making the necessary preparations? *Anticipate* is a wounded word. (Another
trouble with the sample is the shift in
tense: "said [past] he anticipates [pre-
sent]." *See* **Tense,** *2.*)

ANTIDOTE and ANECDOTE.
See **ANECDOTE and ANTIDOTE.**

ANXIOUS. To be *anxious* is primarily to feel anxiety or anxiousness; that is,
apprehension, concern, foreboding, or
uneasiness of mind. "I'm anxious about
the verdict." / "The people are anxious
for the war to end." / "She's anxious to
get the test over with." This adjective
comes barely changed from the Latin
anxius, meaning distressed.

The word often is watered down, particularly in informal conversation, so
that the main idea behind it—the anxiety—is lost. "I'm anxious to see the Yan-
kees play," Joe tells his friend. Pleasant,
not worrisome, anticipation, is all that
his "anxious" implies. He might find *eager,* the pedagogue's alternative, too
fancy for him. One of these, however,
should express his meaning and keep
him grammatical to anyone's satisfac-

tion: "I can hardly wait to see" / "I want very much to see" / "I'm excited about seeing" / "I'm keen on seeing" / "I'm looking forward to seeing. . . ."

Although the use of *anxious* in those carefree senses is widespread in colloquial speech, authorities are divided as to its propriety. One who is writing has more resources and less cause to take liberties with the word than conversing friends have. A book says:

> There is a tendency among Europeans to romanticise the nomads, which I was anxious to avoid.

There was no cause for anxiety. The author could write what he wanted. If he did not want to romanticize the nomads (or romanticise them, using the British spelling), he did not have to do so. Instead of *anxious,* one of these phrases would have served him well: "determined to avoid" / "eager to avoid" / "hoping to avoid" / "inclined to avoid" / "seeking to avoid" / "desirous of avoiding" / "intent on avoiding."

ANY. *1. In general. 2. With BODY or ONE. 3. With MORE. 4. With PLACE. 5. With TIME. 6. With WAY.*

1. In general

It is a mistake to think that *any* must always be joined to *body, one, place, time,* or *way* whenever the two words appear next to each other.

In general, *any-* combined with the other element stresses just the *any* in meaning and speech; as separate words, both get stress, in meaning and speech. *Any* and *more* should not always be joined either, even though *more* is stressed in *anymore.* Each pair will be considered in the sections below.

Anyhow, anything, and *anywhere* are invariably single words.

Anywhere should have no *s* attached. "Anywheres" is substandard.

Any and all, as in "Any and all violators will be prosecuted," is legalese and redundant. Pick *any* or *all*—or neither.

Sometimes *any* is wrongly used in a comparison, such as "The Acme widget has more features than any widget on the market." Any *other.* As it stands, Acme illogically remains in the same class as all the others; *other* would set it apart.

The use of *any* with a superlative, e.g., "the biggest ears of any animal," bothers some critics, who would prefer "of *all animals.*" Others defend the expression as idiomatic and established. You may choose.

Any as an adjective has these meanings: one, of several, no matter which one ("Any brand will do"); some ("Have you any mangoes?"); even a bit of ("I don't have any wool left"); and every ("Any child knows that").

Any can be an adverb, meaning at all ("I can't make it any tighter"). When it does not precede a comparative adjective ("It can't hurt any"), it is regarded as informal.

Furthermore, *any* can be an indefinite pronoun ("I don't have any of those books"). As a pronoun, *any* may be construed either as singular, in the sense of *any one* ("*Is* any of these pictures to your liking?"); or as plural, in the sense of *some* ("*Are* any of them for sale?").

See also **Double negative; ONE as pronoun,** 3.

2. With BODY or ONE

Anybody and *anyone* have the same meaning. As a single word, each is a pronoun meaning *any person.* "Anybody [or "anyone"] can do it." / "Does anyone [or "anybody"] have a knife?" The choice depends on personal preference. If rhythm or conciseness matters, the additional syllable and letter in *anybody* can make a difference. In the pronunciation of either word, the first syllable is stressed.

Occasionally the adjective *any* is separate from the noun, *body* or *one*.

Any and *body* are kept separate when both words are important and both are stressed when spoken, as in mentions of *any* (human) *body* or *any body* of water.

Any and *one* are kept separate when the meaning is any single thing or person and both words are stressed when spoken: "Pick any one." / "Any one of them can do the job alone."

Some critics consider it unreasonable to combine a superlative with *anyone* in an expression of this order: "He is the smartest person of anyone I know." They would replace *anyone* with *all* or omit "of anyone." Others consider the combination a time-honored idiom. It is your decision.

See also ONE as pronoun, *3*; Pronouns, *2C*.

3. With MORE

The writers of these sentences wrongly connected *any* and *more*:

"If I never get anymore, I'm happy," she says, explaining her fear of becoming an obsessed collector.

. . . Travis said, "Come ON, Dad, we're not gonna see anymore trees, are we?"

You cannot go wrong keeping *any* and *more* separate. Some authorities insist on *any more* in all uses.

When *any more* means an indefinite additional amount, degree, or number (serving as an adjective)—the meaning in the sentences above—its words must be kept separate.

When it concerns time (serving as an adverb)—when it suggests from now on, since a certain time, or now—it is either *anymore* or *any more*. Then it goes in a more or less negative statement ("He promised not to do it *anymore*" or "*any more*" / "I hardly go there *anymore*" or

"*any more*") or a question ("Do you visit her *anymore?*" or "*any more?*"). And note that it always ends a thought.

In some regions "any more" is used colloquially in positive statements as a synonym for *now*. An example comes from a radio talk show, whose host asked, "Has the ——— Church gotten so out of touch with reality that it's just a big joke any more?" Sometimes it even starts a sentence: "Any more we don't see them." Such uses are not standard.

4. With PLACE

An architectural critic was quoted as saying, "I'd never seen anyplace so beautiful" (as San Francisco in the forties). It should be: "I'd never seen *any place* so beautiful." (*Any* serves as an adjective, *place* as a noun.)

As one word, *anyplace* (adverb) means at, in, or to any place. It shares that meaning with *anywhere*, although *anyplace* is more informal. Some authorities scorn *anyplace* or *any place* used as an adverb.

Insofar as *anyplace* is acceptable, it is interchangeable with *anywhere*, as in the sentence "I'll go anyplace for a good job." You cannot substitute *anywhere* for "anyplace" in the opening quotation.

5. With TIME

Any time is preferably used as two words. The one-word form has not gained general acceptance. A critic writes, "The one-word *anytime* is nonexistent in the English language"; yet dictionaries list it: "*adv.* at any time." Britain does not use *anytime*.

Street signs say, "No Parking Anytime." Telephone books say, "You can call it [an information line] anytime." Those uses can pass; but *any time* or, strictly, *at any time* is better, allowing *time* due emphasis. As a rule, *anytime* is tolerable when *at any time* can be substituted.

The words unquestionably must be kept detached in this sentence: "I can't find any time for my hobby nowadays." There *any* serves as an adjective; *time* is the noun that it modifies. The single word must be an adverb.

6. With WAY

As a word (adverb) *anyway* means nevertheless or in any event. "Aware of the risks, they embarked on the expedition anyway." / "He probably didn't do it, and anyway there's no law against it." As a phrase (adjective and noun), *any way* means in some manner, no matter which. "Make the repair any way you can." (Some dictionaries confusedly give such a definition for the single word.)

Anyway should have no *s* attached. "Anyways" is substandard.

APE and MONKEY.
When a movie character calls a chimpanzee "bad monkey!" and a pair of movie reviewers repeatedly refer to it as a "monkey," someone ought to speak up for the degraded creature.

Let it be said here that a chimpanzee is not a "monkey." It is an *ape,* one of the *great apes* at that. *Apes* do not have tails; *monkeys* do. *Apes* have more complex brains and can stand and walk nearly upright. They are our closest relatives in the animal kingdom.

Other *great apes* (family *Pongidae*) are the bonobo, gorilla, and orangutan. The gibbon and siamang are *lesser* (smaller) *apes* (family *Hylobaeidae*). The so-called Celebes black ape and Barbary ape (of Gibraltar) are really macaque *monkeys,* misnamed in the belief that they lacked tails; their tails are tiny.

Both *ape* and *monkey* belong to the order *Primates;* so do the lemur and man. The designation of all nonhuman *primates* as "monkeys" is a hoary colloquialism; note the sobriquet of the Scopes ("Monkey") Trial of 1925.

See also **PRIMATES.**

Apophasis. *See* **Verbal unmentionables.**

Apostrophe. *See* **Punctuation,** *1.*

APPARENT, APPARENTLY.
Apparent (adjective) has two nearly contradictory meanings. It can mean open to view ("The damage to the building was immediately apparent") or obvious ("It is apparent from these figures that our financial situation is perilous"). The word can also mean seeming, based on appearance but not necessarily so. ("The apparent art treasure has turned out to be a fake.")

Dictionary definitions of *apparently* (adverb) include plainly or obviously, but now its most common meaning is seemingly. ("The magician apparently sawed a woman in half.")

News media use *apparent* or *apparently* often. Its purpose is not always apparent. This is from a nine-sentence news story:

> Two men were apparently killed in separate shooting incidents, one occurring Tuesday night and the other Wednesday morning. . . . A driver had apparently lost control and crashed his vehicle. . . . Police are investigating the apparent homicide.

"Apparently killed" is absurd. If the "apparently" was meant to apply to something else ("separate" or "shooting"?), it was misplaced. (Incidentally, "one occurring" and "the other" are unnecessary.) The other "apparently" and "apparent" are acceptable.

"Apparently" was misplaced and misleading in another story:

> Tenant power apparently defeated Proposition E, which would have lifted rent controls. . . .

"Apparently defeated" implies doubt that the proposition was defeated. Perhaps this was meant: "What appeared to be tenant power defeated Proposition E. . . ."

A police chief and a victim of a purse snatcher both died "of an apparent heart attack." Such journalistic use of the word has been called ambiguous. It could signify that the diagnosis was obvious; that the fatal ailment merely gave the appearance of being a heart attack; or that a heart attack was *evidently*, *probably*, or *possibly* the cause of death.

Evident or *evidently* applies to that which facts point to. It stresses evidence, whereas *apparent* or *apparently* stresses appearances. *Probable* or *probably* applies to that which is likely to be true; *possible* or *possibly*, to that which may or may not be true.

A news service reported that William Colby, a former CIA director, was "missing and presumed drowned in an apparent boating accident" in Maryland. That he had gone canoeing on a river would have been a more accurate detail than a conjecture about an accident, even though qualified by "apparent." After the body was found, a medical examiner determined that Colby had drowned following a heart attack.

APPENDIX. *See* **Plurals and singulars.**

Apposition, appositive. *See* **Nouns, *1;* OR.**

APPRAISE and APPRISE. To *appraise* is to evaluate or estimate as to worth or quality. "The house was appraised at a million dollars."

To *apprise* is to inform or notify. Often *of* follows. "We must apprise the president of this news."

A woman said in a television interview about her divorce, "I was not appraised that our marriage was having some rocky points." A man calling a radio advice program said, "He was dying and I never was appraised of this." The word needed in each instance was *apprised*.

APT. *See* **LIABLE.**

"AREN'T I?" This expression enters casual remarks and profound writings alike: ". . . Porter said with a grin, 'I guess I am a little detail-oriented, aren't I?' " / "Aren't I equally determined by the grand unified theory?"

Many people who never would say "ain't I?" are drawn to "aren't I?" To point up the absurd character of that genteelism, let us turn the phrase around, making a declarative sentence out of it: "I aren't." Or let us expand the contraction: "Are I not?" In the declarative form: "I are not." In short, *I* and *are* do not mix.

Until the widely maligned "ain't" acquires respectability or *amn't* (a contraction of *am not*, used colloquially in Scotland and Ireland) gains general acceptance, our best recourse may be the phrase *am I not?*—and what is wrong with that?

"I guess I am a little detail-oriented, *am I not?*"

"*Am I not* equally determined by the grand unified theory?"

See also **"AIN'T."**

ARGUE. *See* **ADVOCATE.**

AROMA. An editorial complains about panhandlers at rail stations: Some obstruct the passageways; others are aggressive. "And sometimes in the halls and entrances there is the aroma of human waste."

"Aroma" does not describe what the writer is talking about. An *aroma* is a good smell. It may be spicy or pungent, but it is never bad.

Any of four other words could have been chosen: *Smell* and *odor* can be good or bad or neither. *Stink* and *stench* emphasize badness, just as *fragrance* and *aroma* emphasize goodness. *Scent* suggests an identifying and usually delicate emanation.

We have discussed seven nouns. Adjectives are related to five of them: *Aromatic* and *fragrant* refer to pleasant-smelling odors. *Odorous* usually is unpleasant; *smelly* and *stinking* always are.

AROUND. *See* **ESTIMATE, ESTIMATED.**

ARRANT and ERRANT. *See* **Confusing pairs.**

ARREST WARRANT. *See* **WARRANT.**

Articles (parts of speech). *See* **A and AN; THE.**

AS. *1. Ambiguity. 2. Excessive use. 3. Lack of a pair. 4. With NOT. 5. With WELL.*

1. Ambiguity

The little word *as* can cause a great deal of confusion. It starts many an unclear phrase, an example of which appears in the sentence below. By trying to jam a bunch of different ideas into one sentence, the writer may have saved some space but lost his readers.

> While Wan is not seriously ill and cut short a U.S. trip for political and not medical reasons, as was stated last week, he too is said to be receiving medical treatment, for a heart condition.

We are forced into a guessing game. What "was stated": (1) everything before "as," (2) that Wan "cut short a U.S. trip for political and not medical reasons," or (3) "medical reasons"? (The third choice seems the most plausible, but "medical reasons" and "was stated" do not go together.) And who "stated" it: (1) someone in a foreign government, (2) the writer, or (3) somebody else?

The best repair for such a defective sentence is rewriting. Put each idea into a separate sentence. A possible revision follows. (We are guessing what the facts are.)

> Wan too is said to be receiving medical treatment, for a heart condition. Last week a spokesman in the Chinese government stated that Wan had cut short a U.S. trip for medical reasons. Actually the reasons were political. Wan is not seriously ill.

"As was," seen in the initial sample, is a form that looks artificial and invites ambiguity. So is any phrase combining *as* and a misplaced verb, like "as are" or "as did." A news story described a program drafted by an African political party.

> It refers to the party as the vanguard "of the Mozambique people" rather than "the worker-peasant alliance" as did the program approved at the previous party congress.

The previous program "did" what? "Did" does not hook up with any verb. Perhaps the writer was trying to reuse "refers," but "did refers" would not be grammatical." Here is first-aid: ". . . as the program approved at the previous party congress *referred to it*." That would still leave a double use of "as" and a complex sentence. Again we turn to the two-sentence solution. The quoted sentence could end with "people." A second sentence could read as follows:

> The program approved at the previous party congress called Frelimo [the party's short name] "the worker-peasant alliance."

It can be uncertain whether *as* is intended to mean *because* or *at the same time that*: "As the rain began falling, I went inside." Rephrasing is needed, e.g.,

"The rain began falling, so I went inside" (cause); or "I went inside just as the rain began falling" (time).

(*As* is used as a conjunction in the examples above. It is also classified as an adverb, pronoun, and preposition.)

2. Excessive use

A mere two letters long, *as* is a workhorse in the press. In journalese it is a favorite conjunction for stringing together ideas, related or unrelated. Newspaper writers do not restrict themselves to just one *as* per sentence:

The assessment was borne out by youthful protesters today as they surveyed wrecked banks as plumes of cobalt-blue tear-gas smoke rose in the narrow streets.

Why does everything need to be packed into one sentence? Try chopping the sentence in two.

The assessment was borne out by youthful protesters today. They surveyed wrecked banks as. . . .

The message becomes less unwieldy. (Let us pretend that we know what "The assessment" is.)

3. Lack of a pair

One *as* is usually not enough when a sentence likens two things in a simile or contrasts them in a comparison. Idiom calls for an *as . . . as* pair: "as happy as a lark" or "twice as high as last year's price."

A television newscaster told what researchers knew about left-handedness:

They do know that men are three times as likely to be left-handers than women.

"As . . . than" is wrong. A correction: ". . . men are three times as likely as women to be left-handers." It replaces

"than" with *as* and moves those being compared closer together.

Several words must sometimes separate the first *as* and the second. This is from another TV program:

Costs of health plans are climbing nearly twice as much at midsized companies than at larger companies.

Change "than" to *as*. (The sentence needs more fixing. Just what it means to climb twice as "much" is unclear. *Fast* or *high,* depending on the facts, would be clearer.) *See also* **THAN**, 2A.

Another problem is the faulty "as . . . or . . . than" construction. It is illustrated by a business executive's remark that the decisions made by workers can be "as good or better than" the decisions made by management. The necessary second *as* is missing: "as good *as* or better than. . . ." It may be clearer to put the *or* phrase at the end of the sentence: "as good *as* the decisions made by management, *or better.*" Another possible correction: "at least as good *as*. . . ." Similarly, a history book says:

The new law would permit the company to send its tea directly to America from India, and sell it at a tax of but three cents a pound, making this American potable as cheap, or cheaper, than smuggled tea.

The sentence can be fixed in either of two ways: (1) "as cheap *as* smuggled tea or cheaper"; (2) "as cheap *as* or cheaper than smuggled tea." (All of the commas except the second one are unnecessary. Commas are acceptable in this way: "as cheap *as,* or cheaper than, smuggled tea.")

The examples above each lacked the second *as* of the *as . . . as* pair. In the example below, the first *as* is missing.

It may be hard to imagine Walken—often as not a slick villain in his movie roles—tromping around in farmer's boots and overalls.

Change the phrase in dashes to "*as* often as not. . . ." The sentence appeared in a newspaper's television review. Was the omission of a two-letter word meant to save space? Plenty of it remained at the end of the paragraph.

Sometimes the *as . . . as* pattern is copied when it is not needed: "As hot as it was, I shivered." The opening "As" is unnecessary (and archaic). There is no simile or comparison here. The second *as* means *though*.

"As best as" is not a legitimate form. *See* **AS BEST**.

A personal pronoun following *as . . . as* can be subjective or objective: "He is as big as *I*" (that is, as big as I *am*). But "They pay Sam as much as *me*" (that is, as much as *they pay* me). *See also* **Pronouns**, *10E*.

A sentence may need only a single *as* if one of the two things being compared came up in a previous sentence. "It sells for $1,500. The competing product is twice as expensive" or "just as expensive." *Just as* appears to be the model for redundancies in the press like "equally as speedy." *Equally speedy* would be correct.

4. With NOT

In a negative comparison, switching to *so . . . as* is an option. You can say either "Charles is not *as* tall as his sister" or "Charles is not *so* tall as his sister." A few grammarians prefer the latter form.

A construction that can be confusing goes as follows: "The line-item veto is not an economy device, as a number of reformers think." Do they think it *is* or it *is not?* Literally the sentence is expressing the negative, but that may not be the intended meaning. Similarly, a lexicographer writes:

. . . Orm had not used *unntill* (as the editors of the work and of the *OED*

believed) but its northern variant *inntill*. . . .

Literally the parenthetical clause says the editors believed the negative, although the context suggests the reverse. A clearer wording would be "the editors . . . believed that he had done so."

(What follows "but" does not make grammatical sense. Either add a verb, e.g., "but *had used* its northern variant," or place "not" after "used." *See* **BUT**, *6*.)

This was stated in a news broadcast on a radio network:

The VA considers alcoholism willful misconduct, not a disease, as most of the medical profession does.

"Does" ties in with nothing; but since the only other verb in the sentence is "considers," the second clause seems to say that most of the medical profession also considers alcoholism willful misconduct. An opposite message may have been intended, although there was no explanation. Whatever the message was should have been in a separate sentence.

5. With WELL

The phrase *as well as* has primarily meant *and not only*. Though forced to bear the extra sense of *and in addition*, it has not fully adapted itself to that role. Classified as a conjunction, it is considerably weaker than the conjunction *and*.

This is an example of its distinctive use: "Gertrude, as well as I, is going to the meeting" (not "are" going or "am" going). The number of the verb remains singular, and the person of the verb conforms to the main subject. *As well as* implies the addition of a new fact (that Gertrude is going) to a fact already known (that I am going).

A dictionary's sole example is "skillful *as well as* strong," which illustrates the newer use, that of simple addition.

The phrase becomes merely a drawn-out replacement for *and*. Sometimes one cannot tell which meaning was intended.

When *as well as* is put between two verbs, the verb form is the same. In this sentence, from a biography, one word could well be changed:

> In the three days they covered at least fifty miles as well as climbing two mountains of around 3000 feet.

To match *covered*, change "climbing" to *climbed*. *Besides* would go with *climbing*.

The grammarian H. W. Fowler took it on himself to "come to the rescue of the phrase *as well as* [a conjunction] . . . being cruelly treated" like the preposition *besides*. Among examples: "His death leaves a gap as well as creating a by-election in Ross"—make "creating" *creates*, or replace "as well as" with *besides*. "You were there as well as me"—make "me" *I*.

Both should not go with *as well as*. See **BOTH**, 2.

As well, without the second *as*, can mean *in addition* ("He wins the money and a car as well") or *with similar effect* ("We might as well give up"). It should not open a sentence, as it did on the radio: "As well we've got another [road] closure." Although unnecessary, "as well" would have been more idiomatic at the end of the sentence.

AS and LIKE. *1. Confusion. 2. Incomparability.*

1. Confusion

Like is proper in this sentence: "Sometimes I feel like a motherless child." Or this one: "He looks like you." It conforms to the rule: *Like* (a preposition) may be followed by a noun or pronoun that is not allied to a verb. *As* (a conjunction) introduces a clause, a group of words with a subject and verb.

Like is not acceptable in these sentences, from radio and daily press:

> Tonight it will cool off, like it always does.

> Like they did last week before the Assembly Judiciary Committee, judges were expected yesterday to ask for a delay in legislative action.

> . . . He looked like he had put on some of the weight he had lost.

In the first and second of the three samples, change "like" to *as*. In the third, change "like" to *as if* or *as though*.

The "like"—after "likes"—looks even worse in the sample below, from a book. Change "like" to *as*.

> At other times, he likes to produce spectacular effects, like when he puts an imposing beret made of crumpled paper onto his picture of *The Student with a Pipe*. . . .

Sometimes when *like* is needed, people who have become afraid of it substitute "as." Comprehension can suffer: "Harold, as his brother, appeared in a movie." If the message is that both were in movies, not that Harold portrayed his brother, change "as" to *like*.

One may reasonably take issue with the rule, on grounds of literary history. Shakespeare and other celebrated, long-gone writers did not avoid *like* with verb. Nor do most people in colloquial speech. Some authorities defend such usage. But after generations of insistence by grammarians, editors, and teachers, a writer or careful speaker today emulates Shakespeare et al. at the risk of having his literacy questioned.

2. Incomparability

Simply following the rule will not rescue an error in logic. When you liken one thing to another, they must be comparable. This sentence is defective:

> Like the days before interstate travel . . . Albuquerqueans are using Albuquerque's main street.

The writer seems to be likening a time to what people are doing, but the two concepts are incomparable. Change "Like" to *As they were doing in.*
See also **LIKE**, 2; **UNLIKE**, 2.

AS BEST.
"As best as could be determined, no dailies failed to print . . ." (from a report on a flood, in a magazine for the newspaper industry).

"As best as" should be removed from one's vocabulary. No superlative, such as *best, longest, happiest,* or *bravest,* belongs in the *as . . . as* form. A phrase like "as brave as a lion" expresses the degree of a quality, but a superlative per se expresses that; the degree is the highest. No one would say, "He was as bravest as a lion."

The sample could well begin "*As far as*" (and, to be still more idiomatic, "*it* could be determined" or "*anyone* could *determine* . . .").

The error typically appears in this form: "She painted as best as she could." It can be corrected in any of three ways: (1) change "best" to *well;* (2) change "as best as" to *the best;* "She painted the best she could"; (3) omit the second "as": "She painted as best she could." The single *as* there means *in the manner that* (she could paint best).

See also **AS**, 3; **BETTER and BEST** (etc.); **Comparative and superlative degrees.**

"AS EVERYONE KNOWS" or "AS IS WELL KNOWN." See OF COURSE, 3.

AS FAR AS. See FAR.

AS MUCH AS. See Numbers, 2 (end).

ASPIC. See JELL-O.

ASSAULT. See Crimes, 1.

ASSISTANT.
The abbreviation of *assistant* is *asst.* Do not omit the *t* and the period, as a television station did. In a report on a fire, the station interviewed an assistant fire chief, identifying him with a caption on the bottom of the screen that placed the title of "Ass Chief" before his name.

ASSURE, ENSURE, and INSURE.
1. *The differences.* 2. *More about AS-SURE.*

1. The differences
To *assure* is to make (someone) sure of something, to give confidence, or to promise confidently. Usually the word is directed at people, not things; and it implies the use mainly of words, not deeds, to set one's mind at rest. "We assured them of our support for this worthy cause."

To *insure* is to make (something) sure or certain, to guarantee, to make safe or secure, to protect (against), or to agree to pay money in the event of loss. Usually this word is directed at things, not people; and it implies deeds, rather than mere words, to make something certain or secure. "We must observe our budget strictly to insure that we stay solvent."

Except in the sense of indemnify, when *insure* is the only verb to use ("The company insures my property against fire" or, intransitively, "The company insures against fire"), *ensure* has the same meaning as *insure* and usually is pronounced the same (in-SURE). The spelling of *ensure* is less common. The British prefer *ensure* in every sense except the financial, but almost no American authorities insist on such discrimination.

The related nouns are *assurance* and *insurance.* Again, it is a matter of words and deeds. "You have our assurance that the product is safe." / "The scrupulous testing we do is the best insurance of our product's safety."

Life assurance is a term traditionally used by British insurance companies. *Life insurance* is the American term, notwithstanding the Equitable Life Assurance Society of the United States, whose archaic name insures its distinction.

2. *More about ASSURE*

You *assure* a person or a group. (*Assure* is a transitive verb). You do not just "assure" in general, contrary to the belief of a reporter. This statement is both unidiomatic and misleading: "The President had assured the troops would not be sent into the city." At first it looks as though he "assured the troops" of something. The sentence should have read something like this: "The President had assured *the senator that* the troops would. . . ." (The journalistic avoidance of *that* contributed to the trouble. *See* THAT, *1, 2.*)

AS TO. *See* IN TERMS OF, *1;* TO, *1.*

AS WELL AS. *See* AS, *5.*

ATE and EATEN. *See* Tense, *5A.*

ATOMIC. *See* NUCLEAR.

ATTENDANCE. *See* IN ATTENDANCE.

"AT THIS POINT IN TIME."

The televised hearings in the Watergate scandal of the seventies popularized a wordy and roundabout adverbial phrase. More than twenty years later, a spokesman for major league baseball said, upon announcing a concession to end a strike, "We are happy to have this done at this point in time." And a motor vehicles dealer said, in commenting on the settlement of a trade dispute with Japan, "At this point in time we've all got a lot more cars than we need."

Before Watergate, they might have used *at this time* or *at this point* or, if inclined toward plainer talk, *now* or *right now* or no adverb at all. Just leaving out "at this point in time" would give such messages more punch and not impair them any. Obviously the time is the present.

A variation came from an ex-congressman: "I think at that point in time that I admitted I broke the House rules." *At that time* or simply *then* would be a good replacement. (The second "that" would make more sense after "think" but could be omitted.)

ATTORNEY and LAWYER. "The parents' lawyer, . . . a Corte Madera attorney who specializes in suits against school districts said. . . ." The writer has reversed the two terms. The sentence ought to read, "The parents' attorney, . . . a Corte Madera lawyer who. . . ."

Attorney often serves as a pompous synonym for *lawyer.* In its narrower sense, however, *attorney* means a person who has been appointed or empowered to act for another in a legal or business matter. One who acts as an *attorney* is usually—but not necessarily—a *lawyer.* A *lawyer* is a person whose profession is the practice of law. Smith, a *lawyer,* is Brown's *attorney.* Brown, a *layman,* is Smith's *client.* Each is an *attorney* or a *client* in relation to the other person. *Lawyer* may be used in the more specific sense too: Smith is Brown's *lawyer.*

A lawyer in a trial is often spoken of as *counsel.* "In all criminal prosecutions, the accused shall enjoy the right . . . to have the assistance of counsel for his defense" (Sixth Amendment, U.S. Constitution). *Counsel* can be singular or plural. The judge in a trial often addresses a lawyer as *counselor.*

See also Titles, *3.*

Attributive adjective. *See* **Adjectives and adverbs,** *2.*

Auxiliary verbs (helping verbs). *See* Adjectives and adverbs, *2;* Infinitive, *4* (end); Verbs, *1, 4.*

AVENGE and REVENGE. *See* Confusing pairs.

AVERAGE. *See* Collective nouns, *2;* LIFE EXPECTANCY (etc.); MEAN (noun); Numbers, *10E;* PER CAPITA.

AVERSE and ADVERSE. *See* Confusing pairs.

AVOID and EVADE. *See* Confusing pairs.

AWAKE, AWAKEN. *See* WAKE, AWAKE (etc.).

AWARD. Organizations and governments *award* people honors and money. That is, they give them things as a result of judgment. An *award* (noun) is that which one is *awarded* (verb).

A transit district's newsletter reported that a committee had "awarded four bus operators . . . with plaques recognizing their excellent aid to seniors and disabled passengers." Omit "with." The committee *awarded* the operators plaques. One could say instead that it *presented* the operators *with* plaques or that it *honored* them *with* plaques. It is simply a matter of idiom.

AWAY and AWEIGH. *See* Homophones.

A WHILE and AWHILE. Some have the notion that whenever they find the words *a* and *while* next to each other, they must stick them together as one word, regardless of meaning. Not so.

Awhile means *for a period of time.* It is an adverb, not what the four samples below need. Each should have been given the indefinite article *a* with the noun *while,* meaning *a period of time.* (Three

are from daily newspapers; the fourth is from an annual book for writers.)

> It was awhile before Mr. Pietsch, who is from Ohio, the son of a minister, entirely recovered his sense of humor.

> "After awhile it becomes easy to know things. . . ."

> Once in Awhile, First Time Can Be a Charm

> For most writers it takes awhile to get the knack.

Change each "awhile" to *a while.* For example, let us correct the first sentence: "It was *a while* before Mr. Pietsch entirely recovered his sense of humor." (What does his Ohio origin or his kinship to a minister have to do with his sense of humor? *See* Modifiers, *2.*)

Never write "for awhile." *For* is part of the meaning of *awhile.* Each of the following three samples contains that error. *Awhile* can stay in each, but not preceded by "for." (They are by a columnist, a news service, and a history book respectively.)

> Koppel let it slide for awhile, but finally he whacked Bush with it.

> "So she played the slot machines for awhile, then got a bite to eat."

> In Virginia the assembly actually gained the upper hand for awhile.

Omit each "for": e.g., "let it slide awhile." As an alternative, keep the "for" but sever *a* and *while:* "let it slide for *a while.*" In the sample below (by another columnist) "awhile" cannot stay; make it "For *a while.* . . ."

> For awhile, victory would seem within his grasp.

A while is not often used adverbially, in the manner of the final sample (from another book for writers). Using it that way is acceptable to some authorities but not to others.

Every agent who's been in business a while has been contacted by writers unhappy with their present agents.

Either *awhile* or *for a while* would be unquestionably correct.

B

BACHELOR and SPINSTER. A movie review said, "William Hurt plays Graham Holt, a male spinster who shocks neighbors when he decides to adopt a 10-year-old."

"Male spinster" is as contradictory as "female bachelor." A *spinster* is a female by definition: She is a woman beyond the usual age for marrying who has not been married. (In some contexts, like British law, *age* is not relevant. Neither is sex on rare occasions: in a primordial use of *spinster* as a professional spinner of fiber.)

The actor described in the movie review plays a *bachelor*. Numerous dictionaries define *bachelor* as "an unmarried man." That definition is incomplete. The word often implies that the man (1) is of the usual age for marrying, or beyond, and (2) has never been married. At least two dictionaries recognize *bachelorette* and the synonymous *bachelor girl*. Of course a college graduate of either sex may be a *bachelor* of arts, science, or some special field. But only a male can be a plain *bachelor*.

One who is unmarried as a result of divorce is a *divorcée* (woman) or *divorcé* (man), pronounced dih-vaur-SAY either way. A divorced person, without regard to sex, is a *divorcee*, pronounced dih-vaur-SEE. One who has been bereaved of a spouse and who has not remarried is either a *widow* (woman) or a *widower* (man). Any unmarried status is com-

monly called *single*, although the Bureau of the Census has long defined *single* as "never married."

BACK(-) prefix and pairs. A news article described a drug trial in Florida and added, "Locally it took a backseat to news of the crack cocaine epidemic in Jacksonville. . . ." When used as a noun, the term *back seat* consists of two words: "Locally it took a back seat . . ." or "The passenger sat in the back seat." The two words are hyphenated when used as an adjective, usually in *back-seat driver*. (The article's joining of the phrase contradicted the newspaper's own style rule.)

The same goes for *back room*: two words as a noun ("Come into the *back room*"), hyphenation as an adjective ("It was a *back-room* deal"). It has to do with pronunciation. Unifying the words would indicate that the first syllable should be stressed. Actually, each syllable gets about equal stress in *back seat*, and the same is true for *back room*. It is also true for the two-word nouns *back road* and *back yard*. The latter is often spelled "backyard," although the noun *front yard* is always two words. The Associated Press understandably calls for *back yard* as a noun, *backyard* as an adjective. In a phrase like *backyard barbecue*, the stress shifts to the first syllable.

As nouns, *back door* and *back stairs*

give the syllables about equal stress. As adjectives, when each initial syllable is stressed, they become single words: *backdoor, backstairs.* Both adjectives can mean secret or underhanded, in addition to their literal meanings. The latter has an alternate form: *backstair.*

These twenty nouns are all single words, stressing the first syllable: *backache, backboard, backbone, backcourt, backdrop, backfield, backfire, background, backhand, backlash, backlog, backpack, backrest, backside, backspace, backspin, backstop, backstroke, backwash, backwater.*

Backstretch and *backwoods,* which stress the syllables about equally, are anomalies.

Generally either *backward* or *backwards* may be used as an adverb ("The car went backward[s]"), though some press organizations avoid the latter. Only *backward* serves as an adjective ("a backward glance").

BACK (time). *See* FORWARD and BACK (time).

Backward writing. *1. Looking-glass syndrome. 2. Some causes and cures. 3. "Upcoming": Germanisms.*

1. Looking-glass syndrome
Backward run often sentences. Turvy topsy turned are idioms. Reversed are phrases. Journalese is it.

The compulsion to write backward is not known to reach such an extreme, except in Lewis Carroll's *Through the Looking Glass,* but newspapers from coast to coast are replete with sentences like these:

Suspected are cadmium, nickel, copper, mercury and hydrocarbons.

Affected were eggs, vegetables, sugar and pork—the staple meat in the Chinese diet.

Trying for a comeback is Maurice Ferre, a polished Puerto Rican businessman who was Mayor for six consecutive terms. . . .

Fishing for trout with Baker during the week of the July 18 Democratic conclave in Atlanta will be veteran California political consultant Stu Spencer . . . and Rep. Richard Cheney of Wyoming.

The normal sequence of a declarative sentence is (1) subject, or noun, and (2) predicate, or verb. All of the samples above reverse the normal sequence.

Inversions, as they are called, are necessary in questions ("Where am I?"). They suit the Bible ("Blessed are the meek"), poetry ("While follow eyes the steady keel"), and old-style prose ("To the victors belong the spoils"). They are found in exclamations ("How forceful are honest words!"), commands ("Get thee to a nunnery"), and hypothetical clauses ("Had I only known"). An inversion can provide a transition between thoughts ("Next comes the matter of finances"), emphasize a negative idea ("Never . . . was so much owed by so many to so few"), and set a scene ("In a village of La Mancha . . . there lived . . .").

Reasonable inversions of other types appear now and then, formed with style, in idiomatic English. The idiom sampled earlier is quintessential journalese. Not only does the sentence structure appear awkward and depart from the standard manner of speech, but also it may shift the emphasis away from that which is most important. In the fourth example, is "Fishing for trout" more significant than the meeting of three politicos?

Often the first part of a sentence is a normal quotation, direct or indirect, but the attribution that follows is inverted: ". . . charges a supervisor" / ". . . pointed out Eve" / ". . . explains Bunny." The people are not being charged, pointed out, or explained; they are performing the actions. Simple, unambiguous phrases like "said Tom" or "replied Mrs. Green" are tolerable when not overused.

2. *Some causes and cures*

The persistence and ubiquity of inverted writing may have several causes: perhaps widespread imitation of a *Time* magazine idiosyncrasy, perhaps a belief that distorting sentences helps to make writing readable. Another explanation is that journalists often see the distorting as the solution to a problem:

In a typical case, a reporter has the names and individual details of people caught in a police raid. His problem is to put them in a coherent sentence. Rather than start with a tedious list and end with the words "were booked," he begins with "Booked were" and then gives the list. But he could start with a phrase like *Those booked were* and not have to contort the sentence at all.

Our first two examples can be repaired easily by preceding "Suspected are" and "Affected were" with short phrases: "*The chemicals* suspected [of toxicity] are cadmium, nickel, copper, mercury and hydrocarbons" and "*The foods* affected [by price rises] were eggs, vegetables, sugar and pork. . . ."

An effort to crowd too much into one sentence is often a factor. Our third quotation in section *1* is brief but abridged; the sentence in the newspaper was fifty words long. Instead of putting forty-five words ahead of "is trying for a comeback," the reporter wrote: "Trying for a comeback is Maurice Ferre, a polished Puerto Rican businessman who. . . ." A better course would be to turn that inverted structure right-side up and add a sentence: "Former Mayor Maurice Ferre is trying for a comeback. He is a polished Puerto Rican businessman who. . . ."

In an article about attitudes toward divorce, a paragraph begins this way:

"Comments Marion Solomon, a Westwood therapist and author of. . . ." The title and subtitle of her book and the name of its publisher intervene before we get to read her comment. The reporter could have written something like "Marion Solomon, therapist and author, comments: . . ." and postponed the details.

3. *"Upcoming": Germanisms*

Sometimes a simple phrase containing a verb and an adverb is twisted around, joined together, and used in a manner that is more Germanic than English. Examples are "ongoing" and "upcoming" used as verbs in place of *going on* and *coming up. See* ONGOING; OUTPUT; PLAY DOWN and DOWNPLAY; UPCOMING.

See also "PROOF POSITIVE"—not Germanic but an expression that reverses the normal positions of adjective and noun.

BACTERIA and BACTERIUM.

Bacteria is a plural word, denoting two or more of the microscopic, single-celled organisms that cause disease, putrefaction, and fermentation. In speaking of just one specimen of those organisms, that is, one cell, use *bacterium,* the singular. It is New Latin, from the Greek *bakterion,* small stick.

The excerpts are from a television feature, an article by a news agency, and a statement by a biologist, respectively.

One resistant bacteria can become sixteen million in twenty-four hours.

It should start: "One resistant *bacterium.*"

. . . Any method that sets the white and causes the yolk to begin to congeal will kill the bacteria unless it's present in high numbers.

"It's" should be *they're* or *they are.*

For this bacteria . . . there's practically no effect on any of them.

"For *these* bacteria . . ."

We may also speak of a single *strain* (or *form* or *colony*) *of bacteria:* "A new strain of bacteria has caused the outbreak of influenza."

BAD and BADLY. A local reporter and a Senate leader made essentially the same mistake on television. The first was following up a crime; the second was describing reaction to a change in the president's budget policy:

> Merchants and residents feel badly about what happened.

> Some Democrats who want to play politics and not address the issues feel badly.

Change "badly" to *bad*. One who is ill or unhappy feels *bad*, not "badly." And people, or things, may look *bad*, not "badly." *Feel* or *look* (a linking verb) links the person or persons (the subject) to *bad* (adjective) and is not modified by it. Similarly, one feels *sad*, not "*sadly*."

Theoretically someone could feel *badly* if he lost his sense of touch. Then *feel* (verb) would be modified by *badly* (adverb). This is more likely: "My foot hurts *badly*." *Badly*, this time meaning *intensely*, modifies *hurts* (verb). To say "My foot hurts bad" would be as ungrammatical as saying "I feel badly." Either remark would be enough to make a grammarian or English teacher feel bad.

See also FEEL.

BAIL and BALE. *See* Homophones.

BAN. *See* FORBID, PROHIBIT, and BAN.

BAND-AID. *Band-Aid* is a brand of adhesive bandage with gauze in the center, used for small wounds. Being a trademark, it should not be written in lower case, the way it appears in a book of English instruction for newcomers. In sample dialogue, a pharmacist asks a customer, "Do you need any band-aids?" Capital *B*, capital *A*. Competitors call their products *adhesive bandages*.

BASE and BASS. *See* Homophones.

BATHROOM. Calling a room with no facility for baths a "bathroom" is not a serious shortcoming. It is common in conversational speech, less so in the press:

> The mother of two young sons, she usually finds herself having to take them into the women's public bathroom while shopping.

> The east wing will be radically altered and will contain two movie theaters, . . . bathrooms and a coat check room, among other conveniences.

But *bathroom* is more specifically applied to the type of room that contains a bathtub or shower or both, a sink, and a toilet.

The public place that everyone seeks at some time is often called a *rest room* (although few go there to rest) or a *men's* or *ladies' room* (less often a *gentlemen's* or *women's room*). The *ladies' room* is also a *powder room*.

Even though frankness, if not vulgarity, generally abounds these days in the media of mass communication, Americans remain squeamish in referring to that type of room. Our standard terms are all euphemistic.

In American culture, unlike the convention in some other cultures, it is not considered refined to call the public room a "toilet." But it is proper to use *toilet* in speaking of the plumbing device as such. *Toilet* itself used to be a euphemism. It once meant *dressing table*.

Some use *lavatory*, literally a washing place. *Latrine* is a communal toilet place in a military type of setting. Each word traces to the Latin *lavare*, to wash (*latrine* via *lavatrina*, bath).

What soldiers call a *latrine*, sailors call a *head*. If the enclosure is a small, outdoor shack with no plumbing, it is an *outhouse* or *privy*. The *john* and the *can* are slang.

In Britain you can ask for the *w.c.*, the initials of *water closet*. An informal synonym there is the *loo*.

BAZAAR and BIZARRE.   *See* Homophones.

BE, AM, IS, ARE, WAS, WERE.
See Active voice and passive voice; "AIN'T"; "AREN'T I?"; Collective nouns; DUE TO; Pronouns, *10D*; Subjunctive; Verbs, *1, 3*; WAS and WERE; WHO, *3*.

BECAUSE.   *1. Ambiguity. 2. Incompatible pairs. 3. Who is talking?*

1. Ambiguity
Because needs to be handled with care in a sentence containing more than one idea. Take this sentence, from a newspaper:

> Only 20 percent of Californians would vote to re-elect Senator Alan Cranston because of his involvement in the Lincoln Savings and Loan scandal, a new California Poll shows.

It could be interpreted as saying that only 20 percent of Californians would vote for the senator "because of his involvement . . ." and that others would do so for other reasons. The context suggests that the sentence would be better recast in this way, separating two ideas:

> A new California Poll shows that only 20 percent of Californians would vote to re-elect Senator Alan Cranston

and that his support is so small because of his involvement in the Lincoln Savings and Loan scandal.

The word causes particular confusion after a negative clause.

> The witness said that the case was not brought before the committee because of the incident the night before.

Did the witness testify that as a result of "the incident" the case was not brought before the committee? Or did he deny that "the incident" caused the case to be brought before the committee? We do not know.

Another quotation illustrates the hazardous use of *because* after a negative and, secondarily, the ungainly use of *because* twice in one sentence. In a trade journal for the newspaper industry, an article tells of a British newspaper that increased its circulation by cutting its price. The writer comments:

> This cheers me up because it suggests that circulation is not declining because readers are morons who don't care.

By itself, the sentence is ambiguous. One could rationally interpret it in either of these ways:

1. The information suggests that circulation is not declining, the reason being that readers are morons, who don't care how bad their newspaper is. Thus I am cheered.
2. The information suggests this: The reason that circulation is declining is not that readers are morons, who fail to appreciate how good their newspaper is. I am cheered to know that it is another reason.

The context points to the second interpretation. (The message is that the industry has no control over the intellect of its readers, but it can control price, quality, and marketing.) Either way, the readers do not come out very well.

2. Incompatible pairs

Because is teamed up at times with the wrong partners. "The reason is because" is a redundant partnership. *See* REASON, *1*. "Why . . . because" is another.

"Why the alarm sounded was because a fire broke out on the ninth floor." Omit "why" and "was" ("The alarm sounded because a fire . . .") or change "because" to *that* ("Why the alarm sounded was *that* a fire . . ."). Otherwise it is like saying "The reason that . . . was for the reason that." *See also* REASON, *2*.

Because normally is a conjunction. It should not be used as though it were a noun, e.g., "Because he's the boss gives him the right to boss us around." These are incompatible: "because . . . gives." Change (1) "Because he's" to *Being,* or (2) "gives him" to *he has,* following a comma, or (3) "Because" to *That.*

3. Who is talking?

The lead paragraph of a newspaper article will follow. Not avowedly an editorial, it is identified as "**NEWS ANALYSIS.**"

ZAGREB, Crotia [sic]—In twice bombing Serbian positions around the Muslim enclave of Gorazde, the United States and its Western allies have wagered that force will bring the Serbs back to the negotiating table because force is the one thing Serbian soldiers in Bosnia understand.

It is not necessary to delve into the substance of the final clause, introduced by "because." Some readers will recognize it, recycled from past wars, hot and cold. The point is that the writer, whatever his intention, is expressing that opinion. It is attributed to no one, although later in the article he refers vaguely to "One American official" (the one who fed it to him?).

The conjunction *because* means *for the reason that,* not "on the supposed grounds that." Unless it is qualified—e.g., "because, in the words of one American official, who refused to be identified"—the writer or speaker is liable to be stuck with what follows.

BED as verb. *See* CHAIR, *2*.

BEFRIEND. From its looks, one might assume that the verb *befriend* means to be friendly with somebody. A book on advertising advises any reader who is confused about scheduling radio spots: "Call the media rep you befriended in Chapter Three." That chapter discusses dealings with radio salesmen.

To *befriend* is not merely to be friendly with someone or even to be someone's friend. It is to act as someone's friend in time of need. A family that takes in a war refugee is *befriending* the person.

BEGET. It is a poetic verb (transitive), literally meaning to be the father of. It can be used figuratively, meaning to cause something to exist, e.g., "Hunger begets crime." But do not forget the literal meaning, as a politician did when she wrote in an op-ed essay, "Teenage pregnancies beget teenage pregnancies. Welfare mothers beget welfare mothers."

The normal past tense of *beget* is *begot.* An archaic past tense, found in the Bible, is *begat.* A headline over a letter to the editor erroneously said, "Violence begats more violence." *Begets*—there is no "begats."

See also SIRE.

BEGIN, BEGAN, and BEGUN.
The past tense of the verb *begin,* to start, is *began:* "It began to rain." The past participle is *begun:* "Construction has begun."

A reputable newspaper used one for

the other: "The 'night float' began in most New York State hospitals as a grueling rite of passage ended." *Begun* would be right. (Commas or dashes should precede it and follow "passage" to set off the explanatory matter. By the way, "night float" was a thirty-six-hour shift for new doctors.)

BELLY. *See* STOMACH.

BEMUSE, BEMUSED. Some writers confuse "bemuse" with *amuse*. The meanings of the two words are not at all similar now, although they once were. The *-muse* part of each can be traced to the Medieval Latin word for snout, *musum*.

Bemuse (verb, transitive) means (1) to daze or muddle someone, or (2) to cause one to muse or be deep in thought. It may take the form of *bemused* (past tense and past participle) and *bemusing* (present participle). Examples: "He blamed the alcohol for bemusing his head." / "Bemused by his equations, the professor paid no heed to the bell."

Amuse (verb, transitive) now means to entertain or appeal to one's sense of humor. At one time it meant to beguile or bemuse.

An autobiography describes a general's reaction to a barroom brawl.

> Gunfighter must have noticed that several of his officers sported shiners, bruises, and puffed lips. He said nothing. But I detected on his seamed face a bemused smile.

Could it have been "an *amused* smile"?

Another book of recollections tells of a motor trip in Africa. To get fuel to cross the Sahara, the author willingly detoured for several days.

> I thought, bemused, of the times in my pre-Africa life I had fumed and ranted over late planes and traffic jams.

Was he really so deep in thought or just *amused* by the thought?

In a similar book, another author recalls a visit to an oil company's camp in the Sahara during a choking dust storm.

> The Europeans working there asked whether we would like showers and then some lunch. Such questions were almost bemusing after weeks in the desert.

Later he describes the privation after weeks of desert travel and adds:

> Then there is a town; and the abundance of everything is almost bemusing.

"Bemusing" fits neither context. *Amusing* fits each.

In the excerpt below, from a financial newspaper, the meaning is not clear.

> "You can't find anyone to bribe here," says a bemused American developer, Joseph T——, who is negotiating to build a hotel on the Red Sea and apartment blocks in Asmara.

The context gives no reason why the developer should be stupefied or engrossed. Was he amused, confused, surprised—or what?

BESIDE and BESIDES. *See* Confusing pairs.

BESIDES and AS WELL AS. *See* AS, 5.

BEST. *See* AS BEST; BETTER and BEST (etc.).

BETTER and BEST, WORSE and WORST. The rule is simple, though often disregarded in conversations and by ring announcers who say "May the best man win": When the merits of two things are compared, one thing is *better* and one is *worse* (unless they are equal in merit). Only when there are three or more items for comparison can one be the *best* and another the *worst*. Thus these sentences, uttered by a political candidate and by a senator (who used to be a journalist) are wrong:

Which of the two candidates for your nomination is best qualified to be president of the United States?

The policies of the president are the best of the two [sets of policies].

Correction: "is *better* qualified" / "are the *better* of the two."

See also **AS BEST; Comparative and superlative degrees.**

BETWEEN. 1. *AMONG and BE-TWEEN.* 2. *"BETWEEN EACH" or "EVERY."* 3. *"BETWEEN ... OR" or "TO."* 4. *"BETWEEN YOU AND I."*

1. *AMONG and BETWEEN*

In school many of us were taught to distinguish between the prepositions *between* and *among:* The former applies only to two things, the latter to more than two. That is so in a good many cases. "It was a conversation between Tom and Dick." / "The two talked only between themselves." But "It was a conversation among Tom, Dick, and Harry." Each converser addressed the other two. The Constitution authorizes Congress "To regulate commerce . . . among the several States. . . ."

The rule is too sweeping, however. There are exceptions, and our educators may have considered them too subtle for us. *Between* applies to three or more things when the relation is essentially between pairs. For instance: "Conferences are going on *between* Canada, Mexico, and the United States to consider future migration." That means three separate two-party conferences are taking place. But when "A conference is going on *among* Canada, Mexico, and the United States," all three are meeting together.

Similarly, one may have many pieces of cheese to sandwich *between* many slices of bread. The bread slices are considered as pairs. The same sandwich principle permits "He paused *between* sentences" and "Commercials are broadcast *between* innings." (But *see* 2, below.)

Between can refer to the combined possession of two people or other entities. "John and I had fifty dollars between us." Use *among* when speaking of three or more. A TV newscaster was talking about three baseball-playing brothers: "Between them the Alou brothers played forty-seven major-league seasons." Change "between" to *among.*

2. *"BETWEEN EACH" or "EVERY"*

Although it is fairly common in colloquial use to pair *between* with "each" or "every," it is absurd from a logical standpoint. That such a combination appears occasionally in serious literature does not make it any more sensible. Examples: "He paused between each sentence" and "Commercials are broadcast between every inning."

Something cannot be "between" one thing. *Between* generally applies to two, sometimes to more than two. *Each* and *every* are singular words, meaning one of a group considered individually. In the examples, change each "between" to *after;* or follow "each sentence" or "every inning" with *and the next;* or use plural forms (*see* 1, above).

3. *"BETWEEN ... OR" or "TO"*

When *between* is followed by two specified things, only *and* can connect them. Sometimes *between* is combined with "or," pitting a dual word and a singular word: "It's a choice between right or wrong." Right *and* wrong, or else *a choice of.* The words *choose, decide,* and *decision* also lead people astray.

From goes with *to,* just as *between*

goes with *and*. Sometimes those idioms are carelessly confused. "Between 10 to 15 percent of the population is believed to be affected by the disease." Either change "Between" to *From* or change "to" to *and*. A variation of that error is to use "between" with an en dash: "He ruled between 664–600 B.C." Make it "*from* 664 *to* 600 B.C." Merely changing the dash to *and* would correct the grammar but leave the meaning uncertain. (*See also* **Punctuation**, 4C.)

4. "BETWEEN YOU AND I"

In speaking confidentially, no one is likely to say "between I and you." The common version, with the pronouns switched around, is essentially the same mistake, a form of overrefinement. As the object of a preposition, any personal pronoun following *between* must be in the objective case: between you and *me*; between *him* and *her*; between *us* and *them*. (*You* can be either subjective or objective.) *See also* **Prepositions**, *1*; **Pronouns**, *10*.

BEVY. A *bevy* of quail is a hunter's term for a flock of those birds. This noun is also applied to larks, roe deer, and some other groups. It may once have meant a drinking group, after the Old French noun *bevee*, an act of drinking.

Writers habitually mate *bevy* with the phrase "of beauties" in picture captions and television continuities pertaining to displays of young females. In two installments of an entertainment news series, co-hosts (female and male) referred to "this year's bevy of beauties" at the Miss Universe pageant and said "James Bond's back with a bevy of beauties."

BI- and SEMI- prefixes. The prefix *bi-* indicates two, double, or twice, depending on the word it begins. It comes from the Latin *bis*, meaning twice, and is used in that very form as a musical instruction.

Bi- is part of nouns, verbs, adjectives, and adverbs. Some are general words: *bicycle*, a pedal vehicle with two wheels; *bifurcate*, to separate into two parts or branches; *bilingual*, pertaining to two languages. Some are technical: *bicuspid*, having two points, and a tooth of that sort; *bifocal*, having two different focal lengths, and a lens ground that way; *bivalve*, having two hinged shells, and a mollusk of that sort.

The chief problems with *bi-* lie in designations of frequency. *Bimonthly* (adjective and adverb) means appearing or taking place every two months. A *bimonthly* is a periodical published every two months. *Biweekly* means appearing or taking place every two weeks. A *biweekly* is a fortnightly, a periodical published every two weeks.

Semimonthly is twice a month; *semiweekly*, twice a week. At times "bi-" words have been used instead. "Loosely," said *The Random House Dictionary*, first edition. "Nonstandard" was the label in *The American Heritage Dictionary*, first edition. Later editions of those dictionaries and *Webster's Third* contain no such labels. By including among their definitions of *bimonthly* and *biweekly* "twice a month" and "twice a week" without qualification, they foster confusion. "The ambiguous usage is confusing," *The Oxford English Dictionary* says. It offers *semi-monthly, semi-weekly*, etc. (preferring hyphenated forms).

Biennial (adjective) means taking place every two years or lasting two years. *Biennially* (adverb) is every two years. A *biennium* (noun) is a two-year period. Twice a year is *semiannual(ly)* or *semiyearly*. (*The Oxford* gives *half-yearly*.)

Two other *bi-* words related to year cause confusion and could well be abandoned: *biannual*, which is commonly defined as twice a year; and *biyearly*, which is sometimes defined as every two years and sometimes as twice a year (depending on the dictionary).

All this can be perplexing. To make

sure of being understood, try doing without the *bi-* words that pertain to frequency, or at least explaining them. While it may seem verbally expensive to speak of, say, "the meeting that is held every two years" instead of just "the biennial [or "biyearly"] meeting," it avoids misunderstanding. Similarly, a biweekly or bimonthly does well to explain that it is published "every two weeks" or "every two months."

Semi-, as in "the semiannual meeting," should not cause any problem in the context of time. Latin for half, *semi-* can mean half (*semicircle, semiquaver*) as well as twice during a given period. More often it means partly (*semiautomatic, semiclassical*).

BIBLE. *See* Clichés; COVET; Expletives; Infinitive, *4;* -MAN-, MAN; NONE, *1;* NOR, *1;* Subjunctive, *2;* SUCH, *2;* WHO and WHOM, *2.*

BIG TIME. *Big time* is a colloquial noun for the highest status in any business, occupation, or competitive field: "My athletic friend has made the big time." The phrase came out of vaudeville, where it denoted performances in the big cities, which offered relatively high pay for few performances.

A related adjective, *big-time,* means successful or important or pertaining to the *big time:* "That contractor is a big-time operator."

In recent years it has become a faddish phrase, used in still another way: as an adverb. The lead paragraph of a newspaper's main story, about police powers, said:

> As fear of crime continues to grip the public mind, there's new evidence that a key tactic of the get-tough-on-crime campaign is paying off—big time.

What does "time" contribute to the sentence, except the superfluous message that the writer knows the latest slang?

Not a fragment of information would have been lost if he had saved a word (and an unnecessary dash) and written: ". . . a key tactic . . . is paying off big." Better yet: ". . . a key tactic . . . is paying off."

The same expression, hyphenated, appeared in a banner headline about the success of a young Hollywood performer: "Actor's success now flowing big-time." The use of the word "flowing" is understandable in view of the actor's then latest film, *A River Runs Through It.* One might expect the stream image to continue; for example, "Actor's success now flowing *in torrent.*" To introduce instead that expression from the vaudeville stage is almost to mix metaphors.

BIKE, BIKER. *Bike* is primarily a colloquial shortening of *bicycle,* meaning (noun) the pedal-operated, two-wheeled vehicle or (verb, intransitive) to ride a bicycle. *Biker* is the corresponding term for *bicyclist* or *bicycler,* one who rides a bicycle.

As a comparable term, motorcycle and motorbike riders have borrowed *bike* for either of their motor-driven two-wheelers and *biker* for one who rides it. A problem arises when someone uses *bike* (noun or verb) or *biker* without making it clear which vehicle is meant.

A news broadcast told of a gathering of "100,000 bikers," repeatedly using that word and never once explaining that they were *motorcyclists.* Bicyclists may gather in groups too. *See* **NOT TO MENTION** for a similar example.

BILLIARDS and POOL. The scuttling of a "plan to locate a pool hall" in a mostly residential neighborhood was summarized in the lead of a newspaper story. The second paragraph said "the billiard parlor would have replaced a neighborhood restaurant." Loath to repeat "pool hall," the reporter chose "billiard parlor" as a synonym.

Many owners of *pool halls* or *pool-rooms,* apparently aware of the seamy reputation of those places, prefer the terms "billiards" and "billiard parlor," even though they may own no *billiard* tables, only *pool* tables. Both games use hard balls, rods called *cues,* and oblong, green-felt-covered tables with raised, cushioned edges. But *pool* usually has six pockets and sixteen balls, whereas *billiards*—or *three-cushion billiards,* the favorite version—has no pockets and three balls. What the industry calls *pocket billiards,* players call just *pool.*

BILLION. *Billion* can be ambiguous, especially in the United Kingdom. To Americans, it is a thousand million, or 1,000,000,000, or 10^9. It is the unit that congressmen often toss around when discussing the federal budget. But a British *billion* is traditionally a million million, or 1,000,000,000,000, or 10^{12}— what Americans call a *trillion.* What is called a *billion* in the United States is a *milliard* in the United Kingdom.

In a book, a cosmologist, physicist, and professor of mathematics presents the theory of inflation in the early universe, "an increase by a factor of at least a billion billion billion. . . ." Later in the book he suggests the possibility of the universe's "recollapsing in a hundred billion years or so." The book was published in the United States by an American publisher for American readers, but the author is British and his discussion of the future of the universe is taken from a lecture at the University of Cambridge, England. Unless the book version was edited for American readers, they may not be receiving exactly the intended message.

Under such confusing circumstances, it is well to specify which *billion* is meant, for example "a hundred billion (U.K.) years . . ." or "1.7 billion (U.S.) sales." Fortunately the particular example of ambiguity is not critical; a confusion between a hundred *billion* and a

hundred *trillion* years is not likely to affect life on earth to any measurable extent.

The earliest use of *billion* quoted in *The Oxford English Dictionary* was by John Locke, 1690. The dictionary says that *billion, trillion,* and *quadrillion* were purposely formed in the previous century to denote the second, third, and fourth powers of a million respectively. French arithmeticians later redefined the words so that *billion* represented a thousand million, *trillion* a thousand thousand million, and so on. In the nineteenth century, the United States adopted the French system, and in 1948 France adopted the British system. In later decades there has been a trend toward use of the U.S. values in Britain, especially in technical writing.

See also **NANO- prefix.**

BIT. *See* **MUCH.**

BIZARRE and BAZAAR. *See* **Homophones.**

BLACKMAIL. *See* **Crimes,** 2.

BLAME. 1. *Blame ON and blame FOR.* 2. *BLAME or CREDIT?*

1. Blame ON and blame FOR

The moving of industrial plants to Mexico is "a factor Democrats blame on the nation's unemployment," in the words of a local television newscaster. He got it backward. Nobody says U.S. unemployment causes plants to move to Mexico.

You *blame* something *for* an ill. But you *blame* an ill *on* something, or, as an alternative, *place* the *blame for* the ill *on* something. (Something or someone, that is.)

Thus, "The moving of plants to Mexico is a factor Democrats *blame for* the nation's unemployment." Or they "*blame* the nation's unemployment in part *on* the moving of plants";

or they "*place* some *blame for* the nation's unemployment *on* the moving of plants. . . . " (Changing "the nation's unemployment" to *unemployment in the United States* would clarify the identity of the nation.)

A few critics do not want the verb *blame* to be followed by *on*. They complain that a construction like "He blames the disease on an insect" misplaces the blame. They would approve of "blames the insect for . . ." or "puts [or "places"] the blame for the disease on. . . ." Only 18 percent of the usage panel of *The American Heritage Dictionary* objected to the *blame . . . on* construction. It is doubtful that anyone would misunderstand a sentence like "Don't blame it on me."

2. *BLAME or CREDIT?*

To *blame* is to place responsibility for a fault or a mistake, not for something good or laudable. This was said on a medical talk show:

> Asian women have the lowest rate of cancer in the world and we have blamed it on their lower fat consumption.

Change "blamed it on" to *credited it to* or *attributed it to*.
See also **CREDIT; THANK, THANKS.**

BLITZKRIEG.

Blitzkrieg is a German word adopted by English. It means lightning war, from *blitz,* meaning lightning, and *krieg,* meaning war. It was used by Hitler to describe a sudden, massive attack, designed to conquer a country swiftly. It can also denote a sudden, swift, massive attack of a nonmilitary nature.

Seeking an exciting noun, a writer chose *blitzkrieg* for a story in a metropolitan newspaper. Was she right?

But in his 18 years of defending the industry, Walker Merryman has never seen anything like the current blitzkrieg against cigarettes and people who smoke them.

She was grammatically correct but factually incorrect. The story described several, separate antismoking actions that had taken place within several weeks: enactment of laws by states and cities, bans by restaurant chains, and federal measures. The "blitzkrieg" later became a mere "assault" and still later just a "movement" that "appears to have gathered momentum in recent weeks." Furthermore, "it has been several years in the making and is the result of a complex set of pressures and events." So it could not veritably be described as a lightning war, however metaphorically.

BLOC and BLOCK.

A book dealing with Britain's acquisition of destroyers from the United States in 1940 quotes the minutes of Churchill's war cabinet in this way:

> It might well prove to be the first step in constituting an Anglo-Saxon block or indeed a decisive point in history.

Did those minutes (which, presumably, indirectly quoted Prime Minister Churchill) actually read "Anglo-Saxon block"? *Bloc* was then and is now the normal spelling of the word in the sense of a group of nations, parties, legislators, or individuals of different loyalties allied in a common cause. In politics of continental Europe, a *bloc* is a group of political parties that support the ruling government.

The *k* and no-*k* versions of the word are used interchangeably in the phrase *bloc vote* or *block vote*. It has two meanings: (1) the vote of a substantial number of people voting as a group; (2) a method of voting at a convention or conference in which a delegate's vote is weighted according to the number of members he represents. In dozens of other senses (as noun and verb), the word is spelled only *block*.

BLOND and BLONDE. Yellowish, golden, or flaxen hair is *blond* (adjective) when it is used in a general sense or pertains to a male, *blonde* (adjective) when it pertains to a female. A man or boy with *blond* hair is a *blond* (noun); a woman or girl with *blonde* hair is a *blonde* (noun).

Among four people advertising in the "Personals" one day for companions of opposite sex, two men identified themselves as

40, 6′1″, blonde hair, blue eyed, slender. . . .

. . . Tall, trim, attractive blonde, 32.

The other two were women who identified themselves as

SWF, 26 / Slim, blue-eyed blond. . . .

Petite blond, big brown eyes, 40s. . . .

Each of the four used the wrong gender.

Apropos to the genders of hair words: brown hair is *brunet* (adjective) in a general sense or pertaining to a male, *brunette* (adjective) pertaining to a female. A male with *brunet* hair is a *brunet* (noun); a female with *brunette* hair is a *brunette* (noun).

As adjectives, *blond* and *brunet* are often used for females.

"BLOW YOUR MIND." This expression is a relic of the hippie era. Recent examples follow.

[A promotion for a TV drama:] Their dreams will blow your mind.

[A student suffering a disease:] It still kind of blows my mind.

[A doctor who saw someone driving while reading:] Does that blow your mind? It certainly blows my mind.

Minds are not blown. The expression is overdue for retirement.

Substitute a verb like *amaze(s), astound(s),* or *overwhelm(s)* (you, me, etc.) or, in the example below, an adjective like *amazing, astounding,* or *overwhelming.*

[An astronomer, on the process of humans' acquiring extraterrestrial atoms:] I find the process completely mind-blowing.

BOIL, BOILED. In dealing with eggs, food writers customarily avoid *hard-boiled* or *soft-boiled,* believing that we *boil* just the water and "cook" the eggs. If the rest of us have any qualms about eggs, they are more likely to concern dietary usage than English usage. *Hard-boiled egg* is a common phrase, which gave rise to the colloquial adjective *hard-boiled,* meaning tough and callous, applied to a person.

A leading cookbook gives instructions for cooking "Soft-Cooked Eggs" and "Medium-Soft-Cooked Eggs" and "Hard-Cooked Eggs." But it does not avoid *boiled* beef, *boiled* potatoes, and New England *boiled* dinner. "Cooked" is less informative. The verb *cook* includes all methods of preparing food for eating by the application of heat.

Water will *boil* (verb, intransitive) at 212 degrees Fahrenheit or 100 degrees centigrade; that is, it will reach an agitated, bubbling state in which it vaporizes. A person is said to *boil* when greatly excited. And to *boil* (verb, transitive) a liquid is to heat it to the boiling point.

One can also *boil* a solid: subject it to the heat of a boiling liquid. That has been a definition of the word since the

Middle Ages. In the fourteenth century, Chaucer wrote in the prologue to *The Canterbury Tales:* "A Cook they hadde . . . To boille the chiknes [chickens] with the marybones [marrow bones]. . . ."

Thinking of all those victuals, dare we consider the unappetizing sense of *boil* (noun) as a skin infection?

BORE, BORNE, and BORN.

Two erroneous substitutes for *borne* appeared in two issues of a newspaper.

> The 40-year-old Cambodian woman . . . has bore a child and lived for 10 years here in a thatched hut. . . .

"Has bore" is wrong. Make it "has borne." *Borne* is a past participle of the verb *bear*. The past tense is *bore*. To use *bore* in that sample sentence, relocate "has" in this way: ". . . *bore* a child and *has* lived for 10 years here in a thatched hut. . . ."

> Asked whether the building had ever born any nameplate, Mr. Formanek replied, "No, the secret police have always been very modest."

In the second sample, "born" should be *borne*. *Born* also is a past participle of the verb *bear* but is used only in the sense of *given birth* and only passively; e.g., "She *was born* abroad."

A little-used noun that sounds the same is *bourn*, spelled also *bourne*. It is (1) a brook or small stream; (2) a boundary, destination, or realm, used in poetry: "The undiscover'd country from whose bourn No traveller returns"— Shakespeare, *Hamlet.*

BORN with name.

An almanac says "William J. Clinton was born William Jefferson Blythe III in Hope, Ark., on August 19, 1946." Not exactly. He was probably just *baby Blythe* before being christened *William Jefferson*. An infant at birth normally has only a surname.

See also **NEE.**

BOTH.

1. BOTH . . . AND. 2. BOTH *with words of togetherness.* 3. *Other principles.*

1. BOTH . . . AND

Sentences that contain *both* with *and* are not always constructed as carefully, neatly, and logically as they should be. For instance, the editor of a local weekly wrote:

> We recently added Elizabeth P—— to our pool of critics—both because we like her writing and her perspective.

That is illogical and ungrammatical. Following the "both" there is a clause: "because we like her writing." One should expect to find a comparable clause after the "and," for example: "because we agree with her perspective." Instead only the phrase "her perspective" appears.

The sentence could be corrected also by relocating the "both," as follows: "because we like *both* her writing and her perspective."

The main point is that when *both* is combined with *and* (forming a pair of correlative conjunctions), what follows one must match grammatically what follows the other. If a clause follows the *both*, a similar clause must follow the *and*. A phrase must be paralleled by a similar phrase, a verb by a verb, a noun by a noun. This sentence, from a news story, falls short:

> Mr. Wan is believed to be caught in a difficult position by the power struggle in China. For he is both a close friend of Mr. Deng—sometimes serving as Mr. Deng's bridge partner—and

is a leading exponent of China's changes in recent years.

Omit either the third "is" or the "both."

2. BOTH *with words of togetherness*

Both, adjective or pronoun, means the one and the other. For instance (as adjective), "Both buses go downtown," or (as pronoun) "Both go downtown."

Both indicates that an activity or state that could apply to only one (thing or person) applies to two. Therefore *both* should usually not go with any descriptive word or phrase or any verb that applies only to two or more. Two such words are *alike* and *same.* One cannot be alike, and one cannot be the same. In "Both dogs look alike," change "Both" to *The.* In "The books are both the same," delete "both."

Words of that sort include *agree, between, equal(ly), joint(ly), meet,* and *together;* phrases include *along with, as well as, combined with, each other,* and to *have in common.* It takes two or more to be *equal,* to be *together,* and so on.

"Both" does not belong in "The brothers have both been united." In "Both agreed on the wording of the contract," *they* should replace "Both." In "I did both my work in addition to his," change "in addition to" to *and.* Although "both" could be omitted too, it is useful for emphasis.

A federal cabinet officer spoke of payments to "both HMOs as well as skilled nursing facilities." Either do without "both" or change "as well as" to *and.*

3. *Other principles*

A. BOTH *with OF*

Both often goes with *of* when a pronoun follows: "Give me both of them." You would not say "Give me both them." But "The referee penalized both them and us" is correct.

Otherwise, *of* is generally optional. A dictionary prefers either "both girls" or "both the girls" to "both of the girls" in formal usage. But "both the girls" might bring to mind "and the boys," whereas "both of the girls" is unambiguous.

B. *Possessive constructions*

Whether *both* can go with a possessive pronoun gets a yes and a no. One authority accepts "both our fathers" (referring to two fathers). Another dislikes "both their mothers," preferring "the mothers of both"; but the former seems to be an established construction: "a plague on both your houses."

When what is possessed is singular, there is no such disagreement. *Of both* is often necessary. Either of these will do: "It is the belief of both" or "It is both men's belief." These are wrong: "both's belief" / "both their belief" / "both of their belief."

C. *Replacing EACH; errors in number*

In "Both praised the other," change "Both" to *Each.* An alternative wording is "They praised each other."

"I see a bus stop on both sides of the street" erroneously places one stop on two sides. Either change "a bus stop" to *bus stops* or change "both sides" to *each side.*

D. THE *with BOTH*

Some authorities object to *the* before *both.* It is at least unnecessary in "She scorns the both of them" and strained in "The both men were disappointed." In each instance, either omit "the" or change "both" to *two.*

E. *Two only*

Both applies only to two things, actions, or qualities, not to three or more. In the sentence "He is both tall, dark, and handsome," leave out "both."

BOUGH and BOW. *See* Homophones.

Brackets. *See* **Punctuation,** 7.

BRAKE and BREAK. *See* Homophones.

BRANDISH. To *brandish* an object is, strictly, to wave or shake it menacingly or defiantly. Did these four assailants (described by four journalists) really do that?

A convicted murderer used a hidden pistol to hijack an airliner . . . brandishing it when he left the plane's rest room. . . .

. . . They were surprised by a man . . . brandishing a .25-caliber handgun.

. . . Mrs. B——— . . . brandished a 10-inch knife in her right hand.

. . . Officers said he appeared drunk and brandished a shotgun at two patrolmen and his daughter.

On weighing the likelihood of such an abundance of weapon-wavers as the public press depicts, we can bet that reporters often choose *brandish* when they mean *hold*, *wield*, or *point*.

BREADTH and BREATH. *See* Homophones.

BREAK and BRAKE. *See* Homophones.

BREAKFAST (verb). *See* DINE.

BREATH and BREATHE. *See* Confusing pairs.

BRING and TAKE. "Please take this money and claim check to Tom's Repair Shop and bring me my lamp." In the sense of physical movement, illustrated by that sentence, the verb *bring* indicates movement toward the speaker or writer, or toward a place associated with him; the verb *take* indicates movement away

from the speaker or writer, or other movement that is not toward him.

It was announced on the radio that a police bomb squad had picked up a suspicious device and "they're getting ready to bring it out of the building." Better: *take* it out. The movement was not necessarily toward the speaker; and anyway, in the sense of physical removal, *take out* is idiomatic.

BROADSIDE.

POPLAR BLUFF, Mo.—A Union Pacific train slammed broadside Sunday into a station wagon driven into the path of the 73-car train, cutting the automobile in half. . . .

The train probably did not slam "broadside" into the station wagon. Unless it leaves its track, a train is not likely to hit anything "broadside."

Broadside (when used as an adverb, as it is used above) means with a broad side facing a given object; that is, a broad side of whatever is performing the action. If an automobile skids sideway on an icy street and hits a parked truck (any part of the truck), we can say that the car hit the truck *broadside*.

A newspaper turned the word into a hyphenated verb of uncertain meaning:

. . . His wife, on her usual biking route, was broad-sided only a few blocks from their Twin Peaks home by a drowsy 20-year-old running a stop sign.

Nothing was said about a motor vehicle. Maybe the 20-year-old was running.

BROKE and BROKEN. *See* Tense, 5A.

BRUTALIZE. The primary meaning of *brutalize* is to make (a person or animal) brutal or like a brute, an animal. That meaning of the verb (transitive), from about 1700, is particularly useful, for it is not duplicated by any other single word.

Another sense of *brutalize* (transitive), from the latter 1800s and lately popular, is to treat (one) like a brute or with brutality. That use tends to render the word ambiguous. An article said the prison system "brutalizes inmates." Does the system make inmates brutal or treat them brutally?

Even when not ambiguous, the word is apt to serve nowadays as a fuzzy substitute for more informative verbs, such as *batter, beat, club, kick, mug, pommel, punch, rape, torture,* or *whip.* Or it becomes a fashionable replacement for various idioms: An article said "a group of them brutalized [attacked?] the woman jogging through the park." A movie reviewer commented on TV, "This monster feels himself like a brutalized [an abused?] child."

A nearly obsolete sense of the verb (intransitive) is to live or become like a brute.

BUCK NAKED. *See* ON, 3.

BUCOLIC. *Bucolic* (adjective) means rural, pastoral, pertaining to the countryside. Therefore it was redundant for the narrator of a documentary on railroad travel to say, "As the train nears Portland, the bucolic countryside gives way to signs of civilization." Either omit "bucolic" or change "countryside" to a word like *scenery.*

See also IDYLLIC.

Bullet. *See* DUM-DUM BULLET; Series errors, 5.

BURGEON, BURGEONING. To *burgeon* is to put forth new buds, leaves, blossoms, etc.; or to begin to grow. *Burgeoning,* used as an adjective ("the burgeoning tree") means budding or sprouting or putting forth new buds, leaves, blossoms, etc.

The verb or adjective may be used figuratively or poetically ("The child's artistic talent burgeoned in kindergarten") as long as it refers to that which is newly emerging. Too often *burgeon* or *burgeoning* is used loosely instead of *increase* or *increasing, expand* or *expanding,* or any of numerous synonyms. These two passages (from a syndicated column and an editorial respectively) illustrate the loose use:

> The congressional flag service sprouted in 1937. . . . By 1955 the demand was so heavy that there was a three-year waiting list. This prompted Congress to establish a more elaborate system to meet the burgeoning demand.

> The burgeoning demand for physician services is reflected in a new study. . . .

Strictly speaking, if the flag service "sprouted" in 1937, that is when the demand for flags *burgeoned;* and the demand for physician services probably *burgeoned* thousands of years ago.

The next two sentences (from news stories) are ambiguous:

> . . . The legislation would authorize spending more than $1.5 billion . . . to provide birth control information in an effort to slow the demand for fossil fuels in burgeoning nations.

> Hungary is growing adept at focusing world attention on its burgeoning refugees.

"Burgeoning" could be interpreted either in the loose way to mean expanding or in a stricter way to mean newly emerging. The latter sentence is doubly troublesome: People do not "burgeon," except perhaps at birth.

BURGLARY. *See* Crimes, 3.

BUT.
1. BUT or AND? 2. "BUT THAT"; "BUT WHAT." 3. Further double negatives. 4. Question of pronouns. 5. With "HOWEVER" etc. 6. With NOT.

1. BUT or AND?

But (as a conjunction) introduces a contrast. Something that was just said will be contradicted or an exception to it will be given. The "but" is unwarranted in this headline bank:

Labor got little from Clinton and Demos, but things look worse now

Where is the contrast? Let us assume that labor had got *much,* instead of "little." A *but* would have been called for. As it stands, what follows the "but" is not very different from what precedes it. Thus the conjunction needed is *and.* Alternatively, replace the comma and "but" with a semicolon: "Demos; things."

Similarly, "but" should be *and* in this sentence from television news. The part after the "but" offers no contrast, just more of the same.

Hong Kong is already one of the most crowded places on the planet, but the population is expected to double. . . .

The opposite error, using "and" instead of *but,* comes from a television interview with a woman in public life. As a teacher, she taught girls "never to raise their hands and interrupt."

It seems to mean that she taught them to be quiescent. "And" implies more of what precedes, carrying the negative force of "never" to "interrupt." However, the context indicates that what she taught them was really the reverse: "never to raise their hands *but to* interrupt."

2. "BUT THAT"; "BUT WHAT"

When a phrase such as "no question but that" or "no doubt but that" is used in place of *no question that* or *no doubt that,* "but" is at best unnecessary. At worst, "but" produces a double negative, thereby reversing the meaning of the sentence. On a television talk show, a politician said:

There is no question but that we are in serious economic trouble in this country.

But can mean *except, other than.* So if there is no question "but" that we are in serious economic trouble, one can say with logic that the only question is whether we are in serious economic trouble. Omitting "but" corrects the sample sentence: "There is no question that we are in serious economic trouble. . . ."

"But what" does not improve on "but that." A member of the press said, in a forum on television:

I don't think there's any doubt but what Congress will permit the aid to continue.

The speaker had no doubt *that* Congress would approve the aid. Such replacement of *that* with "but what" is unacceptable to most authorities (even to some who condone "but that").

See also **THAT,** *3.*

3. Further double negatives

But (as an adverb) means *only, no more than.* A negative should not precede *but,* used in that sense.

In both of these sentences, the "wasn't" or "won't" plus the "but" amounts to a double negative: "The child wasn't but five years old." / "We won't have but a day to spend in the city." If the intended meanings are that the child's age was only five and we can spend only a day in the city, change the sentences to "The child *was* but . . ." and "We *will* have but. . . ."

This sentence is fairly clear: "We can but hope that peace will come soon." It suggests that we can do no more than hope. This one is ambiguous: "We cannot but hope that peace will come soon." Is it intended to mean the same as the other sentence—in which case the "-not" is wrong—or does it mean that just hoping is inadequate?

See also **Double negative**.

4. Question of pronouns

A tricky question of pronouns arises when *but* is used to mean *except*. Do we say that "everyone attended class but *she*" or "but *her*"? Authorities differ. (Some consider *but* a preposition, to be followed by a pronoun in the objective case. Others consider *but* a conjunction that precedes an elliptical clause—e.g., "she did not"—and calls for a pronoun in the subjective case.)

A working rule is to make the pronoun *I, we, she, he,* or *they* (subjective case) before the verb; but make it *me, us, her, him,* or *them* (objective case) after the verb. Thus "Everyone but *she* attended," however "Everyone attended but *her*."

5. With "HOWEVER" etc.

But can be the equivalent of *however, nevertheless,* and *yet*. Normally none of those words should go with *but*. Sometimes carelessness produces a sentence like this: "But we must look ahead to the future, however."

"But . . . however" is redundant. Select one or the other.

6. With NOT

"But" is mistakenly used in place of *as* in an essay: "He was not so much a comic actor . . . but a real comedian." What we see is not so much a contrast as a comparison.

"But" should be dropped from this sentence: "It is not an evergreen . . . ; but its leaves fall in the autumn. . . ." The statements are compatible, not contrasting. This is a proper *but* sentence: "It is not an evergreen but a deciduous tree."

Another defective form goes like this: "They did not get as far as the city but its suburbs." It is defective because the implied clause that follows *but* lacks the service of a verb. The only verb in the sentence is "did not get," which does not apply to "its suburbs." The simplest correction is to insert a verb after *but*: "but *reached* its suburbs."

This similarly flawed sentence may be corrected in two ways: "We have not seen the document but the news." Either place "not" after "seen" or follow the *but* with a verb: "but *have seen* the news." It can be argued that the original sentences are clear enough. Nevertheless, adding balance and logic can strengthen them. See **AS**, 4, for another illustration.

C

CAME. *See* **COME and CAME; COME and GO.**

CAN and MAY. The traditional difference between the two verbs is that *can* pertains to ability, *may* to permission. Thus, "Can you lift this barbell?" asks whether one is physically able to do it. "May I speak?" asks permission; obviously anyone orally asking that question *can* speak. "You may kiss the bride" gives permission; plainly the bridegroom *can* do it.

In informal conversation, *can* is often used in place of *may*, particularly in negative questions or statements. "Why can't I speak?" / "You can't" or "You cannot." When a customer asks a storekeeper, "Can I see that watch?" the latter would do well to say, "Certainly"—not "You can, if you have eyesight."

The writer of "Repair Information" in a telephone directory seemed bewildered by the two words, using each twice:

> If you have a problem with your inside wiring, you have several repair options:
> a. You may do the work yourself.
> b. You can hire someone to do it.
> c. You can hire us to repair your inside wiring. . . .
> d. You may subscribe to our "Per-

Month" Inside Wire Repair Plan.

It is a formal list, calling for consistency and correctness. Change "can" to *may* in *b* and *c*.

See also **MAY and MIGHT.**

CANNON and CANON. *See* **Homophones.**

CANVAS and CANVASS. *See* **Homophones.**

CAPITAL and CAPITOL. An article called Katmandu "the capitol of Nepal." Make it *capital*, not "capitol."

The *Capitol* is the building in which the Congress of the United States meets. A comparable building in which a state legislature meets is a *capitol*.

A *capital* is a city or town that serves as the official seat of government of a country, state, or province. A *capital*, or *capital letter*, is a large letter like *A, B,* or *C*, used to start sentences and proper names. *Capital* (with no article) is a noun denoting assets, investment money, wealth, or those possessing them; and *capital* is also an adjective pertaining to those things or meaning fatal, first-rate, or foremost.

Will this help? Only one building in the United States is the *Capitol* and only one building in each state is a *capitol*—with *o* in the third syllable. The word for an administering city and assets and all the rest is *capital*—with *a* in the third syllable.

Both words originated in *caput*, Latin for head. The ancient temple of Jupiter on the Capitoline Hill in Rome was the original *Capitol*.

Capitalization.

When it does not apply to investment and the financial kind of capital, the term *capitalization* concerns the use of capital letters in writing and printing.

Which words start with capitals (upper-case letters) and which start with small letters (lower-case letters) has been decided by custom in most instances, although differences on many points exist. Questions can often be resolved by a dictionary. (But some dictionaries are not helpful. The otherwise authoritative *Oxford English Dictionary* capitalizes all entries. *Webster's Third* capitalizes almost none, running such entries as "kansas city" and "saint patrick's day" while noting that they are "usu cap"; when are they not? The capitalization scheme for entry titles in our book is described under **General Topics**, near the front.)

Sometimes one's personal preference decides, although in the interest of readers, it ought not to be followed to an extreme. At one extreme is the shunning of all capitals, a quirk of two literary personages of the past; at another is the arbitrary capitalization of words for emphasis, which was common centuries back. A condensed excerpt from the Declaration of Independence follows. The first letter of every noun deemed important is a capital.

. . . All men are created equal . . . with certain unalienable Rights, that among these are Life, Liberty and the pursuit of Happiness.—That to secure these rights, Governments are instituted among Men, deriving their just powers from the consent of the governed,—That whenever any Form of Government becomes destructive of these ends, it is the Right of the People . . . to institute new Government . . . to effect their Safety and Happiness.

Some current principles of capitalization follow.

1. Beginning of a sentence. The first letter of every sentence starts with a capital. So does a sentence fragment that stands alone. "Her answer was brief. 'Yes.' "

2. Colon. A sentence fragment following a colon is not usually capitalized: "I'm eating only three times a day: morning, noon, and night." Whether to capitalize a complete sentence after a colon is up to each writer or publication.

3. Days, times of the year. Days, months, and holidays are capitalized: Thursday, November, Thanksgiving. Seasons are usually not: winter, summer.

4. Derivatives of names. Most adjectives derived from people's names or other proper nouns are capitalized: Euclidean geometry, Georgian architecture, Shakespearean plays, Machiavellian ethics, Roman numerals. Many are not: pasteurized milk, roman type, italic type, french fries, venetian blinds.

5. Heavenly bodies. They are usually capital: Saturn, Milky Way, the star Sirius. The Earth and the Sun may be capital in the context of astronomy, small in general contexts: the greatest show on earth; soaking up the sun.

6. Historical events and eras. They are often capitalized: The Industrial Revolution. World War II. But there is disagreement; it is "the battle of Hastings" in one work, "The Battle of Hastings" in another.

7. Initialisms and acronyms. Most initialisms and acronyms, such as M.D. and AIDS, are all capitals. Doctor of philosophy becomes Ph.D. Abbreviations, like *com.* for committee and *secry.* for secretary, do not need capitalizing.

8. *Names.* Capitalize the name of a person, city, state, country, business, organization, religion, language, nationality, specific institution, trademark, or government body: John Brown, Atlanta, South Dakota, Bank of America, Girl Scouts of the U.S.A., Bulgarian, Purdue University, Pepsi-Cola, the Supreme Court. Institutions or groups referred to in a general sense are not usually capitalized: the medical profession, the middle class.

9. *Personification.* In poetic usage, common words put in human terms are capitalized: "the lute of Hope . . . the voice of Love . . . the wand of Power."

10. *Press differences.* Some newspapers will not capitalize the categorical part of names; they will write, for instance, "Elm street" and "Washington school." The press has been getting away from that "down style." Styles of headlines vary. Some are like titles, the initial letter of each word capitalized ("Cops Catch Robbers"); others are like ordinary sentences ("Cops catch robbers"); a few are all capitals ("COPS CATCH ROBBERS"). The Associated Press and many papers following its style do not capitalize *president* unless it precedes a name. *The New York Times* always refers to the U.S. chief executive as *President.*

11. *Quotations.* A quotation within a sentence typically starts with a capital when the quotation is set off by some introductory words: "Emerson said, 'Life is a series of surprises.' " When the quotation blends with the rest of the sentence, some authorities start the quotation with a small letter: "Emerson said that 'life. . . .' " Others insist on a capital if the original text began with a capital: "Emerson said that 'Life. . . .' " All agree that a fragment of the original after the beginning needs no capital when blended with the rest of the sentence: "Emerson called life 'a series of surprises.' "

12. *Sacred names.* The name of God in all its forms—Allah, Jehovah, the Lord—is always capitalized. A deity in a general sense—the Roman god of war— is not. Sacred terms in any religion are capitalized. Modern Bibles do not capitalize *he* and *his* when referring to God. The adjective referring to the Bible may be either Biblical or biblical.

13. *Sentence within a sentence.* A sentence enclosed in parentheses or dashes within another sentence is commonly uncapitalized: "The accusations (remember that he denied them all) were extensive and damaging." Whether to capitalize a question within a sentence is up to the writer: "I thought, Why am I here?" / "I thought, why am I here?"

14. *Titles.* In the titles of books, shows, works of art, and so on, generally all words are capitalized except articles (*a, an, the*), some conjunctions such as *and* and short prepositions such as *in* and *of.* A small word is capitalized too when it is the first word of the title: *Riders of the Purple Sage* but *The Outline of History* and *A Little Night Music.*

Official titles are capitalized before a name (Secretary of State Robert Smith) but not after a name (Robert Smith, secretary of state). *See also 10.*

15. *Two words always capitalized.* The words *I* and *O* (without an *h,* as in "O God") are always capitalized.

16. *Verse.* Traditional verse capitalizes the first word of every line: "We whirl, singing loud, round the gathering sphere, / Till the trees, and the beasts, and the clouds appear / From its chaos made calm by love, not fear."

CARDINAL NUMBERS. *See* **Numbers,** *11.*

CAREEN and CAREER. *Careen* has been misused so often, confused with *career,* that the misusage has largely taken over. Mark a loss for the language.

To *careen* (verb, intransitive) is to tilt or lean to one side, or to toss from side to side, or to turn a ship on its side in dry dock. It can also mean (verb, transitive) to cause to tilt or tip, or to turn (a ship) on one side. It originates in the Latin *carina,* a ship's keel.

To *career* (verb, intransitive) is to rush or move at high speed, perhaps wildly. In a description of a market scene in Niger, a book of true adventure contains an example of the strict use of *career:*

> A man trying out a camel careered out of control, much to the amusement of the crowd.

The word is no longer used often. We are more likely to hear something like this on our television sets:

> Cable Car Thirteen careened almost out of control down one of the steepest hills in San Francisco.

Or this, broadcast by a competing station:

> . . . Car Number Thirteen went careening down the Hyde Street hill.

In newspapers, this is what we will read ad infinitum:

> . . . The car . . . hit another automobile and careened into Biscoe.

> . . . He and his family were injured as the car careened out of control in the same village.

Apart from cars: an editorial warned of "careening" comets; TV news described roller-coaster fans who "careen the curves"; and in press items, bandits "careened" from a crime scene and a senator "careened around the world." But *The New York Times* used the authentic word in a story about new legs for war veterans:

> Within seconds, the two men were skipping, lurching, careering forward. . . .

Case of letters. *See* **Capitalization; I and i; Pronouns,** *10A* (end).

Case of pronoun. *See* **Pronouns,** *10;* **WHO and WHOM,** *1.*

CAUGHT and CAUGHT UP. For aeons, insects have been getting *caught* in webs. All of us have been *caught* in the rain and *caught* in traffic.

Not long ago it became popular to encumber that simple verb with a superfluous adverb. A network anchorman and two local radio broadcasters provide the examples: "What happens when the telephone company gets caught up in its own web?" / "They got caught up in yesterday's strong earthquake." / "In your case, you'll be going early, so you won't be caught up in the 8:30 dinner crush."

To *catch up* has long meant to come from behind through speed or effort: "The Braves were losing to the Twins by two runs but caught up in the ninth inning."

Another meaning of *caught up,* used only in the passive, adds the implication of gradualness or unwittingness to *caught:* "Many who came to listen to the speech were caught up in the mob hysteria." / "She did not intend to abandon New York but was caught up in the glamour of Hollywood." That adaptation of the phrase is useful.

In the contexts of the broadcast sentences, however, "up" contributes nothing. All it tells us is that the speakers are caught in the web of a fad.

See also **UP.**

CAUSATIVE, CAUSE. *See* **FACTOR,** *1.*

CELEBRANT and CELEBRATOR. *See* **Confusing pairs.**

CELEBRATED. Both are well-known cases, famous cases, some may say infamous or notorious cases, but is either a "celebrated" case? A network anchor man reported during television coverage of a hearing for O. J. Simpson that a limousine driver "found himself in the most celebrated murder case of our time." And a prominent daily newspaper reported:

Two years and three months after it began, the celebrated McMartin preschool child molesting case is teetering on the brink of mistrial.

Celebrated suits a person or thing that has been publicly honored or praised. It comes, of course, from *celebrate,* one of whose meanings is to honor or praise someone or something publicly. Who would want to celebrate a murder case or a "child molesting case"?

In describing a newly published set of cards, a writer for a suburban weekly mischose the first word in this sentence:

Celebrated killers like cannibal Jeffrey Dahmer, Charles Manson, Vietnam War criminal Lt. William Calley (convicted of killing 22 Vietnamese in the Mai Lai [*My Lai*] massacre) and Bonnie and Clyde all appear amid the blood-splattered graphics.

If the writer felt that he absolutely had to place an adjective before *killers,* he could have used *infamous* or *notorious.* But could any adjective enhance the effect of a plain enumeration of those killers?

CENSOR and CENSURE. The two verbs are pronounced somewhat differently, SEN-sir and SEN-shur respectively. They have considerably different meanings, though they both originate in the same Latin root, *censere,* to judge, rate, or assess.

To *censor* a written or dramatic work is for someone in authority to examine it and remove passages that he considers objectionable before it is published or presented. Military *censors*

have *censored* news stories at battle fronts, studying them and cutting out or blacking out whatever they do not want to be made public. Such activity is *censorship.* Banning a work as a whole or refusing to sponsor something is not truly "censoring" or "censorship," although such designations are often bandied about.

To *censure* someone is to reprimand or express strong disapproval of him, particularly in an open or formal manner by a person or body in authority. For example, the U.S. Senate has *censured* several members for misbehavior.

The words get mixed up. While expressing distaste for a rap act that was being banned as obscene, a TV panelist asked, "Should it actually be censured?" He probably meant *censored,* although that word would be questionable too.

On another TV panel show, the moderator reported that a baseball club owner was "reprimanded and censored in the strongest terms" for racial slurs. Doubtless he meant *censured.*

A supporter of a senator charged with sexual harassment said of his private conduct, "If it's inappropriate behavior, then let them censor him." *Censure* was the word she needed.

Two nouns pronounced the same as *censor* are *sensor,* a device that reacts to a particular stimulus of energy (light, motion, etc.), and *censer,* a vessel in which incense is burned.

CENSUS. *See* CONSENSUS.

CERTAIN. *See* SURE.

CERTIORARI. *See* GO OFF and GO ON.

CESSION and SESSION. *See* Homophones.

CHAFE and CHAFF. *See* Confusing pairs.

CHAIR.
1. CHAIR and CHAIR-MAN. 2. CHAIR as verb.

1. CHAIR and CHAIRMAN

A chair is furniture; a human being is not furniture. The statement would be too obvious to make if not for published sentences like these:

> Sen. Joe Biden, D-Del., the chair of the Judiciary Committee, has had a mixed record on abortion. . . .

> Eva has served as president and membership chair. Currently she is the Chair of the Board of Directors of Magic Years Day Care. . . .

Correction: the *chairman* of the judiciary committee, membership *chairman,* and *chairman* of the board of directors.

Although widely used in some circles, *chair* as a substitute for *chairman* is proper only in the jargon of parliamentary procedure; e.g., "I appeal from the ruling of the chair." In general prose, *chair* may signify a *chairmanship* or an academic office, but not an individual holding the office; for example, "The chair is vacant," but not "He was appointed chair."

Chair and *chairman* should be in lower case, except when the latter is affixed to a proper name (e.g., *Chairman Mao*). In the second sample, Eva is both a small "chair" and a big "Chair."

A male chairman is formally addressed as *Mister Chairman,* a female chairman as *Madame Chairman.*

Avoid the ungainly barbarism seen in a headline: "Republicans select their chairpersons." A newspaper editor normally seeks brevity in headlines, so it is surprising that one would choose a seven-letter suffix, "-persons," instead of a three-letter suffix with the same meaning, *-men.*

The New York Times style manual properly instructs staff members to use *chairman* and *chairmen* for both men and women. "Do not use *chairlady, chairwoman* or *chairperson.*" It explains that "chairman (like foreman, spokesman and some similar terms) suffices for both sexes."

The Associated Press, while approving of "chairwoman," rejects "chairperson," unless it is an organization's formal title. But a story dispatched under its name contained a similar barbarism: "Glamour was supplied by the dinner's chairpeople."

2. CHAIR as verb

As a verb (transitive) meaning to place in a chair or to install in a chair of office, *chair* is long established though little used nowadays.

The modern press often uses *chair* as a verb meaning to serve as a chairman. A few authorities object to such use, at least in formal writing. The *Times* style manual says to avoid it. The examples are from two other newspapers.

> . . . Assemblyman Richard Rainey failed to win the chairmanship of the Public Safety Committee . . . but . . . he's happy to settle for chairing the Local Government panel. . . . Assemblyman Curt Pringle . . . will chair the Appropriations Committee.

> [Testimony was heard by] a House Government Operations subcommittee chaired by Rep. Mike Synar. . . .

Utilizing an item of furniture as a verb is not out of the question. To *table* is to put (something) on a table; especially to put (a legislative measure) *on the table,* i.e., postpone indefinitely. To *bed* is to furnish (someone) with a bed, or to put (someone) to bed, or to go to bed. On the other hand, no one is likely to say, "A new governor will desk the state administration" or "A vast empire was throned by the queen."

CHARACTER. This noun has many legitimate meanings, among them integrity; reputation; distinguishing qualities or features; a fictional person; and a symbol. Yet it is often used unnecessarily: "glue of a strong character," instead of *strong glue;* or "the charming character of the painting," instead of *the charm of the painting.* In phrases like "an event of this character," *kind* or *sort* is more fitting.

A colloquial sense of *character* is an eccentric person. The reporter who put it in the item below was not necessarily wrong but seemed to be short of facts.

> Clarence ———, otherwise known as Filmore Slim, a long-time San Francisco character, pleaded guilty to one count of ——— in a plea bargain with the district attorney's office yesterday.

CHARITY. *See* **MERCY and PITY.**

CHAUVINISM. *Chauvinism* (pronounced SHOW-vin-izm) is extreme patriotism, militant glorification of one's country; or, by extension, excessive devotion to any cause or group. It came from Chauvin, the name of a French soldier who was a fanatical admirer of Napoleon.

Male chauvinist has been a common pair since the sixties. Some think that *chauvinism* or *chauvinist* has to do with opposition to or disparaging of a group, particularly women, and they omit the modifier. A topic on a TV quiz show was "chauvinist terms for women": *broad, dame, doll.* They are slang terms, perhaps demeaning terms—far removed from *chauvinism.*

CHECK OUT and CHECK-OUT.
A software company advertises, in a magazine, "Checkout our Web Site. . . ." As a verb, *check out* consists of two words. In the context of the ad (transitive), it means examine or investigate. In another context (intransitive) it can mean to be proven authentic. "His story checks out."

To *check out* (verb, transitive) is also to account for a departure (especially of a guest from a hotel, a customer from a store, or a book from a library). Hotel guests *check out* (verb, intransitive); or they *check out of,* say, the Grand Hotel.

Check-out (noun) is the process or act of departing from an establishment, or a time that a hotel sets for the end of a day. In addition it is a counter where customers pay in a self-service market, also called *check-out* (adjective) *counter.*

The noun, as a single word, *checkout,* is instruction or training given to an air force pilot to familiarize him with a particular aircraft.

See also **Punctuation,** *4D,* for an example of inconsistent use of *check-out* and *check-in,* the process or act of arriving at an establishment.

CHIEF JUSTICE. Misnaming the nation's highest judicial office is a common error, albeit a minor one.

A front-page news summary said, "Died: Warren Burger, 87, retired Supreme Court chief justice."

This was reported on a television network: "Warren Burger served as chief justice of the Supreme Court for seventeen years. . . ."

His successor, William H. Rehnquist, became "the sixteenth Chief Justice of the Supreme Court," a book blurb said. The book itself, by Rehnquist, had it right.

Federal law says: "The Supreme Court of the United States shall consist of a Chief Justice of the United States and eight associate justices. . . ." Each of the eight is a "Justice of the Supreme Court of the United States."

The erroneous appellations often can pass. But surely some occasions, like the ones referred to above, call for the official title to be dusted off.

See also **HIGH COURT.**

"CHILLING EFFECT." This modern cliché does not concern refrigeration mechanics or the meteorological consequences of arctic winds. It does concern an effect of an enforcement action, prosecution, enactment, ruling, policy decision, crisis, or other occurrence, according to some critic or commentator. Seldom is heard a *discouraging, impeding, inhibitory,* or *retardant* word. More often the word is "chilling." A few examples follow; many more could be offered.

[TV news of a crackdown on pornography in Alabama:] What worries civil libertarians is the chilling effect this might have on the people who make movies, even good movies.

[An article on Christian Scientists: A medical ethicist] said that the prosecutions already are having a chilling effect.

[A TV "magazine": Virginia's removal of a physician's medical license] had a chilling effect on doctors throughout the country.

[An article about federal policy on scholarships:] . . . Mr. Wilder said Mr. Williams's ruling would have "a chilling effect on all minority-targeted programs. . . ."

CHINESE (language). Under "Chinese" (noun), at least three dictionaries offer "the language of China" as their second definition. In a strict sense, *the* language of China is a written language only and does not exist as a tongue. One speaks *a* Chinese language. An almanac's statement that "Chinese is the mother tongue of more than 1 billion

people" is imprecise. So are a father's words in a newspaper article about bilingual education: "I see people using language as a refuge, not mixing with other people who don't speak Chinese."

China has various spoken languages of the Sino-Tibetan group, including Mandarin, Cantonese, Wu, Min, Hakka, and others. Sometimes they are called "dialects," but they differ among themselves as much as the Romance languages of Europe do and people from one part of China often cannot comprehend speech from another part. Mandarin is the official and most prevalent language of China.

An uncommon error appeared in a picture caption related to the news story quoted above: "A blackboard in Chor Pang's class at Key elementary shows instructions in both English and Cantonese characters." Make it *Chinese* characters. One array of characters exists for all of China, although there are a few variations in the way some characters are assembled.

The written language has no alphabet and no rules for pronunciation. Characters and their meanings must be memorized. One must learn about 4,000 characters to read a Chinese newspaper. Scholars may know ten times as many. The characters are pronounced according to the words in one's spoken language.

CHORD and CORD. *See* **Homophones.**

CHRISTEN. To *christen* (verb, transitive) used to mean to make (someone) Christian. Now to *christen* an infant is to bring it into a Christian church by baptism; also to give it a name at baptism. By extension, to *christen* also means to name and dedicate (usually a vessel or structure) in a ceremony; or, loosely, just to name (anything).

In a film on Siberian tigers, the narrator said, "They [zoologists] christen the cub Sasha." If a wild beast had to be humanized, "they *name*" should have sufficed. (There was no ceremony, religious or otherwise.)

CIRCUM- prefix. The prefix *circum-* comes from the Latin *circum,* around, and means around, surrounding, or on all sides. Sometimes different *circum-* words are confused.

A high school freshman rose in his civics class to contrast the days of Magellan, when it took three years to go around the world, with contemporary times, when "the world can be circumcised in a few days." Silent pause. The teacher said, "You mean *circumnavigated,* don't you?" / "Yes." Actually I had meant *circumscribed.* That would not have been the right word either.

To *circumnavigate* the world, or an island, means to pilot a ship or airplane all around it. To *circumscribe* something is to encircle, restrict, or draw a line around it. To *circumcise* someone is to excise a certain genital part of him or her. The three verbs stem from *circum* plus the Latin verbs meaning to sail, to write, and to cut, respectively.

A news agency said that many promises made to a Brazilian who pacified Indian tribes were "circumnavigated by the government. . . ." In that context, a better verb would have been *circumvented.* To *circumvent* something, say a law, is to go around it figuratively, to keep it from happening, especially by craft or tricky maneuvering. The word originates in *circum* plus the Latin verb meaning to come.

Three other well-known *circum-* words are the nouns *circumference* (a line or distance around a circle) and *circumstance* (surrounding facts or conditions) and the adjective *circumspect* (prudent, cautious). They come from *circum* plus the Latin verbs meaning to carry, to stand, and to look, respectively.

The accent falls on the third syllable in *circumnavigate,* the second syllable in *circumference,* and the first syllable in the other five *circum-* words.

CIRCUMSTANTIAL EVIDENCE. It is a pervasive myth that *circumstantial evidence* is flimsy evidence. Often "mere" or "only" precedes "circumstantial." A biographer wrote, concerning the evidence against two brothers charged with a fatal bombing:

> It would only be circumstantial evidence, and it was difficult to hang men on circumstantial evidence.

On the contrary, *circumstantial evidence* can be just as strong as, or stronger than, the other type of evidence: *direct evidence.* And men have been executed on the basis of circumstantial evidence.

Circumstantial evidence is information used in court to prove a contention indirectly. Rather than dealing with the main issue head on, it relies on reasonable inference from the surrounding circumstances. *Direct evidence* deals with the main issue directly.

A man is accused of burglarizing a home. No witness saw the crime being committed. The evidence against the defendant is solely *circumstantial:* The victims' valuables were found in his possession and his fingerprints were found at the crime scene. It is convincing evidence.

A witness in a murder trial testifies that he saw Mr. Cain shoot Mr. Abel. Such evidence is *direct.* The defense then brings Mr. Abel into court, alive and well. That too is *direct evidence.*

CLASS. *See* FACULTY; KIND OF, *1, 2;* TYPE, *1.*

CLASSIC. The traditional meaning of a *classic* is a literary, dramatic, or artistic work that has survived the test of time and been generally accepted among the highest in quality. Now we seem to have instant "classics," if advertisers can be believed. "The critics love Disney's newest classic," a TV announcer said.

A book blurb hailed a man who had founded a record company "to churn out hundreds of classic records. . . ." What he recorded were not works by Mozart or Beethoven but rock 'n' roll songs. And a review of a movie musical said, "The tunes . . . —including 'Lola Wants' and 'Shoeless Jo From Hannibal Mo'—are classics." A popular song that remains in the repertoire is a *standard*. Any writer who does not know the difference between *popular* and *classical* music may do well to choose some other topic.

Clause.
A clause is a group of words with a subject (the doer of an action) and a predicate (the verb, the action). Some definers stop there. They would consider the simple sentence "Snow fell" a clause. Others would consider it a clause only in a sentence containing at least two clauses: "Snow fell and streets became slippery."

In the latter example, each clause (connected by *and*) is an *independent clause*. Each could stand alone as a separate sentence.

A *dependent* clause (also called a *subordinate* clause) cannot stand alone. In "I love this ring, which my mother gave me," the part up to the comma is an independent clause and also the *main clause* of the sentence; the part starting with *which* is a dependent clause.

CLAUSTROPHOBIA. *See* HOMOPHOBIA.

CLEAN and CLEANSE. *See* Confusing pairs.

CLEMENCY. *See* MERCY and PITY.

Cliché clash.
By that term we mean a jarring mixture of clichés. Typically it turns up when an impromptu speaker gets confused between two expressions.

For instance, when you do not want to confront a problem, do you sweep it under the rug or do you put it on the back burner? "After the campaign, it'll be swept right back on the back burner," said a senator on the drug problem.

Each of eight samples here contains or hints at two well-known expressions. In the first seven, delivered on the air, the expressions are metaphors or combined parts of metaphors.

A TV network reporter and panelist ridiculed reporters who had said that George Bush lost the Republican nomination: "Where are those reporters today? They're eating humble crow." (Note to gourmets: Combine humble pie with crow—and voilà!)

In a press conference, President Bush commented on the government of Panama. He could not seem to decide whether to use a clock or a board game as a metaphor, so he used them both: "You get the distinct feeling that the clock is not going to be set back to square one."

A man on the street was chosen for a sound bite in an election story on a TV network. Explaining why he was voting against an incumbent, he did not say "A leopard can't change its spots" or "You can't teach an old dog new tricks." He said, "You can't change spots on an old dog."

Do you prefer to play poker with wild cards or with a joker? Interviewed on the radio, a South African commentator said about white rightists in his government, "They are a wild joker in the package."

Another question is whether to give the economy a boost or a shot in the arm. A congressional leader theorized that a tax decrease was "giving the economy a boost in the arm."

A panelist said on a television program of news commentary:

We really have no evidence that Bill Clinton is going to step up to the plate in his first hundred days and really take the bull by the horns.

Maybe the new president would have been inspired by a rousing chorus of "Take Me Out to the Bullfight."

The final example is different, because it appeared in print (in a book review) and because the clash is stylistic, rather than metaphoric.

Her husband, Roger, *freaks out* but the party has momentum enough to keep going and just about everyone, it seems, has enough *carnal knowledge* of Ros to make her, posthumously, an even better conversation piece than she was in life. [Emphasis is added.]

There is a place for hippie slang, just as there is for King James's English—but they are not the same place.

Clichés. The character of Big Brother was an exciting, new idea in George Orwell's novel *1984.* Used repeatedly as a metaphor in discussions and articles (for instance, as the subtitle of a column about new technology to snare violators of federal laws), the appellation loses most of its thrill, although it makes a point.

All clichés were original and fresh expressions at one time but now, by definition, are trite, commonplace, and frequently imitated. That reality does not mean we should always avoid them. It depends on the cliché and the circumstances. This volume contains many examples of expressions considered overused, if not unworthy of use; although admittedly the merit of a particular expression is subject to difference of opinion.

A trite expression need not necessarily be banished, as long as (1) it is needed to convey the desired meaning, (2) it is chosen thoughtfully and makes sense, and

(3) it is used correctly and, if a quotation, is quoted accurately.

These are examples of oft misquoted sayings: "Power tends to corrupt and absolute power corrupts absolutely" (not "Power corrupts")—Lord Acton. "For the love of money is the root of all evil" (not money itself)—Bible, 1 Timothy 6:10. "Music hath charms to soothe a savage breast" (not "beast")—Congreve. "A foolish consistency is the hobgoblin of little minds" (not just consistency)—Emerson. "To gild refined gold, to paint the lily" (not "gild the lily")—Shakespeare, *King John.*

The expressions *as a matter of fact, by the same token, in the final analysis, to all intents and purposes,* and *when all is said and done* have meanings but are rather windy and probably not essential. Some other expressions are irrational, inaccurate, or almost meaningless. (*See* "BLOW YOUR MIND"; "COULD CARE LESS"; "EXCEPTION PROVES THE RULE"; "IDEA WHOSE TIME HAS COME"; "OLDEST PROFESSION"; "RINGING OFF THE HOOK"; "YES, VIRGINIA").

On the other hand (that is a cliché), to tell hikers "It's five miles *as the crow flies* but double that on the road" swiftly imparts useful information; and *"the burden of proof* is on the plaintiff" carries legal significance. All of the following fifty clichés also convey ideas succinctly, even though all those ideas might be expressed differently:

Break the ice, call the tune, clear the air, dark horse, fait accompli, give and take, happy ending, heaven on earth, in the same boat, labor of love, law and order, lethal weapon, lion's share, make ends meet, make good, mean(s) well, miscarriage of justice, moral victory, more or less, mutual attraction, neck and neck, needle in a haystack, now and then, odds and ends, on the fence, open secret, patience of Job, pay the piper, persona non grata, place in the sun, pyrrhic victory, rags to riches, rank and file, sav-

ing grace, see eye to eye, smell a rat, stab in the back, stitch in time, supply and demand, sweetness and light, sword of Damocles, take pot luck, tilt at windmills, tip of the iceberg, tit for tat, under a cloud, under the aegis of, vicious circle, wear and tear, wishful thinking.

English is indebted to French for *cliché* in the sense of a printing stereotype (an electrotype plate in traditional printing). A figurative *cliché* can be considered a figuratively stereotyped expression; i.e., one that is fixed, conventional, and unoriginal.

The word is pronounced klee-SHAY.

CLIMACTIC and CLIMATIC.
See **Confusing pairs.**

CLINCH.
"Giants clinch," a streamer cried. And there on the front page was a picture of baseball players hugging one another.

To *clinch* something (transitive verb: it has an object) is to make it secure or settle it conclusively. The San Francisco team had *clinched* the championship of the National League's western division. But just to *clinch* (intransitive verb: no object) means, in slang usage, to embrace. In boxing, to *clinch* (intransitive) is to hold one's opponent so as to avoid getting punched. A *clinch* (noun) is the act of clinching.

Except for certain nautical and industrial senses, do not confuse *clinch* with *clench*, meaning (noun) a tight grasp or (verb, transitive) to grasp or bring together tightly. *Clinch* and *clench* are used interchangeably when they denote (noun) a particular knot or a secure fastening device, especially a driven nail with its point beaten down, or (verb, transitive) to grip with one of those devices.

COCA and COCOA.
A press column related a scheme to use caterpillars to eat the plants that yield cocaine. The heading said, in part, "The drug warriors try 'scientific' fix: Bug cocoa fields." Was an innocuous drink a target in the drug war? *Cocoa* powder, like chocolate, is made from the seeds of the *cacao* tree. It appears that an editor had confused *cocoa* with *coca*, the tree or shrub whose leaves are the source of cocaine. (The text had it right.)

Another plant of similar spelling is the *coco*, also known as *coco palm* or *coconut palm* or *coconut tree*. The plural of *coco* is *cocos*.

COHORT.
This sample sentence, from *The New Republic,* is entirely correct in its usage:

When Robert Bork's Supreme Court nomination went down in flames, his candidacy vanquished by a well-funded cohort of liberal pressure groups, conservatives deplored the tactics used to defeat him.

In the next sample, from a newspaper, a word that was treated properly in the magazine is put to questionable use.

Looming above the throng at the huge CBS window is the elder statesman of the media, Walter Cronkite, hand over heart as a Metropolitan Opera baritone belts out the national anthem, while his younger cohort, Dan Rather, stands respectfully back. . . .

In words like *co-worker* and *coauthor,* the prefix *co-* indicates one who works jointly with another. So is it not reasonable to assume that a *cohort* is an associate of a "hort"? The trouble is that there is no such thing as a "hort." *Cohort* comes from the Latin *cohors:* enclosure, military company, or multitude. (*Court, courtesy,* and *curtain* also stem from that Latin word.)

The most specific meaning of *cohort* is

that of an ancient Roman military division, comprising 300 to 600 soldiers, a tenth of a legion. *Cohort* has been applied also to any body of warriors. It can denote also any group or band joined in a struggle or common cause. That is the meaning of *cohort* in the opening sample. The other samples illustrate the loosest use, in which the word is applied to individuals. Often its tone is derogatory:

> What other operations beyond those already known were planned or executed by Mr. North and his cohorts in the enterprise?

> The youth . . . is accused of coercing four children . . . into becoming his cohorts in the burglary and torching of an apartment. . . .

> . . . Assistant U.S. Atty. John Gordon . . . prosecuted Browning and 21 alleged cohorts. . . .

The crime story represented by the last example shared an issue of a metropolitan newspaper with an obituary containing this sentence:

> . . . Monroe and his cohorts gave movement to Bugs Bunny. . . .

Such lax use of "cohort(s)" is not generally acceptable, though it is usually condoned in casual speech. If a word like *associate, colleague, companion, co-worker,* or *fellow-worker* is meant, it should be used. For an implication of wrongdoing, one can choose *accomplice, confederate, gangster, partner in crime,* or *ring member.* (Occasionally *confederate* is used in an innocent sense too.)

COKE. See **Trademarks.**

Collective nouns. *1. Group: singular or plural? 2. NUMBER OF, AVERAGE OF. 3. Quantities, measures.*

1. Group: singular or plural?

This question deals with the type of noun that is a collection of people, creatures, or things—a crowd, a team, a committee, a jury, a company, a herd, a flock, an array, or other group. When it is the subject of a sentence or clause, should we treat it as singular or as plural?

It may depend on whether we emphasize the group as a whole or its members. "The crowd was roaring," but "A crowd of fans were fighting one another in the grandstand."

Any doubts are customarily settled in favor of the singular in the United States. Britons have leaned toward plural construction.

A frequent mistake is to construe a subject as both singular and plural within a sentence or clause. The mistaker is likely to choose a singular verb but a plural pronoun. In the following quotations, from metropolitan newspapers on two coasts, emphases are added to point up inconsistencies.

> Protests have been going on at the weapons station since June 10 when a group of demonstrators *was* arrested after *they* successfully caused a train to stop.

"Was . . . they" protesting? No, *they were* protesting. "Was" is singular; "they" is plural. The two words do not mix.

Most users of English have no trouble with simple sentences such as "The demonstrator was arrested" and "The demonstrators were arrested." Noun and verb match in number: singular with singular, plural with plural. But complicate a sentence with an equivocal subject, a clause or two, and a pronoun—then trouble arises.

Is "a group of demonstrators" singular or plural? Presumably the writer fixed on "group" and thought that it had to be singular: "was arrested." So why did she not stick with her decision and write "after *it* . . . caused a train to stop"? Aware that the demonstrators were arrested as individuals, she must have felt a sense of plurality to switch tracks and write "they . . . caused." But then the sentence called for "*were* arrested." (It never needed "successfully.")

When a group is a formal body, the American custom is to construe it as singular: "Congress has agreed. . . ." In Britain it is often construed as plural: "Parliament have agreed. . . ." This passage, from an American newspaper, has it both ways:

> The first way around the wall proved to be in Hungary last August, when the reformist-minded Budapest government decided to take down *its* own barbed-wire fence with Austria and later dropped *their* objections to East Germans crossing from Austria into Hungary.

"Its . . . fence" and "their objections" are inconsistent. "Their" ought to have been *its*. (A factual correction: the Germans were crossing from Hungary into Austria.)

When a group is informal, the writer or speaker often has a choice. Here, again, a press sentence is inconsistent:

> A team of California psychologists *has* developed a sense-of-humor test that *they* believe may eventually shed light on the fundamental nature of human personality.

If the team of psychologists is singular and "has" developed something, then *it believes*. But if "they believe," the team of psychologists, being plural, *have* developed something. Other options are repeating part of the subject ("a sense-of-humor test that *the team believes* . . .") and rephrasing the subject

and a verb ("*Five* California psychologists *have* developed . . .").

The final example in this section illustrates two defects:

> A gang of robbers *has* been charged with holding up 31 banks . . . using the subway for *their* getaway. . . .

If the gang is singular and "has been charged," the pronoun representing "gang" also must be singular: Change "their" to *its*. However, if the gang, as plural, made "their getaway," keep the plural pronoun but change "has" to *have*. Better yet, change "A gang of robbers has" to "*Five men have*." They are not "robbers" until they are convicted.

See also COUPLE; FACULTY; **Nouns, 3;** PAIR; STAFF.

2. NUMBER OF, AVERAGE OF

The word *number* often throws writers and speakers off course when it is part of the subject of a sentence.

> A growing number of researchers is trying to teach former crack addicts to stay away from . . . cues that will make them crave the drug. . . .

"A growing number of researchers *are* trying. . . ." The number is not performing the action; the researchers are. They are separate individuals. "A growing number of" merely qualifies "researchers." If the number of researchers were ten, the writer would not have written "Ten researchers is trying. . . ." It should not make any difference that their number is growing. If the subject were, let us say, a group of researchers, a case might be made for "researchers is," as grating as the phrase is.

What is the reader or listener supposed to focus on? In the quoted sentence, the "researchers" obviously take the spotlight. Another sentence could start similarly but place its emphasis elsewhere: "The growing number of researchers in

America *is* attributed to an improvement in science education." Here the emphasis is on the growing number.

As a rule of thumb, a subject starting with "*a* number of" takes a plural verb; a subject starting with "*the* number of" takes a singular verb.

Other phrases that can be misleading as part of a subject are *an average of, a majority of,* and *a total of.* Using them is more complicated than using *a number of.*

It is grammatically correct to say "An average of 186 million eggs *were* produced daily in the country last year." The focus there is on *eggs,* a plural. It is equally correct to say "The average of 186 million *was* lower than . . ." or "The average . . . *takes* into account. . . ." Generally "*the* average" focuses on the average as such. "An average of $5.50 *is* paid" and "An average of two pounds of sugar *is* needed" are correct too; the items would be singular without any mention of an average.

See also MAJORITY, 2; TOTAL, 2.

3. *Quantities, measures*

Measures of distance, money, weight, volume, and so on are commonly treated as singular, even though plural in form. They take singular verbs: "Twenty-two miles *is* a long walk." / "About $3.7 million *is* owed." / "Six feet, four inches *was* Abe's height." / "A hundred pounds more *makes* a ton." / "Twelve gallons of gasoline *fills* my tank."

See also AMOUNT and NUMBER; FEWER and LESS; MANY and MUCH; Numbers; Verbs, 3.

Colon. *See* Punctuation, 2.

COME and CAME. The basic form of the verb *come* is the same as its past participle: "Come inside." / "She has come a long way." The past tense is *came:* "The rains came."

In a situation comedy, the star delivered this line: "I don't understand why I just couldn't have came here and got my stuff on my own." In a television interview, a military cadet said, "At any time they could have came to me." And a caller to a radio talk show said, "He could've came to his co-workers and said, 'How do you feel about this?' " In each instance, the past tense was mistakenly used instead of the past participle; "have *come*" would have been correct.

The three would have had an excuse for the error if they had looked up *come* in a certain general dictionary. It erroneously indicates that "came" is the past participle as well as the past tense.

See also COME and GO.

COME and GO. Considered separately, the two sentences in the quoted passage (from a front page of a renowned newspaper) are correct. But they are inconsistent—in more than their different lengths, which is a desirable inconsistency.

> Organizers of the second Take Our Daughters to Work Day estimated that about 3 million American girls, most of them between the ages of 9 and 15, took off a day from school yesterday to go to work with their parents or other adults and get a closer look at opportunities awaiting them in the real world of work.
>
> And some boys came along this year.

Why did girls "go" to work while boys "came" to work?

Although the distinction between *come* and *go* blurs at times and each word has many meanings, you should know whether you're coming or going. (That principle did not apply to Groucho Marx, who liked to sing, "Hello, I must be going.")

In a sentence like "Come to papa" or "Come to me, my melancholy baby," the verb to *come* means to advance toward the one speaking. To *come* is also to approach a particular place: ". . . Behold, wise men from the East came to Jerusalem. . . ." Another meaning is to appear, to move into view: "The fog comes on little cat feet." Still another meaning is to follow: "Come with me." It can mean also to be a native or resident of a place ("She comes from Spain"), to happen or take place ("The time will come"), to reach a total ("That comes to exactly ten dollars"), and to arrive at a certain result or condition ("We came to an agreement and the meeting came to a halt").

The verb to *go* often means to depart, to move away from this place: "She has gone already." / "Go and sin no more." To *go* can mean also to travel to a place: "I must go down to the seas again." / "We're going home." It can mean also to be in operation or to move: "The motor is going." / "The car started to go." Among other meanings are to disappear ("The dictatorship must go!"), to be in particular circumstances ("The people often go hungry"), to have a certain tendency ("This state usually goes Republican"), to be known ("He goes by Bubba"), to result ("How did the game go?"), to start ("Wait till I say 'go' "), and to be compatible or sociable ("They go together").

Each of the two verbs figures in numerous expressions. A *come* idiom and a *go* idiom may have a word in common but differ completely in meaning. For instance, to *come along* can mean to advance or proceed toward success: "She has really come along in her studies"; to *go along* can mean to cooperate: "When they offered him a lot of money, he went along with their plans." Some other words similarly in common are *about, by, down, into, off, on,* and *out.*

One sentence (and certainly a pair of sentences) can encompass both *coming* and *going;* this one does. Other examples: "The cat comes and goes" (arrives and departs). "The sun comes and goes"

(appears and disappears). But note that each subject has two contrary activities. In the passage about the girls who missed school to *go* to work with their parents and the boys who *went* along, two subjects did essentially the same thing.

See also **COME and CAME.**

COMFIT and COMFORT. *See* DISCOMFIT and DISCOMFORT.

Comma. *See* Punctuation, 3.

COMMISERATION. *See* MERCY and PITY.

COMMIT, COMMITTED. 1. *Missing objects.* 2. *Recommit.*

1. Missing objects

Something is missing from both of these sentences, extracted from a television newscast and a book about business mistakes:

There isn't the same pressure on President Bush as there was on President Kennedy when he first committed to putting a man on the moon.

If the U.S. firm had committed to a more direct form of involvement such as equity participation, it could have earned greater profits.

President Kennedy "committed" *what* or *whom?* The country? The government? Himself? And what should "the U.S. firm" have "committed"? Itself? Its planning and resources? A quarter of its assets?

In all its meanings—obligate, entrust, consign, refer, perpetrate, and so on— the verb *commit* is transitive. That is, it must transmit the action to an object. Each sample sentence lacks an object.

Headlines need to be terse, yet they are not absolved from the requirements of grammar. This one appeared on a front page of a metropolitan daily: "Syria Commits to Talks, Baker Says." Use of the past participle, *committed*, would have avoided the misuse without being wordy: "Syria [is] Committed to. . . ."

At one time, *commit* was used in an intransitive way (with no object) in the sense of perpetrating an offense. Such use is obsolete. No longer may one say, for instance, "This man has *committed*." One may say, "Many people who should know better *commit* grammatical offenses."

2. Recommit

To *recommit* is to commit again. This verb too is transitive only. It comes up mainly in the context of legislative action, in which it means to send a proposed measure back to a committee: "The Senate decided to recommit the bill."

The main article in an issue of a national daily bore a headline that used the verb as though it were intransitive: "PLO Recommits to Peace, but Reins in Arafat." The headline could be challenged on both grammatical and factual grounds. (The story said the Palestine Liberation Organization, critical of its leader's failure to gain wider Palestinian self-rule, "set specific conditions for the continuation of talks with Israel.") A replacement: "PLO Sets Terms for Peace Talks, Reins in Arafat."

Common nouns. *See* **Nouns,** *1*.

COMMON SENSE. *Common sense* may be defined either as ordinary sound judgment or as the assumptions people are liable to make without special knowledge. "For millennia a flat earth was common sense." Originally *common sense* was supposed to be a master sense that gathered and interpreted the five senses. In practice, the term frequently stands for whatever point of view the user expresses.

When Congress favored declaring Communist China a most favored nation, a spokesman for capitalist groups said, "We see it as a vote for common sense."

A talk show host said, "You [women] can't have it all. It's just common sense." A (male) colleague of his said later, favoring higher prices for women's haircuts than for men's, "Let's try to use some common sense on this"; and favoring compulsory auto insurance, "It's just common sense." A competitor prefaced a discussion of Cuba by saying, "I'm going to give you the kind of common-sense logic that you don't get in most of the media these days."

In a headline, a weekly presented a point of view as "Commonsense Drug Policy. . . ." Used as an adjective in that way, the term should be hyphenated: *common-sense*.

COMMUNIST, COMMUNISM. *See* SOCIALIST, SOCIALISM.

COMMUTE. To *commute* (as an intransitive verb) means to travel between home in one community and work in another. Another common meaning of the verb (transitive) is to change a penalty or debt to a lesser one. For instance, when a governor changes a convict's sentence from life imprisonment to ten years, he *commutes* it. It is the penalty that is *commuted*, not the person on whom it was imposed. This is wrong:

> Mao's widow was sentenced to death, later commuted to life imprisonment, for heading the so-called Gang of Four, blamed for the worst excesses of the 1966–1976 Cultural Revolution.

Not the woman but her *sentence* was *commuted*.

Comparative and superlative degrees. Many an adjective or adverb has three forms, or *degrees* (that is, degrees of *comparison*): the *positive, comparative,* and *superlative.*

1. A word in the *positive* degree describes something—say, as *soft, high, fast, sweet,* or *good*—without comparing it with something else.
2. The *comparative* degree indicates that something exceeds something else. It is *softer, higher, faster, sweeter,* or *better.*
3. The *superlative* degree is the most extreme: *softest, highest, fastest, sweetest,* or *best.* Something is in the top order or surpasses all others in some respect.

Use the superlative only when what you describe is among three or more of its kind. If it is one of only two, use the comparative. "This melon is the *largest* of the three" but "This melon is the *larger* of the two."

It is a common mistake to use the superlative instead of the comparative; for instance, to say that someone is the "tallest" of two. *See* BETTER and BEST (etc.). A talk show host made the opposite mistake: "The three networks were fighting to see who would get the bigger piece of the pie." One network would get the *biggest* piece. (And "who" should be *which. See* WHO, THAT, and WHICH, *1.*)

A book about business mistakes makes a verbal mistake:

The firm encountered legal problems in West Germany, however, because German law dictates that superlatives are not permitted. One product cannot be called better (or stronger) than another.

Better or *stronger* are not "superlatives." They are *comparatives.*

See also COMPARED TO and COM-PARED WITH; Comparison; MORE and MOST; MORE with comparative; MOST with superlative; Numbers, *10B, D.*

COMPARED TO and COM-PARED WITH. *1. Similarities and contrasts. 2. Two other problems.*

1. Similarities and contrasts

Each of these four sentences contains one wrong word:

. . . Detective Tom Lange . . . asked him to bring the glove found outside Simpson's mansion into the middle of the crime scene so it could be compared to the glove found near the bodies.

Typically, community college part-timers earn about half the hourly pay of full-time teachers—$28.38 compared to $53.36. . . .

There were not many words in the first ROGET'S THESAURUS, compared to the number in a volume like this. . . .

There are no published studies that compared the drug to placebo or fake pills.

Each "to" should be *with.*

When we compare something *to* something else, we are likening the two things or pointing out similarities. ("The streaks on Mars used to be compared *to* our canals." / "People have compared Castro *to* Stalin.")

When we compare something *with* something else, we are either contrasting the two ("$28.38 compared *with* $53.36") or examining them to look for differences or similarities ("studies that compared the drug *with* placebo or fake pills").

Is all that just unnecessary fussiness? The use of "to" instead of *with* by a news agency gives a twist to the first sample. The "to" seems to imply that the detective wanted to make the two gloves look like a pair—probably not what either he or the writer had in mind. *With* would have suggested that the detective wanted an objective comparison of the two gloves.

2. *Two other problems*
The sentence below (from an editorial) illustrates two other points.

Four in 10 black men over the age of 20 smoke, compared to only 32 percent of white men.

The grammarian Wilson Follett would have challenged *compared,* as well as *to,* in the last sentence, had he lived to read it: The black men would smoke even if *not* compared with the white men; the two facts are independent and belong in separate independent clauses or sentences. He railed at length against "gratuitous comparison," the statement of independent facts as if they were dependent.

Note also that one of those two statistics was presented on a scale of one to ten and the other on a percentage scale. While some readers may have had no trouble converting "four in 10" to *forty percent,* or "32 percent" to *about three in 10,* the writer's zeal for synonymizing may have obscured the message for other readers.

Comparison. 1. *"More" or "less" than what? 2. What are we comparing?*

1. *"More" or "less" than what?*
In the mythical realm of advertising, the advertiser's product customarily is "better," gives you "more," and costs you "less." What it is better, bigger, and cheaper *than* is left to the imagination. The veracity or mendacity of such vague claims cannot easily be checked. A copywriter is interested in sales, not facts.

Informative writing has to make more sense. When something is said to be bigger, smaller, quicker, more beautiful, less crowded, or the like, one needs to know what the thing is bigger *than,* smaller *than,* and so on. The word *than* does not always have to be in the sentence. ("John weighs 300 pounds. His wife is even heavier.") And the comparison is implied in certain expressions, such as *higher education* and *the upper classes.* In general, though, when *more* or *less* or an *-er* word in the comparative degree is used, it must be made completely clear what is being compared to what. This sentence fails to make it clear:

While residents in the San Francisco metropolitan area—including San Mateo and Marin counties—spent less on food last year, they still rank ninth in total restaurant sales and tops in per capita spending.

They "spent less on food" than what? Than on clothing? Than anyone else? Even if the reporter had written, for instance, "spent less on food last year *than they spent in the previous year,*" the sentence still would have raised questions and contained inconsistencies. (How could the spending of "residents" be distinguished from that of visitors? If the spending was for "food," why are only restaurants mentioned, not food stores? Was "per capita spending" just in restaurants too? On what scale were the residents measured? They were "ninth" or "tops" out of how many units, of what nature, in what geographical category?)

See **Comparative and superlative degrees** and its references for some grammatical problems.

2. *What are we comparing?*
To be compared, things must be comparable. They have to fit the same general category. You do not compare apples with orangutans. Apples and oranges at least are both fruits.

The discussion here deals with logic and style, not the verity of the premise expressed in the newspaper sentence below.

> . . . Japanese investors still need to learn that the tenant is king in America, compared to the landlord's market in Japan. . . .

It seems to be comparing a royal rank and a type of market. Either the first or the second part has to change. Examples: (1) "to learn that *a tenant's market prevails* in America, compared . . ."; (2) "to learn that the tenant is king in America, compared *with his subordinate position* in Japan. . . ." ("To" needs to be *with*. *See* COMPARED TO and COMPARED WITH.)

Instead of *compared with*, the difference could be highlighted by *unlike* or *in contrast to*. A reporter was on the track but got derailed:

> In contrast to 40 years ago the Governors today—Mr. Mabus, 39 years old, Mr. Clinton, 40, and Mr. Roemer, 45—are not set in the segregationist ways of the past.

He seems to be comparing a time in the past with three governors. What he probably meant to say and should have said was of this order: "In contrast to *the governors of their states* 40 years ago, the Governors today . . ." or "*Unlike their counterparts* 40 years ago, the Governors today. . . ."

A columnist, writing about quartet singing, got into double trouble:

> Barbershop was big in the '50s, as big at any time since its Golden Era in the early years of the century.

To insert a second *as*—"as big *as*"—would help but not completely rescue the sentence. It seems to be comparing

size with time. A complete correction: ". . . as big *as it was* at any time . . ."

Although the examples above are not worded logically, at least we know the essential points of similarity or contrast that the writers have tried to express. In the example below, the essential message is not clear:

> Contrary to popular belief, children account for 15% of the homeless population.

What is the "popular belief"? *Contrary to popular belief* usually implies that the adjoining statement is the opposite of the belief. The statement here, a statistic, has no clear opposite.

See also AS, *3;* AS and LIKE, *2;* LIKE, *2;* UNLIKE, *2;* Numbers, *7, 10B.*

COMPASSION. *See* MERCY and PITY.

COMPENDIUM, COMPENDIOUS.
A book is subtitled "A Compendium of Source Material to Make Your Speech Sparkle." An article refers to " 'Outrageous Animation,' a feature-length compendium of cartoons. . . ." In both cases "compendium" is used as though it meant collection.

A *compendium* is a summary, abridgment, or outline of a work. That is one meaning of the word in Latin, its source. Perhaps the *comp-*, as in *compilation* or *comprehensive*, fools people.

Compendium (noun) is related to *compendious* (adjective), meaning summarized, containing all the essentials succinctly. Noah Webster's first general dictionary, 1806, was titled *A Compendious Dictionary of the English Language.* He meant that it was concise.

When a lexicographer sought "to produce a work that would be as compendious as *Webster's Third,*" did he want it to be as *concise?* Other comments of his (references, in an essay, to "The sheer quantity and range of the material" and "the inclusiveness of this huge new dictionary") indicate that he meant as *inclusive* or as *comprehensive*.

COMPLAINANT.

The chairman of a Senate committee asked a witness at a prominent hearing three times whether the "conduct of a complaintant" could be relevant to a rape case.

A person who complains, particularly in the sense of filing a formal complaint in a legal case, is a *complainant*, spelled with just one *t*. One who complains, but not in a formal sense, can also be called a *complainer*, with no *t*. There is no "complaintant."

Complement.

As a term of grammar, *complement* is used in varying ways. In the broadest sense, it is a word or group of words that completes a grammatical construction. Usually the word or group of words goes with a verb in the predicate of a sentence (*see* **Verbs**, *1D*) and makes the meaning of the verb or its object complete.

A *complement* may be a *direct object* ("Jack built the *house*" / "I met *him*") or an *indirect object* ("Give the *boy* his money" / "I will send *her* a letter"). *See* **Verbs**, *1E*. More often *complement* refers to a *subjective complement* or an *objective complement*.

A *subjective complement* (or *subject complement*) accompanies a linking verb and identifies or qualifies the subject. If the complement is a noun, it is called a *predicate noun* (or *predicate nominative*). ("That bird is a *gooney*.") If it is an adjective, it is called a *predicate adjective*. ("They seem *happy*.") *See* **Verbs**, *1F*.

An *objective complement* (or *object complement*) completes the meaning of a direct object. ("His friends call him *Red*." / "Mining made them *rich*." / "John got the clock *to run*.") *See also* **FACT- words**, *2* (*factitive*).

COMPLEMENT and COMPLIMENT.

An advertisement for an apartment complex included this sentence: "Beautiful shade trees compliment these garden apartments and beautifully landscaped grounds." If trees could talk, they might "compliment" the apartments and grounds on their appearance. As it is, the writer should have used the other word, *complement*.

To *compliment* (verb, transitive) someone is to pay the person a *compliment* (noun): an expression of admiration, congratulation, or praise. (Think of beautiful i's.)

To *complement* (verb, transitive) something is to add, or serve as, a *complement* (noun) to it. A *complement* is that which makes something whole or brings it to perfection or completion. (Complete this word with e's.)

A savings bank displayed a sign saying, "ASK ABOUT OUR COMPLEMENTARY MORTGAGE ANALYSIS." If the intended meaning was that the mortgage analysis would be provided free of charge as a courtesy or compliment, *complimentary* should have been the adjective chosen. *Complementary* means acting as a *complement*, completing what is lacking.

COMPOSE.

See **COMPRISE**, *1*.

COMPOUNDS (chemicals).

See **SILICON and SILICONE**.

Compounds (words).

See **Plurals and singulars**, *2B;* **Punctuation**, *4D*.

COMPRISE.

1. "COMPRISED OF." *2.* "INCLUDE, CONTAIN." *3.* The whole and the parts.

1. "COMPRISED OF"

To *comprise* (verb, transitive) is to consist of, to be composed of—*of* is part of the meaning.

In four press samples, the word's past

participle, *comprised,* is misused as though it meant "composed." (In the first two, it opens an appositive phrase. In the latter two, it serves as a main verb.)

> The special panel, comprised of seven senators on the Judiciary Committee and two from Foreign Relations, also meets privately.

> The author will develop the plot in consultation with the committee, comprised of Mr. Clarke and two other lawyers.

"Comprised of" is wrong. Changing it to *comprising* would correct both sentences: "comprising seven senators . . ." / "comprising Mr. Clarke and. . . ." Another way is to change "comprised" to *consisting, composed,* or *made up,* keeping *of.*

> The court is comprised of eight active judges.

> . . . Our research team was comprised of women.

To fix those two sentences, change "is comprised of" to *comprises* ("The court *comprises* eight active judges") and reduce "was comprised of" to *comprised* ("Our research team *comprised* women"). There are other ways: "The court *consists* of" and "Our research team *consisted* of" / "The court is *composed* of" or "*made up* of" and "Our research team was *composed* of" or "*made up* of." (We assume that the composition of each group was given in its entirety.)

2. *"INCLUDE, CONTAIN"*
At least three dictionaries misleadingly give as one of their definitions of *comprise* "To include, contain." The meanings are not the same.

Using *comprise* implies that all the items making up the court or team or other body are being enumerated. ("A water molecule *comprises* two atoms of hydrogen and one atom of oxygen.") But using *include* implies that not all the items are being enumerated. ("A water molecule *includes* one atom of oxygen.")

Contain can have either meaning, depending on the context. ("This can *contains* only tomatoes. That one *contains* salt and spices.")

3. *The whole and the parts*
The whole *comprises* its parts, not the other way around. Congress *comprises* two houses. Two houses do not "comprise" Congress.

This passage appears in a medical dictionary, under "fat":

> Three fatty acids, oleic acid . . . stearic acid . . . and palmitic acid . . . comprise the bulk of fatty acids present in neutral fats found in body tissues.

A correction that keeps the word *comprise* is as follows: "The bulk of fatty acids present in neutral fats found in body tissues *comprise* three fatty acids: oleic acid" etc. An alternative correction is to change "comprise" to *make up:* "Three fatty acids . . . *make up* the bulk," etc.

Concrete noun. *See* **Nouns,** *1.*

CONDITION. *1. Accidental drollery. 2. Contradictory meanings.*

1. Accidental drollery
Do you want to get into condition? People do it in a variety of ways. We hear on television that a man is "in good condition after falling twenty feet from a gondola at Disneyland," and we read in a newspaper that an ex-president is "in excellent condition after . . . he was thrown from a horse. . . ."

Warning: Those methods are not recommended for everyone. You are better off with good food and normal exercise.

If anyone really concludes from such reports that accidents bring about physical fitness, blame a combination of two journalistic locutions: (1) reversal of the chronological order of events, often with *after,* in an effort to update the news; and (2) use of *condition* in a special sense, that of a medical prognosis, a prediction of a patient's chance of recovery. A patient who is sore, bruised, and hurting may not feel in "good"—let alone "excellent"—condition, but that is what the reporter got from his medical source.

Sometimes the word *condition* or a synonym is omitted from a headline dealing with someone's health, and readers may be told that the person "is critical" or "serious" or "good." The result may be an ambiguity or, at least, a temptation to wags.

See also **AFTER; CRITICAL.**

2. *Contradictory meanings*

Condition (noun and verb) has dozens of meanings. Two of its popular meanings are contradictory: To be in or get into *condition* refers to physical fitness or good health, but to have or suffer a *condition* refers to an ailment or disease. Neither application is suitable in writings on scientific or medical topics. In "He suffers from a heart condition," the last word would bother many editors, even in the popular press. Its use is your choice.

Conditional sentences. *See* **Subjunctive; WAS and WERE.**

CONDOLENCE. *See* **MERCY and PITY.**

CONFESS. The primary meaning of *confess* is to acknowledge or admit one's crime, misdeed, or fault. The implication is that what is confessed is bad or faulty, or so perceived.

The only perceptible fault in the following sentence, the lead of an article, is its final word:

> "Four times they asked me to play Kate, and four times I refused," Carole Shelley confessed.

What is so bad about turning down a part in a play that an actress has to "confess" it?

In colloquial speech, *confess* and *admit* often are used interchangeably. When a formal, written confession of a crime is made, *confess* is more precise.

In the sense of acknowledging wrongdoing, *confess* is both a transitive verb ("He confessed the burglary") and an intransitive verb ("He confessed"). In that sense, *admit* is transitive only. With the sanction of several dictionaries, one may either *confess* a crime or *confess* to a crime. Some grammarians consider "confess to" clumsy and not idiomatic.

In religion, *confess* can mean to declare one's faith or belief, or to make one's sins known to a priest; the priest is said to *confess* someone.

See also **ADMIT.**

CONFIDENT. *See* **SURE.**

Confusing pairs. A list of sixty word pairs that can be troublesome follows below. The words (or combining forms) in boldface in each paragraph have different meanings, spellings, and pronunciations but are subject to confusion because they look or sound similar. They are presented in alphabetical order and briefly defined, with illustrations of use in most instances.

Other groups of the same kind, enumerated at the end of this list, are dealt with as separate entries. *See also* **Homophones,** listing pairs of words that are spelled differently but pronounced the same. **Punctuation,** *1 B*, deals with confusion related to apostrophes.

Adverse, unfavorable; "an adverse result." **Averse,** opposed; "averse to gambling."

Allude, to refer (to something or someone) indirectly or by suggestion, with no specific mention; "alluding to his opponent but never mentioning him by name." **Elude,** to avoid or slip away from, especially by crafty means; "eluding the police for years."

Alternate (noun), a substitute, "an alternate at the convention"; (adjective) every other, or first one and then the other, "alternate years" / "alternate boxes." **Alternative** (noun), a choice, "the alternative to ice cream"; (adjective) providing a choice, "an alternative dessert."

Ambiguous, able to be interpreted in two or more ways; "an ambiguous sentence." **Ambivalent,** having conflicting feelings, e.g., love and hate; "his ambivalent attitude toward her."

Arrant, out-and-out; "arrant nonsense." **Errant,** wandering, deviating; "a knight-errant" / "an errant golf ball."

Avenge, to inflict punishment for, emphasizing justice; "avenge the crime." **Revenge,** to inflict punishment for or on behalf of, emphasizing retaliation; "revenge my abused daughter."

Averse, see **Adverse** in this list.

Avoid, to keep away from; "avoid the crowd." **Evade,** to escape by devious means; "evade taxes."

Beside, alongside; "a nightstand beside the bed." **Besides,** in addition (to); "other performers besides the star."

Breath (noun), respiration or an inhalation of air; "a deep breath." **Breathe** (verb), to inhale and exhale air; "breathe deeply."

Calvary, the place of, or a representation of, Christ's crucifixion. **Cavalry,** combat troops, formerly on horseback, now in armored vehicles.

Celebrant, strictly speaking, a participant in a religious ceremony, particularly the priest celebrating the Eucharist. **Celebrator,** one who celebrates; "New Year's celebrators."

Chafe, to rub or irritate, "shoes that chafed her feet." **Chaff** (noun), grain husks separated from seeds, "separate the wheat from the chaff"; (verb) to tease in a friendly way, "chaffed by his wife for watching too much sports."

Clean (verb), to literally remove dirt, debris, stains, or impurities; "to clean the bathroom." **Cleanse,** in a figurative sense, to clean, purge, or purify—applicable to religion and ceremony; "to cleanse ourselves of sin."

Climactic, pertaining to a climax; "the climactic scene." **Climatic,** pertaining to climate; "climatic data."

Corps (pronounced like *core*), a military or other group. **Corpse,** a cadaver.

Credible, believable; "a credible actress." **Creditable,** deserving credit; "a creditable achievement."

Dairy, a place that produces or sells milk products. **Diary,** a private record book. (The *a* and *i* are sometimes inadvertently transposed.)

Delusion, a false belief; "a delusion of grandeur." **Illusion,** a misleading image or false perception; "an optical illusion."

Deprecate, to express disapproval of, or to plead against; "to deprecate the proposed merger." **Depreciate,** to lessen the value of, or to decline in value; "the peso is depreciating."

Dialectal, of a dialect; "a dialectal word." **Dialectic,** a method of logic; "the philosopher Hegel's dialectic."

Disassemble, to take apart; "The repairman has to disassemble the machine." **Dissemble,** to disguise the real nature of something by means of a false appearance; to act hypocritically; "He dissembled his hostility by feigning friendship."

Efficacy, effectiveness; "efficacy of the drug." **Efficiency,** competency, speed, and economy in a job; "the workers' efficiency."

Elemental, of or pertaining to an element or force of nature; "elemental particles." **Elementary,** fundamental, introductory, presenting the rudiments; "elementary school."

Energize, to give energy to, or to rouse; "energize the circuit" / "energize the audience." **Enervate,** to deprive of energy, to weaken; "enervated by the tropical climate."

Entomology, the study of insects. **Etymology,** the study of word history or an account of a word's origin and development.

Errant, see **Arrant** in this list.

Evade, see **Avoid** in this list.

Fiscal, financial or pertaining to revenue; "fiscal year." **Physical,** pertaining to the body or to material things; "physical exercise."

Forceful, full of force, effective; "a forceful speaker." **Forcible,** carried out by force; "forcible entry."

Glance (noun), a quick look, "a glance at her face"; (verb) to take a quick look, "to glance back." **Glimpse** (noun), a very brief, incomplete view or sight, "a glimpse of the Pope"; (verb) to catch a glimpse of, "to glimpse at a meteor."

Hyper-, excessive or too high, as in *hypertension,* high blood pressure, and *hyperthermia,* high temperature. **Hypo-,** inadequate or too low, as in *hypotension,* low blood pressure, and *hypothermia,* low temperature.

Illusion, see **Delusion** in this list.

Inter-, among or between, as in *interstate,* among states. **Intra-,** within, as in *intrastate,* within one state.

Judicial, pertaining to or befitting judges or courts; "the judicial system." **Judicious,** prudent or showing sound judgment; "a judicious decision."

Laudable, praiseworthy; "a laudable achievement." **Laudatory,** expressing praise; "presented with a laudatory plaque."

Lightening, reducing a weight or a load. **Lightning,** an electric discharge in the atmosphere.

Luxuriant, abundant, profuse; "luxuriant vegetation." **Luxurious,** of, providing, or characterized by luxury; rich, pleasurable; "a luxurious hotel."

Marital, pertaining to marriage. **Martial,** pertaining to war. (The *i* and *t* are sometimes inadvertently transposed.)

Material, the substance(s) that a thing is made of; "raw material" / "fine material." **Materiel** (or matériel), munitions in war or things needed in any undertaking; "men and matériel." (In pronunciation the *-el* is stressed.)

Moral (noun), the lesson of a tale, "the moral of this fable"; (adjective) concerning right and wrong, "a moral obligation." **Morale,** mental spirits; "the soldiers' morale."

Ordinance, a law or regulation, often minor; "city ordinance." **Ordnance,** weaponry, particularly artillery; "army ordnance."

Oscillate, to swing back and forth regularly; "an electric fan that oscillates." **Osculate,** to kiss each other; "lovers osculating."

Parameter, primarily a mathematical term: a symbol (such as *a* or *t*) representing a quantity that is constant in a particular case but whose value varies in different cases, e.g., a radius, varying with different circles. **Perimeter,** the border of a two-dimensional figure; "the perimeter of the room."

Persecute, to oppress (people), typically because of religion, race, or politics; "China's effort to persecute the Tibetans." **Prosecute,** to institute or conduct court proceedings, particularly criminal, against (someone); "the decision to prosecute him on perjury charges."

Perspective, a technique of representing three dimensions in two-dimensional art, or one's viewpoint; "the perspective of the painting" / "from my perspective." **Prospective,** in the future, likely; "prospective customers."

Physical, see **Fiscal** in this list.

Practicable, workable, able to be carried out; "testing the device to see if it's practicable." **Practical,** effective, utilitarian, put to a useful purpose; "the first practical electric light."

Precede, to go before; "to precede the discussion with a brief introduction." **Proceed,** to continue on; "to proceed cautiously up the mountain."

Presumptive, presumed; providing ground for belief or acceptance; "presumptive evidence" / "heir presumptive." **Presumptuous,** quick to presume, venture, or take liberties; too forward; impudent; "a presumptuous student who contradicted his teachers."

Proceed, see **Precede** in this list.

Prospective, see **Perspective** in this list.

Prostate, a male gland. **Prostrate** (verb), to have (oneself) bow down; or (adjective) lying down full length.

Revenge, see **Avenge** in this list.

Sanction, (noun) authoritative permission, or (verb) to allow or approve; "sanctioning my activities." **Sanctions,** action taken against a country to force compliance with certain standards; "the sanctions against South Africa."

Saving, a reduction in expense (or labor, time, etc.) or its result; "a saving of 20 percent" / "daylight-saving time." **Savings** (plural), sums of money that have been saved and laid away; "to have savings in the bank."

Scrip, a certificate or other paper to be held temporarily and exchanged for stock, money, services, etc., or such issuance in general. **Script,** handwriting; or the written form of a dramatic work or oral program.

Seasonable, suitable to the time of year; "a seasonable cold spell." **Seasonal,** affected by the season, or coming at regular times of the year; "seasonal work" / "seasonal planting."

Sentiment, opinion, emotion, tender emotion, or thought influenced by emotion; "my sentiment is" / "logic, not sentiment." **Sentimentality,** an excess of sentiment or emotion; "a melodramatic play, marred by sentimentality."

Serve (verb), to perform service, to help; "to serve our customers" / "to serve my country." **Service** (verb), to repair or render (something) fit for service, or (for a male animal) to mate with (a female animal); "to service cars" / "to service cows."

Sewage, waste water and solids carried off in sewers and drains; "excess sewage from the heavy rains." **Sewerage,** a system of sewers, or the removal of waste through such a system; "improving the city's sewerage" / "efficient sewerage."

Simple, not complicated, easy to understand or deal with; "simple directions." **Simplistic,** oversimplified; "a simplistic answer to a complex problem."

Specie, money in the form of coin, as distinguished from paper money; "issued in specie." **Species** (singular and plural noun), a biological class, ranking after a genus, consisting of animals or plants able to interbreed; "an endangered species."

Systematic, based on, forming, or characterized by a system, plan, or method; methodical; orderly; "a systematic study" / "systematic work habits." **Systemic,** affecting the body as a whole, not just one organ or location; "a systemic disease" / "a systemic drug."

Trustee, pronounced trust-EE; a member of an institution's governing board, or one who holds title to property for the benefit of another. **Trusty,** pronounced TRUST-ee; a prisoner considered trustworthy and granted special privileges.

Turbid, opaque, dense, or muddled; "turbid water" / "turbid smoke" / "turbid mental state." **Turgid,** swollen, inflated, or pompous; "turgid foot" / "turgid style of writing."

Venal, subject to corruption, "venal officials." **Venial,** easily forgiven, excusable; "a venial sin."

Vicious, wicked; "a vicious crime." **Viscous,** slow-flowing; "a viscous liquid."

See also the following entries:

ADAPT and ADOPT
ADVICE and ADVISE
ANECDOTE and ANTIDOTE
APPRAISE and APPRISE
CAREEN and CAREER
CENSOR and CENSURE
COCA and COCOA
DESERT and DESSERT
DISCOMFIT and DISCOMFORT
DISINGENUOUS and INGENUOUS
DISINTERESTED and UNINTER-
   ESTED
DISQUALIFIED and UNQUALIFIED
EMIGRATE and IMMIGRATE
EMINENT and IMMINENT
EXERCISE and EXORCISE
FARTHER and FURTHER
FLAUNT and FLOUT
FLOUNDER and FOUNDER
FOREWORD and FORWARD
FORTUITOUS [and FORTUNATE
   or FELICITOUS]
FULSOME [and FULL]
FUROR and FURY
GANTLET and GAUNTLET
HARDY and HEARTY
HINDI and HINDU
HISTORIC and HISTORICAL
IMPLY and INFER
INCIDENCE and INCIDENT
LIGATION and LITIGATION
LOOSE and LOSE
MASTERFUL and MASTERLY
NAUSEATED and NAUSEOUS
NAVAL and NAVEL
OPTOMETRIST and OPTICIAN
PALPATE and PALPITATE
PENCHANT and PENSION
PERQUISITE and PREREQUISITE
PRESCRIBE and PROSCRIBE
PROPHECY and PROPHESY
REBUT and REFUTE
REMUNERATION and RENU-
   MERATION
RESPECTABLE and RESPECTFUL
REVOLT and REVOLUTION
RUIN and RUINS
SCALD and SCOLD

SET and SIT
SHIMMER and SHIMMY
SILICON and SILICONE
SPAT and SPATE
TEMBLOR and TREMBLER
TESTAMENT and TESTIMONY
THAN [and THEN]
TORTUOUS and TORTUROUS
WENCH and WINCH
WHEREFORE and WHEREOF
WITHER and WRITHE
WREAK and WRECK
WREST and WRESTLE

**CONGRESSMAN, CONGRESS-
MEN.** *See* PEOPLE as a suffix; PER-
SON, *1*.

Conjunctions. *See* AND; AS; AS and
LIKE; BECAUSE; BOTH, *1;* BUT; EI-
THER; NEITHER; NOR; NOT ONLY;
OR; Series errors; THAN and THEN;
THAT; WHETHER; WITH (misused).

CONNIVE. This verb stems from the
Latin *connivere:* to close the eyes. The
strict meaning of *connive* is to pretend
not to see a wrong or evil, thereby tacitly
consenting to it. It goes with *at.* For instance, "The president connived at the
crimes of his men."

The word (in the form of a gerund)
was not used strictly when a broadcaster
said the movie *Wall Street* conveyed the
message that "lying, cheating, and con-
niving are bad things." Nor was its use
(as a verbal adjective) strict in an article
about a lottery winner, whose "conniv-
ing relatives . . . tore his work clothes to
shreds to keep him at home. . . ."

"Connive" is often used loosely in
place of *contrive* or *conspire,* "conniv-
ing" in place of *contriving, conspiring,*
or *cunning.* Popular confusion probably
arose from the words' superficial similarity. Their roots (Old English for *cunning,*
Latin for the others) differ completely.

**CONSECRATE, CONSECRA-
TION.** *See* DESECRATE, DESECRA-
TION.

CONSENSUS. A question for two critics and a reporter follows these excerpts:

> Here is a man [Scorsese] who, by general consensus is the best American director of the last twenty years.

> When the Chicago group played New York last fall, the general consensus . . . was that the dancers did a swell job.

> But there has always been a general consensus of some kind of Mafia involvement in the crime. . . .

What other kind of *consensus* is there? It is general by definition: general agreement. Sometimes *consensus* is defined as unanimity, although it can describe also a collective view or majority agreement.

The phrase "consensus of opinion" is common. Various authorities frown on it, considering "of opinion" redundant. Some others justify a *consensus of opinion,* particularly when it needs to be distinguished from a *consensus of authority,* of evidence, of faith, of taste, of testimony, and so on.

In any case, "consensus of" does not go with "some kind of Mafia involvement" (in the third example). You can test the sentence by substituting *agreement* for "consensus." Among possible corrections: change the first "of" to *that there was* or change "consensus of" to *belief in.*

Consensus sometimes is misspelled "concensus" and occasionally is confused with "census." *Consensus,* like *consent,* originates in the Latin *consentire,* to agree. It has nothing to do with *census,* an official counting of inhabitants, which comes unchanged from Latin.

CONSENT. *See* CONSENSUS.

CONSUL, COUNCIL, and COUNSEL. *See* Homophones.

CONTAIN. *See* COMPRISE, 2.

CONTINUAL(LY) and CONTINUOUS(LY). *Continuous* (adjective) or *continuously* (adverb) means without interruption; going on steadily, either in time or in space. "The dam provides us with energy continuously." / "I use a continuous roll of paper in my printer."

For centuries *continuous* was the meaning of *continual,* and dictionaries still include the former as one of the definitions of the latter. In modern times, though, a useful distinction between the two arose. *Continual* (adjective) or *continually* (adverb) now means frequently repeated, taking place again and again. "Old Faithful's continual spraying of water and steam into the air fascinates visitors to Yellowstone." / "Our neighbors are continually playing music loudly." To substitute "continuous" or "continuously" would change each meaning.

Sometimes the words are mistakenly or carelessly interchanged, as in this pair of examples: In the Arctic in December "it is dark continually." / "A continuous use of 'miracle' to describe any coincidence or amazing happening is vulgar." Make it *continuously* in the first sentence (the darkness persists without interruption), *continual* in the second sentence (the use is repeated, not steady).

"Our goal at any given time is to strive continually to be 'the best,' " the director of an institute wrote. She probably meant *continuously* strive, rather than strive only at intervals. (*See also* **Quotation problems,** 3.)

Contractions. *1. Errors in number. 2. Informality. 3. Quotation. 4. Perplexity.*

1. Errors in number

A *contraction* is a shortened version of a word or phrase, such as *can't* in place of *cannot* or *it's* in place of *it is.*

Its use does not relax any grammatical requirement. Subject and verb must still agree in number, just as if no contraction were used. Both samples below contain errors in number.

> There's even gossip, advice columns and TV listings [in a Polish weekly].

"There's" is meant to contract *there* and *is*. But *is* does not go with the enumerated features. Change "there's" to *There are*.

> Scientists say it's "usually impossible" to predict when an earthquake occurs but there's been "tremendous advances" in predicting where one occurs, said Gore.

This time "there's" purports to contract *there* and *has*. But *has* (singular) disagrees with "advances" (plural). Change "there's" to *there have*.
See also **DON'T and DOESN'T.**

2. Informality
Usually contractions are acceptable in spoken English. They may also fit writing that is informal or that aims at simulating speech. They are standard in some expressions, "*It's* a boy." / "It *can't* happen here." / "*Aren't* we all?" / "*Isn't* it time?"
An *-n't* in a question is especially common and often desirable, e.g., "*Won't* you come home?" (rather than "Will you not come home?"). But eloquence may call for the complete *not:* "If you prick us, do we not bleed?" (rather than "don't we bleed?").
Except where speakers are quoted using them, contractions can stand out conspicuously in formal writing or accounts of grave events, weakening the writing and giving it an inappropriate informality. Two examples from the press follow.

> He's accused of trying to blow up his disabled parents and grandmother by rigging a natural-gas leak in the basement of their Russell Street home.

> Witnesses reported tank movements Monday, but the reports couldn't be officially confirmed.

Why "He's" and "couldn't" instead of *he is* and *could not?* Did the reporters think a chatty style fit those stories? The latter sentence would be particularly unsuitable for oral delivery, in which "-n't" is not always articulated.

3. Quotation
Contractions may or may not be warranted in quotations. If a speaker did not utter any contraction, its use can border on misquotation. The excerpt below is from a published account of a rally in Moscow.

> "The *agenda's* already been decided," said Boris N. Yeltsin, the popular maverick deputy-elect. "*It's* been prepared by the apparat. . . . If we allow ourselves to be dictated to by the apparat, we will sink into a morass that *we've* only now begun to climb from," he said. [Emphases are added.]

Yeltsin spoke in Russian, a language with few contractions. It has nothing like "agenda's" / "It's" / "we've." What do they contribute to the report that *agenda has, It has,* and *we have* would not?
Far from putting fanciful contractions in their quotations, some writers go to the opposite pole and eliminate contractions that were uttered. President Nixon was widely quoted as saying, "I am not a crook." His precise words were, "Well, I'm not a crook [emphasizing "not"]. I've earned everything I've got." Note the three contractions.

4. Perplexity
Contractions can be confused with possessive forms. Even professional writers sometimes mix them up. See **ITS and IT'S; Punctuation,** *1;* **WHOSE,** 2 (confusion with *who's*).
During the national Democratic con-

vention in San Francisco, a newspaper there ran a banner with this phrase: "Mondale's halfway home." Was the paper running an exposé of a term spent by the vice-president in a house for rehabilitation? The headline raised that question in my mind. But no; the story underneath said he had acquired half the delegates needed to win the presidential nomination. The apostrophe-*s* meant *is*.

If contractions can confound those of us who are native to English, pity the newcomers and foreign visitors trying to decipher them. The contractions in these three passages are emphasized:

> *What's* puzzling is that Mrs. Cheney, *who's* performed ably in her job, applauds the Public Library's "considerable success in recent years in achieving increased support...."

> But if the people who make up America's work force are more diverse than ever before, *it's* men who are still in charge—and *who'll* stay that way if they heed Felice S——....

> ... W—— is one of about 20 youngsters with cancer—or *who've* had cancer—camped at Monte Toyon....

Readers of English must know the possessive -*'s*. They may also know that -*'s* can stand for *is* when attached to a noun or, sometimes, a pronoun. Those who are unfamiliar with American conversational speech may not realize that -*'s* can also stand for *has* or *us* ("Let's eat"). And they may not know what to make of some creations—like "who'll" and "who've," in which half of *will* and half of *have* are expunged for no obvious reason.

CONTRARY TO POPULAR BELIEF. *See* Comparison, 2; NOT, 1C.

Contrast. *See* BUT, 1; COMPARED TO and COMPARED WITH, 1; Comparison, 2; Irony; NOT, 1C; UNLIKE.

CONUNDRUMS. *See* FESTOON, FESTOONED.

CONVINCE and PERSUADE.
Convince deals with **concepts**. It is to cause (someone) to believe something. *Persuade* deals with **performance**. It is to cause (someone) to do something.

If "We convinced the governor of Smith's innocence" or "We convinced him that Smith was innocent," only the governor's belief changed; the man was not yet freed. If, however, "We persuaded him to pardon Smith" or "He was persuaded to pardon Smith," ah, then there was action.

Note that *convince* (verb, transitive) may be followed by *of* or *that,* never by "to." *Persuade* (verb, transitive) is commonly followed by *to.* Literature of the past shows also *persuade into* or *unto* plus noun.

In practice, the two words are often interchanged. In a typical mixup, an anchor man said on network television:

> He has convinced the Food and Drug Administration to change the food-additive laws.

He, a doctor, has *persuaded* the FDA to change the rules. One could also say the doctor has *convinced* the FDA *that it should* change the rules. However, the *persuaded* phrasing is terser and makes it clear that rules—not just minds—have been changed.

COOK. *See* BOIL.

COOL. This word's popularity among juveniles as an all-purpose adjective of approval has spilled over to their elders. Not even a book on computer technology is immune to such jargon:

Some of the multimedia software available on CDs is soooo cool. . . . How totally cool I thought text-based adventure games were. . . . Developers are turning out improved drives, and (coolest of all) some of the funkiest software. . . . [A movie] was cute—very cool, even. . . . The very cool sound programs . . . [Etc.].

Cool is perfectly proper in describing that which is moderately cold; or makes one feel that way, as a *cool* suit or *cool* colors; or is calm, as a *cool* head or a *cool* bandit; or lacks cordiality, as a *cool* reception. But if everything that pleases you, from mild diversion to sublime ecstasy, is "cool," then you are talking kiddie talk.

See also NEAT.

COPE. The issue is not whether one can *cope* with something but whether one can just *cope*—with nothing in particular. An example is excerpted from a journal of business and finance:

> Faced by the pent-up demand created by neglect during Ethiopian rule, barefoot doctors from the front lines couldn't cope.

"Cope" with what? With anything? With everything? With all the medical problems of the civilian population of Eritrea?

Cope (verb, intransitive) came to English from the Old French *couper*, to strike, which came from *coup*, a blow. Usually *cope* is followed by *with*, in a phrase meaning to struggle with or contend with, (something) either with some success or on fairly even terms.

Cope without *with*, meaning to deal with or manage some situation or other, is a relative innovation, described as "colloq." by the *Oxford English Dictionary*. It did well in the title of a musical show, *Don't Bother Me, I Can't Cope*,

but its use in more formal contexts meets with objections from various writers, speakers, and editors. Three-fourths of the *American Heritage Dictionary*'s usage panel found it unacceptable.

Omitting the *with* phrasing shrinks the word's informative value. Unless the context makes it clear, such use of *cope* generates questions.

Copula or copulative verb (linking verb). *See* BAD and BADLY; FEEL; GOOD and WELL; Pronouns, *1*0D; Verbs, *1*F.

COPY-EDITING, COPYREADING. *See* PROOFREAD, PROOFREADING.

CORPORATION. *See* FIRM.

CORPS and CORPSE. *See* Confusing pairs.

Correlative conjunctions. *See* BOTH, *1*; EITHER, *1*; NEITHER, *1*; NOT ONLY; Prepositions, *5*.

"COULD CARE LESS." An expression that once made sense, however overused, has become a cliché in mutilated form. Educated users are uttering the very reverse of what they think they are saying. These include a school principal in a newspaper interview and a columnist in a television forum:

> "I could care less if people never smoked again, but smokers have their viewpoint," said Bill R——, principal. . . .

> Let's assume that Ms. Brown is as sane as a senator. I could care less.

If the speaker could care less than he does now, he still cares. The expression originally was *I couldn't care less*. By the sixties, people began dropping *-n't*s.

Among broadcast variations: "Americans could care less" (instead of *could not* or *couldn't*) and "Some can care less" (*cannot* or *can't*).

COULD HAVE, COULD'VE, and "COULD OF." *See* HAVE, HAS, HAD, 2.

COUNSEL. *See* ATTORNEY and LAWYER; Confusing pairs (*council* etc.).

COUNT and COUNT ON. *See* ON, 2.

COUP D'ÉTAT. *See* REVOLT and REVOLUTION.

COUPLE. *1. Inconsistency in number. 2. Plural construction. 3. Use as modifier.*

1. Inconsistency in number

The journalists who wrote the four sentences below seem unable to make up their minds.

The couple . . . was the crown prince and princess of Sweden . . . on their honeymoon.

. . . The couple has agreed to annul their stormy marriage. . . .

. . . The couple wants to demolish a unique contemporary home on their property.

Couple enjoys reclusive life on their mountain.

What the writers cannot decide is whether to regard husband and wife as one or two. In each sentence, *couple* is regarded as both singular and plural. The verb, such as "was" or "wants," is singular while the pronoun, "their," is plural. Any logic behind such inconsistency fails to emerge.

An old editors' tale holds that *couple* must be singular. If you wish to follow that path, at least do so all the way through a sentence. Accordingly, "their" becomes *its* in each of the four samples. When you construe *couple* as singular, be prepared to say, "The couple *was* on *its* honeymoon." Does the phrasing look or sound odd? Then try a plural construction.

2. Plural construction

In general, the noun *couple* denotes two of the same kind, whether closely related or not. It may be treated as singular or plural, depending on the kind. When it refers to a man and woman who are united in some way, *couple* is more likely to be plural. Most of the time you cannot go wrong with sentences like the following; they are corrections of the four samples:

The couple . . . *were* . . . on their honeymoon.

. . . The couple *have* agreed to annul their stormy marriage. . . .

. . . The couple *want* to demolish a . . . home on their property.

Couple *enjoy* reclusive life on their mountain.

If the man and woman are named, often *they* can replace "the couple."

3. Use as a modifier

As a modifier, *couple* is usually preceded by *a* and followed by *of*: "a couple of kids." An article said "there are a couple ways" to reduce the state's liabilities. Make it "a couple *of* ways."

When *a couple* precedes certain adjectives, including *more* and *less*, no *of* follows: "a couple more oranges."

A *couple* means *two* of something. Using it in place of *a few*—"Go a couple of miles and turn right"—should be left to loose speech.

COVET. To *covet* is to crave or long for something. It may imply craving something that belongs to another. The Ten Commandments say that one shall not covet a neighbor's wife and goods. *Covet* is a verb (transitive and intransitive), pronounced KUV-it.

The news media frequently use *coveted,* the past participle, along with *award* or *prize* in the manner of these excerpts: "Solectron . . . won the coveted Malcolm Baldridge National Quality Award in 1991." / "Now we hear that Dilbert and his hapless colleagues are up for a coveted Reuben Award. . . ."

The award is often one that most people have never heard of. Who is doing all that coveting?

Creatures, plural. *See* **Plurals and singulars,** 2C.

CREDIBLE and CREDITABLE. *See* **Confusing pairs.**

CREDIT. A three-column headline over a letter to the editor of a large daily said, "Credit Reagan for Destroying Social Programs." From the standpoint of grammar and not politics, the verb should be *blame,* not "credit." If the letter writer had opposed social programs (which was not so), *credit* might have been appropriate. (Then it would have been more idiomatic to "Credit Reagan *With the Destruction of* Social Programs.")

In both financial and nonfinancial senses, *credit* (noun) is positive, not negative. To *credit* a financial account is to add to one's *credit:* the amount in one's favor. To *credit* a person with something is to give him *credit,* in the nonfinancial sense: worthy approval, commendation, honor, or praise.

Another large daily made a wildly inappropriate use of *credit* as a noun in a main headline: "Bomb Rips Apart Israeli Bus, Kills 22; ——— Takes Credit." One takes *credit* for, say, founding an institution or creating an invention, not for committing a massacre. *Accepts Responsibility* would have been right. (The headline named the group, thereby granting it the notoriety it craved. Just "Group" would have been preferable.)

See also **BLAME,** 2.

CREDITOR and DEBTOR. A national television show devoted to the trying of monetary claims should be able to distinguish a creditor from a debtor. Yet its announcer said about a woman who was sued for money, "She is accused of dodging a debtor." If she owed the debt, *she* was the *debtor.* The one seeking payment was the *creditor.*

A weekly paper said that someday Iraq's "bank accounts will be unfrozen and it will have to pay its debtors." *Creditors.*

CRESCENDO. No one with a knowledge of music is likely to have written any of these passages:

> Clark's mounting annoyance with the witness reached a crescendo in redirect questioning.

> But with cocaine, dopamine is not absorbed and continues to excite nerve cells. The result is that the nerve stimulation rises to a crescendo with no relief, causing the feeling of euphoria.

> When troubled at home, seek solace—and photo opportunities— abroad. President Nixon offered a prototypical example with his jaunt to Egypt in 1974, as Watergate reached a crescendo.

Crescendo does not mean a high point. It is a musical term that means (as an adjective or adverb) gradually getting louder or (as a noun) a gradual swelling of volume or a passage that gradually gets louder. *Crescendo* tells us nothing about the sound level, only about the process of increasing it. In musical scores, *crescendo* usually is expressed by a symbol (<) or an abbreviation (*cresc., cres.,* or *cr.*).

To say that a piece of music "reached" or "rises to" a *crescendo* would be meaningless. A *crescendo* may, however, reach a *forte,* a loud passage; a *fortissimo,* a very loud passage; or even a *piano,* a soft passage, if the music is very soft at the start. The opposite of *crescendo* is *diminuendo* or *decrescendo,* meaning gradually getting quieter. *Crescendo* in Italian means increasing. All of the italicized words were adopted, full blown, from Italian.

Crescendo may be used figuratively, in a nonmusical sense, to mean an increasing or intensifying, not a peak of intensity: "the market's crescendo of activity as the morning progressed."

Two television networks made the same kind of mistake on the same evening in reporting the same speech. Describing the increasing support for Bill Clinton for president, one newscaster said:

> It reached a kind of crescendo with Mario Cuomo's speech.

The anchor man on the other network said about that speech:

> Particularly did Cuomo do a good job of building to a crescendo.

The sentence below does have a dynamic *crescendo,* but one word needs to be omitted.

> The Reagan administration, amid a rising crescendo of questioning about the U.S. role in policing the sea lanes of the war-torn gulf, strove to adopt a business-as-usual posture. . . .

"Rising" is redundant. Rising is what makes a *crescendo.*

CRIME, MISDEMEANOR, and FELONY.

The title of the Woody Allen movie *Crimes and Misdemeanors* reflected the popular notion that a "misdemeanor" is not a "crime." The *misdemeanor* is one of the two main categories of *crime,* the less serious category. The more serious one is the *felony*—the kind we worry about.

A *misdemeanor* is usually punishable by a fine or a term of less than a year in a county jail or both. The punishment for a *felony* is usually a term of a year or more in a penitentiary, but in some jurisdictions the maximum can be death.

Larceny or *theft,* which is stealing (without personal contact or forcible entry), can be either a *misdemeanor* or a *felony,* depending on the value of the loot. Statutes, varying in the fifty states, determine which category a crime fits. (In some places, traffic or other minor misdeeds are variously categorized as *infractions, offenses,* or *violations.* They bring only fines and often are not considered crimes.)

In popular usage—and even in some formal contexts—"crime" means felony. Any talk about "the crime issue" or "crime on the streets" or "a life of crime" is not likely to concern the commission of *misdemeanors.* Just be aware that *crime* and *misdemeanor* are not opposites.

The U.S. Constitution uses the term *high crimes* for what are usually called *felonies.* It requires the removal from office of any federal officer impeached for and convicted of "treason, bribery, or other high crimes and misdemeanors." So *misdemeanors* are in infamous company.

See also **Crimes (various felonies).**

Crimes (various felonies).

1. *ASSAULT* and *RAPE.* 2. *BLACKMAIL*

and EXTORTION. 3. BURGLARY, ROBBERY, and THEFT. 4. MAYHEM, MURDER, and MANSLAUGHTER. 5. TREASON and ESPIONAGE.

1. ASSAULT and RAPE

If Joe tries to strike Mary but misses or if he merely threatens to hurt her physically and Mary has a reasonable fear that he will carry out the threat, he has committed *assault*. If he actually strikes her, he has committed *assault and battery*.

Unlawful sexual intercourse imposed by a male on a female against her will or without her consent is *rape*. It is *rape* also if the female, willing or not, is under an age specified by law. (In some states, forcible sodomy on either sex also is considered *rape*.) The press long avoided that word, substituting various imprecise terms, like "assaulting" and "molesting." Readers in modern times usually, but not always, get more precision. This is from the lead paragraph of a news story:

> At an emotional hearing Friday, a 36-year-old Los Angeles man dubbed the "Flat-Tire Rapist" was sentenced to 113 years and seven life terms for assaults on 11 women. . . .

To say that a man who forcibly copulated with eleven women committed "assaults" is at best a gross understatement. Nobody would be sentenced to a lifetime in prison for simply *assaulting* people.

The next paragraph recounts the man's conviction on "36 counts of kidnaping, robbing and attacking women. . . ." *Kidnapping* (also spelled *kidnaping*) and *robbery* are criminal charges. "Attacking" is not a criminal charge. Although its use as a euphemism improves upon "assaulting," which carries a legal meaning, consistency and precision would have been best. The writer braced up initially to mention the culprit's sobriquet but otherwise seemed to be too squeamish to display any form of *rape* in the article's seventeen paragraphs, so he let "attack" and "assault" fill in five times.

2. BLACKMAIL and EXTORTION

"When to Stop Oil Blackmail: Now." A headline over an editorial in a prominent daily so declared.

"There isn't any question that there was blackmail," the governor of Wyoming said about his state's raising the drinking age from 19 to 21 to avoid losing federal highway funds.

"The only reason we've got any speed limit at all is Federal blackmail, pure and simple," a Montana state senator said.

"It is blackmail, pure and simple," the host of a news commentary program said of the so-called Unibomber's demand for publicity.

In each case, no "blackmail" had been committed. Strictly speaking, *blackmail* is not just any kind of pressure or coercion. It is not limiting oil production to raise prices. It is not using federal funds to induce states to enact certain laws. It is not threatening violence to exact a payment or an action.

Blackmail is an attempt to obtain money by threatening to disclose information about someone. Jane commits *blackmail* when she demands $5,000 from John for not telling his wife about his double life. The payment too can be called *blackmail*. A popular synonym is *hush money*.

People often loosely use "blackmail" when they are talking about *extortion*. The exact meaning of *extortion* varies from state to state. It may be limited to an official's misuse of his position or power to obtain money or property, or it may encompass any person's obtaining of payment through coercion, intimidation, or threat. Some states use the term *blackmail* only when the threat of disclosure is in writing; when it is oral, the crime is considered a form of *extortion*.

Related verbs (transitive) are to *black-mail* (someone) and to *extort* (money from someone).

3. BURGLARY, ROBBERY, and THEFT

All of these excerpts from news stories show the same confusion:

> . . . Two of those patrons were police officers in search of a burglary suspect. . . . [They] later found out the robbery call was a phony.

> LIMA, Peru—Slum dwellers tied a man accused of burglary to a 40-foot wooden cross. . . . A—— had been caught robbing a home . . . the report said.

> . . . While she and her husband were away from home . . . burglars entered their house. . . . In the previous month there had been 32 similar robberies in just that one suburban neighborhood.

The search for a "burglary suspect" would not be prompted by a "robbery call." The Peruvian "accused of burglary," even if guilty, had not engaged in "robbing." And if the "burglars" had committed similar crimes, the crimes were not "robberies." It is a common mistake to call a *burglary* a "robbery" or to say "I've been robbed" when one's home has been *burglarized* and no *robbery* has been committed.

If someone breaks into your house or apartment with intent to commit a crime, he is committing a *burglary,* which is a felony. Depending on the state, breaking into a commercial establishment also may constitute *burglary.* The standard verb (transitive) is to *burglarize.* To *burgle* (verb, transitive and intransitive), a relative newcomer, has been used mostly in humorous contexts, such as the title of a novel by P. G. Wodehouse, *Do Butlers Burgle Banks?*

Robbery, another felony, is theft from a person, or in one's presence, by violence or the threat of violence. If a criminal steals someone's money or property by striking the victim or threatening to harm him, with or without a weapon, he has committed a *robbery.* A perpetration that begins as a *burglary* can become a *robbery* as well if the culprit confronts an occupant of the building he has entered and threatens or harms him.

A person or place is *robbed;* that which is taken is *stolen.* If *robbers* prey on a bank, for example, they *rob* the bank and *steal* a sum of money. The bank is *robbed* of the money. If the culprits are armed, they can be said to *hold up* an establishment or a person. It or he is *held up;* there has been a *holdup* or *hold-up.* Slangy synonyms are *stick up* (verb) and *stickup* or *stick-up* (noun). What go *up* are victims' hands.

Another example shows the two crimes confused in another way. On Halloween a sign at a convenience store requested that customers not wear masks when entering. A television newscaster tried to explain: "They want to make sure that burglars don't take advantage of the holiday." *Robbers,* not "burglars."

"What you're about to see is robbery in broad daylight," a television reporter said. What he showed was not a "robbery" but a pocket-picking. As long as force is negligible, it is a form of *larceny,* which is common stealing or theft. If the pickpocket jostles his victim or uses other substantial force, the crime becomes a *robbery.* In some states, the term *larceny* or *theft* includes more elaborate schemes for stealing, such as embezzlement, obtaining property by false pretenses, and swindling. *Larceny* or *theft* is usually divided into two grades, depending on the value of the property stolen: *grand,* a felony, and *petty* (or *petit*), a misdemeanor.

A *mugging* is an unexpected, violent attack on a person with the intent of committing robbery. To *mug* someone is to assault and batter the person with intent to rob. It is not a synonym for *rob,* as it was misused in a news story: "The students and parents . . . told tales of being . . . mugged of the chocolate they were selling as a school fund-raiser. . . ." They could be *robbed* of the chocolate. However, one is not "mugged of" anything; and the story did not say if a surprise attack preceded the robbery, making for a *mugging*.

4. MAYHEM, MURDER, and MANSLAUGHTER

In a preview of a local news telecast, an announcer spoke of criminals' "anger at society exploding in murderous mayhem." Then a newspaper columnist described violence on New Year's Eve and commented that "this kind of mayhem" could not be blamed on freedom. Next, readers of an editorial were told, "Senseless mayhem is no monopoly of the Japanese cult" (as though there could be sensible mayhem). Last, a reporter on national television, outdoing others in alliteration, said the Colombia drug cartel dealt in "money, murder, and mayhem." The newscasts, the column, and the editorial told of no case of *mayhem;* no one seemed to know what it meant.

Although some use it vaguely instead of words like *havoc, violence,* or *destruction, mayhem* is a particular felony. It is the act of intentionally depriving a person of a bodily member or function, or otherwise crippling, disfiguring, maiming, or mutilating him. For instance, one who willfully blinds another is guilty of *mayhem*. The crime may become *murder* if the victim dies as a result of the attack.

Murder is the malicious and unlawful killing of a human being with intent to kill, or without intent to kill but done during the commission of another felony, such as robbery. It makes no difference if the one killed was not the intended victim.

An unlawful killing, even if it is intentional, is not *murder* but *manslaughter* if the perpetrator had reasonable provocation and felt no malice toward the victim. An unintentional killing is *manslaughter* if it is committed in the course of a misdemeanor, say the disregarding of a traffic signal.

Homicide is the killing of one human being by another, whether unlawful or lawful. The term takes in *murder, manslaughter,* and legally justifiable killings. Statutes condone *homicide* when it is committed in self-defense, or by an insane person, or as a necessary duty by a law-enforcement officer. (Of course, all those definitions pertain to American law. Military acts have to do with jungle law.)

5. TREASON and ESPIONAGE

A columnist quoted a senator, who was challenging a nominee for secretary of defense:

> "He knew the confidential negotiating positions . . . right after he got through [participating in arms control negotiations], he immediately went to work for defense contractors."
>
> I put that latest charge to John Tower after Sunday's televised broadsides: Did he sell that confidential information about fallback positions to clients, as Senator Nunn clearly implied?
>
> "That would be treason," said Mr. Tower sharply.

For an American to sell confidential U.S. military information to American military contractors would not be "treason." *Treason* is an act of armed revolt or wartime betrayal. If an American sold such information to a foreign representative, either in wartime or in peacetime, he could be charged with *espionage,* a form of spying.

In another incident, the Central Intelligence Agency discovered that one of its spies was also a spy for the Russians. A television interview with a newspaper reporter specializing in intelligence matters produced this dialogue:

[Host:] Why don't they execute him?

[Guest:] We don't have a death penalty for treason.

"Treason" had nothing to do with it. *Espionage* was the crime. The statement is also wrong on a second score: The maximum penalty for *treason* is death, under a federal statute. Another such statute provides a maximum penalty of death for *espionage* too, but only when the information obtained has been delivered to a foreign government.

Two network news women, within three months in 1997, made the erroneous statement that Julius and Ethel Rosenberg were "executed for treason" in 1953. Actually the couple were convicted of *espionage,* not "treason." The alleged deed was the passing of atomic secrets to the U.S.S.R., when it was an ally of the U.S. (One speaker was prefacing an interview with a one-time member of the Soviet spying agency, who said that no atomic secrets were passed and that Ethel was not a spy.)

Espionage is the obtaining—and often the delivery to a foreign government as well—of secret American military or defense information with intent to injure the United States.

In many a country, "treason" or its linguistic equivalent is whatever the ruler says it is. In the United States, *treason* is what the Constitution says it is: only "levying war against them" (the United States) or "adhering to their enemies, giving them aid and comfort." Conviction, under the Constitution, requires "the testimony of two witnesses to the same overt act" or "confession in open court."

Despite the constitutional prescription, those seeking to stain adversaries sometimes apply the "treason" brush with broad strokes. Senator Joseph R. McCarthy once accused the Democratic Party of "twenty years of treason." A former federal administrator called American lawyers for foreign drug cartelists "traitors." A letter in a newspaper termed the campaign of the religious right "treason." Protesters against President Clinton carried signs accusing him of "treason" for actions concerning China.

Treason has to do with war. In miscellaneous decisions, courts have ruled that all these circumstances are essential for conviction: (1) a person either takes up arms against the United States or supports the enemy after a war formally begins; (2) in the latter event, he both takes the side of the enemy and gives the enemy aid and comfort; (3) the aid and comfort is in an overt act; (4) he intends to betray this country; (5) he is a U.S. citizen; and (6) the war formally begins with a declaration of war by Congress.

CRISIS. *See* **CRITICAL.**

CRITERIA and CRITERION. The noun *criteria* is a plural form of *criterion,* a standard or rule on which one bases a judgment or decision. An alternative plural is *criterions.* It is incorrect to speak of "a criteria" or say "the criteria is."

Thus it was a mistake to report on a radio network that "the Chinese have a very strict criteria for what they want" in trade. Depending on the meaning intended, the reporter should have either omitted the "a" ("the Chinese have very strict criteria") or used *criterion* ("the Chinese have a very strict criterion").

When a TV panelist said, about a ban on discrimination by some New York clubs, "I think the criteria is 400 members," unquestionably "criteria" should have been *criterion.*

Criterion comes from Greek and retains the Greek plural ending. *See also* **Plurals and singulars,** 2E.

CRITICAL. 1. *Concerning crises.* 2. *Concerning criticism etc.*

1. Concerning crises

A mayor was shot in Japan, and a story in a New York newspaper included this sentence:

> The Mayor, Hitoshi Motoshima, was reported in critical condition but out of danger tonight after two hours of surgery.

If he was in "critical" condition, how could he be "out of danger" at the same time? *Critical* in such a context normally means dangerous; it pertains to a *crisis,* a crucial point when the course of a disease—or anything else—can turn in either a favorable or an unfavorable direction. Could the report have lost something in translation?

2. Concerning criticism etc.

Critical (adjective) has an assortment of other meanings, among them crucial, decisive, perilous, and referring to important products or materials that are in short supply.

In the sense of judging, *critical* is not necessarily negative. It can mean characterized by careful and objective judgment or it can pertain to formal criticism. Popularly it is more often construed as judging unfavorably or inclined to judge unfavorably.

A Nevada newspaper ran the headline "Man is critical after car goes into canal." The text beneath it indicated that the only person in the car was a woman. Maybe that critical man was the owner.

See also **CONDITION.**

CRY. *See* -Y ending.

CULMINATE. To *culminate* means to reach the highest point or the climax of something. How not to use this verb is illustrated by a press excerpt.

> The razing of the International Hotel . . . culminated a crisis that

eventually touched virtually every agency. . . .

Change "culminate" to *ended*. The example is wrong on two scores: To *culminate* does not mean to end or to be the outcome. Moreover, it is an intransitive verb, not transitive; one does not "culminate" something.

Although *culminate(d)* does belong in the sentence below, the preposition that follows it is not idiomatic.

> . . . A growing body of scientific evidence on the dangers of so-called secondhand smoke has culminated with an influential Environmental Protection Agency report declaring environmental smoke a "Class A Carcinogen." . . .

Make it "culminated *in.*" The verb is normally followed by *in,* not "with."

CUM. *Cum,* Latin for *with,* appears in hyphenated combinations in this manner: "En route, don't miss St. Francis Fountain, a Mission landmark lunch-counter-cum-candy shop, founded in 1918." It becomes a high-flown substitute for *together with* or simply *and,* mystifying many readers who would understand "lunch counter *and* candy shop." (The piling up of two modifiers as well as the compound further complicates the sample. *See* **Modifiers,** 4.)

The *u* in *cum* may be pronounced the short way—inviting confusion with *come*—or like the *oo* in *book.*

CUSTOM. As an adjective, *custom* means specially made for an individual customer (a custom suit) or doing work to order (a custom tailor).

A label and a leaflet accompanying a mass-produced blanket say the product was "CUSTOM LOOMED" by a certain manufacturer. As used in commerce, the word is usually empty puffery.

D

Danglers. *See* **Modifers,** *1*.

DARING. A radio network broadcast this phrase: "A daring escape from a medium-security facility outside of Pueblo." It lacks *Colorado* and a verb. (*See* **Sentence fragment**). The main trouble, though, is that *daring* is a word of praise; it commends one's adventurousness, initiative, boldness, and fearlessness in a risky endeavor. Take the "daring young man on the flying trapeze," the subject of song since 1868.

Although no adjective was really needed, a better one would have been *brazen* or *imitative*. (The method of escape, by helicopter, had been used before and, still earlier, portrayed in a movie.)

In a comparable nonsentence, "A daring daylight robbery on a busy San Francisco street" was reported on local television. The same crime was "a daring holdup" on local radio. And when criminals stealthily murdered a guard and wounded two people before robbing a bank, a newspaper described "a daring holdup." If those crimes required an adjective, *ruthless* would have been preferable, but why did the facts have to be embellished at all?

Dash. *See* **Punctuation,** *4*.

DATA. A historian is quoted, by a book critic, on newly revealed records of the erstwhile Soviet Union:

"On the other hand, the data in the archives doesn't reveal the sense that there's a broad plan afoot to take over Eastern Europe."

Is the sentence right or wrong? As a Latin plural, *data* traditionally was strictly a plural in English. Thus "The *data* in the archives *don't* reveal . . ." *Data* are pieces of information, particularly raw facts or figures used as the basis for conclusions or judgments.

Many educated people, particularly in the United States, now use the word as a collective singular (as the historian uses it); many do not. You cannot go wrong construing *data* as plural, particularly in any formal use.

The traditional singular of *data* is *datum,* which is used much less often than circumlocutions like *an item in the data*. "A data" will offend many pairs of eyes or ears. And "this data" can be ambiguous: Does it mean one item or all the items? *Fact* or *figure* usually will do for a singular.

If you do choose to use *data* as a collective singular, at least be consistent. These two sentences appear in two consecutive paragraphs in a scientific journal:

The demographic data obtained from the present updated sample is very consistant with that found in the initial reports. . . .

These data represent a two-edged sword.

After using "data" as a singular in that write-up, the scientist changes his mind and uses it as a plural. (He is consistent in his misspelling of *consistent:* A little later he writes of "a consistant finding.")

Dative. *See* **Pronouns**, *10B.*

DEBTOR. *See* **CREDITOR** and **DEBTOR.**

DECIMATE.

She [Princess Pauahi] saw native Hawaiians literally decimated—reduced in number from 400,000 to 40,000.

If Hawaiians had been "literally decimated," as a speaker said on television, they would have been reduced in number from 400,000 to 360,000.

The literal meaning of *decimate* is to destroy a tenth part of something; specifically, in Roman times, to kill one in every ten of an army or a group, each victim having been selected by lot. The word comes from Latin, in which *decimus* means tenth. *Decimal* has the same source.

If the word "literally" and the numbers had been left out, *decimated* could have been used in a looser sense: to destroy a substantial part of something measurable by number.

This appeared in a letter to the editor:

The shortsighted exploitation of a rain forest like that of Sarawak—a 160-million-year-old ecosystem that has been decimated by 50 percent in only a few decades and will be gone forever in another 10 years—is not the right of any country.

In the light of its origin, *decimate* should not go with a number—unless used literally to mean eliminate 10 percent. Numerous other verbs are available in place of "been decimated" in the second sample: *diminished, dwindled, been cut, been reduced, been halved* (omitting "by 50 percent"), and so on.

A senator wrote a colleague that the latter's "wish to decimate the bill by an additional 20 percent cut in acreage is unacceptable." Perhaps *weaken* or *enfeeble* was meant.

Decimate should not be used in lieu of *annihilate* or *demolish* or modified by *completely, totally,* or the like; nor should it be applied to something abstract or incalculable. To "decimate his argument" or "decimate their enthusiasm" is meaningless.

Declarative sentence. *See* **Backward writing;** (-) **EVER**, *1.*

DECRESCENDO. *See* **CRESCENDO.**

DEER, plural. *See* **Plurals and singulars**, *2C.*

DEFAMATION. *See* **LIBEL** and **SLANDER.**

DEFEND. *See* **Verbs**, *1C.*

Defining clause. *See* **THAT** and **WHICH.**

Dehumanization. A writer does not consciously aim to dehumanize someone in writing but can do so through fuzzy thinking that equates a human being with an abstraction or a statistic. The example is from a newspaper column:

Smith, by the way, was the first endorsement under the new POA policy of polling all of the station houses before making a decision.

A person is not an "endorsement." The sentence can be improved: "Smith, by the way, was the first *person endorsed* under . . ." or "*Smith's endorsement,* by the way, was the first under . . ."

This is from a front-page news story in another paper:

He was the 14th homicide of the year in the crack-ridden 34th precinct.

"He was the 14th homicide *victim* of the year . . ." or "*His killing* was the 14th homicide of the year. . . ." A victim is not a homicide. *Homicide* is the killing of one human being by another. (General dictionaries contain a secondary definition of homicide as a person who kills another, a meaning that is nearly obsolete.)

In an autobiography, a general draws on military jargon to describe plans for a bombing attack on Baghdad:

The hour was also selected to minimize collateral damage, since most Iraqis would be at home. . . .

By "collateral damage" he means the killing of civilian people.

See also DETERIORATE; FATALITY; FEWER and LESS, 2.

DELUGED. *See* INUNDATE, INUNDATED.

DELUSION and ILLUSION. *See* Confusing pairs.

DEMOCRACY, FREEDOM, and INDEPENDENCE. The three words are not synonymous, contrary to the implication of this sentence, from an editorial:

Students in communist China sought a bit of independence and democracy and paid with their blood to learn that freedom is not in a dictator's dictionary.

The part of the sentence about "freedom" does not follow reasonably from

the part about "independence and democracy." Three concepts have been confused.

Democracy, in theory, is a political system in which the people rule. The term also denotes a system of government by elected representatives of the people.

Freedom means the state of being free from restraints or being free from official oppression or being able to do what one wants.

Independence means complete autonomy, nationhood, not being under foreign rule.

The world has many *independent* dictatorships. Citizens of some autocracies have a degree of *freedom,* perhaps economic or religious, without *democracy.* Citizens of some politically *free* countries may lack certain *democratic* rights, such as the control of foreign relations. And sometimes people democratically decide to curb some *freedoms,* say, for certain businesses or offenders.

DEMOCRAT and DEMOCRATIC. It is ungrammatical to use the noun in place of the adjective, yet it is frequently done intentionally. A rhetorical question posed by a Republican leader in the House of Representatives is typical: "When did we start signing on to any Democrat agenda?" *Democratic.*

The adjective ends in *ic,* whether we use *democratic* (with lower case *d*), pertaining to democracy, or *Democratic* (with capital *D*), pertaining to the Democratic Party. The word *democrat* is a noun only, meaning one who believes in democracy; the name *Democrat* is a noun only, meaning one who adheres to the Democratic Party.

In the fifties, certain Republican politicos began mangling the name of the opposition party by referring to the "Democrat Party" or the "Democrat candidate," on grounds that no one should think of it as the only democratic party. So far the Democrats have not reciprocated the suffix-scrapping by speaking of the "Republic Party."

The silliness has persisted and spread beyond Republican politics. A headline in a national newspaper read, "Democrat Sluggers Are Benched." There was enough space to add two letters, so the newspaper had no excuse for truncating the proper adjective. The normally non-partisan moderator of a news forum on television wrongly referred to a "Democrat plan" instead of a "Democratic plan" or a "plan by Democrats."

Actually, Americans give scant thought to any meaning behind the names *Republican* and *Democratic*, which offer no clue as to current ideological differences. Both parties favor a democratic republic. The party that is now *Democratic* was called *Democratic Republican* in our republic's youth, when such terms had more meaning.

DEMOLISH. When you *demolish* an object, you tear it to pieces, burn it up, or knock it into a shapeless mass. A qualification like "entirely," in the following sentence, or "completely" or "totally" is superfluous; it is implied in *demolish(ed)*. "The front end of his car is reported to be entirely demolished."

Demolish (verb, transitive) implies violent destruction; *destroy*, completeness of ruin or wreckage and the ending of something's usefulness, if not existence; *raze*, leveling to the ground; and *ruin*, spoiling and badly damaging but not annihilating.

Demolition (noun) is a demolishing, a destruction. A synonym, less common, is *demolishment*.

See also **DEVASTATE, DEVASTATING; RUIN and RUINS.**

DEPRECATE and DEPRECIATE. *See* Confusing pairs.

DESECRATE, DESECRATION. The Latin *sacrare*, to make sacred, or holy, is the root of this word. Prefixed by *de*, removal or reversal, *desecrate* (verb, transitive) literally means to divest of sacred character or to use in a profane way that which is sacred. A church has been *desecrated* if it is turned into a private house. A religious emblem has been *desecrated* if it becomes a T-shirt design. To treat with sacrilege, or lack of reverence, also is to *desecrate*. A man who wears a hat in a church (or no hat in a synagogue) could be accused of *desecrating* it. So could one who burns it.

The opposite of *desecrate* is *consecrate*, to establish as sacred. The related nouns are *desecration* and *consecration*, respectively.

When Congress discussed a proposed constitutional amendment that would authorize legislation "to prohibit the physical desecration of the flag of the United States," it was essentially considering the physical *consecration* of that flag, its establishment as a sacred object. One can *desecrate* only that which is sacred. Probably what the sponsors had meant was the malicious *destruction* or *damaging* of an American flag.

DESERT and DESSERT. *Desert* is the sandy wasteland, pronounced DEZ-urt. When we insert an *s*, we get *dessert*, the sweet end of a meal. It is pronounced dih-ZURT, the same as the verb *desert*, meaning to abandon.

The words are mixed up sometimes. In a manual of English for newcomers, this was printed: "*Waitress:* What would you like for desert?" (The answer could have been "sand tarts" but was not.)

Later, a celebrated anchor man announced that Gerald Ford, newly retired as president, was visiting Southern California's warm "dessert country." (It was not announced whether Ford was given an executive sweet.)

See also **SAHARA.**

DESTINY. It is impossible to do what these writings talk of doing. A political ad: "Let the people of New York choose their own destiny." A history book: the world was "bereft of confidence in its ability to control its own destinies." An article: an Iranian official affirmed "the right of every nation to decide its own destiny." (Making the final word *future* would have corrected each example.)

Literally, one cannot choose, control, or decide one's *destiny*. Nor can *destinies* be withheld or changed. A book quoted a professor as saying, "We have been denied our Polish destiny" (*heritage?*). A big headline proclaimed "HONG KONG'S NEW DESTINY." (There was new *rule*, predetermined by two nations.)

By definition, *destiny* is one's inevitable lot; or, in a broader sense, a predetermined course of events or a power that predetermines events. (Explaining the meaning of *destiny* does not imply that there really is such a thing.)

Synonyms for *destiny* are *fate* and *fortune*. However, they have additional meanings that bypass the question of predetermination. *Fate*, like *destiny*, often is used loosely to signify merely an outcome or final result or future; sometimes it specifically means an unfavorable outcome. *Fortune* often denotes good or bad luck, particularly the good; it can also mean financial success or wealth.

The verb *destine* (transitive), usually used in the passive, *destined*, can imply predetermination, or it can suggest no more than intend(ed) for a particular end or head(ed) for a particular destination. *Destination* occasionally means a predetermined end or a destining. More often it is merely a place toward which a traveler or a moving object is headed.

See also **INEVITABLE.**

DESTROY. *See* **DEMOLISH.**

DETERIORATE. The verb *deteriorate*, meaning to make (something) worse or to become worse, has five syllables (pronounced dih-TIER-ee-uh-rate).

The adjective *deteriorating*, becoming worse, has six syllables (dih-TIER-ee-uh-rate-ing).

Omitting the *o* syllable and the *r* sound is a fault of some speakers: On TV, a visitor to a zoo said "it started to deteriate" years ago and a senator said about the North Koreans, "They are a deteriating economy." (They are not an economy. Better: "They *have* a deteriorating economy.")

Deterioration, noun (dih-tier-ee-uh-RAY-shn), is the process of deteriorating or the condition of having deteriorated.

DEVASTATE, DEVASTATING. "A devastating earthquake on Guam," a newscaster announced on television (in a nonsentence of the type so beloved by newscasters). "Nobody was killed and nobody was left homeless," she added.

To *devastate* (verb, transitive) is to lay waste. *Devastating* (adjective) means utterly destructive. The two words imply widespread ruin and desolation. If an earthquake took no lives or houses, how could it be "devastating"?

It was announced on another television program: "An American city has been totally devastated." A qualification such as "totally" or "entirely" is superfluous; it is implied in *devastated*.

See also **DEMOLISH; RUIN and RUINS.**

DEVOTE. *See* Gerund, 3A.

DIALECTAL and DIALECTIC. *See* **Confusing pairs.**

DID. *See* **DO, DID, DONE.**

DIFFERENT. 1. *The preposition that follows.* 2. *Unnecessary use.*

1. *The preposition that follows*

When a preposition follows *different*, normally it is *from*. This usage is not standard:

New York City is different than other cities. . . .

. . . Tragedies . . . have led many South Africans to suspect that the new South Africa is no different than the old.

Change "than" to *from* in both statements (uttered by network television reporters). *Than* generally follows only comparative words—*bigger* than, *faster* than—and *different* is not one of them. It is a positive adjective, except in rare cases.

Grammatically, you cannot go wrong with *different from*. Yet some writers and grammatical authorities have found *different than* acceptable under certain circumstances, perhaps even preferable from the standpoint of style. They allow *than* when a clause or implied clause follows and when using *from* properly would result in a more complicated sentence. For example: "The practice of medicine takes a different form in Japan than [it takes] in the United States." Instead of *than,* you could substitute "from that which it takes," or something of that sort, remaining technically correct but complicating the sentence.

The choice is not just between *from* and *than.* The message can always be expressed differently. "Japanese physicians do not practice medicine in the same way that American physicians do."

Few disagree that when we differentiate individual nouns, noun phrases, or pronouns—"Meteors are different from meteorites" or "Big cats are much different from little cats"—the only preposition to use is *from,* except in Britain, where "different *to*" sometimes is used.

The adverb *differently* is likewise followed by *from:* "Canadians do not speak much differently from Americans."

In listing differences between British English and American English, two English lexicographers present "different

from or to" as the British way and "different than" as the American way. It is not the standard American way.

2. *Unnecessary use*

Sometimes "different" contributes nothing. Omitting it from an advertisement for a newspaper, posted on the side of transit vehicles, might have strengthened the message:

It takes over a million different people over a million different places every day.

Different emphasizes unlikeness: "The French and the Germans are much different people." If multiplicity is to be emphasized, *many, several, various,* or a number, like *nine* or *a million,* probably is a better adjective to use: "Many knights attempted to slay the dragon," not "different knights. . . ."

Digits spelled out. *See* **NO WAY,** *1;* **Numbers,** *11.*

DILEMMA. A *dilemma* is a situation that requires a choice between two equally unpleasant alternatives. The word was borrowed from Greek, *di-* meaning double and *lemma* meaning proposition. Where is the dilemma in the following sentence?

The social dilemma of teenage pregnancy is growing in Wyoming while the state ranks third in the nation, according to a study initiated by Wyoming's Commission for Women.

Neither that sentence nor the rest of the article it is extracted from presents us with a "dilemma." Teenage pregnancy may be a *question, predicament, plight, problem,* or *social ill,* but the writer fails to explain why it is a "dilemma." (Nor does he explain in what way Wyoming ranks third in the nation.)

The paragraph below does present a true dilemma, one faced by a political party in Israel, although the paragraph has other troubles.

> Political analyst Shlomo Avineri foresaw a double-edged dilemma for Labor: Leaving the government opens the party to an unpredictable electoral test, he said, but staying in would mean submission to its direct ideological opposite, the right wing of Likud.

"Double-edged" is superfluous; it describes all *dilemmas*. (Moreover the two alternatives are inconsistent in their moods. Either change "opens" to *would open* or change "would mean" to *means*.)

See also **HOBSON'S CHOICE**.

DIMINUENDO. *See* **CRES-CENDO.**

DINE. When you *dine,* you eat dinner. When you eat breakfast, lunch, or supper, you *breakfast, lunch,* or *sup,* as the case may be. In a magazine article about British tea drinking, this sentence appeared:

> Anna, the seventh Duchess of Bedford, typically dined on a huge breakfast, virtually no lunch, and then again at about eight o'clock.

One cannot "dine" on breakfast and lunch, let alone "virtually no lunch." (The sentence also contains a faulty series: "breakfast . . . lunch [both nouns], and then again [adverbial phrase]. . . ." And then again *what?* The misshapen sentence breaks off, and we have to guess whether another oversized repast or another bird's portion was in store for the duchess. *See* **Series errors.**)

DISASSEMBLE and DISSEMBLE. *See* **Confusing pairs.**

DISASTER. A *disaster* is a great misfortune, such as a destructive earthquake, famine, or flood. It is a happening, typically sudden and unexpected, that causes extraordinary loss of life or property.

A news magazine's treatment of an attempted coup in Moscow reduced the word to triviality. It said of a press conference by the conspirators, "Their performance was a disaster." It was a *failure* or *fiasco* or an *inept* or *bungling* performance or, in colloquial terms, a *flop* or a *dud.* The article perfunctorily added, "Three demonstrators were left dead. . . ."

A book comments on an airline company's change of name: "It was widely greeted as a disaster." If that was an airline "disaster," the word has lost its meaning. Its loose use to describe any failure may be harmless in informal conversation but is inappropriately transferred to serious writing or discussion.

Disaster (from the Old French *desastre,* from the Old Italian *disastro*), reflects a faith in astrology. Latin provided the negative *dis-* and *astrum,* from the Greek *astron*: a star.

See also **TRAGEDY.**

DISCHARGE. *See* **LAY OFF** and **LAYOFF; LET GO.**

DISCOMFIT and DISCOMFORT. Inasmuch as the two verbs look similar and sound similar, it is not surprising that people confuse *discomfit* and *discomfort.* But the words have different meanings and different Latin roots via the old French *desconfire,* to defeat (past participle: *desconfit*), and *desconforter,* to discomfort.

Originally *discomfit* (verb, transitive) meant to defeat (an enemy) completely in battle. Its strictest use today is still to defeat completely, though not necessarily in battle.

It can also mean to frustrate (someone), to foil one's plans. Such an action is likely to leave a person disconcerted, perplexed, dejected, or humiliated. Opinions diverge on whether (1) the defeat or frustration is essential to the meaning or (2) the mental state alone is enough.

At the loosest level we find "discomfit" used as a mere variation of the verb "discomfort." You be the judge of whether the latter *d*-word in this excerpt from a book has any special reason for being:

> While most buyers of literature don't think twice about ads that appear in magazines, they find the same ads discomfiting in books.

Discomfort (verb, transitive) means to make uncomfortable, either physically or mentally; to distress mildly. It is also a noun: an uncomfortable or mildly distressing condition or feeling. The opposite is *comfort* (verb, transitive): to make comfortable, to soothe; and (noun): a comfortable or soothing condition or feeling, or that which produces it.

The noun related to the verb *discomfit* is *discomfiture*: a state of being *discomfited* or, sometimes, the act of *discomfiting*. In Shakespeare's day the noun also was *discomfit*. (This is from *Henry VI, Part 2*: ". . . Uncurable discomfit / Reins in the hearts of all our present parts.")

Comfit is not the opposite of *discomfit* but a type of confection, a sugared fruit or vegetable.

DISCREET and DISCRETE. *See* Homophones.

DISHONOR. *See* HONORABLE, HONORARY, HONORED.

DISINGENUOUS and INGENUOUS. *Ingenuous* (adjective) means candid, straightforward, unsophisticatedly frank.

Two talk show hosts, intending to impugn statements made in a murder case, used that word instead of its antonym. A TV host called a remark "a little bit ingenuous," and a radio host said of another remark, "That was ingenuous."

Both needed *disingenuous:* not candid, not straightforward, insincere.

Perhaps the *in-* (which can mean *in* as well as *not* in Latin) is a source of confusion. *Ingenuous* comes from the Latin *ingenuus,* meaning native, free-born, noble, or frank.

Ingenuous has been confused with *ingenious,* which means clever or cunning and originates in the Latin *ingenium:* innate ability.

DISINTERESTED and UNINTERESTED. What do a book on old Flemish painting and a situation comedy have in common?

> He [Brueghel] rejected literal imitation of the Italians, ignored their subject matter, was disinterested in idealized beauty, had no more taste for nudes than for palatial architecture.

> No matter how disinterested I am, the driver won't stop yapping away.

The answer is the wrong use of "disinterested." Change it to *uninterested* (or, in the first instance, to *not interested*): "He . . . was *uninterested* in idealized beauty . . ." (or "He . . . was *not interested* . . ."). / "No matter how *uninterested* I am . . ."

The prefixes *dis-* and *un-* both mean *not*. Both adjectives, *disinterested* and *uninterested,* mean *not interested*. But two different meanings of *interested* apply:

1. The *interested* following *dis-* means possessing a financial interest or a share or seeking personal gain or advantage (in or from something, either stated

or implied). "All interested parties attended the hearing on the proposed rezoning."

2. The *interested* following *un-* means having a fascination or curiosity or being concerned or absorbed (for, about, or by something). "She is interested in antique collecting."

These are typical sentences using *disinterested* and *uninterested:* "Members of a governmental board must be disinterested in its affairs." / "She is interested in antique collecting, but her husband is uninterested."

A synonym for *disinterested* is *impartial.* A synonym for *uninterested* is *indifferent.* For 500 years *indifferent* meant impartial. Now it commonly means apathetic, not caring—which *disinterested* meant in the seventeenth and eighteenth centuries. We change the quotations again: "He was indifferent to idealized beauty." / "No matter how indifferent I am. . . ." *Indifferent* can also mean mediocre: "Was the movie good, bad, or indifferent?"

The noun related to *interested* is *interest.* It has the meanings of both (1) financial or personal involvement and (2) fascination or concern. The noun related to *disinterested* is *disinterest,* meaning lack of interest in the first sense. "Disinterest is an essential quality in a judge." A noun meaning lack of interest in the second sense is *indifference.* "Our congressman displays indifference to his less affluent constituents."

DISMISS. *See* LAY OFF and LAYOFF; LET GO.

DISMISSED WITH PREJUDICE and WITHOUT PREJUDICE. *See* WITH PREJUDICE and WITHOUT PREJUDICE.

DISMISSIVE. *See* SUPPORTIVE.

DISQUALIFIED and UNQUALIFIED. A TV panelist said an appointee

to a seat on the state supreme court had "received a 'disqualified' rating" from the state bar. Actually the bar's rating was *unqualified;* the governor was not obligated to observe it and did not.

Disqualified means rendered unfit, declared ineligible, or deprived of legal right or power. (One is *disqualified* from entering a contest by being related to the sponsor. A prejudiced juror may be *disqualified* from service.) *Unqualified,* as used above, means lacking proper or necessary qualifications. In another context, it can mean not modified or without limitation (*unqualified* support) or complete or downright (*unqualified* success).

Disqualified is the past participle of *disqualify* (verb, transitive). *Unqualified* (adjective) has no corresponding verb. Its antonym is *qualified* (adjective).

DISSEMBLE and DISASSEMBLE. *See* Confusing pairs.

Division of words. The division of a word between lines slows down a reader a bit. With few exceptions, it should be resorted to only in typesetting or calligraphy and only when the division is necessary to justify the right-hand margin (that is, to make it straight) without big gaps in a line.

In manuscripts for publication it is best not to divide words at all, lest it be unclear whether the hyphens belong in print or not. To indicate that a hyphen at the end of a line should be printed, an editor underlines the hyphen.

Sometimes grotesque divisions are seen in print. A newspaper divided *bootstraps* into "boots-" and "traps." One line should have contained *boot-* (the first syllable plus a hyphen) and the next line *straps.* Nowadays words are usually divided automatically by computers. An editor can correct a bad division or disregard it. No one corrected that one.

Another newspaper divided *probe* into "pro-" and "be." A one-syllable word should never be divided. The division can throw readers off track, particularly when the pieces have other meanings, as *pro-* and *be* do.

Any word should be kept intact if dividing it might mislead readers. When isolated, a part of a word like *hasten* and *often* tends to form a word in itself with a different pronunciation (*has-ten* and *of-ten*).

A hyphenated compound, such as *hang-up* or *send-off*, should be divided at the hyphen and nowhere else. Yet one was published as "han-" and "gup" and the other as "sen-" and "d-off" in two newspapers. A solid compound, such as *nearsighted* or *woodpecker,* is divided between the two words of which it is composed.

Two-syllable words should be divided between the syllables. However, a single letter is not split off from the rest of a word. A word like *adroit* should never be divided, inasmuch as its two syllables are *a* and *droit.* One newspaper divided that word into "adr-" and "oit."

The rules, and their exceptions, go on at length, dealing with prefixes, suffixes, consonants, vowels, and double letters. And the American and British systems vary. Words divided according to pronunciation in the former (*knowl-edge, democ-racy*) are divided according to derivation in the latter (*know-ledge, demo-cracy*).

General dictionaries show possible division points by means of centered dots. The dictionaries do not always agree on where those points are, sometimes because pronunciations differ. It is hi•er•o•glyph•ic in one dictionary, hi•ero•glyph•ic in another; tel•e•phone in the first dictionary, tele•phone in the other. One dictionary makes it gon•a•do•trop•ic, a second go•na•do•tro•pic, a third gonado•trop•ic, and a fourth go•nad•o•trop•ic.

Any division of abbreviations, initials, or figures can be confusing and should be avoided. *See* Numbers, *3.*

DIVORCÉ, DIVORCÉE, and DIVORCEE. *See* BACHELOR and SPINSTER.

DO, DID, DONE. The catch phrase "I dood it" belonged to the comedian Red Skelton. Much later, a big-city police chief said, "I think I've did a good job," and a restaurant reviewer said, about meat that one could cut with a fork, "I know because I've did it." Neither man was being funny. Each probably made a slip of the tongue and knew the correct form, "I've *done* it," meaning I've performed it or carried it out, and all these forms of the verb *do:*

Present tense: I, you, we, they *do;* he, she, it *does.* Past tense: I, you, etc. *did.* Future tense: I, you, etc. *will do.* Perfect tenses: I, you, we, they *have* or *had done;* he, she, it *has* or *had done.*

A helping verb (such as *has* or *is*) usually precedes the past participle *done.* This broadcast sentence, "What he done was impossible to do"—instead of "What he *did*" (dig out of an avalanche)—is ungrammatical. It is also contradictory; what is *impossible* cannot be done.

When it is not ambiguous, *done* is acceptable as an adjective meaning completed: "My work here is done." However, in a sentence like "The work will be done next month" it can be understood to mean *performed;* so if *completed* or *finished* is meant, it is better to use one of those words.

A facetious term for a mystery tale is a *whodunit.* This slang noun was coined from the ungrammatical phrase "Who done it?" Had the coiner been more scrupulous about his grammar, people might be reading or watching *whodidits.*

See also DON'T and DOESN'T; USE TO and USED TO (regarding *did*).

DOESN'T. *See* DON'T and DOESN'T.

DONE. *See* DO, DID, DONE.

DON'T and DOESN'T. A syndicated radio psychologist said she was sad to return home from vacation, "but that don't mean I don't want to go home." And a congressman disputed the idea of encouraging everyone to vote: "I don't want some damn fool idiot that don't know the time of day marking a ballot." Let us not argue any issues or judge who is an idiot but merely consider why "that don't" was wrong each time though "I don't" was right.

Don't is the contraction of *do not*. It agrees with all plural nouns and with the pronouns *I, you, we,* and *they.* "I don't want" is correct in each quotation, for it is like saying "I *do not* want." Similarly you, we, or they *don't* want it, just as antelopes, the Browns, or congressmen *don't* want it.

The contraction of *does not* is *doesn't.* It agrees with all singular nouns and with the pronouns *he, she,* and *it* and other singular pronouns except *I* and *you.* So "that [feeling] *doesn't* mean." And there is an "idiot that *doesn't* know." Similarly, he, she, or it *doesn't* know, just as an antelope, Mr. Brown, or a congressman *doesn't* know. Of course, the full *does not* may be used instead of each *doesn't.*

The psychologist said, in a later broadcast, "their child don't look so good." *Doesn't* or *does not.*

See also **DO, DID, DONE.**

"DON'T LET'S." *See* **LET, LETS,** 2.

Double entendre. *See* **Double meaning.**

Double genitive. *See* **Double possessive.**

Double meaning. In choosing words and expressions, beware of the danger of double meaning. A sentence can be interpreted in a way that was not intended. Even when nobody actually misunderstands it, the result can sometimes be ludicrous, as in the illustrations below. They include boners by seven newspapers, three advertisers, two television networks, and others.

Among the words in double trouble are *appeal, cut, crash, dog, liquidate, poach, spot,* and *spawn.* The trouble may amount to an unperceived coincidence, the lurking of a literal meaning behind a figurative use, an overambitious metaphor, the intrusion of a different meaning for the same word, an unfortunate juxtaposition, a metaphoric contradiction, or the emerging of a true meaning from a corrupted meaning.

Take the contemporary newspaper headline that said: "U.S. Grant Will Help Vets in State Get Jobs." How much help can he give? He has been out of office since 1877.

A banner headline in another newspaper told of "Governor's Plan to Cut Gas Lines." It appeared during a gasoline shortage, when motorists were lining up at service stations. But one could visualize the governor, a critic of the gas company, wielding an ax and whacking away at the company's pipes.

Telling of a $20 million show in New York conducted by General Motors, the automobile maker, a TV network reporter said, "GM went on a crash program to put this one on fast." It is doubtful that the company appreciated his use of the word "crash."

After John DeLorean's car company had run up a $50 million debt, some 400 creditors petitioned for liquidation. One newspaper's coverage of the story included a picture of the gentleman and a headline reading: "Judge asked to liquidate DeLorean." Shades of Stalinism!

The main headline in another newspaper read: "PLO appeals to U.S." But probably few in the U.S. found the Palestine Liberation Organization very appealing.

In the Southwest, the efforts of a local

emergency coordinator to warn of a tornado were the subject of a newspaper article, which reported: "He said his office sounded the sirens because it was alerted by 911 emergency telephone operators." That is a lot of operators.

An article on caring for Christmas plants closed by advising, "Keep the soil moist at all times, but reduce a bit during the winter." And just below, a health spa ad urged women to "SHAPE UP NOW!"

"HAVING AN AFFAIR?" a restaurant menu asks. "We cater all events . . . pick-up or full service." Just the place to take her or him.

A newspaper's television critic wrote: "I must confess that I find cooking shows addictive. There is something magical in the 'act' of taking a wide variety of ingredients and—voilà!—later pulling from the oven a rabbit that bears a remarkable resemblance to an exquisitely broiled fish or a thoroughly forbidding dessert." A broiled rabbit that resembled a fish and could pass for a dessert would be remarkable indeed, even to a nonaddict.

What did the Japanese prime minister report and why did an American newspaper insult him? It ran a four-column headline: " 'Womanizing' reports dog Uno."

A news service reported that a five-inch-long egg, laid by a condor at the Los Angeles Zoo, "was spotted early Easter Sunday morning"—with colorful polka dots for the day's festivities?

In reporting on teenage pregnancy in Wyoming, a newspaper told of activities of the state's Commission for Women: "Conferences like the one in Riverton have spawned other action in Lovell, Cody, Riverton and Thermopolis." Was the commission prepared for all that spawning?

An article by an Alaskan senator protesting the catching of salmon off North America by fishermen from the Far East was headed: "Save the Salmon From Poachers." It raised an obvious question to gourmets: What's wrong with poached salmon?

Another headline said, "Official rips textbooks under review." One could imagine her sitting at a desk and tearing pages from a pile of school books.

This was heard on a national TV newscast: "In the forefront of women's golf, fame is the name of the game." I thought the name of the game was *golf*.

Within several days, three commercials for motor vehicles treated the television audience to an unusual demonstration of truth in advertising. An announcer said 2,000 Dodge vans were for sale, "but they won't last long." He did not state the precise life expectancy of each vehicle. Another man, speaking for Acura, forecast an "old-fashioned, year-end blowout," though presumably the tires would hold for most of the year. And a third said, "Chrysler Corporation announces an incredible lease opportunity on the Chrysler Concord." Some commercial claims are indeed incredible.

See also **Metaphoric contradiction.**

Double negative. 1. ANY, NO, NOTHING. 2. *Carelessness.* 3. *Unsound effects.*

1. ANY, NO, NOTHING

In some languages double negatives are considered proper. For instance, "I have no money" in Spanish is *Yo no tengo ningún dinero*. The literal translation is "I don't have no money," which in English is considered ungrammatical; to make it grammatical, either scrap the "don't" or change "no" to *any*.

The English-speaking tradition is that a double negative is vulgar and improper, unless the speaker wants one negative to cancel the other and thereby produce a positive. A sentence like the sample above can have only one negative: either before the verb or before its object.

Thus a radio host, wanting listeners to stay tuned, erred by saying, "Don't go *nowhere*," instead of *anywhere*.

An investigative correspondent was in error when he told a television audience that the cause of a plane crash did not appear to be mechanical; there was "no distress call, no 'mayday,' no nothing." Two decades earlier, Jimmy Carter had made a similar mistake during a debate with President Ford:

> If the Arab countries ever again declare an embargo . . . I would not ship . . . [them] anything—no weapons, no spare parts . . . no oil pipe, no nothing.

In both instances, the last "no" should have been scrapped. (Another mistake is in mood. Either make "declare" *declared* or change "would" to *will*. See **Subjunctive; Tense,** 4C.) Carter's grammar did not noticeably hurt him; he was narrowly elected. Ford's verbal blunders had been worse.

H. L. Mencken wrote: "Like most other examples of 'bad grammar' encountered in American, the compound negative is of great antiquity and was once quite respectable." Chaucer used it freely. It appears in some Shakespeare plays. (*Romeo and Juliet:* "I will not budge for no man's pleasure.") Mencken had kind words for it:

> Obviously, "I *won't* take *nothing*" is stronger than either "I *will* take *nothing*" or "I *won't* take *anything*." And equally without doubt there is a picturesque charm, if not really any extra vigor in the vulgar American . . . "She *never* goes hardly *nowhere*" [a triple negative] . . . and "*Ain't nobody* there. . . ."

Note that Mencken's own negative is properly singular. Despite his finding of strength and charm in the multiple nega-

tive, it is significant that he did not use it in his own writing.

See also **BUT,** 2, 3; **NEITHER,** 2.

2. *Carelessness*

The double negative is sometimes a result of carelessness or hastiness, hence understandably more common in speaking than in writing.

A television weatherman said, "I wouldn't be a bit surprised if we didn't find some anomalies there." The literal meaning of the sentence is that complete normality (in the weather) would not surprise him at all. Probably he meant the opposite: "I wouldn't be a bit surprised if we found some anomalies there," or "I would be surprised if we didn't find some anomalies there."

This was heard in television coverage of rural fires: "No smoking bans were in effect." It was ambiguous. If the "no" applied to "smoking bans," the sentence meant that no bans on smoking were in effect. If the "no" applied just to "smoking," there was a " 'no-smoking' ban," which, logically, would be the opposite of a *smoking* ban. The newscaster probably meant to say, "Bans on smoking were in effect," which would have avoided the double negative of "no" and "bans."

A university's journalism dean was criticized for hiring a prominent person as a teacher. A newspaper trade magazine quoted the dean on his hiring practices:

> We do not pay our outsiders nowhere near what they are worth and in somewhat different amounts.

"Not" and "nowhere" together make a double negative. Furthermore, the "not" carries over to "in somewhat different amounts," negating the phrase. Omitting the "not" (or, better, "do not") corrects both problems. Alternatively, change "nowhere" to *anywhere;* and after "and," insert *we pay them.*

See also **NOT,** 1G.

3. Unsound effects

A newspaper story (about computer interviews) carried the headline "I can't get no interaction." Perhaps the writer of the headline knew better and was trying to achieve some kind of effect, besides the effect of making the newspaper seem illiterate and causing hundreds of English teachers to grimace in pain.

A two-word sentence fragment with two negatives was put in a column and a book. (The column complained about the poor quality of television "pool" coverage of the U.S. invasion of Panama. The book looked askance at the popular use of a word.)

> Amateur photographers subbing for the big guys? Not hardly.

> I'm sure you are (it is, they will, etc.). Is the sayer really sure? Not hardly.

Hardly would have been enough, for in such contexts it means *probably not*. Preceding it with "not" doubled the negative.

Not all sentences with multiple negatives are no good; the present one is grammatical though graceless. "We are not unmindful of your problem, but . . ." is not so much graceless as heartless. A brave, bleeding athlete remarks, "It's nothing," and his coach responds correctly, "It's not 'nothing.' " And an old song that went "No, no, a thousand times no!" got the negative message across effectively.

Even when used correctly, perhaps as a device for deliberate understatement, a sentence with multiple negatives may not be instantly comprehensible. "I would not be unhappy if the people did not endorse his leadership" is more clearly expressed in a positive way. "I would try to remain cheerful if the people rejected his leadership," or other words to that effect, would be easier to grasp.

See also **NO WAY.**

Double possessive. Joseph Priestley was a scientist and the discoverer of oxygen. He was also a philosopher, politician, and theologian, and in the 1760s he wrote *The Rudiments of English Grammar*. In clear prose that holds to this day, he pointed out an accepted anomaly of English usage:

> In some cases we use both the genitive [possessive] and the preposition *of*, as, *this book of my friend's*. Sometimes, indeed, this method is quite necessary, in order to distinguish the sense. . . . *This picture of my friend*, and *this picture of my friend's*, suggest very different ideas. . . . Where this double genitive, as it may be called, is not necessary to distinguish the sense, and especially in grave style, it is generally omitted.

The *double possessive*, also known as the *double genitive*, remains idiomatic.

Literally the *'s* in a phrase like *that cat of his sister's* is redundant, inasmuch as the *of* has already indicated possession, and a few writers on usage look askance on the form. Roy H. Copperud advises those finding *a friend of my uncle* neater and more logical than *a friend of my uncle's* to use the former even though the latter is long-established idiom and not considered wrong.

Nobody minds when the possessive is a pronoun instead of a noun: *friends of mine* and *a dress of hers*. Nobody is likely to say "friends of *me*" or "a dress of *her*."

In writing, (1) *an opinion of the doctor* and (2) *an opinion of the doctor's* have two different meanings. First, the opinion concerns the doctor; second, the opinion is held by the doctor. In speaking, the possessive form would be ambiguous, "the doctor's" sounding like "the doctors." Better: *an opinion held by the doctor.*

In the view of Eric Partridge, scrupulous writers avoid that form when the possessive is a noun, especially a plural noun; they remember "the very sound rule that a piece of writing should be as clear to a listener as to a reader"; at least a writer or speaker must be sure that the context makes the reference clear.

Doubling of letters. *See* **Spelling,** *3B.*

DOWN. *See* **Numbers,** *1.*

"DOWNPLAY." *See* **PLAY DOWN and "DOWNPLAY."**

DRAFT. *Draft* or *draught* (British spelling) comes from the Old English *dragan,* meaning to draw, pull. When applied to a beverage, *draft* is the drawing of liquid from its receptacle, as beer or ale from a cask. The beverage is available *on draft.*

"GENUINE DRAFT" as seen on beer cans and in ads is meaningless. To see a genuine *draft,* go to your nearest tavern. By definition, *draft beer* is not bottled or canned.

Draft has another connection with fluid: Among many other meanings (like an air current, a check for money, military conscription, a preliminary text, etc.), it is a swallowing or the portion of liquid swallowed.

DRAGGED and "DRUG." The past tense of *drag* is *dragged.* A television interviewer said two competing presidential candidates went to Dallas, Texas, and "drug along a bunch of advisers." His "drug" use was dialectal.

DRAMA, DRAMATIC, DRAMATICALLY. *1. "Drama" everywhere. 2. Alternatives.*

1. "Drama" everywhere
A *drama* is primarily a stage play, or a literary composition that tells a story through dialogue and action. *Drama* or

the drama is (a) the art or profession dealing with plays, (b) the theater as an institution, or (c) plays collectively. By metaphoric extension, *drama* or *a drama* can mean either the nature of a play or a set of events like a play in action, conflict, excitement, or story progression.

Dramatic (adjective) means pertaining to *drama* (noun) or having its characteristics. *Dramatically* (adverb) means in a *dramatic* way or from the standpoint of *drama.* For example, conflict between characters is a *dramatic* device; a court trial sometimes is more *dramatic* than a stage play; the show last night was thought-provoking but *dramatically* inadequate; he orated and gesticulated *dramatically,* like an old-time Shakespearean actor.

"Dramatic" verbiage has proliferated of late. That it does not take a drama critic to find things "dramatic" will be amply illustrated below. First comes a set of extracts from a book by a leading judge.

The country had changed *dramatically* indeed from the time during the Civil War. . . . The income of individual farmers rose *dramatically.* . . . The stock-market crash . . . *dramatically* slowed down industrial expansion. . . . In the short run the effect of the change in membership on the Court's decisions was immediate, *dramatic,* and predictable. . . . When I moved . . . I was delighted with the *dramatic* change in my view. . . . Finally, both the commercial activity and the population of the United States continued to increase *dramatically.* [Emphasis is added.]

Within eight days, television reported that a woman's illness had "dramatically worsened," that local test scores had "dramatically increased from last year," that "a dramatic shift in wind direction" could imperil aircraft, that prosecutors in a murder case had "unveiled some dramatic photos," that Miami had "cut crime against tourists dramatically," and that people could "dramatically reduce their risk of heart attacks." In an ensuing week, there came television reports that test scores in the nation's schools had "improved dramatically," that a reservoir had "dropped dramatically," that a woman with the AIDS virus who took the drug AZT could "dramatically reduce the chances of her baby getting AIDS," and that chicken was found to be "dramatically better than hamburger" in leanness.

2. Alternatives

In most contemporary uses of "dramatic" or "dramatically," one can either eliminate the word without detriment or substitute a more accurate description. Two lists that follow offer fifty replacements. You may think of more.

Adjectives: big, considerable, dangerous, drastic, encouraging, extreme, great, high, huge, large, marked, mighty, noteworthy, precipitous, public, radical, remarkable, serious, sharp, significant, stark, steep, striking, stunning, substantial, vast.

Adverbs: considerably, dangerously, drastically, encouragingly, extremely, far, greatly, highly, hugely, markedly, mightily, much, precipitously, publicly, radically, remarkably, seriously, sharply, significantly, starkly, steeply, stunningly, substantially, vastly.

Saying that something is *dramatic* or done *dramatically* does not make it so. If it is so, such a label may be superfluous. Sometimes the right choice of verb makes any allusion to "drama" unnecessary. For instance, "the rate dramatically increased" is a cumbersome way of saying *the rate soared.* A more precise way is to use a number, if it is known: *the rate doubled* or *increased 69 percent.*

These seven words made up a paragraph in a newspaper: "The child

language field has dramatically mushroomed." Would the field be any worse off if it just mushroomed?

DROVE. *Drove* is the past tense of *drive* (verb, transitive and intransitive). A *drove* (noun, from the same source, the Old English *drifan,* to drive) is a group of animals being driven as a herd or flock. Someone probably saw the resemblance between the moving animals and a moving crowd of people, for at times *drove* is applied to the latter. Typically the word applies to cattle or sheep.

"Mice appear to be flocking out of the area in droves." That was heard on a news-radio station. To *flock* is to gather or travel in a flock or crowd, so *flocking* would suffice to get across the idea of multiplicity without "in droves."

"DRUG" and DRAGGED. *See* DRAGGED and "DRUG."

DUAL and DUEL. *See* Homophones.

DUE TO. When to use the phrase *due to* and when not to use it can be confusing, although the publisher who wrote the sentence below should have known better.

This price increase has become necessary due to the new state sales tax on newspapers and the increasing costs associated with producing the IJ.

All grammarians approve of *due to* when it means *caused by* or *attributable to* and is helped by a form of the verb *to be:* "His back injury was due to a fall from a cliff."

However, when *due to* means *because of* and follows a clause, it is considered taboo. "He suffered a back injury due to a fall from a cliff." Among acceptable phrases in this type of sentence are *as a result of, because of, on account of,* and *owing to.*

The grammarians have never satisfactorily explained this rule. (They say that *due* is an adjective and should modify a noun. In the taboo form of sentence, it introduces an adverbial phrase, which modifies the verb. But *owing* also is an adjective and *owing to* gets their approval in the same type of sentence.) Careful writers and speakers generally accept the rule, whatever its rationality.

As for the opening quotation: one should expect a publisher to be careful enough to avoid a "due to" snare (and delete an unneeded "t" from *producing*) before he publishes a statement explaining why a paper is worth more money.

DUM-DUM BULLET. A newspaper quoted a public official who had returned from the Middle East:

> "I saw older men and women who had been beaten and had suffered from dumb-dumb bullets."

To avoid that dumb-dumb error, realize that the *dum-dum bullet,* an outlawed, soft-nosed bullet that expands on impact, originated in Dum Dum, India, a town near Calcutta. Another spelling of the place is *Dumdum* and of the bullet is *dumdum,* never "dumb-dumb."

E

EACH AND EVERY. *See* **Twins,** *1.*

EACH, EACH OF. *Each* can be either an adjective, meaning every ("We follow each clue"); or a pronoun, meaning every single one ("To each his own"). Either way, singularness is the essence of *each*.

When the subject of a sentence is or starts with *each,* the subject is considered singular. "Each has a car" or "Each person has a car." Note that the verb (has) is singular too and so is the object (car).

The same is true when the subject is *each of* followed by a plural noun or pronoun. Both of the sentences below are in error. The first was part of a television commentary; the second formed a large newspaper headline.

Each of these ladies this evening are going to be doing such difficult routines.

Each of us should know
and love our cholesterol level

In the first, change "are" to *is* and "difficult routines" to *a difficult routine.* In the second, just change "our" to *his.* An alternative is *his or her,* which may be impractical for a headline.

There is another way: When the subject of a sentence is plural and *each* follows the subject immediately, merely modifying or explaining it, the verb and any following object are plural. "The boys each own cars." / "We each should know our cholesterol levels." (The article beneath the headline did not say to "love" them.)

See also **BETWEEN,** *2;* **Nouns,** *3;* **Pronouns,** *2.*

EACH OTHER. Although *each* alone is singular, the phrase *each other* (a reciprocal pronoun) is considered plural. The following sentence, from a large ad by a government, goes astray in that respect and has four other flaws.

Recently, the British Government which has a similar law [concerning drugs], agreed with the Bahamian government for the reciprocal enforcement of forfeiture orders in each others' country.

The last word should be plural: *countries.* In addition, the apostrophe goes before the *s* in *each other's.* (*See* **Punctuation,** *1.*) "Reciprocal" is redundant; either it or the last four words should be deleted. A comma belongs before "which." (*See* **THAT and WHICH.**) Finally, the two governments deserve the same kind of *G* or *g.*

Whether *each other* can represent more than two persons or things divides grammarians. Some say to use *each other* for two, *one another* for three or more: "Agnes and John love each other." / "The three friends visit one another's homes." H. W. Fowler saw neither utility nor history on the side of such differentiation. Anyhow the use of *each other* for more than two is not common. Using *one another* for two is more common. *One another's* is the possessive form.

EAGER.   *See* ANXIOUS.

EATEN and ATE.   *See* Tense, 5A.

ECLECTIC.   Variety is the essence of this adjective. A descendant of the Greek *eklegein*, to select, *eclectic* means choosing or chosen from a variety of sources, subjects, methods, points of view, or the like. "He was an eclectic student, with broad interests." / "The museum's collection is eclectic." *Eclectic* says nothing about merit or quality and does not mean discriminating, as some people seem to think.

In a newsletter, the director of an institute wrote about a series of educational programs that "have featured a variety of eclectic programs. . . ." Either "a variety of" or "eclectic" should have been discarded.

EFFECT.   *See* AFFECT and EFFECT.

EFFETE.   *Effete* (adjective, pronounced like *a FEAT*) is one of those useful words that have been devalued by misuse and rendered often ambiguous. Primarily it means no longer able to produce offspring or fruit. It can also mean depleted of vitality, exhausted of vigor.

An article about Thomas Jefferson says, "Theodore Roosevelt thought he was effete." The adjoining sentences (telling of others' views of Jefferson) shed no light on the writer's meaning. Other sources suggest that *incapable* and

visionary (Roosevelt's own words) would have been more informative than "effete"; so would *ineffective* or *timid*.

A review of a joint Russian and American art exhibit says, "The American painting, on the contrary, looks effete. It's so well-made that its life is gone." This time the passage offers a clue. By "effete," the writer appears to mean lifeless in creation, not depleted of life but stillborn.

At times *decadent, effeminate, foppish, soft, weak,* or even *elite* has been loosely replaced by *effete.* Spiro Agnew used it to describe the press corps. It is seldom clear exactly what the user has in mind.

Effete came from the Latin *effetus,* that has produced young (from *ex-,* out, and *fetus,* giving birth—the source of the English *fetus*).

EFFICACY and EFFICIENCY.   *See* Confusing pairs.

E.G. (for example).   *See* Punctuation, 2A.

EITHER.   1. *As a conjunction.* 2. *Other functions.* 3. *Pronunciation.*

1. As a conjunction
Either fits four categories. In the sentences below, from two restaurant reviews, it is meant as a *conjunction,* or connecting word, but it is misused.

> Dessert is either vanilla ice cream, spumoni or a respectable caramel custard for $1.50 more.

> . . . Other meals [include] . . . meat-sauced rice and country salads and either five-spice chicken, imperial rolls, or shish kebobs. . . .

As a conjunction, *either* means one or the other of *two* possibilities. Each sample sentence, however, tells of a choice between three. Omit "either" or else change it to *a choice of*.

The *either . . . or* form connects two grammatically equal portions of a sentence. (*Either* and *or* are called correlative conjunctions. Other such pairs are *neither . . . nor* and *both . . . and*.) It is correct to say, "You may choose either soup or salad"—a noun follows the *either* and a noun follows the *or*.

Sometimes the *either* is misplaced, like this: "You may either choose soup or salad." Although you will understand her when a waitress says it, the sentence is not logical: a verb and its object follow the *either* while a noun follows the *or*. *Either* tends to grab the next word or phrase. "You may either choose"—here it makes sense—"or have the choice made for you."

This excerpt, from a book on art history, is ill-balanced:

> Nowadays, Bosch is either considered a surrealist, a painter of repressed desires and human solitude, or a fiery mystic with esoteric inclinations. . . .

It says that the artist "is either considered [verb] . . . or a fiery mystic [noun]. . . ." The sentence can easily be repaired by interchanging "either" and the verb, "considered":

> Nowadays, Bosch is *considered either* a surrealist [noun] . . . or a fiery mystic [noun]. . . .

An alternative solution is to insert a verb after *or*. Example:

> Nowadays, Bosch is either considered [verb] a surrealist . . . or *considered* [or *called*, verb] a fiery mystic. . . .

The problem can be more subtle: "He is either fibbing or has forgotten." *He is* is followed sensibly by *fibbing*

(present participle) but not so by *has forgotten* (auxiliary verb and past participle). These are three alternative repairs: "He is either fibbing or forgetting." / "He either is fibbing or has forgotten." / "Either he is fibbing or he has forgotten."

When each noun is singular, any verb that follows has to be singular too: "Either a hurricane or an eruption comes every few years"—not "come." When each noun is plural, any verb that follows must be plural: "Either hurricanes or eruptions come every few years"—not "comes."

It becomes more complicated when the nouns differ in number. Make the verb plural if it is closer to the plural noun than to the singular noun: "Either Presley or the Jacksons are on that record." If the verb is closer to the singular noun, what then? Some grammarians would permit "Either the Jacksons or Presley is . . . ," but a better procedure is to put the plural noun second, as in the previous example; or to revise the sentence, for example: "The Jacksons may be on that record, or it may be Presley."

See also **NEITHER; OR.**

2. *Other functions*

Either serves as three other parts of speech: *adjective* ("Either entree is satisfactory"); *pronoun* ("Either is satisfactory"); and *adverb,* which follows a negative statement ("If you don't want to eat, I won't either"). *Either,* as an adjective, sometimes means each, one and the other ("She wears a bracelet on either arm").

As an adjective or pronoun, *either* goes with a singular verb, singular noun, or singular possessive, as the case may be: "Either of them is capable of playing the role"—*not* "are capable." / "No more copies were available at either the downtown or the uptown store"—*not* "stores." / "Either woman will do her best"—*not* "their best."

3. *Pronunciation*

H. W. Fowler wrote that EYE, "though not more correct," was replacing EE as the pronunciation of the first syllable of *either* in England's educated speech.

EYE-thur seems to be making progress in America too. Imitation of the British practice or a belief that it is more high-class than EE-thur may help to account for this development.

EKE. In *The Outline of History* H. G. Wells describes the raising of livestock by Neolithic people and credits them with the discovery of milking. Then he correctly writes, "They eked out this food supply by hunting." To *eke out* something is to supplement it, to add to it what it lacks. That which is *eked out* is the original thing (the food supply), not what is added and not what results. That is the primary meaning of the verb (transitive).

A later but now common meaning, disapproved by some critics, is to earn with difficulty. Land pressures are intense in El Salvador, a newspaper says, "because so many people are trying to eke a living out of so small a country." In this sense, that which is *eked out* is what results (a living).

Which sense is intended may not always be clear. In the following sentence, what is the person's occupation? "John eked out his living by selling clothing." We do not know. If we construe the sentence according to the more traditional sense, John's selling merely supplements his income. According to the later sense, sales are John's livelihood.

Eke alone, now archaic, meant to increase or enlarge (something); another meaning was *also*. An Old English version was spelled *ecan, ycan,* etc. So traditionally *eke* or *eke out* is associated with the idea of adding. Contemporary users sometimes have in mind the opposite sense: subtracting, or squeezing out.

These are from a newspaper and a book on law respectively:

> Once a company reneges on its half of the bargain, it will have trouble eking out those sacrifices from its workers.

> Every grant to the President . . . was in effect a derogation from Congressional power, eked out slowly, reluctantly. . . .

Still another sense of *eke out,* found in contemporary dictionaries if not often in use, is to make (a supply) last through economy.

ELECT, ELECTED, ELECTIVE, ELECTORAL. *1. ELECTED and ELECTIVE. 2. ELECTORAL.*

1. ELECTED and ELECTIVE

To *elect* (verb, transitive or intransitive) is to choose. Politically, it is to choose an official by vote. A person so chosen is *elected* (past participle). The office so filled is *elective* (adjective); that is, filled by election. A telecast had an error:

> He told ABC that he is not a candidate for any elected office.

". . . Any *elective* office," not "elected." (*See also* **Tense,** 2.)

The words can be used in nonpolitical contexts. "He elects to throw a curve ball." / "I elected a science course." / "It's an elective course." *Elective* here means optional, not required.

Elect (adjective), in combination with the name of an office, e.g., president-elect, denotes one who has been elected but whose term has not yet begun. It can mean given preference: an *elect* group. In theology it means divinely picked for salvation. Those so picked are the *elect* (noun).

2. *ELECTORAL*

Elective can be a synonym for *electoral* (adjective), pertaining to selection by vote or having the authority to elect. The latter is pronounced i-LEK-tur-ul, not (as mispronounced by the host of a TV quiz show) "i-lek-TAUR-ul." The *Electoral College* is not an educational institution but the body that formally elects the U.S. president. Its members are *electors*.

A State Department spokesman expressed hope that the Nicaraguan leader was not "trying to derail the electorial process." The word is *electoral*. There is no "electorial."

ELEMENT.   *See* SILICON and SILICONE.

ELEMENTAL and ELEMENTARY.   *See* Confusing pairs.

ELLIPSE.   *See* OVAL.

Ellipsis.   There are two kinds of ellipsis. In grammar it is the omission of a word or words that would make a sentence more complete but that can be understood from the context. In punctuation it is the set of dots used when part of a quotation is omitted. Only the first kind concerns us right now. (*See also* **Punctuation,** *5*.)

One need not, and should not, repeat the *is* in this sentence: "The boy is 5, the girl 4." The single verb suffices for both nouns. "I'll be ready when you are." That sentence could end with another *ready*, but it is not necessary.

Sometimes a writer or speaker leaves out too much, perhaps a necessary word. As a result, the sentence sounds awkward or even leaves us guessing. A news story in a prominent daily said:

> The Senate's current version calls for spending $2.6 billion for drug enforcement that the House does not.

"Does not" *what?* Want? Match? Agree with? "Does not" relates to nothing that was said or that is obvious. Whatever the meaning is, the sentence would be far clearer if it were divided into two sentences. End the first with ". . . drug enforcement." Begin the second like this: "The House's version provides . . ." or "does not provide. . . ."

A passage in a book on law and government is even more puzzling:

> Having survived the legal maze, where have we ended up regarding the 1973 bombing of Cambodia? Still in something of a mess, because every time Congress authorized the bombing a number of its members said that they weren't.

"Weren't" what? "Weren't *aware that it had*" would be an adequate ellipsis—if that was the intended meaning. Or perhaps the author meant *hadn't* and wrote "weren't" by mistake. (Neither contraction suits the grave topic. *See* **Contractions,** *2*.)

In an ellipsis, it is enough work for the reader or listener to silently repeat a word or phrase without having to change its form. Any word or phrase to be supplied should be exactly the same as one that has just been used. This is from the daily quoted above:

> The companies include . . . the United Coconut Planters Bank, whose disposition could determine the shape of the coconut industry, one of the countries largest.

"Largest" does not connect with any other word in the sentence. If the coconut industry is "one of the country's largest *industries,*" why not say so? (A careless transformation of *country's* also mars the sentence. *See* **Punctuation,** *1 C*.)

In this example from a book on law and history, the reader is expected not only (1) to supply a word that differs from the word used, but also (2) to supply it before the other is used.

> In 1808 President Jefferson took a very serious view of an attack by one army and several navy officers upon Spanish territory.

The first item enumerated seems to be "one army." The authors meant "one army *officer*" and should have said so.

Lines like these, from two network telecasts, have been uttered in exposés by a number of broadcasters:

> The offer sounded too good to be true, and, as it turned out, it was.

> If it sounds too good to be true, it probably is.

What part are we expected to silently repeat? No doubt, from each context, it is "too good to be true." But someone tuning in late might repeat just the "true," reversing the meaning.

Omitting *hundred* or *thousand* from a number can be misleading. *See* **Numbers,** *1*.

See also **AS,** *1*; **Pronouns,** *10E*; **Verbs,** *4*.

ELUDE and ALLUDE. *See* **Confusing pairs.**

EMBRYO and FETUS. A newspaper article said that courts had upheld a Minnesota law under which a man was charged with "fetal homicide" as well as murder. Allegedly he had shot a pregnant woman, killing both her and her one-month-old "fetus."

A woman who is one month pregnant carries an *embryo,* not a "fetus." An *embryo* is an incipient animal or human being. It is in the early stages of development, unlike a *fetus,* which is in the middle or late stages. Interpretations

differ somewhat. For the human species, some draw the line at two months, others at three months.

Embryo comes from the Greek *embryon,* embryo, fetus, or that which is newly born. *Fetus* traces to Latin, in which it means fetus, progeny, pregnancy, or a giving birth.

EMERITUS. *Emeritus* (adjective) means being retired from service but keeping the title one held. As part of a title, it commonly follows the original title: "Professor Emeritus John J. Doe." Otherwise it can follow or precede the original title: "He is an emeritus professor of law." It is mainly applied to those retired from colleges and universities, occasionally to others retired from white-collar positions.

In ancient Rome *emeritus* (past participle of *emereri,* to earn by service) referred to a man who had served his term as a soldier. The term is never applied to a former or retired member of the U.S. armed forces.

To use *emeritus* indiscriminately in describing a former job can be ludicrous. The lead sentence of a newspaper's main article applied it to a professional politician who had not retired but had been unseated from his last office by a term limitation.

> Assembly Speaker Emeritus Willie Brown continues to hold a slim lead over Mayor Frank Jordan among voters as next month's mayoral election nears. . . .

An *emeritus* (noun) is one who is *emeritus* (adjective). The plural is *emeriti*. Pronunciations: em-MER-it-us and em-MER-it-tie.

One who uses Latinisms strictly will speak of a woman as *emerita* (adjective) or an *emerita* (noun). The plural is *emeritae*. Pronunciations: em-MER-it-uh and em-MER-it-tea.

EMIGRATE and IMMIGRATE.
A book by a prominent judge describes changes in U.S. population, such as an increase of sixty million in fifty years.

Some of this was natural increase, but a good deal of it resulted from *emigration*. In the forty years between 1860 and 1900, 14 million people had *emigrated* to the United States from foreign countries. . . . At the same time that *emigrants* and other settlers were populating the territories in the West, many other *emigrants* were settling in the large cities of the East and Midwest. [Emphasis is added.]

Change "emigration" to *immigration,* "emigrated" to *immigrated,* and "emigrants" to *immigrants.*

Which family of words to call on depends on whether you emphasize migrating in, or migrating out. The author emphasizes migrating in. *Immigrate* originates in the Latin *in-,* in, and *migrare,* to migrate; *emigrate* in the Latin *ex-,* out, and *migrare.* A form of *in-* is *im-* while a form of *ex-* is *e-.* That etymology explains the double *m* in the *immigrate* words, the single *m* in the *emigrate* words.

If you need a memory aid, think of *import,* to bring goods into a country; and *export,* to send goods out of a country.

To *immigrate* (verb, intransitive) is to enter and settle in a country. Often it is followed by *to* and the name of the new country. "The Treskunoffs immigrated to the United States ten years ago." The act or practice of *immigrating* is *immigration* (noun). One who *immigrates* is an *immigrant* (noun).

To *emigrate* (verb, intransitive) is to leave one's home country with the intention of giving up residence there. Often it is followed by *from* and the name of the old country. "The Treskunoffs emigrated from Russia ten years ago." The act or

practice of *emigrating* is *emigration* (noun). One who *emigrates* is an *emigrant* (noun).

Occasionally *immigrate* and *emigrate* are used (as transitive verbs) to mean bring in as *immigrants* or to send out as *emigrants.* "The company immigrated Chinese to work cheaply as laborers."

EMINENT and IMMINENT. 1. The difference. 2. Related terms.

1. The difference
Once, while working as a news reporter, I looked in on the mayor's office, where efforts were being made to negotiate the end of a labor dispute. As I was telephoning my editor from the anteroom, the mayor walked in and told me, "The settlement of the bus strike is eminent." I said, misquoting him, "The mayor says the settlement of the bus strike is imminent." (We had a scoop.)

The mayor knew his business, but what he did not know is that *eminent* (adjective) means prominent, outstanding, or noteworthy, whereas *imminent* (adjective) means impending or soon to occur; sometimes, threatening: said of a danger or misfortune.

Some writers do not know that either. A weekly's review of a Shakespearean play contained this sentence: "Best of all, the language, while still Bard-ese, is imminently comprehensible." In this case, "imminently" should be *eminently* (adverb), meaning to a remarkable degree or in an outstanding way.

Note that *eminent(ly)* has one *m* while *imminent(ly)* has two *m*'s. The words originate in Latin, in *ex-,* out, and *in-,* in, respectively (*e-* and *im-* are forms of them) plus *minere,* to project.

2. Related terms
Eminent domain is the right of a government to take private property for public use in return for compensation.

Eminence (noun) means superiority,

celebrity, or a high place or thing. Preceded by *his* or *your,* it is a title of honor for a cardinal in the Roman Catholic Church.

Imminence (noun) is the condition of being *imminent;* or something that is *imminent,* particularly impending danger or evil.

A superficially similar word, not so common, is *immanent* (adjective). Stemming from the Latin *in,* not, and *manere,* to remain, it means existing or remaining within, particularly within one's mind. In theology, it pertains to the doctrine of *immanence* (noun), under which God dwells everywhere in the universe.

EMPLOY. *See* UTILIZE, UTILIZATION (end).

ENDED and ENDING.

> The Times Poll . . . interviewed 1,618 American adults by telephone for three days ending Sunday night.

Such use is common. But some authorities prefer *ended,* rather than "ending," when the period is over. (It is completely *ended,* not just in the process of *ending.*) Some others accept either word. (Present participles sometimes apply to past events.)

All agree that *ending* is the word to use when the terminal date is in the future.

ENDEMIC. "The problem is the kind of violence that's now becoming endemic to Mexico," a panelist on a television forum said. He spoke in the wake of a revolt and a political assassination in Mexico.

That which is *endemic* to a place is restricted to it or particularly prevalent there. The kangaroo is *endemic* to Australia, the apteryx to New Zealand. Political violence, alas, is a global phenomenon. Thus the panelist's state-

ment was not accurate, particularly if the violence was just "now becoming" common in Mexico.

The main article in a newspaper described economic shortcomings in Shanghai, adding:

> Meanwhile, tax evasion in the Shanghai private sector became endemic, increasing an income gap between state employees and free-market entrepreneurs that has aggravated social tensions.

If the writer wanted to say that tax evasion had become a phenomenon peculiar to Shanghai (a dubious proposition), *endemic* would be appropriate. But if he sought to bring out the rapid and extensive spread of tax evasion there, the word to use would be *epidemic.*

ENDING. *See* ENDED and ENDING.

"END OF AN ERA." *See* ERA, 2.

ENDS JUSTIFY THE MEANS. Having gone to Somalia, Africa, to feed the people, U.S. and allied forces were shooting some of them instead. A TV news correspondent said the question was "whether these drastic means justify the humanitarian end."

He had it backward. The question was "whether the humanitarian end justifies these drastic means." Normally the means do not justify the end; that is a matter of language. The end may or may not justify the means; that is a matter of opinion.

ENERGIZE and ENERVATE. *See* Confusing pairs.

ENORMITY. Residents of the Hawaiian island of Kauai who had been made homeless by a hurricane seemed to be in good spirits, a television newscaster

observed. Either they are used to being close to nature, he said, or "the enormity of what's happened to them hasn't yet sunk in."

Unless he was saying that the hurricane was outrageously immoral, he misunderstood the meaning of *enormity*. He may have confused it with *enormousness*, although *magnitude* or *gravity* might have been a better choice of nouns. *Enormity* denotes monstrous evil or a monstrously evil act. A nonhuman phenomenon like a hurricane is amoral, unless one ascribes it to the devil or an evil spirit.

Flying from England to Cameroun, an author observed the Sahara below. "Hours later, still above the desert, we began to appreciate its enormity." Although some travelers in the desert have found it to be a hell, *vastness* or *immensity* would fit the context better.

On a TV show about famous athletes, a narrator said of a baseball player, "Now, two decades later, the enormity of his accomplishments can be appreciated." Surely the TV man did not intend to associate Hank Aaron's accomplishments with monstrous evil, yet that is literally what he did by using "enormity" when he could have used *greatness*.

A book (of mine) said, ". . . The enormity of the cocktails took them out of the 'social' category." Although some have described alcohol as a wicked demon, in this instance the word should have been *immensity* or *hugeness*.

Some dictionaries offer such words among the definitions of *enormity* without mentioning that many critics scorn its application to mere size. A source of criticism is *American Heritage Dictionary*; 93 percent of its usage panel rejected "The enormity of Latin America is readily apparent from these maps."

At one time *enormous* meant monstrously wicked. It and *enormity* both trace to the Latin *enormis*, meaning out of the ordinary, huge.

-EN, -REN plurals. *See* **Plurals and singulars,** *1, 2D.*

ENSURE and INSURE. *See* **ASSURE, ENSURE, and INSURE.**

ENTHUSE, ENTHUSED. If the colloquial "enthused" ever is acceptable, it is assuredly out of place in a grim article about "the fratricidal carnage" of revolutionary France:

> Baron Armel de Wismes, who puts on a black tie of mourning on the anniversary of Louis XVI's execution, is not enthused about the festivities marking the 200th anniversary of the French Revolution.

The appropriate adjective is *enthusiastic*, meaning ardently interested in something. At times "enthuse" is used as a verb. Most dictionaries call "enthuse(d)" colloquial, informal, or popular, and few writers, speakers, or educators show *enthusiasm* (noun) for it.

"The majority leader enthused over his party's gains," instead of *became* or *waxed enthusiastic*, was disapproved by 76 percent of *The American Heritage Dictionary*'s usage panel. "He was considerably less enthused by signs of factionalism," instead of *enthusiastic over*, was disapproved by 72 percent. The panel did not consider the verb in a transitive sense, for which a case could be made: "Professor Marshall enthused his students," instead of *roused enthusiasm in* or *made . . . enthusiastic*.

ENTOMOLOGY and ETYMOLOGY. *See* **Confusing pairs.**

Enumerations. *See* **Series errors.**

EPIDEMIC. *See* **ENDEMIC.**

"EQUALLY AS." *See* **AS,** 3 (end).

ERA.   *1. Definition; pronunciation. 2. When will it end?*

1. Definition; pronunciation

An *era* is a division of time that is (a) reckoned from a notable historical event, as the Christian era is; (b) distinctive in its character, events, conditions, or leaders, like the Roman "era of the adventurer generals" (H. G. Wells) or the nineteenth-century American "era of good feeling"; or (c) fundamental in geologic history, like the Mesozoic era.

Its customary pronunciation has long been EAR-uh. Many now pronounce it like *error* without the final *r*, possibly risking misunderstanding. Modern dictionaries give both pronunciations.

2. When will it end?

The news media, with a notable sense of history, inform us of all the various eras that we pass through—but only when the eras end; they are perpetually ending.

These were press headlines: "Era in Houston Ends As Chronicle Is Sold" / "Christmas at B. Altman: the End of an Era . . ." / "An era ends: Johnny [Carson] says goodbye."

Broadcasters reported "the end of an era" when a navy yard was shut down, a military base was closed, a gorilla died at a zoo, a hotel was demolished, and another navy yard closed. A news service applied the same phrase to a bookstore's closing.

When the baseball player Jose Canseco was traded, an era did not end; it merely relocated. A main story in a California daily began, "A's general manager Sandy Alderson sent an era to Texas."

EROTIC.   *See* EXOTIC.

ERR, ERROR.   Opening a segment on movie mistakes, a network television program displayed the title "TO ERROR IS HUMAN" on the screen. The network staff itself was in error, mis-

quoting the ancient, proverbial saying "To err is human."

Error is a noun only. It means, of course, mistake. It can also mean wrongdoing, an act or example of deviation from what is right, or any of various defensive misplays in baseball.

The related verb is to *err*, which can mean to make a mistake, to do something wrong, or to go off course. ("The captain chose to err on the side of caution." / "I'm afraid that I have erred in my calculation.") *Err* rhymes with *her* and *sir*.

"To err is human" goes back at least to the Roman philosopher and dramatist Seneca (4? B.C.–A.D. 65). Many others repeated that thought in one form or another, in numerous languages. The version by Alexander Pope, the English poet (1688–1744), "To err is human, to forgive divine," is particularly famous.

ERRANT and ARRANT.   *See* Confusing pairs.

ERSTWHILE.   *Erstwhile* (adjective) means *former*. It is a literary word, not a word to be used regularly in conversation or frequently in writing. When it does surface in casual talk or informal writing, its users often seem unsure of what it means.

In a discussion on television, a panelist wondered whether the vice president's involvement in a controversy over election-campaign financing would affect his presidential ambition. She asked:

Does this hurt him? Does this make his erstwhile opponents lick their chops?

She was literally asking about his *former* opponents. "Erstwhile" should have been *would-be*.

A columnist wrote:

The erstwhile George Shultz and his shattered Department of State seemed to feel the same way [intolerant of wrongdoing].

What the writer had in mind is anyone's guess. To speak of, in effect, *the former George Shultz* made no sense; he remained George Shultz. Ultimately one might describe him as *the erstwhile secretary of state.*

Erstwhile as an adverb, or *erstwhiles,* meaning formerly or some time ago, is archaic.

ESCALATE. *See* Verbs, 2.

ESPIONAGE. *See* Crimes, 5.

ESTIMATE, ESTIMATED. *1. An estimated what? 2. Estimated by whom? 3. Pronunciation; other forms.*

1. An estimated what?

"An estimated" followed by a number and a plural noun is a well-worn pattern in the popular press, although four specimens in one news story is unusual. The story dealt with reactions to China's Tiananmen Square massacre.

On Sunday . . . an estimated 3,000 students and sympathizers rallied at Miyashita Park in Tokyo's Shibuya district. . . .

An estimated 2,000 Chinese students held similar demonstrations Sunday and yesterday outside Chinese consulates in Osaka, Fukuda and Nagoya. . . .

Major travel agencies reported that an estimated 500 Japanese are touring in China. . . .

There are an estimated 3,100 Japanese residents . . . in Beijing.

Nonjournalists are less likely to say "an estimated 5,000 were there" than "*about* [or *around* or *approximately* or *roughly*] 5,000 were there."

No one would say or write, for instance, "an 8,000 marchers." The "esti-mated" is supposed to make it right. It has been said that "total of" is understood. *The New York Times* chose to insert the two words, properly, in an article about Yugoslavia in the 1940s.

An estimated total of 1,700,000 Yugoslavs were killed, both in combat and in atrocities and reprisals by and against civilians.

The Far Eastern article could have said, for instance, "An estimated *total of* 2,000 Chinese students. . . ." The same thought can be expressed in some other way: *A group estimated at* 2,000; or *a crowd estimated* (or *said* or *believed*) *to number* 2,000; or simply *about* or *approximately* or *roughly* 2,000. *Around* is colloquial.

2. Estimated by whom?

When "estimated" is used in a vague sense, one is entitled to ask: "estimated" by whom? It does not tell us much unless we know who has done the *estimating.* If, for instance, the police make an *estimate* of the size of the crowd attending a rally, it may differ wildly from an *estimate* made by the sponsors or by journalists.

It is best to state clearly, "The police estimated that 5,000 attended" or "The sponsors estimated that 15,000 attended."

If the word *estimate* or *estimated* is used, a true *estimate*—that is, an approximate calculation—ought to have been made. Sometimes the figure is just a guess, but one never reads in the newspaper or hears on the air, "A guessed 10,000 supporters attended."

3. Pronunciation; other forms

As a noun, meaning an approximate calculation, *estimate* is pronounced ES-tim-mit. As a verb, meaning to calculate something approximately, *estimate* is pronounced ES-tim-mate.

Estimated, the past tense and past

participle of the verb *estimate,* is commonly used as an adjective in the press. The adjective presented in dictionaries is *estimative:* pertaining to estimating or serving as an estimate. ("The 3,000 is only estimative.")

Estimation can be an act of estimating; a judgment made as a result; a valuation of merit; or esteem, repute. A few critics object to the phrase "in my estimation." Roy H. Copperud writes, "*Estimate* is the judgment, *estimation* the process of forming it." Raising no such objection, *The American Heritage Dictionary* illustrates *estimation* by quoting Thoreau: "No man ever stood the lower in my estimation for having a patch in his clothes."

ET AL. *See* ETC., ET CETERA, 2.

ETC., ET CETERA.   1. *And the rest.* 2. *ET AL.*

1. *And the rest*

In Latin *et* means *and* and *cetera* means *the rest.* As adapted to English, the phrase *et cetera* is the equivalent of *and so on* or *and so forth.* Often it is abbreviated: *etc.* Its user avoids listing all the items in a category. "They hunt small animals: rabbits, squirrels, etc." The *etc.* indicates others in the same category (like gophers and chipmunks, in this instance).

Sometimes the two words are combined in the noun *etcetera(s).* "The sentence ends with a lazy etcetera." / "I packed the main items and let the etceteras go."

Inasmuch as *and* is what the *et* means, "and" or "&" should not precede *et cetera* or *etc.,* although *&c.* is an optional abbreviation. A broadcaster spoke of "alcohol, tobacco, and et cetera" and, in another redundancy the next day, ended a series "et cetera, et cetera, et cetera."

A variant spelling is *et caetera.* However it is spelled, it is pronounced either et-SET-uh-ruh or et-SET-ruh. Occasionally someone mispronounces the *et* "ex" or misspells *etc.*: A printed sign in a store window said, in advertising animals made from plant parts, "Everything is Natural . . . Eyes, Nose, Tail, Ect."

Usage critics have taken aim at *etc.* One called it amateurish and slovenly in literary prose. To another, *etc.* suits commercial or technical writing but its use elsewhere can make a writer seem lazy or ignorant.

While accepting those pronouncements as caveats, we can temper them: *etc.* can either stunt or tighten a sentence; it is a matter of judgment. If *etc.* seems too curt, alternatives are to spell out *et cetera* or follow the series with *and so on* or another indication that the examples given are not exhaustive. Yet if conciseness is desired, particularly when the listing is parenthetical or tabular, *etc.* may be preferable, as long as it is clear what *etc.* is meant to suggest.

When, in highly concise fashion, only one item precedes the *etc.,* a comma need not intervene: instead of "rabbits, etc.," make it *rabbits etc.*

2. *ET AL.*

A phrase of similar meaning, used often in legal writing, is *et al.* It is an abbreviation of the Latin *et alii,* meaning *and others,* or *et alius,* meaning *and another.* For instance, a case may be titled *John Smith* v. *Harry Robinson et al.,* indicating that there are other defendants besides Robinson.

ETERNITY. It is forever. It is time without end. (To state the definition of this noun is not to take any stand on the implicit cosmological question.) Sometimes *eternity* is used metaphorically to describe an extremely long time.

A music critic wrote that a symphony orchestra "proved expert at making a mere 68 minutes of music run on for a small eternity." It was an extravagant way to express his boredom. How would he describe, say, the life expectancy of the Sun?

See also **INTERMINABLE.**

EVADE and AVOID. *See* **Confusing pairs.**

(-)EVER. *1. Apart or together?—the W-words. 2. EVER and EVERY. 3. FOREVER, FOR EVER. 4. HOWEVER. 5. WHYEVER, WHY EVER. 6. With RARELY, SELDOM; definitions.*

1. Apart or together?—the W-words

Two words or one word? That is the question here, whether to write *what ever, when ever, where ever,* and *who ever* or *whatever, whenever, wherever,* and *whoever.*

The answer is brief: one word in a statement, two words in a question. A book departs from that rule:

What ever method you use, however, should be checked out with the local postal officials in your area.

"*Whatever* method you use" would be right. The excerpt is a *declarative* sentence, a statement.

All the four *w*-words should be treated the same. "We visit them whenever we can." / "He goes wherever they send him." / "Whoever did that must have been mad."

In sentences like these, however, the *w*-root and the *ever* part company: "What ever made him do such a thing?" / "When ever will that check come?" / "Where ever did you hear that?" / "Who ever said such nonsense?"

In an *interrogative* sentence, that is, a question, *ever* intensifies the basic word but is not essential to it. The separate *ever* is roughly equivalent to *conceivably, possibly, on earth, the heck,* and *in the world.* For example, "What *ever* made

him . . . ?" and "Who *ever* said . . . ?" mean almost the same as "What conceivably made him . . . ?" and "Who on earth said . . . ?" The *w*-word and the *ever* need not be next to each other: "*Where* was it *ever* written that I have to support your brother?" is similar to "Where the heck was it written . . . ?"

The rule was essentially enunciated by H. W. Fowler, although he restricted the interrogative *ever* to sentences reproducing highly informal spoken speech. (Even then, *who* could not come next to *ever*; he wanted "*Who* could *ever* . . . ?" instead of "*Who ever* could . . . ?" To his reviser, Sir Ernest Gowers, the former was merely "better.")

Wilson Follett sanctioned the separated, interrogative *ever* for any "common use" but not for a "grave style." He wrote that the adverbs "whatever, whoever, whenever, wherever, however, and whyever are rhetorically equivalent and should be treated alike." Follett's approach is recommended. (He noted that dictionaries separated some words, kept some joined, and disagreed on which words to give each treatment. Their unruliness persists.)

Speakers need not worry about a difference between the two forms, although they do tend to give an interrogative *ever* more emphasis than a declarative *-ever.*

2. EVER and EVERY

Ever so is a colloquial phrase meaning very, to an extreme degree or extent: "The sea is ever so calm today." *Ever so often* means very often or repeatedly: "It's been raining ever so often lately."

Ever so often should not be confused with *every so often,* which means now and then or once in a while: "Every so often someone hits the jackpot." Sometimes the "ever" phase is used mistakenly when the *every* phrase is meant.

3. FOREVER, FOR EVER

Forever is infrequently written as two

words, *for ever,* an older style. Either way, it means eternally or continually. *See* FOREVER.

4. HOWEVER

However requires special caution, unlike the two-word form, *how ever,* whose use in questions is clear: "How ever did you accomplish it?"

The one-word form, *however,* used in declarative sentences, bears a dual meaning. It can mean (as an adverb) *no matter how* or *by whatever means:* "However you travel, make sure to arrive on time." It can also mean (as a conjunction) *but* or *in spite of that:* "I didn't get the job, however they said they would keep me in mind." *However* can be ambiguous, as in this sentence: "I want to sail however the winds rage." Is the speaker fearless or fearful?

5. WHYEVER, WHY EVER

Whyever is rather rare. *Why ever* is more common. "He must be punished whyever he did it." But "Why ever did he do it?"

6. With RARELY, SELDOM; definitions

Ever means, among other definitions, *at any time.* "Does he ever do any work?" Popularly used in this way: "He seldom [or "rarely"] ever does any work," it is considered redundant by *The American Heritage Dictionary* and its usage panel and by Roy C. Copperud, although the expression has been around since the mid-eighteenth century. One may use *seldom if ever* or *seldom or never* (substituting *rarely* as needed) or just leave out the "ever." Presumably the critics are concerned that time is built into the words *rarely* and *seldom.* Not so *hardly;* it is perfectly all right to say, or sing, "He's hardly ever sick at sea!"

Ever can also mean always ("We must be ever vigilant"), by any chance ("If there ever was damage, you would be protected"), or repeatedly ("The neighbors are ever throwing parties"). Colloquially it is also an intensive, comparable to *very:* "Was that dinner ever good!"

EVERY. *See* BETWEEN, 2; (-)EVER, 2; EVERY DAY and EVERYDAY; EVERY ONE and EVERYONE; NOT, *1 A*; Pronouns, 2; Verbs, *3*.

EVERY and EVER. *See* (-)EVER, 2.

EVERYBODY, EVERYONE. *1. -BODY and -ONE words. 2. "EVERYONE'S TALKING ABOUT." 3. Exaggeration. 4. Number.*

1. -BODY and -ONE words

Everybody and *everyone* mean the same thing: each person. Similarly, *nobody* and *no one* have the same meaning: no person. So do *somebody* and *someone:* some person. All are pronouns. (A *somebody* is a colloquial noun meaning an important person.)

In each pair, one word is not necessarily better than the other, and the choice is a matter of personal preference.

Sometimes, when rhythm or conciseness is important, the fact that one word of the pair has an additional syllable and an additional letter can make a difference. *Everybody* has four syllables and nine letters, *everyone* three and eight. The second *e* is silent.

Everyone should not be confused with *every one. See* EVERY ONE and EVERYONE.

2. "EVERYONE'S TALKING ABOUT"

The expression "everyone [or "everybody"] is talking about" with a mention of a new establishment, product, publication, service, show, or other thing is a promotional device aimed at making us jump on the bandwagon. If everyone were really talking about something, it would be unnecessary to advertise it. But the expression is rarely true.

An informative television program

opened with an announcement of the evening's topics. Among them would be "the shocking, new book everyone's talking about. . . ." *I* was not talking about it, never having heard of it before, and tuned the program out.

A magazine article, about a technique for exercising, was titled "The Super Ab-Flattener Everyone's Talking About." Were *you* talking about it?

3. Exaggeration

Everybody and *everyone* are often gross overstatements. The question *in what group?* ought to be answered, at least implicitly, unless the pronoun represents every person there is.

An article in the sports section of a national newspaper opened this way:

> One word sums up the NFL draft: need. Everybody talked about it, everybody thought about it, everybody drafted based on it.

There may have been a few people in the world who did not talk, think, or do anything about the need for football players. *See also* **Run-on sentence**, 2.

"Everybody does it," or words to the same effect, is a common rationalization for a questionable action. An entertainer said, concerning a risqué photograph of him and a woman on a record cover:

> "When girls see it they go, 'Oh, that's nasty.' But everybody does the same stuff behind closed doors."

Speak for yourself, please.

4. Number

Both *everybody* and *everyone* are singular. Any pertinent noun, possessive, or verb must be singular.

"Has *everyone* here received *a pamphlet?*" / "*Everybody* pulled *his* weight." / "*Everyone* in these units *is* well prepared."

See also **PRONOUNS**, 2.

EVERY DAY and EVERYDAY.

Just because the words *every* and *day* come close to each other is no cause to unite them.

These three quotations have the same error. [By a news agency:] "Everyday he's feeling better." [By a columnist:] "Editorials like that aren't written everyday." [On the TV screen:] "Kids ride free everyday."

Every day must be kept separate when *each day* can be substituted. Corrections: "*Every day* he's feeling better." / "Editorials like that aren't written *every day.*" / "Kids ride free *every day.*" In such instances, when the pair serves as an adverb, there is no more reason to unite the two words than to unite *every hour* or *every week.*

However, the unitary form, *everyday,* is correct as an adjective, e.g., "Her everyday activities are vigorous." Two companies made the opposite slip. In a magazine ad, a chain of computer stores promised "EVERY DAY LOW PRICES!" Signs in the windows of a thrift and loan company urged the public to "LOOK AT OUR EVERY DAY HIGH YIELDS!" In both sentences "EVERYDAY" would have been right.

In pronouncing *every day,* we emphasize both *ev-* and *day.* In pronouncing *everyday,* we emphasize just *ev-.*

EVERY ONE and EVERYONE.

Just as *every day* should not always be unified, neither should *every one,* although the rules are different. The first example is from a weekly publication.

> "Everyone of our 1,500 personnel should have a flashlight—with extra batteries and extra lights."

In quoting an oral statement, the writer mistakenly united *every one.* (*See also* **PERSONNEL**.)

A form letter to clients from a securities group contained the same type of error.

With the holiday season upon us, we . . . would like to extend our warmest greetings of friendship and thanks to each and everyone of our clients. . . .

Only when *everybody* can be substituted is *everyone* right. It means *each person*. It never applies to things or animals, and it can never be followed by *of*. "Everyone needs a home." / "Everyone must eat" / "Everyone in our house has voted." In speech, the first syllable is emphasized: EV-re-won.

Every one places more importance on the *one*. It means *every single member* of a particular group, which can comprise people, things, or animals. Often *of* follows, as in "every one of our 1,500" and "each and every one of our clients." The *of* and its object may be absent but implied: "Twenty mice were tested and every one proved to be disease-free." When *every one* is spoken, both the *ev-* and the *one* are emphasized.

Both *every one* and *everyone* are singular and any ensuing verb or pronoun must be singular: "*Every one* of the contestants *gives her* all." / "*Everyone looks* out for *himself*."

See also EVERYBODY, EVERYONE; NOT, *1A*; Pronouns, *2C*.

"EVERYTHING FROM." *See* Range, true and false, *4*.

EVIDENCE and PROOF. Although loosely used as synonyms, they are not the same. *Evidence* is not necessarily *proof*, but it takes *evidence* to establish *proof*. In general, the first is tentative; the second is conclusive.

Evidence means data that help to establish a factual conclusion or that are meant to lead to a judgment. In a legal case, testimony of witnesses, documents, and objects typically serve as *evidence* that opposing sides present in efforts to demonstrate opposite contentions. *Proof* means evidence that is sufficient

to *prove* something, i.e., to establish a fact or to show the truth of a proposition. In a legal case, *proof* means evidence that convinces those standing in judgment that a contention is true.

When a chimpanzee was found to have the human immunodeficiency virus, a telecaster introduced the news this way: "There's proof today that AIDS came from chimps." It was premature to describe a preliminary piece of *evidence* as "proof." Better news reports said the disease "most likely came" or "may have come" from simians.

EVIDENT, EVIDENTLY. *See* APPARENT, APPARENTLY.

EVOKE and INVOKE. An art gallery says a certain artist's paintings "invoke a sense of continuum. . . ." They *evoke* it. (**Verbosity** has further quotation.) To *evoke* is to elicit, bring forth, or produce (typically a response, feeling, or image).

According to a news story, a litigant "evoked" an obscure law. He *invoked* it. To *invoke* is to appeal to a deity or higher power for help, to call upon a source of authority, or to conjure (a spirit) by incantation.

EXACERBATE and EXASPERATE. A hill was crumbling, threatening a house on top. When a television reporter spoke of the events that had "exasperated the problem," was she correct or should she have used *exacerbated* instead?

At least five dictionaries vindicate her, approving of the interchangeable use of *exacerbate* and *exasperate* (verbs, transitive). In common usage, though, the words are restricted in this way:

Exacerbate: to make (an illness or other unsatisfactory condition) more intense.

Exasperate: to make (someone) angry or highly annoyed.

So if you use either word with the

other meaning, you will be technically in the clear, but you may not be understood.

EXCEPT and EXCEPTING. *Excepting* in place of *except* is out of style. The *-ing* serves no function in this press excerpt:

> A number of small parties have emerged . . . but none of them, excepting Civic Forum, appears to have the strength or organizational muscle to challenge the . . . Communist Party.

As normally used (as a preposition) *excepting* follows a negative: "All political groups in the city, *not excepting* [not excluding] the Klan, have been invited." In that context "not except" would be erroneous.

When *except* (used as a preposition) is followed by a personal pronoun, the pronoun takes the objective case: "All the members voted for it except [other than] *him* and *me*," not "he and I." *See* **Pronouns,** *10*.

Except can have other nuances. (As a conjunction:) "I would stay except that [if not for the fact that] my time is short." / "He never goes out of town except [for any other purpose but] to gamble." (As a verb:) "The costs of living are not high if you except [exclude] real estate and rent."

When spoken, the verb *except(s)* can be confused with "accept," and *excepting* with "accepting." *See* **Homophones.**

"EXCEPTION PROVES THE RULE." As it is commonly used, this cliché contradicts scientific logic. Yet those invoking it assume that it bolsters their points of view:

A book presents a rule that job promotion "is determined by pull" and a section headed "An Exception That Proves the Rule." A TV commentator stated a rule that caucus winners lose elections and added, "Jimmy Carter, the exception that proves the rule, won Iowa in 1976." A movie reviewer wrote, "Italy is simply not a warlike nation. . . . Mussolini was the exception that proved the rule." In another book, a conductor says making concert suites out of movie scores never works and "Prokofiev's *Nevsky* or Walton's *Henry V* . . . are the exceptions proving the rule."

How can an exception "prove" a rule? Shouldn't the exception **disprove** it?

The answer lies in an archaic meaning of *prove:* to test, originating in the Latin *probare,* same meaning. It survives in some special fields, including mathematics, minerals, and weapons. A scientist may test a rule (or theory, principle, etc.) by seeking an exception; finding one is reason to discard, or at least modify, the rule. Users of the cliché, unaware of its true meaning, cite it as authority to keep the rule despite the exception.

Some rules, in grammar and spelling for instance, are not strict and have exceptions. But those exceptions devaluate the rules rather than validate them.

Exclamation point. *See* **Punctuation,** 6.

EXECUTE. To *execute* someone is to impose capital punishment on him, to put him to death in accordance with a sentence legally imposed by a court of law. When criminals, terrorists, or other lawbreakers kill, it is homicide, if not murder, never "execution." So it is when political leaders, government officials, or police kill outside of the judicial system, or when the military kills outside of a battle in war. *See also* **Crimes,** 4.

After Peruvian soldiers had stormed an embassy to rescue hostages, a news story reported

> accusations that military commandos had *executed* some of the guerrillas who had tried to surrender. . . . [F]ormer hostages and military intelli-

gence officers . . . said they had witnessed or overheard the soldiers *execute* the rebels. . . . Speculation that some rebels were *executed* . . . have been increasing. [Emphasis is added.]

Execute(d) is at best a euphemism in such a context, and it can suggest a degree of legal justification that may not exist. In the sample, it could well have been replaced by *kill(ed)* or *slay* or *slain,* with the qualification that the victims were *captured* rebels.

Another meaning of *execute,* an earlier meaning, is to carry out or put into effect (a law, a plan, an order, etc.).

See also SLAY, SLAIN, SLEW.

EXERCISE and EXORCISE. *Exorcise,* also spelled *exorcize,* means to drive out (an evil spirit). It should not be mixed up with the three-*e* verb *exercise,* meaning to exert, perform, do exercises, and so on. Some dictionaries offer the option of pronouncing the two words the same; others would enunciate the *or* in *exorcise,* a practice that could help to prevent confusion.

When one "Jesus Christ Satan—a local street character" showed up in court, jingled bells, and began to speak in protest against a ruling canceling a special election, the judge cut him off. Thereupon this headline appeared in a newspaper: "J. C. Satan exercised." Although Mr. Satan may have been *exercised,* in the sense of worried or upset, or possibly had worked out in a gymnasium, a more likely explanation for the headline is a copy editor's trying to be clever but not succeeding.

EXOTIC. An exhibition of landscape art elicited a review containing this sentence: "Another theme that turns up repeatedly is the exotic foreign locale." To speak of "the exotic foreign locale" is almost like saying "the foreign foreign locale." *Foreign* is the original meaning of *exotic,* which comes from the Greek

word for *outside.* The sense of *introduced from abroad* and then the senses of *strange* and *rare* branched from that original meaning. Later, implications of aesthetics, charm, excitement, or fascination overworked *exotic* further.

That adjective is a frequent euphemism in the field of "adult" (i.e., sexual) entertainment. An "exotic dancer" may have spent her entire life in the United States and not learned any foreign dance, as long as she is an alluring young woman who dances partly or wholly nude. What may explain the choice of "exotic" is that it looks so much like *erotic.*

EXPECTED. It is hard enough for a reporter just to report the facts without trying to predict the future. Note this front-page headline: "C.I.A. Nominee Expected to Win Senate Backing." But senators' opposition to the nomination caused it to be withdrawn. Similarly a story telling what President Reagan was "expected" to tell the nation was not borne out, nor was a story telling how voters in Washington State were "expected" to vote.

Expected in such a context (the past participle of the transitive verb to *expect*) means considered very likely or practically certain. Of what value was that word? And by whom was each event "expected"?

Expletives. These amount to verbal appendixes. They are words or phrases that fill out sentences but have little meaning in themselves.

In its popular sense, an *expletive* is an oath or swear word, like *hell* or *damn* or the obscene variety of four-letter word.

In a grammatical sense, an *expletive* is a word or phrase that, while not necessary or even very meaningful, may serve a stylistic, rhythmic, or syntactical function. *It is* and *there is* (*are, was, were*) are common *expletives.*

When the pronoun *it* does not represent a particular noun and the adverb *there* does not refer to a place, each word may start a sentence or clause without being the subject. Examples: "It is time now to talk business." / "There's a full moon out tonight." The real subjects there are *time* and *moon*. *It* and *there* in such sentences are called *anticipatory* subjects or *dummy* subjects. Idiom generally accepts them, although the ideas may be expressed in other ways; e.g., "Now is the time to talk business" or "A full moon is out tonight."

Many teachers and editors have long objected to expletives, considering their use weak, clumsy, or superfluous. Sometimes it can be so: "There were six other specimens found" is better rewritten as "Six other specimens were found" or, still better, as "We found six other specimens." Writers of impersonal letters are apt to write, e.g., "It is thought . . ." to avoid "I think. . . ."

Scientists like to write impersonally, so it is not surprising that three studies on the same topic (passive smoking) by different researchers say in summaries, "There was a statistically significant difference . . ." / "There was no evidence of any trend . . ." / "There was no association. . . ."

Yet eminent literature contains many quotable examples: "It is a far, far better thing that I do, than I have ever done . . ." (Dickens). "Behold, there come seven years of great plenty . . ." (Bible, Genesis). "To every thing there is a season . . ." (Bible, Ecclesiastes). *It* and *there* fit the rhythm of many song lyrics and poems: "It was down in old Joe's barroom . . ." / "'Twas [it was] the night before Christmas . . . When out on the lawn there arose such a clatter. . . ."

Note that *there* may be accompanied by a singular or plural verb, depending on the noun that follows. "There *is* a lizard in my living room" but "There *are* two lizards in my kitchen." To say "There were a cake and two pies on the table" is strictly correct but it may sound strange to some ears. Some writers would accept "There was a cake and two pies . . . ," however ungrammatical. The dilemma may be resolved by putting the plural item first: "There were two pies and a cake . . ."

It as an expletive is always followed by a singular verb: "It seems they lost their way." / "It's [it is] good we're together again." In a construction like "It is the showers that bring [not "brings"] the flowers," the verb following *that* agrees with the real subject ("showers"), not with the dummy subject *it*. (*See also* **WHO**, 3.) The purpose of that construction is to emphasize the subject. An article said, "It's their specific traits and biography—their background, their demeanor—that is supposed to make us tune in." That *are*.

EXTORTION. *See* Crimes, 2.

EYE (of a storm).

The *eye* of a hurricane or other tropical cyclone is a fairly calm place. It is an approximately circular area of rather light winds and comparatively fair weather in the center of the storm.

The narrator of a documentary film said, "At the eye of the hurricane, the wind can exceed 200 miles an hour." He, or the writer, was wrong. In the eye, "winds diminish to something less than 15 knots" (about 17 statute miles per hour), a weather almanac says.

That meteorological term is sometimes misused in a figurative way when a person in the center of a controversy or furor is said to be "in the eye of the storm."

F

FABULOUS. *Fabulous* (adjective) primarily means pertaining to a fable or of the nature of a fable. That which is mythical, legendary, or imaginary may be described as *fabulous.* "Baron Munchausen was a real man, but his tales were fabulous."

The word came to have an additional meaning, describing something that is real but so marvelous that it would seem imaginary if you did not know it was real. "The fabulous notion of a trip to the moon became reality in 1969."

In later years it entered popular speech as a slang synonym for very good, well done, impressive, successful, or any of numerous other terms of approval. "The dinner was fabulous." / "He did a fabulous job." Such mundane use has become so widespread that it threatens to bury the specific meanings of *fabulous.*

How is the word used in this sentence?

On almost every other page, we find a classic California painting, such as William Alexander Coulter's horrifying yet fabulous view—from the Bay—of San Francisco burning in "San Francisco Fire, 1906."

Whether the writer meant that the scene was imaginary or that it was well painted is not certain. Contemporary speech has so watered down *fabulous* that when someone does use the word precisely, we may not know it.

See also **FANTASTIC; INCREDIBLE.**

FACT. *1. Definition. 2. "The FACT that." 3. Modifiers. 4. Synonyms.*

1. Definition
A *fact* is a statement that is known to be true or that has been proven to be true, whether by observation, research, or reliable testimony.

Fact, as distinguished from fancy, falsity, fiction, or supposition, denotes actuality, reality, or truth.

2. "The FACT that"
The phrase *the fact that* often is used colloquially, and wrongly, for what is not fact. The expression sometimes appears in serious writing (occasionally without "that"), for instance: "The latest deployment may reflect the fact that the government is thinking of launching a military attack." It is speculation, not *fact.* Change "reflect the fact" to *indicate.*

A radio talk show produced this dialogue:

[Hostess:] If your son made a girl pregnant, would you help her to get an abortion?

[Man calling:] I think I would. . . .

[Hostess:] I'm surprised by the fact that he would help a girl of another family get an abortion.

What surprised her was not a "fact" but an offhand response to a hypothetical question. Leaving out "by the fact" would have sharpened the sentence and not relinquished any meaning.

A week later another man calling the program was questioned:

[Hostess:] Your source for the fact that the Russian army is not being fed is what?

The very question indicated her doubt that his *statement* was a fact.

3. Modifiers

In a book about the book business, we read:

It turns out that the researcher provided his coauthor with incorrect facts.

No, he provided him with incorrect *statements* or with *misinformation*. In strict usage, there cannot be "incorrect facts" or "false facts." It is a contradiction.

Superfluous adjectives like "correct" or "true" should not team up with *facts* either.

[A prosecutor, as quoted in a newspaper:] I only want to see the true facts presented.

[An ex-senator on TV:] Americans in poll after poll, when informed of the true facts [about Medicare], say "Let's fix it."

"True facts" is redundant. A *fact* is true by definition.

While I was in the CIA [an ex-agent said in a magazine piece] I also helped prepare briefings for Congress for Mr. Colby. . . . Very few of the facts in these briefings were true.

Then there were very few *facts*. Either replace *facts* with another noun, like *statements* or *details;* or place an adjective, like *supposed* or *purported*, before *facts*. Such an adjective is almost implied in a popular expression: to get one's facts (that is, one's supposed facts) right or wrong or straight.

Fact(s) can be legitimately modified in many ways. One may speak of a surprising *fact*, a scientific *fact*, encouraging *facts*, all the *facts*, and so on.

4. Synonyms

Fact in some contexts is interchangeable with *actuality, reality* or *truth*. The preposition *in* may precede any of those nouns, but the meanings are not necessarily the same. For instance, *in fact* often serves merely to intensify the statement that is coming, whereas *in reality* is more apt to contrast the truth of what is to come with that of a previous statement.

Information can be used as a synonym for facts, knowledge, or learning. It can be used in a neutral way also, to denote something that is told or a telling of something, regardless of the truth or falsity of what is told. If the information is wrong, it can be called *misinformation*.

A *statement* is an act of setting forth in words; also something stated or said, an account of something. Because it may not be true, it is not the same as a *fact*.

Truth, the state or quality of being true or in accordance with fact or reality, can pertain to a particular statement ("Can you verify the truth of that statement?") or to a generality ("When war is declared, truth is the first casualty").

See also **DATA**.

FACTICITY, FACTION, FACTIOUS, FACTUAL, etc. *See* FACT-words.

FACTOR. *1. General meaning. 2. Special meanings.*

1. General meaning

A medical dictionary says about cancer:

> There are probably many causative factors, some of which are known: for example, cigarette smoking is associated with lung cancer, radiation with some bone sarcomas and leukemia.

"Causative" is unnecessary. A *factor* is causative; that is, functioning as a cause. "There are probably many factors. . . ."

When it is not used in a biological, commercial, or mathematical sense, a *factor* essentially is a cause. It is a circumstance, condition, or element that contributes to an effect or a result. The meanings of *cause* and *factor* overlap, but only *cause* will do if an effect is known to have a single cause; *factor* implies one or more additional causes.

The general sense of *factor* is a figurative use of its mathematical sense defined in 2.

Factor is stuffed in innumerable sentences, either unnecessarily or imprecisely. "Causative" and "causal" are among unnecessary modifiers. Another appears in the phrase "contributing factor." *Factors* contribute. "We have to think of the cost factor" probably can be shortened to "We have to think of the cost."

Touching on the difficulty in unscrambling bad English, an essayist asks rhetorically: "And what about the time factor?" Could "factor" not be omitted, perhaps replaced by *spent* or *wasted?*

Often *factor* is used when a more appropriate word would be *circumstance, component, consideration, element, fact,* *feature, force, ingredient,* or *phase.* In "Let's review the factors leading up to this crime," *circumstances* would be an apt replacement for "factors."

2. Special meanings

In biology, *factor* indicates an antigen, gene, or substance; the word is combined in terms such as *Rh factor.* This is an antigen discovered in red blood cells of rhesus monkeys and most people. Blood containing it is incompatible with blood lacking it.

Factor has several commercial meanings. Often it is a person or company that makes loans secured by accounts receivable or, sometimes, that purchases the accounts. An older sense is that of a commission merchant, an agent for the sale of goods.

In mathematics, a *factor* is one of two or more quantities that form a specified product when multiplied together: 5 and 3 are *factors* of 15. A related verb (transitive) is *factor,* meaning to separate (a product) into *factors.* A synonym is *factorize.*

An obsolete meaning of the noun *factor* is one who does or makes something, its meaning in Latin.

FACT- words. *1. Concerning facts. 2. Not concerning facts.*

1. Concerning facts

When an academic said on television, "The level of facticity has dropped on the part of both of the candidates," was she using a recognized word?

The noun *facticity* is defined in *The Oxford English Dictionary* as "The quality or condition of being a fact; factuality." It dates at least from 1945.

So the speaker used a word recognized by the most reputable dictionary, if not by her entire TV audience. A simpler phrasing: "Both candidates are getting away from facts."

The *Oxford* lists three related nouns.

(The dates represent the dictionary's earliest quotations.)

- *Factuality:* "The quality of being factual; factualness" (1887).
- *Factualness:* "The state of being factual; factuality" (1906).
- *Factualism:* In philosophy, "A predominant concern with facts or natural consequences, especially in moral matters . . ." (1946).

The common adjective *factual* means pertaining to, containing, or made up of facts; "a factual report." In some contexts it implies that something is real, not fabricated, at least in essence; "The movie is factual."

A less common adjective is *factful:* well acquainted with facts (said of a person) or full of facts (said of a literary work).

Faction in the sense of fiction based on fact is a fairly new noun, not to be confused with its homonym below.

2. *Not concerning facts*

Several words that begin with *fact-* have nothing to do with facts. Let us list them.

- *Faction* (noun): a clique or a subgroup of a country, government, party, organization, etc.; also conflict or dissension within such an entity. "The city council has conservative and liberal factions. It is hampered by faction."
- *Factional* (adjective): pertaining to a *faction* or characterized by *faction.*
- *Factious* (adjective): producing or causing faction; also, pertaining to or characterized by faction. "This factious election campaign is almost over." / "The Vietnam conflict was especially factious."
- *Factitious* (adjective): unnatural, artificially produced by effort. "Sales, which had been slow, boomed when Madison Avenue set off a factitious demand for the product." *Factitious* should not be confused with *fictitious,* which means written as fiction or created by the imagination and can, but need not necessarily, imply falsity and intent to deceive. (In the context of advertising, the confusion would be understandable.)
- *Factitive* (adjective): in grammar, pertaining to a type of transitive verb. Its direct object takes a complement, and typically a making or rendering is described. In "They made him their leader," *made* is a *factitive* verb.

A journalist described a political party as "factionalized." If he meant it was characterized by faction, either *factional* or *factious* would have expressed that meaning more economically.

FACULTY. A *faculty* is a staff of an educational institution. It is the entire body of teachers in a college or university ("the faculty of Yale") or in one of its departments ("the mathematics faculty"). Some dictionaries broaden the definition to take in any type of school, and some include administrators as well as teachers.

The writer of a main article in a university newspaper could not decide whether the word was plural or singular. In some sentences he made it plural:

> Some faculty . . . fear and loathe student evaluations of their teaching. . . . Many faculty thought the evaluation process was fine as is. . . . Faculty were not given enough research time. . . . Most faculty are expected to teach the equivalent of four classes per semester.

In other sentences, intermingled with those above, he construed the word differently:

The survey asked 78 faculty members questions. . . . Those faculty members eligible for tenure . . . must have their teaching evaluated by students. . . . Many had feared those faculty members might move on to greener academic pastures. . . .

The plural construction of the first set is not customary. *Faculty* is usually regarded as singular. "The faculty *was* not given. . . ." / "Many faculty *members* thought. . . ." The second set is standard, although the inconsistency was worse than the errancy.

Faculty is a collective noun comparable to *class*. No one says "Some class drop out" and "The class are many" instead of "Some class *members* drop out" and "The class *is large*."

See also **Collective nouns; STAFF.**

FANTASIA. *See* **FANTASTIC.**

FANTASTIC. When a state's education chief called on school districts to toughen academic requirements, the president of a parent-teacher association commented that "talk about higher standards is fantastic." And a member of the U.S. House of Representatives said about its speaker, "He's making fantastic efforts on behalf of the American people."

Were they implying that talk of high standards and the House speaker's efforts were bizarre, capricious, fanciful, grotesque, illusory, imaginary, odd, strange, or unreal? *Fantastic* primarily means pertaining to or characterized by fantasy, and it has those associated meanings.

The contexts showed that each was using "fantastic" in a nonstandard sense to mean something like *admirable, capital, great, noteworthy, remarkable, splendid, superb,* or any of dozens of related words.

A reviewer talked on the radio about the movie *Titanic.* "Only one word can describe it," he said. Is the word *titanic?* No. "It is *fantastic.*" That meant the film was characterized by fantasy, untrue to life, if he was speaking strictly. He probably was not.

In music, a *fantasia* is a free-form composition of nontraditional structure, emphasizing fancy over form. It may either stand alone or serve as the prelude for a fugue.

Before playing a piano rendition of a Bach toccata and fugue on a radio program, a musician described some of its technicalities and called it a "fantastic" piece. In the context in which it was used, the word could have meant characteristic of a *fantasia.* At the end, however, when he remarked, "It's a fantastic thing," it became apparent that his use of the word was not authentic. (But then neither was the music, which Bach had composed for the organ.)

See also **FABULOUS; INCREDIBLE.**

FAR. Discussing car thefts, in a radio interview, a police chief said of the Toyota, "It's a very popular item as far as stripping the inside of the vehicle." Stripping the *as far as* construction of *is concerned* (or another appropriate verb) is unfortunately becoming popular too.

When the meaning is *to the extent that* or *to the degree that,* the noun that follows *as far as* or *so far as* must be followed by a verb: "As far as cats *are concerned,* the law is silent." / "He is not a great actor as far as comedies *go.*"

The same rule applies to the phrase *insofar as,* or *in so far as* (as it is sometimes spelled), also meaning *to the extent that* or *to the degree that.* The noun that follows it must be followed by a verb: "Insofar as business grows, dividends will rise."

When *as far as* is followed by a noun representing a place, it may need no verb: "They rode as far as the border." Nor does a verb have to follow when *as far as* or *so far as* indicates a limit of progress: "He went to school as far as the sixth grade."

As far as or *insofar as* often can be replaced, partly or entirely, by one small word or another: "As *for* cats . . ." / ". . . Actor *in* comedies" / "*If* business grows. . . ."

Two physicians and a congressman made these statements in three broadcasts:

As far as frozen embryos, it's amazing how good they are.

As far as short-term toxicity, they've given human beings up to 6,000 milligrams every night.

As far as the loan, it raises questions.

None of the three sentences accepts the "as far as" phrasing. In each, *as for* makes more sense.

FARTHER and FURTHER.

Do we go *further* or go *farther*? Each is a comparative form of *far*. Each is both adjective and adverb.

Many careful writers and speakers observe a useful rule: Limit *farther* to the meaning of more far in the sense of actual, physical distance that can be measured ("I live farther from my office now"). Use *further* for other, more figurative meanings ("He went *further* into debt"). *Further* thus means more distant or distantly in degree, quantity, or time. The distinction should be encouraged to prevent ambiguities like this one, from an art review:

The farther Cézanne got from the object in front of him, the more trouble he had.

The sentence seems to say that the artist had trouble seeing and could not stand too far from the object he was painting.

But the next sentence suggests that the reviewer is not to be taken literally. ("His allegories . . . are not remarkable paintings.") Evidently he means that the more Cézanne departed from reality, the worse were his pictures. In that case, *further* should have been used, not "farther."

In both examples just below, it is clearer that measurable distances were not in the writers' minds. Each "farther" should be further.

. . . Britain . . . had already gone farther than its community partners by withdrawing its entire diplomatic staff from Teheran. . . .

But as the would-be rebels were soon to be reminded, the farther Mr. Kohl is pushed, the more terrible is his recovery.

Here is an example of a "further" that should be *farther*. A measurable distance is exactly what the writer had in mind.

Novosibirsk, the largest city in the vast expanse of eastern Russia known as Siberia, is more than 1,500 miles southeast of Moscow and even further west of Vladivostok. . . .

Change "further" to *farther*; or, better, change "even further" to *more than 2,000 miles*.

The superlative forms of *far* bear the same relationship as the comparative forms. *Farthest* is most far in a literal sense: "Of the nine planets, Pluto is the farthest from the Sun." *Furthest* is most far in a figurative sense: "Of the paintings on display, those by Dalí are the furthest from reality."

Those cool to the idea of distinguishing the words point to their interchangeable use at times by prominent writers. It is also a fact that neither word originally pertained to *far*. *Further* once was a comparative of *fore* and meant more forward. *Farther* came later as a variation of *further,* having nothing to do with *far.* More far was *farrer,* which became obsolete and was replaced by *farther.*

Of the two words, only *further* is a verb (transitive), meaning to advance or assist: "They want to *further* our cause." Another distinctive sense of *further,* as an adjective, is that of additional: "We need further help."

FATALITY. A *fatality* is (1) an occurrence that results in death, or (2) a death resulting from an unexpected occurrence. The word is misused in the excerpts below, from news items and (the third) an editorial.

> Authorities said Patrick P——, of Kalamazoo, became the first hunting fatality of the season on Thursday when he accidentally shot himself in a cornfield while trying to unclog snow from his rifle.

The unfortunate man fell victim to a hunting *fatality,* or a hunting *fatality* ended his life, or he became the first *fatal* victim of the hunting season. But the man himself could not become a "fatality."

> A 58-year-old New York woman who died of the disorder in September is the first confirmed fatality in the outbreak, and several other deaths are still under investigation. . . .

> The driver of the Mercury became the 26th fatality on Highway 37 in the past five years.

In each case, the *death* was the *fatality,* not the person who died. Changing "fatality" to *victim* or *fatal victim* would be preferable to the present wording, which tends to convert human beings into statistics.

See also **Dehumanization.**

FATE. *See* DESTINY.

FAUN and FAWN. Arthur Fiedler once conducted a symphony concert titled "Pops Family Night at the Zoo." The program included *Carnival of the Animals, Tiger Rag, Under the Double Eagle,* and *Prelude to the Afternoon of a Faun.* That last selection seemed out of harmony with the zoo theme. Debussy's *faun*—not to be confused with *fawn,* a baby deer—was an ancient Roman deity, part man and part goat. To the best of my knowledge, no zoo has ever had one.

FAZE and PHASE. A woman was learning to fly a little airplane and enjoying the experience, except for one thing. She wrote in a book:

> The only thing that phased me was when David [the instructor] demonstrated that Pegasus [the plane's name] had pendular stability and could right herself from any twist; he swung the bar and she dived and soared.

Correction: it *fazed*—not "phased"—her. *Faze* and *phase* (verbs, transitive) are pronounced the same but have different meanings and origins. (*See also* **WHEN, WHERE** in definitions.)

To *faze* is to daunt, disconcert, or disturb one. It is used more often in the negative than the positive. "Winter never fazes the Eskimos." The word has progressed from American dialect to colloquial use, to standard use. It began as a variation of *feeze* (or *feaze*), which came from the Old English *fesian,* to drive away (someone or something).

To *phase* is to plan, schedule, or carry out something in phases or stages or as needed. It came from the Greek noun *phasis,* appearance or phase of the moon, which itself came from the verb *phanein,* to show.

To *phase in* or *phase out* something is to introduce it or eliminate it in phases or stages. A *phase* phrase can be useful, but it carries the flavor of bureaucratic or corporate jargon. If the idea is to *gradually introduce* or *gradually eliminate* something, it may be better to say so.

Phase as a noun is a state of development or a temporary form of behavior or an event in a cycle of events. It can also be the way the moon, or another celestial body, or other body whose appearance changes periodically, appears at a certain time.

FEATURE. To *feature* (verb, transitive) is to present as a prominent attraction, display conspicuously, or publicize (a person, thing, topic, etc.).

A music reviewer wrote, "The concert . . . featured an interminable intermission. . . ." The concert *featured* a noted pianist. It *had* or *included* an intermission or, the critic could say, was *unduly stretched out* by it; but the intermission was never presented as a prominent attraction. (*See also* INTERMINABLE.)

"The current issue features space travel" is a straightforward use of the verb. Occasionally someone reverses the subject and object, so that "Space travel features the current issue." If one is determined to lead off with the highlighted topic, a way to do it sensibly is to replace "features" with a passive form, *is featured in.*

FEEL. A businessman admitted that he had made a $300,000 political contribution in return for a meeting with the president. Thereupon a television commentator asked, "How are voters supposed to feel except incredibly cynically about the process?" *Cynical* (adjective), not "cynically" (adverb), would have been correct.

When *feel* means to experience an emotion or perceive one's own condition, an adjective follows: "She feels happy," not "happily"; and "I am recuperated and feel strong now," not "strongly." (*Feel* then serves as a linking verb. It links the subject, *she* or *I,* to the adjective, *happy* or *strong.*)

Feel itself is only occasionally modified, for example: "We feel strongly that he is the best man for the country." There the adverb *strongly* is right; "strong" would be incorrect.

Some editors and critics have objected to *feel* in the sense of hold an opinion or take a stand. That common use need not be wholly abandoned, although *feel* can be wishy-washy when the import is "We *declare*" or "My *position is*" or "The Court *finds.*" *Feel* suits an attitude, conviction, or opinion tinged with emotion and vagueness, as opposed to reason and clarity.

See also BAD and BADLY; GOOD and WELL.

FELICITOUS. *See* FORTUITOUS.

FELONY. *See* CRIME, MISDEMEANOR, and FELONY; Crimes (various felonies).

-F ending. *See* Plurals and singulars, *2F.*

FESTOON, FESTOONED. To *festoon* (verb, transitive) is to decorate with, or make into, or join, by means of a *festoon.* A *festoon* (noun) is a garland or string of flowers, leaves, ribbons, etc. hanging in a curve or loop between two points. A representation of such a hanging garland, say carved in furniture, may also be called a *festoon.* Does either of the samples (from a magazine and a newspaper) describe either kind of *festoon?*

The walls all around Slonimsky's work table are festooned with a gallery of ghoulish nonsense—bizarre tabloid headlines, M. C. Escher conundrums, a reproduction of an 1853 painting. . . .

The walls may be *adorned, decked, decorated, embellished,* or merely *covered* with those things but are probably not truly *festooned.* (The sentence contains two other questionable uses: "ghoulish," meaning fiendish, horrible, or loathsome, to describe the headlines and pictures; and "conundrums," riddles whose answers are puns, applied to Escher's pictures.)

> Mr. Krasilnikov said the city will still be festooned on holidays with celebratory slogans and multistory portraits of Lenin.

Conceivably a slogan could be formed by letters joined on a *festoon* (although a slogan sign pictured with the excerpted news story was not *festooned*), but it is difficult to imagine the *festooning* of multistory portraits.

FETUS. *See* **EMBRYO and FETUS.**

FEWER and LESS. *1. The difference. 2. Exceptions.*

1. The difference

"We now have 200,000 less students in the state university system." A candidate for governor said that in a question-and-answer segment of a television news show, erroneously using "less" instead of *fewer.*

A legal commentator and a network spokesman made essentially the same error in broadcasts. The first said, concerning a criminal trial, "You're going to see less and less objections." The second said, about a reorganization of his company, "It's fair to say that there will be less jobs."

An article similarly erred: Employers like a hospital's day care for ill children "because it means less days out of work for their employees."

As a rule of thumb: *less* goes with a singular; *fewer* goes with a plural. (Exceptions are coming.)

Less means not so *much.* It is a smaller quantity of a substance ("less helium") or type of object ("less fruit") or a smaller amount or degree of an abstract thing ("less excitement") or descriptive quality ("less brilliant").

Fewer means not so *many.* It is a smaller number of objects ("fewer coconuts" or "fewer heavenly bodies") or other things that can be counted and that are considered individually ("fewer pleasures" or "fewer challenges").

See also **MANY and MUCH.**

2. Exceptions

Even if a word is in plural form, *less* applies if the thing represented is considered as a unit. We commonly regard an amount of money, a period of time, or a measure of weight or distance as a unit.

In the sentence "The book costs less than $20," we think of a single sum, not of individual dollars. In the sentences "She is less than six months old" / "The machine weighs less than nine pounds" / "The station is less than two miles from here," we think of a single period of time, a total weight, and a total distance, not of months, pounds, and miles considered individually.

The distinction is not always clear-cut. Grammatical authorities have not agreed on where to draw the lines. H. W. Fowler favored "*less troops* or *clothes,*" finding such plurals "really equivalent to singulars of indefinite amount." After "*less,*" his reviser, Sir Ernest Gowers, inserted "(or *fewer*)."

A book on word usage quotes this anonymous sentence and says that "less" should be *fewer:*

> "The nation's traffic death toll . . . was 377—thirteen less than the . . . pre-holiday estimate."

But the anonymous writer had regarded the toll as a unit: it "was 377." Had he thought of the human victims represented by that figure and written that "377 people died in traffic accidents," *fewer* would clearly need to follow "thirteen." Perhaps his shortcoming was less grammatical than philosophical.

See also **Dehumanization.**

FICTITIOUS. See **FACT-** words, 2.

FIGURATIVELY. See **LITERALLY.**

Figures. See **Numbers.**

FINALIZE. See **-IZE** ending.

FINE. *1. FINE, FINELY, and FINE-TUNE. 2. Other issues and uses.*

1. FINE, FINELY, and FINE-TUNE
You may *finely* chop onions but not "fine" chop them. A news agency made such an error:

On May 6, the treaty's 75 ratifiers are expected to meet at The Hague to fine tune its management and enforcement provisions.

The simplest correction is to insert the hyphen that belongs in the verb *fine-tune*. As an alternative, change "fine tune" to *refine* or change "fine" to *finely*.
Finely is an adverb, meaning in a fine manner. *Fine* as an adverb ("She sings fine") is acceptable in conversation or casual writing but never before the verb.
Fine is mainly an adjective. Its meanings include tiny (*fine* particles); thin (*fine* thread); sharp (*fine* edge); subtle (*fine* distinctions); pure or up to a standard (*fine* gold); and, colloquially, in good health ("I'm fine—how are you?").

2. Other issues and uses
Fine in the sense of admirable or excellent ("a fine poem") used to draw some objections, but it is widely accepted now. If anything, it is weakened from overuse. People toss off "fine" in conversation when other words—sometimes merely *all right* or *O.K.*—would be more fitting.

Among its uses, *fine* (noun) is a monetary punishment or (verb) to impose it. In music scores, *fine* does not describe the music: it is Italian for *the end* (and pronounced FEE-nay). *Fine* once meant that in English.

Fire. See **FLAMMABLE** (etc.).

FIRE (verb). See **LAY OFF** and **LAY-OFF; LET GO.**

FIRM. Each of these paragraphs, from newspapers, contains a contradiction:

Apple Computer Inc. is expected to unveil its much-heralded "Lisa" personal computer model today. . . . The Cupertino-based firm also said Tuesday that net sales grew 60% for the quarter ended Dec. 31.

In Los Angeles, Northrop Corp. spokesman Ed Smith said yesterday that the firm will cut its B-2 bomber task force drastically. . . .

. . . Maxwell put up $30 million for an 18 percent share of Teva Pharmaceutical Industries Ltd., one of Israel's largest and most profitable firms.

The contradiction is that each company is incorporated—as indicated by "Inc." or "Corp." or "Ltd."—but called a "firm." Being a corporation, it is not a "firm."
A *firm* is a partnership. It is "a business or professional association of two or more persons as distinguished from an incorporated company" (*Encyclopedia of Banking & Finance*). Partners of a firm may be sued as individuals if damages are claimed from the business. That is not so for officers of a corporation.

The law treats a corporation as if it were a separate person.

News editors, concerned with fitting headlines into cramped spaces, may not welcome that information, inasmuch as *firm* is seven letters shorter than *corporation* and appreciably shorter than *business, company, concern, enterprise,* or *house.* There is less justification for calling a *corporation* a *firm* in the body of a serious article or talk, particularly one purporting to explain matters of business and finance.

Ltd. (as in the third sample) is the abbreviation for *limited,* used in names of corporations outside the United States and in Hawaii. It indicates that the liability of a shareholder is limited to his investment in the company.

(In the second sample, "will" should be *would. See* Tense, 4.)

FISCAL and PHYSICAL. *See* Confusing pairs.

FISSION and FUSION. *See* NUCLEAR.

FLAIR and FLARE. *See* Homophones.

FLAMMABLE, INFLAMMABLE, and NONFLAMMABLE. Something that is *flammable* can be burned. A synonym is *inflammable,* which used to be a more common word. Those concerned with fire safety have promoted the use of the adjective *flammable,* because some people think that the other word means nonflammable or noncombustible. The *in-* in *inflammable* does not mean "not"; the word originates in the Latin *inflammare,* to kindle, the origin of the English verb *inflame.*

A manufacturer of woolen products stated in a leaflet, "Wool is . . . light, soft, non-flamable and durable." The statement contains errors in spelling and fact: *Nonflammable,* has a double *m.*

(The hyphen is optional.) And, while wool is considered *flame-resistant,* it can burn.

FLAUNT and FLOUT. Addressing television cameras, a senator said the U.S. administration in its foreign policy "has spent seven years flaunting the law"; a prosecutor said, "No one is free to flaunt the tax laws"; and a journalist said "She [a hotel owner] thought she could flaunt the law. . . ." All were wrong.

To *flaunt* is to show off. ("He became rich and *flaunted* his wealth." / "She profits from *flaunting* her body in public.") *Flout,* meaning to show contempt for or to scoff at, or *flouting* (the present participle), is what should have been used by each speaker. The two verbs (transitive) are poles apart. None of the *flouters* would *flaunt* their *flouting.*

FLOCK, FLOCKING. *See* DROVE.

FLOODED. *See* INUNDATE, INUNDATED.

FLOUNDER and FOUNDER. The main headline in a daily newspaper said, "S.F. kids flounder in math on state test." Could the copy editor have been *floundering* and grasping the wrong *f*-word? The story reported that many public school youngsters in San Francisco had done poorly in the mathematical portion of a statewide academic test. In other words, they had *foundered* in that part of the test.

To *flounder* (verb, intransitive) is to move clumsily, to plunge about awkwardly, or to speak or act in a confused way. Lexicographers are uncertain of its origin. Some assume that it came from *founder.* They do not trace it to the fish, although a snared *flounder* certainly *flounders;* so does a cod, trout, etc. when caught, but if the fish helps one to remember the word, good for it.

To *founder* (verb, intransitive) is to fail, to collapse, or to break down. It can also mean (for ships) to sink, (for horses) to fall or become lame, or (for buildings or land) to cave in. *Founder* (verb, transitive) can mean to cause (something) to *founder.* The verb comes from the Old French word *fondrer,* to sink, which stemmed from the Latin word *fundrus,* bottom.

There is a noun *flounder,* besides the fish, meaning the act of *floundering.* The noun *founder* can mean the act of *foundering;* or soreness in a horse's foot. It has two additional meanings unrelated to the verb *founder:* one who founds in the sense of establishing (e.g., a college) and one who founds in the sense of casting metal.

FLOUT. *See* FLAUNT and FLOUT.

FLY. *See* -Y ending.

FOLLOWING. *See* AFTER.

FOR. *See* FREE, *1;* Guilt and innocence, *5;* Prepositions, *2, 3, 4, 7;* WAIT FOR and WAIT ON; WISH.

FORBID, PROHIBIT, and BAN. *1. FORBID, FORBADE. 2. PROHIBIT; BAN. 3. PROHIBITION; BAN.*

1. FORBID, FORBADE

A narrator on a national TV "magazine" said, "FDA regulations at that time forbid using that blood." He used the present tense; he needed the past. The past tense of *forbid* is either *forbade* (pronounced for-BAD or for-BAYED) or *forbad* (pronounced for-BAD).

When a problem with *forbid* arises, more often it is not in the verb itself (transitive) or its forms but in what follows it. For example:

Luzhkov demonstrated his muscle in 1994 when he forbade the federal

government from privatizing large industries located in Moscow.

Nobody is forbidden "from" doing anything. The preposition that commonly follows any form of *forbid* is *to.* Thus "They forbid us to enter." / "You're forbidden to smoke there" or "Smoking is forbidden there." / ". . . He forbade the federal government *to privatize* large industries. . . ."

2. PROHIBIT; BAN

The verb *prohibit* (transitive) is often followed by *from:* "They *prohibited* the company *from* selling the product" (not "prohibited . . . to sell").

Forbid and *prohibit* have substantially the same meaning: to order a person or persons not to take certain action; or to make a rule against some action. *Prohibit,* however, has a ring of legality to it. A parent tells a child, "I forbid you to leave the house tonight" or "I forbid your leaving the house tonight." An ordinance "prohibits motorists from parking" or "prohibits parking" itself or says that "parking is prohibited" at a certain location.

The verb *ban* (transitive) is similar to *prohibit* and means to proscribe some action or some thing, especially by law or religious authority. *Ban* implies a strong condemnation of that which is proscribed. "They banned the book." / "He was banned from entering the country."

3. PROHIBITION; BAN

Ban is also a noun, meaning an official disapproval, decree, or sentence, aimed at preventing or outlawing something. It can be also a condemnation or excommunication by church authorities, and it can be a curse.

A noun related to *prohibit* is *prohibition.* One speaks of "the prohibition *of* alcohol" but "the ban *on* alcohol.

Nouns related to *forbid* are *forbid-*

ding and, a rare one, *forbiddance.* A related adjective is *forbidden,* as in "forbidden fruit." It is also the past participle of the verb: "They have forbidden him to enter the country."

Forbidding has a much different meaning as an adjective: repellent owing to an appearance of danger or unpleasantness. A music critic wrote of a composer's "distinguished and forbidding reputation," thereby praising and dispraising him in the same phrase.

FORCEFUL and FORCIBLE. *See* Confusing pairs.

FOREVER. The quotation is from an author's account of a flight over Mali. Is anything wrong? "I could ride east from there for miles, the sands went on for ever."

One problem lies in the adverb "for ever." It is not the division of *for* and *ever,* an older style that is just as valid as the union of the two components in *forever* if used consistently. It is that *forever,* or *for ever,* pertains to time, not space. It means (1) for eternity, for all time ("The universe will last forever"), or (2) incessantly, continually ("That dog is forever barking"). The title and title song of the musical play *On a Clear Day You Can See Forever,* an anomaly that alluded to a character's ability to foresee the future, may have helped to spread the wrong idea.

The meaning of the quotation can be expressed in many ways: "The sands went on and on" / "seemed endless" / "stretched to the horizon" / "lay as far as the eye could see," et cetera.

(Another mistake in the sample is the improper fusion of two sentences. Either change the comma to a colon or semicolon, or change it to a period and let *The* start a new sentence. *See* Run-on sentence, 2.)

FOREWORD and FORWARD. The *foreword* of a small book is headed,

in large letters, "FORWARD." No one literate in English should mix up the two words; their confounding is a blunder indeed for an author to make and an editor to overlook. (Perhaps it is poetic license. The book is a rhyming dictionary.)

Another book (this time a cookbook) combines part of each word in "FOREWARD."

Foreword (noun), a front note in a book, is made up of two fairly obvious four-letter words. As commonly used, it represents a nineteenth-century Anglicization of the German word for preface, *vorwort,* which combines *vor,* fore, and *wort,* word.

It should not be confused with *forward* (adjective and adverb), whose suffix is *-ward,* meaning in a certain direction. The prefix has the same meaning in both words, fore or front, though *forward* lacks an *e.* This word descended from the Old English *foreweard.*

"FOR FREE." *See* FREE, 1.

FORMER. *Former* (pronoun) is the opposite of *latter.* The *former* refers to the first of two things—only two—that have been mentioned. "Their ham and eggs are good, particularly the former." Often it is clearer to repeat a word or phrase: "particularly the ham."

When three or more items are enumerated—"We saw zebras, giraffes, and lions"—*former* cannot be used. It is best to repeat the first item: "The zebras were especially plentiful." If it is too long, *the first* or *the first-named* or *the first of those* are possibilities.

Former (adjective) can mean previous, past, taking place earlier, or coming before in order.

The meaning is not always immediately clear. Confusion can enter when *former* refers to something that is mentioned first but came later in time. A book on international law tells of the founding of the Permanent Court of Arbitration in 1899 and a proposal in 1907 to supplement it with a Court of Arbitral Justice:

> The CAJ was ... designed to ... coexist with the PCA. ... The implication was clear that states would quickly grow to prefer adjudication over arbitration since the former institution supposedly more nearly coincided with their vital national security interests. ...

Inasmuch as the 1907 event came later, the Court of Arbitral Justice should have been repeated by name, or initials, instead of described as "the former institution."

Another temporal problem is illustrated by a sentence from a news item. The statement cannot be true:

> Haynsworth was nominated for the U.S. Supreme Court by former President Nixon on Aug. 18, 1969, but the Senate later rejected the nomination on a 55-to-45 vote.

No one can be nominated to the Supreme Court by a "former" president. It would be enough to say, "Haynsworth was nominated ... by President Nixon...." Anyone who read the story (years after the famous resignation) would almost certainly have known that Nixon was no longer president. If in doubt, the writer could have made it perfectly clear by writing, "Haynsworth was nominated ... by *then* President Nixon...."

See also **Anachronism, 3; ERSTWHILE; LATTER.**

FORMIDABLE. *Formidable* (adjective) originates in the Latin *formido,* meaning fear. Dictionaries in the past generally stuck to the ideas of (1) arousing fear or dread of any encounter; (2) being alarming or forbidding in appearance, difficulty, strength, etc. They essen-

tially agreed also on the pronunciation: FOR-mid-a-bull.

In recent decades some users have stretched the word nearly to meaninglessness, without a trace of its original element of apprehension. It has been used in place of *big* and *impressive.* One dictionary even gives "admirable" as a meaning.

While a television documentary pictured Jidda, Saudi Arabia, a narrator commented, "It's the formidable face of a booming economy." Impressive? Handsome? Whatever he meant, aside from empty alliteration, omitting "formidable" would not have hurt. He pronounced it for-MID-a-bull, a nonstandard pronunciation heard at other times from a U.S. senator and three broadcasters.

FORSAKE. The Los Angeles Police Department "forsaked its officers," a lawyer said on television, using a nonword. *Forsook* is the proper past tense of the verb (transitive) *forsake.*

In the context above, *forsake* means to abandon or desert (someone or something). It can mean also to renounce or give up (something). Its other forms: "She has *forsaken* me" (past participle), "They are *forsaking* us" (present participle), and "He *forsakes* you" (present tense, third person, singular).

"FOR THE SIMPLE REASON THAT." *See* **REASON, 3.**

FORTUITOUS. *Fortuitous* (adjective) means coming about by accident or by chance or without plan.

A newspaper article told about a hospital's new, state-supported program to provide schooling for juvenile patients. The head of the pediatrics department was quoted.

> "This program was fortuitous because just in the last 30 days we got new hospital accreditation guidelines

that state that, if we provide treatment for infants and children, we must provide for their education if they are hospitalized for long periods of time," E—— said.

The administrator was mixed up and the reporter probably was too. They may have confused "fortuitous" with a combination of *felicitous,* meaning apt or appropriate, and *fortunate,* meaning lucky. Either word would have been a better choice than "fortuitous."

That which is *fortuitous* may be interpreted as appropriate or inappropriate, lucky or unlucky. Natural disasters are *fortuitous.* Like *felicitous,* it is a four-syllable word beginning with *f* and ending with *-itous.* It shares the first five letters of *fortunate.* Otherwise *fortuitous* has little in common with the other two adjectives. The Latin equivalents and ancestors of *fortuitous* and *fortunate* are *fortuitus* and *fortunatus,* which in the distant past evidently had a common root in *fors,* chance, luck.

A book by two scientific writers appears to suggest that accident and uncertainty pervade the universe. The components of such a universe could truly be called *fortuitous.* In the following example, no problem appears up to the second comma.

For some people, the exceedingly fortuitous arrangement of the physical world, which permits the very special conditions necessary to human observers' existence, confirms their belief in a creative Designer.

In this example, *felicitous* would itself be more felicitous than "fortuitous." *Fortunate* also would pass muster.

A similar problem appears in another book, by a traveler telling about car trouble in Africa.

Within a few moments, the engine fired. The mechanic danced a few

steps and doffed his hat just as the boy on the bicycle returned holding up a tube triumphantly. Never had so many fortuitous omens graced us at once.

This time "fortuitous" would well be replaced by *favorable.*

An adverb related to *fortuitous* is *fortuitously.* A related noun is *fortuitousness.*

FORTUNATE. *See* FORTUITOUS.

FORTUNE. *See* DESTINY.

FORWARD and BACK (time). When daylight-saving time arrives in the spring, we are advised to move our clocks "forward" one hour; that is, move them in the direction in which clocks automatically move. Turning the clock "back," say from 2 a.m. to 1 a.m., is what we are advised to do in the fall when standard time returns. The mnemonic "Spring *forward,* fall *back*" does not help some people, who misunderstand those adverbs and arrive at places two hours late or two hours early.

An announcing of a shift in time requires caution. The new hour or date needs to be stated precisely.

The manager of a television station decided to start its network programs at 7 p.m. instead of 8 p.m. A newspaper reported that she was "moving prime time forward one hour."

Sometimes *forward* (as an adjective) can indeed mean early: "A forward contingent is on its way." But *forward* (as an adverb) can refer also to the future: "From this day forward" / "I look forward to the party." Similarly, *back* can suggest an earlier time to some ("Think back to your school days"), a later time to others (who may recall the movie *Back to the Future*).

If a meeting originally scheduled for May 3 is postponed, or put off, to May 10, is it moved "ahead" one week? The future lies *ahead*, but three comes *ahead* of ten. Stating the new date avoids confusion.

FORWARD and FOREWORD.
See FOREWORD and FORWARD.

FOR WHOM THE BELL TOLLS.
See WHO and WHOM, *1*.

FOUNDATION, FUNDAMENTAL, and FUNDAMENT.
All three words stem from the Latin *fundus*, bottom, yet their meanings are not all similar. The writer of this sentence did not know that *fundament* bears only superficial resemblance to *fundamental*: "That event was the fundament of Polish nationalism."

Foundation, meaning base, basis, or founding, would have been a better choice of nouns. *Fundamental* is a basic principle or (as an adjective) basic or essential. Take away *-al* and we have *fundament*, meaning anus or buttocks.

FOUNDER. *See* FLOUNDER and FOUNDER.

FRACTION.
When the anchor man for a television network placed President Gorbachev's salary at $30,000 a year and remarked, "It's a mere fraction of the $250,000 that President Bush makes," was he saying anything wrong?

Strictly speaking, any number below one is a *fraction*. Nine-tenths or even 99/100 is a *fraction* and it is not small and not subject to the modifier "mere" or "only." (In mathematics, any number with a numerator and denominator can be called a *fraction*, even if it exceeds one; for example, 3/2.) On the other hand, one-twentieth could be described as a *small fraction* of something, one-thousandth a *tiny fraction*.

Therefore it is not reasonable to restrict *fraction* to a small part, a little piece, or a minute fragment. Nevertheless such use is entrenched in popular speech. That fact may acquit the telecaster of verbal malfeasance but not of verbosity. Obviously $30,000 is a fraction of $250,000. Had he made a calculation and reported, "It's a mere *12 percent* of the $250,000," at least he would be imparting information.

A press example also deals with Russia:

> . . . The total of about 7,000 working churches is only a fraction of the 54,000 that existed before the 1917 Bolshevik Revolution.

A replacement for "is only a fraction of" might have been "is only *13 percent* of" or (if the writer could not handle the arithmetic problem) "*contrasts with*."

Another example is in **Gerund**, *3A*.

Fractions. *See* FRACTION; HALF; **Numbers**, *4, 5, 8, 10, 11*; **Verbs**, *3* (end).

FRANKENSTEIN.
This error is a hoary one and very widespread. Even a brilliant scientist-author has made it. He writes that the public distrusts science, adding:

> This distrust is evident in the cartoon figure of the mad scientist working in his laboratory to produce a Frankenstein.

Nobody produces a Frankenstein (except, perhaps, Mr. and Mrs. Frankenstein). Frankenstein in Mary Shelley's 1818 novel of that name was not the monster but its creator, Victor Frankenstein. The monster, which ultimately killed him, had no name.

The term *Frankenstein's monster* or *Frankenstein monster* may be applied to any creation that escapes from the creator's control and threatens to, or actually does, crush him. "Nuclear energy is Frankenstein's monster," or "In developing nuclear energy, man created a Frankenstein monster."

"FREAK ACCIDENT." No news story of a distinctive accident is complete unless the reporter drags in this phrase. It is never a *freakish* or *freaky* accident, to use a bona fide adjective, but a "freak" one.

Sometimes the happening is not even very freakish, freaky, or "freak." For instance, a network anchor man described "a freak accident" in which a tree was blown down upon a van. And a newspaper reported "a freak accident" in which debris on a highway stopped a truck, causing it to be hit from behind by another truck.

FREE. *1. FREE and "FOR FREE." 2. FREE and FREELY.*

1. FREE and "FOR FREE"

Two news magazines, which normally prize conciseness, ran the following two sentences, each containing a useless word.

> Perry planned to lease the planes to Jordan for free. . . .

> Soldiers, trying to build good will, cut hair for free [in China].

"For" serves no purpose in those sentences or in these two, found in newspapers:

> Since Oct. 1, Capital Metropolitan Authority patrons have been riding city buses for free. . . .

> The company has grown from 300 outlets in 1980 in part on its boast it would deliver the pizza for free if its drivers were late.

People are being offered the planes, the haircuts, the bus rides, and the pizza *free* or *free of charge* or *for nothing,* but not "for free." *Free* serves as an adverb, whereas *nothing* is a noun. The preposition "for" makes no more sense with *free* than with the adverb *expensively.*

Whether the illegitimate phrase originated in a mistaken analogy with *for nothing* or in a conscious attempt at cuteness is not known.

(The last quoted sentence, while containing a surplus word, omits a desirable word after "boast": the conjunction *that.*)

See also **Prepositions,** 7.

2. FREE and FREELY

Freely is an alternative to *free* as an adverb meaning in an unrestrained or unlimited manner. *The horses run freely* or *free.* To say "The publication is distributed freely" when *free of charge* is meant can be ambiguous.

Free is also a common adjective: *a free country.*

FREEDOM. *See* **DEMOCRACY, FREEDOM, and INDEPENDENCE.**

FROM . . . TO. *See* **BETWEEN,** *3;* **RANGE, true and false; Punctuation,** *4C.*

"FROM WHENCE." *See* **WHENCE and "FROM WHENCE."**

-FUL ending. *See* **Plurals and singulars,** *2B.*

FULL STOP. *See* **Punctuation,** 8.

FULSOME. *Fulsome* fools some people. It means not just *full,* but distastefully so; offensive to the senses, especially by being excessive or insincere: "Belshazzar's fulsome feast" / "Castro's fulsome promises."

Although in Middle English *fulsom* meant simply full or abundant, it took on a negative connotation. Perhaps *ful* suggested *foul.* Anyway, in modern English it combines the idea of abundance with the idea of excess or insincerity.

One of those fooled was a TV network's chief anchor man. He said, in describing Robert Dole's last day in Congress:

And so the senator leaves the Senate with the most fulsome praise ringing in his ears.

The broadcaster probably did not intend to describe the praise as excessive or insincere, but that is essentially what he said. Although some opposing partisans may have secretly agreed with such an assessment, another expression would have been preferable, say *a lavish chorus of praise*. (That corrects the misuse and ties in with the ear-ringing theme.)

FUN. The first time I heard someone say anything like "It's so fun," I was in Europe and appreciated that the woman talking to me could speak my language at all. But for an American television reporter to speak of "the career that had looked so fun and so glorious" could not be easily condoned. A substitute for "so fun" would have been *like such fun* or *so full of fun* or *so enjoyable*.

Fun is properly a noun, usually meaning enjoyment or merriment, or a source of it. "We had fun." / "This game is fun." (As a noun, it is modified only by an adjective—e.g., "*great* fun" or "*some* fun"—not by an adverb. In a sentence such as "It seems *so* enjoyable" or "*so* funny," *so* is an adverb, modifying a predicate adjective.)

Fun is partially accepted as an adjective before the noun (attributive adjective). Informally people may speak of "a fun trip" or "a fun city." In a superlative misuse, a departing talk show host said, "It was probably the funnest two years I ever spent."

FUND. In the sense of money available for use, *funds* is a plural noun. A company reported to stockholders:

For the three months ended June 30 . . . funds from operations was $45,521,000. . . . Revenues . . . were $62,173,000. . . . Funds from operations for the six months ended June 30 . . . was $85,990,000. . . . Revenues . . . were $12,500,000. . . .

"Funds . . . *were*," just as "revenues were." A singular phrasing would be "*income* from operations was $45,521,000."

A *fund,* singular noun, is a supply of money set aside for a specific purpose (the emergency *fund*); or a supply of something else (a *fund* of knowledge).

FUNDAMENTAL and FUNDAMENT. *See* FOUNDATION, FUNDAMENTAL, and FUNDAMENT.

FURIOUS, FURIOUSLY. *See* FUROR and FURY.

FUROR and FURY. *Fury* (noun) is violent action or violent rage: "the fury of the battle" / "the storm's fury."

A tabloid headline screamed, "FURY OVER CLAIM IKE KILLED 1M GERMAN POWs." The article did not bear out the headline. A book about Eisenhower was not met with "fury" (as *The Satanic Verses* was, for instance). However, on the basis of the article, the book could be said to have created a mild *furor*.

Furor can range in intensity from harmless to violent. It can be a fad, a public commotion or uproar, a state of high excitement, a frenzy, or violent anger or *fury*. (*Furore* is a variation in the sense of a fad. It is mainly British, an import from Italy.)

Both words have the same Latin root, *furere,* to rage.

Furious (adjective) and *furiously* (adverb) can mean full of or with *fury,* implying violence; or it can mean fierce(ly) or vehement(ly) without the implication of violence.

FURTHER. *See* FARTHER and FURTHER.

FURY. *See* FUROR and FURY.

Fused participle. *See* Gerund, 4.

FUSION and FISSION. *See* NUCLEAR.

Future tense. *See* Tense, *1 and 4.*

G

GAL. *See* GUY.

GAMBIT. A chess maneuver in which a player sacrifices a pawn or piece to try to gain an advantage is a *gambit*. Usually it occurs at the beginning of a game and involves a pawn. *Gambit* or *opening gambit* may be used figuratively, outside of chess, to denote an early concession, as in diplomacy or business negotiation.

Looser uses of that noun in place of *opening move, opening remark, maneuver, move, strategy,* have become widespread, dulling the word. Magazines have described a remark to initiate a conversation as a "conversational gambit" and a move in Congress as a "legislative gambit." Those uses omit the main element of a gambit: the sacrifice.

GAMBLING and GAMING. To bet or risk money on the outcome of a contest or of a game of chance is *gambling* (noun). A euphemism for it is *gaming,* used by those who advocate or play a role in legal *gambling.*

The word *gambling* was scarcely used in an initiative measure to make it easy to put gambling devices and games of chance on Indian reservations in California, but "gaming" appeared hundreds of times. The Nevada Gaming Control Board regulates gambling casinos in that state.

The word *gambling* has had disreputable associations; *gaming,* like *games,* sounds clean and recreational. General dictionaries consider them synonyms.

GAMUT. *See* GANTLET and GAUNTLET, 2.

GANTLET and GAUNTLET. *1. The difference. 2. GAMUT. 3. More meanings.*

1. The difference

Confusion between these two words is rampant. The main use of either is in a common expression. The historian Francis Parkman wrote:

> They descended the Mississippi, running the gantlet between hostile tribes.

A radio newscaster said, referring to gun battles between drug dealers:

> Residents have to run a gauntlet just to get to their front door.

And this was in a news agency's dispatch:

> [Kenneth Starr] must run a daily gantlet of reporters and cameras just to leave his driveway.

Is it "gantlet" or "gauntlet"? American tradition leans toward the former. The latter, a British import, has become more common in colloquial use. Both are corruptions. Originally one ran the *gantlope.*

A *gantlope,* from the Swedish *gatlopp,* was used in a punishment of thieves and then of soldiers. It consisted of two rows of men facing one another and holding such objects as sticks and knotted cords. The offender was stripped to the waist and forced to *run the gantlope* as the others struck him.

It was not long before people began confusing *gantlope* with a then familiar word, *gauntlet,* a type of glove, of which *gantlet* was a variant. The first quotation of *gantlope* in *The Oxford English Dictionary* is from 1646; fifteen years later "run the gantlet" appears; afterward we see both *gauntlets* and *gantlets* as well as *gantlopes.*

The phrase was used almost from the start in both a literal and a figurative sense. Today it is nearly always used figuratively, meaning to suffer attacks, particularly from two sides; to risk perils; or even to endure any series of troubles.

Literally "run the gauntlet" is like saying "run the old glove." A *gauntlet* was an armored glove of medieval times. A man who cast his *gauntlet* to the ground was issuing a challenge to fight. If another picked it up, he was accepting the challenge. The custom gave rise to the expressions *throw down the gauntlet* and *take up the gauntlet,* meaning to issue or accept a challenge.

To run the *gantlet* is favored by four works on English usage and the manuals of the Associated Press and *The New York Times.* It was the preferred term in American dictionaries through 1960. Later dictionaries have offered both spellings for each sense. The books have never agreed on pronunciation. The suggestion here is to pronounce the words as they are spelled, GANT-let and GAUNT-let, and to use the former for running and the latter for throwing down. All sources agree that only the *gauntlet* is thrown down.

2. GAMUT

Gamut (noun), which appears in the expression *run the gamut,* usually means the complete range or extent of things; for instance, "The chefs ran the *gamut* of flavors."

It is sometimes confused with the other *g*-words. This was from a news report: "Prisoners were forced to run a gamut." *Gantlet* would be right, not "gamut." The host of a talk show said, "Once someone has served as president, he has run the full gauntlet of accomplishment." *Gamut,* not "gauntlet."

"A complete *gamut* of colors," a dictionary's example, unnecessarily modifies *gamut.* A *gamut* is complete.

Gamut (from *gamma* and *ut,* medieval musical notes) denoted the musical scale in medieval times. It has since been applied to the whole series of recognized musical notes or, sometimes, to just the major scale.

3. More meanings

Gantlet is also a railroad term. It is a section where two tracks overlap, enabling a train from either line to pass in a narrow place.

Gauntlet for glove is not wholly obsolete. Certain types of work and dress gloves and glovelike athletic devices are known as *gauntlets.*

GAS.   1. *Confusion.* 2. *Definitions.*

1. Confusion

An automobile company was selling a low-pollution van, "powered by natural gas instead of gas," a news agency reported.

On its face, the quoted phrase seems to part with logic. *Natural gas* is a *gas.* No doubt the writer meant *gasoline,* for which "gas" is a common, colloquial American term. Displayed in serious writing, it does not fare well. When it is being contrasted with the real *gas,* "gas" is particularly ill-chosen. It can perplex those who are unaccustomed to informal Americanisms and do not recognize it as the British *petrol.*

A newspaper article used the phrase "gas tax" eleven times (counting the headline), never once spelling out the topic: the federal *gasoline* tax.

Even Americans are not always sure what is meant by, say, "I smell gas."

2. Definitions

Gas is a substance that is neither solid nor liquid and is characterized by very low density and readiness to expand and fill its container. The Flemish chemist J. B. van Helmont (1577–1644), who discovered carbon dioxide and distinguished gases from liquids and solids, coined the word, basing it on the Greek *khaos,* chaos.

In colloquial use, *gas* means gasoline; in slang use, empty or boastful talk.

Gasoline is a flammable, liquid mixture of hydrocarbons, obtained in the distillation of petroleum and used as a fuel in internal-combustion engines.

Natural gas is a mixture of gaseous hydrocarbons, mainly methane, found in the earth in oil deposits and used as a fuel.

Petrol, the British term for *gasoline,* is pronounced PET-trull.

GAUNTLET. See GANTLET and GAUNTLET.

GAVE and GIVEN. See Tense, 5A.

GAY. *1. History. 2. The press. 3. Two meanings.*

1. History

Gay is an adjective that, for seven centuries, has primarily meant joyful, light-

hearted, merry, or mirthful. Chaucer, for instance, wrote that a pilgrim "iolif [jolly] was and gay." It can also mean bright or showy. Tennyson: "when all is gay with lamps." Probably of Teutonic origin, the word came to Middle English from the French *gai.*

The use of *gay* in the above senses dates back at least to 1310, antedating Chaucer, *The Oxford English Dictionary* indicates. Records of its occasional euphemistic use to mean a man "of loose and immoral life" begin in 1637; a woman, 1825. Its use as a euphemism for the adjective *homosexual* did not become popular until close to 1970, although rare uses dating from the 1880s are documented.

Used in the sense of homosexual, the adjective *gay* used to be considered slang but now is accepted as standard by all dictionaries. *Gay* as a noun, meaning a homosexual person, has been so accepted by American dictionaries but is considered slang by the *Oxford.*

2. The Press

The publicly sold style manual of *The New York Times* disapproves of *gay* for *homosexual,* although in 1987 the staff was told that the adjective was acceptable. (*Gay* could describe both sexes, but *lesbian* was preferred in specific references to women.) However:

> The noun will continue to be *homosexual(s).* Thus we'll write *gay author,* but not "a gay"; *gay men* (or *homosexuals*) but NOT "gays."

The distinction made grammatical sense. If someone can be "a gay," can someone else not be "a sad" or "a tall"?

Most of the press had been quicker to adopt *gay* in the sexual sense, particularly in headlines, where news essences must be squeezed into small spaces. Being able to replace a ten-letter word with a three-letter word pleases a typical editor. So to see a headline in 1990 in a San Francisco newspaper saying "Homosexual rights law challenged" was surprising, particularly when the text of the article said:

> Federal courts have found that gays are not protected against bias by the U.S. Constitution. Gov. Deukmejian vetoed a bill in 1984 to give gays equal rights under state law. [A misplaced prepositional phrase produces "bias by the U.S. Constitution." See **Modifiers**, *3*.]

The same paper ran the headline "A GAY BASHER ASKS: WHY?" Was he a basher who was gay? No, but that sense results from the adjectival use of a noun adopted from an adjective.

Homosexuals themselves have embraced *gay*, as adjective and noun, although many originally resisted it. Some of them annually celebrate "Gay Pride Day." No one has explained why a euphemism is needed for that which one takes pride in.

3. Two meanings

Harper Dictionary (1985) reported that only 36 percent of a usage panel of 166 members accepted the modern sense of *gay*. Some expressed anger. Isaac Asimov: "This use of 'gay' has killed a wonderful word. . . ." Erich Segal: "It robs our language of a lovely adjective. . . ."

While *gay* in the traditional sense, that of merry or bright, can at times be misunderstood—"It was a gay party" permits two interpretations—reports of its demise have been exaggerated. Anyone who wants to use the word in that way has a perfect right to do so but should see that the context makes the meaning clear. It was clear in a 1990 article in the *The New York Times*:

> But today the only people walking in Red Square were tourists who had come to ogle the gay domes of St. Basil's Cathedral.

See also **HOMOPHOBIA.**

GENDARME. Americans who use the word *gendarme* think it is French for policeman. They are partly right, as right as a European would be in using "constable" or "sheriff" for an American policeman.

A movie guide book describes the plot of the 1963 film *Irma la Douce*: "A gendarme pulls a one-man raid on a back street Parisian joint and falls in love with one of the hookers he arrests." The leading actress recalled in a TV documentary: "I played a prostitute and Jack played a young gendarme who tried to rescue me from the street."

Jack (Lemmon) did not play a "gendarme." One French-English dictionary defines *gendarme* as a policeman "*in countryside and small towns*." Another defines it as a "member of the state police force," approximately equal to a "police constable."

It is possible to speak of a Parisian *policeman* without dragging in "gendarme."

GENDER and SEX. *Gender* is a term of grammar. It is the classification of certain words as masculine, feminine, or neuter. In English those words are nouns and pronouns, the great majority of them neuter, like *table, song, it, its*. Among masculine words are *man, boy, he, his*. Among feminine words: *woman, girl, she, her*.

In English, gender for the most part is natural. That is, most words of masculine or feminine gender represent sexual, or at least human, qualities. But the word *gender* is not synonymous with sex. In various languages it often has nothing to do with sex—or with anything else.

In the Romance languages, grammar

arbitrarily decrees nouns to be masculine or feminine, regardless of any sexual qualities. Thus, in Spanish *el día,* the day, is masculine, while *la noche,* the night, is feminine. In French *la plume,* the pen, is feminine, while *le crayon,* the pencil, is masculine.

Even in English, the feminine pronouns *she* and *her* are often applied to such neuter things as ships and countries. *His* in a phrase like *to each his own,* while masculine in *gender,* is used in a neuter sense.

In recent decades an increasingly popular use of *gender* has been as a euphemism for *sex,* meaning the classification of human beings and animals as male or female. It is not obvious why *sex,* in such an innocent sense, needs a euphemism.

Thus, a magazine chart lists library visits by demographic categories, including "AGE . . . INCOME . . . EDUCATION" and "GENDER." On another page, an essayist criticizes "double standards that have the effect of . . . pitting race against race, gender against gender." *Sex,* rather than "gender," would be quite fitting in both instances and in the newspaper sentences below.

Prosecutors and defense lawyers may not bar a potential juror from serving in a criminal trial solely because of the person's gender. . . .

[Under a proposed bill] a man could sue a woman for a violent attack, arguing it was based on his gender.

Not even an editor's normal penchant for short words in headlines overcomes the squeamishness toward *sex.* The first news story was headed "Potential Jurors Can't Be Barred Because of Gender, Court Rules."

While *gender* has increasingly usurped the role of *sex* in genteel use, the casual use of *sex* as a noun denoting coitus or any sexual activity has become more common. For instance, the message that "We had sexual intercourse" is more likely to take the form of the "slept together" euphemism or "We had sex."

Strictly speaking, all of us have sex all the time. It is either male or female.

Genitive (possessive). See **Double possessive; Gerund,** *4;* **Possessive problems; Pronouns,** *1, 2, 9, 10A;* **Punctuation,** *1.*

Germanisms. *See* **Adjectives and adverbs,** 2; **Backward writing,** 3; **Infinitive,** 4; **Joining of words; ONGOING; OUTPUT; PLAY DOWN and "DOWNPLAY"; UPCOMING.**

Gerund. *1. Definition. 2. Errors of omission. 3. Gerund or infinitive? 4. Possessive with gerund.*

1. Definition

When the *-ing* form of a verb is used as a noun, it is called a *gerund.*

It serves every function of a noun. It may be a subject ("*Laughing* makes me happy"), a direct object of a verb ("Jane loves *kissing*"), the object of a preposition ("By *oversleeping,* John missed the plane"), or a subjective complement ("His goal was *finding* the missing link").

Many *-ing* words are not *gerunds.* "Reinforcements are *coming.*" / "The senator delivered a *stinging* rebuke." / "*Laughing* hysterically, he could barely resume the broadcast." In those examples *coming, stinging,* or *laughing* is a *present participle.* It is a verb form that expresses present action (in relation to the tense of the finite verb) and can serve as an adjective.

Do not confuse a *gerund* with a *present participle.* It appears that an editor did so in program notes for a recording: A music critic "reproached Beethoven for the absence of a great vocal fugue considered traditional in every musical, setting of a religious drama. . . ." A comma does not belong in *musical setting* but fits this sentence, in which *setting* does act as a present participle: "He strode inside, setting the statuette on the floor." (A comma should follow "fugue." *See* **Punctuation,** *3C.*)

2. Errors of omission

One who uses a *gerund* carelessly and fails to indicate the subject of an action can create a dangler. The result may be an awkwardly ungrammatical sentence and worse: the *gerund* may link with a wrong part of its sentence and produce an unintended meaning.

This sentence is typical: "The whales can be protected only by being ever vigilant." It seems to be calling on the whales to take action. The trouble is that "being" is a dangling participle. Preceding it with *our* would make it a *gerund* and indicate the intended meaning.

Although a similar grammatical error did not obscure the meaning of an editorial, it is not what the newspaper traditionally considers fit to print:

It costs only $500 to provide an expectant mother with adequate prenatal care. Yet treating a low-weight infant can cost $180,000 even before leaving the hospital.

"Treating," a gerund and the subject of "can cost," seems to take over—senselessly—as the subject of "leaving" too because the writer failed to indicate any other subject. "Leaving" is a dangling participle. To precede it with a pronoun, "*its* leaving," thereby making it a gerund, would be a correction; *it leaves* would be better still.

The final example in this section, quoted by *Punch* of England, originates in a column of personal items. Grammatically the only subject is the "Muske-

teers." The result is hardly what the writer intended.

Grateful thanks to the three Musketeers who carried Mrs. Pride home after breaking her leg on Wednesday.

The magazine commented, "Least they could do."
See also **Modifiers,** *1.*

3. Gerund or infinitive?

A. Examples

Some people who use our language lack a command of idiom. They do not always know whether a particular construction calls for an infinitive, that is, the basic form of a verb; or a *gerund,* that is, the *-ing* form used as a noun.

The resulting errors are excusable when committed by foreigners who are unfamiliar with English. A Japanese-owned jewelry store displayed a sign that said, "PLEASE GET AN APPOINTMENT BEFORE GO IN." When advised that the sign could stand improvement, especially by inflection of the verb "GO," the management replaced it. The new sign said, "PLEASE MAKE AN APPOINTMENT BEFORE GOING THANK YOU."

Such errors are less tolerable when committed by an English-speaking person, particularly one whose regular job is to communicate information to the public. An example is provided by a news service:

There were 299 rapes, assaults and murders last year on campuses of the UC system, which devotes a fraction of its $6 billion yearly budget to protect students. [*See* **FRACTION.**]

The verb *devote* does not go with an infinitive, such as "protect." *Protecting* would be right. The two made-up examples below will help to explain.

- "The university devotes most of its budget to salaries, buildings, and protecting students." That is, it appropriates funds for certain purposes; each purpose is a noun ("salaries, buildings") or a gerund ("protecting students"). Here *to* introduces the ultimate recipients of the action.
- "The university's police try to protect students." The verb *try,* unlike *devote,* can go with an infinitive: the police *try* to do something ("protect students"). This time *to* indicates the infinitive.

Erroneous analogies may account for some misuses. A book says "the decision . . . contributed notably to redress the constitutional balance. . . ." The unidiomatic "contributed . . . to redress" parallels *served to redress,* which would be correct. "Contributed" can stand if the infinitive is changed to the gerund: "contributed . . . to *redressing.* . . ." Here the *to* does not indicate an infinitive; rather it points to that which benefited from the action.

There is no general rule, except that a writer or speaker needs to be secure in his knowledge of any verb's properties before using the verb. In case of doubt, a dictionary that offers examples of the verb's use may help.

See also **Infinitive,** 2; **POSSIBLE** (etc.), 2; **TO,** 2.

B. Lists

It would be impractical to try to list all the many other words that could pose similar problems of idiom. Here are sixty such words: nouns, verbs, and adjectives. Each is followed by the preposition that usually goes with it, and each is categorized according to part of speech and whether a *gerund* or *infinitive* can follow idiomatically. (Other forms that may follow instead are not listed.)

Noun **followed by** *gerund* (laughing, winning, etc.) *enthusiasm for, fear of, habit of, hope of, idea of, indulgence in, insistence on, love for, possibility of, resistance to*

Noun **followed by** *infinitive* (to sing, to build, etc.) *ability to, determination to, duty to, effort to, failure to, hesitation to, inclination to, obligation to, opportunity to, tendency to*

Verb **followed by** *gerund* *boast of, commit (someone or something) to, despair of, dream of, keep (someone or something) from, look forward to, object to, prevent (someone or something) from, prohibit (someone) from, succeed in*

Verb **followed by** *infinitive* *agree to, dare to, encourage (someone) to, forbid (someone) to, force (someone) to, hope to, neglect to, permit (someone or something) to, persuade (someone) to, pledge to, prepare to, presume to, refuse to, try to, want to*

Adjective **followed by** *gerund* *capable of, grateful for, hopeful of, wary of, thankful for, tired of, worthy of*

Adjective **followed by** *infinitive* *adequate to, competent to, eager to, glad to, inclined to, likely to, pleased to, ready to*

Some words may go with either *gerund* or *infinitive,* depending on context. Examples are the nouns *chance* (*of* or *to*) and *intention* (*of* or *to*), verbs *fail* (*at* or *to*) and *think* (*of* or *to*), and adjectives *sorry* (*about* or *to*) and *sure* (*of* or *to*).

4. Possessive with gerund

Just as nearly every noun may be possessed ("He took *his* suitcase" / "They pledged *their* love"), so may a *gerund*: "She was shocked at *his winning* the money." *His* modifies the gerund *winning*. It would not be strictly correct to say ". . . at *him* winning the money." Not "him" but his *winning* shocked her.

A similar example: "Children's drinking vexes the councilman." Note the apostrophe-*s*. *Children's* modifies the gerund *drinking*. "*Children* drinking vexes . . ." is wrong, the grammarian H. W. Fowler would say: What would be the subject of the sentence, "Children"? But *vexes* is singular. Making it "vex" would be of no help. The *children* do not trouble the councilman; only their *drinking* does. Could the subject be "drinking"? That would leave "Children" hanging there without any grammatical purpose.

Omitting the possessive produces a form that Fowler condemned for "rapidly corrupting English style": a *fused participle*, "a compound notion" resulting from the fusion of a noun or a pronoun in the objective case and a participle. He did not invent the concept of *possessive* with *gerund*, which went back several centuries, but did introduce the name for the questionable form (with his brother in *The King's English*, 1906) and publicize it (in his famous *Dictionary of Modern English Usage*, 1926).

The four examples below come from a book of true adventure, an editorial, an article from a Hong Kong newspaper, and an ad for an aquarium respectively. Corrections are inserted in brackets.

. . . A search and rescue situation . . . could end up in me [*my*] being charged half a million pounds.

He blamed Democrats last year for Susan Smith [*Smith's*] drowning her two young children in South Carolina.

This [Chinese protest to a U.S. visit by Taiwan's leader] is despite Mr Lee [*Lee's*] indicating he would not be travelling abroad for some time to come.

See sharks without it [*its*] costing an arm and a leg.

Sometimes the possessive form does not work. We look at three examples that are technically flawed according to the principles stated above. (Each fused participle is emphasized:)

A. "He wouldn't hear of *that being* possible . . ." (Dickens). You would not say "that's being possible." The sentence is best let alone.

B. "I hate the thought of *any son of mine marrying* badly" (Hardy). You would not say "son's" or "mine's." Besides, as a colloquial sentence, in a novel, it is tolerable.

C. "*This state's metropolis undergoing* chaos is an unhappy sight." If said aloud, "metropolis's" would sound like a plural. Anyway, how desirable are a double possessive and all those esses? The sentence needs rewriting.

In two instances, Fowler's own cure seems worse than the disease: He would "deny the possibility of *anything's* happening" and would not mind "*many's* having to go into lodgings."

Writers on grammar have generally accepted a possessive pronoun with a gerund (*my being charged*) or a proper noun with a gerund (*Lee's indicating*) in a simple sentence. But they have found numerous exceptions, particularly in complicated sentences. Some grammarians (not quoted here) have justified the fused participle as a valid alternative in any sentence.

Not even Sir Ernest Gowers, the sympathetic reviser of Fowler's dictionary, could accept the pure precept. He agreed that "upon your giving" was undoubtedly more idiomatic than "upon you giving." But he found that a more complicated sentence could make a possessive impossible, for example: "We have to account for the collision of two great fleets . . . ending in the total destruction of one of them." He would waive the possessive also when it was possible but "ungainly." (*"Anything's* happening"?)

In literature, the grammarian George O. Curme found, the possessive has been (1) most common when the gerund's subject is a pronoun; (2) rendered useless by modifying phrases or clauses ("Have you heard of Smith, who used to be pitcher, being injured?"); and (3) avoided for an emphatic subject ("She was proud of *him* doing it") or contrasting subjects ("We seem to think nothing of *a boy* smoking but resent *a girl* smoking").

The final example is drawn from a relatively recent book about words. Ironically, the author is praising Fowler, who railed against just such usage:

> Too often a name is legendary without many people knowing about the person.

Fowler would have insisted on *people's.* You may decide for yourself whether it would be an improvement. (*See also* LEGEND, LEGENDARY.)

GHOULISH. *See* FESTOON, FESTOONED.

GIRL. *See* GUY.

GIVE AWAY and GIVEAWAY. A printed election poster attacked a local ballot proposition as "The $100 Million-a-Year Give Away!" From a technical standpoint, it was in error. For one thing, "Give" and "Away" should have been united.

Give away, in two words, is a verb phrase meaning (1) to present (something) as a gift; (2) to disclose (information): "Don't give away our secret"; or (3) to ceremonially transfer a bride from her family to her husband: "Mr. Green gave his daughter away."

Uniting the words yields the informal noun *giveaway,* which means (1) something given away or the act of giving away: "Vote against the giveaway"; or (2) that which discloses: "His fingerprints were a giveaway." A *giveaway show* is a quiz program, usually on television, in which prizes are given away. As an alternative, *give* and *away* may be hyphenated: *give-away.*

The poster also needed to follow "$100" with a hyphen (-) to connect it to "Million-a-Year."

(The ballot proposition, to eliminate public voting on rule changes for city employees, lost by three to one despite its opponents' mistakes in English.)

GIVEN and GAVE. *See* Tense, 5A.

GLANCE and GLIMPSE. *See* Confusing pairs.

GO. *See* COME and GO; GONE and WENT.

GOING ON. *See* ONGOING.

GONE and WENT. "The drug activity has went down in this area dramatically." A police official in an Illinois town said that on nationwide television.

". . . Has *gone*" would have been correct.

"The child had opened the car door, climbed in, and went to sleep," a newscaster said on nationwide radio. ". . . And *gone*" would have been correct.

Has, have, or *had* does not mix with "went." *Went* is the past tense of the verb *go.* The past participle of *go* is *gone.* Therefore a correction of the first example is either "The drug activity *went* down . . ." (in the past tense) or "The drug activity has *gone* down . . ." (in the present perfect tense).

In the second example, deleting "had" would permit "went to sleep." Keeping "had" requires "*gone* to sleep." Someone seemed to have forgotten that "had" applied to three participles: "opened . . . climbed . . . and *gone.*"

See also **COME and GO**; **Tense,** *1, 5.*

GOOD and WELL. A Polish leader was toasting the American president in Warsaw. A metropolitan newspaper in the United States quoted him, in part, this way:

> What is more, we were able to meet in a friendly atmosphere. And I believe we have felt well together.

The defect can easily be forgiven if the Pole was speaking in English. It is more serious if he was speaking in Polish and this was an English translation.

A correction: "we have felt *good* together," that is, happy, content, or optimistic. In the context of feeling, *well* usually pertains only to health. On rare occasions it pertains to touch or the ability to feel things.

"I feel well" means I suffer no sign of illness. (*Feel* is not modified by *well. Feel* acts there as an intransitive verb, also as a linking verb: It links the subject, *I,* to the verb's complement, the adjective *well.* Or, in the sentence "We felt good," it links *we* to the adjective *good. See* **FEEL.**)

In the sense of health, "I feel good" is quite informal; "she's not good" is dialectal. One is *well* or feels *well.*

A baseball umpire said, in an interview on a radio sports program, "We cover the games pretty good." Change "good" to *well.* Here it means properly or skillfully. (In this context *cover* is modified by *well.* This time *well* is used as an adverb. *Cover* is a transitive verb. "Good," not being an adverb, cannot modify a verb. Usually *good* is an adjective, which modifies a noun: *good* boy; the food is *good.*)

Interviewed on a television "magazine," a designer of military aircraft said about one of his planes, "It worked as good or better than we expected." A partial correction: "It worked as *well.* . . ." (*Well,* an adverb, modifies *worked,* an intransitive verb.) A further correction: "as well *as* or better than we expected" or "as well *as we expected or better." See* **AS,** *3.*

An essayist on that program said later, referring to a supposed winner of two monetary prizes, "Mary's doing pretty good." She is doing *well* (adverb), not "good." If she were performing charitable deeds, one could say "She is doing *good.*" (*Good* would be used as a noun. There would be no place for "pretty.")

Still later, a reporter on the same program correctly used both words in the same sentence: "Before he did well [became successful], he did good [performed altruistic acts]."

GO OFF and GO ON. Occasionally the phrase *go off* is ambiguous. It can mean the same as *go on*—even though *off* and *on* are opposites, as anyone who has flipped an electric switch knows.

Go off can have these contradictory meanings: (1) to take place ("The show went off as planned") and (2) to discontinue or go away ("The show went off the air").

The execution of a prisoner was hours away when the news came that the

Supreme Court had agreed to review his case. A television newscaster announced, "Prison officials are proceeding as though the execution will go off."

Did he mean "as though the execution will go *on*" (or "*take place*") or "as though the execution *is off*" (or "will *not take place*")? Probably he meant the former, although the "prison officials" did not explain what good a Supreme Court review would do if the prisoner were dead.

By the way, the newscaster said that the Supreme Court had issued a "writ of certiori." He left out a syllable. It is *certiorari* (sir-she-a-RARE-ee), an order from a higher court to a lower, requesting the records of a case for review.

GRAFFITI and GRAFFITO.
Graffiti is a plural word. It denotes crude inscriptions, drawings, or scrawlings, often on walls, meant to be seen by the public. One such marking is a *graffito*.

The two quotations are from a news agency's dispatch and an editorial respectively:

Stylized graffiti was even scrawled on a sign—the "z" on the Hollywood Freezway ice cream parlor—for a hint of hometown believability.

The city of Dublin is discussing a five-day graffiti-removal program on the theory that the longer graffiti remains, the more publicity it gives the gang that did it.

Both sample sentences are ungrammatical in their mixing of plural and singular. The first sentence refers to only one marking, so change "Stylized graffiti was" to "*A* stylized *graffito* was." If there had been two or more markings, *graffiti were* would be correct. A correction of the second sentence is "The longer graffiti *remain*, the more publicity *they give* the *gangs* that *make them*."

Originating in the Greek *graphein*, to write, *graffito* and *graffiti* come to us from Italian. They used to have archeological and, later, political connotations. Now the words, more commonly *graffiti*, popularly connote the defacing of structures and vehicles by callow vandals.

GRAZE.
A restaurant reviewer tells readers: "Graze on skewers of grilled food—the list spans 27—in this noisy yet convivial yakitori bar."

Animals such as cows and horses *graze*. To *graze* (verb, intransitive) is to feed on growing grasses and similar plants. The verb came from the Old English *grasian*, from *graes*, meaning grass.

Sometimes *graze* is humorously applied to the eating of raw, leafy vegetables. Applying it to the eating of barbecued meat, however, is far-fetched.

Farmers and ranchers use *graze* (verb, transitive) in a variety of ways: to feed on (a type of herbage or the herbage of a particular pasture), to put (animals) out to feed, to tend (feeding animals), and so on.

Graze (verb, transitive and intransitive) means also to scrape, rub, or touch lightly in passing. "The bullet grazed his skin"). The way bees or butterflies skim along the grass of a field could conceivably have suggested this sense.

GREAT.
This adjective, of Old English lineage, primarily expresses magnitude: being large in size, area, amount, number, importance, or other attributes. The Great Lakes and the Great Plains are aptly named.

That traditional sense of *great* can conflict with a newer, informal sense. Talking about cars, a syndicated radio host asked, "Why are prices so great?"—leading some of his audience to assume that prices were high. His own answer was that foreign competition had caused prices to be low. They were "great"—that is, very good—for the consumer.

GRIEVOUS, GRIEVOUSLY. A mistake that some speakers make in uttering *grievous* and *grievously* is inserting an extra syllable. The words are pronounced GREE-vuss(-lee), not "GREE-vee-uss(-lee)." Sometimes they are misspelled "grievious(ly)," with an extra "i."

A newscaster on a radio network said a bill to ban certain abortions made an exception "to save the life of the mother and to prevent grievious harm to her." He got *grievous* wrong.

A congressman said on television, concerning the issuance of rubber checks by colleagues, "There are some people here who may have been grieviously wounded." *Grievously.*

Grievous (adjective) means (1) serious or grave; or (2) causing or expressing grief. It has two syllables, not three.

Grievously (adverb) means (1) seriously or gravely; or (2) in a way that causes or expresses grief. It has three syllables, not four.

GRISLY, GRIZZLY, and GRIZZLED. *1. GRISLY and GRIZZLY. 2. GRIZZLED.*

1. GRISLY and GRIZZLY

While pronounced the same (GRIZ-lee), these two adjectives have different meanings and histories. A newspaper ad mixed the words up. Warning against selling a house without an agent, it said, "The stories are grizzly." A frightening story is *grisly.* (It could possibly be a "grizzly" story if it dealt with bears.)

Grisly (from the Old English *grislic,* terrifying) means gruesome, horrifying, or terrifying.

Grizzly (from the Old French *gris,* gray) means gray or grayish. The *grizzly bear* was named for its grayish coloring, not for its fearfulness.

The misspelling or misuse of *grisly* may be less frequent than its unnecessary use. Technically it was not used wrong in the lead sentence of a news story, quoted here:

> A family member was being held Friday for suspicion of murder in the wake of a grisly stabbing that left four other family members dead. . . .

What fatal stabbing is not "grisly"?

2. GRIZZLED

Writing in a magazine about the frustrations of his job, a news reporter complained that he had become "a cynic" and "a curmudgeon." One paragraph said:

> Another sign I'm become more grizzled, I suppose, is I used to call my wife excitedly to tell her I'm on a breaking story. Now I call and say, "Damn it, I can't get away."

If he thought that *grizzled* meant anything like cynical or ill-tempered, he was mistaken. *Grizzled* (adjective) means gray or streaked with gray, or gray-headed. A picture of the reporter showed a rather young man with an abundance of dark hair. (The sentence is otherwise defective. "Another sign . . . is" heralds a noun or nounal phrase, such as "my reaction to a breaking story." Instead, we get the clause "I used to call my wife excitedly. . . .")

Grizzled is related to the verb *grizzle,* meaning (transitive) to make gray or (intransitive) to become gray. In British English, *grizzle* can mean to worry or fret.

GROUP OF. *See* Collective nouns.

GROW. The farmers *grow* artichokes. Hilda *grows* kumquats. Wilbur *grew* a beard. As a transitive verb, *grow* means *cultivate* or *raise* (a plant or crop) or cause (something natural) to arise. Its object should not be an artificial object or abstraction.

Although figuratively a house, a town, a business, or an economy can itself *grow* (intransitive verb), that is, become larger, people do not "grow" it.

The promise by a gubernatorial candidate "to try and grow this economy"—instead of *broaden, expand,* or *strengthen* it—was an anomaly. So was the headline "Netanyahu promises to grow West Bank settlements." A better verb was in the story, which said he would *build* there. Other usable verbs: *enlarge, expand.*

A financial company boasts of "helping to grow the future of America." Perhaps people could *brighten* or *insure* or *secure* its future, but the future does not "grow."

Guilt and innocence. *1. Civil vs. criminal. 2. Guilty vs. not guilty. 3. Innocence presumed. 4. Pleas and charges. 5. Some words to watch.*

1. Civil vs. criminal

The difference between *civil* and *criminal* cases escapes some people who are supposed to inform others about such matters.

Prop. 51, the only initiative on the ballot, would change court rulings that now require someone who is partially responsible for an accident to pay all the victim's damages if the other guilty parties have no money.

That statement confuses *civil* and *criminal* law. The proposition (on the California ballot) that the news story cites deals wholly with *civil* actions. Nobody is found "guilty" in *civil* trials, which mainly settle lawsuits in private disputes. Guilt is a concept in *criminal* prosecutions, which are meant to enforce public laws by bringing their violators to justice. The newspaper writer properly used *responsible* but quickly traded it for an incorrect adjective.

An announcer invited television viewers to "Join Judge Wapner in his struggle to separate the guilty from the innocent." The program being promoted was "The People's Court," an unofficial imitation of a small claims court and strictly *civil.* A small claims judge does not "separate the guilty from the innocent" but settles disputes about modest amounts of money and property.

A network newscaster announced: "A jury has found Carroll O'Connor not guilty of slander. . . ." He was not *responsible for* it. The trial was civil. Verdicts of "guilty" and "not guilty" were not options.

2. Guilty vs. not guilty

Under the American system of justice, nobody needs to prove himself innocent. Unless convicted, a person accused of a crime is presumed to be innocent. The prosecution has the burden of proving him guilty beyond a reasonable doubt. If he is not found *guilty,* the verdict must be *not guilty.* The latter is no synonym for "innocent" but means that the prosecution has failed to prove the defendant guilty beyond a reasonable doubt. There is no other verdict.

President Clinton showed misunderstanding of that legal principle when he said, "Some of these [aliens] are found guilty and some innocent of the crimes with which they are charged." He may have got the idea from news items like the following.

In an ironic turn of court procedure, a young man pleaded guilty Tuesday to a drug-trafficking charge in the same courtroom where jurors in 1988 found him innocent of murdering his mother.

Three former candidates for Sweetwater County public offices were found guilty and one was found innocent of failing to file campaign financial reports in time.

Members of the jury had said they found the former automaker innocent because they felt government agents had lured him into illegal activity.

Nobody is found "innocent" in American courts. Nor is there such a plea—except in the news media:

> Marine in Spying Case
> Enters Plea of Innocent

> Suspect pleads innocent
> in deadly shooting spree

Every "innocent" should be *not guilty.* Now let us explain the reason for the distortion.

A hoary newspaper superstition has it that if anyone ever is reported to be "not guilty," terrible things will happen: Maybe the "not" will disappear or the *t* in "not" will change to a *w,* the person on trial will sue, and the paper will go out of business.

The odds against such a procession of events must be huge. The news media should consider whether the perpetuation of that superstition is worth the distorted picture of our judicial system that it fosters.

(As for the incident reported in the first sample: was it "an ironic turn of court procedure" or "an ironic turn of *events*" or not very ironic at all? *See* **IRONY, IRONIC, IRONICALLY.**)

What is worse than using an imprecise term is changing the term in mid sentence.

> B—— was found innocent of involuntary manslaughter in the deaths of two other patients and not guilty of five counts of dereliction of duty.

Some readers may have wondered about the difference between being found "innocent" and being found "not guilty."

3. Innocence presumed

The presumption of innocence is a principle that some journalists have yet to learn. A criminal charge is far from a conviction. A suspicion is further removed yet.

> In the last 18 months, serious damage has been done to national security by convicted or suspected spies in the CIA, the NSA, the Navy's antisubmarine warfare program and Navy communications and Middle East intelligence operations.

Lumping together as "spies" both those who have been convicted in court of spying and those who have merely been suspected of spying, the writers (the story has two by-lines) in effect find them all guilty and declare that all have done "serious damage . . . to national security."

(Style fares no better than substance in that passage. The listed items are jumbled. There appear to be five, but it is hard to tell. Inadequate punctuation and perhaps an unnecessary "and" befog the series. *See* **Series errors,** 7.)

4. Pleas and charges

Two additional points are illustrated by each of these two samples (each the lead paragraph of a fourteen-paragraph news story):

> A former soldier from Pearl was sentenced to 30 years in prison Monday after pleading guilty to kidnapping a Jackson teenager and shooting at a police officer who tried to arrest him.

> Michael D—— . . . pleaded guilty yesterday to having engaged in bogus stock transactions with a British broker to evade Federal laws requiring brokers to maintain minimum amounts of capital.

First, one does not plead to a crime. One pleads to *a charge of* a crime or *a count of* an indictment.

Second, in any criminal proceeding, someone is accused of violating the law. Which law? Neither article tells us exactly. The first alludes to two charges (in stating the penalty for "kidnapping" and "assault"). The second refers to "Federal laws" without specifying them. A summary of the charge might be something like "violation of the Securities and Exchange Act by failing to maintain adequate net capital and by falsifying records."

Another news story says, "He has been charged with setting a dynamite bomb that caused extensive structural damage" to an abortion clinic (identified by name and address). That is typical; the story details what the arrested man is supposed to have done but not what law he is charged with having broken.

A news service report tells about a police chief who "was arrested for allegedly taking cocaine from the police department evidence room to support his 5-year-old addiction." The sixteenth and last paragraph says, "If convicted" the chief "could face more than 20 years in prison." If convicted of what crime? The report fails to say. A possible charge might be "unlawful possession of cocaine," but a reader must guess.

5. Some words to watch

A possessive pronoun can be incriminating, as in the sentence "Doaks has denied his guilt." The pronoun "his" juxtaposed with "guilt" seems to imply that the man is guilty. (Of course, "her" or "their" would have the same effect.) Conversely, "Doaks proclaims his innocence" displays an apparent bias in his favor. An impartial version is *Doaks has denied the charge* or *Doaks insists that he is innocent.*

A network television reporter identified a man who had not been arrested but who was being investigated in connection with a bombing in a park. The reporter said, "J—— continues to deny his guilt." It would have been far better to say, "He denies any involvement" or "He says he had nothing to do with the bombing" and to leave out the name as long as the man was not charged with a crime. In the end, he was exonerated and compensated by news companies for slander and libel.

The preposition *for* can appear prejudicial in a context like this: "Doaks was arrested for robbing the First National Bank on May 1." The "for" juxtaposed with "robbing" links him to the crime. This is impartial: *Doaks was arrested on a charge of bank robbery. The police allege . . .* (or *an indictment alleges . . .*). Some news media justifiably forbid any combination of *for* and a legal charge or complaint.

"Police said" and "police reported" are two of the most common phrases in crime reporting. A multitude of misstatements have followed. Such attributions do not shield news media against claims of defamation, particularly if no formal charges have been filed.

See also ACCUSED, ALLEGED, REPORTED, SUSPECTED; Pronouns, 5.

GUNNY SACK. *See* HINDI and HINDU.

GUY. The colloquial word for a man came from Guy Fawkes, conspirator in the Gunpowder Plot of 1605. To commemorate its thwarting, the English established the holiday Guy Fawkes Day and each November 5 would display and burn grotesque effigies of him. People called them *Guys. Guy* became a noun for an odd-looking or strangely dressed man, also a verb meaning to jeer at or ridicule. In the United States it began to be used in the nineteenth century as a slang synonym for chap, fellow, or man.

For generations, popular speech distinguished between *guys* and *gals* (or even *Guys and Dolls,* as in the musical play). TV reflected changes: In 1988 the moderator of a forum informed his panel, four women, that time was up by saying "Gotta go, guys." In the 1990s a female doctor asked five female patients, "Do you guys believe the [estrogen] research that is out there?"; and in sitcoms, men said to women, "Hi, guys" and "Come on, guys," and women said to women, "Ready, you guys?" and "Look, you guys."

Why women would want to take over the word got this answer in an op-ed article, "Women Aren't Guys," by a woman president of an advertising agency:

Why is it not embarrassing for a woman to be called "guy"? We know why. It's the same logic that says women look sexy and cute in a man's shirt, but did you ever try your silk blouse on your husband and send him to the deli? It's the same mentality that holds that anything male is worthy (and to be aspired toward) and anything female is trivial.

Maybe. Or perhaps some women turned to the male term because it was more terse and colloquial than *ladies* or *women* and they perceived *girl(s)* and its colloquial variation, *gal(s),* as taboo by feminist rules. Anyway, it remains unanswered why men would surrender a word that had been associated with males for so long.

H

HAD, HAS, HAVE. *See* HAVE, HAS, HAD.

"HAIRBRAINED." *See* HARE-BRAINED.

HALF. *1. With A. 2. With ONE.*

1. With A

A *half* is right at times, *half a* at other times; sometimes either phrase is right. But "a half a" is never right.

A restaurant review said a shrimp plate contained a garnish of shredded cabbage and carrots "and a half a sliced strawberry." The "a" before "half" was superfluous. Better: "and half a sliced strawberry."

Half is part of some terms, like a *half brother* or a *half-life*. You do not normally speak of "half a brother" or "half a life." Nor do you put *half* immediately before an adjective (as in "a half-sliced strawberry") unless *half* applies to the adjective ("sliced").

Either *half a dollar* or a *half-dollar* is correct; either *half an hour* or *a half-hour;* either *half a portion* or a *half-portion.*

When *half* adjoins a noun, the use or nonuse of a hyphen is often a matter of personal preference. Some terms are usually hyphenated, some usually unhyphenated; dictionaries differ on others.

2. With ONE

One and one-half miles (feet, days, etc.) is seen also as *1½ miles* and *a mile and a half.* A mixture of word and figure, "one and 1/2," is not standard.

Either *half of the land* or *one-half of the land* (population, weight, etc.) is correct, although the latter may add a shade of emphasis or precision.

Half can mean 50 percent of something or close to it (*half note, half-moon*); or partial(ly) or incomplete(ly) (*half crazy, half asleep*). It can serve as adjective, adverb, or noun.

See also **Verbs,** 3.

HANGAR and HANGER. *See* **Homophones.**

HAPPEN, OCCUR, and TAKE PLACE. Announced in a network radio broadcast: "The Senate vote is expected to happen Thursday." If the vote is expected, it will not "happen." It will *take place.* The latter is preferred when the action is prearranged or foreseen. An alternative correction is to leave out "to happen": "The Senate vote is expected Thursday."

Happen usually implies that the action has come about by accident or chance ("Something has happened to the plane") or that it is unforeseen ("How could it happen to such a strong man?").

In the words of an institute's executive, educational monthly programs "have been happening for about a year. . . ." They have been *taking place* or have been *presented*.

Occur often means the same as *happen;* that is, come about by accident or chance. From a broadcast: "The same road work that occurred yesterday afternoon is occurring today." The work was planned, so "occurred" and "occurring" are unsuitable. *Took place* and *taking place* are possible, but more often work is *done* or *performed*. "The same road work that *was done* yesterday afternoon is *being done* today."

Occur usually goes with more information than *happen*. "Find out what *happened*." / "The accident *occurred* at about 2 a.m. today at Hollywood and Vine." *Occur* can apply to a foreseen event: "The eclipse will occur at 9:17 this evening."

Other senses of *occur* are to come to mind ("It never occurred to them that they were in danger") and to appear or exist ("This flower occurs throughout the southern states").

HARD-BOILED. *See* BOIL.

HARDLY. *See* **Double negative,** *3;* (-) **EVER,** *6;* **THAN,** *2E.*

HARDY and HEARTY. *Hardy* means able to resist hardship, robust ("Astronauts must be hardy souls"), or, said of garden plants, able to get through the winter without special care. It is used in error here:

> Cooler weather and football season make a perfect time for hardy food.

Hearty is closer to the mark. In the context of food, it means ample, nourishing, and satisfying ("a hearty dinner") or requiring plenty of food ("a hearty appetite"). Food aside, it can mean cordial, genial ("a hearty greeting").

The two words have different ancestries. *Hardy* is traced to the Old High German *hartjan,* to make hard. *Hearty* is composed of *heart,* from the Old English *heorte,* plus the common suffix *-y.*

The sample sentence led an article on condiments in the food section of a large newspaper. Nothing more was said about football, and just how it was pertinent is not obvious.

HAREBRAINED. To be *harebrained* (adjective) is to have or reflect the brains of a *hare* (e.g., "a harebrained idea"). Some people mistakenly spell it "hairbrained." *Webster's Third Dictionary* legitimates the misspelling, making it an entry.

One who displays no more intelligence than that long-eared animal can be called a *harebrain* (noun).

Hare-brained and *hare-brain* are optional spellings.

HAVE, HAS, HAD. *1. Ambiguity. 2. Corruption. 3. Passive sense. 4. With TO.*

1. Ambiguity

The verb *have* has dozens of meanings. Its particular meaning in a sentence needs to be made plain. How do we interpret *have* in the following sentence of a radio broadcast?

> Half the mothers who have abused children were abused themselves as children.

That "have" can be a synonym for *are parents of* (if "abused," a past participle, is construed as an adjective modifying "children"). However, "have abused" can be construed as a verb phrase, as in the sentence "You *have abused* your power." (There *have* functions as an auxiliary verb, *abused* as a main verb, in the present perfect tense.) The speaker should have phrased the sentence better, perhaps in one of these ways, depending on her meaning: ". . . mothers who have abused their children . . ." / ". . . mothers with children who have been abused . . ." / ". . . mothers who are responsible for the abuse of children. . . ."

Some hasty readers may have been fooled by the second "had" in the extract below.

"But I cannot understand how each of these missiles could possibly have cost anywhere close to what they did, had this been an efficient operation," added Percy, who said he had "falsified time cards to support his argument."

The skimmers, interpreting "had falsified" as a verb phrase, may have concluded that a senator had admitted falsifying documents. Changing the second "had" to *held* or *possessed* or *could produce* would have eliminated the ambiguity. (Splitting that unwieldy sentence into two sentences also would have aided comprehension. The second sentence: "He said he held falsified time cards to support his argument.")

The sense of the sample below is easier to conjecture than the two previous samples, yet the sentence has faults. It deals with the detention of a Dutch visitor with AIDS.

Mr. Verhoef, who is 31 years old, was detained Sunday after Customs officials learned he has acquired immune deficiency syndrome when he stopped over at the Minneapolis-St. Paul International Airport.

Because "has" and "acquired" adjoin, they tend to form a verb phrase, as in the sentence *She has acquired money.* One who knew that AIDS stood for *acquired immune deficiency syndrome* could backtrack and reinterpret "has" as denoting possession. (Those misinterpreting the sentence might be fooled further by the placement of the phrase "when he

stopped over at the Minneapolis-St. Paul International Airport," which could make it appear that the visitor acquired the disease when he stopped over at the airport. *See* **Modifiers**, *3*. The tense would be wrong, but the tense is questionable however the sentence is interpreted: "learned [past] he has [present] . . ."? *See* **Tense**, *1, 2*.) Here is one way to rephrase the sentence (omitting one phrase):

Mr. Verhoef was detained Sunday when he stopped over at the Minneapolis-St. Paul International Airport and Customs officials learned that he suffered from acquired immune deficiency syndrome.

(The phrase "who is 31 years old" was irrelevant to the essential message of the sentence. One could wonder what the age had to do with the detention. A better location for that phrase, or for just the number 31, was four paragraphs earlier in the story, when the man was identified.)

See also **TENSE**, *5*, concerning the perfect tenses, which use *have, has,* or *had* as an auxiliary verb.

2. Corruption

Following the auxiliary verb *could, may, might, must, should,* or *would,* sometimes the *have* is wrongly replaced by "of"; for instance, "I could *of* gone fishing" and "They would *of* beaten us" (in place of *have gone* and *have beaten*). The misuser may be confusing "of" with the contracted *have,* as in *could've* and *would've,* which is acceptable in colloquial speech.

In another corruption, the *have* turns into an "a" attached to a helping verb: "Sheila *shoulda* come" and "Monty *musta* seen it" (instead of *should have come* and *must have seen*).

3. Passive sense

Nobody objects to the causative *have,*

or *had.* "She had her hair done." / "The company is having the store remodeled." The subjects cause things to happen.

What a few critics object to is this: "They had their house damaged in the storm." / "I'm tired of having my property defaced." The form is the same; it is active, yet the meaning is passive. The subjects do not cause the action; it is thrust upon them.

The passive use of the verb *have* is not new; it is found in the writings of Shakespeare and Dickens. An old *Webster's Dictionary* gave as one definition of *have* (verb, transitive) "to suffer or experience from an exterior source." Its example was "he *had* his leg broken." Sentences like that and "He broke his leg" have drawn ridicule from pedagogues, newspaper editors, and some grammarians.

A critic deplored such use of *have* as a "counterfeit" of the causative *have,* more feeble than the true passive. Among "depraved" examples: "The Newark team . . . had six . . . games rained out last spring." The suggested correction: "Six . . . were rained out"— scant improvement. The passive *have* has some reputable defenders. One found the meanings clear and the objections erroneous and pedantic. Another called the critics "lint pickers" but favored the rewriting of any ludicrous sentences.

A sentence like this does demand rewriting: "While she had her hair done, she had her car smashed by a truck." The second *had* is absurd; although it is supposed to have a different meaning, it parallels the first *had.*

4. *With TO*

Two sentences, from a folder issued by a hospital and from an essay by a political scientist, each misuse *to.* (In addition, both err in their pronouns.)

Every patient receiving general anesthesia or medication must have a re-

sponsible adult to accompany them home.

He [President Jefferson] wished, he said, to have Congress, who "exclusively" had the power, to consider whether it would not be well to authorize measures of offense.

In the first sentence, omit "to." In the second sentence, omit the second "to." When *have* is causative—when you *have* someone do something—"to" does not follow idiomatically. "I'll *have* [or "I *had*"] the plumber fix the sink"—not "to fix." / "Have an adult accompany him home." / "Have Congress authorize measures of offense."

(The other errors: [1] referring to a singular subject, "Every patient," with a plural pronoun, "them"; and [2] representing a thing, "Congress," by "who." *See* Pronouns, 2; WHO, THAT, and WHICH, 1.)

Have may go with *to* in other contexts. "I have a key to get inside" is correct. There *have* indicates possession and *to* indicates purpose. And *have to* is a proper phrase indicating obligation or necessity: "I *have to* [or "She *has to*"] go home."

See also TO.

HAVOC. *See* WREAK and WRECK.

Hawaii. Hawaii seems to be a foreign country to the copy editor who wrote a headline reading "Amfac [a conglomerate] says 'aloha' to U.S. divisions to focus on Hawaii" and a caption reading "Amfac will shed domestic units to stay in Hawaii."

Some people remain unaware that Hawaii has been the fiftieth U.S. state since 1959, the *Aloha State.* (*Aloha* is Hawaiian for *goodbye, hello,* or *love.*) A former kingdom, it was annexed by the United States in 1898 and became a U.S. territory in 1900.

It is composed of the Hawaiian Islands, once called the Sandwich Islands, a chain some 2,000 miles southwest of San Francisco. Hawaii is the most southerly state of the United States. It is not the most westerly; Alaska is.

Hawaii is properly pronounced Ha-WHY-ee—never Ha-WHY-uh, which some dictionaries condone; and never Ha-VIE-ee, which some people mistakenly believe is authentic. Its main islands are Hawaii; Kauai (cow-EYE); Maui (MAO-wee); and Oahu (owe-AH-who), on which the capital city, Honolulu (hano-LOO-loo), is situated.

A person lives *in* Hawaii, if you are referring to the State of Hawaii. One could live *on* Hawaii, i.e., on what is locally known as "the Big Island," the largest of the Hawaiian Islands in area, but it is better to specify "the Island of Hawaii" to avoid confusion.

Hawaii residents never call themselves "Hawaiians" unless they are descendants of the original Hawaiians, members of the Polynesian race. ("Race" is not a common word there; the people prefer "nationality.") Few pure Hawaiians survive, but many islanders are considered "part Hawaiian." To call anyone else a "Hawaiian" is to betray one's unfamiliarity with the islands.

The mainland's mass media seem incapable of dealing with Hawaii without sticking in the "paradise" cliché. Articles in two newspapers and a magazine were typically headed "Hawaii: Pint-size paradise" / "Debate in Paradise—Who's Hawaiian" / "Hawaii: Telecommuting from Paradise."

The use of that word to describe the Hawaiian Islands goes back at least to 1888, when a magazine called *Paradise of the Pacific* was founded in Honolulu. (It would last seventy-eight years.) *Paradise* means the kingdom of heaven, the abode of eternal bliss; and understandably that scenic, flowery, subtropical kingdom suggested it to some.

Notwithstanding the one-sided picture presented in travel promotions, Hawaii residents complain of many of the same problems that beset other Americans: problems concerning the environment, health, the law, living costs, population pressures, and so on. Then there are some distinctive troubles.

A volcanic eruption on one of the islands was the subject of TV news on the mainland. An anchor woman said, "There is more trouble in paradise tonight. Another home went up in flames on the Island of Hawaii." Isn't it odd that a land where lava consumes houses should remind her of heaven and not of the other place?

HEAD ON and HEAD-ON. *See* **Joining of words; Punctuation,** 4D.

HEADQUARTERS. *Headquarters,* meaning a center of operations, usually is treated as a plural noun. Below it is construed as singular.

> But already now, even while the Civic Forum searched for a headquarters and Mr. Adamec looked for new ministers, the faint outlines of the future were taking shape. . . .

The article "a" is not necessary. Yet few would flatly declare a singular construction of *headquarters* to be incorrect.

What is more disputable is using the word, sans *s*, as a verb. Nine-tenths of *The American Heritage Dictionary* usage panel rejected "The European correspondent will headquarter in Paris" and "The magazine has headquartered him in a building that houses many foreign journalists." The use of the past participle has become a fairly common colloquialism, especially in the passive ("is headquartered").

HE and HIM. *See* **Pronouns,** 10.

HEARTY. *See* HARDY and HEARTY.

HEBREW. *See* JEW, JEWISH, 2; YIDDISH.

Helping verbs (auxiliary verbs). *See* Verbs, *1, 4*.

HER and SHE. *See* Pronouns, *10*.

HER, HIS. *See* Possessive problems, *4*; Pronouns, *2*.

HEROIN and HEROINE. The two words are pronounced identically. Except for the *e* at the end of one, they have the same spelling. They are similarly rooted in Greek. But their meanings are vastly different.

A *heroine* is a female hero or the main female character in a work of fiction. It originated in the Greek *heroine*, feminine of *heros*, hero (via the Latin *heroina*).

Remove the *e* and we have *heroin*, a highly addictive narcotic, a derivative of morphine. Once used as an analgesic and sedative, it is now prohibited by the U.S. government. *Heroin* began as a German trade name in the late nineteenth century. It was adapted from the Greek stem *hero-*. Perhaps the coiner had the original sense in mind, but the modern perception is that one who takes up that drug is less a hero than a fool.

A weekly paper said a state law "permits the use of heroine, LSD and methamphetamines" when prescribed. *Heroin. Webster's Third Dictionary* inexplicably accepts the wrong spelling along with the right.

HERSELF. *See* Pronouns, *3, 4, 5*.

HETEROPHOBIA. *See* HOMOPHOBIA.

"HIGH COURT." The highest court in the United States is the Supreme Court. What are we to make of the following?

> The state of Missouri appealed the case to the High Court.

> . . . The High Court . . . ruled that . . . the Federal Tort Claims Act . . . did not protect officials who may have been negligent. . . .

Contrary to such writings, there is no American court called the "High Court." It is a term concocted by journalists in their perpetual search for synonyms.

Inasmuch as *high court* is not a real name, it makes no sense to capitalize it. (A better case can be made for using a capital *S* in "State of Missouri.")

HIM and HE. *See* Pronouns, *10*.

HIMSELF. *See* Pronouns, *3, 4, 5*.

HINDI and HINDU. A dictionary says, "*Gunny* comes from the Hindu word 'goni'. . . ." Correction: it is a *Hindi* word (meaning gunny sack). *Hindu* pertains to Hinduism, the religion that is predominant in India. The language is *Hindi*. It is the official language of India, a literary language based on a group of northern Indian vernacular tongues, to which the term *Hindi* sometimes is applied also.

A *Hindu* is a believer in the *Hindu* religion. Westerners used to erroneously apply that name, or "Hindoo," to any Indian. A *Hindi*, a less common term, is a northern Indian whose native language is in the *Hindi* lingual group.

HIS, HER. *See* Possessive problems, *4*; Pronouns, *2*.

HISPANIC. *See* LATIN(-)AMERICAN.

"HISSELF."   *See* **Pronouns,** *5.*

HISTORIC and HISTORICAL.   *1.*
The difference. 2. HISTORIC news?

1. The difference
The two adjectives are not synonyms.
The *-al* makes a difference.

An event that is famous or important
in history—such as Columbus's discovery in 1492 or the first trip to the moon,
in 1969—may be called *historic.* Sometimes the word is used more loosely to
describe a contemporary event that one
thinks or hopes will prove *historic.*

That which pertains to the topic of
history or contributes to the record of
history—a society, a document, etc.—is
historical. So is a book, a show, etc.
based on historic events. Dickens's story
of the French Revolution, *A Tale of Two
Cities,* is a historical novel. However, in
referring to the academic subject, *history*
usually serves as an adjective: a *history*
teacher, course, or textbook.

When an indefinite article precedes either word, it is usually *a,* as in "a historic
voyage" or "a historical movie." *See
also* **A and AN.**

2. HISTORIC news?
The word *historic* is used freely in the
press. There it often pertains, not to an
event of long ago, but to a current event,
usually one that has been anticipated.

A main headline proclaimed a "Historic Global Trade Pact." Another, in a
second newspaper, announced: "Historic anti-crime bill passed by the Senate." Did the editors possess a deep
knowledge or sense of history? Or was it
just their way of letting readers know
that the issues those events resolved—after prolonged and prominent debate—
were important?

The historical importance of a "historic" current event is open to argument.
This was broadcast: "NASA today
called off an historic space mission." To
apply "historic" to something that does
not even happen may be going too far.

HOBSON'S CHOICE.   A *Hobson's
choice* is a take-it-or-leave-it offer. It is
the choice of taking either that which is
offered or nothing at all. All three quotations misuse the term.

> [A news magazine:] King Fahd . . .
> faced a Hobson's choice: he could go
> it alone, leaving his small and scat-
> tered army to answer Iraq's battle-
> hardened troops, or he could call in
> the U.S. and lay bare his ties.

> [A talk-show host on the choice be-
> tween a child and a career:] A lot of
> women have to make that decision
> and it's like a Hobson's choice, isn't it?

> [A poll taker, as quoted in a newspa-
> per:] "Both candidates appear to be
> highly flawed. . . . For Democrats, it's
> a real Hobson's choice."

Each statement describes a *dilemma,* not
a "Hobson's choice."

The expression is said to have originated in the practice of Thomas Hobson,
of Cambridge, England, who died in
1631. He let horses and required each
customer to take the horse nearest the
stable door or none.
See also **DILEMMA.**

HOLD.

> Hey, voters, get
> ahold of yourselves

Get *what?* What is that strange amalgam, displayed prominently in a headline on the op-ed page? Could it be a
typographical error? No; there it goes
again, in the text of the article:

> It's time for the American elector-
> ate to get, as they say, ahold of itself.

Regardless of what "they say" to the writer and his editor, the proper idiom is to *get* (or *catch* or *lay* or *take*) *hold of* something. It means to seize or grasp it.

A *hold* is (among other things) a grip or an act of holding. Under no circumstances should *a* and *hold* be stuck together.

To *get* (or *lay* or *take*) *hold* of something can also mean to acquire it.

HOLD UP, HOLDUP, HOLD-UP. See **Crimes**, *3*.

HOME and HOUSE. The first paragraph of an article deals with "homes"; the second, with "houses." Then "homes" are mentioned several times more.

> Low mortgage interest rates and a smaller supply of homes for sale in the last six months helped break what had been a free fall in Alameda County home prices.
>
> Houses in a few neighborhoods even increased in values since the last survey. . . .
>
> Livermore has a stock of relatively smaller and older three-bedroom homes [and so on].

What is the difference? Not much to the writer, who has largely accepted the word pushed by real estate people (although the second paragraph may indicate a twinge of journalistic conscience). They prefer to call a residential *house* for sale a "home," bare and unoccupied though it may be, thereby helping to convey the notion that they sell security, comfort, happiness, and the like.

To Edgar A. Guest, there was a good deal of difference between the two words. He wrote in his poem *Home:* "It takes a heap o' livin' in a house t' make it home."

People have made their *homes* in other than *houses*—in caves, cliff dwellings, hogans, huts, igloos, lake dwellings, lean-tos, pueblos, tepees, wickiups, wigwams, yurts, and of course apartments. On the other hand, a *house* in which nobody lives is nobody's *home*.

On national television one saw flames consuming *houses* in Glendale, California. Firemen in helicopters dropped chemicals on what a voice called "the homes." They were now hardly "homes."

Homographs and homonyms. See **Homophones.**

HOMOPHOBIA. The Greek *phobos,* a fear, is the origin of the noun *phobia,* a morbid, or unhealthy, fear; an intense, persistent, irrational dread of a thing, being, or situation. The suffix *-phobia* is part of many words that indicate types of morbid fear, such as *acrophobia,* fear of heights; *agoraphobia,* fear of being in a public place; and *claustrophobia,* fear of being in a confined place.

A dictionary of psychology defines *homophobia* as (1) "A morbid fear of homosexuality" and (2) "A morbid fear of mankind." (The combining form *homo-* is from the Greek word *homos,* meaning same; while *Homo,* the genus including mankind, is from the Latin *homo,* meaning man.) An encyclopedia of phobias defines *homophobia* as "Fear of homosexuality or becoming a homosexual." An approximate antonym is *heterophobia,* "Fear of the opposite sex. . . ."

The common element in all the definitions is fear, yet that element is often lacking in the current use of the word, as in an editorial:

> Who cares who Ellen is sleeping with? . . . Those rock-ribbed Americans who'd sooner puke than applaud Ellen's lesbianhood. . . . This show . . . will just harden their homophobia to tensile strength.

When the meaning is a dislike of homosexuals or opposition to homosexual practices and there is no fear, let alone phobia, it is better to explain what is meant than to miss the mark with *homophobia*. If a lone noun is needed, a possibility is *antihomosexuality* (adjective *antihomosexual*); another, which would fit the editorial, is simply *hatred*.

Homophones. The English language contains an abundance of words (or linguistic units) that are pronounced or spelled like other words but have different meanings. Let us define three such categories:

- *Homographs,* words that are spelled alike but pronounced differently (e.g., *wind,* moving air; and *wind,* to coil or turn).
- *Homonyms,* words that are spelled and pronounced alike (e.g., *bear,* an animal; and *bear,* to carry or withstand).
- *Homophones,* words that are spelled differently but pronounced alike. In the following examples, writers have absent-mindedly replaced correct words with their homophones.

According to a news item, an editor "said he hoped the former aide to Richard Nixon would right an afterword" for a book by Nixon. Plainly *write* (to compose sentences) was confused with "right" (which also can be a verb, e.g., to right a wrong).

A famed lexicographer wrote in a letter that he had sunk "waste deep" in snow in the Alps. He meant *waist* (the narrow part of the torso), not "waste" (refuse or an act of wasting).

Under a proposal by the president, "overall Federal spending would be held constant accept for inflation." Someone at a newspaper confused *except* (a preposition meaning other than) with "accept" (a verb meaning to take something offered). The pronunciations differ slightly.

An op-ed piece about telephone solicitors said "their ought to be a law." Make it *there* (the adverb), not "their" (the possessive pronoun). Sometimes *they're,* the contraction of *they are,* is confused with one or the other.

A movie review said "he crawls into a construction sight. . . ." *Site* (a place) would be right, not "sight" (a view). A third word that sounds the same is *cite,* to quote, refer to, or officially summon or mention.

Forty other groups of homophones are listed below in boldface, a pair or triplet in each paragraph. They are arranged alphabetically and briefly defined, many with illustrations of use. Additional homophones are dealt with in other entries, listed after this list. *See also* **Confusing pairs.**

Ad, a short form of *advertisement;* "a classified ad." **Add,** to combine numbers; "to add or subtract." **Ad,** Latin for *to,* found in terms like *ad hoc* (literally *to this*), meaning for this specific purpose; and *ad infinitum* (literally *to infinity*), meaning endlessly.

Altar, an elevated place for religious rites; "the couple standing at the altar." **Alter,** to change or modify; "to alter the pants."

Ante- (prefix), before; *antedate, anteroom.* **Anti-** (prefix), against, *antifreeze, antitrust.* **Auntie** or **Aunty,** aunt, an affectionate or familiar form.

Away, in another direction, from a place, from one's possession; "turned away" / "went away" / "gave it away." **Aweigh,** clear of the water's bottom, said of an anchor; "anchors aweigh."

Bail, a security payment to insure a defendant's appearance in court; "released on $5,000 bail." **Bale,** a large bundle, compressed and tied; "a bale of hay."

Base, a foundation, fundamental ingredient, headquarters, or starting point; "paint with an oil base" / "our base of operations." **Bass,** a low-pitched voice or musical instrument; "The singer is a bass" / "He plays the double bass."

Bazaar, a market place or benefit sale; "a Middle Eastern bazaar" / "a church bazaar." **Bizarre,** strange, grotesque; "a bizarre sight."

Bough, a large branch of a tree. **Bow,** a respectful lowering of the head or body; also the front of a ship.

Brake (noun), a device for stopping a vehicle; (verb) to stop a vehicle. **Break** (noun), a fracture or pause; (verb) to fracture or pause.

Breadth, width, extent; "traveling the length and breadth of the land." **Breath,** air inhaled; "a deep breath."

Callous (adjective), hardened, insensitive; "a callous attitude." **Callus** (noun), a hardened part of the skin; "calluses on their hands."

Cannon, a big gun. **Canon,** a rule or principle; a body of church law.

Canvas, heavy cloth; "painted in oil on canvas." **Canvass** (noun), an inspection or solicitation, "the candidate's canvass of the district"; (verb) to inspect or solicit, "to canvass the district."

Cession, a formal yielding; "cession of territory under the treaty." **Session,** a meeting or sitting; "Court is now in session."

Chord, a combination of musical notes; "a G-major chord." **Cord,** a string or thin rope; "tied with a cord."

Council, a group of people serving as an assembly for advice, legislation, discussion, etc.; "the city council." **Counsel,** advice, "wise counsel"; attorney(s), "defense counsel." **Consul,** one who represents a foreign government in a particular city; "the Danish consul in Seattle." (Its first vowel rhymes with *Don;* that of the other two words rhymes with *down.*)

Discreet, prudent, acting properly reserved; "a discreet witness." **Discrete,** separate, having distinct parts; "four discrete sections of the work."

Dual, double, related to two; "dual engines." **Duel,** a fight, often under traditional rules; "shot in a duel."

Flair, a natural ability; "a flair for sports." **Flare** (noun), a blaze of fire, or a signal of fire or light, "Rescuers saw the flares"; (verb) to blaze or burst out, "Tempers flared."

Gamble, to risk money on a game of chance; "gamble on the lottery." **Gambol,** to frolic, to skip about; "children gamboling in the garden."

Hangar, a structure for housing airplanes. **Hanger,** a frame for hanging clothes.

Idle, not active, not kept busy; "idle hands." **Idol,** an image of a deity; "a Polynesian idol."

Lama, a Buddhist priest or monk of Tibet or Mongolia. **Llama,** a woolly, domesticated animal of South America.

Lesser, smaller, less important or serious; "the lesser evil." **Lessor,** an owner of property who lets it under a lease to a *lessee.*

Manner, a way of doing; "I am native here and to the manner born." **Manor,** a landed estate; "an English manorhouse."

Medal, a small piece of metal cast or awarded in someone's honor; "a gold medal." **Meddle,** to interfere in a matter that is not one's business; "Don't meddle in our private affairs."

Metal, a class of hard, elemental substances or alloys such as iron, silver, and bronze. **Mettle,** quality of character, spirit, or courage; "Both fighters showed their mettle."

Miner, one who works at extracting minerals from the earth. **Minor** (noun), one who is not yet a legal adult; (adjective) lesser, the opposite of *major,* or (in music) related to a minor scale.

Passed, the past tense of *pass;* "I passed the exam." **Past** (noun or adjective) time before the present; "remembering the past" / "in the past month."

Peace, absence of hostility; calmness. **Piece,** a fragment or part.

Pedal (noun), a foot-operated lever; (verb) to operate such a device, "to pedal a bicycle." **Peddle,** to work at selling goods carried from place to place; "to peddle brushes."

Plain (noun), a level, treeless region, "the midwestern plains"; (adjective) obvious, simple, unadorned, "plain talk." **Plane** (noun), airplane, carpentry tool, flat surface, or level, "a higher plane"; (adjective) flat, "a plane figure."

Pore (noun), a small opening, as in the skin; (verb) to gaze at or study carefully; "He pored over the volume." **Pour,** to let flow; "pour the tea."

Rain, water condensed from atmospheric vapor that falls to earth in drops, or its falling; figuratively a shower of anything, "a rain of sparks" / "a rain of blows." **Reign,** rule, sovereignty, or dominance; "the reign of George III" / "a reign of terror." **Rein,** a strap for controlling a horse, attached to a bit in its mouth and held by the rider; figurative restraint or guidance, or the means thereof, "a tight rein on government spending."

Role, a part in a performance, or a function; "to play a role." **Roll** (noun), something rolled up, a list of names, a small bread loaf, a swaying motion, or a loud sound; "a roll of tape" / "honor roll" / "sweet roll" / "rock and roll" / "roll of thunder"; (verb) to revolve, move by repeatedly turning over, or move on wheels, or to cause such movement; "to let the ball roll" / "to roll the ball."

Session: see **Cession** in this list.

Sole (noun), a shoe bottom or a fish; (adjective) lone, only, "the sole heir." **Soul,** human spirit, "bless her soul."

Stationary, not moving, not changing; "stationary equipment" / "stationary philosophy." **Stationery,** writing paper and related supplies; "sold in a stationery store."

Trooper, a mounted policeman or soldier, or a state policeman. **Trouper,** a member of a troupe of performers, a performer of long experience, or (informally) a loyal worker.

Vice, a wicked practice. **Vise,** a clamping device.

Weather, the condition of the atmosphere. **Whether,** in either event; either; if.

See also the following entries:

AFFECT and EFFECT
ALL TOGETHER and ALTOGETHER (etc.)
BLOC and BLOCK
BORE, BORNE, and BORN
CAPITAL and CAPITOL
COMPLEMENT and COMPLIMENT
EXERCISE and EXORCISE
FAUN and FAWN
FAZE and PHASE
GRISLY, GRIZZLY, and GRIZZLED
HEROIN and HEROINE
INCIDENCE and INCIDENT
ITS and IT'S
LEAD (verb) and LED
LOATH and LOATHE
MARSHAL
NAVAL and NAVEL
PRINCIPAL and PRINCIPLE
Pronouns, 8.
Punctuation, *1*B.
RACK and WRACK
SHEAR, *1*.
TO, TOO, and TWO
TROOP, TROOPS, and TROUPE
Verbs, 2 (medal)
WHOSE, 2
YOUR and YOU'RE

HONORABLE, HONORARY, HONORED. *1. HONORABLE. 2. HONORARY; HONORARIUM. 3. HONORED IN THE BREACH. 4. TIME-HONORED.*

1. HONORABLE
Honorable, usually in its abbreviated form, *Hon.,* often precedes the names of high public officials, despite the dishonorable records of some. It is used in let-

ters and formal documents in this way: *Hon.* (or *the Hon.*) *John Doe, secretary of state.*

It goes with the full name, not with the surname alone as in "Hon. Doe." It is a term of respect, not a true title. *Hon. Senator and Mrs. Richard Roe* is right. "Hon. and Mrs. Richard Roe," as used sometimes, deprives him of his title.

Honorable is an adjective only, literally meaning characterized by, possessing, or worthy of honor. "Brutus is an honorable man." (*See also* **REVEREND.**) The related adverb is *honorably.* "You performed honorably."

2. *HONORARY; HONORARIUM*

Usually *honorary* (adjective) describes either (1) a title or position granted as an honor with no payment, duties, or privileges, as *honorary chairman,* or (2) something else given solely as an honor without any actual utility, such as an *honorary degree* conferred by an educational institution (sometimes to honor the institution more than the official honoree).

Honorary originally meant of honor or conferring honor, the word's meaning in Latin; e.g., "The simple crown of olive, an honorary reward" (in ancient Greece).

A word that sounds similar but has a much different meaning is *honorarium* (noun), a voluntary payment to a professional person for special services when no fee is set or legally required.

3. *HONORED IN THE BREACH*

A custom or rule that is more honored in the breach than in the observance is one for which a person deserves more honor for breaking than for observing.

A book on English usage says a certain grammatical rule "is honored now more in the breach than in the observance." The intended meaning is that the rule is broken more often than it is kept.

This illustrates a common misapplication of the saying.

The source is Shakespeare's *Hamlet,* in which Hamlet, the Prince of Denmark, says, "it is a custom / More honor'd in the breach than the observance." The reference is to the custom of wassail, revelry with spirituous toasts to health. (*See also* **Prepositions,** 4, end.)

4. *TIME-HONORED*

"Negative campaigning is a time-honored tradition in this country," a network broadcaster said. A story that followed described political mud-slinging since the days of Jefferson, tending to disparage it.

Perhaps he meant "time-honored" as irony. The practice of defaming one's political opponents is commonly *dishonored,* not *honored.* To *honor* (verb, transitive) something or someone is to treat it or him with *honor* (noun): esteem, regard, respect, or reverence. To *dishonor* something is to insult it or treat it with disrespect, as the broadcaster did to mud-slinging.

Anyway, "time-honored tradition" was redundant. One dictionary's definition of *tradition* is "A time-honored practice. . . ." *Time-honored* means honored, observed, or carried on because of antiquity or long continuation.

HOPEFULLY. Nobody denies that the adverb *hopefully* can mean in a hopeful manner, showing hope, feeling hope, or with hope. "Striding hopefully to the betting window, I slapped down my twenty-dollar bill."

However, a controversy goes on between those who would restrict the word to its primary meaning and those who would allow it to serve as a synonym for "I hope" / "let us hope" / "it is hoped" / or "we can hope." Such use has become increasingly popular since the sixties.

A radio newscaster tells of a standstill

at the airport and adds, "The fog is lift-ing and hopefully things will be return-ing to normal." The "things" are not doing any hoping. Then who is? The newscaster is, but she is not in the sen-tence. Her "hopefully" modifies noth-ing. It just dangles there.

Hopefully may eventually be admitted to the elite society of absolute construc-tions, words and phrases that are per-mitted to dangle; but its time has not yet arrived. See **Modifiers,** 1D.

HOUSE. See HOME and HOUSE.

HOW. *How* (adverb) means in what manner or way ("How did the accident happen?"), by what means ("I wonder how he does that trick"), in what condi-tion ("Tell me how she is"), or to what amount, degree, extent, etc. ("How ex-pensive and how good a car do you want?"). It can be used as an intensive or as part of an exclamation ("How sweet!") and colloquially it can amount to *why?* ("How so?")

One thing it is *not,* at least in standard usage, is a substitute for *that.* Such use of "how," or sometimes the phrase "as how," is highly informal or regional. So is the phrase "being as how" or "seeing as how" in place of *because* or *inasmuch as.*

An urban daily newspaper devoted a front-page article to a family's display of wooden sheep on a hillside.

It has something to do with how K—— once kept live sheep there and how he and his wife, J——, are ex-pecting their second child.

The article says nothing about the man-ner in which he kept live sheep (e.g., loose on a hillside, watched by a shep-herd) and nothing about the manner in which the couple are expecting their child (e.g., cheerfully with monthly cele-brations). The newspaper people seem to

have used "how" as a substitute for *the fact that* (or, the second time, for *that*). How can they do it? In a substandard manner with little thought.

HOWEVER. *See* BUT, *5;* (-)EVER, 4.

HUSH MONEY. *See* **Crimes,** 2.

HYPER- and HYPO- prefixes. *See* **Confusing pairs.**

Hyphen. *See* **Punctuation,** 4.

HYPOTHESIS and **THEORY.** Some people use the two words inter-changeably, encouraged by some dictio-naries. That is how a certain book on English usage uses the words (emphases added):

> Among the various other *theories* concerning the alphabet are the *hy-potheses* that the alphabet was brought by the Philistines from Crete to Palestine, that the various ancient scripts of the Mediterranean countries developed from prehistoric geometric symbols [etc.]. . . . Another *hypothe-sis,* the Ugaritic *theory,* evolved after an epoch-making discovery. . . .

Among "theories" are several "hypothe-ses"? Another "hypothesis" is a "the-ory"? The writers seem more intent on avoiding repetition of a word than avoiding confusion among readers.

Those who want to be precise or sci-entific distinguish between the two words in this way:

A *hypothesis* is much more tentative. It has much less evidence to support it or no evidence at all. It is an unproven proposition, supposition, or plain guess that is accepted tentatively to explain some facts or to serve as the basis for study, investigation, or experimentation.

A *theory* is bolstered by a good deal of evidence and usually is more elaborate.

It is a system of principles to explain certain phenomena that have been observed; the principles have been at least partially verified.

The *nebula hypothesis* and the *planetesimal hypothesis,* for example, are alternative, unproven explanations for the origin of the solar system. On the other hand, Einstein's special and general *theories of relativity*—dealing with space, time, mass, energy, and gravitation—have been repeatedly tested in experiments and are generally accepted by the scientific community.

In view of the abundance of alternative explanations for the creation of the alphabet, *hypothesis* would seem to be an apt label for each.

I

I and i. The letter *i* should be dotted in lower case and only in lower case. A capital *I* should never get a dot. Although dotted capital *I*'s are seen on innumerable homemade signs, they offend the eyes of professional sign painters, calligraphers, typographers, and others sensitive to the letters of our alphabet.

In the opening episode of a television comedy series, a learned professor chalks the word "HUMANITIES" in capital letters on a blackboard. A coed tells him impudently: "When you write the letter *I*, the dot is supposed to go over the *I*. They teach you that in the first grade." Actually his letters are perfectly correct (though nobody putting on the show seems to know it). The episode ends as the professor dots the capital *I* in "RENAISSANCE"—erroneously.

I and ME. *See* **Pronouns,** *10.*

"I COULD CARE LESS." *See* **"COULD CARE LESS."**

-ICS ending. *See* **Plurals and singulars,** *2G.*

"IDEA WHOSE TIME HAS COME." This phrase dates from 1943 at the latest, and its time should have expired by now. Instead it is going strong as a cliché. Example:

[From a lecture:] Mind-body medicine is an idea whose time has come.

Or, put in the past:

[From a book:] But book clubs were an idea whose time had come.

It amounts to a fancy way of saying that the idea is or was popular. (For those taking the cliché literally, questions arise: Does every idea, even a trivial one, have a "time"? What determines it? What about conflicting ideas, wrong ideas, bad ideas?)

In 1943 a circular from *The Nation* attributed this sentence to Victor Hugo's diary: "There is one thing stronger than all the armies in the world; and that is an idea whose time has come." Its origin was probably *Histoire d'un crime* by Hugo: "An invasion of armies can be resisted; an invasion of ideas cannot." (Source: *The Home Book of Quotations.*)

Some still combine Hugo's thought about the invincibility of ideas with the timeliness notion. In an article about the Romanian revolution of 1989, a professor of political science wrote:

The luminous courage of [the Rev. Laszlo] Tokes and his supporters proved, yet again, that no force can resist an idea whose time has come.

The particular idea discussed was that of political freedom. In the same year, a similar idea came to Communist China, but lethal force resisted it.

IDENTICAL. *1. Modifiers. 2. Prepositions. 3. Related words.*

1. Modifiers
An author describes a visit to a remote village in Niger, Africa.

> Looking at the young men, all of pure blood, I noticed their faces were indeed somewhat identical.

". . . Their faces were indeed *similar*" would make more sense. "Somewhat identical" is impossible.

Somewhat (adverb) means rather, or to a limited extent or degree. *Identical* can mean the very same or exactly alike. Either way, *identical* cannot be diminished by modifiers like "a bit" / "rather" / "slightly," and "somewhat," any of which contradicts it. Some modifiers, such as *almost* or *completely,* which leave the second sense at least mostly intact ("The two paintings are almost identical"), are acceptable. *Identical* in the first sense ("He is the identical man who robbed us") may not be modified at all.

2. Prepositions
Is this picture identical *with* that picture? Or is it identical *to* it? Grammarians have disagreed.

Theodore Bernstein would accept either preposition. Wilson Follett would not use *to:* "a thing [has] identity *with,* not *to,* another." That is so, and that is the British tradition, but American idiom accepts either, and you may choose.

3. Related words
Words related to the adjective *identical* include the adverb *identically,* the nouns *identicalness* and *identity,* and the verb *identify.* All are traced to the late Latin *identitas,* identity.

In mathematics, an equation that is satisfied for all values of its symbol(s) is called an *identical equation.*

In logic, a proposition whose subject and predicate amount to the same thing ("Nonexistence is not existence") is an *identical proposition.*

In poetry, an *identical rhyme* uses words or syllables that have the same sound, such as *beat* and *beet.*

Identical twins are siblings who developed from the same ovum and look the same.

Identic is an archaic version of *identical* as well as a diplomatic term. It may be defined as the same in form and substance though not the same in wording; for example, *identic* communiqués issued by the United States and Russia.

IDLE and IDOL. *See* Homophones.

IDYLLIC. *Idyllic* means rural, naturally charming or picturesque, or suitable for an *idyl* (also spelled *idyll*), a pastoral poem. What is *idyllic* here?

> . . . His friends believed that the youngest of the Elliotts spent an idyllic childhood: growing up with his father, his mother, Lee, one brother and three sisters in Manhattan. . . .

If the boy had grown up in, say, the Catskills, his childhood could have been described as *idyllic.* The adjective hardly seems appropriate when associated with modern Manhattan.

An author writes about his experiences:

> The days had been idyllic and made for strolling, for sitting at sidewalk cafes, for sipping wine under a canopy.

The author was in Paris, a metropolis of some two million people and, however pleasant, no more *idyllic* than New York City.

In response to a suggestion that youngsters be taught to ride motorcycles properly, the host of a talk show said on television:

That's a great idea in an idyllic world, but that's not the way we live.

Did he really think that motorcycles would improve a pastoral setting?

People often use "idyllic" mistakenly in place of *ideal,* a word that would fit all three quotations.

The two sentences that follow do have pastoral elements, but they are overwritten.

Still, if The Avalanche [a Texas newspaper] mostly reflects an idyllic rural life style, it's also a revealing indicator of change.

It [an anti-American poster in Moscow] has been replaced by a new poster with drawings of a young American boy and a young Soviet girl in an idyllic, pastoral scene.

"Idyllic rural" and "idyllic, pastoral" are both redundant. ("Revealing indicator" is no model of terseness either.)

See also BUCOLIC.

I.E. (that is). *See* Punctuation, 2A.

IF AND WHEN. *See* UNLESS AND UNTIL.

IF clauses. *See* Subjunctive; WAS and WERE.

ILK. A grammar says, "The indefinite pronouns are *one, someone, anyone . . .* and others of this same hazy ilk."

If you must use *ilk* in that way, at least never do so in Scotland, and leave out "same." *Same* was the original meaning

of *ilk,* in the Middle Ages, and remains its meaning in Scotland, at least in a narrow way. As an adjective, *ilk* used to appear in a phrase like this: *the ilk night,* meaning the same night.

In modern times, *ilk* serves mainly to identify someone. It is used in a phrase like *Macduff of that ilk,* meaning of that same (*name* is understood). It signifies that the person has the same name as the place he owns or comes from. It is like saying *Macduff of Macduff.*

In the United States and England too, *ilk* is used loosely—*The Oxford English Dictionary* says "erroneously"—as a noun meaning class, kind, or family. It is usually meant to be facetious or derogatory.

A comedian said in an interview, "It's an unwritten rule among people of the same ilk." The same *ethnic group?* (The "rule" presumably is that they may deride their group while outsiders may not.)

ILLUSION and DELUSION. *See* Confusing pairs.

IMMANENT, IMMANENCE. *See* EMINENT and IMMINENT.

IMMEMORIAL. A candidate had accused an opposition party of dirty tricks. The leveling of such a charge is "a method that has been tried since time immemoriam," a commentator said on television.

The nonword that came forth seemed to be a mixture of *immemorial* (the word that he probably was aiming at) and *in memoriam.* The former means back in time beyond recorded history or human memory. The latter is a Latin phrase used in epitaphs and obituary notices, meaning *in memory.*

IMMIGRATE and EMIGRATE. *See* EMIGRATE and IMMIGRATE.

IMMINENT, IMMINENCE. *See* EMINENT and IMMINENT.

IMPACT. *1. A forceful noun. 2. IMPACT as a verb. 3. IMPACTED, an adjective.*

1. A forceful noun.

A forceful word is being enfeebled. Blame the increasingly sloppy and pretentious ways in which people who ought to know better are tossing it around these days.

An *impact* is a violent contact or a striking of an object against another, or the force or shock of that contact or striking together.

Too often it serves as a fancy synonym for *effect, importance, influence, result,* or the like.

Interviewed on television, an economist was asked about the effect of Midwestern floods on prices. He answered that it would have "a very small impact, almost unnoticed by the consumer."

Strictly speaking, "a very small impact" is a contradiction. If an effect is so small that one can hardly notice it, "impact" is not the word to choose.

Use *impact* to suggest violence or power in the way things come together. When a giant meteor struck the earth, there was an *impact.* When two speeding cars collide head on, there is an *impact.* When a leaf falls gently to the ground, or when we talk about an economic *effect,* there is no impact.

A television reporter made the following statement. (Emphasis is added to it and the ensuing examples.)

> Zebra mussels have already had a great *impact* on ways of doing business. Until scientists control their numbers, that *impact* will continue to grow.

Those passive, immobile mollusks literally have no "impact" on anything (with the possible exception of minute organisms that enter their systems). Even if a creative commentator could devise a way in which zebra mussels entered into a figurative "impact," that "impact" would not "continue to grow." An *impact* does not grow.

The popular press is as accountable as anyone for the enfeeblement of the word. These are excerpts from three successive paragraphs of a news story:

> Other press analysts argued that reporters' party registration had no *impact* on the fairness of coverage. . . . Even inside journalism's most influential institutions there are sharp divisions on the *impact* personal views may have on coverage. . . . He [an editor] said he feared political affiliations "could have an *impact* on coverage."

A learned professor of political science used the noun "impact" 100 times in an otherwise illuminating, 289-page book. He used "impact" 4½ times as often as the combination of *effect* and *influence,* two words that he could well have substituted throughout.

> Collectively, they [elements of the environment] have a substantial *impact* on the Court's decisions, an *impact* that merits examination. . . . It is likely that Congress has exerted a subtle *impact* on the Court's policy choices. . . . Of course this kind of subtle *impact* is difficult to ascertain. . . .

An *impact* is not "subtle." It is forceful. More examples from the same book:

> We can gain a fuller sense of the Court's *impact* on society and the forces that shape that *impact* by looking at a few areas of the Court's activity. These examples provide reminders that the Court's *impact* is complex.

. . . Until the late 1980s it generally gave them [civil rights laws] expansive interpretations that enhanced their potential *impact*. There is evidence that the federal laws against employment discrimination have had a significant *impact* on the economic status of black citizens; this *impact* can be ascribed primarily to the other branches.

And so on and on.

2. IMPACT as a verb

Now that *impact* has been weakened, the next step in its ruination is the misuse of it as a verb. Two newspaper examples follow.

So the question on many people's mind is how will the downtown/waterfront ballpark impact our already congested streets and roadways?

She expressed concern about how providing the initial medical treatment service . . . might impact other services at the hospital.

Change each "impact" to *affect*. (In the former sample, also change "mind" to *minds* and the virgule, or slash, to a comma and space.) The writers not only used "impact" in the wishy-washy sense but further misused it as a verb. The noun and the verb express considerably different ideas and are pronounced differently.

Impact (noun), a violent contact, was discussed in the first section. It is pronounced IM-pact.

To *impact* (verb, transitive) is to squash something or to press things together tightly, the way a garbage truck *impacts* garbage. It is pronounced im-PACT.

The writers must have gone to school. What accounts for such slovenly English? An article quoted a Massachusetts superintendent of schools turning the word in question into an intransitive verb. As a teacher, she had tried to tame an unruly little pupil, and "the time I had spent with him impacted on the other children." She may have meant it *affected* them. It probably did not squash them.

This example is from a form letter to bank customers:

From a customer's perspective, this general decline in interest rates has favorably impacted mortgage interest rates, which are at their lowest level in many years.

Does the letter contain metaphor—a vision of interest rates being squeezed down—or merely a piece of roundabout prose?

3. IMPACTED, an adjective

Impacted (adjective), pronounced im-PACT-ed, means jammed together, packed tightly in, or firmly wedged. It is used correctly in this sentence from a book, concerning an airplane flight in northern Africa:

The firmest sand for our runway was the impacted Land-Rover track.

Impacted has technical meanings in dentistry and medicine, denoting teeth or fractured bone ends that are abnormally wedged, or trapped dejecta. A dentist may say, "You have an impacted tooth," perhaps speaking of a wisdom tooth that is firmly wedged in its socket and cannot emerge through the gum. An *impacted* condition is an *impaction* (noun).

This is from a book on marketing:

Any purchase is basically made on impulse, and response levels can be seriously impacted if the potential respondent does not act within a short time span.

The author presumably means that sales may be few if ad readers do not act soon. Would he advertise a bug killer by saying, "Pest levels will be seriously impacted"?

On a radio talk show, a lawyer presented the type of final argument that he thought the prosecution should make in a current murder trial. The hostess responded with an adjectival creation, "It's an impactful statement to have been made," as though the misuse of the *i*-word as a noun and a verb were not enough.

IMPARTIAL. *See* **DISINTERESTED and UNINTERESTED.**

IMPEACH, IMPEACHMENT. A news announcement on a radio network and a headline in a newspaper reflected a popular misconception that "impeachment" meant removal from office:

The Senate impeached him [a federal judge] on charges stemming from a perjury conviction—kicked him off the bench.

Hatch predicts Senate
won't vote to impeach

"Impeached" and "impeach" should have been *convicted* and *convict*. The Senate does not "impeach" anyone. The Constitution says:

The House of Representatives . . . shall have the sole power of impeachment. . . . The Senate shall have the sole power to try all impeachments.

To *impeach* a public official is to present him with official charges of wrongdoing in office. Following *impeachment,* he goes on trial. If he is a federal official of the United States, the Senate tries him. If the Senate convicts him, in a two-thirds vote, the penalty cannot exceed re-moval from office and disqualification to hold a federal public office, although the convicted person remains liable to prosecution elsewhere.

The House of Representatives impeached two presidents: Andrew Johnson in 1868 and William J. Clinton in 1998. The Senate tried both but convicted neither. In 1974 President Richard M. Nixon avoided impeachment, for which the House Judiciary Committee had voted, by resigning as president.

To *impeach* (verb, transitive) in a general sense is to discredit or impugn (a person or his motives, testimony, etc.).

Imperative. *See* **Mood; Subjunctive,** *1.*

IMPLICATION. *See* **IMPLY and INFER.**

IMPLY and INFER. The difference between these two words is like the difference between saying and thinking. A speaker or writer *implies.* A listener or reader *infers.*

To *imply* (verb, transitive) is to say indirectly, to hint or suggest. "The writer implies that the mayor is crooked."

To *infer* (verb, transitive or intransitive) is to conclude from evidence, to reason on the basis of something known or assumed. "From the facts in the article, a reader infers that the mayor is crooked."

At times "infer" is used by mistake when *imply* is meant. Misunderstanding can result. "He inferred that Charlie was the culprit" indicates that he drew such a conclusion from evidence. "He implied that . . ." indicates that he made a suggestion that may not have been backed by evidence.

The second edition of *Webster's Dictionary* gave as the (fifth) meaning of *infer:* "Loosely and erroneously, to imply." *Webster's Third* substitutes "to give reason to draw an inference concerning: HINT." That is a meaning of *imply.* Two misuses are quoted, including this from a

British weekly: "did not take part in the debate except to ask a question *inferring* that the constitution must be changed." *Implying*.

Something implied or the act of implying is an *implication* (noun). Something inferred or the act of inferring is an *inference* (noun).

A political commentator evaluated the performance of Jack Kemp in a so-called vice-presidential debate: "In no way did he buckle Al Gore's knees or, by inference, Bill Clinton's." Kemp would have involved President Clinton by *implication*. It would have been up to listeners to draw an *inference*. The speaker would be hinting, suggesting, *implying*. The listeners would be reasoning, concluding, *inferring*.

IN. *See* **DISINGENUOUS and IN-GENUOUS; EMIGRATE and IMMIGRATE; EMINENT and IMMINENT; INTO,** *1;* **LIVE,** *2;* **ON,** *3;* **Prepositions,** *1, 2, 6;* **TO,** *2.*

IN ATTENDANCE. This phrase enters accounts of meetings and other gatherings; for example:

> Responses to a four-page questionnaire given to those in attendance . . . will be taken into consideration in developing the education reform package. . . .

"In attendance" is not wrong but somewhat stilted and drawn out. *Present* or even *attending* would be crisper in that example.

One writer seems fond enough of the phrase to use it three times in one article:

> Those in attendance last night . . . might have been years removed from the segregated world that Robinson challenged. . . . [*See also* **MAY and MIGHT**.] Branch Rickey III . . . was in attendance. . . . Also in attendance

were Sandy Koufax, Lou Brock and Reggie Jackson.

Chaucer had no need for "in attendance" when he wrote "A Shipman was ther" / "A good Wyf was ther," and so on. "About 100 were in attendance at the meeting" can be simplified to "About 100 were *there*" or "100 *attended*" or "100 were at the meeting."

IN A WORD. This sentence appears in a book by a law professor:

> In a word (though requiring many qualifications), the laws and policies of the federal government are made by the Congress (even if largely, now, on Executive initiative), are carried out and enforced by the President, and applied by the courts in particular cases.

A word? Forty words follow "in a word."

The phrase can make sense when used by a person of few words: "How was the show?" / "In a word, lousy." One who is verbose can render it ludicrous, as in the sample sentence. (That sentence has another failing: an inconsistent series. Either leave out the second "are" or insert a third *are* just before "applied." *See also* **Series errors,** *9.*)

INCIDENCE and INCIDENT. The nouns *incidence* and *incidents* sound alike. They confused a congressman, who said, in a widely broadcast speech to the Senate, "she related these incidences"—instead of *incidents*.

An *incident* is a particular occurrence or happening, sometimes relatively trivial ("There was an amusing incident at work today"), sometimes troublesome ("A border incident could set off a war"). It can also be an episode in a literary work. ("The final incident in the play comes as a surprise.") Those who use *in-*

cident without qualification as a euphemism for a criminal, violent, or other unpleasant event ("Opponents booed the marchers, but there was no incident") may be overstretching the word.

Incidence can mean occurrence in general or in the sense of extent, range, or manner of occurring. ("The incidence of the disease is widespread in this area." / "I'm surprised at the incidence of this species so far north.") It can also mean a falling on or striking, or the way in which something falls on or strikes something else. ("The angle of incidence was 45 degrees.") The word is not usually made plural.

Two adjectives are *incident,* meaning likely to occur in connection with ("the dangers incident to a fireman's life"), and *incidental,* occurring or likely to occur by chance or as a minor result of something ("incidental expenses"). A related adverb is *incidentally,* meaning in an incidental way, apart from the main matter, or by the way. The spelling *incidently* is obsolete and now usually considered wrong.

INCLUDE. *See* COMPRISE, 2.

Incomplete sentence. *See* Sentence fragment.

INCREDIBLE. If an announcer shouts about an "incredible offer," take him at his word and don't believe it. *Incredible* (adjective) primarily means not believable. It is from the Latin *incredibilis,* based on *in-,* not, and *credibilis,* credible, from *credere,* to believe.

Many people came to use the word in a second way, to express not skepticism but amazement. Thus one might call a strange story or sight *incredible,* finding it hard to believe but still believing it.

Still looser lips have diluted the word to an insipid slang sense, far removed from that of unbelievable. When a broadcaster said, "These are some of the authors that are incredible," his intention was to recommend their works. "Incredible" to him probably meant very good, great, superb, or any of dozens of synonyms. Yet he was literally condemning their veracity.

See also **Double meaning** (end); **FABULOUS**; **FANTASTIC**; **INCREDULOUS**.

INCREDULOUS. *Incredulous* (adjective) means skeptical, disbelieving, or unable to believe. That meaning applies only to people. "Despite his aggressive sales talk, she remained incredulous." *Incredulous* can also refer to something one does to express disbelief: "With an incredulous wave of the hand, she left the show room."

Incredulous should not be confused with *incredible,* meaning not believable, which applies either to things or to people. The use of *incredulous* to mean incredible is obsolete and now generally considered erroneous.

The defendant in a prominent lawsuit had just testified. Emerging from the courtroom, a man commented on television, "It was totally incredulous, everything he said." Correction: "It was totally *incredible* [or "*unbelievable*"] ..." or "*I* was totally incredulous *about* everything he said."

The word is barely changed from the Latin *incredulus,* from *in-,* not, and *credulus,* credulous.

See also **INCREDIBLE**.

INCREMENT. Sharing the first five letters of *increase* and its basic idea as well, *increment* derives from the Latin *incrementum,* meaning growth or increase. The quotations, from newspapers, show some skewed uses of our word.

If a horse pays $2.40 for $2 to show at the track, the OTB bettor gets only $2.20 for $2—supposedly a 5 percent surcharge but effectively as much as 50 percent because payoffs are rounded to the nearest 20-cent increment.

According to a billing statement inadvertently submitted by Root to the FCC in a Sonrise case, the money provided for Root would be kept by Sonrise and parcelled out to him in $1,500 increments as he billed the firm.

The first sentence seems to use "increment" to mean point; the second, to mean installment. *Increment* (noun) does not mean either. It is an increasing, or something that is added, or the amount of gain, or the amount by which something is growing. The idea of increase goes with *increment*.

Increment as a verb (transitive and intransitive) is not used often. A technical manual says:

The line feed counter will be incremented one count for each line advance.

The word is used there correctly, although "be incremented" is a roundabout way to say *add*.

INDEPENDENCE. *See* DEMOCRACY, FREEDOM, and INDEPENDENCE.

INDESCRIBABLE, UNDESCRIBABLE. In the wake of a hurricane on the Hawaiian island of Kauai, a television reporter was on the scene. "It really is undescribable," he said. Somehow he managed to describe it anyway, having been sent there to do so.

On another program, a historical documentary, the narrator said "the storm swept down with a grandeur and power that are indescribable." She was thereby describing it.

Undescribable is not wrong, although it is much less common than *indescribable*. They are paradoxical. It is hard to think of anything that is impossible to describe—perhaps some of the ultimate secrets of the universe?—yet that is what those adjectives mean. Nevertheless, when either is used, it is liable to accompany some kind of description. Even "indescribable joy" is a description.

A synonym is *inexpressible,* less often *unexpressible* (adjectives), not subject to expression. An *inexpressible* (noun) is something that cannot be expressed. At one time *inexpressibles* applied to trousers. So did *unmentionables* (noun), which denoted underwear also and occasionally is still so used, in a jocular way. An *unmentionable* is that which should not be mentioned. *Unmentionable* (adjective) means unfit to be mentioned.

Another synonym is *unspeakable* (adjective), meaning beyond speech, unfit to be spoken, or extremely bad or objectionable.

See also **Verbal unmentionables.**

INDIAN (AMERICAN). *See* MISNOMER; RACE and NATIONALITY.

Indicative. *See* Mood; Subjunctive; Tense, 1.

INDIFFERENT, INDIFFERENCE. *See* DISINTERESTED and UNINTERESTED.

INELUCTABLY. *See* Range, true and false, 2.

INEVITABLE. It is easy to say about something that has already happened that it was "inevitable." Who can prove that it was not? Part of a main story in an eminent newspaper said:

After the legislation had staggered under its own weight and the withering attacks of Republicans and insurance interests for months, Senator George J. Mitchell, the majority leader, bowed to the inevitable and announced that Congress would not pursue the issue any further this year.

"The inevitable" seems to have been ascribed supernatural power and station: One bows to it. The supporters of the bill (dealing with health care) probably did not know that it had been doomed by that mystic force, so they tried for months to pass it. The writer would have saved them all that trouble by informing them earlier of its fate.

That which is *inevitable* (adjective) is certain to take place. It cannot be avoided, evaded, or prevented. Few events in society are like that.

An example of the fallacy of attributing inevitability to past events is a statement in a paper written by a collegiate freshman. Upon researching the Populist movement of the 1890s, I penned the vacuous sentence "It was inevitable that the farmers would revolt." Think of all the oppressed people of the world who do not "revolt."

Decades later, a network broadcaster commented, "It was probably inevitable that Hollywood would team up with Michael Jordan." At least the "probably" left some room for doubt, but think of all the sports stars with whom Hollywood has *not* teamed up.

Applying *inevitable* to future human events is especially dubious. (Some schools of thought deny the existence of free will, but who can predict the future with certainty?)

The word was part of an exhortation to Congress and radio listeners by President Franklin D. Roosevelt on December 8, 1941:

> With confidence in our armed forces, with the unbounded determination of our people, we will gain the inevitable triumph, so help us God.

That "inevitable triumph" was conditioned upon two variables, those of "confidence" and "determination." Yet even their fulfillment must not have ensured inevitability; otherwise why was God entreated to "help us"?

In a historical documentary on television, a narrator made the statement "But American participation in the war [World War I] was inevitable." In place of "was inevitable," *came in 1917* or *was declared by Congress* or almost any other pertinent fact would have been more informative.

During the height of the so-called Cold War between the United States and the Soviet Union, one often heard the sentence "War is inevitable," anticipating an atomic war between the two nations. Such a war did threaten on many occasions, but now that the Soviet Union is no more, the speakers of that phrase are proved wrong. Nevertheless, it was a dangerous phrase, fostering as well as reflecting a grim fatalism.

See also DESTINY.

INEXPRESSIBLE. *See* INDESCRIBABLE, UNDESCRIBABLE.

INFER, INFERENCE. *See* IMPLY and INFER.

Infinitive. *1. Definition; description. 2. Gerund versus infinitive. 3. Perfect infinitive. 4. Split infinitive.*

1. Definition; description

The *infinitive* is the basic form of a verb: for instance, *know, leave, run,* and *stop.*

The word *infinitive* comes from the Late Latin *infinitivus,* unlimited. The *infinitive* is not limited by tense, person, number, etc. (that is, not *inflected*).

It is identical with the imperative form, *go* or *help;* also with the form of the ordinary present tense in the third person plural, they *speak* or they *walk,* and in the first person singular (except for I *am*), I *think* or I *see*.

Usually an *infinitive* is indicated by *to:* "He wanted *to know*."/ "She needs *to leave*."

Infinitives without *to* regularly follow some verbs, such as *can, let, may, might, must,* and *should* ("The man can *run*" / "You should *try*"), and appear in certain constructions ("A crowd watched them *fight*" / "I will quit rather than *move*").

To plus *infinitive* may act as a noun, either in the subject ("*To build* is a noble art") or in the predicate ("Maria loves *to sing*"). It may also act as an *adjective* ("John has an ambition *to fly*") or as an *adverb* ("They came *to help*").

One *to* normally suffices for multiple infinitives of similar construction: "I want *to finish* my work and *go home*"— the second *to* is understood. But a subsequent *to* may be desirable for emphasis: "I come *to* bury Caesar, not *to* praise him."

The use of *to* to indicate the infinitive ("I want *to* buy a pig") should not be confused with any other use of *to*, e.g., to indicate direction or purpose ("I'm going *to* town *to* buy a pig"). *See* TO.

See also Verbal, *3;* Verbs, *1.*

2. Gerund versus infinitive

When to use the *gerund* and when to use the *infinitive* puzzles some writers and speakers. It is the difference between *seeing* and to *see,* between *laughing* and to *laugh*. The first is the *-ing* form of a verb when it serves as a noun. The second is the basic form of a verb, preceded by *to*. For instance, a broadcaster said:

Not all dry cleaners share Robin B——'s enthusiasm to protect the environment.

A more idiomatic phrasing would be "enthusiasm *for protecting* the environment." Some other nouns would go with the infinitive: e.g., "*desire* to protect" /

"*wish* to protect." Still other nouns would go with the gerund: e.g., "*concern* for protecting" / "*idea* of protecting."

An infinitive is needed in this sentence, by a news agency:

HELSINKI—President Boris N. Yeltsin of Russia yesterday acknowledged his failure in winning President Clinton's promise that no former Soviet republic will ever be allowed to join NATO.

"In winning" should be *to win.* A correct example of the former: "She is encouraged by her success in winning the tournament."

There are no rules pointing to one form or the other. It is a matter of idiom and knowing how each verb is used. Dictionary examples can be instructive.

See also Gerund, *3.*

3. Perfect infinitive

A form that borrows the term *infinitive* but should not be confused with the form defined in *1* is the *perfect infinitive.* Examples are *to have gone, to have made,* and *to have sung.* Using *to have* and a past participle, it normally expresses action that is, was, or will be completed before another action or event indicated in the same sentence. "I'm happy *to have won* your confidence." / "The office seemed *to have been* ransacked." / "They plan *to have built* the house by the end of the year."

Sometimes the *perfect infinitive* is unneeded, as in this sentence from a novel: "He would have liked *to have hugged* his father." Probably at that moment he would have liked *to hug* his father.

Another example of a misuse of the *perfect infinitive:* "I planned to have moved." It reverses the logical time sequence. Make it "I *had* planned to *move*"; the planning had to precede the moving.

"He wants to be the first to have

bought a ticket" can be trimmed to "He wants to be the first to *buy* a ticket."

4. *Split infinitive*

To walk typifies the normal infinitive form. *To quickly walk* is a *split infinitive.* It is an infinitive form in which *to* and the verb are separated by a modifier (an adverb in the preceding example).

Grammarians differ on the matter. One writes, "Don't split your infinitives. They'd rather remain intact" (Karen E. Gordon). Another writes that "the split infinitive is an improvement of English expression" (George O. Curme).

Split infinitives can be awkward, especially when separated by more than a word or two. They can also be helpful at times in communicating one's meaning.

The two quotations that follow contain awkward splits. A radio announcer said, about the temperature, "It's supposed to Sunday night drop lower." The end of the sentence would have been a better place for "Sunday night." Worse yet: in a sentence from a book, telling the author's purpose, fourteen words separate *to* and the verb. (Those two words are emphasized here.)

Its main idea is *to* historically, even while events are maturing, and divinely—from the Divine point of view—*impeach* the European system of Church and States.

On the other hand, the fear of splitting infinitives results in ambiguities like this:

Some of the stones . . . failed completely to melt before they reached the ground.

It was quoted by Sir Ernest Gowers, whose comment cannot easily be improved upon:

Did the hailstones completely fail to melt, or did they fail to completely melt? The reader has to guess, and he ought never to have to guess.

In a book on lexicography, a seeming effort by its authors to avoid a split infinitive has resulted in something worse:

General lexicographers were commonly content to use the *Dictionary* as a mine, without attempting greatly to extend its limits, at least until Richardson and Webster.

Did the lexicographers make no great attempt or did they not attempt a great extension? That is, which verb was the adverb "greatly" meant to modify: "attempting" or "extend"? More likely the authors intended the latter but wanted to steer clear of *to greatly extend.* They could have written "to extend its limits *greatly,*" if they did not mind giving *greatly* more emphasis.

. . . Linguistic stiffness . . . is a factor [in air accidents] that the NTSB investigators, because of their own verbal awkwardness, have been unable quite to recognize.

The writer of a magazine article failed to recognize the verbal awkwardness of "quite to recognize" instead of "*to quite* recognize."

The style books of The Associated Press and *The New York Times* call for generally avoiding split infinitives but sometimes making exceptions. The latter condones "He was obliged *to* more than *double* the price" but forbids "*to* clearly *show.*" In the following sentence, from a *Times* article, an infinitive has been justifiably split in the manner of the forbidden example (emphasis added):

A special prosecutor said in court papers made public today that she would urge the Supreme Court *to* quickly *overturn* a Federal appellate decision Friday that struck down the Federal law on special prosecutors.

Where else could the adverb go? "To overturn *quickly* . . . a decision" would separate verb from object, in Germanic fashion. "She would urge the Supreme Court *quickly*" could be misleading.

Sometimes a *split infinitive* is hard to avoid: "*to* half *surmise* the truth" (Robert Browning); "his fortune being jeopardized, he hoped *to* more than *retrieve* it by going into speculations" (Theodore Roosevelt); "I've heard enough *to* about *do* for me" (Willa Cather). Furthermore, it can contribute to poetic rhythm.

In his grammatical treatise, George O. Curme devoted five pages to examples of split infinitives by such writers as the poets Burns ("to nobly stem tyrannic pride"), Wordsworth ("to still further limit the hours"), and Byron ("To slowly trace the forest's shady scene"). Curme said that inserting an adverb between *to* and the infinitive was a six-century-old practice that "cannot even in the strictest scientific sense be considered ungrammatical." Yet he drew the line in some cases: "Almost everybody, however, puts *not* before the *to* of the infinitive. . . ." For example, "He promised *not to* do it again," rather than "*to not* do it again." His explanation: *not* is felt as modifying, not the verb, but the infinitive phrase as a whole, *to do it again.*

One writer seemed unable to decide between splitting and not splitting negative infinitives, so she split the difference:

Once called the loneliest man in America because of his agreement *to not* only integrate the major leagues but agree *not to* lash back at those who assailed him, he knew the importance of his task.

Make it "*not only to* integrate." (In addition, omit "agree," which is redundant; and substitute *also,* which is missing. *See* **NOT ONLY.** A question of style is whether the twenty-nine words before the comma belong with the seven words after.)

The splitting of infinitives, by adverbs and also by pronouns, goes back to the fourteenth century. A Biblical translation by John Purvey in 1388 said, "It is good *to* not *ete* fleisch and *to* not *drynke* wyn." (The Revised Standard Version says, ". . . It is right not *to eat* meat or drink wine. . . .")

The practice, not common over the centuries, spurted in the nineteenth century; it was then that grammarians drummed up opposition to the form. Their knowledge of the classical languages of Greek and Latin, in which the infinitive is a single word, may have influenced them. The term *split infinitive* came later, near the end of the nineteenth.

The infinitive was a single word in Old English. It was a verbal noun (what the gerund is today), indicated by the suffix *-an* (or *-ian*); for instance, "Ongan he *writan*": he began to write. The *to* going with the infinitive originally meant *toward.* Thus *to do* in the sentence "Anger drove him *to do* it" would be construed as *toward the doing of.*

Nowadays the *to* that goes with the infinitive, while categorized as a preposition, often is not felt as a preposition and serves merely as a signpost pointing to the infinitive word or phrase. Yet many consider it to be part of the infinitive.

The reality today is that the unsplit infinitive remains the norm, and doubtless there are more than a few people who find the split kind somewhat discomforting. But you need not avoid splitting an infinitive if you have good reason to split it. A good reason is that it either expresses your meaning more clearly or sounds more natural.

Bear in mind that a phrase like "*to be*

adequately financed" or "*to have* slightly misjudged" is *not* a *split infinitive*. It is not wrong for an adverb (*adequately*) to separate an auxiliary verb (*be*) from a main verb (*financed*). Grammatical authorities agree on that.

An excessively finicky British official wrote, "They appeared completely to have adjusted themselves to it." He had evidently put the adverb in that abnormal position in the belief that "*to have* completely adjusted" would split an infinitive. It would not. The infinitive would have been split by "*to* completely *have* adjusted."

INFLAMMABLE. *See* FLAMMABLE, INFLAMMABLE, and NON-FLAMMABLE.

Inflected and uninflected forms. *See* Infinitive, *1*.

INFORMATION. *See* FACT.

INGENIOUS, INGENUOUS, and DISINGENUOUS. *See* DISINGENUOUS and INGENUOUS.

-ING form of verb. *See* Gerund; Participle.

Initials. *See* Abbreviation.

IN MEMORIAM. *See* IMMEMORIAL.

INNOCENT. *See* Guilt and innocence.

INNOVATION. When a radio announcer said "There's been a lot of new innovation in the area of laser surgery," she was using a redundant *new*. All *innovation* is new.

Innovation (noun) is something that is newly introduced; a change in method, device, or mode of doing things; or the act of *innovating*. To *innovate* (verb, in-

transitive) is to introduce something new or change that which is established.

IN NO WAY, IN NO WISE. *See* NO WAY.

IN ORDER TO. *See* TO, 2 (end).

IN PERSON. *See* PERSON, 2.

INSECT. The word *insect* properly applies only to a minute animal with six legs in the class Insecta. A book on first aid uses it loosely when it says:

> Insect bites and stings are not usually dangerous except from the black widow spider, the brown recluse spider, and the scorpion.

A spider, scorpion, tick, or mite is an *arachnid*, in the class Arachnida; each has eight legs.

Popular speech often lumps all tiny creatures together as "insects" or "bugs." A news magazine reported, under an article titled "INSECT ASIDES," that "all sorts of bugs are making news." Its first example concerned Japanese panic over an infestation of spiders—*arachnids*.

A *bug* is a crawling insect or, more specifically, a type of crawling insect with a mouth adapted for piercing and sucking.

INSIDE. *See* INTO, *1*.

INSOFAR AS, IN SO FAR AS. *See* FAR.

INSTINCT. A book by a lexicographer says, "We can all, by instinct, construct sentences more or less effortlessly." By "instinct"? Although definitions vary, most sources agree that what the term *instinct* concerns is essentially inborn rather than learned. One learns a language. Perhaps this is what the author meant: "We can all construct sentences without much conscious effort."

Instinct is often loosely used when *aptitude, impulse, intuition, reflex, skill,* or *the subconscious* is meant.

The Random House Dictionary ably defines *instinct* primarily as "an inborn pattern of activity or tendency to action common to a given biological species." A migratory pattern of a bird or a mating pattern of a fish may be termed an *instinct.* The tendency to act in such a manner or even the presumed force behind that tendency is also at times called an *instinct.* The choice of behavior is innate, although environmental events may trigger it and modify it.

Related words are *instinctive* (adjective) and *instinctively* (adverb). A newspaper article said:

> The driver of the Redman car instinctively braked when he saw the boulder flying toward them. . . .

"Instinctively" should have been dropped or perhaps changed to *reflexively.* A *reflex* is an involuntary response to a stimulus.

INSURANCE and ASSURANCE, INSURE and ENSURE. *See* ASSURE, ENSURE, and INSURE, *1.*

INTER- and INTRA- prefixes. *See* Confusing pairs.

INTEREST, INTERESTED. *See* DISINTERESTED and UNINTERESTED.

INTERMINABLE. *Interminable* (adjective) literally means not terminable, unending, lasting forever. Few things last forever, if anything does. One could strictly speak of the *interminable* universe, although some cosmologists believe that even the universe will end eventually.

The word can be extended to mean unending for practical purposes ("the sun's interminable energy") or seeming to last forever ("the country's interminable fiscal troubles"). However, it does not make sense to apply it to something that plainly has an end, as a college teacher did:

> Moving up the state's presidential primary would only lengthen the already interminable period of presidential selection.

Logically, that which is *interminable* cannot be lengthened. Anyway, to apply that word to a period of presidential selection is absurd. The period terminates on the day that a president is elected.

A critic called a film a "brain-numbing barrage . . . that lasts nearly two hours," and he ridiculed a scene at "the end of this interminable picture." It terminated after nearly two hours. "The end of this interminable picture" is a contradiction.

A music reviewer wrote of a symphonic concert with "an interminable intermission." The conductor "filled the second half of the concert with . . . extroverted tone painting. . . ." Inasmuch as the concert had a second half, the intermission was not *interminable.*
See also ETERNITY.

IN TERMS OF. *1. Legitimate and illegitimate uses. 2. Need for another preposition. 3. Need for rewriting or rethinking.*

1. Legitimate and illegitimate uses

The phrase *in terms of* is encountered often in speech and writing, and usually it is empty verbiage. It has a legitimate use; it introduces a translation to another language, jargon, or way of speaking:

"The buyer must beware—or, in terms of Latin, *caveat emptor*." / "In terms of baseball, our fund drive enters the ninth inning and to win we need a home run with the bases loaded." / "To win back her love, you have to start talking in terms of endearment."

More often its use is either a slovenly way of tying together two dissimilar ideas or a pretentious substitute for a simple word or phrase that is more to the point. Frequently one of these will do the job better than "in terms of": *about, as, as for, as to, by, concerning, of,* and *regarding.* Even the three-word phrases *with regard to* and *with respect to* may be preferable.

2. *Need for another preposition*

Expressing something in other terms through mathematical equation is what science does continually. Yet the loose use of "in terms of" is not absent from scientific writing.

In a book on contemporary physics, the authors use "in terms of" three times in as many pages. (Emphasis is added to the excerpts.)

> Though we have described the process of electron scattering *in terms of* the exchange of a single photon between two charged particles, there is also the possibility that two, or more, photons will be exchanged.

> These [nuclear] forces each have their associated fields, which can be described *in terms of* messenger particles, analogous to photons.

> The existence of similar descriptions of all three forces—electromagnetic, weak and strong—*in terms of* messenger particle exchanges has encouraged the belief that a common unified description of the forces might be found.

In the first and third sentences, they could have replaced "in terms of" with *as;* in the second sentence, with *as exchanges of.* Again, there are valid uses for *in terms of.* The authors explain forces and fields *in terms of* quantum electrodynamics.

Occasionally all one needs to do is leave words out. A medical researcher is explaining the close relationship between human immunodeficiency virus and simian immunodeficiency virus:

> "*In terms of* the target cells they enter, *in terms of* the known modes of transmission, and *in terms of* the disease caused, they are very similar."

Except for the first "In," the emphasized words could be scrapped with no sacrifice to the message.

3. *Need for rewriting or rethinking*

Sometimes no first aid will help; the sentence must be recast or the ideas must be rethought. This newspaper sentence concerns a breaking and entering at a political campaign office in Washington, D.C.:

> Last night's "vandalism," the word preferred by Martin D. Franks, executive director of the committee, according to Mr. Johnson, was so insubstantial, in terms of what were termed "sensitive files" that remained locked in undisturbed cabinets, that the committee denied permission today for photographs.

". . . In terms of" is bad enough. ". . . In terms of what were termed" compounds the trouble. The sentence could have been patched up by replacing "in terms of" with *inasmuch as* and throwing out the first "that." Other faults would remain, however. (The story mentions "Mr. Johnson" four times, never saying who he is. Moreover, by the placement of the phrase "according to Mr. Johnson," it tends to apply only to the "word preferred" phrase. And the clause about photographs is almost a non sequitur.) So the story was revised for a later edition:

> "Vandalism" was the word preferred by Martin D. Franks, executive director of the committee, to describe last night's incident, according to Mark Johnson, the campaign committee's press secretary. . . .
> What he described as "sensitive files" were still safely under lock and key, he said.

The revised story (saying nothing about photographs) is an improvement. (But "What he described as" is unnecessary, inasmuch as "sensitive files" is in quotation marks and the sentence ends with "he said.")

The passages below are from a biography. Nothing but thorough recasting of the sentences could help them.

> In terms of the prosecutor's future philosophy, there seemed not to be one word in the controversy about the freedom of the press provided under the First Amendment.

> In terms of professional memberships, moreover, nothing succeeded like success, as Black himself noted in an interview published after his death—"I was trying a lot of cases against corporations, jury cases, and I found out that all the corporation lawyers were in the Klan. . . ."

Sticking an "in terms of" into a sentence is no replacement for clear thinking. No one can be expected to speak in terms of a future philosophy or otherwise foresee the future. (Besides, there cannot be one word about press freedom; it takes at least two words.) The first sample sentence from the biography could be rewritten this way:

> The prosecutor's arguments did not foreshadow his future philosophy. There seemed to be nothing in the controversy about. . . .

The latter quotation from the book is unwieldy and obscure, somehow tying professional memberships to the cliché about success and tacking on a quotation with still another idea. A rescue attempt would be futile.

INTERNECINE. *Internecine* (pronounced inter-NIECE-sin, among other ways) is a useful adjective in the sense of mutually destructive. It comes from the Latin *internecinus,* meaning murderous. A word so derived should be expected to bear the concept of deadliness. Indeed *internecine* originally meant characterized by bloodshed or slaughter.

It came to mean deadly to both adversaries in an armed conflict. This is a useful interpretation, for no other single word expresses the idea.

Still later, it was given another twist. Evidently assuming that the first six letters came from *internal,* some began applying *internecine* to internal conflicts, e.g., "America's internecine struggle of the 1860s."

Now we often find the element of deadliness, the essence of *internecine,* slighted or forgotten altogether and the word serving merely as a synonym for *internal* in connection with verbal, political, or other harmless disagreements within a group.

In a TV forum, a newspaper publisher was discussing South Africa's leadership:

> Botha and his successor, de Klerk, are apparently having internecine warfare.

They were not actually shooting at each other; they simply disagreed on policy.

This is from a prominent newspaper:

The prospect of a Warner defection in two years could shatter the party unity . . . and throw Republicans into an internecine war.

No weapons would be discharged in the so-called war, only words.

To adapt that distinctive and powerful adjective to such unexceptional uses is like resorting to a pistol to dispatch a cockroach.

Interrogative sentence. *See* (-)EVER; Punctuation, 9.

INTO. *1. IN and INTO. 2. IN TO and INTO. 3. Slang use.*

1. IN and INTO

The preposition *in* indicates position, location, or condition. Among its various senses, it means inside; within the area or confines of (the house, the city, the deal, etc.).

The preposition *into* indicates motion, direction, or change in condition. It often means to the interior of (a place); from the outside to the inside of (the place).

"The children are jumping *into* the pond" clearly indicates their movement from the banks to the water. "The children are jumping *in* the pond" is less clear; they may have already been in the water when they started jumping.

"We walked *into* the house" clearly indicates that we entered the house. "We walked *in* the house" is less clear; we may have already been in the house when we decided to tour the place.

Some contexts in which *into* is right allow *in* as an option. "They let him into [or "in"] the country." / "Throw the peel into [or "in"] the trash can."

The verb *put* goes with either *in* or *into*. ("Put the dishes in [or "into"] the cupboard.") But idiom dictates the companionship of the verb *place* and *in*. ("Place the dishes *in* [not "into"] the cupboard.")

Into can also mean against ("The truck crashed into a utility pole"), to a certain form or condition ("The vase broke into little pieces" / "Matter can change into energy"), to an occupation ("She is going into real estate"), or toward ("We must look into the future").

2. IN TO and INTO

When *in,* serving as an adverb, comes in contact with the preposition *to,* a writer may erroneously unite them. The resulting "into" can grossly distort the meaning.

Such a mistake could cause alarm. "The ship came *in* to the pier" simply means that it docked. "The ship came *into* the pier" means that it crashed.

The mistake could cause just mirth. "A man wanted as an army deserter for fifteen years turned himself into the sheriff's office last night." Unless the reporter was describing a magical transformation, the *in* and the *to* should have been separate.

3. Slang use

"Fred is *in* sales" indicates that selling is his occupation. "Fred is going *into* sales" indicates that he intends to enter that occupation. The era of "flower children" and "Do your own thing" brought the use of *into* in the sense of a continuing participation in a vocation or avocation. One would say "I'm into painting," instead of "I do painting" or simply "I paint."

The term persisted, and a daily paper said a designer of science exhibits was "so into tornadoes" that his contribution to a testimonial dinner was a chocolate tornado. "Into" was a columnist's slangy substitute for *absorbed in, con-*

cerned with, enthralled by, interested in, or *taken by.* Prepositions are not normally modified, yet "so" was forced to modify "into."

INTRA- and INTER- prefixes. *See* Confusing pairs.

Intransitive and transitive verbs. *See* Verbs, *1.*

INTRIGUE, INTRIGUING. Did the writer of this headline (ten years after the Watergate scandal) intend to convey a double meaning? "Why Nixon Is Still Intriguing."

Intriguing can mean plotting *intrigue.* Intrigue as a noun means secret or underhanded scheme or scheming. It can also denote a secret love affair (one thing that Nixon was not accused of). The verb *intrigue,* in its most settled meanings, means (intransitively) to engage in *intrigue* and (transitively) to plot, to cheat, or to achieve or get through intrigue. The present participle is *intriguing.*

Commonly the verb *intrigue* (transitive) is used as a synonym for enchant, excite, fascinate, interest, make curious, mystify, puzzle, or perplex; *intriguing* as an adjective meaning enchanting, exciting, fascinating, etc. Such use is not accepted by all.

H. W. Fowler pooh-poohed it as a Gallicism (it came from the French transitive verb for puzzle, *intriguer*) "confusing the sense of a good English word." His reviser, Sir Ernest Gowers, wrote that a reason for its popularity was that it could convey the meanings of two words at once; he cited *puzzle* and *fascinate.* "But," he went on, "it is still true that *intrigue* is often used in place of a simpler and better word. . . ."

Theodore Bernstein found the verb turned into "a fuzzy, all-purpose word" in place of various precise words. Just 52 percent of *The American Heritage Dic-*

tionary's usage panel approved of the popular use of the verb. On the liberal side, Roy H. Copperud called such use "well established . . . despite carping by some pedants."

These are excerpts from a book by the editors of a news magazine:

What made Gorbachev a truly intriguing Man of the Year was that . . . so little was known about him. . . .

This reassuring rhetoric was intriguingly . . . similar to what liberal Western strategists had accepted as conventional wisdom for decades. . . .

But Gorbachev's choice [of a constituency] was intriguing. . . . Economic stagnation and political torpor [under Brezhnev] seemed to hatch corruption and intrigue in the highest places.

Following the contestable use of *intriguing* twice and *intriguingly* (adverb), finally *intrigue* is used strictly in the last quoted sentence.

INUNDATE,   INUNDATED. While television cameras focused on a huge fire in southern California, a reporter called attention to some houses "just about to be inundated by the flames." Not burned, consumed, or destroyed, but "inundated." His choice of verb could hardly have been further from the mark. To *inundate* is to flood, to cover with water in the manner of an overflowing river. Drought and water shortage had contributed to the fire disaster.

Inundated can equal *deluged, flooded,* or *swamped.* Used figuratively, any of those words is drenched with metaphor.

When the moderator of a forum said, "At this point in time, the American people are completely inundated with polls," he overdid it. Scratch "completely." (*See also* "**AT THIS POINT IN TIME.**")

The pronunciation is IN-nun-date(d) or, less often, in-NUN-date(d).

Inversions. *See* Backward writing.

INVERTED COMMAS. *See* Punctuation, *10.*

INVITE and INVITATION. When a boy in a situation comedy said, "I got a special invite [pronounced IN-vite] tonight to a dance at Hamilton High," he was perfectly in character. The word is most informal though. Its use was questionable when a broadcaster on a specialized news program boasted of an "exclusive invite" to a TV wedding.

A courteous request for a person to attend an event or to participate in an activity is an *invitation.* So is a note used in extending it. To extend an *invitation* is to *invite* (someone), pronounced in-VITE.

INVOKE. *See* EVOKE and INVOKE.

Iran. A factual error mars this passage, from a newspaper:

The [Persian Gulf] crisis has shaken the Mideast regional power balance. Egypt has moved to the forefront, and Syria and Iran have moved toward the Arab mainstream.

Iran is not "Arab." Its official and predominant language is not Arabic but Farsi, which uses the Arabic alphabet plus four additional letters. Formerly *Persia,* this sizable southwest Asian country has its own culture and traditions. It does share the Muslim religion with the Arab countries, like Egypt and Syria, although Iranians mostly belong to the Shiah sect whereas the Sunni predominates in most Arab countries. *Iran* is pronounced either ih-RAN or, more authentically, ee-RON.

IRONY, IRONIC, IRONICALLY.
1. Contrast essential. 2. SARCASM, SATIRE.

1. Contrast essential
Upon reporting that a maritime collision had cost a company a vessel, a newscaster told the television audience:

Ironically it's the same company that lost a boat in a collision ten years ago.

There was nothing *ironic* (adjective) about it. The two incidents were parallel. Contrast is the essence of *irony* (noun). *Ironically* (adverb) would have been an appropriate word if, for example, the maritime company had been known for ads promoting safety afloat but then caused a collision.

Irony can be a noteworthy incongruity of events, a glaring contrast between what one could have reasonably expected and what actually happens. *Irony* is also a literary style, a rhetorical figure, or a humorous device. The contrast then is between the apparent meaning of words that are written or spoken and a far different meaning beneath the surface.

2. SARCASM, SATIRE
Sarcasm is similar to *irony* in the contrast between literal meaning and intended meaning, but *sarcasm* implies overt ridicule or taunting; *irony* is milder and subtler. Related words are *sarcastic* (adjective) and *sarcastically* (adverb). "This is a fine time to be telling me!" is a sarcastic remark.

Satire (noun) is a literary or dramatic style using *irony* to attack or ridicule something held to be wrong or foolish. Related words are *satirical* (adjective) and *satirically* (adverb). A writer of classic satire was Jonathan Swift, best known for *Gulliver's Travels.*

"IRREGARDLESS." *See* REGARD-LESS.

IS, AM, ARE (etc.). *See* BE, AM, IS (etc., cross-reference).

IS and ARE. *See* Verbs, *3.*

-ISE ending. *See* -IZE ending, 2.

IS IS. Many a speaker follows *is* with an echo of the word, as though he has forgotten that he just uttered it.

A double *is* can be deliberate. "Whatever is, is right" appears in the works of Dryden and Pope and is also attributed to the Greek philosopher Democritus. Dryden wrote also, "Whatever is, is in its causes just." The poet Ella Wheeler Wilcox wrote that "whatever is—is best." This is a translation from Hegel: "Everything that is, is reasonable." A more recent example is President Clinton's reply to a question in testimony, "It depends upon what the meaning of the word *is* is."

Usually, however, as the following quotations from television suggest, the echoed word is not the product of thought. A member of Congress: "The fact is is that there's nothing there" (in an investigation of the president). An astronomer: "The problem is is that we've got an enormous amount of work to get done right now." An appraiser: "The good news is is it's worth three to five thousand dollars." A writer and TV panelist: "The fact of the matter is is that he [the president] is in deep trouble." Each second "is" was superfluous.

ISRAELI. *See* JEW, JEWISH.

Italic(s). *Italic* type, or *italics,* is a form of printing type or lettering, used for emphasis and special purposes. The letters slant to the right (and use fewer serifs than *roman,* the common book type).

Writers and editors underline those words in manuscripts that they want to be italic. Thus this is a sample becomes *this is a sample.*

Among other functions, italics indicate that a word is not playing its usual role, that of contributing to meaning, but is being considered as a word. For instance, this book discusses *me* and *I.* It deals also with *and* and *but.*

Names of books, dramatic works, works of art, publications, and genera and species go in italics: *Moby-Dick* by Melville; *The Glass Menagerie* by Williams; Leonardo's *Mona Lisa;* Mozart's opera *The Marriage of Figaro;* an article in *Time;* the lion, *Felis leo.* (*See also* **Punctuation**, *10.*)

Italics serve also to distinguish foreign words or phrases that are not also considered part of English, such as *semper fidelis* and *et tu, Brute!;* introduce new terms: "*Automatic speech recognition* (ASR) is developing . . ."; and enumerate points, principles, or questions that an author wishes to stress.

Italics call attention to a particular word or phrase. It may be one that would be emphasized if the sentence were spoken:

> "When *I* use a word," Humpty Dumpty said, in rather a scornful tone, "it means just what I choose it to mean—neither more nor less."

The highlighted word may be one that is not usually emphasized, as in this example from a book on economics:

> The discovery that man needs stimulation as well as comfort is not new. After all, the ancient Romans clamored for bread *and* circuses.

It may be an unexpected word: "Are the wages of sin *wealth*?" Or two words may be contrasted: "If *he* will not do it, *she* will."

Italics are effective when used in moderation. A few writers overdo them, italicizing passages here and there in efforts to gain readers' attention.

The word *italic* (adjective and noun) is so named because it first appeared in an Italian book (an edition of Virgil printed in Venice in 1501). The word *italics* (noun) is often construed as plural, sometimes as singular.

Styles of italic go with the various roman styles. When a word in an italic passage needs emphasis, it may be printed in roman. Another device for emphasis is the heavy form of type known as **boldface**. Italics and boldface are sometimes combined in ***boldface italics***.

IT, anticipatory. *See* **Expletives.**

"IT GOES WITHOUT SAYING." *See* OF COURSE, 3.

IT IS I (HE, SHE) and IT'S ME (HIM, HER). *See* **Pronouns,** 10D.

IT IS I (YOU) WHO. *See* WHO, 3.

IT, ITS, neuter pronoun. *See* **Pronouns,** 2B.

ITS and IT'S. *Its,* the possessive, as in "The cat licked its paws," has no apostrophe.

It should not be confused with *it's,* the contraction. Like every contraction, this does have an apostrophe. *It's* is usually a contraction of *it is,* as in "It's a good day"; sometimes a contraction of *it has,* as in "It's been a long time."

An apostrophe was erroneously inserted in each of the four passages that follow (from newspapers and a notice to shareholders). "It's" should be *its.*

"It would be more racism showing it's ugly head again."

We would also like to applaud the cafe for it's non-smoking policy.

". . . They shouldn't have the right to decide the future of the lion or risk it's extinction."

. . . Shareholders may now treat a portion of the distributions paid by the Fund as interest income from obligations of the United States and it's possessions. . . .

The example below (from an ad in a trade magazine) shows the opposite error: the omission of a necessary apostrophe. "Its" should be *it's.*

Ask any talent agent or A&R person. They'll tell you that, without the right production values, its hard to make great music stand out in a world of mediocrity.

(Another mistake is the use of a plural pronoun, "They," with a singular antecedent. *See* **OR; Pronouns,** 2. What about "mediocrity"?)

See also **Punctuation,** 1B.

ITSELF. *See* **Pronouns,** 3, 4.

"IT STANDS TO REASON." *See* REASON, 3.

I WHO. *See* WHO, 3.

-IZE ending. 1. *Excessive use.* 2. *-ISE.*

1. Excessive use

The practice of using the suffix *-ize* to make verbs goes back to the Middle Ages. Both nouns and adjectives are turned into verbs by tacking on the suffix.

Hundreds of legitimate words have *-ize.* At some time, most of us *emphasize, memorize, recognize,* and *sympathize.* Finance leads many to *amortize, equalize, itemize,* and *minimize.* Some people professionally *criticize, organize, specialize,* and *theorize.* Miscreants *bur-*

glarize, scandalize, terrorize, and *victim-ize.* Substances *energize, fertilize, neu-tralize,* and *vaporize.*

Nevertheless, the practice has long been overdone. H. L. Mencken wrote in *The American Language:*

> I reach into my collection at random and draw forth such monstrosities as *to backwardize, to fordize, to belgium-ize, to respectablize, to scenarioize, to moronize, to customize, to featurize, to expertize, to powerize, to sanitize, to manhattanize* and *to colonize;* I suppose I could dredge up at least a hundred more.

Colonize is accepted now as a standard word. *Customize, featurize, sanitize, and manhattanize* have reached acceptance at least as jargon. Mencken later, in the first supplement to his work, listed forty more that had been coined "in recent years." By then, he had learned that *-ize* words dated to the Middle Ages, and he no longer called them "monstrosities." But we can be glad that few of them survive. Those on his list that have been generally accepted (excluding trade names) are *glamorize* and *publicize;* two others, *finalize* and *moistureize* (now without the first *e*), have reached the status of jargon.

Many seem attracted to *-ize* because it appears impressive, official, or technical. But it is often weak and unnecessary, and the multiplication of *-ize* verbs adds monotony to the language.

"Finalize," for instance, serves more often as a bureaucratic and pretentious synonym for *complete, finish,* or *end* than as a necessary verb. "Moisturize" essentially says *dampen* or *keep moist,* although it can imply the use of a commercial product.

A candidate for district attorney said in an election statement:

> We must prioritize the prosecution of violent, repeat offenders.

"Prioritize" is no fist-pounding verb. Among stronger choices would have been *make our top priority* (if that is what he meant), *emphasize,* and *stress.*

A local legislative body argued in support of a ballot measure:

> By allowing less than prevailing wage standards . . . the City can maximize scarce job training funds.

Did "maximize" exceed *extend, pro-long, spread,* or *stretch* in clarity or just in pomposity?

Clarity may not have been uppermost in the mind of a business executive on a news telecast as he tried to justify a government subsidy for his prosperous corporation:

> When they [U.S. officials] want an industry to succeed, they incentivize it.

A physician sought to tell a huge TV audience that some health plans were harming patients' health; that holding down doctor costs, à la merchandising, was replacing the practice of ethical medicine. What he said was:

> We are being commoditized and our patients are being commoditized.

Perhaps unaware of the verb *meta-morphose*—to transform (something) or be transformed, as by magic or metamorphosis—a journalist said a politician who changed jobs had "metamorphosized."

See also **FACT-** words, 2 (end).

2. *-ISE*

In Britain the American *-ize,* the original British spelling, usually is spelled *-ise* (after the modern French practice of changing the Greek *-izo* to *-iser*). For instance, the American *realize* is spelled *re-alise. The Oxford English Dictionary* finds no good reason for *-ise,* "in opposition to that which is at once etymological and phonetic."

Some verbs (not part of the Greek tradition) always end in *ise* though possessing the *ize* sound. Among them are *advise, apprise, arise, chastise, comprise,* *compromise, demise, despise, devise, enterprise, excise, exercise, improvise, revise, supervise, surmise, surprise, and televise. Advertise* and *merchandise* are infrequently spelled *advertize* and *merchandize.*

J

JELL-O. As a brand of gelatin dessert, *Jell-O* is a trademark and should not be used in lower case, the way a manual of English for newcomers uses it: "Waitress: You have your choice of pudding, ice cream, or jello."

If that particular brand is meant, use capital *J*, hyphen, and capital *O*. Otherwise *gelatin* (or *gelatine*) is likely to describe the jellied dessert, salad, or mold in mind. A cold dish of meat, fish, vegetables, or fruit in gelatin is an *aspic*.

JEW, JEWISH. *Jew* denotes either a descendant of the Hebrews or one who adheres to the Judaic religion, whether through birth or conversion. The name comes from the Hebrew *yehudi*, originally a member of the tribe of Judah.

Two critiques, in a reference book and an editorial, bear criticism themselves. Each contains an unacceptable word.

An author objected to careless use of the terms *Jew* and *Jewish* in connection with Israel:

> Although that nation is closely identified with the Jewish race and religion, the expressions *Israeli* and *Jewish* are not interchangeable.

An "Editorial Board" expressed reservations about a presidential candidate that it was endorsing:

> We don't endorse anti-Semitism of any kind, and we're not happy about some of Jackson's racial slurs and insensitivity toward Jews.

In the first sample, the objectionable word is "race." (A good substitute would have been *people*.) In the second sample, the word "racial" should have been scrapped.

When there are African Jews, Chinese Jews, and Jews of just about every race, it makes no sense to refer to Judaism in racial terms. Contrary to Hitler's doctrine, there is no Jewish race.

The point made in the book about the separateness of *Israeli* and *Jewish* is valid. It is incorrect to speak of the *Israelis* as "the Jews," the way some adversaries of Israel have done. Only about 30 percent of the world's 14 million Jews live in Israel, and about 18 percent of the Israelis—that is, the citizens of the State of Israel—are non-Jews, mostly Moslems.

Jew is a noun only (e.g., "Jesus was a Jew"). The related adjective is *Jewish* ("a Jewish temple" / "a Jewish woman"). Using "Jew" in its place is derogatory.

Hebrew is the name of a language and an ancient people. It is not "in modern usage interchangeable with *Jew*," contrary to a dictionary's statement.

See also **YIDDISH.**

JOBLESS. The average newspaper editor is unlikely to put *unemployment compensation* in a headline when he can save space with "jobless pay," even though "jobless" misses the mark in that phrase. An unemployed person can be called *jobless;* it is not the "pay" that lacks a job. *Joblessness* is comparable to *unemployment,* but the press does not use the former often; it saves only one letter.

"Jobless" has branched out from the headlines into the bodies of news stories and into newscasting. A news agency reported:

> Blue-chip stocks fell in subdued trading Tuesday as investors stood on the sidelines waiting for Friday's key jobless numbers for September.

A TV newscaster announced a "jump in jobless claims." Another reported that "the number filing jobless claims dropped. . . ." Still another: "California's jobless rate has also dropped slightly."

So far the word has not entered the vernacular. A laid-off worker is likely to say, "I got my unemployment [not "jobless"] check today."

Joining of words. Some writers feel compelled to join pairs of words that are perfectly comprehensible when left separate. The result can be misleading. A newspaper item said an ex-president had thanked "the secret serviceman credited with saving his life after an assassination attempt. . . ." Although an intelligence agent in the armed services could possibly be described as a "secret serviceman," the recipient of the thanks was a *Secret Service man.*

Usually the reader is unlikely to be actually misled by unwieldy fusions, such as "Assemblymember" for *Assembly member,* "autoworkers" for *auto workers,* or "eightmillion" for *eight million.* More likely such behemoths will just

look like mistakes and stop the reader momentarily.

Because two words often go together, the writer may think they are wedded. The phrase *damn yankee* has been so common in the South that some people have thought it is a single word.

Printed works can be inconsistent in their choices of words to unite. This is from an autobiography: "We were introduced to the great military thinkers and their ideas—Mahan on sea power, Douhet on airpower. . . ."

Another author practices orthographic discrimination by writing, in a book of reminiscences, "Blackamericans are different from white Americans."

Phrases that have been published in fused form include these thirty-five: *ad writers, auto maker, best seller, break even, business folk, cab driver, care givers, catch phrases, child care, common sense, decision making, dining room, down payment, drug war, face down, front lines, full text, fund raising, good will, hard cover, home care, house cleaning, job seeker, market share, news writers, night watchman, park land, phone book, round trip, trap doors, word games, word play, work force, working women, work station.*

The innumerable "-person" and "-people" monstrosities can be added to the list. *See* **PEOPLE as a suffix; PERSON.**

Sometimes hyphenated adjectives like *cold-blooded; head-on; hour-long, month-long,* etc.; *long-time; short-lived; small-town;* and *worn-out* are divested of their hyphens and jammed together. A restaurant announces "HOMESTYLE COOKING" on its sign and "Home Style Cooking" on its menus. The adjective is *home-style.* A headline, "Barry Goldwater Is Dead at 89; Conservatives' Standardbearer," omitted the hyphen in the noun *standard-bearer.* (*See also* **Punctuation,** 4D.)

The combining of moderately sized

words to build giant words may be proper in the German language. Any advantage of imposing such a system on English, other than the saving of a minute amount of space, fails to come to mind.

In many instances the first word is not emphasized, so sound is no rationale for joining the words. Each of these nine phrases gives somewhat more emphasis to the second word; joining the two words obscures that fact: *best seller, common sense, down payment, front lines, full text, good will, night watchman, round trip,* and *trap doors.* In each of the nine hyphenated adjectives, both syllables get emphasis.

It is true that a long-range trend toward the solidification of phrases and hyphenated compounds has been observed. That any need exists to hasten the process has not been shown.

Consult the entries below for notable examples of wrongly joined phrases. Some of the phrases are supposed to become single words at times; others are not.

ALL RIGHT
ANY
A WHILE and AWHILE
BACK(-) prefix and pairs
CHECK OUT and CHECK-OUT
EVERY DAY and EVERYDAY
EVERY ONE and EVERYONE
HOLD
INTO, 2
LAY OFF and LAYOFF
LOT
NEVER MIND
ON, 3 (end)
PICK UP and PICKUP
ROUND UP and ROUNDUP
RUN AWAY and RUNAWAY
SET UP and SETUP

JOKE, JOKINGLY. *See* QUIP, QUIPPED.

JUDICIAL and JUDICIOUS. *See* **Confusing pairs.**

JURIST. A *jurist* is one who is well versed in the law. He may be a judge, a lawyer, a legal scholar or writer, or none of the above. The popular press generally misunderstands.

. . . The incident raised questions about whether K—— had violated a judge's rule that says a jurist "should not lend the prestige of his office to advance the private interests of others."

The rule applied to a *judge;* it said nothing about a "jurist." Evidently the reporter, thinking it was a synonym for *judge,* used "jurist" to avoid repeating "judge."

In another newspaper, a columnist appeared to do the same thing:

. . . The Senator, himself a former jurist, wondered out loud if Judge Bork was really a true conservative. . . .

If the senator is a "former" jurist, he must have forgotten what he knew about law.

Here is a similar example but with a little puzzle: who is the "jurist"?

Neither California nor U.S. judicial rules of misconduct appear to apply to a questionable $1 million legal fee awarded lawyer E—— W—— by a San Francisco judge before the jurist's appointment to the federal bench.

Either man could be a "jurist." The context verifies that the judge was the one. There is nothing wrong with "the judge's appointment." If the writer found the prospect of repeating a word too dreadful, he could have written "the latter's appointment." A reappearance of "the jurist's," six paragraphs later, could easily have been avoided:

... The time limit to investigate a matter of alleged impropriety for a sitting judge is six years prior to the start of the jurist's current term.

Replace "the jurist's" with *his*. (And make those "judicial rules of misconduct" the *Code of Judicial Conduct*.)

Another story indirectly quoted a judge on the reinterpretation of principles by "successive generations of jurors." The writer probably knew the difference between judges and jurors, members of juries, but mixed up his j-words.

The examples above come from general newspapers. One might think that the staff of a newspaper for the legal profession would know better than to run anything like "Review Calendar Forces Jurist to Do Double Duty" (headline) and "the assignment has passed to several jurists" (text underneath). The article was about a judge. So why not say *judge*?

Juvenile language. *See* ALSO, *1;* COOL; MOM, MAMA, MA; NEAT; STOMACH; WEIRD; WHEN, WHERE in definitions.

K

KIND OF. *1. Combined with plural.*
2. Improperly used with A or AN. 3.
Properly used with A or AN. 4. Replac-
ing RATHER or SOMEWHAT. 5. Used
"vulgarly."

1. Combined with plural

Kind (noun), meaning class, sort, or
variety, is singular. To qualify it with a
plural word is not generally accepted as
correct. An example, "These kind of
birds live . . ." instead of *Birds of this
kind live* or *This kind of bird lives.*

Kind itself may be made plural, in
representing more than one class or variety: *Many kinds of fruit grow / All kinds
of tools are sold.* In these examples, *fruit*
is regarded as an abstract category; *tools*
are regarded as concrete items.

The grammarian H. W. Fowler for-
gave irregular uses of *kind of* just "in
hasty talk." Confusion is common, even
in more careful use. A U.S. president
spoke publicly of "those kind of tests,"
instead of *tests of that kind.*

To use a word like *all, many, some,
these,* or *those* with *kind* and a plural
noun and verb used to be generally acceptable. Wyclif wrote: ". . . Alle kynd
of fishis gedrynge" (gathering); Shakespeare: "These kind of knaves I know"
and "To some kind of men . . ."; and
Flatman: "Such kind of Pamphlets work
wonders with the credulous Multitude."

The Oxford English Dictionary says

of the amalgam of *kind of* and plural:
"This is still common colloquially,
though considered grammatically incorrect." *The Random House Dictionary,*
pointing out the objections to that form,
offers the historical explanation that
kind once was an unchanged plural
noun like *sheep* and that the *s*-plural developed later.

The usage panel of *The American
Heritage Dictionary* rejected "Those
kind of buildings seem old-fashioned"
(90 percent) and "that kind of buildings
seem" (75 percent) for formal writing
but approved "What kind of books are
these?" (76 percent). A question beginning with *what* or *which* is a more acceptable deviation.

Although the second edition of *Webster's Dictionary* said *kind of* was used
with a plural "incorrectly," *Webster's
Third* accepts the disputed forms without qualification or mention of any objections.

What is said about the singularity of
kind of goes for *class of, sort of,* and
type of. See **TYPE.**

See also **THEM and THOSE.**

2. Improperly used with A or AN

Another source of criticism is the intrusion of *a* or *an* in "That kind of *a*
song" or "this kind of *an* apple," where
kind means variety, class, or the like.
The indefinite article does not belong

204 KISS OF DEATH

there, inasmuch as *song* or *apple* stands for a category (of which *kind* is a subdivision), not just one specimen. (But *see also* 3.) These follow the acceptable form: "She likes that kind of plant." / "This is my kind of meal." / "It's a rare kind of stone."

The same principle holds for *class of, sort of,* and *type of.* "A gnu is a type of antelope."

3. Properly used with A or AN

Kind of in another sense may go with *a.* Being *a kind of* or *a sort of* critic, poet, vagabond, or something else can be the same as being *something of a* critic etc. It often implies that the person possesses the characteristics of the specified class to a certain extent but not fully. "She's a kind of butterfly." / "George is a sort of expert."

The same goes for *kind of a* (or *an*) or *sort of a* (or *an*). "My boss is kind of a tyrant." / "They say Fred is sort of an animal at home."

Either way, a second indefinite article—"*a* kind of *a*" or "*a* kind of *an*"—is redundant. (It does appear in old writing: ". . . my master is a kind of a knave," Shakespeare; and "I thought myself a kind of a monarch," Defoe.)

4. Replacing RATHER or SOMEWHAT

Kind of is used colloquially (as an adverb) to mean *rather, somewhat, in a way,* or *to some extent:* "We were kind of surprised by the news." / "The weather is kind of brisk today" / "I kind of miss her."

Sort of is used similarly. Neither is suitable for careful writing.

5. Used "vulgarly"

The *of* in *kind of* is "vulgarly" slurred (the *Oxford*'s label). The result may be spelled "kind o' " / "kind a' " / "kinda" / "kinder," or otherwise. Dickens put "Theer's been kiender a blessing fell upon us" in a character's mouth.

The same is done to the *of* in *sort of,* producing "sorta" and so on.

KISS OF DEATH. *See* WHICH.

KNOT.
When a mariner speaks of a ship's going, say, forty *knots,* he is indicating speed, not distance. A knot is one nautical mile per hour.

Television narrators said, over films of ships, "The cruising speed is fifty knots per hour" and "The Starship will do twenty knots an hour on the open ocean." With *knots,* "per hour" or "an hour" is superfluous. A phrase like "fifty *nautical miles* per hour" would be acceptable—at least for landlubbers.

A *nautical mile,* also known as a *geographical, sea,* or *air mile,* is used by ships and aircraft. It equals one minute of a great circle of the earth, about 6,076 feet, or about 1.15 *statute* miles. A *statute mile,* also known as a *land mile,* is the ordinary mile, about 5,280 feet.

KODAK.
Kodak is a trademark, originally the name of a popular camera, now more often associated with camera films and photocopying machines.

Old dictionaries contain two words derived from the camera's name: the verb *kodak,* to take a snapshot, and the noun, *kodaker,* one who takes snapshots. H. L. Mencken called them, along with *kodak fiend,* "familiar derivatives." All are now obsolete. He repeatedly used Kodak and other trade names in lower case, but they should be capitalized.

George Eastman coined the name of the camera he invented, registering it in 1888. He said the name was arbitrary. It has not been tied to *Kodiak* island or the *Kodiak* bear. The *K* probably came from his mother's maiden name, Kilbourn.

KUDOS.
This noun originated as Greek for glory and fame. It can convey that meaning or a shallower sense: credit or acclaim for a particular act or achieve-

ment. Its life as an English word began as British university slang, and when used casually to signify a transitory compliment, it retains a sophomoric air.

An editorial said that a competing paper, impressed by the mayor's housing policy, had given him a compliment—"perhaps the first such unadulterated kudo" since he took office. "Kudo" is not a legitimate word. The editorial writer probably thought of *kudos* as plural. It is singular. A movie reviewer on television similarly erred when he said, "The greatest kudos go to Martin Landau." It *goes* to him.

The second edition of the *Random House Dictionary* granted the misbegotten "kudo" the status of an entry, leading a reviewer to ask whether one instance of *pathos* would now be a "patho."

The first syllable of *kudos* is emphasized and pronounced CUE or COO; the second syllable is pronounced *doss* or *dose*.

Let no one confuse that word with *kudu* (KOO-doo), an African antelope, or its plural, *kudus* (KOO-dooz).

L

LAID and LAIN. *See* LAY and LIE.

LAMA and LLAMA. *See* Homophones.

LARCENY. *See* CRIME, MISDEMEANOR, and FELONY; Crimes (various felonies), *3*.

LAST (in a series). *See* LATTER.

LAST NAME and SURNAME. In a newspaper article with a Budapest dateline, a sentence said:

> A Hungarian named Laszlo, who declined to give his last name, earns 10,000 forints a month in his government job as a repairman. . . .

Laszlo *is* his last name. What we do not know is his *surname,* or family name. In Hungary a citizen's surname comes first; his given name comes last. If that fact surprises some people who know something about Hungary, it is because writers in English switch the names around. For instance, the composer known as Béla Bartók was really Bartók Béla. The practice is so pervasive, it may be futile to try to change it. Just do not call his *surname* his "last name."

In China and Japan too the surname comes first, then the given name. In English writing, names of Chinese are usu-

ally left in the traditional order (Mao Tse-tung), but names of Japanese are usually reversed (Akira Kurosawa). Most immigrants to the United States adopt its customary order of names.

LATIN(-)AMERICAN. *1. LATIN AMERICA and SPANISH AMERICA. 2. LATINO, HISPANIC, SPANISH, MEXICAN, and CHICANO.*

1. LATIN AMERICA and SPANISH AMERICA

A columnist criticized the U.S. invasion of Haiti for, among other reasons, its lack of approval by "Spanish-speaking" countries of the Western Hemisphere. "So much for 'Latin American' support," he remarked.

What do Spanish speakers have to do with Haiti? The Haitians speak French.

Latin America is by no means synonymous with *Spanish America.* The former includes those countries of the Western Hemisphere south of the United States where Spanish, Portuguese, or French is the official language. The latter excludes Brazil, where Portuguese is spoken, and French possessions as well as Haiti. Neither term should be applied to the countries of Belize and Guyana, where English is the official language, and Suriname, where Dutch is the official language.

A person from Latin America is a

Latin American, with no hyphen. Used as an adjective, as in *Latin-American* country, the term takes a hyphen.

2. LATINO, HISPANIC, SPANISH, MEXICAN, and CHICANO

Latin(-)American used to be colloquially shortened to *Latin.* This has given way to a use of the Spanish word *latino,* capitalized. In Spanish it primarily means of the Latin language (adjective) or a scholar in the Latin language (noun). It is often used in the United States to mean a person here with any ethnic tie to Latin America. It is used also as an (attributive) adjective, "this country's Latino population," an un-Spanish form. (Spanish would say *la población latina.*)

Another popular term, older and somewhat more formal, is *Hispanic.* As an adjective, it has long meant Spanish, in the sense of pertaining to or originating in Spain. In the popular use of *Hispanic,* the adjective includes Spanish America and the word serves also as a noun, meaning a person with ties to either place.

A *Spanish* person is one from Spain and nowhere else, although a *Spanish-speaking* person may be from anywhere else. It is incorrect to use the adjective "Spanish" in lieu of *Mexican,* although such use has sometimes been quietly encouraged by Americans of Mexican origin as a response to discrimination. In recent decades they have more prominently used *Chicano* to describe themselves (from an elision and dialectal pronunciation of *Mexicano,* meaning Mexican); however, some Mexican-Americans object to the term.

LATTER. *1. As adjective. 2. As pronoun. 3. With number.*

1. As adjective

The latter refers to the second of two things or persons mentioned. The com-

parable term for the first of the two is *the former.*

Latter is used correctly as a comparative adjective in this way: After two choices have been offered, one might say, "The latter choice is more practical." Or, if one has been asked to choose between two paragraphs: "I prefer the latter paragraph."

The word is used incorrectly to refer to the last of three or more things. Furthermore, its use can have other drawbacks.

An article enumerates six local political meetings that took place in one night and adds: "It was the latter event that drew the most political luminaries." *Last,* not "latter," would be grammatically correct; so would *last-mentioned* or *last of those events.* But any of the terms could slow down readers by sending them back to find out what it pertains to. Although the writer did not need to repeat the thirty words used to describe the particular event, he could have made a capsule reference to it: "The birthday dinner drew the most political luminaries."

The "latter" device, aimed at verbal economy, sometimes brings verbosity. This passage is from a book on computing:

> If you're looking for an inexpensive printer, your best bet is an HP DeskJet, which is small, light, and whisper quiet. The latter attribute may not seem very important unless, like me, you once had your nerves . . . shattered daily by the jackhammer clanking of a dot matrix or daisy wheel printer.

Last instead of "latter attribute" would be correct but still roundabout. If the author had replaced "latter attribute" with *quietness,* he would have been correct, saved a word, and avoided a conspicuous circumlocution.

This passage is from an article in a financial newspaper:

> The quarry gang was the macho crew. They never wore shirts, vied for the deepest tans, walked with a distinctive "strut," and clinched their belts unbelievably tight to accentuate a "Scarlett-O'Hara"-type waistline. (This latter habit the camp physician believed to be at least partially responsible for the four cases of appendicitis during the year I spent at Henryville.)

Changing "latter" to *last* would improve the third sentence but not completely fix it. A "habit" is a noun, whereas the previous sentence enumerated a series of verbs. Better: "The camp physician believed the belt-tightening habit to be. . . ."

Latter can also mean later, in time or sequence. It should not pertain to an earlier event. There should never be any doubt what *latter* refers to. *See* **FORMER.**

2. As pronoun

The latter may be used without a noun; so may *the former.* An illustration of correct usage (though bad poetry): "Jack and Jill went up the hill to fetch a pail of water. The former fell down and broke his crown, and the latter came tumbling after."

Latter denotes the second of two things. It should not be used in the manner of the following passages.

> In ensuing weeks, Mr. Momper won from the environmentalists an agreement on three basic principles— the presence of the allies, legal ties to West Germany and the government's monopoly on the legal use of force. The latter was a singularly West Berlin issue.

If there are three principles, the third is not "the latter" but *the third,* or *the last* or *the last of those* or something similar.

> Among the items kept there are the diary of Nazi propaganda chief Joseph Goebels, an X-ray of Adolph Hitler's skull and the first edition of Pravda, the newspaper of the Soviet Communist Party.
> The latter is so rare that even Soviet officials don't have an original; they had to photocopy the Hoover Institution's edition.

Change "latter" to *last* or *last of those* or—best of all—*newspaper.* (Two names are misspelled: *Goebbels* and *Adolf.* And "edition" at the end should be *copy.*)

Latter is commonly used—or misused—to avoid repeating something. Many journalists are averse to repetition. But repetition is not necessarily bad. There is nothing wrong with repeating a word or short phrase to be clear or grammatical.

> D'Amato owns [?] the Republican, Conservative and Right to Life lines, and the latter got more than 130,000 votes in the 1978 gubernatorial election, displacing the Liberals as the fourth strongest party in the state.

Replacing the erroneous "latter" with *last-named* or the like would correct the error. A better solution is to turn the sentence into two sentences. End the first with "lines." Start the second: "The Right to Life Party got. . . ."

The writer of the next sample seems baffled by grammar as she switches chaotically between the comparative and the superlative in a book on calligraphy:

> It [vermilion] is obtainable in several shades—in vermilion, scarlet vermilion, orange vermilion and Chinese vermilion; this latter, being the deepest shade, is considered the more reliable.

Change "latter" to *last* and "more" to *most*.

3. With number

Use of *the latter* implies the existence of *the former,* in the same category. If you speak of *the latter choice,* you are implicitly distinguishing it from *the former choice.* Similarly, if you speak of *the latter three* (days, games, etc.), there must be *the former three.*

This passage, from a news article, contains an illogicality:

> . . . He [President Bush] would permit abortion only in cases in which a continued pregnancy would threaten the life of the mother, or when a pregnancy results from rape or incest. But he has also said that he opposes the use of federal funds in the latter two cases.

"The latter two cases" would be proper if one could speak of "the *former* two cases," but only three categories are mentioned altogether. The writer would have done well to grit his teeth and repeat three words: "in *rape or incest* cases."

LAUDABLE and LAUDATORY.
See Confusing pairs.

Law, courts, legal terms.
See ACCUSED, ALLEGED (etc.); ATTORNEY and LAWYER; CHIEF JUSTICE; CIRCUMSTANTIAL EVIDENCE; Confusing pairs (*judicial, prosecute*); CRIME, MISDEMEANOR, and FELONY; Crimes (various felonies); EVIDENCE and PROOF; EXECUTE; Guilt and innocence; "HIGH COURT"; JURIST; LIGATION and LITIGATION; Numbers, *9;* PAROLE and PROBATION; Pronouns, *2A;* PURSUIT of HAPPINESS; Quotation problems; REGULATION, STATUTE, and LAW; Reversal of meaning; REVERT; RULE, RULING; SAID; TESTAMENT and TESTI-MONY; Twins; UNLESS and UNTIL; VENUE; Verbs, *1C;* WARRANT; WITH PREJUDICE and WITHOUT PREJUDICE.

LAY and LIE.
You *lay* your pen down. You *lie* in bed.

The verb *lay* is transitive. (That is, it transmits the action from subject to object; and the object is essential for the verb to have full meaning.)

The verb *lie* is intransitive. (It does not transmit the action. Just the subject participates in the action.)

Thus a U.S. president spoke ungrammatically when he declared that "a new world of freedom lays before us." It *lies* before us. A manual said incorrectly that envelopes "should lay flat." They should *lie* flat. A newspaper columnist was wrong to write, "I was laying on my back. . . ." She was *lying* on her back. *Lying* was needed also in radio and TV reports of a truck "laying there on its side" and a crime victim "laying in the street."

There are a few exceptions to the rule that *lay* is a transitive verb. A hen can *lay* and a sailor can *lay* aft, for example. But *lie* is always intransitive.

The past tense of *lay* is *laid;* the participles are *laid* (never "lain") and *laying.* Examples: I *laid* my pen down yesterday. I have (or had) *laid* it down often. I am *laying* it down now.

Lie becomes *lay, lain* (never "laid"), and *lying.* Examples: I *lay* down last evening. I have (or had) *lain* on the bed occasionally. I am *lying* on it now.

"He lied down," a radio host said incorrectly. He *lay* down. *Lied* is the past tense of *lie* (verb) in another sense: to tell a *lie,* a falsehood.

LAY OFF and LAYOFF.
". . . Management still planned to layoff Teamster delivery drivers"; so said an article (by two writers quoting "sources" quoting a union representative quoting a management negotiator). It was in error: man-

agement would not "layoff" anyone. The correct verb is *lay off,* two words.

Layoff as a single word is a noun only, for example: "The layoff of workers will start next week." The verb (transitive) has two words: "The company will lay off workers starting next week" or "Workers will start being laid off next week."

To *lay off* someone is to suspend or discharge him from employment for an impersonal economic reason.

To *discharge, dismiss,* or *fire* an employee is to stop employing him, usually for cause, such as performance on the job. In that sense, *fire* is an informal verb, probably originating in a humorous analogy with *discharge;* both also mean to shoot a gun.

A *layoff* used to occur typically during a slow period for an industry or at a troubled time for a particular company, and it was often temporary. Now its only reason may be to save money, and it is usually permanent.

When not describing lingerie, *pink slip* is a colloquial term for a notice of layoff, dating from the 1920s.

See also LET GO.

LEAD (noun). While the television screen depicted a group of miners at work, an announcer remarked that for a century "Idaho has been producing lead for pencils or whatever else lead is used for." He thereby publicly announced his ignorance of the difference between a pencil's graphite, a form of carbon that is colloquially called "lead," and the real *lead,* a metal used in alloys, bullets, piping, printing type, and so on. Both are elemental substances and both are pronounced LED, but the similarity ends there.

A writer for a metropolitan newspaper also confused the two:

> What if they come out with a study that claims the best way to fight cholesterol is to pump more lead in your diet?

Pretty soon people would be tossing their oat bran in the trash and chewing on No. 2 pencils.

At a time when warnings about *lead* and health are common, the first sentence leads us to thoughts of the metal. Only when we read to the last word of the second sentence do we realize that the writer had a different "lead" in mind.

(Among shortcomings is an inconsistency in mood. Either change "come . . . claims . . . is" to *came, claimed,* and *was* [subjunctive], or change "would" to *will* [indicative]. *See* **Mood; Subjunctive.** By the way, why would people necessarily pick the No. 2 pencils? I prefer the No. 1.)

See also LEAD (verb) and LED.

LEAD (verb) and LED. An otherwise tightly written novel contains this sentence: "Pierce Bascomb lead the way up a slight hill and then down another." Bascomb "*led* the way."

The past tense of the common verb *lead*—pronounced LEED and meaning to direct, go first, or be the head of—is *led* and only *led,* pronounced LED. The same goes for the past participle: She has *led* the cause for years. He had *led* the army to defeat.

An article in a legal newspaper quotes a lawyer as telling the Supreme Court that "jurors could be mislead by the anti-sympathy instruction." Evidently a thought of *lead,* the metal, pronounced LED, *misled* the writer.

There is an uncommon verb *lead,* pronounced LED and meaning to put lead in or on; or, in traditional printing, to create spaces by placing lead strips between lines of type. Its past tense and past participle is *leaded.*

See also **Homophones;** LEAD (noun).

LEAP, LEAPED, LEAPT. A music critic, reviewing a symphonic performance of a Bartók piece, wrote that "the middle Elegy lept into prominence." Although it may be pronounced LEPT, the verb he needed is spelled *leapt*. It is a variant of *leaped*, past tense of *leap:* to spring, bound, or jump. Another way to pronounce *leapt* is LEEPT, the same way *leaped* is pronounced.

LEAVE and LET. *See* LET, LET'S, *1*.

LECTERN and PODIUM. The stand for a speaker's notes or papers is a *lectern*. In a broadcast, an autobiography, and a grammar, it was confused with something else seen in an auditorium:

> We want to return to the podium for this evening's featured speakers.

> . . . When I walked into the auditorium . . . to meet the press for the first time, I noticed that the thirty or so microphones on the podium left me no room for my notes.

> . . . The new audio-visual system self-destructed while the CEO stood helplessly at the podium.

A *podium* is a small platform on which the conductor of an orchestra stands.

The roots of the two words, shared by *lecture* and *podiatrist,* are Latin and Greek for *read* and *foot* respectively.

LED. *See* LEAD (verb) and LED.

LEGATION and LIGATION. *See* LIGATION and LITIGATION.

LEGEND, LEGENDARY. *1. Ambiguity. 2. Before and after. 3. Other meanings.*

1. Ambiguity

The trouble with the contemporary practice of applying "legend" or "legendary" to real people or activities is that it has created ambiguity and threatened a distinctive pair of words. Now we cannot always be sure whether a user is talking about fact or fiction.

A book (which purports to clarify words) tells us that "Too often a name is legendary" while few people know about the person. The same book says:

> It was a legendary television talk-show host who once said of his nightly performance, "I just keep talking until I have something to say." . . . The British upper-class stammer (or traulism) is a legendary mannerism.

Does "legendary" imply that the person, the story, and the stammer are of doubtful authenticity? Or is "legendary" simply the author's synonym for *famous?*

2. Before and after

In the BC era—before corruption—*legendary* (adjective) primarily pertained to a *legend* (noun): a traditional story, usually about a famed personage, that was popularly believed to have a factual basis but could not be accepted as historical fact. It might be partly true or wholly fictional. Examples are the legends of Don Juan, Saint Nicholas, and King Arthur. Longfellow wrote: "Listen to this Indian legend / To this Song of Hiawatha!"

Then someone was described as being so famous that he was "a legend in his own time." A strikingly fresh phrase at first, it became a cliché. After a while "in his own time" began to be dropped.

When a baseball player changed teams, a big headline said "A legend departs." A blurb for a book on science called one of its authors "a teaching legend," and the author wrote that "legendary chefs of the past have gone to thirteen doublings" (of dough in making noodles). The introduction of another science book said, "Stephen Hawking was a legend even then." On TV news: "His [David Packard's] story is legendary and it all began here. . . ." A magazine said, "Senator Robert Byrd . . . is legendary for directing wasteful spending in West Virginia." To another magazine, " 'Louie, Louie' . . . is one of the most legendary songs in music history." And a newspaper told "a story that became an instant Broadway legend" (about a Sondheim show).

The language has plenty of synonyms for *famous* and *famous person.* It cannot afford to lose *legendary* and *legend.*

3. Other meanings

A *legend* is also an inscription on an object like a coin or monument; a tablet or identification accompanying an exhibit or picture; or a key to symbols used in a map or chart.

Legend, not preceded by an article, denotes a body or collection of popular stories handed down from earlier eras; or myth or traditional story in general; or popular belief as distinct from fact or scholarship.

In the distant past, a *legend* was supposed to represent historical truth. It was a medieval story of the life of a saint; a collection of stories about saints or other admirable figures; or in general an account or history of a person's life.

LENIENCY. *See* **MERCY and PITY.**

"LEPT." *See* **LEAP, LEAPED, LEAPT.**

LESS. *See* **FEWER and LESS.**

LESSER, LESSOR, and LESSEE. *See* **Homophones.**

LET GO. As a verb phrase meaning to terminate employment, *let go* suits informal contexts, unlike an article in a newspaper's normally staid financial section. It reported that the news division of a broadcasting company, to cut costs, "let many senior people like Mr. P—— go." Obviously they did not want to go. To say they were "let" go when they were

ousted from their jobs is euphemistic. *See also* **LAY OFF and LAYOFF.**

The main standard meanings of *let go* are to release from confinement ("Let my people go"), to release one's hold ("He let go [or "let go of"] the rope") and to abandon or relinquish ("Ah, take the cash and let the credit go").

LET, LET'S. *1. LEAVE and LET. 2. "LET'S DON'T." 3. With pronouns.*

1. LEAVE and LET

The chorus of a once-popular song presents the words "leave me alone" a dozen times. It reflects a widespread usage. To *leave* one *alone* commonly means to refrain from disturbing the person. But some strict writers and speakers apply *let alone* to such a sense. For them, the meaning of *leave alone* is to go away and leave one in solitude.

To say, for instance, "She wants to be *left* alone" instead of "*let* alone" is not incorrect, but it can be ambiguous. Does she want to be alone or does she just want to be undisturbed? Unless the context makes it clear, distinguishing between *let* and *leave* (or *left,* its past tense and past participle) can be useful.

Leave, aside from its companionship with *alone,* should never be substituted for *let* in the sense of allow or permit. "Leave" is improper in such sentences as "Let us be merry" / "Let me go" / "Let it cook" / "Let John speak."

2. "LET'S DON'T"

A letter to the editor of a financial newspaper was headed "Let's Don't Endanger the Truth." To demonstrate why "Let's Don't" is bad English, we expand the contractions, producing "Let Us Do Not." The editor who wrote the headline could have either omitted the "Let's" ("Don't Endanger the Truth") or changed the "Don't" to *Not* ("Let's *Not* Endanger the Truth") without endangering the English language.

Sometimes the first two words are switched around: "Don't let's take a chance." It suits only casual conversation. *Let us not* or *let's not* is the preferred phrase.

3. With pronouns

No one is likely to say, "Let I decide." Mistakes are liable to enter when another noun or pronoun is introduced. After the verb *let,* any personal pronoun has to be objective, not subjective (nominative): "Let Agnes and me [not "I"] finish it." / "Let you and him [not "he"] make the arrangements." / "Let him and her [not "he and she"] know." *See also* **Pronouns,** *10.*

These are right: "Let us walk" / "Let's walk" / "Let you and me walk" / "Let's all walk." But "Let's you and me walk" and "Let's all of us walk" are redundant sentences.

LIABLE.

This adjective primarily means legally bound or responsible, or obligated by law: "One who lies under oath is liable to prosecution." / "The jury found the driver liable for Smith's injuries." / "Parents are liable for the support of minor children."

In addition, *liable* means susceptible to something undesirable; or likely to do, experience, or be exposed to it. "Accidents are liable to occur in this storm." / "Your house is liable to be flooded." / "We're liable to get complaints."

In its first edition, *The Random House Dictionary* said, "LIABLE should not be used to mean 'probable' " in place of "the true meaning, susceptibility to something unpleasant, or exposure to risk." The second edition says "LIABLE is often interchangeable with LIKELY . . . where the sense is that of probability." Its example is "The Sox are liable (or likely) to sweep the series"—but *liable* would be wrong on the basis of the restriction in the first edition; *likely* would be right.

Likely does mean probable or probably going (to be, do, have, happen, etc.). It does not in itself suggest unpleasantness; its context may or may not. *Likely* is more general than *liable* or *apt* and can often substitute for either.

Apt is similar to *liable.* It suggests not only that unpleasantness is likely but also that a bent or characteristic of the subject is contributing to the outcome, and it carries a hint of apprehension by the speaker. "He's *apt* to pick a fight" but "She's *likely* to receive a big ovation." / "The old tire is *apt* to blow out soon" but "This new tire is *likely* to last for years."

LIBEL and SLANDER.

An untrue communication about someone that injures his reputation or holds him up to hatred, contempt, or ridicule is a *defamation.* When the *defamation* is expressed in writing or print, it is *libel.* When it is spoken, it is *slander.*

Journalists should know all that. Yet a newspaper headline read, "Hughes ruined me—Maheu tells libel jury." The jury found that Howard Hughes had defamed his former assistant in a news conference conducted by telephone. The suit was not for "libel" but for *slander.*

See also **ACCUSED, ALLEGED** (etc.); **Guilt and innocence,** *5;* **Quotation problems,** *1.*

LIE. *See* **LAY and LIE.**

LIFE EXPECTANCY and LIFE SPAN.

It is a fairly common misconception that a long life span is a modern phenomenon and that in past centuries people did not live to ripe old ages. A statistical misunderstanding and a confusion of terms both appear to be at the bottom of it.

It is written that two centuries ago the average life expectancy, at least in some countries, may have been in the thirties. Some forget that such an average includes a high infant mortality rate and deadly childhood diseases. One who survived the first decade might expect a half-century more of life. Some individuals lived even longer. In the fifth century B.C. the Greek writer Sophocles lived to about ninety when the average life expectancy was probably in the twenties.

This passage by a prominent writer of popular science, who must have understood the statistics, uses the term "life span" loosely:

> . . . Until the coming of modern medicine human beings did not have a long life span on the average. Most people, even in comparatively good times, were dead of violence or infectious disease before they were 40. . . .
> . . . The average human life span has reached 75, in many parts of the world. . . .

Change "span" to *expectancy*. Students of longevity distinguish between *life expectancy* and *life span*.

Life expectancy is the number of years that a newborn or an individual of a given age in a particular population is expected to live, based on statistical probability and the likelihood of mortal illness or trauma.

Life span is the maximum number of years that a human being or animal can live under ideal conditions, in the absence of illness or trauma. The human *life span* is not known, but one authority estimates it to be 120.

See also **Numbers**, *10E*.

LIGATION and LITIGATION. A

woman calling a radio talk show said that mothers on welfare should be forced to have "tubal litigation." *Litigation,* pronounced lit-ih-GAY-shun, is a legal action or the carrying on of legal action. Although intending to sic the doctors, not the lawyers, on the hapless mothers, the caller put an extra syllable in *ligation*. Pronounced lie-GAY-shun, it means an act of binding, a state of being bound, or a thing that binds. In medicine it is the application of a *ligature*, LIG-a-choor, any material that is tied around a blood vessel or other structure to constrict it. To so tie the part is to *ligate* it, LIE-gate. *Tubal* in the context of *ligation* pertains to the Fallopian tubes.

A word that looks similar is *legation*, lih-GAY-shun, a diplomatic establishment in a foreign country, below the status of an embassy; also a mission on which an envoy of the pope is sent.

LIGHTENING and LIGHTNING. *See* **Confusing pairs**.

LIGHT YEAR. What is wrong with this statement (by a national press service)?

> On Aug. 23, the telescope's faint-object camera took an image of supernova 1987a, a star that exploded about 160,000 light years from Earth in February 1987.

The latter half of the statement is impossible. It takes about 160,000 years for light to reach us from that distance. If the "star . . . exploded" in 1987, nobody would know about the explosion until approximately the year 161,987. It is more likely that 1987 was simply the year in which telescopes picked up the event. In that case, it must have occurred about 160,000 years before, in approximately the year 158,013 B.C.

A *light year,* or *light-year,* is the distance that light travels through space in a year, at its speed of about 186,000 miles per second: about 5.878 trillion (5.878×10^{12}) miles.

LIKE. *1. Ambiguity. 2. Incomparability. 3. Sense and senselessness.*

1. Ambiguity
The meaning of sentences combining *not* and *like* can be uncertain; for exam-

ple: "Farnsworth is not a lawyer, like his predecessor." Was his predecessor a lawyer or a nonlawyer? Depending on the answer, one might either (a) change "like" to *unlike* or (b) place "Like his predecessor" first, followed by a comma. An alternative way to correct the example is to change the comma to a period and start a new sentence: "His predecessor was. . . ." *See also* **NOT,** *1C, E.*

A fear of misusing *like* leads occasionally to an ambiguous use of *as. See* **AS and LIKE,** *1.*

2. *Incomparability*

Like primarily likens one thing to another. The things need to have a similarity, albeit not the equivalence of a mathematical equation.

A weekly's review of a recording purports to equate a voice with certain people:

Like all great hip-hop MCs, Keith's voice has natural personality.

It seems to say that the man's voice is like masters of ceremony. They are not compatible ideas. Change one or the other; for instance:

A. "Like *the voices of* all great hip-hop MCs, Keith's voice has natural personality." Here voice is like voices.
B. "Like all great hip-hop MCs, *Keith has a voice with* natural personality." Here person is like persons.

A news story of a (revised) theory by two geochemists about a prehistoric collision is headed:

Asteroid once rocked Earth
like 10,000 megatons of TNT

The headline seems to say that what an extraterrestrial body did (verb) equaled an explosive force (noun). The ideas are at odds. Among possible corrections: "*Force of asteroid crash was* / like . . ."

Now one force is likened to another. An alternative: "Asteroid *hit Earth with force* / *of* 10,000 megatons of TNT."

A large daily almost gets it right but appears to go astray:

Like most of the other successful farmers on formerly Mfengu land, he struggled at first and later was divorced by his wife during the hard times.

It is right through "he struggled at first." End the sentence there—unless most of the man's colleagues were divorced by their wives too—and start a new sentence: "His wife divorced him. . . ."

See also **AS and LIKE,** *2;* **UNLIKE.**

3. *Sense and senselessness*

Like, while a legitimate word, is perhaps used more often in a slang sense or senselessly.

In standard usage, *like,* as a preposition, means similar to ("She's like a doll"), similarly to ("He worked like a horse"), in the usual manner of ("It's just like him to joke about it"); desirous of ("I feel like eating"), or indicative of ("It looked like rain"). *Like,* as an adjective, means equal or similar ("three pounds of potatoes and a like amount of carrots"); as a noun, something similar (with *the:* "squirrels, chipmunks, gophers, and the like"); or, as a verb, to be fond of ("I like Mike").

Like, the preposition, can also mean *for example, for instance,* or *such as.* Sometimes it is redundantly used with one of those expressions. A columnist in a television panel spoke of the weighty issues that the president was attending to, "like, for instance, the poison gas treaty." Either *like* or *for instance* would have been enough.

While not a conjunction in strict usage, *like* often is casually used in place of *as* or *as if.* A correction is inserted in each of these remarks: "Like [*as*] I told the team, 'Keep gnawing at 'em. . . .' " /

"It was like [*as if*] she had been picked up and put there." The distinction is covered in **AS and LIKE.**

Like figures in various informal expressions: "like a bat out of hell," very fast; "like crazy," wildly or violently; "like hell," never, not at all, strongly, or rapidly; "like a hole in the head," not at all (needed); "like a million bucks," very good (looking); "like there's no tomorrow," avidly; and so on.

On a still lower level, it substitutes for *approximately* ("It lasts like three hours"), *for example* ("They have like steaks there"), *perhaps* ("They went, like, to the store"), and *unfortunately* ("I accidentally, like, broke the dish"). The word serves also as a verbal crutch, in the manner of a pause or a grunt. ("Mary doesn't want to, like, come." / "He was, like, terrific.")

Like undergoes further maltreatment in a faddish replacement of *I think, I thought, she said, he said,* etc. An actress displayed minimal artistry when scriptless in a television interview:

I just came from a big dinner and I'm like I shouldn't have had that wine. . . . He said, "How much?" I'm like okay.

And a university student showed limited grasp of his language in a magazine interview:

There are days where I'm like, "Oh, my God, I'm so happy I'm living the life I'm living." . . . And I'm like, "What if they offer me this job?" . . . To my dad, I'd be like, "I gotta find myself. . . ."

"Like" could have been removed from each of the following remarks without any loss of meaning:

[The student again:] OK, like, here's the deal. . . . Like, how can I start working when I don't know who I am yet[?].

[A man praising a car for a commercial:] You are [able to go] from zero to like sixty in no time.

[A mother calling a radio psychologist about a baby:] She was getting up like four or five times a night. . . . She's waking up like a lot.

[A woman calling a general talk show:] Cars think that I'm like a target.

LIKELY. *See* **LIABLE.**

LIMERICK. One word does not belong in the following sentence, from a book:

Gelett Burgess, who invented the word "blurb" and was the creator of the limerick about "the purple cow," once tried to smuggle "huzzlecoo," a word he coined, into English.

"The Purple Cow" by Burgess is a quatrain, a verse, a nonsense poem—but not a "limerick." Here it is:

I never saw a purple cow,
*   I never hope to see one;*
But I can tell you, anyhow,
*   I'd rather see than be one!*

A *limerick* is not just any humorous verse, but one with five lines and a strict form. Many are ribald. This one is not:

A flea and a fly in a flue
Were imprisoned, so what could they
*   do?*
*   Said the flea, "Let us fly!"*
*   Said the fly, "Let us flee!"*
So they flew through a flaw in the flue.

(Technically, the first, second, and fifth lines of a *limerick* have three feet each; the third and fourth lines have two feet each. The rhyme scheme is usually A, A, B, B, A.)

Dating from the early eighteenth century, limericks were popularized by Edward Lear, English humorist and artist, in *The Book of Nonsense* (1846). The word *limerick* is said to have developed late in the century from a communal nonsense song that included the words "come up to Limerick [Ireland]."

LIMITED, LTD. *See* **FIRM**.

LIMP. To *limp* (verb, intransitive) is to walk unevenly, haltingly, or as one walks with a lame leg or foot: favoring the other.

The first time some writer tried out the word in describing a disabled ship or airplane, it may have been an effective metaphor. Now that innumerable craft have been limping about in the press for decades, it has turned into a lame cliché. A newspaper's use is typical:

> Later, planes limped back from a dozen secret arms drops inside Nicaragua on one engine, with smoke and oil spewing behind.

In the following passage, from a book of true adventure, the word is turned into a transitive verb.

> . . . As I hurtled along at full power into lift-off, the motor spluttered and one cylinder conked out. . . . We limped the plane back to the apron.

(It is not clear whether the plane was still flying when they "limped" it.)

Linking verbs. *See* **BAD and BADLY**; **Complement**; **FEEL**; **GOOD and WELL**; **Pronouns**, *10D*; **Verbs**, *1F*.

Lists. *See* **BACK(-) prefix and pairs**; **CAN and MAY** (example); **Clichés**; **Confusing pairs**; **DRAMA** (etc.), *2*; **General topics** (near the front); **Gerund**, *3B*; **Homophones**; **Introduction** (to the book), *Wounded Words*; **Joining of words**; **Plu-** rals and singulars; **Prepositions**, *7*; **Reversal of meaning**; **Series errors** (principles of listing); **Spelling**; **Twins**.

LITERALLY. Picture the amazing sight described by this headline:

> Literally waltzing on air
> Jesse Winchester comes to town

A television commentator described another weird phenomenon.

> We've seen in this election Ronald Reagan literally change his spots in front of our eyes.

Maybe Mr. Reagan's special-effects department was responsible for that. Anyway, as president he discovered that people were starving in national parks.

> When we took office, we found that . . . the funding for the maintenance and upkeep of our parks had been literally a starvation diet.

One day a gunman invaded the Senate and demanded the approval of stopgap funds before midnight. A senator was quoted as saying on the Senate floor:

> We are literally here today with a gun to our heads.

The senators acquiesced and were spared. But another culprit (we learn from TV news) was not at all merciful.

> . . . He literally made a killing in oil and real estate stocks.

How he perpetrated the deed was not spelled out. Possibly he smothered his victim in a mound of stock certificates.

Because all those things happened *literally*, you could see them actually happen. No metaphor was intended. No imagination was shown. Words were used in their strictest senses.

Had people been speaking poetically or metaphorically or with imagination, they would not have said *literally*. And, if they had any concern that their *figurative* statements would be taken as *literal* truth, they might have explained that they meant "figuratively a starvation diet" or "figuratively here today with a gun to our heads" or "figuratively made a killing."

Poets do not require such explanation for their metaphors, like this one: "Life's but a walking shadow, a poor player / That struts and frets his hour upon the stage." Shakespeare had no need for *figuratively* or, heaven knows, for "literally."

LITIGATION. *See* LIGATION and LITIGATION.

"LITTLE MUCH." *See* MUCH.

LIVE. 1. *Adjective: LIVE and ALIVE.* 2. *Verb: LIVE with IN.*

1. Adjective: LIVE and ALIVE

The adjective *live* (rhyming with *dive*) is not interchangeable with *alive*, although both primarily mean possessing life. "These are *live* flowers" but "The flowers are *alive*." In that sense, *live* goes before the noun; *alive* goes after the noun.

In certain, technical senses, *live* may either precede or follow the noun: "This is a *live* broadcast" or "The broadcast is *live*," meaning it is being made now, not transmitted from a recording. "It's a *live* wire" or "The wire is *live*," meaning it is carrying electric current.

2. Verb: LIVE with IN

This section deals with the verb *live*, rhyming with *give*. An editor wrote, "So it might be the one place I'll ever live that hasn't been 'discovered.' " You do not live a place. You cannot live Chicago

but can live *in* it. Correction: "place I'll ever live *in*" or "place *in which* I'll ever live."

The verb *live* is intransitive in the sense of reside and in most other senses. It is transitive when it means to spend (one's life) in a particular way or to carry out (something) in one's life: "He lived a celibate life" / "They live their religion."

LIVID. Bluish in the shade of a bruise or in any other dull hue is the primary meaning of *livid*, just as it was of *lividus* in Latin.

Some people mistakenly identify *livid* with another primary color, red, and the second *Random House Dictionary* rubber-stamps that misunderstanding. This odd distortion of recent years may have come about in these steps: from blue to grayish-blue, to gray, to pale-faced, to pale with anger, to very angry, to flushed with anger, to red.

Livid in the sense of very angry is termed colloquial by *The Oxford English Dictionary*. It is common in the news media. A four-word paragraph in a newspaper: "Environmental groups were livid" (when Congress refused to support a desert preserve). A quotation from a recording-academy president, in another paper: the trustees "were just livid about the situation" (the discovery that a prize-winning duo did not sing).

LOATH and LOATHE. A computer magazine was discussing desktop publishing programs:

PageMaker users who find their program to be simple will be loathe to tread in new waters.

"Loathe" was wrong. Adding *e* to *loath* (presumably by the article's two writers) was a mistake.

Loath (adjective) means reluctant, unwilling. You should be *loath* to add another letter to it. (Sometimes a letter is taken away: *loth* is found in some old literature.)

To *loathe* (verb, transitive) is to hate intensely, to abhor, to detest. This one has the *e*—as in enemy.

The words appear to have in common an ancient, Teutonic root meaning to hate.

LONGSHOREMAN. *See* STEVEDORE and LONGSHOREMAN.

LOOSE and LOSE. The (transitive) verbs *loose* and *lose* sometimes are confused. The former, pronounced LOOS, means to let loose, to release, or to make less strict. "Did he loose the boat from its moorings?" The latter, pronounced LOOZ, means to suffer the loss of, to be deprived of, or to be defeated. "Don't lose your ticket."

A passage from a book about books is followed by part of a testimonial for a gymnasium in a published ad:

A bright, colorful, attractive cover can only increase the sales of a publication. A poorly designed cover will loose sales.

I always wanted to loose weight and become stronger.

"Loose" is almost the reverse of what both excerpts need: *lose*.

The past tense and past participle of *loose* is *loosed*; of *lose* is *lost*. A verb similar to *loose* is *loosen*, meaning (transitive) to make looser; past tense and past participle: *loosened*. (The three verbs have intransitive senses also.)

LOOT. A radio report said, regarding the theft of money from a truck wrecked in an accident, "Attempts are ongoing to identify others who helped themselves to the loot." To the *money*. It was not "loot" before it was stolen. (*See also* ONGOING.)

To use "loot" as slang for money or valuables is not advisable, unless in private conversation. The owner may object to seeing or hearing what he owns associated with a word for stolen goods.

The noun *loot,* acquired directly from Hindi, originally meant the booty or spoils of war or pillaging. Now it can also be any goods or money stolen or appropriated dishonestly: "The burglars hid their loot in the cellar." It can also be the act of plundering: "He was accused of the loot of the treasury."

Loot is also a verb (transitive and intransitive), meaning to plunder. "The army looted the town."

LOSE. *See* LOOSE and LOSE.

LOT. *1. Meaning MANY or MUCH. 2. Two words.*

1. Meaning MANY or MUCH

Using *a lot (of)* to mean *much* or *many* used to be generally considered just colloquial, and some writers still avoid it in serious writing, although others use it without hesitation. The same is true of *lots (of)*, a synonym.

A reporter said on national television, alluding to statements by Republican election campaigners:

A lot of people is saying, "We're talking about matters of trust."

"People is saying"? The reporter would probably not announce that "many people is saying." A "lot" is not speaking; *people are*. In that context *a lot (of)* means *many*.

A lot (of) can mean *much*. "A lot of money is invested in the project." The verb is singular because "money" is singular.

Similarly, *lots (of)* can mean *many* or *much*.

In other senses, a *lot* is a piece of land; an object used for random choosing, as in, "We'll draw lots"; and a number of people or things considered as a group, as in "They're a sorry lot" and "How much for the lot?" One's *lot* is one's fortune in life.

2. *Two words*
   "There's no need for ice or a glass, you can buy it almost anywhere, and it's the kind of thing you want to drink alot of," Sousa added.

The first time you see that four-letter anomaly in a newspaper, you can dismiss it as a typesetter's error. Perhaps he forgot to put a space between the *a* and *lot* in *a lot*. But in the next paragraph, it appears again, twice:

   "Although wine is also cheap, if you drink alot of wine, you are called a wino; but if you drink alot of beer, you're just a big macho," Sousa said.

After three appearances of the barbarism, it becomes apparent that the reporter did not know any better. If an editor examined the copy at all, he did not know enough to correct it. Possibly a vague memory of the word *allot* (verb), meaning to apportion, had played a part in the muddling. The interviewed man would deserve sympathy if he were not an advertising executive who probably welcomed the free publicity for his client, notwithstanding a lot of errors.

LTD., LIMITED. *See* **FIRM.**

LUNCH. *See* **DINE.**

LUXURIANT and LUXURIOUS. *See* **Confusing pairs.**

-LY ending. *See* **Adjectives and adverbs.**

M

MA. *See* MOM, MAMA, MA.

MAGNETIC POLE. *See* NORTH POLE and MAGNETIC POLE.

MAJORITY. *1. MAJORITY and PLURALITY. 2. Singular or plural?*

1. MAJORITY and PLURALITY

An error in word usage can amount to a factual error, as in this passage from a local newspaper:

> All that was needed to win the election to replace Horcher was a simple majority and, according to tallies, the top vote-getter was Republican Gary Miller, who will take office immediately upon certification of the election. . . .
> Miller . . . garnered 18,304 votes, or 40 percent, in the field of six candidates.

If Miller won with 40 percent, he did not have a "simple majority"—or any other majority. He had a *plurality*.

A *majority* is at least half of the votes cast plus one. If three or more candidates run and none gets more than 50 percent of the total vote, the highest number of votes is a *plurality*.

Under many election laws, a *plurality* is enough to win. Others require a *majority* to win, and if no candidate gets it

in the main election, those with the two highest totals compete in a *run-off*.

2. Singular or plural?

A network's chief anchor man was reporting from South Africa, using a verb inconsistently: The vast majority of black students "is" undereducated. The majority of blacks "are" under twenty-one. "Is" is incorrect. *Are* is correct.

If *majority* signifies a particular number or a numerical superiority as such, it gets a singular verb. "The majority *was* only three votes."

If *majority* signifies the larger of two groups, the verb may be singular or plural. It depends on what the speaker or writer has in mind. When the group's unity is emphasized, the verb is singular. "The majority *stands* solidly behind the bill." But when *majority* refers to most individuals in a category, the verb is plural. "The vast majority of black students *are* undereducated."

This passage is from a special article in a financial newspaper:

> Many middle-ranking Chinese officers have expressed fears of a civil war because recent events have increased the divisions within the army. But the majority believes that the result will be not an army split, but an army controlled by the hard-liners. . . .

Change "believes" to *believe.* "Many . . . officers" foresee a split. But more officers foresee no split. "The majority" refers to most individuals in a category, not to a unified group.

See also **Collective nouns.**

MAMA. *See* **MOM, MAMA, MA.**

-MAN-, MAN. The combining form *-man-* means human being. It is found in words like *mankind* and *manslaughter,* as a prefix; and *freeman* and *woman,* as a suffix. The plural of the suffix is *-men.*

Woman came from the Old English *wifman,* from *wif,* meaning female or woman, and *man,* meaning human being (the meaning of *manu* in Sanskrit). The other meaning of *man,* that of an adult male, developed later.

The sense of *man* as human being or humanity is reflected in the Biblical line

So God created man in his own image . . . male and female created he them.

and in a passage by the philosopher David Hume:

There is in all men, both male and female, a desire and power of generation more active than is ever universally exerted.

Similarly, Jefferson's line in the Declaration of Independence that "all men are created equal" refers to all people.

Man retains that meaning to this day. Man cannot live by bread alone. Man's inhumanity to man. Man's best friend. The dawn of man. God or man. Man or beast. Man overboard!

That millennia-old syllable was threatened in the sixties and seventies when a radical movement arose to fix what was unbroken and break what was fixed. The mistaken belief that *-man-* meant male, coupled with the perverse notion that masculinity was ipso facto

bad, gave rise to several circumlocutions. They pollute the language to this day. One of them has been to substitute other words, no matter how unidiomatic or ludicrous the result.

Taking politic license, a book reviewer wrote:

It's a visiting firefighter type that drew understandable derision from Safer and other correspondents stationed in Saigon at the time. . . .

"Firefighter" stands out embarrassingly. Although that word may be an acceptable job title, the expression that the reviewer corrupted is *visiting fireman.* It means a visitor who is catered to because of his importance or money.

Some have chosen to change *mankind* to the windier *humankind,* unaware that *human* derives from the Latin *homo,* meaning man or a man.

Another circumlocution has been to drop *-man:* to give a *chairman* the name of a piece of furniture, a "chair." (*See* **CHAIR.**)

Then there are the "person" and "people" monstrosities, in which the offending monosyllable in almost any word is replaced with a disyllable. For example, *manhole* gets corrupted to "personhole," *airman* to "airperson," and *congressmen* to "congresspersons" or "congresspeople." (*See* **PERSON; PEOPLE as a suffix; SPOKESMAN.**) Turning *woman* into "woperson" has even been suggested. Unfortunately for male-haters, *person* has a *-son.* A few choose to misspell *woman* "womyn," as if to fool the English-speakers of the world.

The words *virtual, virtue,* and *virtuoso* do stem from the Latin word for a male, but thus far there has been no movement to resist them. *See* **VIRTUE.**

MANNER and MANOR. *See* **Homophones.**

MANSLAUGHTER. *See* **Crimes, 4.**

MANY and MUCH. "You won't get much extra sales if you throw in a pencil with every purchase of a car," says a book on marketing. Change "much" to *many*: "many extra sales. . . ."

Use *much* when you talk about a large amount of something ("much money") or a large degree ("much wisdom") or a large extent ("much devastation"). It goes with a singular noun.

Use *many* when you talk about a large number of things ("many trees" / "many people" / "many sales"). It goes with a plural noun.

Occasionally, in a more or less poetic vein, *many* is followed by *a* or *an* and a singular noun. "And many an eye has danced to see that banner in the sky." The meaning of *many* remains the same: a large number of things, though represented by one thing.

In that construction, any verb should be singular, e.g., "*has* danced." The narrator of a travel series on television erred in saying, "Many an amusing anecdote have been born" on a railway. It *has* been born. In a more common construction, the verb is indeed plural: "Many amusing anecdotes *have* been born" / "Many brave hearts *are* asleep in the deep."

See also **MUCH.**

MARGINAL, MARGINALLY. In general, *marginal* (adjective) pertains to a *margin* (noun). A *margin* is an edge or border of something. It can be literal, as the margin of a page; or figurative, as a *margin* for error or the line between being able or willing to carry out an activity and not.

The terms are used in various ways in business and economics. We may regard *margin* as the line between being in the black and being in the red. A *marginal* business barely meets its costs. The receipts for a *marginal* product barely cover the cost of production. A producer in that situation operates *marginally* (adverb).

Writers and speakers in the popular media often use "marginal(ly)" when all they mean is *small, slight(ly), a little*—or any of numerous synonyms. Perhaps they think that it has a more learned ring to it. A columnist wrote:

> Mr. Marchais has presided over a decline of the French Communists' vote by well over half, from a powerful force that blocked alternating politics to a marginal role on the national scene.

If she meant a *small, slight,* or *modest* role, she could well have said so.

Here is a part of a news dispatch from Luxembourg:

> . . . Appreciation of the United States is overshadowed these days by nervous talk of sabotage and snubs in this bucolic land, which is marginally smaller than Rhode Island.

"Marginally smaller" is better changed to "*somewhat* smaller" or "*a little* smaller." A still better way is to be specific: "*18 percent* smaller."

A report said that ten staff members of a university had found a management training program to be "a beneficial experience, but only marginally so." That roundabout wording—apparently laudatory at first but reversing course midway—could perhaps have been boiled down to "a *slightly* [or "*barely*"] beneficial experience."

MARIJUANA. *Marijuana,* sometimes spelled *marihuana,* is a complex drug produced from the *Cannabis sativa* plant and used illicitly, usually by smoking, for its intoxicating effect. It consists of any part of the plant that has been prepared for smoking, primarily by dry-ing. Containing at least 426 compounds, it produces thousands more when burned.

These headlines distorted the facts:

U.S. OK's marijuana pills

Legal marijuana capsules on way to 4 cancer victims

The first story described the contents of the pills as "synthetic marijuana," which is impossible. The second described the contents as "federally grown marijuana," which was erroneous. The pills contained no marijuana. Their active ingredient was synthetic THC (delta-9-tetrahydrocannabinol). THC is the principal mind-affecting ingredient in marijuana but it is just one of the 426 compounds.

Headlines like these went further in disseminating misinformation:

Pot—a New Prescription for Cancer?

Pot for cancer available

"Pot," which is slang for marijuana (as is "grass" / "weed" / "dope" / "herb" / "tea" / and "Mary Jane"), does not cure or ameliorate cancer and never has been used to treat cancer. Its smoking provides no medical benefit that is recognized by the medical profession or the federal government and, according to thousands of scientific studies, causes many injurious effects. These effects include transportation accidents, lung ailments, and probably cancer.

Marijuana cigarettes and, more often, synthetic THC in capsule form were tried out as an antiemetic, a drug for curbing nausea and vomiting, in some patients taking anticancer drugs. The THC was found to be effective. In 1986 the federal government approved the commercial production, not of marijuana, but of the encapsulated THC in

an oil base (under the trade name Marinol) and its dispensation by prescription to cancer patients unresponsive to conventional antiemetics.

MARSHAL. This word traces to the Old High German *marahscalh*, meaning horse servant. Originally a *marshal* was a groom, one who took care of horses. Later *marshal* was applied to the master of horses in a medieval royal household, then to the official in charge of military affairs for a sovereign. In various countries today, a *marshal* is the highest ranking military commander or a commander of a particular military branch. In the United States, officers of different kinds bear the title *marshal:* one who carries out federal court orders; a municipal functionary, such as a *fire marshal;* and the head of a parade.

The verb *marshal* means (transitive) to arrange in order ("marshal the troops"); to direct as a *marshal;* to lead, someone, ceremoniously; to enlist and organize for action; or (intransitive) to take up positions in proper order, particularly in military formation. The past tense or past participle is *marshaled* and the present participle is *marshaling.* The British prefer *marshalled* and *marshalling.*

Whatever the meaning, the noun or basic verb *marshal* is properly spelled with one *l* and should not be confused with the name *Marshall* (as borne by two Supreme Court justices, a vice-president, and a general and statesman). Confuse them is what *Webster's Third Dictionary* has done, indicating that the spelling is "also *marshall.*" It is if you are a grade-F speller.

Marshal is pronounced the same as *martial,* warlike or related to war. This adjective derives from the Latin *martialis,* of Mars, the god of war.

MASTERFUL and MASTERLY. When a political party spokesman told a television audience that the president "has handled this crisis in a very masterful fashion," he was saying in effect that the president had acted in a very dictatorial, arbitrary, domineering fashion, as a master acts toward a servant. Being of the same party as the president, the spokesman would not have uttered such a verity on purpose. Perhaps, had he known better, he would have used the word *masterly,* meaning like a master of a skill or discipline; possessing or exhibiting the ability, knowledge, or skill of a master.

Centuries back, *masterful* and *masterly* were both used in either sense. The distinction between the two was a useful development, but there has been retrogression. Now "masterful" is mistaken for *masterly* so often that modern dictionaries have rubber-stamped the misuse and accepted it as a secondary meaning without comment, thus contributing to confusion rather than to clarity.

Masterful is an adjective; *masterfully* is the related adverb. *Masterly* is both an adjective and an adverb.

From an autobiography: "He gave a masterful speech, greeted by a thunderous ovation." Befitting a foreign dictator, the sentence actually was meant to praise a U.S. president (another one).

MATERIAL and MATERIEL. *See* **Confusing pairs.**

MAXIMIZE. *See* **-IZE ending,** *1.*

MAY and MIGHT. *1. Fact versus supposition. 2. Other distinctions.*

1. Fact versus supposition

A comment by a government official that "The accident at St. Louis may have been prevented" was a mistake on its face. *May have* deals with fact, with what was possible. The speaker needed *might have* to express what was hypothetical, a supposition contrary to fact.

To say "He may have won all four" tournaments, as a golf authority said of the late Ben Hogan, is tantamount to saying "I'm not sure if he won all four or not." The intended meaning was "He *might* have won all four" had he played in them.

The opposite error enters this sentence (from an article):

Those in attendance last night, as well as a national cable audience, might have been years removed from the segregated world that Robinson challenged in such a public, yet lonely, fashion.

"Might" should be *may,* expressing what is possible.

These two sentences illustrate correct uses of *may* and *might* with *have:*

- "I *may* have attended the meeting, but I don't remember if I did." It discusses a question of fact, something that could have happened.
- "I *might* have attended the meeting if my health permitted." It deals with the hypothetical, presenting a supposition contrary to fact.

See also **Subjunctive.**

2. Other distinctions

These are some other distinctions between the two words (used as auxiliary verbs):

A. *May,* expressing permission in the present tense, as in "The boss *says* we *may* take the holiday off," becomes *might* in the past tense: "The boss *said* we *might* take the holiday off."
B. *May,* expressing possibility in the present tense, as in "The Browns *say* they *may* buy a house," becomes *might* in the past tense: "The Browns *said* they *might* buy a house."

C. *Might* can be used to express possibility in the present tense: "She *might* sue him." When it is used in that way, it is less forceful than *may:* "She *may* sue him"; the likelihood is greater here.

D. *May* can express a purpose or result, in a clause beginning with *that* or *so that:* "I work hard so that my children *may* be cared for." *Might* expresses a more forlorn hope: "We struggle that someday our people *might* be free."

E. *Might* in a courteous request as in "*Might* I say something?" is weaker and hence more humble than *may.*

MAYHEM. *See* Crimes, 4.

MEAN (adjective).

Mean in the sense of inhumane, malicious, or unkind often gets a tail these days, as in this snip from a movie review: "She is a mean-spirited, dishonest, highly judgmental individual. . . ." Followers of the fad would not be satisfied to call Simon Legree *mean;* he was "mean-spirited." The "-spirited" is not wrong, just often unnecessary.

So far the appending has not extended to *mean* in the sense of humble, low-grade, paltry, or petty.

MEAN (noun).

Three books on word usage misleadingly define the statistical term *mean* as "the midpoint" or "the middle point." In addition, a book on press style calls *mean* "a figure intermediate between two extremes." It gives 45 as the "mean temperature" between a high of 56 and a low of 34.

In a general sense, the noun *mean* does denote a middle point or medium. In a statistical sense, a *mean,* also known as an *arithmetic mean* or *arithmetical mean,* is what people commonly call an *average.* It is the sum of a set of figures divided by the number of figures in the set.

The definitions coincide only for a set of two figures. The mean of 56, 36, and 34 is 42.

A statistical term in which the middle point is essential is *median.* It is a figure midway in a set of figures arranged in order of size. In the set of three just above, the *median* is 36. (When the number of items is even, the *median* is the mean of the two figures in the middle.) Technically, the *mean* and the *median* are both *averages.*

ME and I. *See* Pronouns, *10.*

ME and MYSELF. *See* Pronouns, *3, 4.*

Measures, quantities. *See* AMOUNT and NUMBER; Collective nouns, *3;* FEWER and LESS; MANY and MUCH; Numbers; Verbs, *3.*

MEDAL and MEDDLE. *See* Homophones; Verbs, *2.*

MEDIA and MEDIUM. *1. Mass MEDIA. 2. Other MEDIUMS.*

1. Mass MEDIA

Radio is a *medium* of mass communication. Television is another such *medium.* So is the newspaper. So is the magazine. They are *media* of mass communication—and people in those *media* should know that, but not all of them do:

[Radio:] They pulled it off secretly [setting a killer free on parole]. No media was on hand.

[Television:] How well does the news media cover the story?

[Newspaper:] However, in this generation, the media is not so meek.

[Magazine:] While the argument that the media has become too powerful is plenty convincing . . . a majority of the public (54 percent) believes the media is fair. . . .

When bitten, the media has a habit of biting back.

The quoted sentences may be corrected as follows: "No media *were* on hand" or "No *news medium* was on hand." / "How well *do* the news media cover the story?" / ". . . The media *are* not so meek." / ". . . The media *have* become too powerful . . . the media *are* fair . . . the media *have* a habit of biting back."

Media is a plural of *medium*. Except in sentences like that one and this one, *media* is improper in the singular. There is no such word as "medias."

Agencies of mass communication have become known as *the mass media*. Those agencies in general, or at times just the *news media,* are colloquially called *the media*.

A talk show host used *media* wrong and right in the same sentence when a listener complained about excessive interest in O. J. Simpson.

To some extent the media is responsible, because they're covering all of this.

Make it "the media *are* responsible. . . ." *They're* is correct.

This sentence appears in a book, another *mass medium:*

Direct marketing is not restricted to any one media.

There cannot be "one media." Make it "one *medium*."

2. Other MEDIUMS

Mediums is another plural of *medium* and the only plural of the word when used in the sense of a person claiming the power to communicate with the de-

ceased. "She is superstitious and has gone to fortune-tellers and mediums."

The use of *media* rather than *mediums* is more common in designating agencies of mass communication.

A *medium* is also a means or instrumentality through which an effect is produced; an environment in which something exists and functions; or a nutritive substance in which organisms can grow. On a television news program, a physician tried to use the word in that last sense.

It's the water in the ear that makes a nice media for bacteria to grow.

"Media" should have been put in the singular: "a nice *medium*."

A *medium* is also something that is intermediate between two extremes. It is like the more common *medium* (adjective—the others are nouns), meaning intermediate or average, as in "small, medium, and large sizes." The last two *mediums* resemble the Latin *medium,* meaning middle, which English adopted.

MEDIAN. *See* **MEAN (noun).**

MEMORANDA and MEMORANDUM. A U.S. senator at a hearing kept referring to a written record as "a memoranda." It was *a memorandum*.

A participant in a television forum said, "North drew up memorandas. . . ." They were *memoranda* or *memorandums*.

Because *memoranda* is plural, "a memoranda" and "memorandas" are wrong.

MERCY and PITY. Heavy rains had swelled streams and caused widespread flooding. When the deluge subsided, a banner headline across a newspaper's front page read, unidiomatically: "Rivers take mercy." It looked as though a confused editor had combined a part of two common phrases: *take pity* and *have mercy*. Sometimes a creative writer departs from idiom, but a serious headline calls for communication more than creativity, and the humanizing of rivers is literary license enough.

Mercy and *pity* are not synonyms, though aspects of each are related. Often *mercy* is more active. It can suggest (1) an extraordinary act of kindness, possibly toward someone whom one is in a position to harm; (2) compassionate treatment, such as the relief of suffering; or (3) an inclination to be kind, to forgive, or to pity. Often *pity* (noun) is less active. It denotes a feeling of sorrow, sympathy, or compassion for another's misfortune or suffering. It may imply an attitude of condescension toward someone considered inferior or weaker.

Some words associated with *mercy* are *charity,* alms-giving, benevolence, or tolerance in judging one; *clemency,* a reprieve or lenient act by someone in authority; and *leniency,* mildness in dispensing justice or administering rules.

Some words associated with *pity* are *compassion,* sorrow for one's suffering with a desire to help; *commiseration,* a feeling or expression of sympathy with a person in distress; *condolence,* an expression of such sympathy; and *sympathy,* an understanding of and a sharing in one's grief, pain, or other feelings.

METAL and METTLE. *See* **Homophones.**

METAMORPHOSE. *See* -IZE ending, *1* (end).

Metaphor. *See* BEGET; BIG TIME; Cliché clash; Double meaning; LITERALLY; Metaphoric contradiction; SIRE.

Metaphoric contradiction. Instead of saying "What bad luck I'm having!" a poetically minded person might say "I am drowning in a sea of trouble." The statement would be a *metaphor,* a figure of speech in which one thing is likened to another. Often a concrete object (e.g., the sea) is used to describe an abstraction (trouble).

If that poet's main trouble is a drought that has dried up his vegetable garden, his metaphor is compromised—or it does not hold water, to use another metaphor. If it stirs mirth in his listeners or readers, he has defeated his purpose. Thus one needs to think of the literal meaning of a metaphor before using it for a particular purpose.

A newspaper story about health risks in restaurants pointed out that "a diner does not always know how long food has been sitting unrefrigerated" and it quoted thus a Food and Drug Administration spokesman: "If it's lukewarm, they're just playing with fire." Calling for a vision of lukewarm fire, the metaphor fizzled.

A news story about the tunnel under San Francisco Bay bore this lead: "BART will pull out all the stops today to try to locate the spot where water is still leaking into the trans-Bay tube at the rate of eight gallons an hour." It made one want to dash into the offices of the Bay Area Rapid Transit and shout, "Wait! Don't pull out the stops! Do you want to flood the tube?"

The topic on a national TV news program was skin cancer. A physician said, when asked about the safety of the tanning salon: "If people use it, they should use it with their eyes open." The interviewer missed a chance to ask: "Wouldn't people be safer using it with their eyes closed?"

Metaphors can be single words, just as they can be phrases. The same admonition applies. The task may be harder, inasmuch as the words are often used without regard to their literal meanings. A few examples:

- *Bottleneck*—"The biggest bottleneck in housing" fails as a metaphor. Its purpose is to describe the worst problem, so an analogy would be the narrowest, most constricting bottleneck, not the biggest.

- *Breakdown*—"The breakdown of patients by . . . departments . . . should be strictly followed." / "The houses should be broken down into types." Nobody is accused of promoting patient breakdowns in a hospital or broken-down houses in the real estate business, but *classification* or *classified* would have been preferable.
- *Depression*—A board was urged to promote industrial development before "a depression . . . arises." Literally a *depression* is a sunken area; to *arise* is to move upward. A related contradiction is the use of "as much as" together with "less." *See* **Numbers**, 2 (end).
- *Inundate*—Someone or something may be figuratively *inundated,* or flooded, but not by flames. *See* **INUNDATE, INUNDATED.**
- *Spawn*—A newspaper reported that one conference had "spawned" (that is, prolifically given birth to) others throughout the state. The conferences dealt with the prevention of teenage pregnancy. *See* **Double meaning.**

Two metaphoric words or expressions that are close by may contradict each other, even if they are individually satisfactory: "This is a virgin field, pregnant with possibilities" (a pregnant virgin?). "We must not allow ourselves to be stampeded into stagnation" (no place for a stampede).

Additional examples of ludicrous metaphors are in **BEGET; Cliché clash; LITERALLY.**

METEOR, METEORITE, and METEOROID.
A television news man described sightings of a blue, scintillating object in the sky, attributing to the National Weather Service that "it proba-

bly was a meteorite and it probably fell into the ocean."

Meteorites are not seen in the sky. A *meteorite* by definition is a body from space that has survived the trip to earth.

While it was traveling through the earth's atmosphere, it was a *meteor.* The term is applied also to the luminous streak produced by the *meteor's* friction with the atmosphere.

Before reaching the atmosphere, the object was a *meteoroid,* a small body that travels through outer space. A newspaper's science writer was imprecise in writing:

More precise radioactive dating methods have fixed the age of the oldest meteorites orbiting the Sun at about 4.53 billion years.

Those bodies are *meteoroids,* not "meteorites"—except in the loosest of language, unbefitting a science column.

MIDNIGHT. *See* **A.M., P.M., NOON, MIDNIGHT.**

MIGHT. *See* **MAY and MIGHT.**

MILE. *See* **KNOT.**

MILLIARD. *See* **BILLION.**

MIND. *See* **NEVER MIND.**

MINER and MINOR. *See* **Homophones.**

MINIMIZE. To *minimize* something is to reduce it to a minimum ("We must minimize our cost") or to place it at the lowest or smallest estimate ("I minimized my estimated tax") or to make it appear as small or trifling as possible ("Smith, the attorney, minimized his client's responsibility for the accident").

Minimize (verb, transitive) is an absolute term, several authorities agree. It is not properly qualified by adverbs like *considerably, greatly,* or *somewhat.* They can qualify a verb such as *belittle, diminish, reduce,* or *underrate,* none of which is the meaning of *minimize.*

Even when used properly, the word can be misunderstood. In isolation, this press sentence permits two interpretations:

> In his session with the Tower commission, McFarlane said he had acquiesced in a White House effort to minimize the president's role in the affair.

Was the effort (1) to make sure that the president would play as small a role as possible or (2) to make the president's past role appear as small as possible in the eyes of the public? The context shows that it was the second.

A related adjective is *minimal,* the least possible (cost, tax, role, etc.).

MISCHIEVOUS, MISCHIEVOUSNESS.

Discussing a case of sexual harassment on the job, the host of a nationally televised talk show said, "It really seems that it went from a kind of mischeviousness to a much more malicious acting out."

"Mischevious" or "mischeviousness," with the emphasis on the second syllable, is not a legitimate word. It is a distortion of the proper word *mischievous* (adjective) or *mischievousness* (noun), pronounced MISS-chuh-vuss (ness).

Mischievous means causing mischief; *mischievousness,* the inclination to cause mischief. *Mischief* is vexing action or conduct, or its result. Depending on the context, it can vary from a child's impishness to destruction or violence by a miscreant or nonhuman agent. A related word is *mischievously* (adverb), in a mischievous way.

MISDEMEANOR. *See* CRIME, MISDEMEANOR, and FELONY.

MISINFORMATION. *See* FACT.

MISLEAD and MISLED. *See* LEAD (verb) and LED.

MISNOMER.
A guest on a TV interview show said that Henry Kissinger was born in the United States, not in Germany as many people thought. "It's a common misnomer," he said.

An incorrect idea may be a *misbelief,* a *misconception,* or a *mistake,* but it is not a "misnomer." A *misnomer* is a name or epithet that is wrongly or inappropriately given to a person or thing; or an error in a name, particularly in a legal document.

For instance, the term *Indian* when applied to an aborigine of the New World could be called a *misnomer.* Columbus was said to have used it for natives of the Bahamas in the erroneous belief that he was in India.

(As for Mr. Kissinger's country of birth: five reference books say Germany.)

Misquotation. *See* Clichés; Quotation problems, *1.*

MISQUOTE. *See* QUOTE and QUOTATION.

MISS, MR., MRS., MS. *See* Plurals and singulars, *2H;* Titles, 2.

Modifiers. *1. Dangling. 2. Extraneous. 3. Misplaced. 4. Piled up. 5. Restrictive. 6. Senseless.*

1. Dangling

A. Dangling participles

> Although widely used by the men, Bashilange women were rarely allowed to smoke cannabis.

One might think that the topic was female abuse rather than drug abuse. The sentence, from a book about cannabis, literally says that the women were "widely used by the men."

It is an example of a *dangler,* a phrase that does not fit the rest of a sentence and does not accomplish what the writer thinks it does. It may apply to the wrong person or thing or to nothing.

As a rule, *modifiers* adjoin the words they *modify.* (*See* **Modifying.**) In the example above, the writer wanted a phrase at the beginning of the sentence to modify the word at the end, "cannabis." The placement of the phrase and its lack of subject and verb encourage its bonding with the nearby subject of the sentence, "Bashilange women." Here is a possible correction: "Bashilange women were rarely allowed to smoke cannabis, although it was widely used by the men."

In each of the four examples coming next, the noun that is supposed to be modified is not even there; it exists only in the mind of the writer or speaker. The dangling phrase affixes itself to the subject that is there.

A news report on national television about a car accident included this sentence:

> Severely burned and nearly an invalid, her lawyer expects that any agreement with General Motors will require secrecy.

If any who heard it sympathized with the lawyer, blame the opening phrase. Grammatically it applies to the subject, "her lawyer." The description could have been placed in another sentence: "*The girl is* severely burned and nearly an invalid. Her lawyer expects. . . ."

This was on the radio:

> After being hit by the spray, the officers called the fire department and an ambulance.

Anyone who had just tuned in could reasonably gather that officers had been hit

by spray. Just before that, the newscaster had announced that it was a seemingly drunk man who had been pepper-sprayed. Change the opening phrase to "After *hitting the man with* the spray" or "After *the man was sprayed.*"

A newspaper example follows. The writer had escaped an earthquake.

> Now, finally, overlooking the Golden Gate Bridge, tears started to fall, tears of gratitude.

This seems to say that the falling tears overlooked the bridge, a senseless statement unless "tears," the subject, is a metaphor for rain. Change "overlooking" to *as we overlooked,* or else change "tears started to fall" to *we started to shed tears.*

A dangler can appear at the end of a sentence. The example is from an article about alcoholic policemen.

> Termination is recommended if found drunk on the job.

The subject is "Termination," which of course cannot be "found drunk" though the sentence literally suggests otherwise. After "if," insert *an officer is.*

The examples above illustrate what textbooks and teachers call the *dangling participle* and have derided for generations. Whoever coined the term evidently visualized a participle dangling precariously from a sentence. H. W. Fowler called them *unattached participles.* As he saw them, they were not even dangling. They have been called also *confused, disconnected, misrelated, suspended,* and *wrongly attached participles.* (*See* **Participle** for a definition.)

B. Some other danglers

The problem goes beyond participles. *Danglers* come in different varieties, such as adjectival, adverbial, and nounal phrases. Examples follow, first a caption that appeared under a picture of a cartoon character.

> At 52, the feisty little black duck's star may finally be on the rise.

The subject is the duck's "star," which, we are literally told, is 52 (young for an astronomic object). If that is the *duck's age* (an advanced age for a fowl), one way out of the dangling would be to scrap "At 52." A sentence could be added after "rise": *Daffy Duck is 52.* (That pile-up of adjectives is dubious too. Commas would help: "The feisty, little, black duck's. . . .")

This was broadcast on a national radio news program:

> Travelers checks may protect you against thieves while on vacation.

It seems to imply that traveler's checks, if not thieves, are on vacation. After "while," insert *you are.*

Up to now, the examples all have contained phrases applying to the wrong words. But sometimes a phrase just dangles there, applying to nothing in the rest of the sentence. This example is from a restaurant review:

> More culinary independence was shown with what the menu called "Pork, Chicken and Veal Spiedini" ($7.50) with Polenta. Basically a grilled brochette, there was no chicken anywhere in sight.

The latter sentence makes no sense. The first part of it has nothing to do with the second part grammatically or logically. Splitting it into two sentences helps to correct it: "It was basically a grilled brochette. There was no chicken anywhere in sight."

C. Journalistic danglers

There is a similar type of dangler, so common in newspapers that it might be called the *journalistic dangler.* It is a descriptive noun phrase that comes at the end of a sentence and bears no grammatical relationship to the rest of the sentence. Often it deals with a precedent or a record. It may follow a dash. Five illustrations from the press follow.

> By the time the last valve is in place, the tunnel's price tag is expected to total $5 billion—the most expensive project financed by the city.

The phrase following the dash does not connect with anything. One expects it to modify "$5 billion," for it immediately follows it. Now "$5 billion" is an amount, a cost, or a sum, but it is not a "project." Change the phrase to something like this: "—the highest sum for any project ever financed by the city."

> Sister Francis Russell has co-founded a home for needy men, women and children, resettled Cambodian refugees in Denver, Cubans in Cheyenne, and recently received the Social Worker of the Year award from the National Association of Social Workers—the first recipient to have been active in the anti-nuclear movement.

The phrase following the dash ought to modify the "award," but "the first recipient . . ." does not do it. Either make the phrase a separate sentence ("She is the first recipient of the award . . .") or rephrase it ("—the first such award presented to someone active in . . ."). By the way, the sentence has other faults, including a bad series and confusing punctuation. (Omit the comma after "Denver" and substitute *and.* Change the commas after "children" and "Cheyenne" to semicolons. *See* **Punctuation, 11; Series errors.**)

> For a while it appeared that the parties would simply be canceled,

a multibillion-dollar disaster for Tokyo's hotels and restaurants.

What does "a multibillion-dollar disaster" modify? Nothing visible. Preceding it with a verb, say *causing*, rescues the sentence.

A newspaper and a news agency covered the same event, and the lead paragraphs of both stories contained *journalistic danglers* of similar wording:

> Residents of Sacramento, Calif., voted Tuesday to shut down their utility's only nuclear power plant, the first time voters have decided to close a working reactor.

> Residents of the capital area have voted to shut down the trouble-plagued Rancho Seco nuclear power plant, the first time such a facility has been closed by voters.

What does "the first time" modify? Not the nearest noun, "plant"; not "Residents"; not anything obvious. Again, the dangling phrase may be placed in a separate sentence, for instance: "This is the first time. . . ." Or else: "For the first time, voters have decided to close a working nuclear reactor. Residents of the Sacramento area voted Tuesday to shut down. . . ." (It was the first time *where?*—in the world, in the U.S.A.? Neither story explained.)

D. Absolute constructions

Some expressions resemble danglers, yet they have won the right to exist alongside their grammatical cousins. They are *absolute constructions*. A word or phrase in that category is not grammatically connected with the sentence it appears in. Referring to no specific thing or person, it modifies a thought in a general way.

Here are some examples: "*Strictly speaking,* the stomach is an organ of digestion." The opening phrase is very

common, and nobody will think that the stomach is speaking. "Let's play one more game, *winner take all.*" There the unconnected phrase comes at the end. "*The storm having ended,* we set sail on the third of May." / "*My secretary being ill,* I hired a temporary employee." That form is well established, though considered artificial by some. One difficulty is that someone may be tempted to insert a comma, incorrectly, after the first noun (*storm* or *secretary*).

Absolute constructions include adverbs, such as *admittedly, conceivably, happily,* and *thankfully;* participles, *assuming, barring, concerning, considering, failing, following, given, granted, judging, provided,* and *regarding;* participial phrases, *all things considered, depending on, generally speaking,* and *speaking of;* and other phrases, *after all, by and large, on the whole, in the long run, in the final analysis, to be frank,* and *to be honest.*

This is acceptable: "*Considering the era,* it was a remarkable accomplishment" *Considering* is not connected with the subject. But this is a dangling participle: "*Considering his merits,* my cat deserves to win the contest." The cat seems to be engaged in an intellectual pursuit.

E. Danglers that dangle

Let us end our discussion of *danglers* with a couple of sentences from news stories (about the Amazon Basin and Kennedy Airport) in which things are said to really *dangle.*

> As the boats swerved among palms, rosewood and wild fruit trees, the rescue team kept ducking to avoid vines and aerial roots, dangling like dangerous nooses overhead.

> A cigarette dangling from his mouth, he said he wanted to sit down with the Port Authority management to

discuss his "plan" to legalize Smarte Carte hustling.

To keep the rescue team from "dangling," make it *which dangled*. And to avoid equating the man at the airport with a dangling cigarette, precede the latter sentence with *With*.

See also **Gerund**, 2 (more dangling participles).

2. Extraneous

The newspaper article quoted below is referring not to four governors (the diminutive governor, the conservative governor, etc.), but to only one.

> Mr. Mecham's decision . . . provoked a constitutional confrontation between the Legislature and the first-term Republican Governor. . . .
> After his statement, the 63-year-old Governor agreed to answer questions posed by the committee. . . .
> The diminutive Governor arrived at the hearing dressed in a powder blue suit. . . .
> The recall campaign and a boycott of the state by many convention groups began almost as soon as the conservative Governor took office.

This illustrates a peculiar journalistic practice. Instead of devoting a sentence or paragraph to a description of a person, the writer sticks in descriptions at irrelevant places.

Sometimes an extraneous modifying phrase interrupts a sentence: "Marceca, *a civilian Army employee*, refused to testify at a Senate hearing Friday." At times it starts a sentence: "*Born in . . . Australia . . .*, Mr. Mitchell served as a Royal Canadian Air Force pilot. . . ." / "*A West Point graduate from Bridgeport, Conn.*, Mr. Mucci ran unsuccessfully for Congress. . . ." Neither of the forms represented by the quotations is necessarily wrong. Either is acceptable when the

facts are related: "Murphy, *an amateur astronomer*, discovered a comet last year." / "*A corporate executive*, he is well to do."

See also **HAVE, HAS, HAD**, *1*; **WHO**, 2.

3. Misplaced

A. Ludicrous placement

This sentence appeared in a restaurant "guide" in a neighborhood newspaper:

> Enjoy Scallops Provencal or fresh salmon cooked to order while watching football.

If the fish's last request is to see the Super Bowl on TV, the phrase "while watching football" is in the right place. More likely, it belongs at the beginning of the sentence.

A modifier tends to bond with a nearby word or phrase. When the modifier is placed too far from what it is supposed to modify, the result can be ludicrous, like the example above or the four examples that follow.

The moderator of a television forum ended the program by saying, "Thank you all for watching very much." Was he thanking people for watching very much television? More likely the phrase "very much" was misplaced, belonging immediately after "all."

Interviewed on television, a lawyer told families of homicide victims:

> You have the right to recover, the same as if someone ran over your little girl in the street who was drunk.

He was not implying that they would give their small daughters booze. Again, the final phrase was misplaced. Here is where it should have been: ". . . the same as if someone *who was drunk* ran over. . . ."

A heading in a postal brochure reads:

Let everyone know you're
moving ahead of time.

Literally it says to announce a premature move. To make it say what was intended, put "ahead of time" ahead of "you're moving."

This message seems to be a fixture on so-called noncommercial television:

With twelve billion dollars in annual sales, your broker knows McKesson.

No doubt he would love to do that much business. The phrase preceding the comma belongs after "McKesson."

Excerpts from a newspaper and a magazine are reminiscent of Groucho Marx's tale of the time "I shot an elephant in my pajamas."

Police said he was convicted . . . of a misdemeanor . . . after he was stopped by police in a stolen truck.

Face and hands greasepainted gold, . . . he collects a hefty amount of money from European tourists in a gold can.

Groucho wondered what the elephant was doing "in my pajamas." We can wonder what the police were doing "in a stolen truck" and what the European tourists were doing "in a gold can."

B. *Ambiguous or misleading placement*
As absurdly as the above examples are worded, their meanings are nonetheless understandable. The six press quotations below illustrate that separating a modifier from what it is supposed to modify can obscure or transform the message. We start with three headlines; in each the modifying phrase was wrongly placed last.

Readers of the headline "North learned he was fired from TV" could reasonably deduce that North had worked in TV. But the story under the

headline said he had *learned from TV* that the President had announced his dismissal as a staff member of the National Security Council. The phrase *from TV* needed to modify *learned*, not "fired."

"Torture Is Depicted in Turkey" implies that someone in Turkey has described the matter in pictures or words. Actually the description took place in England, where a group (Amnesty International) had issued a report that accused Turkish authorities of harming political prisoners. "Torture *in Turkey* Is Depicted" would have been right. The phrase *in Turkey* needed to modify *Torture*, not "Depicted."

"Children gather to celebrate life at Mount Zion Hospital" boosts the hospital. But the story said that former patients in the intensive care nursery had attended a party "to celebrate the gift of life," not life at the hospital. The headline's last four words need relocation, as in this version: "Children gather *at Mount Zion Hospital* to celebrate life."

The rest of the city relies on Staten Island mainly as a garbage dump; more than three-quarters of the city's garbage is disposed of in a vast landfill on the island known as Fresh Kills.

A reader might wonder: is "the island known as Fresh Kills" off the coast of Staten Island, or did the writer put the phrase "known as Fresh Kills" in the wrong place? A possible editing: ". . . a vast landfill, *known as Fresh Kills,* on the island."

This excerpt deals with a concert in Prague:

Mr. Neumann, who conducted with a large Civic Forum button in his lapel, was joined on the stage after the last movement, the "Hymn to Joy," by Vaclav Havel, the playwright who is the Forum's leader and presidential candidate.

Havel would not have appeared to get credit for a Beethoven composition if the sentence had begun, "After the last movement, the 'Hymn to Joy,' Mr. Neumann. . . ."

This one deals with health records of nuclear weapons workers:

> Last month, the Department of Energy halted an agency letter from being sent to the group that officially denied its request.

Taken alone, the sentence seems to say that a certain "group that officially denied" a certain request of the department almost received some kind of letter. A study of the context suggests this reinterpretation:

> The Department of Energy had prepared to send the group a letter that officially denied its request, but the department decided last month not to send it.

This version, bringing the letter and its message together, would have averted the confusion (and left no one wondering what an "agency letter" was and how it differed from any other letter).

C. Unidiomatic placement

Adverbs can get misplaced in unnecessary efforts to avoid split infinitives or the division of verb phrases. *See* **Adjectives and adverbs, 2; Infinitive, 4; Verbs, 4.**

D. *Intrusion between THE and noun*

The, the definite article, pertains to what is already known. A common defect in the press is to intrude an adjective with new information between *the* and its noun. *See* **THE,** 2C.

4. *Piled up*

The practice of piling up modifiers on top of a noun is a journalistic practice that results from an effort to be terse. In a typical example, a press item identified a man as "South Oklahoma City Chamber of Commerce executive vice president Jim Crosby." The standard construction would be "Jim Crosby, executive vice president of the South Oklahoma City Chamber of Commerce." The writer's purpose seemed to be to save the space of *of, the,* and a comma. It can get more confusing, as in this item from a magazine:

> What was O. J. *Simpson white knight* Johnnie Cochran doing popping into the fraud trial of Robert Maxwell's sons in London recently? [Emphasis added to modifiers.]

At first the item seems to be about Simpson. While the style saves a minute amount of space, it may waste a bit of the reader's time by obliging him to reread a passage to understand it.

Seven words, a figure, and an initialism intervene between "purchase" and "buses" in this sentence from a newsletter:

> In January 1996, the Golden Gate Bus Transit Division got the go ahead to purchase 30 *newly designed Motor Coach Industries (MCI) "Commuter Special"* buses. [Emphasis added.]

A neater and clearer sentence would get to "buses" sooner, deferring part of that description (and putting a hyphen in *go-ahead*).

To avoid a mere two-letter word, someone writes, "Police arrested him on *receiving stolen goods* charges," instead of "charges of receiving stolen goods." Then there are the strings of hyphenated nouns used as adjectives, such as "the workers' *50-cents-an-hour wage-*

increase demand," instead of "The workers' demand for a wage increase of 50 cents an hour."

See also **Nouns,** *5;* **Prepositions,** *6;* **Titles,** *1;* **UNLIKE,** *1.*

5. *Restrictive*

This is the last paragraph of a crime story distributed by a national news service:

> After Mr. L—— was arrested, he confessed to the Monday burglary.

On reading the sentence above, one might wonder if there was a Sunday burglary, a Saturday burglary, and so on. Slipping in the word "Monday" tends to restrict the meaning. It implies that burglaries were committed on more than one day but that the arrested man confessed only to the one on Monday. That is not the case; only one burglary was under investigation. The essential fact is that the man confessed it.

Four paragraphs above, the story mentions that the man was arrested on a Tuesday. That might have been a good place to make known that the arrest came a day after the crime. Instead, the writer waited until the end to stick the fact about Monday in a place where it did not belong.

Here is a similar example, by a newspaper writer:

> The patient was reported in stable condition after the 7:30 a.m. operation.

The qualifier "7:30 a.m." could make a reader wonder if there was, say, a noon operation or a 6:45 p.m. operation too. Three paragraphs earlier, the story says that the operation lasted more than six hours. That would have been an ideal place for the time.

Two variables becloud the sentence below, broadcast on network television.

Of the several special-education students aboard the bus, only one suffered minor injuries from flying glass.

A person who had tuned in late and heard that sentence alone might reasonably wonder: Did the others suffer *major* injuries from flying glass? Minor injuries from *other* causes? *Major* injuries from other causes? The problem lay in the modifiers of the noun "injuries" that the telecaster had jammed into the sentence. Those modifiers, "minor" (adjective) and "from flying glass" (prepositional phrase), tended to restrict the meaning. One who had heard the whole piece, of which the above excerpt is the final sentence, might guess that this message was intended:

> . . . Only one suffered any injuries. They were minor wounds, caused by flying glass.

Here each fact is isolated, not confused by any other fact.

6. *Senseless*

Announcements like this make one want to talk to the television set:

> We will be back two weeks from tonight. Until then, this is Dan Rather.

Who will you be then, Dan? "Until then" made no sense and could easily have been left out.

Phrases of that sort often conclude broadcasts, their purpose evidently being to connect sentences and provide smooth transitions. They have little or no meaning.

Radio disc jockeys typically utter lines like this: "You're listening to KAZOO, Zanyville, where the time is 7:39 a.m." What time is it elsewhere in town?

Modifying. To *modify* in grammar is to qualify or limit or alter the sense of (a word or group of words). In "the red mill," for instance, the adjective *red* modifies the noun *mill*. In "They run fast," the adverb *fast* modifies the verb *run*.

A *modifier* is a word or word group that modifies another word or word group. It may be an adjective, an adverb, a participle, a phrase, etc. *See* **Modifiers** for a catalogue of misused varieties, such as danglers.

MOISTURIZE. *See* **-IZE ending,** *1*.

MOM, MAMA, MA. *Mom* originates in baby talk. It is short for *mama,* also spelled *mamma* and *momma,* which is a doubling of *ma. Ma* is an infantile utterance that is common internationally.

Such terms are expected in children's vocabulary and among the appellations by which adults address their mothers. They appear increasingly in other colloquial speech. Except in quotations, none of them has any place in more formal speech or writing, particularly in an otherwise solemn piece like an obituary:

> K——'s mom said he loved to surf so much that he will have a surfer's funeral with an ocean ceremony off Stinson at sunset on Friday. . . . Services will be held at 4 p.m. Friday at his father's house in Stinson Beach.

Note that the quoted obituary does not say "his pop's house" or his "papa's" or "dad's" or "daddy's" house. "Mom" stands out conspicuously and undignifiedly. Only one word takes its place: *mother.*

MONKEY. *See* **APE and MONKEY.**

Mood. The word *mood* as used in grammar is a set of verb forms. It does not have anything to do with the happy or sad type of mood. The grammatical

mood is just a variation of *mode.* It shows the mode, or manner, in which a speaker or writer wants to represent an action, whether factually, commandingly, or otherwise.

Grammarians call the moods *indicative, imperative,* and *subjunctive.*

By far, the most frequently used one is the *indicative* mood. It is the ordinary verb form. It suggests that one is presenting a fact or asking a question about fact. Every sentence in this entry up to now is in that mood.

In the *imperative* mood, one gives a command or tells someone to do something. Examples of sentences in that mood are "Come here" / "Stop, look, and listen" / "Friends, Romans, countrymen, lend me your ears."

The *subjunctive* mood is for various statements or questions in which the actions are doubtful, hypothetical, conditional, or otherwise not factual. It is the mood that is used least often. *See* **Subjunctive.**

MORAL and MORALE. *See* **Confusing pairs.**

MORE and MOST. It is a rather common error to use "most" in place of *more.* A news article produced the example.

> Foreign analysts here are undecided over which version [of events in China], the official or the foreign, is most believed.

"Most" should be changed to *more,* because only two versions are mentioned.

The rule is that when just two things are compared, *more* (comparative) is the word to use; and when three or more things are compared, *most* (superlative) is the word.

See also **Comparative and superlative degrees; MORE with COMPARATIVE; MOST with superlative.**

MORE THAN and OVER. *See* OVER and MORE THAN.

MORE THAN ONE. Although a logical case could perhaps be made for its plurality, the phrase *more than one* is usually treated as singular. "More than one union claims jurisdiction." / "There is more than one way to skin a catfish." (*One* draws the next word, the subject noun [*union* or *way*], into its singular sphere of influence; and the predicate verb [*claims* or *is*] agrees with the noun.)

It is different when the phrase *more than one* is split up. "More unions than one claim jurisdiction." / "There are more ways than one to skin a catfish." (The plural implication of *more* makes the subject noun that follows it [*unions* or *ways*] plural; the predicate verb [*claim* or *are*] agrees with the noun.)

In the journalistic sample below, the trouble transcends the question of singular versus plural.

> More than one out of five Hispanics in HISD [Houston Independent School District] drops out of school.

If the statement had said that "one out of five Hispanics in HISD drops out . . . ," it would not be arguable. But the "*more than* one" phrasing is an absurdity. *More than one* person is at least *two* persons; you cannot have, say, a person and a half. Presumably the writer meant not *two* (or she would have said so) but something like "22 percent of Hispanics" or "more than one-fifth of Hispanics."

MORE with comparative. *More* does not go with the comparative form of any descriptive word. The radio speakers who slipped up as follows probably knew that elementary rule.

> Sometimes it [purple asparagus] can be a little more sweeter than the green asparagus.

> There is a way to empower your children and make them far more better and powerful students.

> . . . You have canker sores and that's going to let the organism get in a little more easier.

In the first quotation, omit "more." In the second, relocate it ("far better and *more* powerful"). In the third, keep it but change "easier" to *easily* ("a little more *easily*").

More and the *-er* ending, which means *more,* are redundant together. One speaking standard English does not normally say "more sweeter" / "more better" / "more easier," and so on. (Speakers of Hawaiian pidgin do say such things.)

"More preferable" is another redundancy. "More" is usually superfluous, because *preferable* is a comparative form.

See also **Comparative and superlative degrees; MOST with superlative.**

MOST and MORE. *See* MORE and MOST.

MOST with superlative. An article about selecting meat appeared with this mistake (or shall we say "mis-steak"?): "The filet mignon, he said, is the most tenderest but also has the least flavor."

You may say that something is the *most tender* or the *tenderest* but not that it is the "most tenderest." *Most* (as an adverb) does not go with any word containing the suffix *-est,* which means the same as *most.* Someone can be the *most clever* or the *cleverest,* the *most happy* or the *happiest,* the *most silly* or the *silliest,* and so on.

Certain superlatives take only the *most* form. *Most* regularly precedes adjectives and adverbs of three or more syllables (such as *astounding* and *terribly*) and sometimes those of fewer syllables (such as *dreadful* and *aptly*).

Some other adjectives and adverbs take only the -*est* form (for example, *few* and *fast,* which become *fewest* and *fastest*). Still others are irregular (*good* and *less* becoming *best* and *least*).

See also **Comparative and superlative degrees; MORE with comparative.**

MOTHER. *See* MOM, MAMA, MA.

MUCH. *1. "A BIT MUCH." 2. "MUCHLY."*

1. "A BIT MUCH"

The contemporary cliché represented by these press excerpts seems a bit contradictory: "His IRA penalties seem a bit much" / "Houseman says the success of his S-B ad has become a bit much" / "The Government began to fear that the reaction was a bit much."

When "bit" and "much" are juxtaposed, the idea of smallness or moderation clashes with the idea of largeness or notableness.

Such a clash occurred also when "a little" became the modifier, in a television forum: "To be shocked that this is going on [charging people money to dine with the president] is a little much."

Too much means an excessive amount, degree, or extent. That amount etc. may be only slightly excessive: *a little too much* or a *bit too much.* To omit the *too* is to create a contradiction.

In the first example, a headline, there is also a conflict between the plural "penalties" and the singular "much." *See* **MANY and MUCH.**

2. "MUCHLY"

Occasionally someone attaches a superfluous -*ly* to *much,* either mistakenly or facetiously ("Thank you muchly"). H. W. Fowler dismissed "muchly" as worn-out humor in 1926, and it has not grown funnier since then. Centuries back it was used seriously and deemed proper. *Much* is now the standard adverb. "We

don't depend *much* on the government" is synonymous with "We don't depend *greatly* on the government."

Much can be an adjective ("It gives me much pleasure"). It can also be a noun, meaning a large amount or quantity ("Did you find much"?) or a great thing ("The job is not much").

MUNCH.
Dictionaries do not agree on how *munch* originated. Some say it was an imitation of chewing. Others say it came from the French *manger,* to eat, plus the English *crunch* by way of the Middle English *munchen.* To most of them, *munch* suggests the sound of chewing. The chewing is at least ample and vigorous and perhaps steady. Is *munching* really going on in the press examples below?

Wednesday evening at the Opera House, Dance Theater of Harlem invited the community to munch on a bit of birthday cake. [Only "a bit of" cake for the whole community?]

The streets of the city still are filled with people of money munching bran muffins as they push their way through the crowd. [A strange portrait of San Francisco.]

Too late for a prime table, they seemed to be happy in a tiny corner spot[,] munching on steak sandwiches and beer.

You *munch* raw carrots and crisp toast, not a typical, fluffy birthday cake. A bran muffin is not likely to be *munched* either. Sandwiches on toast may require *munching,* but how on earth does anyone *munch* beer?

MURDER. *See* Crimes, 4.

MUST HAVE and "MUSTA." *See* HAVE, HAS, HAD, 2.

MUTUAL. The adjective *mutual* describes a relationship between two persons or things in which there is an interaction or exchange: *mutual admiration, mutual assistance, mutual fear.*

An old use of the word to describe something held in common was popularized by the Dickens novel *Our Mutual Friend.* A dictionary's rationale for "mu-

tual friend" is that the adjective *common,* connoting "low" or "ordinary," would be a stigma. But *a friend in common* would not. If Jack and Jill like climbing hills, they have a *common*— not "mutual"—interest.

MYSELF. *See* **Pronouns,** *3, 4.*

N

Names of products. *See* **Trademarks.**

Names, plural. *See* **Plurals and singulars,** *2H, K.*

NANO- prefix. *Nano-* is a combining form meaning billionth (in the American sense: one part in 1,000,000,000). It is used in scientific contexts. A *nanocurie* is one billionth of a curie. A *nanogram* is one billionth of a gram. A *nanometer* is one billionth of a meter. A *nanosecond* is one billionth of a second. Although it is a theoretical unit and brief beyond perception, it has been seized by nonscientists for displays of verbal extravagance.

A journalist said, in a TV forum, that a political adviser had worked for a candidate, not for a day or a week, but "for a nanosecond." The host of a radio talk show said, "Anyone who can think for more than a nanosecond knows how specious that whole line of argumentation [for natural birth control] is." A headline in a full-page, full-color magazine ad for an employment service read, "Opportunity Knocks Every Other Nanosecond In Silicon Valley." Perhaps the company felt that "Every Nanosecond" would be overdoing it. Still, a hint of 500 million jobs every second depreciated the ad's credibility.

Nano- was drawn from the Latin *nanus,* which came from the Greek *nanos.* The words mean dwarf.

See also **BILLION.**

NATIONALITY. *See* **RACE and NATIONALITY.**

NATURAL GAS. *See* **GAS.**

NAUSEATED and NAUSEOUS. The title "Feeling Nauseous" flashed on the television screen several times to announce a forthcoming report on motion sickness. *Nauseated* was needed. "Nauseous," although common in conversation, is improper for more formal use.

Nauseated (adjective) means suffering from *nausea* (noun), a feeling of sickness in the stomach. "I feel nauseated."

That which is *nauseous* (adjective) produces nausea. "It's a nauseous gas." A synonym is *nauseating.*

A person can be *nauseated* without being *nauseous* in the same way that a person can be endangered, periled, or poisoned without being dangerous, perilous, or poisonous.

To *nauseate* (verb, transitive) someone is to produce nausea in the person. "The gas nauseates me." / "The rough sea has nauseated us." Less common relatives are *nauseation* and *nauseousness* (nouns) and *nauseatingly* and *nauseously* (adverbs).

All those *n*-words come from the

Greek *nausia,* meaning seasickness. It stems from *naus,* ship, the origin of our word *nautical.*

NAUTICAL MILE. *See* KNOT.

NAVAL and NAVEL. Three food stores sold "NAVAL" oranges. So indicated a newspaper advertisement, a window sign, and sales receipts. None of the stores suggested any connection between the navy and the oranges. (For instance, "These vitamin-rich fruits are good for the high C's, a sweet treat for the fleet!") Hence we can assume that they all misspelled what should have been *NAVEL.*

A seedless orange that bears a depression resembling a *navel* is called a *navel orange.* The *navel* (noun) is the mark on the abdomen representing the place where the umbilical cord was connected to the fetus. *Naval* (adjective), as in naval officer, pertains to a navy. If you need a memory aid, you can think of the *a*'s in anchors aweigh.

NEAR MISS. "Canadian Jet in Near-Miss," a headline said. The incident may be described as a *near-accident,* a *near-disaster,* or a *near-tragedy,* but it was an actual *miss.*

When *near* is tied to the noun with a hyphen, it implies that the accident, disaster, tragedy, or other incident *almost* occurred. It came *close* to occurring but was barely avoided. The *miss* was not avoided. What should have been avoided was the hyphen—or, better yet, the whole phrase.

What about these two headlines, with no hyphen?—"Near Miss for Elizabeth Dole" and "Near Miss Reported in Smoke." *Near* can also mean *narrow.* As an example, at least four dictionaries give "near escape." So we cannot condemn whoever wrote those two headlines. But why use an expression that can be confusing? Some readers may not know whether a "near escape from

prison" was an escape or not. As for listeners: oral reports have no punctuation.

There are better ways to express the idea of a narrowly averted air accident, or other mishap, as in the following examples. An article was headed, "Planes Just Miss Collision Over Sea." One sentence of the text said, "Both crews planned to file official near-collision reports with the F.A.A." The Dole story said that a plane carrying her "was involved in a near-collision with another aircraft."

NEAT. Nothing is wrong with a *neat* home, desk, or person—one that is spick-and-span, orderly, uncluttered. A *neat* trick or job is performed with adroitness, deftness, precision. And if you drink whiskey *neat,* undiluted, you can get drunk quickly.

On the other hand, "neat" in the juvenile sense is slang: like "cool," an all-purpose adjective of approval, synonymous with "keen," "groovy," and "swell" from earlier eras. Adults have been perpetuating the childish use of "neat."

In response to a news report of a robot designed to save lives by destroying land mines, a young woman at a TV anchor desk made this penetrating comment: "That's pretty neat."

On the same day, also on TV, a noted critic expressed his discerning appraisal of the Theremin, the electronic musical instrument: "It sounds neat."

A book instructs computer users that a certain program "has a neat way to change text" and that "you can do all kinds of neat things with headers. . . ."

See also COOL.

NEE. *Nee* or *née,* pronounced NAY, means born, as it does in French. It is used to introduce the maiden surname of a married woman, for instance "I am Gladys Goldman, née O'Brien." In strict use, it is not followed by the woman's

given name, only by her name at birth: her family name.

A legend under a published photograph identified a governor with "Mrs. Thomas Pattinson, nee Marcy Taylor," who under her original name gained celebrity for a valorous act. *Formerly* would have been preferable, because the given name needed to be mentioned but did not properly go with "nee."

See also **BORN with name.**

NEEDLESS TO SAY. *See* **OF COURSE,** *3.*

Negatives. *See* **"AIN'T"; "AREN'T I?"; AS,** *4;* **BECAUSE,** *1;* **BUT,** *6;* **Contractions,** *2;* **Double negative; Ellipsis; FLAMMABLE** (etc.); **Infinitive,** *4;* **LIKE,** *1;* **NEITHER; NEVER MIND; NO CHOICE; NO WAY; NONE; NOR; NOT; NOT ABOUT TO; NOT ONLY; NOT TO MENTION; PROOFREAD** (etc.); **REALLY** (end); **Reversal of meaning,** *1;* **THAT, ALL THAT; TOO,** *1;* **TO SAY NOTHING OF; UNLIKE; WHICH,** *1;* **WILLY-NILLY.**

NEITHER. *1. Equation. 2. Negativity. 3. Number and person.*

1. Equation

Neither . . . nor must connect two equal things. So must *either . . . or* and similar forms (correlative conjunctions). One side must be grammatically parallel to the other. If a verb follows *neither,* a verb follows *nor;* if a noun, a noun; and so on. This quotation is aberrant:

In a news conference, the Pravda editor, Ivan T. Frolov, also vowed that under his direction Pravda would neither cater to conservatives nor radicals. . . .

The sentence is not logical. It says that Pravda would neither "cater" (verb) nor "radicals" (noun). "Neither" and "nor" are followed by different parts of speech.

The simplest way to fix the sentence is to exchange the positions of "neither" and "cater to," thereby equating noun and noun: ". . . Pravda would cater to neither conservatives [noun] nor radicals [noun]. . . ." Another way is to exchange "neither" and "cater" and add another *to* to the "nor" side, thereby equating prepositional phrases: ". . . Pravda would cater neither to conservatives nor to radicals. . . ."

Neither does not go with "or." However, if *nor* introduces two closely related nouns, *or* may connect them: "Neither Bennett nor Johnson *or* his wife was in the house when the fire broke out."

See also **NOR.**

2. Negativity

Neither without *nor* means *not either* (adjective) or *not either one* (pronoun). Respective examples: "She selected neither suitor" and "She selected neither."

Inasmuch as *neither* carries a negative meaning, it is wrong in a sentence like this, which has another negative: "I didn't go neither." Use *either* to avoid a double negative.

Two dialogues from a situation comedy follow. Each response has two words, both wrong.

[Elaine:] I haven't been eating anything different.
[Jerry:] Me either.

[Mother:] I've never seen your arm move like that.
[Father:] Me either.

The negative does not carry over from the first speaker to the second. The latter needs his own negative, whether *neither* or another *n*-word. Among correct responses that could have been put in the script are "I neither" / "Neither have I" / "Nor have I" / Jerry: "I haven't either" /

Father: "I've never seen it either." ("Me either" might at best be defended as an ellipsis, or a short form, for a sentence that nobody would be likely to utter: "Me haven't been eating anything different either" or "Me have never seen it either." Maybe Tarzan could get away with "Me" instead of *I* for the subject of a sentence, but native speakers of English should know better. *See* **Pronouns**, *10*.)

3. *Number and person*

Neither without *nor* is construed as singular. A verb that follows must be singular: "Only two of the suits are left and neither *fits* me" (not "fit").

Any object of the verb also is singular if it would normally be singular for an individual subject. This is from a news article:

> Neither of the women, who were said to be babysitting the children, was wearing seat belts. . . .

The verb, "was wearing," is correctly singular; but the object is inconsistently plural: "seat belts." Neither was wearing *a seat belt*. (The material between the commas is irrelevant to the main thought and belongs in another sentence.)

Neither without *nor* pertains to only two things or two persons, not to three or more. "Neither of the two boys" / "neither of the couple" / "neither of the pair" are correct. "Her feelings were very hurt that neither of the three of us showed up" (said by a caller to a radio psychologist) is incorrect. *See* **NONE**, *1*.

The *neither . . . nor* construction sometimes applies to more than two things or two persons: "Neither snow, nor rain, nor heat, nor gloom of night stays these couriers. . . ." Note that *nor* is repeated for each item. This excerpt from a book is not idiomatic:

> . . . Neither the President, Congress as a whole, nor either of its houses may

constitutionally defeat action by the rest of the government to meet the country's responsibilities abroad.

When nouns that immediately follow *neither* and *nor* are singular, the verb is singular: "Neither Jim nor Al *earns* much money" (not "earn"). When both nouns are plural, the verb is plural: "Neither gems nor precious metals *were found* in the wreckage."

When the nouns differ in number, should the verb be singular or plural? If the plural noun is nearer to the verb than the singular noun, the verb should be plural: "Neither his wife nor his sisters *like* his politics." But if the singular noun is nearer, a problem arises. In the sentence, "Neither his sisters nor his wife ———his politics," some authorities would allow *likes,* others *like.* The advice here is to place the plural noun ("sisters") second, as in the former example, or to recast the sentence, e.g.: "His wife and sisters dislike his politics."

Any possessive pronoun that follows *nor* also must agree in number with the verb: "Neither Charles nor Susan owns *his* or *her* own home" (not "their").

A final puzzle concerns the verb following a personal pronoun. An authority lets the nearer subject govern the verb: "Neither he nor I *am* at fault." / "Neither I nor he *is* at fault." But revision may be better: "He is not at fault, and neither am I."

See also **EITHER.**

NEVER MIND. A weekly's front page contained the headline "Nevermind the English" (referring to competition from New Zealand in popular music). In a column in a daily, one read, "Nevermind that I had repeatedly been warned . . ." (not to lean too far back in a chair).

Never mind is a phrase of two words: the adverb *never,* meaning at no time or not at all; and the verb *mind,* meaning to pay attention to or care about someone or something (transitive) or to take notice or be concerned (intransitive).

The journalists were probably unfamiliar with the song "Never Mind the Why and Wherefore"—stressing *mind*—from Gilbert and Sullivan's *H.M.S. Pinafore*.

NEVERTHELESS. *See* BUT, *5*.

NEW RECORD. *See* RECORD.

NICKEL. The metallic element symbolized by *Ni* is *nickel*. The five-cent piece is a *nickel,* after one of its metals. Both end in *-el* only.

In defining "nickle," *Webster's* has been fickle. It was a local British term for "the green woodpecker" in the second dictionary. *Webster's Third* ignores the bird and calls "nickle" a "var of NICKEL," instead of the misspelling it is.

NIL and NILL. *See* WILLY-NILLY.

NISEI. A biography harks back to World War II and

> the case of the 112,000 Nisei, over 75,000 of them native-born American citizens, who were removed from their homes on the West Coast and sent to "relocation centers" in the mountain states. . . .

Those who were born in Japan should not be called "Nisei." An immigrant to the United States from Japan is an *Issei;* the word is Japanese for first generation. *Nisei,* meaning second generation, refers to a U.S.-born child of those immigrants. A U.S.-born grandchild of the immigrants is a *Sansei,* which means third generation. Each term may be used unchanged as a plural, or *s* may be added: *Isseis, Niseis,* and *Sanseis.*

If all of that looks too complicated, one may refer to Japanese immigrants, children or grandchildren of Japanese immigrants, or Americans of Japanese ancestry.

NOBEL PRIZE. Two scientists at the University of California School of Medicine were being honored for a discovery concerning cancer cells. "Today they won the Nobel Peace Prize for Medicine," a newscaster announced on television. She was confused. The Dalai Lama of Tibet won the *Nobel Peace Prize* that year. His activities had nothing to do with medical discoveries, and the research of the scientists, Bishop and Varmus, had nothing to do with the promotion of peace.

The peace prize is decided and awarded in Norway; the prize in medicine or physiology, in Sweden along with separate prizes for accomplishments in chemistry, economics, literature, and physics. A bequest of Alfred B. Nobel, Swedish chemist and the inventor of dynamite, established the *Nobel Prizes* in five fields. They were first awarded in 1901. The Bank of Sweden added the economics prize in 1969. Winners get money and medals.

NOBODY. *See* Pronouns, 2C.

NO CHOICE. A restaurant may offer *no choice* of soups. A dictatorship may offer *no choice* in an election. But "I had no choice"—or "We have no choice" or a variation on that theme—is also a hoary excuse for gory acts.

Hitler said, on launching World War II, "I have no other choice" than to fight Poland. In the United States, "We have no choice" was Theodore Roosevelt's rationale for the nation's asserting its power abroad.

At a time of supposed peace, a national newspaper reported that U.S. planes had attacked Serbian planes. Its explanation was that the Serbs had flown contrary to the United Nations' wishes, leaving the Americans "little choice but to blow them out of the sky" (a non sequitur). "Little choice"? The Americans had the choice of *not* blowing them out of the sky; the choice of talking instead of shooting; the choice of going home. Life presents most of us with innumerable choices, and national leaders generally have more choices than the rest of us.

A local newspaper reported that the mayor "felt he had no choice but to fire almost his entire Library Commission. . . ." The headline read, "Jordan Didn't Have Choice in 'Massacre.' " But as a city's chief executive, he had the choice of *not* doing it. By the way, to quote a politician's self-serving blather is excusable; to headline it without attribution, thus presenting it as fact, is not.

Nominative case. *See* **Pronouns,** *10.*

Nondefining clause. *See* **THAT** and **WHICH.**

NONE. *1. Number. 2. Other uses.*

1. Number

None (pronoun) may be construed as singular or plural or either, depending on its meaning in a sentence. A pedagogic and journalistic rule has long held it to be singular only. Indeed its original version, in Old English, *nan,* meant *not one:* it was a fusion of *ne,* not, and *an,* one.

Yet most authorities accept both constructions, and literature records both. In the Bible we find both "trouble is near and there is none to help" and "none come to the appointed feasts." Dryden wrote that "none but the brave deserves the fair" and Tennyson, "I hear a voice, but none are there."

None may mean *not one,* emphasizing singularity: "I asked each person, and none was aware of the problem." Instead of *none,* however, using *not one*

or *not a single one* may be a stronger way to make the point. Unquestionably *none* is singular when it means *not any amount* or *part:* "None of the merchandise is domestic." / "She says none of the advice helps her."

None may be plural when it means *not any (people or things):* "Of all the people in our town, none appear more industrious than the Lees." At times it must be plural: "None of these contenders have much fondness for one another." Using "has" would conflict with "one another," which is plural. "None of the troops were completely prepared for their mission abroad." Nobody would be speaking of one "troop."

At times *none* may be regarded as either singular or plural. "Of the models advertised, none *suits* me" or "none *suit* me." Singularity is possible in this sentence: "None of the houses *is* for sale." But "houses *are*" has fewer s's, a consideration if the sentence is to be spoken.

Whichever construction is selected, any related verb and pronoun must agree in number. "None of the machines still *works* as well as *it* used to" or "*work* as well as *they* used to" / "None of the men *has his* orders yet" or "*have their* orders yet." (*See also* **Pronouns,** *2.*)

Whether you deem *none* to be singular or plural in a particular sentence, stick with your decision. The quotation is from a short story in a magazine.

> None of these players was over 18, and they were trying too hard either for the $100 prize or to impress the girls gathering behind them.

Were should replace "was," which is inconsistent with "they were" and "them."

None meaning *not any* applies to three or more people or things, not to two. The phrase "none of the three cats" is right but "none of the two cats" is wrong. *See* **NEITHER,** *3.*

2. Other uses

None (adjective) meaning *no* is an archaic use that survives in the phrase *none other.* "The winner was none other than my sister."

A paragon, someone or something without equal, may be called a *nonesuch* (noun). "Caruso was a nonesuch among singers."

None, as an adverb, appears in the following expressions:

* *None the less.* The phrase *none the less* or word *nonetheless* means *nevertheless* or *however.* "Small in stature, he was none the less [or "nonetheless"] skilled in basketball."
* *None the* plus comparative. In a sentence like "They were none the wiser," *none* means *not at all* or *to no extent.*
* *None too.* In its understatement, this phrase serves as mild sarcasm. It can mean *not sufficiently:* "This horse is none too fast." Sometimes it is ambiguous, meaning either *barely enough* or *not quite enough:* "We arrived none too soon." *See also* TOO.

NONESUCH, NONETHELESS, NONE TOO, etc. *See* NONE, 2.

NONFLAMMABLE. *See* FLAMMABLE, INFLAMMABLE, and NONFLAMMABLE.

"NO NOTHING." *See* Double negative, 1.

Nonrestrictive clause. *See* THAT and WHICH.

NOON. *See* A.M., P.M., NOON, MIDNIGHT.

NO ONE. *See* ONE as pronoun, 3; Pronouns, 2C; Reversal of meaning, 1.

NOR. 1. How it is used. 2. NOR and OR.

1. How it is used

Nor (conjunction) often serves as the negative version of *or.* It is most common in the construction *neither . . . nor:* "This is neither fish nor fowl." In such a construction, *nor* is always right. It is no more correct to say "neither . . . or" than to say "either . . . nor."

Nor, like *or,* links alternatives. When the alternatives make up the subject of a sentence and each alternative is singular, the verb too must be singular. Example: "Neither Dan nor Tom speaks French" (not "speak"). When the alternatives are plural, the verb is plural. When the alternatives differ in number, complications arise. *See* NEITHER, 3.

A sentence without *neither* may still take *nor.* Example: "The telephone has not rung, nor has any mail arrived." Such a sentence contains two thoughts, or ideas, and the negative force of the *not* would not carry over to the second thought without help. *Nor* furnishes that help. (Some may find this construction difficult to master or too formal for their tastes. The second clause may be expressed in other ways, e.g., "and no mail has arrived.")

"Will you condemn him . . . who shows no partiality to princes, nor regards the rich more than the poor . . . ?" In that Biblical example, the *no* unaided would have no effect on the idea about the rich and the poor. *Nor* negates the action of the verb *regards.* "Or" would not do it.

See also NEITHER, 1, 2.

2. NOR and OR

A rather common error is to use "nor" redundantly in place of *or.* Generally you use *or* when (1) the sentence is a simple one (that is, it has essentially one thought) and (2) the negative word or phrase fits each item.

A book says a little airplane "didn't have a rudder, nor a tailplane." Many grammarians would disapprove of the sentence, considering it to contain a double negative. (Literally *neither . . . nor* amounts to a double negative; nevertheless it is well established.) A better phrasing is "didn't have a rudder *or* a tailplane." The sentence is simple, and the one negative ("didn't have") fits each item (each aeronautic part).

An alternative phrasing is "didn't have a rudder, nor did it have a tailplane." The sentence no longer is a simple one (a clause has been added), and no longer does the one negative cover it all. Under those circumstances, *nor* is the conjunction to use.

In another book we read: "His son's literary success would never cheer Lord Auchinleck nor improve relations between them." Change "nor" to *or*. The sentence is simple, and the first negative ("never") fits each item ("cheer" and "improve").

Some grammarians would condone the use of *nor* in each excerpt as a way of stressing a difference between the two items. It conforms with the practice of some past writers, including Shakespeare and Shaw. Except for those who fancy themselves in that class, the safest course is to follow the rules.

See also **OR.**

NORMALCY. A myth that "President Harding coined 'normalcy' from ignorance of 'normality' " has been perpetuated since the twenties. Two authors of a handbook for writers repeated it (in the above quotation). So did a history teacher of mine in high school. It dates at least from 1929, when a writer alleged in a tract of the Society for Pure English:

If . . . 'normalcy' is ever to become an accepted word it will presumably be because the late President Harding did not know any better.

The Oxford English Dictionary traces *normalcy* to a mathematics dictionary published in 1857—eight years before Harding was born.

It is the persistent objection to *normalcy*, not the use of the word, that is based on ignorance. The word is a valid alternative to *normality*, but be advised of that objection.

The statement below was uttered in 1920 by the man who occupied the White House from 1921 to 1923. It is technically impeccable, perhaps too slick; it has the earmarks of a speech writer.

America's present need is not heroics but healing, not nostrums but normalcy, not revolution but restoration.

NORTH POLE and MAGNETIC POLE. At a national meeting of mathematics teachers, a salesman was selling compasses. "These compasses draw circles; they won't point to the North Pole," a columnist wrote.

The magnetic compass, the type of compass that he probably was alluding to, does not point to the *North Pole*. It points to the *North Magnetic Pole* (or *Magnetic North Pole*). The location of the latter varies from time to time, but atlases published in the 1990s place it amid the Queen Elizabeth Islands in the waters of northern Canada, some 800 miles from the true *North Pole*. (There is another type of navigational compass, the gyroscopic compass, used on large ships, which does point to the true North Pole, although no one would expect it to be for sale at a teachers' convention.)

Just as the earth has two poles, north and south, it has two *magnetic poles,* north and south. Either end of a magnet also is called a *magnetic pole*.

NOT. *1. Ambiguity. 2. Problems of placement.*

1. Ambiguity

The use of this adverb requires care. Usually *not* is definite in its meaning: negation, refusal, in no way, to no degree, no. Yet in some contexts, as indicated below, *not* can permit widely varying interpretations.

A. NOT ALL and ALL . . . NOT

Not all . . . are is different from *all . . . are not*. The latter invites confusion. Normally the place for *not* is immediately before the word or phrase that it qualifies.

These two sentences do not have the same meaning:

- Not all lawyers are truthful.
- All lawyers are not truthful.

The first means that some are untruthful. The second means that all are untruthful; that is the literal meaning, although it may not be the intended meaning.

The problem is essentially the same when *not* is separated from *every* plus noun, *everyone,* or *everything.* "Not every applicant is qualified" (some are unqualified) is far different from "Every applicant is not qualified" (literally, all are unqualified).

A book says (about writing an article): "Everything that will go into it is not in your notebook." The authors meant: "*Not* everything that will go into it is in your notebook."

B. NOT TOO

The standard meaning of *not too* is *not excessively.* It can be confused with a colloquial meaning: *not sufficiently.*

"That chinaware is not too fancy for a holiday dinner," says Gertrude. Does she approve or disapprove of the dishes? The standard meaning is that they are not excessively fancy. The colloquial meaning is that they are not sufficiently fancy.

Fred, a farmer, says, "We haven't had too much rain this year." (Of course -*n't* is a contraction of *not.*) He could be either pleased or displeased by the weather. If rain was excessive last year and flooded his farm but has been normal this year, Fred may be speaking literally and expressing his relief. On the other hand, if there is a drought, "haven't had too much" may be his way of saying "haven't had *enough.*"

See also **TOO.**

C. NOT *with AS*

It can be confusing to follow *not* with *as,* in the manner of this example: "Columbus was not the first European to discover America, as many people believe." Do "many people" believe that he *was* or that he *was not?* Rephrase it. Depending on meaning, you might either begin with the phrase "Contrary to popular belief, . . ." or end the sentence with "America" and add a sentence: "Many people now believe that other Europeans arrived earlier."

See also **AS,** 4.

D. NOT *with BECAUSE etc.*

Whether *not* applies just to the next word or to more can be a puzzle. The sentence is apt to include *because.*

"He was not hired because of his background." Was he hired for another reason? Or was he turned down, and, if so, was the reason something in his background? In either case, rephrasing is desirable. For example: "He was hired, not because of his background, but because . . ." or "He was not hired, and the reason was his background." If a sentence has two ideas, they should be clearly distinguished.

An explanatory phrase without *because* can create a similar ambiguity.

"The bill was not introduced for political reasons." / "We did not file at Grant's request." Does "not" modify all that follows or just the verb ("introduced" or "file")?

See also **BECAUSE,** *1.*

E. NOT *with* LIKE

This is a problem similar to that of *not* with *as*, though less common. "Alice is not married, like Betty." Is Betty married or single?

See also **LIKE,** *1;* **UNLIKE,** *1.*

F. *Omission of* NOT

The fear of omitting *not* leads the press to misrepresent legal proceedings. It usually reports pleas and verdicts of *not guilty* as "innocent." *Not* is infrequently forgotten; **Reversal of meaning,** *1,* gives examples.

See also **Guilt and innocence,** *2.*

G. *Superfluous* NOT

In a complicated sentence, *not* is sometimes introduced unnecessarily, producing a double negative.

". . . He had found nothing to make him doubt that H—— was not rightly convicted." In other words, he firmly believed that the person was wrongly convicted. That is the opposite of the intended meaning: Actually he believed that the conviction was justified. But a *not* was erroneously slipped into the sentence, canceling the negative effect of *doubt* and reversing the meaning. Omit *not,* or rephrase the sentence; for instance: ". . . He had found no reason to question H——'s conviction."

See also **Double negative.**

H. *Uncompleted* NOT

Sometimes it is unclear what *not* pertains to. Whatever that is has been omitted.

"The Senate's current version calls for spending $2.6 billion for drug enforcement that the House does not." The House "does not" *what?* The writer has left out a necessary verb.

See also **Ellipsis.**

2. *Problems of placement*

Referring to the two sides in a labor dispute, a television reporter said, "They have been not making any progress." The statement is clear, but "have *not* been making" would be more idiomatic. Perhaps he was under the erroneous impression that splitting a verb pair, like *have been,* was wrong.

Putting *not* in the wrong place can throw a sentence out of kilter; witness this complex example from a newspaper's front page:

It was an attempt not to change President Bush's mind, which the organizers of the march consider improbable if not impossible, or to persuade Congress to pass a law, which they deem unnecessary.

Better: "It was *not* an attempt to change. . . ." Thus *not* modifies "was an attempt." The news writer misplaced "not," modifying "to change"; a reader could at first think the organizers attempted to avoid changing the president's mind. The "which" clauses (with unclear antecedents and four negatives, including a second "not") contribute to the muddiness.

When a sentence has multiple verbs, it may not be clear which one *not* modifies. It takes some effort to interpret this press example correctly:

Defense attorney Nancy G—— asked the court to dismiss that charge because the ruling involved a third party who struck a pregnant woman, *not the mother herself* [emphasis added].

Does the emphasized phrase contrast with "involved a third party" or with "struck a pregnant woman"? A reader at first could reasonably think it refers to the latter, because "woman" immediately precedes "not." However, the story suggests that the other interpretation is correct. It would be less ambiguous to say that "the ruling involved, not a pregnant woman, but a third party who struck a pregnant woman." (The writer encouraged confusion by following "pregnant woman" with "the mother," instead of repeating "pregnant woman." One could take them to be two people, for a pregnant woman is not necessarily a mother. *See* **Synonymic silliness.**)

A fad based on a disconnected "not" appears to be fading away, fortunately. Someone first makes an outlandish statement; for example, "The President has ditched his wife and moved in his girl friend." After a pause, the single word "not" follows, supposedly canceling the fib. If a listener does not stick around for the "not" or fails to recognize it when so grossly misplaced, a rumor can take wing.

Not goes before the *to* of an infinitive: "She swore *not to* reveal their secret," instead of "to not." *See* **Infinitive,** *4.*

Among entries dealing with *not* are **BECAUSE,** *1;* **BUT,** *6;* **Contractions,** *2;* **Double negative; NOT ABOUT TO; NOT ONLY; NOT TO MENTION; PROOFREAD, PROOFREADING** (example); **Reversal of meaning,** *1;* **THAT, ALL THAT; WHICH,** *1* (example).

NOT ABOUT TO.   The subtitle of a magazine article about hotel maids was a long one:

> If they were going to clean rooms, they were going to be well paid—so they struggled for their union. And they're not about to give it up.

The phrase "not about to" in the sense of *determined not to* or *unwilling to* (do something) is colloquial and regional. It was curious to find it displayed prominently in a reputedly sophisticated publication representing a city where that expression was alien.

The standard meaning of *about to* is *ready to* or *soon to* (do something). In the negative, the encroachment of the nonstandard meaning brings problems of ambiguity. "He is about to leave for home" is fairly clear. "He is not about to leave for home," as broadcast nationally, is ambiguous. Does it mean that he will not leave soon (the standard meaning) or that he is determined not to leave at all (the nonstandard meaning)?

Even when the meaning is clearer, the nonstandard phrase is not appropriate in writing, unless the writer's intent is to reproduce colloquial, regional speech; and it can be risky. In the press sample below, a foreign correspondent used the phrase in the nonstandard way (the context indicates), using it inappropriately and—as it turned out—inaccurately:

> But the reaction by the authorities indicated that the Czechoslovak [Communist] leadership is not about to take the path chosen in East Germany.

The leadership in Czechoslovakia was indeed "about to take the path chosen in East Germany." Four weeks after the article appeared, it resigned.

NOT ALL THAT.   *See* **THAT, ALL THAT.**

"NOT HARDLY."   *See* **Double negative,** *3.*

NOTHER.   As a legitimate variation of *other, nother* is obsolete. It is now dialectal and nonstandard.

A radio announcer, advertising recorded products, said, "Video is a whole nother thing." Correction: "Video is a whole *other* thing," or, better,

"Video is *another* thing entirely." *Another* equals *an other*. The *n* is needed only when the indefinite article adjoins the *o*. *See* **A and AN**.

NOT JUST, NOT MERELY, NOT SIMPLY. *See* NOT ONLY.

NOT ONLY. In using the phrase *not only*, watch out for three pitfalls. This sentence (from a book on marketing) illustrates them:

> The franchise not only buys training, but a recognized brand name.

1. Misplacement of *not only*. The word *only* tends to attach itself to whatever immediately follows. In the sample, the word following "only" is "buys." The writer did not intend to emphasize "buys," but that is what he has done. He meant to emphasize "training." (*See also* **ONLY**.)
2. Grammatical imbalance. *Not only* and *but also* are sister (correlative) conjunctions. The grammatical structures following them must match. In the sample, the phrase following "not only" is a verb and its object ("buys training") whereas what follows "but" is a noun phrase ("a recognized brand name"). The phrases do not match grammatically.
3. Omission of *also* (or a synonym). A sentence like the following does not need *also* (or a synonym): "Today I choose *not* steak *but* lobster." An item is substituted for another. However, the next sentence needs the *also*: "Today I choose *not only* steak *but also* lobster" (or "*but* lobster *too*" or *as well* or *in addition*). An item is added to another.

We correct the quotation by interchanging "not only" and "buys" and by inserting *also*:

> The franchise *buys not only* training but *also* a recognized brand name.

Now noun matches noun, and *also* (adverb) announces an addition. (The comma is not necessary.)

"The franchise not only buys training but" would be acceptable if followed by another verb and its object, e.g., "*buys* a recognized brand name also."

The next (newspaper) example properly contains "also," but it too misplaces "not only," producing a grammatical imbalance.

> The fact that the army fired on Chinese citizens not only shocked the Chinese people but also large segments of the army. . . .

Again "not only" is followed by a verb and its object ("shocked the Chinese people") whereas "but" is followed by a noun phrase ("large segments of the army"). The sentence may be corrected most simply by interchanging "not only" and "shocked":

> . . . *shocked not only* the Chinese people but also large segments of the army.

This way, noun matches noun.

Occasionally *not only* does not need to be followed by *but* or by *also* (or synonym):

- *But* is unnecessary if the contrast that it expresses is indicated in another way; for instance: "Protecting the environment is not only good public policy: It can be good business too."
- *Also* (or synonym) is unnecessary when what follows the *but* does not add something substantial but merely intensifies what came before; for instance: "He was not only a poet but a great poet."

The principles that apply to *not only* apply also to similar phrases, like *not just, not merely,* and *not simply.* "What helps agriculture benefits not just farmers but the nation as well."

NOTORIETY, NOTORIOUS. A person who is *notorious* (adjective) is well known for something bad or objectionable. "The accused is notorious for his drug dealing." / "He's a notorious liar." The condition of being notorious is *notoriety* (noun).

A Wall Street analyst was introduced on television as "one man who has achieved some notoriety for his predictions." *Fame, prominence,* or *repute* would probably have expressed the meaning intended by the host, without insulting his guest.

The featured words should not be confused with other words beginning with *not-*: A person of *note* has achieved some *notice* or *notability* (nouns), that is, distinction, eminence, or importance, but not "notoriety." The person is *notable* or *noteworthy* (adjectives) but not "notorious."

The implication of badness may or may not apply to inanimate objects: "a notorious gambling house" / "a notoriously [adverb] soft metal."

NOT REALLY. *See* REALLY.

NOT THAT. *See* THAT, ALL THAT.

NOT TO MENTION. Should we mention this expression at all? It was used as follows in a telecast and a newspaper:

These were bikers [motorcyclists] for Dole, not to mention it was a great day to go biking.

One of the many oddities in this battered capital is that a son of Gen. Mo-hammed Farah Aidid, the Somali faction leader who humiliated the United States in 1993, was a naturalized American citizen, not to mention a United States marine.

Another oddity is the expression "not to mention." If one is not to mention something, why does one mention it?

At times the phrase is a colloquial substitute for *and by the way* (which would have suited the first example) or *let alone.* At other times its purpose is unclear; the item or point that it introduces might better be joined to the main idea by *and* or *or.* The second example could have said the son "was a naturalized American citizen *and* a United States marine." A book on word usage says of an adverb:

. . . *Where* may also be a pronoun or a noun (not to mention a conjunction).

How about "a pronoun, a noun, *or* a conjunction"?

See also TO SAY NOTHING OF; Verbal unmentionables.

NOT TOO. *See* TOO.

Nouns. *1. Definition. 2. Noun creations. 3. Number. 4. Omission. 5. Using nouns as adjectives.*

1. Definition

A *noun* is the name of something or someone. These are the main kinds:

- *Proper noun* (also called *proper name*)—the name of a specific person, place, or thing, spelled with an initial capital (Gertrude, Chicago, Acme Laundry).
- Its opposite: *common noun* (also called *common name*)—a name that represents no specific thing, place, person, etc. but rather a category

with multiple specimens (antelope, planet, noise).

- *Abstract noun*—the name of an idea, quality, or state (patience, length, merriment).
- Its opposite: *concrete noun*—the name of an object that one's senses can perceive (apricot, robin, telephone).
- *Collective noun*—the designation of a group of things or people (team, gang, army).

Besides being single words, *nouns* may be hyphenated words or groups of words (will-o'-the-wisp, human being, scarlet fever).

Among other uses, nouns may be subjects ("*Rain* is falling"), objects ("He hit the *target*"), complements ("That lady is her *mother*"), and appositives ("Jim, the *guide*, has arrived"). An *appositive* is a word or group of words in *apposition*, i.e., placed beside another to identify or explain it. (*Guide* is a noun in apposition with *Jim*. See also **Punctuation**, *3A*, on commas.)

Some words, like *love* and *set*, are classified both as nouns and verbs. Other words, although not classified as nouns, can serve the function of nouns. In the sentence "I love *eating*," the last word is a gerund, a verb form acting as a noun. (*See* **Gerund**.) A word or group of words that serves the function of a noun, whether it is a true noun or its equivalent, is called a *substantive*.

2. Noun creations

Using an adjective as a noun in place of a legitimate noun is a contemporary fad, illustrated as follows.

A commercial for a shampoo said, "You really can feel the clean." Asked what an R movie rating meant to him, a child said, "It means in some ways more intense. We like intense."

Perhaps one cannot expect an advertiser to care about using the noun *clean-* *ness* or *cleanliness* properly or a ten-year-old to know the noun *intensity*. However, a radio psychologist should know *politeness*. She advised a caller to "Just turn on the polite." And a stand-up comedian should know *humility* (even if he does not practice it): He called Parisians arrogant and added, "If you want humble, go to Paris, Kentucky."

Those who put on situation comedies are guilty of similar distortions, such as a comedienne's comment, "It's not about cute. It's about pitiful." Could she and her writers all have been ignorant of the nouns *cuteness* and *pitifulness*? Another comedienne said, "I think there are different types of pretty"—instead of *pretti-* *ness* or *beauty*. Her counterpart on another show instructed sonny in the different types of "proud." She needed *pride*. A supporting actor on still another show said, "If you want common, you name a kid John." The noun is *commonness*.

Clean, intense, polite, humble, cute, pitiful, pretty, proud, and *common* are all adjectives, modifiers of nouns but not nouns themselves. Some words that are primarily adjectives legitimately double as substantives; the nouns they would modify are understood: a *commercial* (announcement); a *musical* (comedy); the *rich* and the *poor* (people). One may speak of *the humble,* but not of wanting "humble."

The nouns are ripped more painfully from some adjective-noun phrases, including *classified ads, personal ads,* and *gay man;* and the adjectives are dubiously made plural: "classifieds" / "personals" / "gays." (*See also* **GAY**, *3*.)

News people create some nouns of their own. In traffic reports, "the roadway is blocked by an overturn" (instead of *overturned vehicle*) and "we do have a stall on Highway 24, eastbound" (not a place for a horse but a substitute for *stalled vehicle*).

"There are more layers of pretend in

'Waiting for Guffman' than in most movies," a critic wrote. "Pretend" is a verb. Pertinent nouns include *pretense, pretending,* and *make-believe.*

Nouns are sometimes forced into verbal roles. *See* **Verbs,** 2.

3. Number

An elephant has a trunk. Two elephants have two trunks. Who could disagree? Yet the choice between singular and plural nouns seems to baffle some people, who figuratively attempt to force two elephants to accept one trunk. For example:

> Both were from Central America and had a visa, but they didn't have a work permit.

A newspaper erred. Two visitors would not share one visa or one work permit. They had *visas.* They lacked work *permits.* The thing possessed would be singular if the subject of the sentence were singular; for instance: "Each man had a visa but neither had a work permit." Another paper made a similar mistake:

> SEG Technologies Inc. in Philadelphia even invites people to watch their PC being assembled.

Just one "PC" for all to share? Make it "their *PCs.*" A number of people have a number of the devices, which are, after all, *personal* computers.

A newscaster said, "Cats seem to have a mind of their own." There is no collective feline mind. "Cats seem to have *minds* of their own" or "*A cat seems* to have *a mind* of *its* own."

An author believes that "editors should be required to write a novel." They would not all collaborate on the same novel. Either "editors should . . . write *novels*" or "*an editor* should . . . write a novel."

The rule that plural subjects possess plural things has exceptions:

- Individuals that constitute a subject may possess something in common: "The Smiths had a lease." / "Agnes and John met at their college."
- If what is possessed is not a concrete item but an abstract quality, the singular will do: "The cars gained speed." / "The boys' anger subsided."

Propriety of number is more than a matter of tidiness. It makes a difference whether Tom and Mary are looking for *apartments* or *an apartment.*

A grammar rightly points out a bad shift in pronouns: ". . . A [job-seeking] person who interviews a company is more successful . . . than *one* who waits for a company to interview *them.*" This is given as correct: ". . . People who interview companies are more successful . . . than *those* who wait for a company to interview *them.*" But the second "company" should be made plural too.

Two statements on the radio exemplify an occasional mistake: "We can provide that [neutering] service for dog and cats." / "Doctors have more bag of tricks. . . ." *Dogs* and cats. *Bags* of tricks. Making the final noun plural is not enough.

See also **Collective nouns; ONE OF,** 3.

4. Omission

In a complicated sentence telling of multiple actions, sometimes it is not immediately clear who or what is performing one of the actions. The writer or speaker has left out a *subject* (the doer of an action), either a noun or a pronoun, leaving a disconnected *predicate* (the part of a sentence or clause that tells about the subject).

A TV network's anchor man spoke of an explosion on a train in Pakistan:

> Pakistan said it has proof Indian intelligence agents planted the bomb and linked the attack to tensions over nuclear testing.

Who did the linking? The sentence seems to say the agents, but the speaker probably meant Pakistan. A noun (e.g., *Pakistan*) or pronoun (*it*) should have preceded "linked." (And "has proof" should have been "*had* proof." *See* **Tense**, 2.)

See also **Pronouns**, 6.

5. Using nouns as adjectives

Nouns often serve as adjectives: *fire* insurance; *snow* removal; *spring* cleaning. Such use is not necessarily objectionable. What can be criticized are uses like these:

- "The Senate consent to the treaty and its rejection of four amendments . . . was a disappointment to conservatives . . ." (from a news dispatch). "Senate" should be possessive—*Senate's*—just as *its* is possessive. "Senate consent" is headline language.
- "She displays both dramatic and music skills." *Dramatic* ought to be matched by *musical*. A standard adjective does not mix well with a noun-adjective.
- ". . . Exotic species invasions" / "the biggest selenium discharger" / "a multimillion-dollar aid package" (by two men of science and a news service). Better: *invasions of exotic species / discharger of selenium / package of aid.*

See also **Modifiers**, 4; **Prepositions**, 2, 4.

NOW. *See* **Anachronism**, 2; **PRESENTLY.**

NO WAY. Years ago I asked a former flame if she cared to renew our relationship. "No way!" she exclaimed. I responded, "Where there's a will, there's a way." She amended her answer: "No will." At least I had the satisfaction of winning her concession on a point of English usage.

In popular use, "No way" often substitutes for a more straightforward negative like *no* or *not*. At times it stands alone as an interjection. At other times it is stuck onto sentences crudely—often inaccurately as well, for frequently there *is* a way.

The form in which the expression reached my ears at the start of the seventies was "in no way." Before long, the "in" was being dropped and the uttering of "no way" became a fad. The example is from a restaurant review:

> No way am I hungry after this meal; not for at least 8 hours.

An improved version, "*In* no way am I hungry after this meal for at least 8 hours," adds *in* and deletes "not." (*See* **Double negative**.) A still better version scraps "no way" and relocates three words:

> I am *not* hungry after this meal for at least eight hours. [Most publications spell out the digits.]

The following sentence opens a news brief:

> There's no way Reagan will accept an invitation by leaders of South Africa's neighboring black states to visit the region in an attempt to end the violence.

To keep the first three words but make the sentence minimally grammatical, extra words are needed to connect the noun phrase "no way" to the verb "accept"; for instance: "There's no way *in which* Reagan will accept . . ." or "There's no way *to get* Reagan *to* accept. . . ." But was there truly no possible condition under which he would accept? The best solution might be to toss out the first three words and insert *not*:

Reagan will *not* accept an invitation by leaders of South Africa's neighboring black states. . . .

Unless *no way* is used to mean *not a proper way*—"This is no way for a lady to behave"—its unqualified use should be reserved for impossibilities: "There is no way to travel faster than the speed of light."

An even clumsier opening than "There's no way" is "No way there's," heard in a TV report:

No way there's enough money in the education budget to pay for all this.

It is simpler and neater to say, "There's *not* enough money. . . ."

The columnist who wrote the sample sentence below (on how a comedian tried to help a New York mayoral candidate) seemed hell-bent on using the phrase, at the cost of a confusingly convoluted sentence with two double negatives.

No way he wouldn't say something offensive and no way it wouldn't be picked up, set aside and then repeated just when it would hurt the most.

This is simpler and clearer:

He would say something offensive and it would be picked up, set aside, and then repeated. . . .

Noway or *noways* is an old adverb, meaning in no manner or by no means and pronounced with stress on *no-*. The two-word version either stresses *way* or gives the two words about equal stress. These are correct examples from *The Oxford English Dictionary*: "They were tied up and could noways appear" (1702). "I have lived a virgin and I noway doubt I can live so still" (1875). A synonym of *noway* is *nowise* or, more commonly, *in no wise*.

NUCLEAR. *Nuclear* is pronounced NOO-klee-urr. Sometimes it is mispronounced "NOO-kyuh-lurr," and some of the mispronouncers are people who should know better: a secretary of defense was heard uttering it the latter way seventeen times in one interview. President Eisenhower was said to have habitually given the word the same twist. (Maybe there ought to be a law saying that nobody shall have any control over weapons that he cannot pronounce.)

Nuclear, in the sense of pertaining to weapons and energy, its predominant sense, is now more common than its synonym, *atomic*, the original term. Basically *nuclear* (adjective) pertains to a *nucleus* (noun): a center or core around which things are collected. The *nucleus*, in biology, is a body of protoplasm within an animal or plant cell that is essential to such functions as growth and reproduction. In chemistry and physics it is the central part of an atom, includes protons and neutrons among its parts, and makes up nearly all the atom's mass. Either *nuclei* or *nucleuses* serves as a plural.

Two terms that look and sound rather similar but have significant differences are *nuclear fission*, the principle of the atomic bomb and civil atomic energy, and *nuclear fusion*, the principle of the hydrogen bomb. In *fission*, the nuclei of atoms are split; in the process, part of their mass is converted to energy. In *fusion*, the nuclei of atoms fuse into heavier nuclei (e.g., tritium, or heavy hydrogen, into helium), but the total mass is less and the balance is converted into energy. *Thermonuclear*, pronounced thur-mo-NOO-klee-urr, pertains to the *fusion* process, which is conducted at high temperatures. *Thermo-* means heat.

NUMBER and AMOUNT. *See* AMOUNT and NUMBER.

Number (grammatical). *Number* in a grammatical sense is mainly (1) the distinction between singular and plural words; that is, between words that apply to one thing or person and words that apply to more than one; or (2) a form of a particular word or phrase that indicates such singularity or plurality. *Tree, woman,* and *this* are in the *singular number,* whereas *trees, women,* and *these* are in the *plural number.* A subject and its verb must agree in *number;* for instance, "*A tree stands* in the yard" but "*Two trees stand* in the yard."

Among entries dealing with number in a grammatical sense are the following: AMOUNT and NUMBER; BE-TWEEN, 2; Collective nouns; Contractions, *1;* COUPLE; EACH, EACH OF; EACH OTHER; EITHER, *1, 2;* EVERY-BODY, EVERYONE, *4;* EVERY ONE and EVERYONE; Expletives; FEWER and LESS; LATTER; LOT, *1;* MAJOR-ITY, *2;* MANY and MUCH; MORE THAN ONE; NEITHER, *3;* NONE, *1;* NOR; Nouns, *3;* ONE OF; OR; PER-SONNEL; PLUS; Pronouns, *2;* STAFF; TOTAL, *2;* TRIO; Verbs, *3;*

See also **Plurals and singulars** with references listed in *2L.*

The entry **Numbers** concerns figures and statistics.

NUMBER OF. *See* **Collective nouns,** 2.

Numbers. *1. Ambiguity. 2. Contradiction. 3. Division between lines. 4. Impossibility. 5. Inaccuracy. 6. Inanity. 7. Incomparability. 8. Incompleteness. 9. In lawsuits. 10. Misinterpretation. 11. Spelling out.*

1. Ambiguity
"Building permits were down six point eight percent in October," a newscaster announced. "Down" from what? Were they down from what they had been in September, or were they down from what they had been in October of the previous year? The newscaster, on network television, failed to say. Further-

more, was she referring to the total number of permits or to the total of estimated costs? We do not know. The "six point eight percent" hinted at a precision that was not there.

When comparisons are made, it must be clear what is being compared to what. When totals are presented, it must be clear what items have been added up. *See* **Comparison,** *1.*

A man saw "between four and five hundred people" at a place. What was the smallest number of people he saw there at any time? It is plausible that if he was the fifth to arrive, he saw four there at first. The context, in a biography, indicates that the writer meant four *hundred* but omitted *hundred.*

This was heard on television news: "Estimates range from 250 to 400,000." This time we cannot figure it out. We must guess. It is likely that the speaker meant 250 *thousand* but omitted *thousand.*

To save one word, the author and the news man each risked misinterpretation.

2. Contradiction
It is a serious problem when numbers contradict their interpretation, as in the two press examples that follow.

. . . The southwestern neighborhoods rejected the ballot measure 9,323 votes against to 17,251 in favor.

The number of marriage licenses is also down in Louisiana, the only other state that requires premarital AIDS testing. In the first quarter of 1988 776 marriage licenses were issued in New Orleans, the only parish monitored by the State Department of Health, as against 628 the previous year. . . .

In the first excerpt, the figures contradict "rejected." The second excerpt shows the figures going up, not "down." (It has three lesser flaws: For one thing, running two successive figures risks confusion; *this year* could have replaced the date. Then too, "the previous year" is not usually used for *last year*. Anyway, it lacks a qualification, like *during the corresponding period*.)

It is equally troublesome when two numbers contradict each other, as in the next two extracts.

An article attributes a number to "industry analysts" and a second number, ten paragraphs later, to "some estimates":

> They estimate, however, that there are fewer than 20,000 fax machines in American homes. . . .
>
> By some estimates, there are more than 20 million people working at home with a facsimile machine. . . .

The two estimates differ by a factor of more than 1,000. Yet we are offered no explanation of that remarkable discrepancy (let alone how 20 million people can share "a facsimile machine"—*see* **Nouns,** *3*).

Where was the copy editor when the following passage went into the paper?

> A 31-year old man fell six stories from a window ledge down a light well while attempting to gain access to his apartment early yesterday.
> San Francisco Police said that T—— G——, 27, of 250 F—— Street either locked himself out or had been locked out by his roommate.

The four-year discrepancy is glaring, granted that a harrowing experience can age one. (By the way, a hyphen is missing after "31-year." And we may wonder why a news story has to begin with such an insignificant detail, particularly when the very next sentence includes that detail. A far more important fact, the victim's "guarded condition," was relegated to the third paragraph.)

Although the final example does not leave us readers puzzled, the way it is expressed may be questioned.

> In addition, Mr. Dukakis's administration announced last week that tax revenue would be as much as $77 million less than anticipated, creating a potential deficit in the nearly $11 billion budget for 1988.

"As much as" lifts us. "Less than anticipated" drops us. That roller-coaster effect could have been avoided, for instance by changing "would be as much as" to *could fall to* or by simply changing "much" to *little.*

3. Division between lines

When a figure and a word together represent a number, particularly a dollar amount (like $3 billion), both elements should go on the same line, unlike these two examples:

> By last month, more than $2 million of this fiscal year's $2.5 million overtime budget had already been paid out. . . .

> . . . He does not know how much of a subsidy the east hotel would get but it would not be "significantly less" than the $17 million awarded to the Hilton.

Separating "$2" or "$17" from "million" is likely to impede readers.

See also **Division of words.**

4. Impossibility

The statements quoted below cannot literally be true. They imply calculations that are impossible. First an excerpt from a news article:

> . . . Tests of apple products from two education department warehouses showed that they contained

levels 400 times lower than federal limits.

. . . Some tests showed the products at 1,000 to 10,000 times lower than allowable limits.

Inasmuch as *one time lower* is zero, "400 times lower" defies the imagination, let alone "1,000 to 10,000 times lower." Could the levels (of a pesticide) found in the tests have been *one four-hundredth of* the limits, *one thousandth of* the limits, and so on?

A magazine ad for a computer company (not Apple) makes a similarly impossible claim:

. . . Our latest microprocessor technology requires each transistor to be 100 times thinner than a human hair.

The statement is corrected by a caption elsewhere in the ad: "1/100th the thickness of a human hair."

A book on science says that a film of oil was "on average ten or twenty times thinner" than gold leaf. One-tenth or one-twentieth as thin? Later the spacial separation of atomic layers of gold is judged to be "two dozen times less than the minimum thickness we found so easily for an oil film upon water." One twenty-fourth as large? (The consistency of "on average" [a mean?] and "ten or twenty" [a range?] is a lesser question.)

A well-known anchor man announced to the nation the incredible news that "U.S. farm exports declined more than 300 percent last year" (presumably from the year before). If farm exports had declined *100* percent, all farm exports would have ceased. Could someone have typed an extra zero in the copy that he read?

5. Inaccuracy

What we see in print is not necessarily so. Most of us know that and still tend to trust the printed word. Like everyone else, a professional writer can get a fact or figure wrong. Usually a copy editor reviews his work, but errors do sneak by, particularly those that cannot be corrected without specially researched background information.

The cause of a mistake may be absent-mindedness, carelessness, faulty memory, haste, ignorance, inadequate research or thought, miscalculation, misunderstanding, repetition of another's error, slip of the keyboard, or a combination of the foregoing. It may be "just one of those things" and truly "everyone makes mistakes," as we often say. Whatever the reason, it does not justify infecting readers with misinformation, which can be passed on to others in viral fashion.

A news service circulated a factual mistake far and wide:

Syria, along with Egypt and Jordan, lost territory to Israel in the 1967 seven-day war and was known to have adopted a hard line on getting the lost ground back.

The Israelis fought the war in *six* days, hence the well-known appellation the Six-Day War. (On the seventh day they rested.)

The same news service reported this startling intelligence: "Seven out of every ten married Italians commit adultery." It based its report on a survey of 1,000 families by the weekly magazine *L'Europea* showing that "49 percent of the men and 21 percent of the women" admitted the sin. The service was wrong, even if we assume that the survey was reliable, that it represented all Italians, and that half of them were men and half women. Adulterers then would make up 35 percent of married Italians, or seven out of *twenty*. Evidently someone had simply added 49 and 21, forgetting that 100 percent of each sex made up only 50 percent of the total.

A newspaper item told of nuns with a convent at the scene of the former Auschwitz death camp, "where they pray for the thousands who died in the Nazi Holocaust." How could any writer or editor on the staff of a large metropolitan daily be ignorant of the fact that the Nazis murdered *millions?*

The sentence below is extracted from an earlier issue of the same newspaper. What the writer apparently lacked (and his copy editor failed to provide) was not factual knowledge but the ability to divide sixty-five by six.

> There are about six phones per 100 persons in the Soviet Union, which is less than one-fifth the American ratio of 65 per 100.

But then they probably surpassed us in arithmetic.
See also 10B.

6. Inanity

Some writers can find no other way to compare figures than to state the obvious. The first example deals with Nicaragua.

> ... The country's per capita gross domestic product has fallen to roughly $300 a year. That figure is less than the comparable figure of $330 a year for Haiti, long the hemisphere's poorest nation.

> Industrial accidents in the Soviet Union killed 14,377 people last year. ... That's more than the 13,833 troops the Soviets say they lost in eight years of fighting in Afghanistan.

Can there possibly be any reader who does not know that $300 is less than $330 or that 14,377 is more than 13,833?
See also FRACTION.

7. Incomparability

The quoted sentence, from a well-known work, purports to compare the incomparable.

> Among the browsers, for example, was the *Diplodocus carnegii*, which measured eighty-four feet in length. The *Brachiosaurus* was still more colossal—it had a live weight of about fifty tons!

We could compare the two dinosaurs in length if we knew how long the Brachiosaurus was. We could compare them in weight if we knew how much the Diplodocus weighed. All we have is the length of one and the weight of the other, and how can these be compared?

In the following example, from a press article, the problem may lie in the writing, rather than in the data.

> ... U.S. postal employees handle an average of 190,000 pieces of mail per year, compared to just 50,000 pieces of mail per employee in West Germany.

It appears that U.S. pieces "per year" is being compared with German pieces "per employee." A year and an employee are incomparable. Probably the writer intended to compare the number of mail pieces per U.S. employee per year with the number of mail pieces per German employee per year. But he did not say so.

When numbers are to be compared with one another, it must be made clear that they are in the same category. One should not assume that the reader or listener will make the proper assumptions. *See also* AS and LIKE, 2; Comparison, 2; LIKE, 2; UNLIKE, 2.

Anyhow, the 190,000 cannot be compared "to" the 50,000. *See* COMPARED TO and COMPARED WITH, 1.

8. *Incompleteness*

Percent, or *per cent,* as it is also written, or *%,* as it is symbolized, means parts of 100. In any pie chart, or its equivalent in prose, all 100 parts must be accounted for. Someone in an editorial office should have performed a little simple arithmetic:

> Already 76 percent of Bergen's land is covered by private and public development. With 15 percent preserved as golf courses and public parkland, only 5.9 percent, or 9,000 acres, remains in private hands, still open to either development or preservation.

Those percentages total 96.9. Nothing is said about the remaining 3.1.

(The paragraph is otherwise unclear. "... Only 5.9 percent ... remains in private hands" produces confusion. Part of the 76% is land in private hands too. This may be what the writer meant: "... Only 5.9 percent, 9,000 acres in private hands, remains open to either development or preservation.")

An editor doubtless did not intend to put a misleading headline on a front page: " 'Friendly fire' killed 1 in 5 GIs in gulf war." It suggests that about 100,000 of the approximately half a million U.S. servicemen in the war died at the hands of their comrades. It fails to indicate that "1 in 5" is a fraction of U.S. battle deaths, said to total 148. This is one of many possible amendments (taking up no additional space): "U.S. fire hit 1 in 5 GIs slain in gulf war."

The ranking of entities as *first, second, ninth,* and so on can be too short of explanatory facts. *See* **Comparison,** *1.*

9. *In lawsuits*

In filing lawsuits, lawyers routinely inflate the damages. They do not seriously expect to win the full amounts requested. They know that a judgment for the plaintiff or a settlement almost always sharply cuts the amount sought in the complaint.

News reporters and editors generally do not know this. They tend to rate the importance of a suit according to the sum of money requested. So ordinarily the best way for a lawyer to get a suit in the news is to ask for absurdly exorbitant damages. The amount of the suit will appear in the opening sentence of the story—each of the sample sentences below—and often in the headline as well.

> Dr. Sam Sheppard's former wife has filed a $10 million lawsuit against the National Broadcasting Co. over the television network's dramatization of her husband's murder trials.

> A Marina service station operator filed a $20 million damage suit against Texaco Inc., accusing the oil company of coercing him into selling only Texaco products.

> Financier J. William Oldenburg has filed a $400 million suit against three newspapers ... alleging libel. ...

> Real estate investor Richard Traweek, his legislative attempts to convert 720 apartments to condominiums blocked, filed a $800 million lawsuit against San Francisco yesterday. [*See also* **A and AN.**]

The point here is not that any suits are unjustified or justified but that journalists are dupes for lawyers.

10. *Misinterpretation*

A. *Percentage of increase*
An editorial said, erroneously:

> Carousel expenditures will soon go up 400 percent. ... The 25-cent ticket would be eliminated for children, who

would pay the same dollar fare as their moms.

When an item costing a quarter doubles in price, it rises another quarter, or one time, or 100 percent. When it triples in price, it rises 50 cents, or two times, or 200 percent. A 25-cent ticket that increases to a dollar goes up 75 cents, or three times, or *300* percent—not "*400*." (Incidentally, the writer seems uncertain whether it "will" [definitely] or "would" [maybe] go up. *See* **Mood; Subjunctive.** *See also* **MOM, MAMA, MA.**)

The same erroneous percentage appeared in a periodic column:

The current fee for a basic, minimum plumbing permit is now $15.75. The fee, starting Sept. 4, will be $65.25, and up—a 400 percent increase.

When a fee of $15.75 goes up $49.50, the increase is *314* percent—not "*400*."

B. Comparison

Henry earns $500 a week. Wendy earns $1,500. These are two ways in which one may compare the two numbers:

- Contrast the totals, figuring the number of times $500 goes into $1,500. ("Wendy earns three times as much as Henry earns" or "His earnings are a third of hers.")
- Emphasize the difference, $1,000. ("Wendy earns two times more than what Henry earns" or "Her earnings are 200 percent higher than his.")

X times *more* or *bigger, higher, greater,* etc. (*than*) is not the same as X times *as many* or *as big, as high, as much,* etc. (*as*). Either type of description is valid if used consistently and accurately. The defective example below is from a newspaper's main story.

. . . The Bush proposals would require the Warsaw Pact to destroy eight times more planes and four times as many helicopters [as NATO].

The proposals called for the destruction of 4,850 and 577 planes respectively. One bloc would destroy 7.4 times *more planes* than the other, or roughly seven times—not "eight" times. The helicopter part was correct.

More means greater in number, amount, etc. Thus X "times more planes" deals only with the times that are greater than one time. In the example above, the 577 NATO planes amount to one time. The first 577 planes of the other side are numerically the same, not "more," so they should not be counted.

As many implies that the larger number has been divided by the smaller number. A proposed NATO destruction of 419 helicopters goes into the other side's figure of 1,700 about four times. So the latter would indeed destroy "four times as many helicopters" or *four times the number of helicopters* or would be bound to a *fourfold* destruction of helicopters compared with NATO's obligation.

An advertisement for a silver medallion said:

The standard American Eagle weighs merely one troy ounce. . . . "Silver Eagle" is an astonishing 16 times heavier . . . (16 Oz. Troy . . .).

Correction: 16 times *as heavy* but 15 times *heavier.*

The moderator of a television forum said, and it was simultaneously displayed on the screen, that Indonesia was "Three times bigger than Texas" in land area. Correction: Indonesia, with about 741,000 square miles, is about 1.8 times *bigger than* Texas, with about 267,000 square miles. Indonesia is about 2.8 times *as big as* Texas.

This sentence, from a book of popular astronomy, is inconsistent in its terms (and contains several other errors):

Uranus is 15 times as far from the sun as the Earth; Neptune, 17 times; and Pluto is 50 times farther.

The sentence uses "as far as" twice and then switches to "farther." Is there a reason for the switch, or is the writer simply unaware of the distinction? A reader cannot tell. (Anyway, all the numbers are wrong. On the average, the three planets are 19, 30, and 39 times as far from the Sun as the Earth is. An *is* after "Earth" is desirable to clarify that only distances from the outer planets to the Sun, not to the Earth, are being compared. An "is" after Pluto is superfluous when no "is" follows Neptune. *See also* **Series errors, 9; STAR and SUN.**)

C. CHANCES, PROBABILITY, ODDS

Does the retired general who is quoted here approve or disapprove of the operation?

I would have rated Desert One's chances of success at a hundred to one. . . .

He seems to be estimating a hundred chances of success to one chance of failure. But the sentence concludes by calling the chances

foolhardy odds for a military operation.

He meant to have rated the chances of *failure* at a hundred to one (chance of success), or the chance of success at about *one in a hundred*.

The context in the following sentence, by a scientist, explains what he had in mind, although literally the sentence says the opposite.

The probability of all the gas molecules in our first box being found in one half of the box at a later time is many millions of millions to one, but it can happen.

The probability of winning the state lottery is *one* (chance) *in* millions. The probability that the sun will come out tomorrow somewhere in the world is many millions of millions (of chances) *to one* (chance that it will not)—the same as the probability of gas molecules being in both halves of the box.

The meaning in the sentence below is harder to discern. First of all, the sentence makes no sense grammatically. Changing "were" to *at* would help the grammar. But something more is wrong.

He [a state criminalist] also testified that the combined test results put the odds that the blood on socks found in Simpson's bedrooms [sic] was not that of his ex-wife were 21 billion to 1, up from the 9.7 billion to 1 odds Cotton gave last week.

Odds means probability, likelihood, or chances of a given event happening or a given thing being. If the chances of the blood *not* being his ex-wife's were "21 billion to 1" (chance of its *being* his ex-wife's), it would seem to be almost certain that the blood was someone else's. Contrasted with previous testimony, it would mean improved odds for Simpson. But the source of the figures was testimony for the prosecution, and the headline read "State's odds against O.J. keep growing." Here is one way to revise the sentence:

. . . Test results put the likelihood that the blood . . . was not that of his ex-wife at only one chance in 21 billion—less than half of the one chance in 9.7 billion that Cotton estimated last week. In other words, the probability that the blood came from the murdered woman appeared even greater now.

The chances, probability, or odds of one's misunderstanding numerical information of this sort are high enough to warrant a cautious treatment by the writer or speaker.

D. *The superlative*

It pays to think twice before describing a number by a superlative, like the *biggest,* the *smallest,* or the *highest.* Adding a modifier like "ever" or "of all time" is especially risky. Too often someone comes along to point out something bigger, smaller, higher, etc.

A main headline described an action in the House of Representatives: "Assault Weapons Ban OKd By the Narrowest of Margins." The narrowest of margins would be one vote. The story reported a tally of 216 to 214. Thus the winning margin was *two* votes—twice as large a margin as the "Narrowest."

E. *AVERAGE*

Average in a numerical sense does not mean *typical. Average* (noun) is the common term for what is, more precisely, a *mean* (also called an *arithmetic mean* or *arithmetical mean*): the result of adding two or more quantities and dividing the sum by the number of quantities added.

It does not necessarily resemble any individual quantity. If four employees out of five are paid $25,000 a year each and the fifth is paid $100,000, the *average* (adjective) or *mean* salary is $40,000, an amount unlike the salary of any employee in the company. That statistical reality is not always grasped by those interpreting numerical facts.

See also LIFE EXPECTANCY (etc.); MEAN (noun).

11. *Spelling out*

When should numbers be represented by words, when by figures? To answer that question and others, the press has style rules that aim at consistency, but their mindless enforcement can lead to inconsistency. This is from an account of a baseball game:

> Twenty-seven Dodgers came up, 27 Dodgers went down. There were 17 groundouts, five strikeouts, two foul outs, and only three fair balls hit out of the infield.

It seems that the Dodgers came up as words but went down as figures. The explanation lies in an age-old press rule: Do not start a sentence with a figure. No rationale for that rule is ever advanced. Headlines often start with figures; for example: "36 hours of work piled on average desk."

The second "27" and the "17" are expressed in figures, the remaining numbers in words, because of another style rule, common among newspapers: It requires figures for numbers above nine (except at the start of sentences) and words for numbers of nine and under. The rule includes both *cardinal* numbers (nine planets, a family of 10) and *ordinal* numbers (the fourth dimension, the 18th hole). Exceptions are made for decimal numbers (a 3.7 average), sums of money ($8), statistical tables, and so on.

Book editors often follow *The Chicago Manual of Style,* which calls for figures for 100 or more but also rejects them at the start of sentences, giving no reason.

When spelled out, compound numbers through ninety-nine and fractions commonly take hyphens: "Three hundred forty-seven residents" / "About two-thirds of all animals." *See also* HALF.

When *a hundred* or *a thousand* serves as an adjective—"a hundred yards" / "a thousand clowns"—it should be spelled out. "A 100" or "a 1,000," as writers sometimes put it, is the equivalent of "a one-hundred" or "a one-thousand."

Apart from the use of numbers, the first sentence of the baseball quotation is defective. It contains the makings of two sentences (two independent clauses) divided by a comma, an inadequate punctuation. (*See* **Run-on Sentence,** 2.) Below, we fix the punctuation, strengthen the message by expressing it in parallel sentences, and still observe the initial-number rule:

Twenty-seven Dodgers came up. Twenty-seven Dodgers went down.

(There is still another inconsistency in the passage. While "groundouts" and "strikeouts" take one word each, two words are allotted to "foul outs." In an adjoining box, tabulating the statistics of the game, it is "foulouts.")

O

Object(ive) complement. *See* Complement.

Object, objective case. *See* Complement; Prepositions, *1*; Pronouns, *10*; Verbs, *1, 5*.

OBSCENE, OBSCENITY. While
the courts have labored over the precise meaning of *obscenity* and the definition has determined whether people are sent to jail, the mass media, some public officials, and others have been stretching their constructions of the word to the point of inanity.

A banner headline proclaimed "An 'obscene' state deficit." The story underneath quoted a state treasurer: "The 'obscene surplus' I spoke of four years ago has turned into an 'obscene deficit'. . . ." An interviewer asked people on the street for "An Example of Obscene Wealth." A legislator said that revenues should not accumulate to "obscene levels." A columnist wrote of "obscene profits" from drugs, and another columnist wrote that "total compensation of top execs at some corporations is so large it borders on the obscene."

In the examples above, "obscene" was forced to serve as a general pejorative for a variety of monetary conditions. But money or the lack of it is not "obscene" (even though people may speak of "filthy lucre"). Nor is, say,

theft, although it may be bad, wrong, evil, vicious, or vile.

In the pair of examples below, "obscene" and "obscenely" are made to deal with people's ingestion of substances. To a food writer, being "obscene" seems to be a good thing: She credited an intensified flavor and sweetness of homemade jam to "the obscene amount of sugar that goes into its making." In a discussion of vitamins, a radio doctor asked, "Are we doing any good by taking obscenely large amounts of the chemicals?"

A television exposé of fake going-out-of-business sales included this comment: "What made it a sham was that the sale ran an obscene length of time, almost eleven months."

The *o*-words have nothing to do with money, consumption, or time. *Obscenity* (noun) is that which is *obscene* (adjective): offensive to generally accepted standards of modesty or decency; in particular, filthy, disgusting, or indecent in representing sexual or excretory parts or functions by word, deed, or illustration. *Obscenely* (adverb) means in an obscene way or to the point of obscenity. Exactly where the lines are drawn and what is placed within them and by whom are up to the judiciary.

You can be accused of "obscenity" even if you do nothing. The verbal manhandling took this form in a bookstore's newsletter: "We're shocked, saddened, and generally PO'ed by the obscenely low turnout of voters in U.S. elections. . . ." Ironically the quoted sentence itself bordered on obscenity: "PO" did not stand for *post office.*

Two nouns associated with *obscenity* are *vulgarity,* meaning coarseness, poor taste, impropriety, or an act or expression with those characteristics; and *profanity,* strictly speaking, irreverence to that which is sacred, or an instance of such irreverence, popularly used as a synonym for *obscenity.*

OBSESS, OBSESSED, OBSESSION.
To *obsess* someone is to besiege, beset, dominate, haunt, or trouble the person. Nowadays it always pertains to the way a persistent feeling, idea, thought, or the like can act on the mind. Often it is in the passive voice: "Gertrude was obsessed with guilt." / "Edison was obsessed by the vision of his lamp." It may be in the active voice too, as in this press example:

> . . . The show looks at how the concept of stardom can inspire or obsess an artist. . . .

One thing the verb *obsess* may not be is intransitive, as it was forced to be on two national television programs:

> [News:] BBC viewers are obsessing about something else [besides the Beatles: Princess Diana].

> [Drama:] It's that dog he's been obsessing about.

Change "obsessing about" to *obsessed by* or *with.* The verb is transitive. Something *obsesses* one, or (more often) one *is obsessed by* or *with* something. One does not "obsess" any more than one "besieges."

Obsess once meant besiege in a literal sense. It came from the Latin *obsessus,* past participle of *obsidere,* to besiege or beset.

The noun is *obsession:* the action of obsessing (someone) or the state of being obsessed; or the influence of the persistent idea etc.; or the idea etc. itself. "His obsession with presidential politics endured for decades." / "Fashion obsessions afflict many girls."

OCCUR. *See* HAPPEN, OCCUR, and TAKE PLACE.

OCTOPUS. *See* Plurals and singulars, *1.*

OCULIST, OPHTHALMOLOGIST, OPTICIAN, and OPTOMETRIST.
All are concerned with eyes. *Oculist* is an old term for an *ophthalmologist,* a medical doctor who specializes in treating eye disorders. An *optometrist* is not a physician but a person holding the degree of Doctor of Optometry (O.D.) who tests the eyes for vision problems and prescribes eyeglasses. An *optician* makes or sells optical products. A *dispensing optician* deals in prescribed eyeglasses.

The Greek word for eye, *ophthalmos,* gave rise to numerous technical terms. Medical dictionaries contain more than fifty of them, including *ophthalmia,* severe inflammation of the eye; *ophthalmic,* pertaining to the eye, e.g., the *ophthalmic nerve; ophthalmology,* the science and medical specialty of the eye and its diseases; and *ophthalmoscope,* an instrument for examining the interior of the eye. Note that all have at least two *h*'s. (A few, like the twenty-letter disease *ophthalmoblennorrhea,* have three *h*'s.) The first one was missing from *ophthalmologists* in an op-ed article of mine. The editor had knocked the *h* out of it.

OD. Probably not everyone understood him when a newscaster on a na-

tional radio network mentioned a certain actor's "OD'ing on cocaine at his home in Malibu." The strange-sounding word, the lack of a complete sentence, and the failure to place Malibu in California all detracted from easy comprehension.

OD (noun or verb, which looks odd but is pronounced OH-DEE) means *overdose* in police and medical jargon, not in standard English. *OD'ing* means *overdosing*.

The Random House Dictionary oddly fails to include any definition under *overdose* (which it dates from the seventeenth century); instead it refers readers to OD (1955 to 1960) and defines that.

OD as an abbreviation (often with dots) can stand for many things, including doctor of optometry, officer of the day, Old Dutch, ordnance department, outside diameter, overdraft, overdrawn, and the right eye (from the Latin *oculus dexter,* used on prescriptions).

-ODD. *See* SOME.

-O ending. *See* **Plurals and singulars,** *2J.*

OF. *See* **COMPRISE; HAVE, HAS, HAD,** *2;* **OFF and "OFF OF"; ON,** *3;* **Prepositions; SUPPORTIVE.**

OF ANY, OF ANYONE. *See* **ANY,** *1, 2.*

OF COURSE. *1. Benefit. 2. Drawback. 3. Other expressions.*

1. Benefit

Sometimes a statement seems obvious but needs to be stated anyway. The common phrase *of course* lets us state the obvious without sounding pedagogic or preachy or insulting anyone's intelligence.

What is stated may be a fact or truism that puts things into perspective or leads

up to one's main point: "He made his discovery in 1776, which of course was the year of our Declaration of Independence." / "Of course, you shouldn't put all your eggs in one basket. Farnsworth did so and this is what happened to him."

Using *of course* in that way tells the reader or listener, "You're smart enough to know this, but it is helpful to the discussion if I mention it anyway."

2. Drawback

Occasionally, instead of avoiding insult, the use of "of course" produces it. A listener asks a speaker a question; the answer should be "yes," but the speaker answers "of course," as though to say: "You're a dummy for asking." Or a writer attaches an "of course" to an obscure fact or arguable proposition, thereby implying to a number of readers that they are dolts for not knowing what the writer knows.

The three quoted statements that follow, from three books, are scarcely the epitome of everyday conversation. None gives any clue as to why it warrants "of course." First, a traveler describes an Algerian repast of which he partook: "We started with dates, of course, and drank milk." (Why must a meal start with dates?) A musicologist tells the general public, ". . . Berlioz, of course, made liberal use of the instrument," the harp. (Why is that presumed to be an obvious fact?) Last, a cosmologist writes about a theory of multiple universes:

Only in a small number, with conditions and parameters like our own universe, will it be possible for intelligent life to develop and ask the question, "Why is the universe as we observe it?" The answer, of course, is that if it were otherwise, there would not be anyone to ask the question.

It is unclear why that answer should be accepted as a matter of course. Maybe the question could be answered in an astronomic, rather than philosophic, way. Possibly celestial events could have made the (or a) universe "otherwise" but still observable. This is a deep matter. Must discussion be cut off so soon?

3. Other expressions

There are some other phrases that are similar to "of course" in patronizing character but less useful, if indeed they should be used at all. One of them appears in a renowned book. (Emphasis is added to the excerpts below.)

> The English, *as everyone knows,* usually put a comma after the street number of a house, making it, for example, 34, *St. James's Street.*

If everyone knew it, would the author have felt it necessary to give the example? Related phrases are "as everybody knows" and "as is well known."

Another expression in a similar vein is found in a widely used manual for authors and editors:

> It *goes without saying* that author-date citations in the text must agree exactly with the list of references.

If something really "goes without saying" or, to use a related expression, is "needless to say," why say it? What the manual says, however, seems worth saying. *See* **Verbal unmentionables.**

Two other expressions of a comparable, patronizing character are "for the simple reason that" and "it stands to reason." *See* **REASON, 3.**

OFF and "OFF OF." A talk show host objected to giving driver's licenses to anyone illiterate in English. What if you can't read the signs on the freeway and "don't know what exit to get off of?" In his comment, he displayed less than full proficiency in English himself. The "of" should have been *at.*

"Off of" is a substandard phrase. "Of" is superfluous; its sense is included in *off.* The "of" intrudes often in conversations and at times in broadcasting and print.

A reporter on a TV network said, "Moving people into jobs and off of welfare demands that there be jobs to go to." The "of" was wrong; *off welfare* would have been right.

The mistake glared in a front-page headline: "Gingrich wants wealthy retirees off of Medicare." *Off Medicare* needed no "of." Nor should "of" have intruded in this sentence, from a dispatch by a news agency: "That [infusion with carbonate grains] would have happened during the impact that knocked the meteorite off of Mars." *Off Mars.*

The four extracts below from newspapers all contain the same error: "Martinez's car hit the rear of one car, glanced off of it and struck another car." / "That limits the number of objects off of which radar energy can bounce." / "Mr. Courter's campaign, coming off of a tough primary . . . , suffered from poor organization. . . ." / "The Department . . . added staff to help General Assistance clients get off of local welfare rolls. . . ." In every instance, *off* is enough: ". . . glanced *off* it . . ." / ". . . objects *off* which . . ." / ". . . coming *off* a tough primary . . ." / ". . . get *off* local welfare rolls. . . ."

The final example, from a column, is a bit different: "Gabbert broadcasts off of Mount San Bruno south of The City. . . ." Change "off of" to *from.* (And insert a comma after "Bruno." As for the capital *T* in "The," not the writer but a quirk of his newspaper was to blame.)

OFF and ON. *See* **GO OFF** and **GO ON.**

"OLDEST PROFESSION." This bromide is liable to be dragged into any

popular discussion of harlotry and accepted without thought as though it were established wisdom. It made typical appearances in announcements of two television programs to be shown and in an argument by the host of a radio talk show: "plus a new look at the world's oldest profession, prostitution" / "a provocative look at the world's oldest profession . . ." / "The idea of trying to outlaw the world's oldest profession is ridiculous."

Is there any truth in the "oldest profession" cliché? First of all, prostitution, the selling of sexual services, is not a *profession* in the standard sense: a vocation requiring much advanced study and training, in the practice of which one is relied on for one's knowledge and judgment. *The professions* once meant theology, law, and medicine.

That leaves the question, What is the oldest vocation or occupation? Writings in anthropology suggest that the earliest beings that walked upright subsisted by scavenging, gathering, and hunting. Fishing and animal husbandry entered at some points, tillage later. Prostitution was not in the running. Anyway, could prostitutes have gone into business if there were not men who had earned the money to pay them?

ON. *1. Missing. 2. Superfluous. 3. Unidiomatic.*

1. Missing

The preposition *on* gets pushed around: left out when it should be in, put in when it should be out, and overworked when another preposition would do a better job.

To omit *on*, as newspapers are apt to do, can make a sentence unclear: "He met Billy Sunday." / "He hired his man Friday." If we are referring to days and not people's appellations, precede each day with *on*. A press example follows.

State court Judge Lawrence Weiss Friday sentenced Mr. B—— to 10 years in state prison. . . .

"*On* Friday" would clarify that "Friday" is not the judge's last name. The sentence would read still more smoothly if it began "*On Friday*. . . ." *On* would suit the start of the following press sentence too.

His first day as principal of South Boston High School, Jerome W—— received a poetic greeting from white residents opposed to desegregating their neighborhood's school.

The meaning is clear, but it would be more idiomatic to say "*On* his first day. . . ." Without the *on*, the reader could start out on the wrong track, expecting something like "His first day as principal was exciting."

On does not always need to precede a day or date, but it cannot hurt. "He came Thursday" or "He came *on* Thursday." / "The fiscal year ends June 30" or "The fiscal year ends *on* June 30."

A faddish expression at this writing is "Get a grip." A grip on what (on a problem? on oneself?) is not explained. It is literally telling someone to obtain a suitcase.

2. Superfluous

The needless appearance of "on" plays a part in contemporary slang. *Up* often gets "on" added when *up* would be enough by itself.

A column of letters to the editor was headlined "U.S. Should Stop Beating Up on Cuba." And this was said in a televised documentary: "Orson constantly picked up on those things [reports of his genius] and accepted them as true." In each case, *on* could have been dropped with no detriment to the meaning. (*See also* **PICK UP and PICKUP**, 2.)

When a congressman sought a presidential panel to restudy veterans' complaints of illness, a news item said "more than 75 House members signed on to his letter. . . ." They *signed his letter*. There was no need for "on to."

A witness was quoted: "He was waiting on every second for the police to arrive. He couldn't wait to see them." Dropping *on* would help the first sentence. (But if "he was waiting," how is it that "He couldn't wait"?)

Seeking a home for a cat, a humane society ran an ad that began, "Cat lovers should count on their blessings." *Count their* (*our, your,* etc.) *blessings* is the expression. "On" was ill chosen. To *count on* is to depend on (something or someone).

3. Unidiomatic

On has become a highly popular tool of the press, usurping functions that most of us would reserve for other prepositions. In headlines it is nearly an all-purpose preposition. Take this headline, across a page:

> Shelley backs off on Brown's ballot measure

Off and "on" seem contradictory. A more normal preposition with *back off* (meaning to retreat) is *from*.

Here are five more headlines (with possible replacements in brackets):

> U.S. to take Russia
> to task on [for?] Chechnya

> RUSSIA TELLS NATO
> IT ACCEPTS OFFER
> ON [OF?] A FORMAL LINK

> Wilson backs floor
> fight on [over?] abortion

> Ruling lets activists pursue
> warning on [of?] mercury fillings

> Ex-Klansmen to Take
> Classes on [in?] Civil Rights

Space limitation only partly explains the press's fondness for *on*. In print it is slightly longer than *of* and *in*, two prepositions that it sometimes supplants. Reliance on *on* seems to be habitual with some copy editors, easier than having to select the best preposition. Equally unidiomatic "on" phrases are sometimes found in other media. This is from a scholarly book:

> [E]vans said its [a dictionary's] purpose was to give the reader help on spelling, pronunciation, and the meaning and proper use of words.

Would we not want "help *in* spelling" et cetera?

To stand or wait *on line* is a regional idiom of New York City, seen in writing produced there. Most of the country speaks of standing or waiting *in line*.

A certain actress "has never before been 'butt naked' onscreen," an article said. *On* and *screen* do not require union. (And *buck* [stark] *naked* is the colloquial expression.)

See also 2 (end); **GO OFF and GO ON; ONGOING; ONTO; Prepositions**, 7; **SPEAK TO, TALK TO; WAIT FOR and WAIT ON**.

ONE ANOTHER. See EACH OTHER.

ONE as pronoun. *1. The indefinite ONE. 2. The I ONE. 3. Some other ONEs.*

1. The indefinite ONE

One serves as a pronoun, most often legitimately, sometimes less so. It is acceptable to let *one* stand for a person in general or any of us or an average person: "One must earn a living." / "One needs to watch one's weight." In this use, which we may call the *indefinite one,* inconsistency is a problem that crops up fairly often. A sentence written for a newspaper by a dietitian will illustrate:

> . . . When one is occupied with good food, you don't miss some of the foods you thought you would.

The "one" that appears early in the sentence soon shifts to "you." Inasmuch as "you" shows up three times, the simplest correction would be to change "one is" to *you are* or *you're.* Anyway, keeping the first "one" would require "one" three more times ("one doesn't miss" etc.) and the sentence would look stilted.

A sentence from a magazine article also shifts from "one" to "you":

> It [Vancouver] is compact and one has little need of a car if you are staying in one of the downtown hotels.

It should all be either in the second person, ". . . and *you have* little need of a car if you are staying . . ."; or in the third person, ". . . and one has little need of a car if *one is* staying. . . ." If the latter is chosen, another improvement would be to change "one of the downtown hotels" to "*a* downtown *hotel.*" It is not just a matter of conciseness: When the indefinite *one* is used, it is best to avoid *one* in another sense.

An excerpt from an op-ed article about telephone solicitors contains a glaring error and two subtle defects.

> Such calls were always intrusive, but when one receives one or two of them almost daily (or nightly), I really begin to think, "Their ought to be a law."

"Their," of course, should be *there.* Another mistake is the shift from third person to first person—"one . . . I." A better way would be either "when *I receive* one or two . . . I really begin to think" (first

person); or "when *you receive* one or two . . . *you* really begin to think" (second person). The indefinite *one* does not suit this sentence, which uses *one* in another sense ("when one receives one"). *See 3* (end).

See also **Pronouns,** 7.

2. The I ONE

A less legitimate use of the pronoun is what we call here the *I one* but could as well call the *coy one.* Some people treat the word as a substitute for *I,* out of coyness, modesty, evasiveness, or affectation. Its other forms are "one's" in place of *my* and "oneself" in place of *myself.*

A few quotations with translations: "His accounts . . . are the best one has seen"—the best *I have* seen. ". . . One's efforts will now be more fully and adequately supported"—*my* efforts will. ". . . One was almost beside oneself with joy . . ."—*I* was almost beside *myself* with joy.

This mannerism is associated mainly with British writing, although it is not rare among Americans. A "presidential spokesman" was quoted as saying:

> We have not solved problems related to discrimination in the workplace and sometimes one wonders whether those who advocate abolishing affirmative action understand that clearly.

Which "one" wonders? The forthright course would be to say "*I wonder . . .*" or "*the president wonders.*" But to be forthright is not the function of a presidential spokesman.

3. Some other ONEs

The pronouns *anyone, everyone,* and *someone* need to be distinguished from the phrases *any one, every one,* and *some one.*

The three pronouns refer only to people and mean any person, every person, and some person. ("*Anyone* can enter the building." / "I wish *everyone* a happy holiday." / "*Someone* is at the door.")

Each of the three phrases is made up of an adjective and the pronoun *one*, can refer to either things or people, and emphasizes a single item or person. ("Any *one* of the jurors can thwart a conviction." / "Every *one* of the envelopes contains a bill." / "The check is in some *one* of the drawers.")

No one does not present such a problem. It is always a two-word phrase.

The common reflexive form of the indefinite *one* is *oneself,* with only one *s* and no apostrophe ("College study is a way to advance oneself"), although *one's self* is its meaning and its variation.

The pronoun *one* can represent a person or thing of a kind or group mentioned or understood. "Sing one of the songs." / "I've seen those machines and plan to buy one." / "That one should fit you." / "Give me the blue one." / "Is this the one you want?"

See also ANY, 2; EVERYBODY, EVERYONE; EVERY ONE and EVERYONE; Pronouns, 2 C.

ONE IN EVERY. *See* ONE OF, *1*.

ONE OF.   *1.* ONE OF EVERY, ONE OUT OF, *etc.*   *2.* ONE OF THE, IF NOT THE, *etc.*   *3.* ONE OF THE . . . WHO *etc.*

1. ONE OF EVERY, ONE OUT OF, etc.

"One of every four persons in this state have been hit hard by the flooding," a governor said on television. Change "have" to *has*. The essential subject is *one*, which is singular. *One* remains singular even when it represents millions.

Similarly: "About one out of every six adults is a college graduate." / "One in every forty children displays the symp-

toms." / "Only one in a thousand wins a prize."

See also MORE THAN ONE.

2. ONE OF THE, IF NOT THE, etc.

The desire to avoid repetition is at the root of this problem, an example of which goes: "She was one of the best, if not the best, teacher I had." It takes many forms, such as the form of this quotation, attributed to a medical investigator: "It is one of the, if not *the*[,] most egregious case I've ever seen."

If the parenthetical phrase in each example is removed, neither sentence makes grammatical sense. The "one of the" part does not go with the singular noun: "one of the best . . . teacher" / "one of the . . . most egregious case." Making the singular noun plural would add no sense; the pronoun and first verb, both singular, would not go with it: "She was . . . the best teachers." / "It is . . . *the* most egregious cases."

This is a solution: Tell what group the individual or item is "one of," before you consider that one as a lone superlative. And do not worry about a little repetition. "She was one of the best teachers, if not the best teacher, I had." / "It is one of the most egregious cases, if not *the* most egregious case, I've ever seen." Even limiting the parenthetical phrase to "if not the best" or "if not *the* most egregious" would be preferable to the original version: It is easier for someone to mentally extract a part of a word that has been mentioned (*teacher* from *teachers,* or *case* from *cases*) than to imagine something that is not there.

Another option is rewriting; for instance, "This case is as egregious as any I've seen in ten years, perhaps more so." The rewritten version might be an improvement. Those "if not" sentences can get repetitious themselves.

3. ONE OF THE . . . WHO etc.

The question here is whether singular

or plural words go with phrases like *one of the, one of a, one of those,* and *one of six* (or another number). Such a phrase gives no trouble in a simple sentence: "One of the women wears a hibiscus in her hair." But when it appears in a sentence with a clause, usually a clause containing *who* or *that,* people often go astray (as a newspaper did):

> . . . The son is now a Senator from Connecticut himself and one of a handful of Democrats who has not said how he will vote. . . .

That senator is one of those Democrats who *have* not said how *they* will vote. *Who* pertains to the people just mentioned, not to "one." Ask the question What is he one of? The answer: "a handful of Democrats who *have* not said how *they* will vote. . . ."

Similarly, in each of the three examples below (from a radio feature, a biography, and a TV documentary) a singular verb is erroneously used in place of a plural verb: "He's one of the five [Polish conspirators] who gets away." / "One of the few Gilbert diaries that survives is of this year." / (This pride of lions is) "one of six prides that lives here." Change "gets" to *get,* "survives" to *survive,* and "lives" to *live.* What is the man one of? ". . . The five who *get* away." What is the diary one of? ". . . The few Gilbert diaries that *survive.* . . ." What is the pride one of? ". . . Six prides that *live* here."

An obituary opens with a singular noun that should be a plural noun: "Judith Somogi, one of the first women to become a conductor, died . . . Wednesday morning." She was not the first woman to become a conductor but "one of the first women to become *conductors.*"

Here is a similar error, the failure to use a plural pronoun and noun: *their husbands.* The erroneous sentence (from

network TV news) can be interpreted whimsically.

> She [the princess] is one of the few Japanese women who will have her husband home for dinner at night.

Does she know about the others?

See also **Nouns,** *3;* **Verbs,** *3* ("is among senators who").

ONE OUT OF. *See* ONE OF, *1.*

ONESELF. *See* ONE as pronoun, *3;* Pronouns, *3.*

ONGOING.

Several dictionaries define *ongoing* as an adjective that means *progressing, evolving,* or *growing.* More often it is used as a synonym for *continuing,* as in "the ongoing operation."

Ongoing or *on-going* came out of the nineteenth century. It appeals to those of our contemporaries with taste for bureaucratic jargon. Use it if you will (as an adjective before the noun), but not as a substitute for *going on,* in the Germanic manner in which it was used below (as a verb following an auxiliary verb).

> [A metropolitan mayor:] It [an investigation] is ongoing as we speak.

> [A journalist in a TV forum:] There's a Justice Department investigation ongoing.

> [A newspaper:] . . . He said negotiations with the developer were ongoing.

> [A news service:] . . . Poindexter several times misled him by asserting that the Iran arms operation had been closed down, when in fact it was ongoing.

Changing "ongoing" to *going on* would fix all four examples. An alternative in the fourth example is *continuing;* this would particularly suit the sentence below (from a TV news report):

> That sort of construction is going to be ongoing for a number of years.

An idiomatic replacement for "ongoing" in this sentence (from a radio news report) is *being made:*

> Attempts are ongoing to identify others [who stole money]. . . .

Still better: "The police are attempting to. . . ."

A folder issued by a utility company on the effects of magnetic fields contained the subheading "Research Is Ongoing." The text said research studies were *under way,* which would have been an ideal substitute for "Ongoing."

Related noun forms, all little used, are *on-going,* the action of going on; *ongoings,* goings on or doings; and *ongoingness,* the quality or condition of going on.

See also **Backward writing,** *3.*

ONLY. *1. In general. 2. Misplacement.*

1. In general

Normally *only* affects the word or phrase that immediately follows. "Only time will tell." / "The only thing we have to fear. . . ." (When exceptions will arise, "God only knows.")

The meaning of a sentence can hinge on the location of *only.* To illustrate, let us put it in different places in four otherwise identical sentences.

A. *Only* he sells watches in town. (Nobody else sells them here.)

B. He *only* sells watches in town. (He does not make or fix them.)

C. He sells *only* watches in town. (They are his sole merchandise here.)

D. He sells watches *only* in town. (He sells them nowhere else.)

Only is classified as (1) an adjective, meaning sole or single one in a category; (2) an adverb, meaning merely, solely, or exclusively; and (3) a conjunction, meaning but or except that. Some disparage that third function; 85 percent of *The American Heritage Dictionary*'s usage panel found this sentence unacceptable in writing: "They would have come, only the automobile broke down."

2. Misplacement

A sign in a window of a clothing store announced: "Large Assortment of 100% silk ties only 2 for 14.90." It seemed to be emphasizing that customers could have "only 2" ties (not three or four) at that price. Most people probably understood the offer, despite the misplacement of "only"; but "2 for *only* $14.90," clearly emphasizing the price (with the $) would have presented it better.

A developer planned to turn a historic farm into a village in Princeton Township, New Jersey, a newspaper reported.

> However, Princeton zoning permitted only houses on three-acre sites on the White Farm.

The sentence says zoning allowed no structures other than houses on those sites; but was that the intended meaning? More likely the writer was referring to the required acreage for each property. In that case, *only* belonged elsewhere: ". . . permitted houses *only* on three-acre sites. . . ." The wording could be still clearer: "However, on the White Farm, Princeton zoning permitted houses *only* on sites of [at least?] three acres each."

The writer of an opinion piece told newspaper readers that he would have loved Ronald Reagan if the president had kept all of his campaign promises of 1980.

> During his campaign he promised us lower taxes, limited government and an administration that would only spend the money it collected.

To say that the administration would "only spend" the money seems to imply that it would never *save* any of the money. Interchange "only" and "spend." The proper phrase does appear elsewhere in the piece: "If Reagan had stuck to his promise to *spend only* what government collected, we would not have a $4.1 trillion debt today" (emphasis added).

The problem in the press example below is not ambiguity but absurdity.

> New York is only one of two states in the nation that now rely exclusively on the S.A.T. to determine eligibility for their state-scholarship programs.

Obviously New York is "only one" state. Make it "one of *only* two states. . . ."

See also **NOT ONLY.**

ONLY TO. *See* **TO**, 2.

ONTO. *1. ON and ONTO. 2. ON TO and ONTO.*

1. ON *and* ONTO

The relation between these two prepositions resembles that between *in* and *into*.

On indicates position or location. Among its many senses, it means in contact with (a surface), e.g., a fly *on* a wall; or above and supported by (a surface), a dish *on* a table.

Onto signifies motion to a position on (a surface). A frog hops from a tree *onto* the grass, then hops along *on* the grass.

Sometimes *on* can fill the role of *onto* without confusion (Snow dropped *on* our heads); at other times, it cannot. If children throw a ball *on* the roof, they may be up there themselves; they are not if they throw the ball *onto* the roof. *Onto* is unequivocal.

Among the early uses of *onto* was this by Keats, 1819: "Please you walk forth Onto the terrace." Since the sixteenth century, the preposition had been treated as two words, *on to*, a use that persisted in Britain into the modern era.

2. ON TO *and* ONTO

When *on*, serving as an adverb, adjoins the preposition *to*, the two words should not be joined. These are correct examples: "I walked on to the next village." / "Take one copy and pass the rest on to your neighbor." / "Hold on to the rope." / "We'll fight on to victory!" In each instance *on* is an adverb, closely related to the verb.

This is an erroneous use from a contemporary book of essays: "I'd given this company, a bank, all my money to hold onto for me until I needed it." Make it "hold *on to* for me . . ." or simply "hold for me . . ."

To be *on to* something like a plot or scheme is an informal term meaning to be aware of it. *The Oxford English Dictionary* quotes an old editorial comment as an example of an erroneous joining of *on* and *to*: "It is a very pretty game, governor, but the people are onto it." Two other dictionaries present that term as "onto" without identifying it as a misspelling.

As separate words, *on* and *to* get about equal stress. *Onto* stresses the first syllable, *on-*.

OPHTHALMOLOGIST. *See* **OCULIST, OPHTHALMOLOGIST** (etc.).

OPINE. Once used in serious writing, *opine* now usually serves journalistic writers seeking to be mildly funny or facetious. *Opine* (verb, transitive and intransitive) is an economical way to say *express an opinion.* Nowadays it tends to make light of the opinion expressed.

Thackeray wrote in the 1850s, "He opined that the rich should pay." An article in a daily paper praises a work of print and television even though it

> "pours fuel on the smoldering election-year rage of the middle class," *USA Today* opined.

A magazine article says of a performer's supposed bodily insecurities:

> "I think . . . she looks in the mirror and sees a girl with big thighs," opines [the] *Striptease* director. . . .

On those infrequent occasions when *opine* is uttered orally, it is pronounced oh-PINE.

OPTOMETRIST and OPTICIAN. *See* OCULIST, OPHTHALMOLOGIST (etc.).

OR. A columnist criticized passive verbs, remarking:

> If your doctor or lawyer write that way to other doctors or lawyers, fine.

If a writer uses a singular subject with a plural verb in a column on word usage, it is not so fine. Change "write" to *writes.*

Whenever the subject of a sentence or clause consists of two or more alternatives—that is, words or phrases linked by *or* or *nor*—and each alternative is singular, the verb too must be singular.

Example: "Either Mary *or* Jane *has* the key"—not "have." It is held by one person, either this one or that one. The subject expresses oneness, and so must the verb express it.

Any related pronoun also is singular: "Abe *or* Charles, whichever one goes, will have to pay *his* own way"—not "their."

Whenever *or* links plural alternatives in a subject, the verb is plural. It gets complicated when the alternatives differ in number. *See* EITHER, *1.*

Using *or,* like using *nor,* shows us some limitations of English. Which form of the verb goes in the following sentence? "Settle your quarrel before you or Joe get[s] hurt." Both "you . . . gets" and "Joe get" are ungrammatical. A number of grammarians tolerate whichever verb goes with the nearer noun or pronoun, in that example "gets." If the sentence is to be written, one can usually rephrase it, evading the dilemma; e.g., "Settle your quarrel before you get hurt or Joe does" / ". . . before someone gets hurt" / ". . . before you two get hurt." Rephrasing may be the best option.

Instead of an alternative, *or* may introduce an appositive, an explanatory word or phrase. When it does, a comma precedes *or:* "The bird is a rock dove, or pigeon."

See also **NOR; Series errors,** *6.*

ORAL. *See* VERBAL.

ORDINAL NUMBERS. *See* **Numbers,** *11.*

ORDINANCE and ORDNANCE. *See* **Confusing pairs.**

OSCILLATE and OSCULATE. *See* **Confusing pairs.**

OTHER. *See* ANOTHER; NOTHER.

OURSELVES. *See* **Pronouns,** *3, 4, 5.*

OUTPUT. The noun *output* is more or less technical. It means the quantity of a product turned out in a given period of time, or the amount of energy or power that a device can produce, or the data that come out of a computer.

The verb *output* flowered in the fourteenth to seventeenth centuries with several general meanings, and it persisted as jargon for *produce* or *put out*: "to output coal" or to "output some 1,200 tons of flour per day." Computer technology assigned *output* another sense: to give out, print, or transfer processed data.

No one objects to the technical use of a technical term. Adapting such a term to general use, however, may not be necessary. A common word or phrase may bring out the meaning as well or better.

A boy doing poorly in school was described, in a newscast, as handicapped in "his ability to output the information" he was taught. To *express* it? To *recall* it? To *write* it *down*?

Let that Germanic-sounding verb remain a technical term in computing and industry, not replacing common words or phrases like *put out*. If we are lucky, nobody will ever "output" a fire, "output" a batter, "output" to sea, or "output" the cat.

See also **Backward writing**, *3*.

OUTRAGEOUS, OUTRAGEOUSLY.

The adjective *outrageous* (and its adverbial relative *outrageously*) can mean disgraceful(ly), harmful(ly), immoral(ly), indecent(ly), offensive(ly), shocking(ly), or violent(ly). Those meanings apply to criminal or other antisocial deeds. ("We've got to curb that drug lord's outrageous activities.") Does a single one apply to the event described below?

> More than 17 million visitors were attracted to the 1939 Golden Gate Exposition, held on man-made Treasure Island, dredged from the Bay bottom to house the outrageously spectacular exhibition. . . .

Just why the writer thought he was improving on "spectacular" is murky.

The producer of a computer show advertised "OUTRAGEOUS DEALS UNDER ONE ROOF!!" Was that a warning?

OVAL. *Oval* (adjective and noun) originates in *ovum,* Latin for egg. English adopted *ovum* in the sense of egg cell, female reproductive cell. From the foregoing, one could reasonably assume that *oval* has something to do with eggs, and so it has. *Oval* means (as an adjective) egg-shaped, whether solidly or planely; or (as a noun) an egg shape.

What is the shape of an egg? Anyone who has ever seen a common hen's egg is probably aware that it is rounded and somewhat elongated, with one end broader than the other. The disparity between egg ends is likely to be impressed on the minds of those who have read Swift's *Gulliver's Travels* and recall the violent ideological conflict in the empire of Liliput: It pitted the Big-Endians, the heretics, who broke their eggs at the big ends, against the Little-Endians, the orthodox egg-breakers.

Oval may be distinguished from *elliptical* (adjective) and *ellipse* (noun). An *ellipse* is an elongated circle, the shape of the numeral 0. (More technically, it is a symmetrical closed curve, the path of a point that moves in a way that the sum of its distances from two fixed points is constant.) A planet's orbit is sometimes called its *ellipse,* inasmuch as the planetary orbits are approximately elliptical. An American football is an *ellipsoid,* a solid object whose plane sections are all ellipses or circles. The adjective is *ellipsoid* or *ellipsoidal*.

More often than not, the public confuses an *oval* and an *ellipse*. Usually an *ellipse* is called (an) "oval." Occasionally it is the other way around. A number of modern dictionaries have legitimated the misemployment, thereby contributing further to it.

A national TV "magazine" broadcast a portrait of a tycoon in the chicken industry. After visiting the White House,

> he redesigned his office to look like the president's. But instead of "oval," he calls it "egg-shaped."

That is exactly what *oval* means. (Exactly what the shape of each office is, we do not know.)

Scientists do not necessarily use the terms with any more precision than laymen. The quotation is from a book on cosmology and pertains to a theory of cosmic history.

> Other regions, which did not happen to pick up a rotation, would become oval-shaped objects called elliptical galaxies.

It contains a contradiction. If the galaxies are *elliptical,* they are not "oval," at least in strict usage—and if a scientist is not strict in his usage, who is? Anyway, "shaped" is redundant; it is part of the meaning of the adjective *oval.*

OVER and MORE THAN. "Over
50 years in business," says an ad for an auto painting company. Is the phrase "over 50 years" correct?

People who work in the mass media frequently avoid *over* in that sense. An editor of mine insisted that *over* could only mean *above* in a literal, geometric sense: "I see the balloon over the building." (He expressed no such objection to *under.*) Many an editor, despite a penchant for conciseness, will omit the word *over* in a sentence like "Over 2,000 attended" and change it to the two-word phrase *more than. More than* is perfectly proper, but it has been one of the meanings of *over* since the Middle Ages. *The Oxford English Dictionary* offers eight quotations, from the fourteenth century on, to illustrate that *over* can mean "In excess of, above, more than (a stated amount or number)."

What caused the odd aversion to phrases like *over a ton, over a million,* and *over 50 years* after all those centuries of use? The only visible answer is a little book from 1909 called *Write it Right* by Ambrose Bierce. He subtitled it

"A Little Blacklist of Literary Faults," and one item was "*Over for More than.*" He gave an example, "A sum of over ten thousand dollars," but no reason for his stricture.

Bierce also damned such uses as "*Over for About, In, or Concerning*" (e.g., "Don't cry over spilt milk" and "He rejoiced over his acquittal") and "*Over for On*" ("The policeman struck him over the head"), uses that are generally accepted.

Although Bierce did not say anything about *over* in the sense of across ("Let's walk over the bridge"), some others have condemned it. The *Oxford,* again, supports such use, offering quotations dating from the ninth century.

For better or worse, *over* has numerous meanings and it has had them for centuries. *The Random House Dictionary* gives sixty-one definitions of the word, as preposition, adverb, adjective, noun, verb, and interjection (in radio communication, as in "Over and out").

OVERLY and OVER- words. *1. Is
OVERLY unnecessary? 2. Misuse of OVERLY.*

1. Is OVERLY unnecessary?
Several grammarians have objected to any use of *overly* as superfluous, contending that the *over-* words have taken its place. They would, for instance, say *overcautious* and reject "overly cautious."

The Random House Dictionary lists about 1,500 *over-* words. *The Oxford English Dictionary* has 83 pages of *over-* words, many of which it prefers to hyphenate, *over-cautious,* for instance. Such a word is a little more concise than an *overly* phrase and usually just as good.

Overly is an "Americanism" to Britons, although the *Oxford* traces it back to A.D. 10. (It was *oferlice* in Old English.) Before burying the word, let us consider two points:

- The language is full of synonyms. That the same idea may be expressed in two ways is not a strong reason to discard one of them. *Overly* means *excessively* (a word preferred in British English), yet the critics are not advocating the latter's elimination.
- On a few occasions *overly* can contribute to clarity or grace. It outdoes *over-* in this sentence: "The fight was over money and overbrutal." *Overly overt* beats "overovert," although *too overt* may be the best choice. And a behemoth like *overgesticulative* or *overindividualistic* may not suit a particular sentence, speaker, or writer. In a poem titled "The Second Voyage," Kipling wrote: "Yet caring so, not overly we care / To brace and trim for every foolish blast." Was he expected to force "overcare" into his iambic pentameter?

2. *Misuse of OVERLY*

Overly is not misused often, but a columnist did wrongly insert it in an opening sentence:

> When an overly weight man came into my office wanting a notary I noticed his shoe was untied.

The phrase "overly weight" is wrong. Change it to *overweight* or some other *over-* adjective. Alternatively, to keep "overly," change "weight" to an adjective referring to the man's avoirdupois: *overly heavy, overly stout*. (The sentence also could use a comma after "notary.")

Overly is an adverb, a word that modifies an adjective, a verb, or another adverb. It cannot modify a noun, such as "weight."

(The anecdote was leading to a historical sketch: The portly one could not bend enough to tie his shoe; he would not have faced such a problem when the region was a ranch and men wore laceless boots.)

OWING TO. *See* DUE TO.

OXYMORON.

A panelist in a political discussion on television probably intended this question to be rhetorical: "If a 'paid volunteer' is not an oxymoron, what is?"

The answer is that an *oxymoron* is a figure of speech in which contradictory words or ideas are intentionally combined. The striking effect produced by the juxtaposition of incompatibles is designed to make a point. Some popular examples are *agreeing to disagree, deafening silence,* and *killing with kindness*. The *oxymoron* was a favored device in Latin and Greek literature. The word entered English from the Greek *oxumoron,* literally meaning pointed foolishness.

If the contrariness of the terms is accidental or unintentional, other words can describe it. If a bureaucrat comes up with a phrase like "paid volunteer"; a novelist writes that "they had found increasingly little to talk about"; or a diplomat remarks, "The situation in Iraq is clearly very confused," there may be a *contradiction,* an *incompatibility,* or a *paradox*. The word *oxymoron* should be reserved for the figure of speech.

P

PACHYDERM. *See* **Synonymic silliness**, *1*.

PADDY. *Paddy* is rice. It comes from the Malay *padi,* meaning rice in the husk, and in the strictest sense *paddy* denotes such rice, whether it is growing or has been harvested. By extension, the word can also mean rice in general. Used loosely, it means rice field.

Describing an Egyptian oasis, a book explains that the growing of rice there is forbidden for fear of malaria, because "mosquitoes thrive in paddy fields." *Paddy* is used admirably. On the contrary, these press samples show no understanding of it:

> Across the rice paddies, several hundred men from leftist organizations carried red banners. . . .

> The dilapidated brick villages and bright green rice paddies in this corner of southern China sometimes seem as American as chop suey.

> Many Cambodian houses are built on stilts near the rice paddies that line the road.

"Rice paddies" is redundant. Change all the "paddies" to *fields,* or at least omit "rice."

Rice is totally absent in a piece about Maui, Hawaii, by a travel editor: "White-haired old men and women return from their taro paddies, their legs spackled with mud." The people work in taro *fields.* Taro is an edible plant that has nothing to do with *paddy.* (Moreover *speckled* is misspelled and "old" is superfluous editorializing.)

PAIR. *Pair* (noun), like *couple,* concerns two of the same kind. *Pair,* however, often stresses their close association, perhaps their mutual dependence: a *pair* of pants, a *pair* of scissors. *Pair,* like other collective nouns, may be either singular or plural. It depends on which gets the emphasis: the group as a unit or its individual members.

If you say, "A blue pair of pants does not go with a brown pair of shoes," you are emphasizing the oneness of each pair. But "A pair of soldiers were guarding the entrance to their post." To say "was guarding . . . its" post would be ridiculous. When *pair* refers to people, it is normally plural.

A nature film depicted two dangerous animals of Africa, the cape buffalo and the hippopotamus. The narrator said, "When the pair clashes, the outcome is uncertain." The two *clash.* They could not do so if they were *one.* Besides, *pair* has special meaning when applied to animals: it denotes two that are either mated or yoked for labor.

A news story said: "In a rare finding, a pair of twins has been shown to have different fathers." Make it either "*have* been shown to have different fathers" or "*has* been shown to have *two* fathers." That which is one unit cannot differ from itself.

See also Collective nouns; COUPLE.

Pairs of words. *See* BACK(-) prefix and pairs; Confusing pairs (with lists); Homophones (with lists); Joining of words; Twins.

PALPATE and PALPITATE. One physician spoke about another on a television "magazine" program and made what may have been a slip of the tongue: "The doctor palpitated a mass, but nothing was done to rule it out." The "it" that the speaker referred to was cancer, but he should have ruled the "-it-" out of "palpitated." The word he needed was *palpate,* to touch a part of someone's body for medical diagnosis.

To *palpitate,* said of the heart, is to beat unusually fast or intensely or with abnormal flutter.

The two words have a relationship. They come from different forms of the Latin verb *palpare,* to touch.

PANTS. *See* PAIR; Plurals and singulars, *1;* Verbal unmentionables.

PARADISE. *See* Hawaii.

Paragraph. Almost every piece of writing is divided into paragraphs. They are orderly collections of sentences. The main function of a paragraph is to group related points, ideas, or statements.

A new paragraph says in effect, "Here comes something a bit different." The eye recognizes it because each paragraph starts on a new line and is commonly indented (begun a little distance in from the margin), except that publishers often do not indent the first paragraph of a book chapter, magazine article, etc.

A paragraph may have one sentence, if its message stands alone; or multiple sentences, if they all go together in sequence. But it should not have too many. A secondary purpose of a paragraph is to give the reader a momentary rest, a chance to absorb a particular point before moving on to the next point. Sometimes a paragraph, though properly homogeneous, is too long. It may then need to be divided more or less arbitrarily, for the brain can weary of overlong blocks of writing. An extreme example is seen in *Webster's Third Dictionary,* where paragraphs reach lengths of some four thousand words (*take* and *turn*).

Newspapers often go to the opposite extreme. Journalists know that the usual newspaper column, being narrow, does not lend itself to long paragraphs. Many turn nearly every sentence into its own paragraph, thinking that they are furthering readability. They are hindering it, failing to fully organize the material, and defeating the main function of a paragraph.

PARAMETER and PERIMETER. *See* Confusing pairs.

PARANOIA, PARANOID. *Paranoia* (noun) is a psychosis characterized by a delusion of persecution or grandeur or both. Usually the delusion centers on one theme that is elaborated with logic, and the person is otherwise rational and intelligent.

Paranoid (adjective) means characteristic of, relating to, or exhibiting the psychosis. Often "paranoid" and sometimes "paranoia" are used loosely to refer to a feeling or showing of worry, fear, distrust, or suspicion. Who among us has never had real cause for such thoughts?

A book says to "trust your agent— don't get paranoid if you don't receive an instant response." Was *distrustful* or *fearful* meant? You are unlikely to lose your mind from a delayed letter or call.

"You are paranoid," a physician conducting a syndicated talk show on radio told a caller who had expressed the view that breast implants were unsafe. Was he diagnosing her as psychotic on the basis of one statement? No, he too was using "paranoid" in the loose way.

Parentheses. *See* **Punctuation, 7.**

PAROLE and PROBATION. A woman had been convicted of murdering a well-known singer. Jurors now were deliberating on the penalty. "They could decide on a penalty ranging from parole to life in prison," a radio news report said. "Parole" was wrong. *Probation* would have been right (from the standpoint of English usage). The penalty, by the way, turned out to be life in prison.

Parole is the conditional release of an imprisoned convict. One who is on *parole* must exhibit good behavior and follow certain rules during the period of *parole.*

Probation is the conditional freedom that sometimes is allowed a convicted person instead of imprisonment. The sentence of someone on *probation* is suspended as long as he behaves well and fulfills any conditions that the court sets.

A *parolee* or *probationer* is under the supervision of his parole officer or probation officer and may be imprisoned for violation of his conditions for freedom.

Laws governing *parole* differ from state to state. A term of *parole* may be fixed and follow each completed prison term; or it may be determined by a *parole* board, vary with each convict, and reduce prison time.

Participle. A *participle* is a word that is derived from a verb, has the properties of both verb and adjective, and can go with an auxiliary—*has, had, is, was,* or the like—to indicate tense.

Two types are *past participle,* such as *fallen* and *thrown;* and *present participle,* such as *falling* and *throwing.* Some

examples of use: "The city has *fallen* to the rebels." / "He was hit by a *thrown* ball." / "I see a *falling* star." / "They're *throwing* darts."

General dictionaries customarily list a verb's infinitive, past tense, past participle, and present participle, in that order, e.g.: *ring, rang, rung, ringing.* If the past tense and past participle are the same, they parsimoniously allot one word between them: *make, made, making.*

Occasionally participles are ambiguous. An article about gambling on Indian reservations was headed "Cheating Indians." Did the present participle describe Indians who were *cheating* or mean that some people were *cheating* Indians? (Probably the latter.)

Combining *have* with a past participle sometimes creates an ambiguity. A news report dealt with "mothers who have abused children." Did it mean simply that the mothers were parents of *abused children* or was it alleging that the mothers themselves *have abused* children? *See* HAVE, HAS, HAD.

The combination of *having* and a past participle forms a *perfect participle.* "*Having done* the work, I went home."

Among entries that consider participles are BEGIN, BEGAN, BEGUN; COME and CAME; DO, DID, DONE; Gerund, *1;* GONE and WENT; Infinitive, *3;* LAY and LIE; Modifiers, *1A* (dangling participles); SLAY, SLAIN, SLEW; TEAR, TORE, TORN; Tense, *5;* THINK, past participle; Verbs, *1B.*

PASSED and PAST. *See* **Homophones.**

Passive voice. *See* **Active voice and passive voice.**

Past tense. *See* **Tense.**

PAY. An exhibit of ceramics at a college tells viewers, "These exhibition cases were . . . payed for with funds donated by the artist."

A friend writes that he is working for the government and "Though I have next to nothing to do, I am well payed for that."

Paid is the past tense of *pay* (verb, transitive and intransitive) in the sense of compensate for services or goods. The writers of the quoted sentences forgot the irregularity and followed the pattern of *played* and *prayed*.

Pay has nautical senses (transitive): to let out (a line) and to coat with a waterproof material. The past tense in those senses is *payed*.

PEACOCK. "Why do peacocks— male peacocks—have such beautiful tails?" A radio host asked listeners that question, as part of a short discussion of natural selection. "Male peacocks" is a redundant phrase. The *peacock* is male. It is a male *peafowl* (plural *peafowl* or *peafowls*), a type of pheasant of either of two species, native to southern Asia but widely domesticated. The female is a *peahen,* which lacks the *peacock*'s spectacular tail.

A vain person may be called a *peacock,* and sometimes the word is used as a verb (intransitive): to *peacock* is to display oneself vainly.

PEDAL and PEDDLE. *See* **Homophones.**

PENCHANT and PENSION. A book describes a Briton's sculptures of the royal family: Art lovers admired his rendering of the queen's expression but found the figures to be dressed like tramps, for "his pension did not run to the sort of garb in which Royalty is normally kitted out." Instead of "pension," the word should be *penchant,* a persistent liking or a strong inclination. *Pension* is a retirement benefit or a European boarding house. (We should not be too critical of the book, inasmuch as it is *The Incomplete Book of Failures:*

The Official Handbook of the Not-Terribly-Good Club of Great Britain.)

PEOPLE and PERSONS. An article on labor problems in London said, "More than 150 people were injured, mostly police officers, and 67 persons were arrested." Why were the injured called "people" and the arrested called "persons"? Either one would have been acceptable, but using both raises that question.

When in doubt, you will probably not go wrong using *people* as the plural of *person. Persons,* especially popular with lawyers and journalists, can seem stilted at times, although it has a proper use.

Persons emphasizes individuals. It applies to a specific but not large number: "The group honored seven persons." *People* can be used in that way too; but, of those two words, only *people* is correct in referring to human beings in general, or in a large group, or indefinitely. No one should remark that "persons are funny," speak for "the American persons," or sing about "persons who like persons."

PEOPLE as a suffix. *People* is a word, a noun. It is not a suffix, though it has been rudely forced into that role of late. Some of the outlandish creations are less informative than the legitimate words they replace.

Two reviews on one tabloid page referred to "waitpeople" at restaurants, not saying whether they were *waiters* or *waitresses* or both.

A national-parks functionary seeking funds was quoted as saying, "I hope people will write their congresspeople." There are no such officials. The members of Congress are *senators,* in the Senate; and *representatives,* in the House of Representatives, unofficially known as *congressmen.*

See also **PERSON.**

PER CAPITA. In English, *per capita* is a statistical term meaning *for each person*. It came from Latin, in which the same phrase means *by heads*. In English it expresses an average: a total number or amount divided by the number of people in the population being considered. For instance, "The state's income per capita last year was about $14,000."

A radio reporter said that San Francisco's transit system was transporting some 700,000 riders a day, "more per capita than any other city. . . ." Substitute *population* for "capita." Obviously the number was not an average but a total.

Percent, per cent. *See* **Numbers,** *1, 4, 5, 8, 10.*

Perfect infinitive. *See* **Infinitive,** *3.*

Perfect tenses. *See* **Tense,** *1, 5.*

Period. *See* **Punctuation,** *8.*

PERPETRATE. "He joined with Chief Justice Warren and perpetrated a revolution in the fifties and the sixties." The intention of a TV moderator was probably to honor Justice Brennan, not to condemn him. Yet one could draw the opposite conclusion from "perpetrated."

To *perpetrate* (verb, transitive) something is to commit or carry it out; usually it is a felony or immoral deed, but it can be a repugnant action that is not felonious or immoral, say a blunder or hoax. Although a descendant of the Latin *perpetrare,* to accomplish, *perpetrate* is not a neutral word and no vehicle for praise.

PERQUISITE and PREREQUI-SITE. A *perquisite* (noun) is a benefit that goes with a job in addition to money, or a privilege expected by virtue of one's office. "Use of a mansion is a perquisite of the governorship." A colloquial short form is *perk* or *perq.*

A *prerequisite* (noun) is a prior condition that must be fulfilled before something that one desires is available. "A high school diploma is a prerequisite of college admission." *Prerequisite* (adjective) means required in advance. "Latin 1 is prerequisite to Latin 2." Note that *of* follows the noun and *to* the adjective.

A news story described Suharto's new cabinet, including a tycoon friend with "a lot to lose if Indonesia adopts stringent economic reforms to satisfy the perquisites of the IMF's 50-point, $43 billion bailout package." *Prerequisites.*

PERSECUTE and PROSECUTE. *See* **Confusing pairs.**

PERSON. *1. As a suffix. 2. Meanings.*

1. As a suffix

Articles told of "a first baseperson for the Cubs" and "university freshpersons" and said "most of the cost goes to the middlepersons." A national column referred to "the clergyperson at the wedding festivities," and a local column mentioned people who subsisted "from their salespersonship." Most of us would hesitate to substitute those corrupted forms for the correct nouns *first baseman, freshmen, middlemen, clergyman,* and *salesmanship.*

Few words so innocuous have figured in as much linguistic pollution as *person.* The harm is done when the word is tacked to some other word, usually out of ignorance. Misunderstanding of the origin and meaning of *-man* has led to various circumlocutions, of which *-person* is one. *See* **-MAN-, MAN.** So far, it appears, nobody has sought to replace the *-son* in *person.*

A columnist criticized a candidate for "congressperson from the Fifth District," and a big ad protesting against a foreign leader said to write "Your Congressperson." There is no such official. A member of Congress is either a *senator* or a *representative*. Each state has two senators in the Senate. Each local, congressional district has a representative in the House of Representatives, often unofficially called a *congressman*.

An editor's normal drive for conciseness was not evident in this headline: "A Handyperson's Guide to Reducing Hazards." A caption described an electric hammer to "GIVE YOUR HANDYPERSON A BANG," and a columnist chose to call himself "MR. HANDYPERSON." The rest of us can use the correct word, *handyman*.

A news item said two financial establishments were "held up by female gunpersons" and "a male gunman" held up a store. Presumably males did not qualify as "-persons."

A column referred to the "hostessperson" at a restaurant, in case anyone might think the hostess was not a person.

Among other clumsy and needless combinations seen in print have been these: "airperson" / "anchorperson" / "draftsperson" / "foreperson" / "foreignperson" / "newsperson" / "pressperson" / "salesperson." Some are perversions of well-established words, such as *airman, draftsman, foreman,* and *pressman*. Some might pass as phrases. *Foreign person* makes sense unjoined. *News person* or *sales person* is more ungainly and no less insipid when joined. Would Arthur Miller have written *Death of a Salesperson*?

A classified ad seeking a "WAITER/WAITRESS" was followed by one for a "WAITPERSON." No normal restaurant patron is likely to say to his waiter, "Waitperson, we're ready to order."

See also CHAIR, *1;* PEOPLE as a suffix; SPOKESMAN, *1.*

2. *Meanings*

Person now is a bland synonym for *human being*, but its ancestral meaning had little humanity in it. It comes, via Old French, from the Latin *persona,* literally a mask used in Roman drama, also a character or role.

The sense of a mask did not make it into English, but that of character or role did. The import of *person* has varied from one of distinction to one of inferiority. *Person* was used contemptuously for some time. It stood for a lower-class man ("a person in the trade") and for a young woman. It has also denoted a living body or bodily form, appearance, or presence.

Person has had special meanings in religion, where it is one of the three manifestations of the Trinity; in philosophy, a rational being or human personality; in law, an individual or an organization; and in grammar, a classification of pronouns and corresponding verb forms. *See* ONE as pronoun, *1;* Pronouns, *7.*

In person, meaning physically present, can be a useful phrase. In "The actor will appear in person," it emphasizes that the appearance will be bodily, not pictorial. But it is probably unnecessary in "The president cannot attend in person." Attendance is in person.

See also PEOPLE and PERSONS; PERSONAL.

PERSONAL. *Personal* (adjective) means of or pertaining to a certain person; private; intimate; bodily; or like a person.

A book on English usage reproves the use of *personal* to qualify words that can be nothing else: mainly *charm, friend,* and *opinion*. Yet elsewhere it says, "The comments in this article reflect a personal opinion. . . ." One can assume that the writer's opinion is personal.

A "personal opinion" may occasionally be valid in distinguishing it from an official opinion. So may "Personally, my view is. . . ." However, the adverb is superfluous in "I cannot attend personally." *See also* PERSON, 2.

Some publications with personal ads

turn them into "personals." *See* **Nouns, 2.**

PERSONALITY. Strictly speaking, *personality* is an abstract noun that usually pertains to a person's pattern of traits or to one's character: "a dual personality" / "her pleasant personality." To say "She has personality" without describing it is a colloquial use, not very informative except to imply that the speaker likes her personality. Everyone has it.

In a news story, the word served as a nondescript tag for a television performer:

> . . . The evening's host, "Entertainment Tonight" personality Mary Hart, presented 14 distinguished service awards for Holocaust remembrance in the performing arts. . . .

Using *personality* as a job title is quite informal and not suitable for a straight news account of a rather somber banquet. If the writer did not know the woman's function on the show (co-host), he could have written "Mary Hart of 'Entertainment Tonight.' " (It would have improved the awkward form too. *See* **Modifiers, 4; Titles, 1.**)

Person (grammatical). *See* **ONE as pronoun, 1; Pronouns, 7.**

Personification. In his poems, the poet Shelley asks questions of Earth, Star, Moon, Wind, Sea, and Skylark. They do not answer, but he does carry on a two-way conversation with Sleep; Dawn instructs her children, the Hours; Indignation answers Pity; and a crowd vows allegiance to Anarchy as it rides by, crowned and sceptered.

To regard nonhuman things as people is a time-honored poetic device. Their investment with human attributes but not full human status is a closely related de-

vice and equally reputable, though disparaged by John Ruskin as the "pathetic fallacy." A prose example is the caption of a cartoon by James Thurber: "It's a naive domestic Burgundy without any breeding, but I think you'll be amused by its presumption."

Those devices are less honored in matter-of-fact writing or speaking. A news photo showed private vehicles using a lane meant for buses; meanwhile, a caption said, "One bus chose to use an adjacent lane." The power of choice belonged to the driver, not to the bus. News stories telling of the suffering of vehicles or buildings in mishaps are disputable too. *See* **SUFFER; SUSTAIN.** A woman tells what cars think, in **LIKE** (last quotation). Sympathetic rivers are headlined in **MERCY and PITY.**

To apply the pronoun *she* or *her* to a country or ship is a traditional personification. *It* or *its* is an acceptable alternative. What is unacceptable is mixing those treatments: "Japan . . . accepts responsibilities . . . which *it* cannot abandon; *her* frontier is no longer the sea." Change either "it" to *she* or "her" to *its.*

PERSONNEL. *1. Number. 2. PERSONAL and PERSONNEL.*

1. Number

Personnel does not pertain to an individual or individuals. It is a collective noun denoting a body of people who work in a business or organization.

A law professor used it wrong on the radio when he explained an action by the judge in a prominent criminal trial:

> Probably he was going to have a court personnel go along [with the lawyers to another court for a special procedure].

Changing "personnel" to *officer* would repair the sentence.

One could also object to a fire commissioner's reference to "our 1,500 personnel." Whether any number goes with *personnel* is debatable. Better: "our department's 1,500 members."

Personnel may be construed (1) as a unit, taking a singular verb ("Our personnel is ready to serve you"), or (2) as a collection of individuals, taking a plural verb ("Personnel of this company have varied backgrounds").

The word may also, as a noun, denote a department or office concerned with employees ("Mr. Carey is the head of personnel") or, as an adjective, refer to employees or the managing of employees ("Please get me these personnel files").

2. *PERSONAL and PERSONNEL*

Personal (adjective), meaning private or pertaining to a particular person, should not be confused with *personnel* (adjective), referring to employees or their managing. The first is pronounced PER-son-null, the second per-son-NELL; and note the second *n* and second *e* in *personnel*. Sometimes the two words are indeed confused, even by those who should know better, and the fact that both come from the Late Latin *personalis*, meaning personal, is no excuse.

A woman sought a personnel job with a community college. A student on a hiring committee said to her, "Tell me about your personal experiences." She assumed that he was inquiring about her experiences in the *personnel* field, not her religious or sexual experiences, "otherwise I could have sued them for harassment."

PERSONS and PEOPLE. *See* PEOPLE and PERSONS.

PERSPECTIVE and PROSPECTIVE. *See* Confusing pairs.

PERSUADE. *See* CONVINCE and PERSUADE.

PETROL. *See* GAS.

PHASE. *See* FAZE and PHASE.

PHENOMENA and PHENOMENON. A *phenomenon* is (1) an observable occurrence or circumstance, (2) a scientifically notable natural event, or (3) an extraordinary, prodigious, or marvelous thing or occurrence. *Phenomenon* is singular. Of Greek origin, it has a Greek plural, *phenomena*. "Earthquakes and tsunamis are related phenomena."

Two talk show hosts on a radio station used the wrong form: "I don't know if this [fading interest in disasters] is uniquely American or if this is an international phenomena. . . ." / "The American Revolution was in large part a minority phenomena." On television, a gerontologist, a journalist, and a newscaster respectively did likewise: "It's the most complex biological phenomena that we know." / "We had this strange phenomena of the president speaking but his mike turned off." / "Geologists say that what they see is a new phenomena." Every "phenomena" should have been *phenomenon*.

Phenomenons is an alternative plural of *phenomenon* in the third sense (extraordinary thing etc.). The adjective *phenomenal* commonly applies to *phenomenon* in that sense.

See also **Plurals and singulars,** 2E.

PHOBIA. *See* HOMOPHOBIA.

Phrase. *See* Sentence fragment.

PHYSICAL and FISCAL. *See* Confusing pairs.

PICK UP and PICKUP. 1. *Confusion of verb with noun.* 2. *Unneeded hyphen and preposition.*

1. *Confusion of verb with noun*

To *pick up*, as in "Pick up the trash," is a compound verb. No one should confuse it with the noun *pickup,* as in "This car has good pickup." That is what the writer of a promotional pamphlet did.

> These mics will not pickup as much noise and radio frequency interference (RFI) as high impedance microphones will. . . .
> Microphones pickup everything, to greater and lesser degrees, within their directivity patterns.

Change each "pickup" to *pick up.*

In the context of recording or broadcasting, to *pick up* is to take sound or light into the system, for conversion into electrical energy. *Pickup* is the process or the apparatus.

The primary meaning of *pick up* is lift up. It has several other meanings, among them to accelerate, to acquire or learn casually, to improve, and to stop for and take along.

Pickup has about as many meanings: acceleration, the act of picking up passengers or objects, a phonograph arm, a pickup truck, and special senses in the jargons of agriculture, broadcasting, journalism, and music. In slang, it is a stranger met casually with the aim of lovemaking.

(Two minor points: The logic of shortening *microphone* before spelling it in full is obscure. And the pet name is better spelled *mike,* if it is to rhyme with *like* and not *tic.*)

2. *Unneeded hyphen and preposition*

Sometimes a hyphen is placed between *pick* and *up.* For the noun, it is unnecessary, though not objectionable: "This car has good pick-up." For the verb, it is erroneous. A sign in a national park tells people to "pick-up" their dogs' dirt. They should *pick up* the stuff. *See also* **Punctuation,** 4C (near end).

An article in a Mississippi newspaper said about high school dress codes: "Some schools are already picking up on new fashion trends." *Picking up* is enough. The "on" serves no purpose, except perhaps to demonstrate that a writer can *pick up* new trends in slang. *See also* **ON,** 2.

PITY. *See* **MERCY and PITY.**

PLACE (verb). *See* **INTO,** *1.*

PLAIN and PLANE. *See* **Homophones.**

PLANET. *See* **STAR and SUN.**

PLAY DOWN and "DOWNPLAY." To *play down* something is to make little of it or to minimize its importance. "The press played down the event."

A Germanic-sounding inversion of it is "downplay," which probably originated in telegraphic messages between correspondents and editors. By reversing and combining two words, a journalist saved the cost of a word. Such jargon was not intended for use in any newspaper story: "Hospital officials downplayed the investigation." / "The counties also allege the industry fraudulently misled the public . . . by downplaying the potential health risks."

Nor was it meant for a broadcast interview: "The Administration had downplayed any real prospects" (of Russia's agreeing to an expansion of NATO). Or a forum: "I don't want to downplay what they're doing" (referring to academics' criticism of the news media). Or an almanac: "Over time . . . fascist elements were downplayed" (in the Franco regime).

John Chancellor, the late broadcaster, and Walter R. Mears, journalist, wrote that "the news business has coined its share of dreadful nonwords. Take 'downplay.' . . . It does not save words, and it ought to be banned." We need not go so far as to criminalize nonwords, but a case can be made for putting that one on the most-unwanted list for speakers of English.

The opposite of *play down* is *play up,* to emphasize the importance of something, to give it prominence. "The news media played up the scandal." So far it has not been Germanized.

See also **Backward writing,** *3.*

PLAY UP. *See* **PLAY DOWN** and **"DOWNPLAY."**

PLEAD. *See* **ADVOCATE.**

PLEONASM. *See* **Tautology.**

PLURALITY. *See* **MAJORITY,** *1.*

Plurals and singulars. *1. Errors. 2. Principles and problems.*

1. Errors

A circus menagerie included lions, tigers, and "rhinoceri," a radio reporter said. And at a zoo "the approach of the rhinoceri did give us a start," a TV host said. Perhaps they deemed an "i" ending for *rhinoceros* an elegant Latinism. They were wrong. The plural is *rhinoceroses* or just *rhinoceros.* The word came from *rhinokeros,* Greek for *nose-horn.*

Some swear that the plural of *octopus* is *octopi,* in Latin fashion. But not all Latin *-us* singulars change to *-i* plurals, and anyway the word came originally from Greek, in which *oktopous* meant eight-footed. One is on firmer ground using *octopuses* or, to be fancier, *octopodes* (pronounced *oc-TOP-a-deez*), even though dictionaries condone the misconception.

A common mistake is to use an exotic plural as a singular: e.g., "a criteria" / "a memoranda" / "a stimuli." Another mistake is to add *s* to one of them, producing a double plural: "criterias" / "memorandas" / "stimulis." In a regional idiosyncrasy, *s* or *es* is added to common plurals: "folkses" / "lices" / "oxens" / "sheeps" / "geeses."

In dealing with plurals and singulars, affixing the wrong ending is one pitfall; another is omitting the right ending.

When "The Ultimate Pant" flashed on television screens, it was not referring to someone's last gasp. It purported to advertise a particular brand and style of *pants.* The word has no singular when applied to an article of clothing.

People have been known to omit the plural endings of *calves, corps, hooves, measles,* and *summons,* thinking that "calv" / "corp" / "hoov" / "measle" / "summon" are singular. *Appendix* (a singular whose plural is *appendices* or *appendixes*) has been turned into "appendic."

Other nonstandard colloquialisms are singulars used as plurals ("many bushel" / "foot" / "mile" / "pair" / "year") and plurals used as singulars ("a woods" / "grounds" / "stairs" / "ways").

2. Principles and problems

A. Basic

The principle is simple for most nouns: To turn a singular into a plural, add *s* or *es.* Add the *es* if the word normally ends in a sibilant (a *ch, j, s, sh, x, z,* or *zh* sound).

The *s* is voiceless after a voiceless sound (*cats*) but pronounced *z* after a voiced sound (*dogs*). The *es* is pronounced *iz* (as in *foxes*).

Problems lie in the minority that are irregular nouns.

B. Compounds

What to do about hyphenated words, like *mother-in-law,* or sets of words, like *consul general,* is a common puzzle. The traditional principle, increasingly disregarded, is to assign the plural ending to the part that is normally a noun; or, if there are two nouns, to the more important one.

Thus these are plurals: *adjutants general, aides-de-camp, attorneys general, daughters-in-law, men-of-war, mothers-*

in-law, *consuls general*, *courts martial*, *notaries public*, *sergeants major*, and *tugs of war*. The noun goes first in each of those; it goes second in these: *judge advocates*, *lieutenant generals*, *major generals*. Many compounds that do not end in nouns get simple s endings, particularly if they are single words: *breakthroughs*, *forget-me-nots*, *knockouts*, *ne'er-do-wells*, *takeoffs*, and words ending in *-ful*, like *cupfuls* and *spoonfuls*.

C. Creatures; peculiarities

English has a variety of peculiar changes to perplex newcomers. *Louse* and *mouse* change to *lice* and *mice*. *Blouse* and *house* become *blouses* and *houses*, but the s sound in *house* changes to a z sound in the plural. You have one *goose* or two *geese*, but *mongoose* becomes *mongooses*, and *moose* remains *moose*.

Fish remains *fish* for individual specimens but becomes *fishes* for different types. Many fishes and beasts have simple s plurals, but sometimes the singular is treated as a plural, particularly by fishermen and hunters: two *flounders* or *flounder*; three *pheasants* or *pheasant*. Other creatures are unchanged in the plural, except for different types or varieties. John buys two *salmon* or studies the different *salmons* of North America. I saw two *deer* and wondered which *deers* inhabit this region. *Coffee*, *fruit*, *silk*, *steel*, *tea*, *wheat*, and *wool* are treated as singular except when different types or varieties are considered; then s is affixed and it becomes plural. An orchard produces lots of *fruit* and five different *fruits*.

D. -EN, -REN

The *-en* and *-ren* forms are descended from Old English. They turn *brother*, *child*, *ox*, *man*, and *woman* into *brethren* (the archaic version of brothers), *children*, *oxen*, *men*, and *women*.

E. Foreign derivations

Some words preserve the forms of the foreign languages they were derived from. As in Latin, the singular words *addendum*, *alumnus*, *datum*, *genus*, *minutia*, *ovum*, *stimulus*, and *stratum* change to the plural *addenda*, *alumni*, *data*, *genera*, *minutiae*, *ova*, *stimuli*, and *strata*. As in Greek, *analysis*, *criterion*, *ellipsis*, *phenomenon*, and *thesis* change to *analyses*, *criteria*, *ellipses*, *phenomena*, and *theses*.

Other words adopted from foreign languages present a choice between the original plural and an Anglicized plural. *Beau* may become either *beaux* (French) or *beaus*. *Cactus*: either *cacti* (Latin) or *cactuses*. *Carcinoma*: either *carcinomata* (Greek) or *carcinomas*. *Cherub*: either *cherubim* (Hebrew) or *cherubs*. *Curriculum*: either *curricula* (Latin) or *curriculums*. *Formula*: either *formulae* (Latin) or *formulas*. *Index*: either *indices* (Latin) or *indexes*. *Libretto*: either *libretti* (Italian) or *librettos*. *Matrix*: either *matrices* (Latin) or *matrixes*. *Nucleus*: either *nuclei* (Latin) or, occasionally, *nucleuses*. *Opus*: either *opera* (a possibly confusing Latinism) or *opuses*. *Radius*: either *radii* (Latin) or *radiuses*. *Virtuoso*: either *virtuosi* (Italian) or *virtuosos*.

F. -F ending

Words that end in the f sound in the singular may have a *-ves* ending in the plural. *Calf*, *half*, *knife*, *leaf*, *life*, *thief*, *self*, *wife*, and *wolf* become *calves*, *halves*, *knives*, *leaves*, *lives*, *thieves*, *selves*, *wives*, and *wolves*. But *wharf* may become either *wharfs* or *wharves* and *hoof* either *hoofs* or *hooves*. *Roof* becomes only *roofs*. And *still life* becomes only *still lifes*.

G. -ICS ending

Words that end in *-ics* may be construed either as singular or as plural. It depends on meaning.

Considered as sciences, subjects, or occupations, *acoustics*, *acrobatics*, *athletics*, *ethics*, *mathematics*, *physics*, *politics*, *statistics*, *tactics*, and so on are usually treated as singulars. Considered as qualities or activities, they are usually treated as plurals. Thus *"mathematics is* emphasized at that school" but "my *mathematics are* rusty." / *"Accoustics has* become his business," but "The *accoustics* here *impress* me."

H. Mr. and Mrs.

Mr. and *Mrs.* use the French in the plural: *Messieurs* and *Mesdames* respectively, abbreviated *Messrs.* and *Mmes.* and pronounced MESS-errs and may-DAM or may-DOM. *Miss* becomes *Misses* or *misses* (with no name). *Ms.* has no plural. (*See* Titles, 2.)

I. No plurals

Most words that represent abstractions, generalizations, or qualities, rather than concrete items, are singular only. Examples are *amazement, courage, eating, fondness, happiness, ignorance, learning, nonsense,* and *vindication.*

J. -O ending

Add *s* to any word ending in *o* after a vowel: *patios, radios, stereos, studios* and *tattoos.*

Most words ending in *o* after a consonant also take *s* (*altos, egos, pianos*), but several take *-es* (*echoes, heroes, potatoes, tomatoes*). Several others go either way: *buffaloes* or *buffalos, cargoes* or *cargos, dominoes* or *dominos, zeroes* or *zeros.*

K. -S ending

Some nouns that normally end in *s* may be considered either plural or singular: *alms, barracks, corps, forceps, means, scissors* (also pair or pairs of *scissors*). Some other nouns that end in *s* are plural in form though singular in meaning: *blues* (music), *checkers, overalls, measles, pants, remains, tongs, trousers.*

Chess, kudos, and *news* are singular only. The plural of *lens* is *lenses.* The plural of *gallows* is either the same or, occasionally, *gallowses.* Names ending

in *s* add *es: Barnes—*the *Barneses. Davis—*the *Davises. Jones—*the *Joneses.*

L. Other entries

Among entries dealing with plural and singular matters are these: BACTERIA and BACTERIUM; COHORT; CRITERIA and CRITERION; DATA; EMERITUS; GRAFFITI and GRAFFITO; HEADQUARTERS; KUDOS; MEDIA and MEDIUM; MEMORANDA and MEMORANDUM; NONE, *1;* Nouns, *3;* PHENOMENA and PHENOMENON; Pronouns, *2;* Punctuation, *1H* (apostrophe); RAVIOLI; RUIN and RUINS; Verbs, *3;* VERTEBRA and VERTEBRAE; WAY and "A WAYS"; -Y ending, 2.

See also **Number (grammatical)** with a list of references.

PLUS. *Plus* is not always a synonym for *and.* The sentence "Talent *plus* luck *accounts* for his success" correctly has a singular verb. But "Talent *and* luck *account* for his success" correctly has a plural verb. *Plus,* meaning *added to* or *increased by,* is a preposition, like *with.* It is not a conjunction, a connecting word, like *and.*

"Four *plus* three *equals* seven" is right. Each number is construed as singular, so the total is singular. In that context *and* is synonymous with *plus.* "Four *and* three *equals* seven" is idiomatic.

"The potato *plus* the apple *costs* fifty cents," but "The *potatoes* plus the apple *cost* a dollar." In the latter sentence, the verb, *cost,* is plural because *potatoes* is plural, not because of the *plus.*

That brings us to an item about a father's concern that his son is close to driving age.

The Vice President's Observatory Hill mansion grounds have private roads on which the teen-ager can learn to drive. "Plus you have a police car in front," Quayle said, "and a concrete wall around the place and an ambulance following behind. . . ."

Usually "plus" does not start a sentence or clause, except in the most casual speech. Better: *in addition, furthermore,* or *and.*

Plus can be also an adjective ("a plus sign" / "the plus side of the account" / "a grade of D plus") and a noun ("This is a plus: +" / "The contract is a plus for our company").

P.M. *See* **A.M., P.M., NOON, MIDNIGHT.**

PODIUM. *See* **LECTERN** and **PODIUM.**

POINT OUT. To *point out* is to direct one's attention to (certain information or a particular situation). The phrase is not impartial. It suggests that what is *pointed out* is true.

Unless the information is clearly factual ("He pointed out a defective leg of that chair") or you are prepared to vouch for its truth ("Let me point out my client's long record of altruism"), use a more neutral word or phrase.

A TV newscaster's announcement that a utility company "points out that Proposition 9 is not needed" in effect supported the company's position. Replacing "points out" with *says* or *contends* would have maintained the impartiality of the television station.

POOL. *See* **BILLIARDS** and **POOL.**

POPULIST. A minor factual error is found in the following passage from a book by a chief justice. The same error is made by an encyclopedia and a dictionary.

The Farmers' Alliances joined together with other splinter factions to put the Populist party on a national basis in 1892. . . .

The Populist party nominated James Weaver of Iowa for president in 1892. . . . Four years later the Populist party fused with the Democratic party. . . .

The party was the *People's Party.* A supporter of that party, but not the party itself, was called *Populist.* Weaver, for instance, was a *Populist.* The farmer's movement of that era was known as the *Populist* movement or *Populism.*

PORE and **POUR.** *See* **Homophones.**

Positive degree. *See* **Comparative and superlative degrees.**

Possessive problems. 1. *Can a thing possess something?* 2. *Multiple possessives.* 3. *Possessive or not?* 4. *Possessive pronouns.* 5. *Various questions.*

1. *Can a thing possess something?*

A grammatical tradition has it that the possessive ending in 's applies only to animate beings. An extreme view reserves the 's possessive to human beings, with few exceptions. Thus a grammarian holding that view rejects "Florida's governor." It would have to be *the governor of Florida.* Presumably *the governor's signature* would be acceptable.

But the exceptions that have become standard are many and getting more numerous. They are in innumerable common expressions: *a day's work; for heaven's sake; in harm's way; my mind's eye; my wit's end; a stone's throw; today's paper.* Literary uses abound: *A Midsummer Night's Dream* / "the dawn's early light . . . the twilight's last gleaming" / "the pangs of despised love, the law's delay" / "the wheel's kick and the wind's song" / "The world's great age begins anew."

The extreme view is not recommended here. Nevertheless, the use of artificial possessives in the news business has long been rampant. Some, like *the nation's capital* in place of *the national capital,* have become familiar. Others are unidiomatic combinations such as "Spain's King Juan Carlos" instead of *King Juan Carlos of Spain,* designed to save minute amounts of space. One typical paragraph in a news magazine contains phrases like "the group's new leader . . . the group's founder . . . Jihad's representative in Tehran warning that Iran's Ministry of Foreign Intelligence believes. . . ."

Let inanimate objects or animals possess things, if they can do so gracefully. Few will complain about "The town's only theater" / "The value of Apple's stocks" / "a dog's age" / "horses' hoofs." But let no one speak of "the century's turn," write that "I'm having my life's time," or wish anyone the "morning's top."

2. Multiple possessives

"Your and my boss are friends" and "My and her children play together" sound strange, because in each instance the first possessive pronoun is separated from the noun. Placing one possessive pronoun before the noun and the other after the noun solves the problem: "Your boss and mine . . ." / "My children and hers. . . ." If we have something in common, there is no problem: "our building" / "our country."

How to make two nouns possessive depends on whether possession is separate ("The plaintiff's and the defendant's attorneys") or joint ("Laurel and Hardy's films"). *See* **Punctuation,** *1E.*

3. Possessive or not?

Whether a noun is possessive or merely acting as a modifier can be a subtle distinction. One can write about the *United States' population* and a new *United States citizen* or about *General Motors' plants* and the *General Motors*

Building. Note that it is never "United State's" or "General Motor's."

The names of organizations are highly variable in their use or nonuse of the apostrophe. It is the *Boys' Clubs of America* but the *Girls Clubs of America;* the *International Backpackers' Association* but the *National Campers and Hikers Association;* the *Sheet Metal Workers' International Association* but the *Transport Workers Union of America;* the *National Sheriff's Association* but the *Music Teachers National Association.*

The apostrophe is necessary in *Children's Aid Society* and *Women's Christian Temperance Union.* Without an apostrophe, it makes no sense to add an s to *children* or *women.* The same is true for any other word that is plural without an added *s.*

The apostrophe is traditional in phrases like *ten years' imprisonment* and *thirty days' notice.* Some critics would omit the apostrophe in such phrases. No one would want possession in such variations as *a thirty-day notice* or *notice of thirty days.* It would be *a thousand dollars' worth* or, in figures, *$1,000 worth.*

4. Possessive pronouns

Let nobody tamper with a word like *hers, his, our, ours, your,* or *yours.* It takes no *'s,* no apostrophe. It is already possessive. Sometimes "her's" and "our's" and "your's" are seen, and they are wrong (although they were deemed correct centuries back). So is "his'n" or "hisn," a dialectal version of *his,* which is heard or seen in some regions.

A word like *his, hers,* etc. may be regarded as a *personal pronoun* in the *possessive* case. There are two types:

• The type that goes *before* the noun (e.g., "This is *her* house"). It takes in the singular words *my, your, his, her,* and *its* and the plural words *our, your,* and *their.*

- The type that goes *after* the noun ("This house is *hers*"): the singulars *mine, yours, his, hers,* and *its* and the plurals *ours, yours,* and *theirs.*

(Words of the first type are known also as *possessive adjectives.* Some grammarians assign that name to *my, your his, her,* etc. because they go before nouns, as adjectives do: "This is a *fragrant* flower." But adjectives too follow nouns: "This flower is *fragrant.*")

The *indefinite pronoun* is a class of pronoun that can be made possessive, e.g., *anybody's, anyone's, either's, everybody's, everyone's, nobody's, one's, somebody's,* and *someone's.*

5. Various questions

Is this correct? "I have Elisabeth Schwarzkopf, the soprano's, records." What is made possessive when an appositive, or an explanatory word or phrase, follows a person's name? The appositive is. That example is correct, and so is this one: "They showed Douglas Fairbanks, Jr.'s, first film." But "records of Elisabeth Schwarzkopf, the soprano" and "the first film by Douglas Fairbanks, Jr." are smoother ways to express the same thoughts.

How is a compound noun like *brothers-in-law* and *attorneys general* made possessive when it already has a plural *s*? Add an apostrophe and another *s*. "Guess what my brothers-in-law's occupations are." / "He spoke at the attorneys general's meeting."

Which is right, "They ask for our first name" or "names"? The latter; we have separate *names.* But "John and Agnes are selling their *house,*" if they own it jointly. *See* **Nouns,** *3*.

Is it "the painting of my daughter" or "the painting of my daughter's"? It is the first if the picture shows her; the second if it was painted by her. Some critics find the double negative illogical, however old and established. Nobody objects to it

when the possessive is a pronoun: "a colleague of mine." *See* **Double possessive.**

What is the *genitive case*? It is the *possessive case,* the form of a noun or pronoun that indicates someone's or something's possession, characteristic, product, etc. *See also* **Pronouns,** *10A.*

See **Punctuation,** *1,* the apostrophe, for problems such as the confusion of possessive forms and contractions (*B*), omitted and superfluous apostrophes (*C* and *D*), possessives of possessives (*F*) and sibilant endings (*G*).

See also **Gerund,** *4;* **Pronouns,** *1, 2, 9.*

POSSIBLE, POSSIBLY, POSSIBILITY. *1. Meaning of POSSIBLE. 2. Preposition with POSSIBILITY.*

1. Meaning of POSSIBLE

Possible (adjective) means capable of being, doing, or happening. It is *possible* for an imprisoned burglar to be elected president on a platform of legalized crime; not likely, highly improbable, just *possible.* Were broadcasters talking about the realm of *possibility* when they made the following statements?

[Woman:] Public TV stations need your support.
[Man:] Support that makes programs like *Nightly Business Report* possible.

The Fresh Grocer is made possible by Lunardi's Market.

Express Traffic [is] made possible by the California Lottery.

Monetary contributions *finance* the public TV programs. The radio programs are *sponsored* by the market and the lottery. All of those programs were *possible* before the stations went seeking contributions or sponsorship. The contributors and sponsors help materialize or make feasible or sustain that which is *possible.*

Journalists often misuse *possible* in this way: "He suffered a possible broken leg." If it were *impossible,* no one would suffer it. Better: "He *may have* suffered a . . ." or "*It is possible that* he suffered a . . ." or "He *possibly* [adverb] suffered a. . . ."

A less frequent journalistic misuse appears in crime stories. "Police arrested a possible suspect. . . ." Omit "possible." They arrested a suspect. A suspect is *possibly* the *culprit.*

See also APPARENT, APPARENTLY.

2. *Preposition with POSSIBILITY*

When *possibility* (noun) is followed by a preposition, it is *of.* Then comes a gerund, an *-ing* word used as a noun. This sentence was part of a statement to the voters of a city from its legislative body:

> Every time San Franciscans face the possibility to enact candidate spending reform, hired gun campaign consultants and weak-willed candidates try to snow the voters.

"The possibility to enact" is not idiomatic. Make it "the possibility *of* enact*ing.* . . ." (And insert a hyphen after "candidate.") See Gerund, *3.*

POUR and PORE. See Homophones.

PRACTICABLE and PRACTICAL. See Confusing pairs.

PRECEDE and PROCEED. See Confusing pairs.

PREDECESSOR and SUCCESSOR. A magazine publisher, leaving to take another job, wrote to his readers, "I . . . know you will be as kind and thoughtful to my predecessor as you were to me." Someone's *predecessor* is one who preceded him, one who served

earlier in the same capacity. The opposite word was needed: *successor,* one who succeeds another. "My successor" is the person who will take my job when I leave.

Predicate. See Clause; Complement; Nouns, *4;* Prepositions, *4;* Sentence fragment, *1;* Verbs, *1D.*

Predicate adjective. See Adjectives and adverbs, *2;* Complement.

Predicate noun (predicate nominative). See Complement; Nouns, *1.*

Prediction. See EXPECTED; NOT ABOUT TO; Reversal of meaning, *1.*

PREFER. See THAN, *2D.*

Prefix. See BACK(-) prefix and pairs; BI- and SEMI- prefixes; CIRCUM- prefix; FACT- words; NANO- prefix; PRE- prefix; Punctuation, *4D* (hyphenated forms); SELF- prefix; Spelling, *3;* UP, *3.*

PREJUDICE. See WITH PREJUDICE and WITHOUT PREJUDICE.

Prepositions. *1. The ABC's of prepositions. 2. Ambiguity. 3. Ending with a preposition. 4. Insufficient prepositions. 5. Misplacement. 6. Omission. 7. Selection of a preposition. 8. Superfluous preposition.*

1. The ABC's of prepositions

The preposition is a deceptive part of speech, simple on the surface while troubling to learners of English and sometimes to native speakers as well. It is everywhere; it appeared in the last sentence five times. It includes some of the shortest words—*at, by, in, of, on, to, up*—but properly choosing and using it can be illogical, dictated by idiom.

A preposition shows the relation of a word or phrase in a sentence to a noun or pronoun in that sentence. In the sentence "She lives in Providence," the preposition *in* relates the verb *lives* to the noun *Providence*. In "The cat came to me," the preposition *to* relates the verb *came* to the pronoun *me*.

A preposition may relate an adjective to a noun ("young at heart"), one noun to another ("the sound of music"), one pronoun to another ("Are you with him?"), and so on.

The choice of a preposition can determine the meaning of a sentence. "He ran *into* the building" and "He ran *from* the building," though differing by only one word, have opposite meanings.

In many cases idiom, not meaning, dictates which preposition to use. "Visitors are forbidden *to* enter" but "prohibited *from* entering." (*See* **FORBID, PROHIBIT, and BAN; Gerund,** *3*.)

Depending on how it is used, the same word may go with different prepositions. "Twelve is equivalent [adjective] *to* a dozen" but "Twelve is the equivalent [noun] *of* a dozen." / "I agree *to* the deal" but "I agree *with* you." (The first *agree* means to give approval; the second means to concur.) More examples appear in *7*.

Prepositions are not all tiny words; they include *against, around, between, during, through, toward, without,* and some that comprise more than one word, such as *according to, because of, by means of, in regard to,* and *on account of.*

The noun or pronoun (or other substantive) that the preposition pertains to is called the *object* of the preposition. A pronoun that serves as the object takes the *objective case*. "The town stood behind *him*," not "he." (*See* **Pronouns,** *10*.)

The preposition plus the object (and any modifier of it) is a *prepositional phrase*, e.g., *behind him* in the last example and the following emphasized words: "Violin *with guitar* makes a pleasant

sound." / *Under that tree* is a good place to rest." The phrases are acting as adverb, adjective, and noun respectively.

2. *Ambiguity*

One might expect the little prepositions *of* and *for* to be clear in meaning, and usually they are. But each has many meanings and can become cloudy in certain contexts.

" 'They have a valid complaint,' said Dawis of the squatters." Was Dawis one of the squatters? "Of" could mean *from* or *belonging to*. However, the context (a news story) indicates that *about* was meant; it would have been a more suitable preposition.

A book on words mentions "*achthronym,* a word H. L. Mencken used for an ethnic slur. . . ." Those unfamiliar with the combining form *-onym,* used in classifying words and names, could get the idea that the writer Mencken used the word as a slur against an ethnic group. "For" could give that impression. *To mean* or *to denote,* a verb, would be more precise.

An almanac says that Boris Yeltsin urged fast reform and "championed the cause for national reconstruction. . . ." Was "the cause" reform? It was probably "national reconstruction," but the *for* is ambiguous; it could mean *in the interest of*. ". . . The cause *of*" would be clearer and more idiomatic.

The headline "Guards Use Rifles in Quentin Killing" suggests that prison guards shot someone to death. Actually, one inmate stabbed another, whereupon a guard fired at and wounded the attacker. The copy editor evidently had a peripheral role for "in" in mind; instead, it drags the using of rifles smack into the "Killing." He probably avoided anything as straightforward as "San Quentin Inmate Is Fatally Stabbed" because a competing paper got the news first.

See also 6.

3. Ending with a preposition

The word *preposition,* a relative of the Latin *praepositus,* meaning placed in front, should not be taken literally. Sometimes a preposition goes at the end of a sentence.

A newspaper quotes an eyewitness as saying on Israeli radio: "Everybody was hysterical, and nobody knew where the bullets would come from." There is nothing wrong with the quoted sentence (as long as it was quoted and translated correctly).

Anyone who says you cannot end any sentence with a preposition does not know what he is talking about. He would probably change the foregoing to ". . . does not know about what he is talking."

The notion was called by H. W. Fowler a once "cherished superstition" and by Winston Churchill "an arrant pedantry up with which I will not put." It originates in the Latin language.

Placing a preposition at the end may weaken a sentence, strengthen it, or do neither. It depends on the sentence. ". . . Nobody knew from where the bullets would come" is a weakened version of the opening sample.

Many great writers have ended sentences with prepositions. Shakespeare wrote: "It is an honor that I dream not of" (*Romeo and Juliet*) and "It would be spoke to" (*Hamlet*).

Prepositions end various common expressions, such as to have or not have "a leg to stand on" / "to be reckoned with" / "that's what —— are for" / "where I come from."

4. Insufficient prepositions

One preposition may or may not be enough for a compound predicate; that is, a predicate with more than one verb. (The predicate is the part of a sentence that expresses the action.) One preposition is enough in this compound sentence: "He ranted and raved *about* his wife's alleged unfaithfulness." The next one, from a telecast, has one correct preposition but lacks a second:

He was treated and released from a nearby hospital.

Released goes with *from* but "treated" does not. A person is treated *at* or *in* a hospital, not "from" a hospital. This is one possible correction: "He was treated at and released from a nearby hospital." Better: "He was treated at a nearby hospital and released."

Two similar sentences, from newspapers, are likewise inadequate:

Another victim was transported to St. Francis Memorial Hospital, where he was treated and released for minor injuries.

Mike K——, 38, was treated and released from Marin General Hospital for smoke inhalation and first- and second-degree burns on his head. . . .

The first sentence of that pair says the victim was "released for" injuries, an absurd juxtaposition. Here is a correction: "Another victim was transported to St. Francis Memorial Hospital, treated there for minor injuries, and released."

In the second of the pair, "treated" does not go with "from" and, again, "released" does not go with "for." Try this: "Mike . . . suffered from smoke inhalation [etc.]. . . . He was treated at Marin General Hospital and released."

H. W. Fowler called attention to what he labeled "CANNIBALISM," a sad practice in which "words devour their own kind." For instance:

The most vital problem in the etymological study of English place-names is the question as to what extent personal names occur in place-names.

"As to" and "to what" need separate *to*'s, but one *to* is missing—swallowed by the other one, as Fowler would say.

A sentence by Fowler himself evidences a swallowed preposition:

> . . . It means, beyond a doubt, a custom that one deserves more honour for breaking than for keeping. . . .

A *for* has been swallowed, so to speak, immediately after *honour* (the British spelling of *honor*). If *for for* is not to one's liking, an alternative correction is to change "that" to *for which*. (*See also* HONORABLE [etc.] *3*.)

More examples appear in TO, *1*.

5. Misplacement

An adjective and a preposition that commonly go together, like *similar to* or *different from,* should not be split apart. This sentence, from a computer book, splits them apart:

> . . . The Toolbox has its own title bar and System menu, with similar properties to the publication title bar and System menu.

A correction is "properties *similar to* the publication. . . ." (The sentence needs more fixing, for it compares unlike things. Make it "properties similar to *those of* the publication. . . .")

Prepositions are liable to be misplaced in sentences containing correlative conjunctions like *both . . . and* and *either . . . or.* "The bill has been passed both by the Senate and the House of Representatives." Make it *by both.* "He has no faith either in the Democrats or the Republicans." Make it *in either.* Now in each sentence the preposition (*by* or *in*) affects both nouns, not just the first; and we uphold the rule of correlative conjunctions: The same grammatical form that follows the first conjunction of the pair must follow the

second, somewhat in the manner of a mathematical equation. *See also* BOTH, *1;* EITHER, *1;* NEITHER, *1;* NOT ONLY.

6. Omission

The casual speaker or writer sometimes omits *on* and *of* when they are needed and sticks them in when they are not needed. "*On* the first day" and "a couple *of* kids" are typical phrases in which prepositions are subject to omission, contrary to idiom. *See* ON, *1;* COUPLE, *4*.

This sentence, from a book of travel adventure, omits another idiomatic preposition:

> Mid-afternoon we passed a ruined hamlet of stone and shortly after it reached an ancient and revered mosque.

It would improve the sentence to start it with *In.* Adverbs representing times of day do not usually open sentences. (Another improvement would be to drop "it," which tends to fuse with "reached.")

A similar omission impairs a sentence by a food critic:

> Multiply your weight times 13 to get a rough idea of how many calories you can consume a day. Divide the total by 4, and that's how many fat calories you can handle.

You can "consume a day" repairing your house or operating your computer. As for the sample sentence, it would be improved either by "how many calories you can consume *in* a day" or by "how many *calories a day* you can consume." An *a* or *an* may be enough when sandwiched between the nouns denoting units and time. But the preposition *in* should precede *a* when units and time are further apart. The statistical preposition *per* fits either context: "calories *per* day" or "calories you can consume *per* day."

Prepositions, especially *of,* are often omitted in efforts to be concise. The result can be ambiguity. "A small sculpture collection" could mean either "a collection *of* small sculptures" or "a small collection *of* sculptures." A more complicated example: "The curbing of public meetings and the publication of newspapers eliminated most opposition to the regime." As it stands, "the curbing of public meetings" and "the publication of newspapers" may appear to be parallel factors. But if "curbing" controls the latter phrase (a more likely assumption), precede the phrase by *of:* "The curbing of public meetings and *of* the publication of newspapers . . ."

If the meaning is clear, omission of prepositions is tolerable in headlines, such as the following, which appeared in one newspaper edition: "Police seek Netanyahu indictment" / "Oil industry fights gas additive ban" / "Group urges tough rules for hydrofluoric acid use" / "Panel OKs flood aid package." In texts, clarity and grace call for ". . . indictment *of* Netanyahu / ". . . ban *on gas additives*" (or, better, "*gasoline* additives") / ". . . *use of* hydrofluoric acid" / ". . . *package of* flood aid."

7. *Selection of a preposition*

Learning which preposition goes with each verb, adjective, noun, or pronoun is a daunting task for the foreign student of English, sometimes for the native speaker too. The choice of preposition often depends on idiom, rather than logic. The same word may go with two prepositions, depending on meaning: *Agree to* means to consent to or approve something; *agree with* means to be of the same opinion as, or to be suitable for. *Belong to* means to be a member of; *belong with* means to deserve being classified among. *Capacity for* means apti-

tude for; *capacity of* means the most that can be contained in. *Compare to* means to liken to; *compare with* means to contrast with. (*See* **COMPARED TO and COMPARED WITH,** *1.*) *Concur in* means to express approval of (an opinion or joint action); *concur with* means to agree with (someone). *Correspond to* means to match; *correspond with* means to exchange letters with. *Differ from* means to be unlike; *differ with* means to disagree with. *In behalf of* means in the interest of; *on behalf of* means as the agent of. *Liable for* means responsible for; *liable to* means apt to. *(In) sympathy with* means in agreement with; *sympathy for* means compassion for. *Wait for* is to be inactive and in anticipation of; *wait on* is to serve (someone food or drink). (*See* **WAIT FOR and WAIT ON.**)

Even when the meaning does not change much, the preposition may vary with context. A conversation *between* two people is a conversation *among* three. (*See* **BETWEEN,** *1.*) A patient is *cured of* a disease but *cured by* a treatment. One is *grateful for* a benefit but *grateful to* a person. One may *intervene in* a dispute but *intervene between* those disputing. A buyer is *in the market* for a product; a product is *on the market.* Someone gains *mastery of* a skill or subject; a ruler or regime gains *mastery over* a country or people. A *report of* an accident appears in the paper; the government submits a *report on* the economy. One may *speak on* a subject but *speak to* a person. (*See* **SPEAK TO, TALK TO.**)

In the press *on* often assumes functions that would be better served by other prepositions. (*See* **ON,** *3.*) In news items about arrests, *for* can be prejudicial. (*See* **Guilt and Innocence,** *5.*)

An occasional error in the choice of prepositions goes like this (numbers added): "He will be in the best possible position for [1] getting the most out of the land and of [2] using it to the best possible advantage." Although *for* would apply to both 1 and 2, the writer chose to precede the second phrase with an extra preposition to be clearer; but instead of repeating *for,* which would make sense, he carelessly copied "of," the last preposition he saw.

See also *1, 2;* DIFFERENT, *1;* Gerund, *3B;* INTO, *1;* RALLY; WITH PREJUDICE (etc.).

8. Superfluous preposition

A newspaper ran the headline "Regulators' beef with selling milk for cheap." The "for" was unnecessary and unidiomatic. ". . . Selling milk cheap" (or *cheaply*) is enough. You do not say "moving for quick" or "coming for soon."

That is an example of a superfluous preposition, one that is used unnecessarily with a particular word. Some prominent examples include "for" before *free,* "of" after *off,* and "from" before *whence.*

A series may be marred by an extra preposition, as in this extract from a news story:

Its history has been reconstructed from ticket stubs found on the floor, dressing room graffiti and from interviews with older black residents of Athens. . . .

The first "from" covers all the three items enumerated. The other "from" is superfluous, inasmuch as no preposition precedes the second item, "dressing room graffiti." *See also* Series errors, *9.*

In numerical ranges, prepositions are liable to pile up: "A high temperature of from 70 to 75 degrees is forecast." Omit *from.* "The gadget is priced at between $40 and $50." Omit *at.*

This example is similar in its causes to the one at the end of *7:* "It could be done without unduly raising the price of coal or of jeopardizing new trade." Omit the second *of;* no preposition belongs there at all.

See also ADVOCATE; FREE, *1;* OFF and "OFF OF"; ON, *2;* WHENCE and "FROM WHENCE"; WISH; WITH.

PRE- prefix. The prefix *pre-* means before, beforehand, early, in advance of, or in front of. An example appears in the noun *prefix* itself (originating in the Latin *prae-,* before, and *figere,* to fix). Other examples are adjectives, such as *preadolescent* (youngsters), *precancerous* (lesions), *prefabricated* (houses); verbs, to *predominate,* to *prejudge;* and more nouns, *prescription, preview.*

If such a meaning is obvious without it, *pre-* is probably unnecessary. These sentences are redundant: "Advance payment of the initiation fee and the first year's dues is a precondition of membership." / "We won't begin operations without careful preplanning." / "On January 2 all students must preregister for courses." / "Before buying the car, have a mechanic pretest it."

Radio commercials for two respected automotive brands have offered "preowned models" and "certified preowned automobiles." The merchandise is what most Americans call *used cars.* A sign at a bookstore: "PREVIOUSLY READ BOOKS & MAGAZINES."

When the prefix *pre-* is followed by *e,* many publications separate the two *e*'s with a hyphen. It indicates that the long vowel sound in *pre-* (PREE) is followed by a short vowel sound: *pre-eminent, pre-emption, pre-existing.* (*Pre-* has a short vowel in some words, including *preliminary* and *preserve.*) A hyphen is necessary when the second element starts with a capital letter: *pre-Columbian.* The Associated Press hyphenates *pre-convention, pre-dawn,* and any combinations that are not in a certain dictionary.

PREREQUISITE and PERQUISITE. *See* PERQUISITE and PREREQUISITE.

PRESCRIBE and PROSCRIBE.
An article says a federal law "proscribed
that the tax on capital gains be the same
as the top rate on incomes." The sentence says the opposite of what its writer
intended. "Proscribed" should be *prescribed.* To *prescribe* something is to establish it as a rule. To *proscribe*
something is to outlaw it. The law established that tax rule; it did not outlaw it.

PRESENTLY. The meaning of
presently seemed to slow down over the
centuries. It used to mean *now* until that
meaning became obsolete, except for dialects, some three hundred years ago.
Later it came to mean immediately; still
later, *soon.* "The queen is expected to arrive presently." / "The small gathering
presently grew into a huge crowd."

The original meaning, *now,* has been
revived. But several authorities prefer to
restrict *presently* to the meaning of *soon,
before long,* or *in a short time,* so as to
avoid any confusion from a second
meaning. They would not look with favor on these press uses: "[His] yearly
salary is . . . presently the highest in the
country. . . ." / ". . . The group is
presently about $30,000 in debt." /
"Presently, a few Monterey
pines . . . grow on the block-long site."
In those sentences "presently" plainly
means *now,* but the meaning can be
blurred: "I believe presently the venture
will be profitable." Does "presently" refer to the speaker's belief or to the future?

One can sidestep the issue, saving two
syllables at the same time, by replacing
"presently" with *now* when that is the
meaning. Those who scorn *now* because
a little monosyllable does not seem important enough can draw upon *currently, at present,* or *at this time.* For
those wishing to drag it out still further,
a phrase associated with Watergate is
available: *See* **"AT THIS POINT IN
TIME."**

Even *now* or a synonym is often unnecessary in sentences that are in the present tense. Delete "presently" from the
three press quotations and it remains obvious that the time is the present.

Now or a synonym is useful for emphasis or for contrasting the present
with the past or the future. "*Now* she
tells me!" / "He's sorry now, but what of
the future?" / "I used to be married, but
I'm not at present."

Present tense. *See* **Tense.**

PRESS (verb). *See* **ADVOCATE.**

**PRESUMPTIVE and PRESUMP-
TUOUS.** *See* **Confusing pairs.**

Preterit, preterite (past tense). *See*
Tense.

PREVENT. To *prevent* (verb, transitive) is to avert or thwart; to keep (someone or something) from doing
something; or to keep (something) from
happening.

All of these constructions are idiomatic: (1) "Run the water slowly to
prevent overflowing"; (2) ". . . *prevent* it
from overflowing"; (3) ". . . *prevent its*
overflowing."

What is unidiomatic is "to *prevent it*
overflowing." *From* or a possessive form
(*see* **Gerund,** 4) should precede the *-ing*
word. Neither of them does in this press
sentence:

The challenge facing the two sides
in South Africa is to find a formula
which incorporates some of these elements into a constitution which will
prevent South Africa going the same
way as the rest of Africa.

It should be "prevent South Africa *from*
going . . ." or "prevent South *Africa's*
going. . . ." (For more clarity, the first
"which" should be *that;* it is used restric-

tively. Whether the reporter meant to use the second "which" in the same way is uncertain. *See* **THAT and WHICH.**)

PRIMATES. A caption under a photograph of two chimpanzees says, "Primates are much more vegetarian in their diet than humans," which is something like saying that rodents run faster than mice.

Humans *are* primates. *Primates* is an order of animals, the most highly developed order. It comprises man, ape, monkey, lemur, loris, and tarsier. As a taxonomic order, *Primates* is capitalized, singular though ending in *s,* and pronounced pry-MAY-tease. A member of the order is a *primate,* pronounced PRY-mate.

An item deals with a "toddler who fell into a Chicago zoo's gorilla pit and was rescued by a 160-pound primate. . . ." The last word is neither wrong nor precise (I have been a 160-pound primate myself) but a synonym obviously chosen to avoid repeating *gorilla.*

See also **APE and MONKEY.**

PRINCIPAL and PRINCIPLE. A political consultant was quoted as saying, "It was a credible message, based on very broad philosophical principal." The last word amounted to a misquotation. A newspaper reporter had heard it right but spelled it wrong.

One speaks of a philosophical *principle* (except in some rare instance of a school principal who is a philosopher). This noun denotes a law of nature, a basic truth or postulate, a cause to which one is dedicated, an essential element or quality, or a rule of conduct. (It might aid one's memory to note the *-le* ending in both *rule* and *principle.*)

The noun *principal* denotes the head of a school, or a main participant, or the amount of a debt or investment without the interest. As an adjective, *principal* means first in rank or importance, pri-

mary, primal. (Note the *-al* ending in both *primal* and *principal.*)

PRIORITIZE. *See* **-IZE ending.**

PRIOR, PRIOR TO. Using "prior to" as a genteel synonym for *before,* in the manner of this press example, serves no useful purpose: "Officer Malcom M—— said prior to last month, the last vehicle to go over the cliff was in 1978. . . ."

In formal writing, *prior to* (adverb) may be used to emphasize that one event is a prerequisite to the other: "Citizens must register prior to voting."

Prior (adjective) without the *to* is more useful. It can mean preceding in importance, in order, or in time: "a prior consideration" / "his prior choice" / "my prior appointment."

(As for the press sentence: "said *that*" would be clearer, unless the officer *said* it "prior to last month." *See* **THAT,** 2. The month should have been stated; the story appeared on the first.)

PRISTINE. A television screen depicted a suburban park. Now it is "pristine" wilderness, but it used to be the site of explosives manufacturing, the narrator said. He was nearly contradicting himself. If it was an industrial site, it is no longer "pristine," although it could have returned to a state of wilderness.

Pristine (adjective) describes an early period, predating the touch of man; or an original, unspoiled condition. It comes from the Latin *pristinus,* former.

On a radio talk show, a commentator on popular culture spoke of television's "very pristine image" of the police and "pristine image of doctors." Perhaps he thought it meant pure. A TV newscaster may have had that idea too; he said the study of Lake Tahoe began four decades ago when the water was "relatively pristine." To qualify *pristine* with "very" or "relatively" is dubious; something either is *pristine* or it is not. In each instance it was not.

Probability. *See* Numbers, *10C.*

PROBABLE, PROBABLY. *See* AP-PARENT, APPARENTLY.

PROBATION. *See* PAROLE and PROBATION.

PROBE. A *probe* is an instrument used by physicians in examining wounds, cavities, or sinuses. Often made of silver, usually thin and flexible with a blunt end, it serves to determine the depth and direction of those depressions. To *probe* (verb, transitive and intransitive) is literally to examine with a probe.

Originating in the Latin *probare,* to test (the origin of *prove*), the English noun dates at least to the sixteenth century; the verb, to the seventeenth. A figurative meaning of the verb, to search into with the aim of exploring or discovering, developed almost at the same time as the literal. The sense of interrogating closely came out of the nineteenth century.

In the mid-twentieth, *probe* became associated with congressional hearings. Headlines used it freely, as both verb and noun; the thirteen letters of *investigation* could not compete with the five letters of *probe*. Though *inquiry* was not much longer, it never caught on. Writers and speakers too adopted that headline word for general use.

Within several days, the national TV audience heard on a newscast that the Senate planned "to launch a widespread probe of voter fraud" in Louisiana; on a news feature program that a "task force conducted a lengthy probe" into customs corruption; on one discussion program that the Louisiana election was "now being probed" and an independent counsel was needed "to probe the White House scandal"; and on another discussion program that "Hillary was the central figure in a probe. . . ."

At *The New York Times,* a creditable standing rule has been "Do not use [*probe*] for *inquiry, investigation* or *investigate*." The rule does not prevent specialized use, as in *space probe.*

PROCEED and PRECEDE. *See* Confusing pairs.

PROFANITY. *See* OBSCENE, OBSCENITY.

PROFESSION. *See* "OLDEST PROFESSION."

PROGNOSIS. *See* CONDITION.

Progressive tenses. *See* Tense, *1.*

PROHIBIT. *See* FORBID, PROHIBIT, and BAN.

PROLIXITY, PROLIX. *See* Verbosity.

Pronouns. *1. Ambiguity. 2. Disagreement in number. 3. Lack of reflexive. 4. Needless use of -SELF. 5. Nonstandard -SELF or -SELVES words. 6. Omission. 7. Shift in person. 8. Superfluous apostrophe. 9. Superfluous pronoun. 10. Wrong case.*

1. Ambiguity

A pronoun is a word used in place of a noun. For instance, "Stand beside *her* and guide *her*" substitutes for "Stand beside *America* and guide *America*" in a famous song. Pronouns are handy devices, enabling us to avoid having to repeat names, words, or whole phrases all the time. (*See also* **Pronouns' classification.**)

Usually, if a pronoun is not to do more harm than good, it must be clear just what it is replacing. Because of defective phrasing or organization, it can be unclear which noun a given pronoun represents (i.e., which is its *antecedent*) or the pronoun can literally apply to the wrong noun. Sometimes it is better to use no pronoun and repeat the noun.

The first sample statement is by a well-known reporter on a TV "magazine" program. It is not clear which person was "he."

> When P—— was hired by H——, he had a criminal record.

The following sentence, a paragraph in itself, is from a news agency's dispatch.

> Another witness, Drazen E——, testified that he had participated in the slaughter of up to 1,200 Srebrenica Muslims in one day.

It seems to say that the witness admitted participating in the crime. But the context indicates that "he" was meant to apply to someone else, an army general identified earlier in the story. Read in isolation, the sentence defames the witness. Its only subjects are the proper noun and the personal pronoun. Hence it is reasonable for a reader to assume that the pronoun represents the noun. Instead of "he," *the general* or the general's name should have been used.

The succeeding illustrations come from newspapers in five cities.

> Rules were changed to open up the nominating process after the 1968 convention, in which Chicago Mayor Richard Daley and other bosses delivered the nomination to Hubert Humphrey while his police beat heads outside the convention.

In "his police," to whom does "his" refer? The meaning suggests that it refers to Daley, but the "his" tends to cling to "Humphrey" because they are so close. The sentence would be improved by changing "his" to *the mayor's*.

A report on the origin of Arabian aid for the Nicaraguan Contras quoted the president, described a congressional investigation into the matter, and followed with excerpts from the testimony of Robert C. McFarlane. Emphasis is added to the questionable pronoun, at the end.

> Sen. William S. Cohen (R-Me.) said he was troubled by "the definition of solicitation" of funds.
>
> Although he has talked of Reagan's meeting with Fahd, McFarlane on Wednesday refused to term any discussion of the contras' needs a solicitation of aid.
>
> "It seems to me that we have been engaged in this exercise of trying to define how many foreign leaders can be made to dance on the head of the President's contra program without calling it a solicitation," *he* said.

Who said? Since McFarlane was the last name mentioned, a reader can reasonably assume that McFarlane is the man now being quoted. But the essence of the message has changed. Actually "he" is Senator Cohen. (I wrote to him and he confirmed that he made the statement.) It would have avoided confusion to interchange the first and second paragraphs. The existing order presents a confusing "he" in the second paragraph too: A reader may at first take it to be Senator Cohen, the person last mentioned, but that "he" is McFarlane.

Here is an excerpt from a news story about speeches made by Jesse Jackson during his second campaign for the Democratic presidential nomination:

> He termed Mr. Dukakis's proposals "very conservative, very cautious, very inadequate."
>
> Today Mr. Jackson said, in reference to Mr. Dukakis, "a cautious approach without commitment will not

satisfy our basic needs." About his proposals, he added, "Democrats in Atlanta will rejoice at this budget."

Whose proposals are "his" proposals? Since "Mr. Dukakis's proposals" were mentioned just two sentences ago and since the story says Mr. Jackson is speaking "in reference to Mr. Dukakis," it is plausible to assume that "his" refers to Mr. Dukakis. Yet it would not make sense for a candidate to predict rejoicing over a rival's proposals, unless the candidate is speaking ironically. The context indicates that "his" probably means Mr. Jackson's. If so, the confusion could have been avoided by the insertion of a three-letter word: "About his *own* proposals. . . ."

This is from an article on the prosecution of parents who depend on faith healing for their children:

Over the years, Christian Science lobbyists have succeeded in either drafting or playing a significant role in the wording of religious exemption statutes in the child welfare codes of 47 states.

And while they insist that the statutes were designed to protect them from exactly the legal nightmare they now face, prosecutors argue that the laws do not cover manslaughter or other serious crimes.

Who are "them" and "they"? If the second paragraph is considered alone, those pronouns seem to stand for "prosecutors," but such an interpretation would not be reasonable. The first "they" could reasonably apply to the "lobbyists" mentioned in the previous paragraph, but "them" and the second "they" could not; the lobbyists would not be likely to argue that the statutes were designed to protect the lobbyists. "Them" and the second "they" probably apply to nobody mentioned in either paragraph.

The writer should have discarded the first two pronouns and used nouns, perhaps in this manner: "And while *the lobbyists* insist that the statutes were designed to protect *Christian Scientists* from. . . ."

The W——s are the Long Island couple cited by Eugene police last month after they offered University of Oregon students money to engage in sex with Nancy W——, 44.

Because "they" soon follows "police," a reader may think that "they" represents "police," although further reading of the article will correct such an interpretation. Instead of a muddy pronoun, the couple's surname should have been repeated.

Meeting reporters later after changing out of her prison clothes, Morgan said her daughter was better off than she was when her mother started the jail term.

Was "Morgan" imprisoned along with her mother? The parallel phrasing of "her daughter" and "her mother" seems to suggest that. However, the full story says nothing about a grandmother being locked up. Probably "her mother" means "Morgan," but another "Morgan" would be awkward. The best solution is to rephrase part of the sentence: ". . . better off than she had been when the jail term began."

By noon, Rosie—surrounded by her mom and dad . . . —had her mare. And this morning when she wakes up, she can run out to her own corral and watch her own horse in her new home.

In "her new home," who or what is "her," Rosie or the horse? "Her" evidently is Rosie the first four times, so no reader can be blamed for assuming that it is Rosie the fifth time. Nothing is said in the article about Rosie's moving, however, so the fifth "her" seems to be the horse. It would have forestalled the confusion to put the horse in the neuter gender: "*its* new home."

Ambiguity in the use of relative pronouns comes up in **THAT and WHICH; WHICH,** *1*; **WHO,** *1*. How misunderstanding can occur when such a pronoun (*that*) is not placed immediately after its antecedent is illustrated in **Modifiers,** *3B* (end).

2. Disagreement in number

A. An individual gets a singular pronoun

This is all about grammar. A spokesman for a group supporting what it called a woman's right to choose (abortion) was quoted in the press as saying, "This is all about an individual's right to make a choice about their individual lives." Plainly "an individual" is singular. What can be more singular? It does not agree with "their . . . lives," which is plural. It would, however, agree with *her* . . . *life*, which is singular. Having erroneously associated "individual" with "their," the speaker proceeded to give that individual a number of "lives."

Disagreement between a noun (such as "individual") and a pronoun pertaining to it (such as "their") is a common mistake in grammar. Usually the mistaker tries to represent a singular noun by means of a plural pronoun. A book of popular psychology says:

It's as if we're waiting for permission to start living fully. But the only person who can give us that permission is ourselves.

A "person" is not "ourselves." One is singular, the other plural. "But the only person who can give *you* that permission

is *you*" would be grammatically correct. Yet the excerpt is part of a paragraph that uses *we, us,* or *our* twenty-one times; a version consistent with all the plurality is this: "But the only *persons* [or "the only *ones*"] who can give us that permission *are* ourselves." (Still more proper: "*are we.*" See *10D*.)

Further examples are taken from a book about English words, a state's tax form, and two news articles:

For the dedicated dictionary browser a new edition is a great joy, but sometimes their pleasure in discovering new words is tempered by the loss of the old.

Did you live with any other person who claimed you as a dependent on their income tax return?

The study . . . found that the older a person is, the faster their infection progresses to AIDS diseases.

. . . if a suggestion is made to an anesthetized patient to make a specific gesture in an interview days later, they will probably make the gesture, although they will not be aware what they have done or why they have done it.

Changing "their" to *his* would correct the first three examples. In the fourth, change "they" to *he* four times and "have" to *has* twice. Singulars will then match singulars.

A *browser,* a *person,* or a *patient* is singular, as is an aviator, the dentist, Aunt Fifi, an infant, the president, Captain John Smith, a thespian, a zoo keeper, or anyone else.

Their is plural. So is *they* or *them.* Each of those *th* words pertains to more than one person or thing.

It is a long-standing rule of grammar that a pronoun referring to a *singular* noun must be *singular;* a pronoun referring to a *plural* noun must be *plural.*

Personal pronouns referring to one person, aside from you and me, are *he* and *she* (in the subjective case); *him* and *her* (in the objective case); and *his, her,* and *hers* (in the possessive case). *It* and *its* are considered in B. *See also* ONE as pronoun.

What if we do not know if the person is male or female, or what if the sex does not matter? *He, him,* or *his* then represents a person of either sex.

The editor and grammarian Patricia T. O'Conner writes in *Woe Is I* that she cringes when she hears a sentence like "Somebody forgot to pay their bill" instead of "pay *his* bill." She perceives good intentions but bad grammar. "The pronouns *he* and *his* have been used since time immemorial to refer to people in general."

That a pronoun in the masculine gender can represent any person when sex is immaterial or unknown has been long established in law as well as grammar. *Black's Law Dictionary* says *he* is "usually used . . . to include both sexes as well as corporations" and *his* too "may refer to a person of either sex." Oxford's *A Dictionary of Modern Legal Usage* says:

> . . . The traditional view, still to be observed in the most formal contexts, is that the masculine pronouns are generic, comprehending both male and female. Thus cumbersome pairs such as *he or she* and *his or her* are usually unnecessary.

Such a pair can be unwieldy in a sentence with several pronouns (like the one about the anesthetized patient). And it can be conspicuous unless the matter of sex is pertinent or, as in the example below, both male and female are mentioned. A college advertised:

> The alternative to night school: Weekend College. The least disruptive way for a working man or woman to return for their degree.

A "man *or* woman" is singular. (*See* **OR.**) Thus "their" should be *his or her* or simply *a.* (We will overlook the lack of a complete sentence.)

While English has riches, it has some shortcomings; it lacks, for instance, a multipurpose possessive pronoun like the Spanish *su.* (In Britain, as Shakespeare indicates, some used an unaccented *a* or *a'* in lieu of *he, she, they, it,* or *I.*) Nevertheless, for anyone who insists on reading sexual significance into his pronouns, there is always the option of rephrasing a thought, e.g.: for dedicated dictionary *browsers* / on *an* income tax return / the faster *an* infection progresses / *the patient* will probably make the gesture, *without being aware of it* / pay *the* bill. It is a better answer to the limitations of our language than childish barbarism.

The errors can be droll. A book on first aid warns of danger from the black widow spider, brown recluse spider, and scorpion, and it says:

> If a person is bitten by any of the three, have them lie down and not walk.

But what if the creatures don't want to lie down?

B. IT, ITS: *pronoun in the neuter gender*
A book of travel adventure says:

> If one has never seen a grand African river their beauty comes as a wonderful surprise.

River is singular. "Their" is plural; it should be *its* (preceded by a comma).

As a rule, an inanimate, nonliving, or

abstract thing takes the singular, neuter pronoun *it* or *its*. Traditionally *she* and *her* have been applied to a ship or country—"Aye, tear her tattered ensign down"—but *it* and *its* will do for either.

In an article, quoted below, a company is regarded, correctly, as singular. Five paragraphs later, it becomes plural and then turns singular again. (Emphasis is added.)

> Procter & Gamble Co., the Cincinnati-based consumer products concern, has begun shipping diamonds with *its* soap powder. . . .
>
> The promotion is unusual for P&G, although the company may have put pearls in *their* bottles of Prell shampoo once. . . . The company *expects* this promotion to do very well.

In American usage, company is singular. Do not speak of "their" bottles instead of *its* bottles—if you are not prepared to say "The company *expect*. . . ."

Here is an example of the singular incorrectly used instead of the plural: a can labeled "PINEAPPLE CHUNKS IN ITS OWN JUICE." The chunks have *their* own juice. (The possessive cannot apply to "PINEAPPLE," which is serving as an adjective. If the label said "CHUNKS OF PINEAPPLE," then "PINEAPPLE" as a noun could possess "ITS OWN JUICE.")

It or *its* may be used for a baby, particularly if it represents babies in general: "A newborn needs its mother."

An article about children's learning of language quotes a linguist:

> Dr. C—— concludes that "a 1½-year-old knows a lot about containers and surfaces, but they don't know the words 'on' or 'in.' "

"A 1½-year-old" is singular and conflicts with "they," which is plural. The final clause may be corrected this way: ". . . but *it doesn't* know the words. . . ."

An alternative correction would start out plural: "*1½-year-olds know* a lot. . . ." (In either case, change "or" to *and;* that will produce a plural to agree with *words. See* **OR**.)

It or *its* applies also to an animal, unless its sex is known and material.

A radio physician advised a caller, "Take the dog to the doctor and give them the penicillin." The dog has no choice, but what if the doctor resists?

C. (-)ONE words and phrases; -BODY words; EACH; EVERY

A school principal might be expected to know the grammatical rules that are taught to children. One principal said, in a speech acknowledging his winning of the title of "educator of the year," it is the job of educators to insure "that every one of those children know more than they knew the year before." This educator may not be up to the job, unless he knows more than he knew at the time of that speech.

Obviously *one* is singular. So is any phrase ending in *one*, including *any one, each one, every one,* and *no one.* So is any word ending in -*one*, including *anyone, everyone,* and *someone.* So are the -*body* pronouns: *anybody, everybody, nobody,* and *somebody.* We say "Everybody *knows*," not "know"; and "Everyone *is* here," not "are." *Each* also is singular, particularly as a subject. (*See* **EACH, EACH OF.**) A possessive that refers to any of the pronouns just mentioned should be singular, just as the related verb should be singular. Similarly the adjective *every* makes what it modifies singular.

Examples: "Is anyone missing his keys?" / "Everyone must buy her own dress." / "I see everybody brought his or her spouse." / "Somebody sends her regards." / "Every man for himself." / "To each his own." (Nobody sings "To each their own.")

Two news stories and a book about

English (quoted earlier) display the same kind of mistake:

> The state Elections Code requires anyone who raises more than $500 to disclose their finances.

> Everybody had their moment. . . .

> To quiz someone was to make fun of them. . . .

Change "their" to *his* in the first two sentences. Change "them" to *him* in the third.

A congressman being interviewed on television was partly right and partly wrong:

> Each candidate has to make his or her own decision on how they play this [the issue of impeachment].

He recognized the singularness of "each candidate" by correctly saying "his or her own decision" but failed to follow through: "on how *he or she plays* this." If he wanted to express the same message more concisely, he could have said "his own decision on how he plays this."

Sometimes there is disagreement in number even when the subject is plainly female or male. In an editorial column, a sentence appeared that should have been deemed unfit to print. A new publisher had just taken over the newspaper, and here was his first statement. Referring to his predecessors—his grandfather, uncle, and father—he wrote:

> Each of these men, in their message upon being named Publisher, quoted the pledge Mr. Ochs made when he took the helm of the Times: To give the news impartially, without fear or favor, regardless of any party, sect or interest involved.

Had the copy gone unedited? If it had been edited, did the copy editor miss the offending "their" in place of *his* or was he afraid to correct the boss? (The publisher added a pledge that the paper would continue to adhere to its traditional "high standards of journalism and business." Its standards of grammar used to be high too.)

See also EVERYBODY, EVERYONE, 4; EVERY ONE and EVERYONE; ONE as pronoun.

3. Lack of reflexive

A pronoun misses the mark in each of these passages (by a lawyer, an anchor man, and two journalists respectively):

> "I ultimately refused to go, thereby depriving me of the ability to participate. . . ."

> What did one man do to land him in court?

> Mr. McCain, for example, must stand for re-election . . . giving him less time to recover.

> A . . . motorist . . . lost control of her car and slammed into two oncoming cars, killing her instantly. . . .

Change "me" to *myself,* each "him" to *himself,* and the second "her" to *herself.* Each of the emphasized words is a *reflexive pronoun.* The action that the subject performs is done to the subject; it reflects back onto him or her. The suffix *-self* or *-selves* indicates reflexiveness.

Other pronouns of that type are the singular words *itself, oneself,* and *yourself* and the plural words *ourselves, themselves,* and *yourselves.*

Often a *-self* pronoun is used when it should not be. "Myself," in place of *me,* is the most common one. *See 4.* Sometimes a nonstandard form, like "theirselves," is used. *See 5.* (In the third example, "stand" is dubious. *See* RUN and STAND.)

4. Needless use of -SELF

Many people are reluctant to use the simple word *me,* possibly fearing that they will be considered ungrammatical or immodest. Their concern may hark back to school days and a confusion about "I" versus "me." So they use "myself," thinking wrongly that it is a safe word. Two books furnish our first pair of examples:

> In late 1965, the Chicago Zoological Park . . . sent an expedition to Mexico consisting of myself and photographer Alan ——.

> Special tools were cut by myself [to bind a book].

"Myself" should be *me* in both excerpts: "consisting of *me*" and "cut by *me.*" In the latter instance, "*I cut* special tools" would be still better.

The suffix *-self* or *-selves* in a pronoun serves either of these two functions:

1. It makes the pronoun reflexive. A reflexive pronoun turns the action back upon the subject (the performer of the action). Examples: "She talks to herself." / "The boy doesn't know what to do with himself." / "We gave ourselves raises." / "The cat is washing itself." / "I cut myself." / "They blame themselves." / "Do yourself a favor."

2. It gives emphasis to the subject. "Instead of calling the plumber, Agnes fixed the sink herself." / "He called for law and order when he himself was a crook." / "Jack himself says he's unqualified for the job." / "No one helped, so I did it all myself."

The "-self" in the following sample serves neither function.

> Dr. Lowery said plans for the classes were not finished but they . . . would probably include two one-hour

sessions with himself and other black leaders.

Change "himself" to *him.* There is no reason for the "-self": it has no effect on the subject of the clause in which it appears. That subject is "they," referring to plans for the classes.

A TV news correspondent in Moscow was reporting on a violent revolution and an author was describing an African trip:

> Myself and other members of the press were pinned down. . . .

> Henry, Ann, myself and Joseph were in the little Renault 12 station wagon.

If no one else had been present, neither narrator would say "Myself was pinned down" or "Myself was in the little Renault." Each would say "*I* was." Bringing in others as part of the subject makes no difference in the use of the pronoun. Change each "myself" to *I.*

5. Nonstandard -SELF or -SELVES words

In California a man and a woman were injured by explosives and then arrested on suspicion of illegal possession of (the same) explosives. A TV newscaster reported the happening and named names. "Police said —— and —— built the bombs theirselves," she announced. Later the two were released for lack of evidence, notwithstanding what "police said." Aside from other misfortune, they had been subjected to the indignity of being defamed with atrocious English.

"Theirselves" is not a legitimate word. The proper pronoun is *themselves.* It is the plural of *himself* or *herself.*

Some illegitimate relatives that occasionally pop up are "hisself" / "theirself"

/ "themself" / "ourself." They are not accepted as English words. The plural of *myself* is properly *ourselves*.

6. Omission

A. Isolation of verb

In a complicated sentence it may not be clear who is performing some of the action. A verb seems to lack a subject. The forty-five-word sentence below offers a good illustration. Grasping all of its meaning calls for more than the usual effort by the reader.

> A party spokeswoman, Brigitte Zimmerman, told reporters that angry citizens recently tried to storm the secret police offices in the city of Erfurt to keep documents from being taken away, and warned of "anarchy and chaos" from "people taking the law into their own hands."

Who "warned"? That verb lacks an obvious subject. We need to figure it out. The previous action in the sentence was by the "angry citizens," so they seem to be the subject. But it would be out of character for them to issue a warning of "anarchy and chaos." We skip backward. "A party spokeswoman, Brigitte Zimmerman," evidently was intended to be the subject of "warned."

Inserting one little pronoun would have forestalled all that effort. Make it ". . . and *she* warned. . . ." Better yet, start a new sentence with "She warned . . ." (after changing the third comma to a period and omitting the "and").

It needs to be obvious who or what is the subject of a verb; that is, who or what is performing the action. That subject may not be obvious when a clause intervenes between it and the verb and when the clause's subject ("angry citizens") threatens to take over the verb ("warned"). In such a case, the verb requires its own subject, either noun or pronoun. The comma does not help; it just sets up another barrier. In the next two samples, the meaning may be easier to figure out, but why stint pronouns?

> In 1983 he sued *The Review* for libel after it published an article criticizing him, but dropped the suit two years later.

> He was foreclosed from the Bush ticket because both men have a Texas voter registration, and probably hoped that Bush would clear the decks for the next GOP generation by choosing an older running mate.

Better: ". . . but *he* dropped . . ." / ". . . *but he* probably *had* hoped. . . ." (*See* **BUT**, *1*; **Tense**, *5B*.)
See also **Nouns**, *4*; **Punctuation**, *3E*.

B. Synonym instead of pronoun

It is a journalistic mannerism to use a synonym for the subject instead of a personal pronoun; for instance: "Mr. Gore's opponents had criticized the Tennessee senator about the secrecy surrounding the loans. . . ." Although readers who did not know that Mr. Gore was "the Tennessee senator" could probably guess it, *him* would be clearer and more natural. *See also* **JURIST; Synonymic silliness; THE**, *2B*.

The avoidance of pronouns in that manner can produce outright confusion. *See* **Synonymic silliness**, *2*, for examples.

7. Shift in person

Much as a ball player must have a particular position, a writer or speaker needs to express a sentence from a particular standpoint—the first person, the second person, or the third person. Straying could mean bungling a play, or a thought.

A rather common error is the mixing of the indefinite *one* with "you" or another personal pronoun. This is typical: "One loses track of the time when you're having fun." One errs when one tries to have it both ways. Either change "One loses" to *You lose* (second person) or change "you're" to *one is* (third person). *See also* ONE as pronoun, *1*.

A radio psychologist said, in reply to a mother who had caught her small daughter drinking beer, "I would just keep your eyes open." The psychologist did not mean that she would literally keep someone's eyes open; the trouble was her switch from first person to second person. The pronouns are consistently in the first person in this sentence: "I would just keep *my* eyes open" (if I were you). Alternatively, the second person could be chosen: (You should) "Just keep *your* eyes open."

Within a single paragraph, a book's point of view shifts wildly from "we" to "one" to "you" and to "my." (Emphasis is added to the pronouns:)

To look more intimately at sand as a substance, *we* may seek the aid of a magnifier. . . . Under the lens *one* can see black grains, pink grains, and clear, whitish grains. Here and there *you* can notice even at a distance that waves and wind have somewhat sorted the diverse grains of sand by motion on a larger scale than in *my* hand.

Although the meaning is understandable, the vacillating style can be unsettling.

A book deals with the future of the universe:

. . . The present density is very close to the critical density that separates recollapse from indefinite expansion. . . . So I am in the well-established tradition of oracles and prophets of hedging my bets by predicting both ways.

The tradition of oracles and prophets is that of hedging *their* bets, not "my" bets.

A syndicated radio host said to a caller, "Jeff, you are somebody who doesn't like to pay your taxes." *Somebody*—third person—doesn't like to pay *his* taxes. Why would somebody want to pay *Jeff's* taxes?

A news story about a senator's ouster from a committee contained the sentence below. It swings from third person to first person and back again as the quotation marks come and go.

"Life goes on," he said drily, adding, "I have a fair amount of things I've been following for 1,000 years" to keep him busy.

A sentence must hold together grammatically, even if part of it is a quotation. " '*I* have . . . things' . . . to keep *him* busy" literally means that I will keep someone else busy. If the second quotation was obscure enough to require an explanation, the writer would have done well to paraphrase it all. (A paraphrase might have avoided "amount of things" instead of "*number* of things." *See* AMOUNT and NUMBER. By the way, *drily* is a variation of *dryly*. Just how illuminating was its use?)

8. Superfluous apostrophe

Its, the possessive ("Our team did *its* best"), should not be confused with *it's,* the contraction of *it is* or *it has* ("*It's* only a penny" / "It's been fun"). And *your,* the possessive ("Is that *your* house?"), should not be confused with *you're,* the contraction of *you are* ("*You're* looking well"). People continually mix up each homophonic pair, often inserting apostrophes in the possessive words, incorrectly.

The pronouns *hers, ours, theirs,* and *yours* have no apostrophes. ("The money is *hers.*" / "It's *ours.*" / "It's *theirs." / "It's yours.")* Often someone sticks an apostrophe in.

See also **Possessive problems,** *4;* **Punctuation,** *1;* **ITS and IT'S; WHOSE,** *2;* **YOUR and YOU'RE.**

9. *Superfluous pronoun*

Occasionally a sentence contains a superfluous pronoun, a word that contributes as much to meaning as a benign tumor to bodily functioning. The first example is from the press.

> . . . No one foresaw the firestorm of . . . criticism . . . that would descend on Oakland—the last school district left in California where a majority of its students are black.

Better: ". . . the last school district . . . where a majority of students are black." The unneeded word is "its." It is plain from "the last school district . . . where" that the "students" are its.

The chairman of a political party said, when queried about allegedly illegal donations:

> If you've done something you can't do that, I don't want you part of my responsibility.

"That" serves no purpose. (Another fault of the sentence is its apparent illogic: How can you do something you can't do? Either change "can't" to *shouldn't* or insert *legally* before "do.")

10. *Wrong case*

A. *"Me and them"—right or wrong?*

A teacher competing in a TV quiz contest said, "Me and my kids live in a dormitory. . . ." Can "me and my kids" or "me and them" or "me and him," or the like, ever be right? The answer is yes, although it was wrong in the example. The contestant chose the wrong *case* for the pronoun representing himself. It should have been *I.*

Case is the form of a pronoun or noun that expresses the word's relation to other words in a sentence; mainly it marks the word as a subject or object.

The pronoun *I* in the sentence "I and my kids live in a dormitory" is correct because it is part of the subject; that is, the doer(s) of the action. Hence it is in the *subjective* case (also called the *nominative* case). *I* is strictly subjective, and so are the pronouns *we, he, she, they,* and *who.*

In the sentence "They evicted me and my kids," *me* is correct because it is an object; it (along with *my kids*) is the receiver of the action of the verb, *evicted.* Hence it is in the *objective* case (also called the *accusative* case). *Me* is strictly *objective,* and so are the pronouns *us, him, her, them,* and *whom.*

You can be either subjective or objective.

(If you think the rules are fussy now, hark back to about 1150–1500. Whereas we have only *you* for the second person, speakers of Middle English had the *subjective* forms *thou,* singular, and *ye,* plural; and the *objective* forms *thee,* singular, and *you,* plural. Making it more complicated, during that period the use of the plural *ye* or *you* as a polite singular developed; *thou* or *thee* became the familiar singular.)

Another case is the *genitive* (or *possessive*) expressing the ideas of possession, origin, characteristic, measure, etc.; e.g., George's shirt, their novels, the voice of the turtledove, a friend of hers. (See *1, 2, 9;* **Double possessive; Gerund,** *4;* **Possessive problems; Punctuation,** *1.*)

Case is used in a wholly different sense in *upper case,* meaning capital letters, and *lower case,* small letters. The terms come from the cases in which the old-time printers kept their type.

B. *"And I" or "and ME"?*

At some time in the dim past, many of us said something like this: "Jimmy and me are going to the park." A correction followed: "No, no. You should say

'Jimmy and *I* are going.' " The lesson must have been incomplete or indigested. Its upshot is sentences like these:

[From a magazine article:] Being forced to operate "differently" has given Judy and I the privilege of publishing whatever we enjoy reading.

[From a situation comedy:] I just know things got better for Jill and I.

[By a TV weather man:] This weather comes as a surprise to you and I.

In every instance, "I" should be *me*. No one would have erred if "Judy" / "Jill" / or "you" had been excluded. No one would have said ". . . has given I the privilege . . ." / ". . . things got better for I" / or ". . . comes as a surprise to I." It would have sounded too bad. The extra person in each sentence seemed to steer each speaker or writer off course. Perhaps the phrase "and I" acted as a false beacon, although the linking of the pronouns by *or* instead of *and* did not prevent a similar error, by the hostess of a radio talk show:

There are only about five minutes left for you or I, Robert.

Again "I" should be *me*. Her competitor, a host on another radio station, erred the other way:

We have revised the plan, just you and me.

It should be "you and *I*," merely rephrasing the subject, "We." A similar mistake, though a more obvious one, was made on TV by a prominent critic:

Halfway into this screenplay even you and me had questions.

The *objective* case includes not only a direct object of a verb, but also:

- An indirect object (which tells *for whom* [or *for what*] or *to whom* [or *to what*] the action is done), for instance, "has given *Judy and me* the privilege." (Some consider these forms a separate case, the *dative*.)
- An object, or goal, of a preposition: "for *Jill and me*" / "to *you and me*" / "for *you or me*."
- An object of a verbal: "Jack loves visiting *her*." / "The court trying *him* has adjourned." / "The doctors want to test *me*." (Gerunds, participles, and infinitives are *verbals*. See **VERBAL,** *3*.)

C. *"Between HE and . . ." or "between HIM and . . ."?*

Just as an unmastered grammar lesson of long ago could have led to the "and I" error shown above, it could explain overgrammatical efforts of the "he" or "she" kind.

Nobody would be likely to say "I gave he the key" or "They elected she," instead of *him* or *her* respectively. Confusion arises with more complicated sentences, particularly when the pronoun is linked with someone or something else. Let us quote a television newscast and a newspaper caption.

Rose said he was glad that all legal action between he and the league was over.

The legal action was between "*him* and the league." They are objects of the preposition *between*.

The Princess of Wales, with Henry A. Kissinger and Gen. Colin L. Powell, was undeniably the center of attention last night at a reception following an awards dinner honoring she and the retired general.

The awards dinner honored "*her* and the retired general." They are objects of the participle *honoring*.

The newscaster and writer would say, "It's just between *us*," not "we" / "Stop harassing *her*," not "she" / "Helen works for *him*," not "he" / "Pay *them*," not "they." The pronoun would have to be in the objective case. That the object has an extra component should not make any difference in the choice of case: "It's just between *us* and the league." / "Crowds kept surrounding *her* and her family." / "John gave the packages to *him* and his wife." / We photographed *them* and the neighbors."

D. *"It's I"* or *"It's ME"*? / *"HE"* or *"HIM"*?

A traditional rule of grammar decrees that the subject of a linking verb and any pronoun linked with that verb be in the same case. The linking verb (called also a *copula*) most often is a form of the verb *be,* and the problem usually boils down to something like this: Which is right, "The winner was *he*" or "The winner was *him*"? The traditional answer would be *he,* on the grounds that the pronoun represents the same entity as the subject. Actually it depends on whether the statement is to be written or spoken.

When your friend or relation responds to your knock with "Who's there?" you will probably not reply, "It is I." You are more likely to respond, "It's me"—and so you should. Grammarians are on your side.

A phrase like *It wasn't me* being colloquial, "such a lapse is of no importance," H. W. Fowler wrote. Sir Ernest Gowers, his reviser, went further: In colloquialisms like that and *It's me,* the use of *me* is "perhaps the only successful attack made by *me* on *I*"; moreover, *That's him* has won "the status of idiomatic spoken English." Wilson Follett wrote that writers and others devoted to sound grammar were "firm in believing that the colloquial *It's me* is acceptable in speech and in writing when the tone is not elevated."

Such usage is far from new. A tendency in popular speech to use the objective case for a pronoun that complements a linking verb "has persisted since the sixteenth century," George O. Curme wrote. He found examples even among "good authors of serious style." He quoted Churchill: "It is not *me* he misjudges." Jonson: "Here be *them* haue beene amongst souldiers." Shakespeare: "And damn'd be *him* that first cries, 'Hold, enough!' " Marlowe was quoted (elsewhere): "Is it *him* you seek?" and " 'Tis *her* I esteem."

Despite literary examples to the contrary, most authorities advocate following the rule in formal writing. But Roy H. Copperud says flatly: "The nominative ('It's I') is stilted and thus avoided."

E. *"Than I"* or *"than ME"*?

A pair of reviewers rejected a movie, although, one of them said on television, "Roger liked it a little more than me." Literally the remark was tantamount to saying, "Roger liked the movie a little more than he liked me." That may have been Roger's sentiment, but more likely the other reviewer was comparing their attitudes toward the movie. Thus he should have said "more than *I.*" It would be an elliptical, or shortened, version of "more than I liked it," in which *I* would be the subject of the clause "I liked it." He would never say "more than *me* liked it." Understandably, newcomers to the language sometimes make the mistake of using the objective case as a subject, e.g., "Me Tarzan." Native speakers of English lack their excuse.

The context may have made the meaning clear to all the television watchers, but in some similar constructions the wrong choice of case can change the meaning or render it ambiguous. "Do you see Jack more often than *I*?" asks whether you see him more often than I do. "Do you see Jack more often than *me*?" asks whether you see him more often than you see me.

The principle is the same in this example: "Helen loves chocolate as much as *he*" means they are equally fond of it. "Helen loves chocolate as much as *him*" means her affection is divided.

F. "WE people" or "US people"?

The preamble to the Constitution starts out, "We the people of the United States. . . ." Perhaps with that phrase in her mind, the wife of a presidential candidate told a gathering in New Hampshire that her husband stood for "more freedom for we the people." Change "we" to *us*. An object of the preposition *for*, the pronoun should be in the objective case. "We the people" is not an immutable phrase. In the Constitution *we* essentially is the subject. The phrase *the people of the United States* is in apposition to it (that is, explains it). A comma often precedes appositive phrases ("Mr. Wilson, the chairman . . .") but not necessarily.

Similarly "we" should have been *us* when a radio announcer said, advertising a wine, "This name is not too difficult for we Americans to say."

A teacher in North Carolina publicly objected to "pay that is not encouraging to we people who have decided to stay in education." Again change "we" to *us*. It is an object of the preposition *to*. She could have got by with *we* as the subject of a sentence, like this one: "We people who have decided to stay in education need the encouragement of better pay."

The reverse error used to appear in ads showing a man supposedly saying, "Us ———— smokers would rather fight than switch." As the subject of the sentence, *we*, not "us," would be grammatical. The advertising agent who wrote the slogan probably knew that.

See also WHO and WHOM.

Pronouns' classification.
Pronouns are customarily classified in eight categories. (*See* **Pronouns** for an enumeration of problems.)

1. *Demonstrative pronouns* point out. They include *this* and *that*, *these* and *those*. "*This* is the forest primeval." / "*These* are the times that try men's souls." (*See* **THIS; THESE and THOSE.**)
2. *Indefinite pronouns* represent no particular person or thing. "*Everybody* loves a baby." / "Take *it* easy." / "*One* never knows." Among them are *all, another, any, anybody, anyone, anything, each, everything, everyone, few, many, most, nobody, no one, none, several, some, somebody, someone,* and *something.* (*See* **ANY; EACH, EACH OF; EVERY ONE and EVERYONE; ONE as pronoun; Pronouns, 2C.**)
3. *Intensive pronouns* end in *-self* or *-selves* and give emphasis to personal pronouns. "I built it all *myself.*" / "He *himself* has said it." (*See* **Pronouns, 4, 5.**)
4. *Interrogative pronouns* ask questions. "*What* did the president know?" / "*Whose* undergarments are these?" *Which, who,* and *whom* are others. (*See* **WHO and WHOM; WHOSE.**)
5. *Personal pronouns* represent particular persons, sometimes things. "*I* now pronounce *you* husband and wife." / "*You* don't scare *me.*"

   Personal pronouns change form depending on *case* (subjective, objective, or possessive); *gender* (masculine, feminine, or neuter); *number* (singular or plural); and *person* (first, second, or third).

   Personal pronouns in the subjective (or nominative) case are *I, you, he, she,* and *it,* singular; and *we, you,* and *they,* plural. Pronouns in the objective case are *me, you, him, her,* and *it,* singular; and *us, you,* and *them,* plural.

   (*See* **Possessive problems, 4,** on the possessive case. *See* **Pronouns, 2,** on number; 7 on person; and 10, mainly on the subjective and objective cases.)
6. *Reciprocal pronouns* show exchanges. "The three brothers joshed

one another." / "Romeo and Josephine despise *each other*." (See **EACH OTHER.**)

7. *Reflexive pronouns* bounce the actions taken by subjects back on the subjects. Like intensive pronouns, they end in *-self* or *-selves*. "Hortensia hurt *herself*." / "Make *yourselves* at home." (See **Pronouns**, *3, 4, 5*.)

8. *Relative pronouns* commonly include *that, which, who, whom,* and *whose.* "The creature *that* lives there is a bandicoot." / "This cheese, *which* comes from Belgium, smells delightful."

Generally a relative pronoun (a) stands for a particular noun (*creature* or *cheese*); (b) connects the noun to a dependent clause that modifies it ("*that* lives there" or "*which* comes from Belgium"); and (c) introduces that dependent clause, serving as the subject of its verb (*lives* or *comes*). (See **THAT and WHICH; WHO, THAT, and WHICH.**)

PROOF and EVIDENCE. *See* **EVI-DENCE and PROOF.**

PROOF OF THE PUDDING. The proverb about proof and pudding perplexes people. Some, it seems, would search through the pudding for the proof, however messy it would be to do so. A senator, contrasting the president's promises and performance, said, "The proof's in the pudding." A TV reporter, summarizing a city official's remarks about proposed transit improvements, said, "The proof will be in the pudding."

No, the proof is not in the pudding. Nor is it in anything as complicated as the following. A chief justice was writing about the problems in drafting a Supreme Court opinion:

Here again, we do the best we can, recognizing that the proof of the pudding will be the reaction of those who

voted with the majority at conference when they see the draft Court opinion.

"The proof of the pudding is in the eating." That is all there is to the proverb.

Proof means *test* in that context. A good cook tastes and hence tests his food. *See also* "**EXCEPTION PROVES THE RULE.**"

"PROOF POSITIVE." English syntax calls for the adjective first, noun second, as in *positive proof.* Nevertheless, a network anchor man said the Nixon tapes offered "proof positive that he knew there was a widespread criminal conspiracy." And an article in a health magazine contained this sentence:

The fact that Asian populations eat a great deal of soy foods and have lower rates of breast cancer is not proof positive that soy is protective. . . .

The reversal may stem from a series of cigarette ads and commercials in the days when they were broadcast. A company claimed to offer "proof positive" of the salutary benefit of its product, thus turning truth as well as syntax topsy-turvy.

See also **Adjectives and adverbs,** *2.*

PROOFREAD,   PROOFREAD-ING. The fact that *proofread* and *proofreading* are each spelled in two different ways in the excerpts below (from a book that purports to instruct writers in self-publishing) is not the main problem. The author evidently did not know what the terms meant.

. . . Rough grammar or duplication of information . . . can be corrected later during the proof reading session. . . .

. . . Allow someone else to proof read it. This someone should not be overly familiar with his subject and who will not be affraid to be biased in their opinion. . . .

Once you have finished all the proof-reading of this draft copy and made any changes you wish to make, you should retype your draft copy. . . .

Now, finish writing your book and proofread it. . . .

A *proof* is a test print of material that has been set in type and is to be published. It permits one to correct typographical errors before the material goes to press. To *proofread* is to check the proof against the manuscript, that is, the pages from the writer and editor, and to make any corrections on the proof. One who works at *proofreading* is a *proofreader*. It is not necessarily wrong to spell each term as a hyphenated word or as two words, provided that the chosen style is used consistently.

Proofreading differs from *copyediting* (also spelled *copy editing* and *copyediting*), which is done before type is set. To *copy-edit* (sometimes spelled *copyedit*) is to edit *copy*, that is, any manuscript to be published, making corrections or otherwise preparing the copy for typesetting. One who does such editing as a livelihood is a *copy editor* (sometimes spelled as one word). In newspaper offices the task is often called *copyreading* and the editors *copyreaders*. Those who *read copy* there also write headlines.

(The sample could have stood some copy-editing. The second paragraph alone has six defects: Change "proof read" to *copy-edit* or *edit*; omit "who"; change "will" to *should*; omit the extra "f" in "affraid"; change "biased" to *unbiased*; and change "their" to *his*.)

Proper nouns (names). *See* **Nouns,** *1*.

PROPHECY and PROPHESY. The noun, meaning prediction, is *prophecy,* pronounced PROF-ih-see. The

verb (transitive and intransitive), meaning to predict, is *prophesy,* pronounced PROF-ih-sy.

Sometimes the spellings are erroneously reversed. *Webster's Third Dictionary* accepts the misspellings as legitimate alternatives.

PROSCRIBE. *See* **PRESCRIBE** and **PROSCRIBE.**

PROSECUTE and PERSECUTE. *See* **Confusing pairs.**

PROSPECTIVE and PERSPECTIVE. *See* **Confusing pairs.**

PROSTATE and PROSTRATE. *See* **Confusing pairs.**

PROVE. *See* **"EXCEPTION PROVES THE RULE"; PROOF OF THE PUDDING.**

PRY. *See* **-Y endings.**

PUDDING. *See* **PROOF OF THE PUDDING.**

Punctuation. *1. Apostrophe. 2. Colon. 3. Comma. 4. Dash and hyphen. 5. Ellipsis. 6. Exclamation point. 7. Parentheses and brackets. 8. Period. 9. Question mark. 10. Quotation marks. 11. Semicolon. 12. Virgule.*

1. Apostrophe

A. Apostrophe's purpose

The apostrophe (') is a widespread source of confusion. Many people have little or no idea of what it is for. We see evidence of that fact constantly in homemade signs, notes, and other writings throughout the country. Even professional writers sometimes misuse this mark, sticking it in where it does not belong and leaving it out where it does belong.

Notwithstanding all the misuse, the

proper use of the apostrophe is not usually very difficult. The mark has two main purposes:

- It indicates possession—for nouns mostly. Usually an apostrophe and *s* are added to a singular noun or to an irregular plural, e.g., *girl's, Jack's, men's.* Only an apostrophe, no *s,* is added to a plural noun that ends in *s,* e.g., *birds', friends'. (See also* **Possessive problems.***)*
- It takes the place of a missing letter or letters when a word or phrase is shortened in a contraction, e.g., *can't* for *cannot* and *that's* for *that is. (See also* **Contractions.***)*

B. Common types of confusion

It's, the contraction of *it is* as in "It's a boy," is often mixed up with the possessive *its* as in "The bird has spread its wings." There tend to be similar mix-ups of *who's,* the contraction of *who is* as in *Who's Who,* with *whose* as in "Whose car is this?"; and *you're,* the contraction of *you are,* as in "You're welcome," with *your,* as in "Bring your lunch." *(See also* **ITS and IT'S; Possessive problems,** *4;* **Pronouns,** *8;* **WHOSE,** *2;* **YOUR and YOU'RE.***)*

Many who understand the possessive function of the apostrophe are uncertain whether to put it before or after the *s.* This is the procedure:

- When a singular noun that does not end in *s* is made possessive, the apostrophe always goes before the *s,* never after. An ad for "One of the citys' 10 best restaurants" misplaced the apostrophe. *City's* is the right way. A plural that does not end in *s* also gets an apostrophe followed by *s:* "the children's hour" / "the geese's wings."
- When a plural noun with an *s* ending is made possessive, it is followed by an apostrophe and no

extra *s:* "the Twin Cities' finances" / "the doctors' offices." *See* **G** for words ending in *s,* a complicated topic.

C. Forgotten apostrophes

A national newspaper promised to run, among other information, "Each teams first pick. . . ." *Team's,* possessive, needs an apostrophe.

Another prominent newspaper later omitted a needed apostrophe from a plural noun in a main headline:

CANDIDATES CLASH
OVER TRADE ISSUES
HEADING INTO VOTE

The first word should have been *CANDIDATES'.* Without the apostrophe, "CLASH" is read as a verb—"CANDIDATES CLASH / OVER TRADE ISSUES"—and the third line does not make sense. With the apostrophe, "CLASH" would be read as a noun and the third line would be comprehensible.

The same publication described the coconut industry of the Philippines as "one of the countries largest." This time, a plural, "countries," erroneously replaced the possessive, *country's. (See also* **Ellipsis.***)*

An apostrophe is omitted also in a book about marketing problems:

The firm encountered additional problems in Italy when it tried to introduce the ladies electric shaver.

Logically it should be "the *ladies' electric shaver.*" The masculine equivalent would be the *gentlemen's* or *men's* (not "gentlemen" or "men") electric shaver. And one would speak of *children's* (not "children") toys.

D. Intrusive apostrophes

Some people seem to think that any word ending in *s* gets an apostrophe.

Even press professionals, who know better, sometimes put apostrophes in simple plurals.

A headline over a man-in-the-street column asked, "Tell About Parent's By Their Kids?" and one answer began, "Kid's are usually a lot different than their parents." Let "Parent's" be *Parents* and let "kid's" be *kids*. One could justify leaving a mistake intact in a quotation ("different than" instead of "different *from*") but not adding a mistake. On the next day, an article in the same newspaper said, "As a matter of public policy, attorney's have a higher duty to the client's cause. . . ." A possessive form was erroneously used instead of the plural. Make it *attorneys* or, better yet, *the attorney has*.

E. Multiple possessives

In making two or more words possessive, here is a rule of thumb: If there is joint possession, use an apostrophe and *s* only after the final word: "Black & Decker's factory" / "Tom and Jerry's antics" / "Peter, Paul, and Mary's music." If possession is separate, however, use an apostrophe and *s* after each word: "Russia's and China's representatives" / "men's and boys' clothing" / "Carson's and Leno's comedy."

F. Possessives of possessives

To have consecutive words with the possessive *s* can be awkward and usually is avoidable. "Jack's mother's friend" is better rephrased "a friend of Jack's mother." This was in a news story:

> But Francis ———, president and chief operating officer . . . , filed a report with the network's affiliate's board president. . . .

Either "the network affiliate's" or "the board president of the network's affiliate" would be an improvement.

G. Sibilant endings

Most words or names ending in *s* are made possessive by adding an apostrophe and *s*: *boss's, James's, duchess's, Gladys's.* An older practice was to add only an apostrophe. Some publishers continue that practice, particularly for poetry and multisyllabic words: *duchess', Gladys'.* Either way, when the word is read aloud, the *s* sound is pronounced twice. If a final *s* is silent, most publishers will add *s*: *Arkansas's, Illinois's.*

Those who prefer to add *s* will not usually do so when two *s* or *z* sounds precede the apostrophe: *princess', Moses', Jesus'.* Similarly, plural words ending in two *s* or *z* sounds get an apostrophe only: *misses'* and *dresses'.* Exceptions are made also for some expressions in which the word following the apostrophe begins with *s*: *for goodness' sake, for appearance' sake.* When pronounced, such an expression usually gets only one hiss.

By any standard, an *s* belonged after the apostrophe here:

- 23 percent believed Marx' phrase, "From each according to his ability, to each according to his need."

It is *Marx's* phrase. Although *Marx* sounds like *Mark's,* an *x* does not replace an *s.*

An apostrophe without an *S* made no more sense in a leading tabloid's main headline that screamed about "LIZ' HUBBY'S DRUG BUST." *LIZ'S* would be right. A *Z* does not replace an *S.* (From the standpoint of the tabloid, maybe the only *S* that counts has two lines through it.)

H. Special uses

The apostrophe is used with *s* to make plurals of letters, numbers, and symbols: *The Oakland A's; two SOS's; three B-2's.* Omitting the apostrophe and using just *s* in such cases is now preferred by many. When the meaning is unmistakable, as in *the 1700s* or *in her 50s,* it is acceptable. But in some cases it can be confusing to omit the apostrophe. For instance, an apostrophe is needed in *A's* to keep it from turning into the word *As.*

The plural of a word cited for its grammar, typography, or the like, takes apostrophe-*s.* For example, "Some writers stint in their *and's.*" If, however, the meaning of the word is important, use only *s* and no apostrophe: "The policy has too many *buts.*"

I. The other APOSTROPHE

The word *apostrophe* is used in another sense: words addressed poetically to a person, thing, or deity as a digression in a speech or literary piece. *See 6.*

2. Colon

A. Functions: mechanical and optional

Essentially, the *colon* (:) gives notice to the reader to expect something. It has both cut-and-dried uses and optional uses.

In the first category, it follows a formal salutation in a letter (*Dear Sir:*); it punctuates clock times and racing speeds (*8:30 p.m.* and *3:59*); it divides a main title and a subtitle in a reference to a book or other work (*Words: The New Dictionary*); and it introduces quotations, especially those that are relatively long (as shown throughout this book), and lists (as illustrated below).

Combine in a skillet:

> ¼ cup olive oil
> 1 tablespoon curry powder
> 1 tablespoon Worcestershire sauce
> ⅛ teaspoon cayenne

If the victim is conscious while you wait for help to arrive:
a. Keep the victim warm . . . and lying down.
b. Give the victim nothing to drink or eat. . . .

In the second category, the colon can put the reader on notice that an elaboration or explanation is coming (as in subheading A); or it can separate a set of one-two punches: When a statement consists of two parts, and the first leads to the second, a colon may well separate the two. In that function it substitutes for *e.g., i.e.,* or *viz.* or the equivalent, *for example, that is,* or *namely* respectively. (Incidentally, the letters stand for the Latin words *exempli gratia,* for the sake of example; *id est,* that is [to say]; and *videlicet,* to see is permitted.)

The two examples below, both proper, come from a book on economics. (In the first, the colon separates an independent clause and a phrase. In the second, the colon separates two independent clauses.)

> In addition, our economy provides a much more powerful antidote to the rule of the rich: the economies of scale.

> Here we have a dilemma: we must choose between pleasure at some sacrifice of comfort and more complete comfort at the sacrifice of pleasure.

In the latter example, the two clauses could be two wholly separate sentences, but the colon clearly relates the first to the second. Views differ on whether or not the second statement should start with a capital letter if it amounts to a complete sentence. It is a matter of style. The lower-case "we" is valid, though the book you are reading would use *We.* (So would The Associated Press and *The New York Times. The Chicago Manual of Style* would allow the "we." But it follows a colon with a capital letter when the colon introduces more than one sentence, a formal statement, a quotation, or a speech in dialogue.)

B. Interrupted sentences

Unless a sentence is meant to be interrupted, a colon should not separate a verb from its object or complement. A newsletter and a newspaper do interrupt their sentences:

> We're pleased to welcome: Lynn B . . . Margaret H . . . Vivian K [etc.]. . . .

> The nine inductees are: Donald B . . . Maurice C . . . Dick M [etc.]. . . .

A writer probably would not insert the colon if only one name followed. "We're pleased to welcome: Mary Richards." / "The inductee is: John Tyler." / "They call me: Mimi." The additional names should not matter.

An interruption may be appropriate if the ensuing enumeration or quotation is long or formal; if it goes in a separate paragraph or paragraphs; or if the introduction heralds the approach of the material. "The president's four main points are the following:" / "The text of the anthem goes as follows:" / "The ten leading companies in the field are these:" / "The pope's full statement said:"

C. Verbless writing

The use of sentence fragments in which colons take the places of verbs is a technique associated with journalism, particularly news magazines. One of them ran this paragraph:

> Year Edison and his aide invented the Kinetoscope: 1889; reason Edison was slow to develop the technology: He thought interest in movies would quickly fade; year he began marketing his own projector: 1896

It takes the same number of words to convey the same message in complete sentences:

> Edison and his aide invented the Kinetoscope in 1889. Edison was slow to develop the technology because he

thought interest in movies would quickly fade. He began marketing his own projector in 1896.

Using colons instead of verbs is not necessarily wrong, but it can be overdone. The device appears in three successive paragraphs of a Sunday magazine section. *Are* and *is* are the words that have been replaced by colons.

> The villains: The out-of-towners, a Newport Beach suburban office developer. . . .
> The victim: Robert D . . . sailor and idea man who three years ago. . . .
> And the mystery man: Arthur C . . . physician and swing vote on this question. . . .

Some 110 words go by with three subjects and no predicates. The style is questionable. (So is the capitalized "T" in the second "The," inasmuch as only a fragment of a sentence follows the colon.)

3. Comma

A. Department of commas

The *comma* (,) provides a bit of separation or a brief pause. Some uses are mechanical: "New York, NY" / "July 4, 1776" / "$4,507,000." Many uses are discretionary, helping to make sentences clear.

The modern trend is to use fewer commas. In 1789 this was high style; the commas would not have been used today: "The enumeration in the Constitution, of certain rights, shall not be construed to deny or disparage others retained by the people." But in modern times an abundance of writing without needed commas suggests that the trend may be going too far.

Commas can be indispensable for clarity. Take this sentence: "Jack, said Sam, took the money." Removing the commas changes the meaning completely: "Jack said Sam took the money." And "Fruit, trees, and flowers" are not the same as "fruit trees and flowers." And it might be confusing to read this one without commas: "According to my brother, George, Washington apples are best."

Commas have many functions. They set off attributions, definitions, explanations, elaborations, and identifications. They divide three or more items in a series. (*See* **Series errors,** 7.) Often they separate phrases. And they indicate pauses in thought.

Their function of setting off part of a sentence resembles that of dashes and parentheses. (*See* 4, 7.) In general, commas least interrupt the flow of the sentence.

When the set-off matter comes amid a sentence, as in this very sentence, a pair of commas is needed. "They moved to Charleston, West Virginia, last month." / "At last, men felt, the ranks of diplomacy were broken. . . ." The second comma of such a pair should not be overlooked. Sometimes it is overlooked, particularly in attributions: "Soon after midnight, police said the blast took place." If that was when it happened, not when they *said* it, commas are needed both before and after "police said."

A comma or pair of commas sets off a *which* clause or a nonrestrictive *who* clause. "Sam's Restaurant, which was my favorite, has gone out of business." / "Do you know Edith Bunker, who used to work here?" (*See* **THAT and WHICH,** *1;* **WHO, THAT, and WHICH,** 2.) A comma or pair of commas can indicate whether a category has only one member or more than one member: "I'm taking my daughter, Matilda" implies that I have just one daughter; the name is incidental to the main message. "I'm taking my daughter Matilda" implies that I have more than one daughter; the name is an integral part of the message.

When a subordinate clause opens a sentence, a comma normally follows: "If you have a loss, check the box that describes your investment." Many phrases are treated similarly: "Having delivered this blow, he departed on the pacific crusade. . . ." Commas separate many other clauses or other parts of sentences, particularly when they diverge in meaning: "He has eyes, yet he cannot see." / "Make love, not war."

When a series of adjectives modify the same noun, commas may or may not follow them. They do if each adjective has an equal effect on the noun, as in "the dark, threatening sky" or "a soft, sweet, juicy fruit." The test is whether *and* can sensibly go between each adjective; if so, a comma can. One can say, for instance, "the dark *and* threatening sky." But in "a gray alley cat" or "a pleasant masquerade party" the adjectives are unequal; *and* or a comma would not go between them. The first adjective ("gray") modifies the second adjective combined with the noun ("alley cat"), two words that function together as a noun.

When used in place of a colon or dash, a comma can be misunderstood: "He received a dollar, a half and two quarters." The total he received could have been either $1 or $2. If "dollar" is a total and not just an item in a series, a comma is not the right mark to set it off. Commas in place of semicolons can be misunderstood too: "We met Harris, the chairman, the treasurer, and the secretary." How many did we meet? If three, change the second and third commas to semicolons.

A comma does not belong between two independent clauses; that is, what could be two complete sentences: "I haven't heard any objections, nobody here has complained." The comma does not do an adequate job of either separating the clauses or uniting them in that published example of what is called a *comma fault* or a *comma splice*. A period (followed by a capital *N*) would separate them into two sentences. A semicolon or a colon would properly unite them. (So would a conjunction, *and,* but the passage is quoting someone.)

See also 2, 8, *11;* **Run-on sentence,** 2.

B. *Missing commas: ambiguity*

The lack of a comma sometimes distorts the meaning of a sentence. When the comma's job of separation is not performed, separate thoughts may appear to be one thought.

An epilogue is summing up the main themes of a book: "In the third essay on mapping the world, another theme enters." It seems to imply that three essays on mapping the world have been presented. Actually the third essay is the only one on that subject. There needs to be a comma after "In the third essay," indicating that "on mapping the world" is separate information and not part of the first phrase.

In each of the two press quotations below, the absence of a comma restricts the meaning. The result probably was not intended by the writer.

House Democrats who've pushed through $93.6 billion in income tax hikes vowed to fight for some of those provisions over the weekend.

Did only those House Democrats who did the pushing do the vowing? That is what the sentence suggests now. If the writer regards all the House Democrats as a unit, the sentence needs a pair of commas: "House Democrats, who've pushed through $93.6 billion in income tax hikes, vowed to fight. . . ." (The "who've" instead of *who have* is questionable too. See **Contractions.**)

Some plasma cells join to cancer cells forming hybrid cells able to reproduce indefinitely.

If the plasma cells and not just the cancer cells are "forming hybrid cells," insert a comma after "cancer cells."

The lack of a comma can result in ambiguity when words meant to be separate form unexpected units.

Four days into the hearing the real estate agent and co-defendants reached an out-of-court settlement with buyers paying an undisclosed sum and taking back the house.

Who paid the sum and took back the house? ". . . Buyers paying" suggests that it was they. But if the writer neglected to put a comma after "buyers," it was the other parties that acted. From the context, the latter seems to be so. The defendants reached a "settlement with buyers, paying an undisclosed sum. . . ."

C. *Missing commas: pauses skipped*

Hundreds of uses of the comma can be summarized this way: It indicates a slight pause. It tells the reader, whether reading silently or aloud, to hesitate or slow down a trifle. Thus it helps communicate the writer's meaning. Let us list a few of the normal points of pause. The illustrative sentences, from books and newspapers, lack commas and are followed by corrections.

- After an initial phrase that is absolute or contrasting:

. . . Neither of us being expert we were well splattered.

Somewhat cruel and ambitious he was nevertheless a strong leader. . . .

Commas after "expert" and "ambitious" would be desirable.

- Where the main thought meets a participial phrase:

[A critic] reproached Beethoven . . . for the absence of a great vocal fugue considered traditional. . . .

. . . The Postal Service still turns a slight profit making daily deliveries. . . .

. . . I hauled on my paddle and the infant did his part back paddling with a broken blade.

Put a comma after "fugue," after "profit," and after "part" (and hyphenate "back paddling"). A comma in the second sentence would have avoided the false phrase "profit making."

- Before a phrase of negation or contradiction:

. . . Scarce resources . . . are rationed not by price . . . but by [corrupt] officials. . . .

. . . This is only bad prose not bad pollution.

Insert commas after "rationed" and "prose."

- After a phrase ending in a negative.

Adding to the new government's problems is the confusion about what is state property and what is not following 10 years of secretive Sandinista rule.

A comma after "not" would keep it from fusing with the next word.

- Where the scene abruptly shifts, often just before *then*:

He was suspended for 30 days without pay then dismissed after he requested a transfer.

A comma should follow "pay." And note this pair of sentences:

Some researchers believe a baby forms concepts about the world and then matches the words it hears to those concepts. Others think a baby hears the words first then matches concepts to those words.

The latter sentence needs a comma before "then"; the former does not, because a conjunction, "and," bridges the gap.

- Before and often after a parenthetical identification, explanation, or appellation.

"Don't be scared baby."

. . . Payne, a legal consultant for Risk Management said . . . the state could reduce the need to pay for judgments. . . .

Put a comma after "scared," just as you would put one in "Won't you come home, Bill Bailey?" One comma is enough when the set-off matter ends a sentence; otherwise a pair of commas is necessary, just as a pair of parentheses is. The latter sentence lacks the second comma of the pair, after "Management."

D. Needless commas

Unnecessary commas occasionally produce as much confusion as the absence of necessary commas can. The commas do so by isolating words or phrases that should not be isolated. This example is from a column:

Although they produced solid evidence that some Temple members, and others who lived outside the city, had voted, it was never proved that their votes made a difference in the outcome.

Two commas set aside "and others who lived outside the city," tending to distinguish that group from the Temple members. If both groups were outsiders, clarity requires removing those commas. (A better treatment would be rewriting. "Although they produced solid evidence that people who lived outside the city, both Temple members and others, had voted. . . .")

Unnecessary commas can make a portion of a sentence appear to be unessential when it is really essential. A noted book on language says:

> Two years earlier the Scottish physician, Alexander Hamilton, traveling along the Hudson, found an immense number of colonels.

The comma after "the Scottish physician" makes the ensuing name seem just an elaboration, unessential to the previous phrase. The implication is that Scotland had only one physician. Removing the comma distinguishes the Scottish physician Alexander Hamilton from all the other Scottish physicians. (But *see* **THE,** *2A,* end.)

A comma generally should not be placed between a subject and its verb. Delete the commas in the two press sentences:

> . . . The seller's only obligation without a written warranty, is to sell you a car that is capable of providing basic transportation. . . .

> . . . The established way to prove a statistically significant improved survival rate in the patients who have taken the drug, is for a certain number in the control group to die.

To place a comma immediately after *is* in either of those sentences (and thereby separate the auxiliary verb from the rest of the verb phrase) would also be a mistake, yet some make such a mistake. *See* **Verbosity** (artist) for an example.

Nor should a comma follow the subject of an absolute construction. "Mangoes, being cheap, I bought a bunch of them." Delete the first comma. *See* **Modifiers,** *1D.*

Normally two items in a series of two in a simple sentence need not be separated by a comma. (*See* **Series errors,** *8,* for the rules in longer series.) Delete the commas in these two samples, from news stories:

> Police said the dead were four construction workers, and the driver of the school van.

> Hungarians were denied jobs, and arrested in inordinate numbers.

Those commas are just unnecessary, slightly impeding communication. Occasionally such a use can mislead. A memo says, "Joe: Tell Fred to draw up the contract, and see me in my office." If Fred is the one to visit the office, the comma is unwanted; it seems to herald an independent clause, in which "see me" is an order to Joe. A more complicated version of that problem comes from a magazine article, which advises parents:

> . . . Insist that your child never give out personal information—home address, phone number, school name— on-line without first asking your permission, and never agree to meet someone in person without a parent being present.

At first, the comma may seem to divide the sentence into two independent clauses, in which you, the parent, are told to (1) "insist that . . ." and (2) "never agree to. . . ." Actually, "never agree" is not an imperative but a present subjunctive; it is subordinate to "insist that your child," just as "never give out" is. Readers can figure out the meaning, but the comma is momentarily misleading. (For emphasis and clarity, the main points could be numbered or even given their own paragraphs.)

E. *Too few and too many*

Missing and needless commas are not mutually exclusive. Each of the following passages (from three newspapers and a book) calls for a comma or two while containing an uncalled-for comma.

> Sometimes, the snow swirls low across the road drifting in from the forests. The world is pine and white prairie, entirely.

A comma is lacking after "road," if it is the snow that drifts in and not the road. The commas after "Sometimes" and "prairie" are unnecessary.

> The Senate passed the bill, but later passed another version requiring that fewer palladium coins be minted.

That one lacks a comma after "version," preceding a separate thought. The comma after "bill" tends to isolate the subject, "The Senate," from the second verb, "passed." (*See also* **Pronouns, 6.**)

> The former self-proclaimed emperor, who ruled this landlocked diamond-rich black African state from 1966–79, returned home unexpectedly, in October 1986. . . .

In stringing together a series of four adjectives without a comma, did the writer intend to restrict the sentence so much (distinguishing this state only from *non*-landlocked diamond-rich black African states)? If not, commas are lacking. A reasonable punctuation gives us ". . . landlocked, diamond-rich, black African state . . ." (treating three adjectives equally but "African state" as a unit). While withholding commas from the adjectives, the writer used an unnecessary comma after "unexpectedly."

(And "from 1966–79" is a faulty mixture. *See 4C.*)

> I have almost total recall, every face is there, every hill and tree and color, and sound of speech and small scenes ready to replay themselves in my memory.

A comma fault follows "recall." (*See 3A,* end.) The third comma would be better after "scenes." (And *scene* and *itself* [in lieu of "themselves"] would agree with "every . . . is . . . every.")

4. *Dash and hyphen*

A. *The difference*

The public often confuses the *dash* (—) and the *hyphen* (-). Occasionally the press mixes them up too. Both punctuation marks are horizontal lines, but a hyphen is very short; a dash is longer. When a typewriter or word processor is used, one stroke of the key to the right of the zero (unshifted) makes a hyphen. Two strokes of that key make what represents a dash.

They have largely opposite functions. A dash separates words. A hyphen unites words, although it may separate syllables of a word.

In the sentence below, from the press, dashes would have been appropriate. Instead, hyphens were used by mistake.

> The Egyptian army has been trying hard-albeit unsuccessfully-to prevent PLO terror squads from crossing the Sinai into Israel.

Hyphens are found in words like *hard-boiled* and *lean-to*. The hyphens in the sample sentence unite words that should have been separated and create the monstrosities "hard-albeit" and "unsuccessfully-to." It makes more sense this way:

> The Egyptian army has been trying hard—albeit unsuccessfully—to pre-

vent PLO terror squads from crossing the Sinai into Israel.

The phrase "albeit unsuccessfully" is a thought within a thought. The two dashes set off that phrase.

Dashes resemble commas (,) and parentheses ( ) insofar as they all set off words and phrases. Dashes tend to give them prominence, however, whereas commas often play them down and parentheses play them down further. Parentheses always come in pairs, whereas a comma or dash may be used singly when the set-off material ends a sentence.

A dash or a pair of dashes may set off an explanation or expansion of the preceding thought: ". . . Tchaikovsky omitted the bass instruments—cellos, double basses, trombones, tuba—as well as trumpets." / "The Gothic—early, middle, and late—extended over centuries. . . ." Or it may set off a contrast or contradiction: "People wanted to laugh, and weep—and could do neither." Or a summary of a series: "Rare, medium, or well done—these are such personal preferences. . . ." And dashes may serve mechanically in lists:

Originally, the four main castes seem to have been:
The Brahmins—the priests and teachers;
The Kshatriyas—the warriors;
The Vaisyas—herdsmen, money-lenders. . . .

Hyphens, besides uniting certain words (e.g., *left-handed, five-and-ten, Spanish-American War*), mark the division of words between lines (*see E*), indicate combining forms (*-ing, anti-*), simulate stuttering or halting ("K-K-K-Katie"), and suggest the spelling of words letter by letter ("M-i-c-k-e-y"). When two hyphenated compounds are used together, a hyphen suspends part of the first compound ("*one- and five-dollar bills*").

B. Problems with dashes

Sometimes a writer squeezes too much stuff between a pair of dashes, and it may not even be pertinent to the rest of the sentence. Writers at times treat dashes as handy devices to dispose of facts that they don't otherwise know what to do with.

In the following sentence, from a newspaper, the use of dashes is not wrong per se, but the twenty-nine-word clause flanked by the two dashes awkwardly separates the subject ("dinner") from its verb ("was described").

Dinner—where they were joined by Mr. Marvelashvili; Georgi Gordodze, who heads the board of the Ministry of Trade in the Georgian capital of Tbilisi; an interpreter and two Americans—was described to the visitors as a "typical Russian dinner," complete with folk music and dancing.

It would be better to dispense with the dashes and place the information now jammed between them in a second sentence: "They were joined by. . . ."

In the excerpt below, from a law book, the material sandwiched between the dashes below is even longer, fifty-four words. It adds a confusing element: separate sentences within a sentence.

There have been at least five other perplexing constitutional questions—Who can start a war? When is a war "over," and who is to end it? What are the war powers of Congress, and to what extent may they be delegated to the President? How independent of the Supreme Court are courts-martial and presidential military commissions? What are the President's powers in conquered areas?—that the Court has been begged to answer with some show of finality.

The first ten words, "There have been at least five other perplexing constitutional questions," appear to complete a thought. So after five complete sentences go by, the reader is utterly unprepared for the tail end: "that the Court has been begged to answer." The divided sentence should first be connected, *then* the five questions introduced. You cannot keep a sentence going if another sentence stops it.

To avoid confusion, no more than one single dash or one pair of dashes should be used in a sentence (except for special purposes; *see* C). Dashes, like other forms of punctuation, should help to bring out meaning; the four dashes in the passage below do more to obscure it.

> The Republican Party was created out of the remnants of the old Whig Party and the dissenters from the Democratic Party who called themselves Independent Democrats.
>
> It was the first party which, for half a century, proclaimed—and campaigned on—a body of "principles," and its victory in 1860 marked it as the first—and the last—new party which has won a presidential election.

The second sentence would benefit by (among other things) a slicing into two or more sentences and an isolation of each main point; specifically, the *firsts* should not be confused with the later history. A possible revision:

> The Republican Party was the first party to proclaim and campaign on a body of "principles"—which it did for half a century. Its victory in 1860 marked it also as the first new party to win a presidential election—and it has been the last new party to do so.

"The dash," as a professor of mine used to say, "is a dashing form of punctuation." Overused, as it is by some writers, it is like too much of any good thing.

A dash may adjoin the words it separates—in this manner. But some publications, especially newspapers, will sandwich a dash between two small spaces — thus.

A hyphen never needs space around it. Often someone will type a hyphen with space to the left and right, in the mistaken notion that to do so makes the hyphen a dash. Such an error was made in a newspaper and a magazine:

> The couple got $17,000 for the bungalow - $20,000 more than the asking price.

> . . . Hassam began . . . among his most important late works - a unique series of powerful, patriotic images. . . . Hassam created around 30 flag paintings in prints, oils, and watercolors - all set in mid Manhattan. . . .

Corrections: ". . . bungalow—$20,000 . . ." / " . . . late works—a unique series . . ." / ". . . watercolors—all set. . . ."

Elsewhere a peculiar headline looked like this:

> Rosh Hashana- the Jewish
> New Year is a time for new
>   beginnings

The hyphen (peculiarly adjoining a word to the left and a space to the right) needs to be a dash. But one dash is not enough to set off a thought amid a sentence. It should be *Rosh Hashana—the Jewish New Year—is. . . .*

The usual computer keyboard has every important punctuation mark except a dash. Some programs enable the user to evoke a dash by means of a special code. Otherwise it is necessary to type two successive hyphens to simulate a dash, the way one does it on a typewriter.

C. Types of dashes

Compositors and printers have traditionally had a variety of dashes besides the ordinary dash, or *em dash* (—), discussed above.

The *two-em dash* is used to indicate missing or omitted letters: "She blurted out, 'Oh s——!' " It may also suggest unfinished sentences or conspicuous pauses:

Mr. Dawson: You're referring there to the backgrounders that Poindexter and Regan have in advance of the November 18——
Mr. McFarlane: I believe that's right.

"Does——the one——that wins ——get the crown?" she asked, as well as she could, for the run was putting her quite out of breath.

The *three-em dash* indicates absent words: "Police said —— and —— built the bombs. . . ." In a bibliography it means the author is the same as in the preceding paragraph.

The shortest dash, shorter than the *em dash,* is the *en dash,* used between dates, times, and page numbers. For example, "1914–17" stands for "from 1914 to 1917 (inclusive)." The shortened form is mainly suitable for lists, tables, notes, and parenthetical mentions. A mistake associated with it is illustrated by these two excerpts from articles:

In six decades, Horowitz had four periods when he gave up public concerts: from 1935-38, 1953-65, 1969-72 and 1983-85.

Wyman and the former president were married from 1940-48.

The mistake of both sentences is not the use of the hyphen, a common substitute when the *en dash* is not available. It is that "from" does not go with the short-

ened form, in which "from . . . to . . ." is implied. Anyway, the latter sentence is better expressed fully: "from 1940 *to* 1948."

The *en dash* has another, subtle function. It is used in a compound adjective (that is, an adjective made up of multiple words) in which at least one element consists of two or more words or a hyphenated word. Examples: "He grew up in the post–World War I era." / "She described her half-Hawaiian–half-Caucasian background."

Contemporary writers do not usually follow a dash with a comma. This shows an exception: " 'But——,' he started to say. . . ." (To follow a dash with whatever punctuation would be there in the absence of a dash is an older style, favored by H. W. Fowler. An example: "If I have caused a problem—and I may have—, I am sorry.")

D. Problems with hyphens

Hyphenation has some rules, although many exceptions exist. In case of doubt, consult a general dictionary. Better yet, consult two; dictionaries do not always agree. One says *vice-president* and *co-worker* while another says *vice president* and *coworker.* When that happens, you take your choice.

". . . A German-born immigrant . . . built the 14-room mansion." The sentence illustrates a correct use of the hyphen: to join the components of a compound adjective. It appeared in a New Mexico newspaper. Note that the phrase *New Mexico* does not get a hyphen, because it is an established unit as two words. Some compound expressions are established in hyphenated form. Examples are *cold-blooded, law-abiding, one-horse* (town), and *ten-gallon* (hat). Such expressions may have multiple hyphens: *out-and-out, dyed-in-the-wool, will-o'-the-wisp.*

A phrase may or not be hyphenated, depending on its position in a sentence.

"It was a *head-on* collision" but "The collision was *head on*." / "I like *small-town* life" but "I like life in a *small town*." / "The state set a *55-mile-an-hour* limit" but "The state set a limit of *55 miles an hour*." / "Why is an *upside-down* car in the street?" but "Why is a car *upside down* in the street?" Hyphenated *before* the noun, the same phrase gets no hyphen *after* the noun.

Hyphens are never affixed to adverbs ending in -*ly*, regardless of position. Thus "The *happily married* couple possessed a *closely guarded* secret." Adjectives combined with participles are hyphenated— "a *funny-faced* comedian" / "the *shy-looking* girl." That is so even for adjectives that end in -*ly*: "that *heavenly-sounding* music" / "a *costly*-looking car." While -*ly* adverbs derive from adjectives (*happy, close*), -*ly* adjectives derive from nouns (*heaven, cost*).

Certain prefixes normally adjoin hyphens, in compounds such as *all*-powerful, *ex*-mayor, *great*-grandson, *no*-fault, *post*-bellum, and *self*-made. Suffixes that adjoin hyphens appear, for example, in president-*elect*, mother-*in-law*, thirty-*odd*, and show-*off*.

A hyphen is essential in *re-form*, meaning to form again, to distinguish it from *reform*, meaning to correct defects. Similarly, a hyphen distinguishes *re-creation*, to create again, from *recreation*, playing.

While not essential, a hyphen is useful in a word like *co-operate* or *de-emphasize* or *anti-intellectual* and is preferred by a number of publications and writers. It keeps the two like vowels from appearing to fuse into *oo* or *ee* or *ii*.

Typically a publication nowadays closes up a word like *antiterrorist* or *progovernment* but hyphenates, say, *anti-European* or *pro-American* to separate the lower-case prefix and the capitalized name. Some writers prefer to hyphenate both forms. They are not wrong, just using an older style.

A person who is a *secretary-treasurer* performs two roles, united by a hyphen; but *secretary general*, which amounts to general secretary, is a single role. A construction such as "vice president-general manager" is confusing; replace the hyphen with *and*.

In the phrase "Japanese American soldiers of the 442nd and the 100th" (from an article) a hyphen is missing: it is *Japanese-American*. A combination of ethnic labels, used as either an adjective or a noun, normally calls for a hyphen (although sometimes an exception is made for *French Canadian* as a noun).

Meaning can depend on a hyphen. A chance to make a sizable profit may be a *big business opportunity*, whereas a chance to deal with large corporations may be a *big-business opportunity*. A beneficial activity by the federal government may be a *good government program*, whereas an organization's plan to reform official abuses may be a *good-government program*.

The hyphens in many compound adjectives, such as *man-eating*, are necessary to prevent ambiguity or, at least, absurdity. A newspaper that resisted the use of hyphens ran a headline that said, "Man eating piranha sold as pet fish." It prompted *The New Yorker* to ask, "Did he *look* like a fish?"

Similarly, two words need to be joined by a hyphen in each of the two examples that follow, from a newspaper and an encyclopedia.

> David was born without any infection fighting blood cells and is suffering from Severe Combined Immunity Deficiency.

To avoid suggesting that an infection should be fighting blood cells, hyphenate "infection" and "fighting." The sentence will read: "David was born without any infection-fighting blood cells. . . ."

> The order contains two families; the small rodent like pikas . . . ; and the rabbits and hares.

Is "the small rodent" one of the families and "pikas" an example of that family? No, "pikas" is the family, but someone neglected to make that fact clear by placing a hyphen between "rodent" and "like." A correction: "the small, rodent-like pikas. . . ." (The comma clarifies that *small* and *rodent-like* equally modify *pikas. See 3A.*)

Half a loaf may be worse than none when it comes to hyphens. A newspaper reported that the secretary of state, visiting Bolivia, had condemned what he regarded as "anti-civilized society." The target of his rebuke was not a society that was anti-civilized but an action that defied civilized society: a bombing. Therefore the phrase needed a second hyphen: "anti-civilized-society."

Using a hyphen or hyphens is not the way to join phrases. A news story referred, twice, to "the Christian Democratic-Free Democratic" coalition running West Berlin. The writer did not intend to suggest that the coalition was free of democracy, but the hyphen tended to do so by joining the words "Democratic" and "Free." Extra hyphens would not help here. An *en dash* in place of the hyphen would clarify the names of the two parties, although a better solution would be to recast the phrase, perhaps in this manner: "the coalition of the Christian Democrats and the Free Democrats."

The press sometimes is inconsistent in its use or nonuse of hyphens, as in this example:

The Travelodge, near the Dallas Market Center, began its 24-hour flexible check-in and checkout at the beginning of the year after a three-month test.

Inasmuch as *check-in* has a hyphen, it is hard to justify the omission of the hyphen in its parallel, *check-out. (See also* **CHECK OUT and CHECK-OUT.**)

So much for the omission of necessary hyphens. Writers are known to insert them unnecessarily too.

In an article about educational decline, two writers decried "a seeming reluctance by educators to tackle the problems head-on." It should be *head on* (an adverb, modifying the verb *tackle*). Compare it with "The cars were in a *head-on* collision." (Here *head-on* is an adjective, modifying the noun *collision*.) Hyphens are unnecessarily stuck into two-word verbs in the two press examples that follow.

They almost never picked-up the phone to tell a supervisor's office what they thought about a law. . . .

The writer of that sentence had never *picked up* the correct verb. The related noun is *pickup.* Neither has a hyphen. (*See also* **PICK UP and PICKUP.**)

Voters . . . turned-down the idea of demolishing the freeway. . . .

It should be *turned down,* with no hyphen.

A book describes someone as a

soft-spoken man who did not mince his words and could put them on paper in a literate, easy-to-read-and-digest style.

Soft-spoken is correct. The problem lies in the five-word compound, which is properly punctuated but awkward. All that information does not have to precede *style;* an alternative: "a literate style that was easy to read and digest."

E. Use of hyphens to divide words

The most common use of the hyphen is to indicate the division of a word between two lines in printed material.

A word of two or more syllables that is too long to fit on a line is apt to be divided. The line ends with a syllable and hyphen together (*sam-*). The line below begins with the next syllable (*ple*). *See* **Division of words.**

5. Ellipsis

A. *Its legitimate use*

The function of the three dots known as an *ellipsis* or *ellipsis points* (. . .) is to show that a writer has left something out of a quotation.

As an example, here is an unabridged quotation from a governmental report: "Despite disagreement—both within the Administration and with the Congress— the policy continued apace." Now here is an abridged version: "Despite disagreement . . . the policy continued apace." The three dots indicate an omission of words from the original sentence.

What if your sentence ends with such an omission? It is a common procedure (followed by this book) to add a fourth dot, a period, to mark the end of the sentence. "We hold these truths to be self-evident, that all men are created equal. . . ." The dot following the last word is the period.

An alternative, when an ellipsis comes at the end of your sentence, is to use just the three dots and no period: "We hold these truths to be self-evident, that all men are created equal . . ."

Several authorities in the four-point school present optional refinements. They call for just the three dots if your sentence ends with a quotation that is grammatically incomplete.

> Amendment IV: "The right of the people to be secure in their persons, houses, papers, and effects, against unreasonable searches and seizures . . ."

A further refinement prescribes a period if your own words blend with the quoted fragment to make a grammatically complete sentence.

> The Fourth Amendment protects "The right of the people to be secure in their persons, houses, papers, and effects, against unreasonable searches and seizures. . . ."

It can be perplexing at times to pursue those distinctions. Whether it is worth the effort is up to you.

Other authorities call for a period at the end of your sentence, full sentence or not. "The only thing we have to fear. . . ."

If you are quoting multiple sentences, the ellipsis can mark an omission of any intervening matter, whether phrases, sentences, or paragraphs. Each of the first two ellipses below represents the omission of whole sentences (from a passage in *Hamlet*); the third ellipsis represents the omission of the latter part of a sentence.

> Be thou familiar, but by no means vulgar. . . . Give every man thy ear, but few thy voice. . . . Neither a borrower nor a lender be. . . .

An ellipsis may open a sentence, indicating that some preceding matter appeared in the original sentence:

> " . . . Government of the people, by the people, and for the people shall not perish from the earth," said Lincoln.

Here is that quotation preceded by an attribution. Some authorities would omit the ellipsis. (A colon may be used instead of a comma for more formality.)

> Lincoln said, " . . . Government of the people" [etc.].

What precedes the quotation, notably *that*, may make the ellipsis unnecessary by blending with the quotation:

Lincoln said that "government of the people" [etc.].

Any other punctuation found in the original quotation may be placed before or after the ellipsis. "Was this the face . . . ?" A period would be excessive in addition to the question mark. Another example is the following verbatim excerpt from an official report; the colon and dash are unnecessary, though not wrong. (The ellipsis is in the report.)

> "At this meeting, Mr. McFarlane, as instructed by the President, stated that: . . . —the U.S. could under no circumstances transfer arms to Iran in exchange for hostages."

Any number of dots other than three or four, such as . . (used by the *Oxford English Dictionary*) or . . . . . , is nonstandard, except that in poetry the omission of any lines of verse is indicated by a line of dots, about the length of a printed line of verse.

An ellipsis should not be broken at the end of a line of type, although an ellipsis may be separated from a period. Some printing fonts and computer fonts have ellipses as units.

In printing, small spaces may separate the dots, or asterisks, from the words or any adjoining punctuation or each other.

Occasionally three asterisks are used, rather than three dots. Again from the report (ellipses unchanged): "I think it was * * * the 18th * * * " Asterisks go above the line, dots on the line.

A very short quotation that is obviously incomplete needs no ellipsis:

> Washington warned his countrymen against "permanent alliances."

The word *ellipsis* is also used in a general sense to mean the omission of words that would be part of a fully expressed sentence but that are not essential to un-

derstanding. An example is *if necessary* instead of *if it is necessary.* That topic is covered under **Ellipsis.**

B. *Varieties of abuse*

Ellipses are abused in a variety of ways. The examples presented here appeared in print with the ellipses that are shown.

A feature article quotes a foreign official. He was asked to provide a picture of his flag so that it could be copied and displayed:

> "Well . . . I'm not sure I can do that, but we bring Byelorussian constitution. Flag described there!"

Seeing the ellipsis in that quotation, we assume that something has been omitted. Has it? Later in the article, a sentence that is not a quotation starts out the same way:

> Well . . . it was just a thought.

Too many writers use the ellipsis thoughtlessly as all-purpose punctuation. In the two sample sentences above, it replaces what should be a comma (,). In the one below, it replaces what should be a comma or dash (—).

> Decisively, Mr. Bush said he supported it . . . with reservations.

Here the ellipsis usurps the function of a dash (—):

> Binoculars, camera, compass and map, field guides to flora and fauna, pedometer, walking stick, telescoping fishing rod, portable games . . . all these things can make your outing more enjoyable.

One writer seems to think that the purpose of an ellipsis is emphasis. The dots bog down his sentence.

But here in a glass-fronted grotto off Columbus Avenue, the damned ignored nature to find exhilaration in . . . coffee.

Using *italic* or **boldface** type would be a wiser means of emphasis than separating a preposition from its object with a misapplied punctuation mark.

Some newspaper columnists use ellipses to separate unrelated items placed in a common paragraph instead of individual paragraphs. "Three-dot journalism" is what one of them called it.

The purpose of the ellipsis in the passage below is obscure. A simple period or a new paragraph would do.

Mr. Wagner, the former Pentagon official, said another reason for the Administration's inaction was a tendency to focus on what turned out to be a much lesser problem, assuring supplies of plutonium for new bombs . . . Plutonium, a radioactive metal, decays very slowly; tritium decays at a rate of 5.5 percent a year.

Merely eliminating the ellipsis would make the next sentence smoother:

Few low[-]budget publications in the history of American journalism have approached its effectiveness . . . or its popularity.

The article in which it appears uses ellipses three times more, in quotations like this one (set off, as explained in *10*):

You know when you start writing a book at 78. . . .

At first, the ellipsis suggests that the quotation was cut short. But the context suggests another interpretation: that the speaker did not finish the sentence. The writer should have used a long dash, instead of an ellipsis (and a comma after "You know").

A manual for authors and editors condones the use of ellipses, even in quotations, to indicate "faltering speech" with "confusion or indecisiveness." Such advice invites indecisiveness by writers and confusion by readers, who may be unable to tell whether a quotation is complete or not. Commas and dashes can handle the task without creating the ambiguity.

Some writers omit parts of direct quotations without inserting the necessary ellipses. They seem to think that it is enough to insert their own words in parentheses or brackets. It is not. *See 7B.*

6. Exclamation point

The *exclamation point* (!) exclaims. It screams. It symbolizes emotion, excitement. It may climax a cry of pain or shock, a fervent demand, or an uproarious laugh.

An exclamation point can change the character of a word or phrase. "No" may just be providing information, whereas "No!" may be expressing shock or vehement refusal. "Oh" may just be acknowledging information; "Oh!" may be indicating surprise. "How big?" merely asks a question; "How big!" expresses surprise or awe, and it would make no sense to end such a phrase with a period.

We use a play by Shakespeare to illustrate some defensible uses of the exclamation point: in an apostrophe, a hailing, a dictate, an alarm, an excited announcement, an expression of grief, an outcry, and an urgent entreaty.

O valiant cousin! worthy gentleman! . . . All hail, Macbeth! hail to thee, thane of Glamis! . . . Methought I heard a voice cry 'Sleep no more! . . .' Awake, awake! . . . Murder and treason! Banquo and Donalbain! Malcolm! awake! . . . Our royal master's murder'd! . . . Woe, alas! . . . Fie, my lord, Fie! . . . Lay on, Macduff, and damn'd be him that first cries, 'Hold, enough!'

H. W. Fowler sought to restrict the exclamation point to "what grammar recognizes as exclamations": interjections ("Golly!"), sentences with the exclamatory *what* or *how* ("What a difference it makes!"), wishes ("God forbid!"), emotional ellipses and inversions ("If only I could!" and "A fine friend you have been!"), and apostrophes ("You little dear!"). He would not permit the mark in statements ("You surprise me"), questions ("How dare you?"), and commands ("Don't tell such lies").

Most authorities today do not set such strict limits but leave the use of exclamation points to the writer's judgment. Nevertheless, they would probably agree that writings of the immature or inexperienced are likely to overuse the mark. The writer imposes it on an unexciting sentence in the belief that it adds excitement, or he appends it to a joke (with or without the "ha ha") lest the reader fail to recognize it as such. He does not realize that understatement can be a stronger device than overstatement.

A presidential candidate tried to make himself seem more exciting by putting an exclamation point after his name, but "Lamar!" failed to excite the voters. The musical show *Oklahoma!* did excite the public, but it probably would have done so without the punctuation.

Some have the notion that using multiple exclamation points, side by side, multiplies the excitement. A real estate ad advertises "RICHMOND DESIRABLE DEVELOPMENT SITE!!" A sign in the window of a restaurant says, "TRY OUR IRISH BREAKFAST!!!" Electric signs at train stations flash, "ATTENTION SAN FRANCISCO-BOUND PASSENGERS!!!! NO DIRECT SERVICE . . . ON SUNDAY." Appending those extra points is like labeling the notice "unprofessional." It is sloshing gold paint over the lily.

Authors vary markedly in their readiness to resort to the exclamation point. F. Scott Fitzgerald was quoted as telling his ladylove, "Cut out all those exclamation points," as he deleted them from a radio script that the public would never see. "An exclamation point is like laughing at your own joke." At the other extreme, a theoretical scientist employed it fifty times in a 198-page book. Some excerpts follow:

> To their great surprise, they found they were exactly the same! . . . Our sun, for comparison, is a mere eight light-minutes away! . . . The farther a galaxy is, the faster it is moving away! . . . Things always tend to go wrong! . . . We have had false dawns before! . . . Four years later, a possible solution, called "supergravity," was suggested! . . . Presumably, he knew what he intended when he set it up! . . . We shall not bridge that gap with particle accelerators in the foreseeable future!

Sometimes we find parentheses, which tone down a statement, combined with an exclamation point, which amplifies it.

> (It is very difficult to make a mark in experimental physics these days unless you are already at the top!) . . . (A lot of prizes have been awarded for showing that the universe is not as simple as we might have thought!) . . . (Of course there would be no one left to observe it!) . . . (One has only to stop making repairs around the house to see that!) . . . (We are, in any case, unlikely to be able to build a larger detector!) . . . (I know, because I have been around the world!)

The exclamation inflation did not harm the book's popularity any. It was a best seller. For those of lesser prominence, restraint is advisable, to afford the mark full value in the relatively few cases in which it is needed. Overuse can amount to a frivolous cry of "wolf!"

See also 9D.

7. *Parentheses and brackets*

A. *Functions of these marks*

Parentheses ( ) are dropped into a sentence to set off an explanatory or incidental word, phrase, notation, figure, or abbreviation.

Dashes or commas may be used instead for that purpose. Dashes, though, tend to give prominence to the inserted word etc. whereas parentheses play it down. Commas are intermediate in prominence.

Brackets [ ] serve the same function as parentheses but are used inside direct quotations. The use of brackets indicates that the person doing the quoting, not the one who is quoted, has inserted the word or phrase.

The first example indicates the correct use of parentheses and brackets. This and the examples in the next section are all quoted precisely; nothing has been added.

> Sen. David Pryor (D-Ark.), chairman of the Senate Aging Committee, said in a letter to King that "a lengthy delay [in halting collection of the premiums] will create a firestorm of protest."

"D-Ark." (Democrat from Arkansas) is in parentheses. The writer's explanation of what is meant by "delay" is enclosed by brackets because it is inside a quotation.

A pair of parentheses or brackets is used to append something to a sentence. Being an appendage, the enclosed matter does not replace any part of the sentence. The sentence must be complete without it and in no way depend on it.

The use of brackets cannot substitute for any part of a direct quotation. If something is left out, an ellipsis (. . .) must be put in its place. A quotation must always be accurate apart from any matter in brackets.

Parentheses do not go inside parentheses, and brackets do not go inside brackets. When you need a parenthetical word etc. within a pair of parentheses, place it in brackets. For example: "(*The Pittsburgh* [Pa.] *Press*)." When you need the parenthetical matter within a pair of brackets, place it in parentheses: "[*The Pittsburgh* (Pa.) *Press*]."

The British have different terminology. Sir Ernest Gowers used the term *parenthesis* to include any of the four devices for inserting extra matter into a sentence: commas, dashes, "round brackets" ( ), and "square brackets" [ ].

B. *Mishandling of quotations*

Four pairs of brackets appear in the press quotation below. All but the second pair are obviously misused.

> "The public is so panicked that [government] is trying to take away their means of defense that they are buying nationwide in record numbers," Kohn said. "I'll probably lose a considerable percentage of business [because of the ordinance], but that's not involved here. [The city] is trampling on the rights of law-abiding citizens for emotional appeal and political mileage."
> Alan C——, an NRA member who repairs guns at a Van Nuys shop, said he will defy the new law because "I think what [the city] did was illegal."

Using four sets of brackets in four successive sentences may be overdoing it. More important, the writer has obviously tampered with the speakers' words, discarding some and substituting his own words three times. When we omit what he has appended, someone is quoted nonsensically as saying, "The public is so panicked that is trying to take away their means of defense"; a sentence begins "is trampling on the rights"; and another reads, "I think what did was illegal." If the speakers did not say "government" and "the city," what did they say and why are their words omitted? And why are there no ellipses at the points of omission? (*See 5.*)

Some newspapers go a step further in the mishandling of quotations by avoiding brackets entirely.

"At no time did the consulate-general approach the (Foreign Ministry) with a request to send an envoy," said Iaan Basson, a spokesman for the consulate-general.

If he did not say "Foreign Ministry," what did he say and why was it left out? And, again, why is there no ellipsis at the point of omission?

The quotations below do not have words missing. They may have words added.

"I must acknowledge that when I look at those figures (tax increases), I see that some of those businesses are going to have to restructure," said Glenn Davis, district director in Kansas City for the Small Business Administration. . . .
"The small businessman is in a vicious Catch-22," Jameson said. "If you eat it (the tax increase), the business has a very slow and painful death."

Using parentheses instead of brackets within quotations raises uncertainty whether the parenthetical words belong to the speaker or the writer.

C. *Other errors*

A New York publisher, in listing a series of art booklets, indicates that the reader will find "Volume numbers in

brackets." What follows are forty-four pairs of parentheses: "(14) . . . (36) . . . (13)" and so on. It is obscure whether the editor who put the list into print was British and neglected to make the correction for American readers or was American and just did not know any better.

The main part of a sentence must be grammatically independent of any parenthetical matter. A general dictionary erred in this definition of *vivisect:*

To dissect (an animal) while living, with a view to exposing its physiological processes.

"Its" lacks an antecedent in the main part of the sentence; instead it refers to "an animal," which is a mere parenthetical phrase. (The sentence is additionally defective in containing a dangler: It is only "while living" that one does anything. ". . . While *an animal is* living" would fix both defects. *See* **Modifiers,** *1,* about danglers.)

The parenthetical material should be in a particular sentence for a good reason. In the next sample, the statement in parentheses is irrelevant. The writer evidently did not know where else to put it.

Napoleon's conversations with Bertrand and Moncholon (it is unfortunate that there are several misprints in the book) are a skillful blending of record and pastiche.

A parenthetical insert may fit smoothly into the rest of the sentence or be a virtual sentence itself. If it is the latter and the insert is too long or too farfetched, it may tear the message asunder and make readers backtrack. Below, the narrative is interrupted by the abrupt quotation in parentheses in addition to the parenthetical matter between the commas.

It is now an accepted fact that Taney, old and worn as he was, or perhaps because he was old and worn and had little to fear ("I was ever a fighter, so—one fight more, the best and the last!"), went from Washington to Baltimore for the specific purpose of entertaining Merryman's application.

Three messages intervene between "Taney" and "went." Putting them into another sentence or two might have improved them all.

Parentheses and brackets should always come in pairs. The use of one parenthesis is not standard, except at the Internal Revenue Service:

> You must include in your income difficulty-of-care payments received for more than:
> 1) 10 children under age 19, and
> 2) 5 individuals age 19 or older.

A comma or semicolon that coincides with a parenthetical or bracketed passage follows the closing parenthesis or bracket: "Although Mercury's year is only one-fourth the length of ours (88 earth days), its day is 59 times as long as ours." See also 8.

8. Period

The single dot called a *period* (.) goes at the end of nearly every sentence that does not end with a question mark (?) or an exclamation point (!); those two marks have built-in periods. (Infrequently a sentence ends with a dash, indicating an unfinished sentence. See 4C.)

Periods go only at the *end* of sentences (or sentence fragments), except in abbreviations or initialisms. Within a sentence, even a complete thought gets no period: "I think perhaps—it's just speculation—he was advised that maybe some of the money was being diverted."

If four dots follow a sentence, the first dot is a period; the next three make up an ellipsis. See 5A.

In the United States, a period goes *before* a closing quotation mark: "Let our drums strike." In Britain, a period—or *full stop,* as it is known there—goes *after* a closing quotation mark: 'Let our drums strike'. See 10.

Periods are not used in isolated titles, headlines, and subheads, except in the manner of the 8 at the head of this section.

No additional period is needed when one used in an abbreviation or initialism ends a sentence. Two dots do not normally go together.

Periods are customarily used in some initialisms, particularly when they spell words without the periods (U.S., A.D., A.M.). The trend, however, is away from them (NY, AMA, YMCA). They are used in abbreviations (Dr., Mr., Lt. Gen., Rt. Rev.) but not in acronyms (AIDS, DOS, NATO). (*See* **Abbreviation,** 2.)

When part of a sentence appears in parentheses or brackets and it ends the sentence, the period goes after the closing parenthesis or bracket, not before. The period is misplaced here: "Peanut oil . . . often can be used for flavoring (I prefer it for stir frying.)" Reverse the order of parenthesis and period: ". . . stir frying)."

The period goes before the closing parenthesis or bracket when the parenthetical or bracketed passage forms an independent sentence: "Peanut oil . . . often can be used for flavoring. (I prefer it for stir frying.)"

9. Question mark

A. Missing

What is missing in the following sentence (from a New York newspaper)?

> The artist had a show in the spring at Farleigh-Dickinson University in Madison, and 20 of the Empire State Buildings are on display in, where else, the lobby of the Empire State Building at Fifth Avenue and 34th Street.

The answer is—what else?—a *question mark* after "where else." The phrase is a question, so the mark (?) must follow. (However, the question would be set off better by dashes or parentheses than by commas.)

Although the question mark commonly goes at the end of a sentence, it may be more appropriate elsewhere. When a question ends before the end of its sentence, the mark can go at the end of the question; it should not be left out, as it was in the excerpt below from a book of criticism.

How are computers going to make craniums smaller—unless, of course, they turn the brain into a recessive organ.

Insert a question mark after "smaller." (*See also* **OF COURSE**, *1*.)

A *rhetorical question* is still a question, albeit meant to emphasize a point, not to obtain information. The two quotations above and the one following illustrate that type of question. A column on an editorial page quotes an official on a goal of U.S. foreign policy and says: "What's wrong with a goal like that." What's wrong with the sentence is the lack of a question mark instead of the period.

"But the sentences can be understood," someone will say, and it is so. But unsweetened lemonade can be drunk; it is about as complete and satisfying as sentences like those.

Sometimes meaning hinges on the presence or absence of a question mark. "Throw it away" gives instruction. "Throw it away?" seeks instruction. "This is a comedy" gives information. "This is a comedy?" expresses doubt. "What?" asks for information. "What!" expresses surprise.

Question mark is sometimes called *interrogation mark* or *interrogation point*.

B. Needless

When a direct question is affixed to a statement, the question gets the mark: " 'What is in the box?' she asked the spirit." Or "She had to know—What is in the box?" But a statement that presents a question indirectly does not get a question mark: "She had to know what was in the box."

Thus the song title "I Wonder Who's Kissing Her Now?" should not have the question mark it was given (although the title phrase got no question mark in the text of the song). It is making a statement, not asking a question. A question would be "Who's kissing her now?"

The noun *question* has several meanings besides a query or interrogation, which is a sentence or phrase that tends to call for a reply. *Question* can denote an issue, a point under consideration, a problem, a proposal to vote on, a query expressed indirectly, a subject for debate, or uncertainty. Calling an expression of any of these other meanings a *question* does not make it one in the sense of an interrogation. A book relates a historical episode:

During the court-martial, Flipper's attorney had put the question squarely: "Whether it is possible for a colored man to secure and hold a position as an officer of the Army?"

The clause in quotation marks is a summary of a *question* in the sense of a problem or an issue. It should get no question mark, inasmuch as it is a declarative statement, not an interrogation. It would be an interrogation if it began *Is it* instead of "Whether it is."

To use more than one question mark, side by side, does not make a phrase or sentence any more of an interrogation. It does make it amateurish. A magazine ad for a computer company bore this headline:

?????? Should - Should Not . . . . . .
Invest in a Computer ??????

All twelve question marks could not turn that phrase into a proper question, such as "Should I, or should I not, invest in a computer?" (Nor could the spacious hyphen or the sextet of dots contribute anything, neither being bona fide punctuation.)

C. *Two opposing views*

Does a request or statement in the form of a question call for a question mark? Grammarians differ.

H. W. Fowler argued the affirmative. Among his examples: "Will you please stand back?" and "Will it be believed that . . . ?"—presenting an incredible fact of sizable length. Because each is in the grammatical form of a direct question, each should end with a question mark, even though it is equivalent in sense to a request or statement.

Theodore M. Bernstein took essentially the opposite view, that no question mark should be used when an answer is not expected or when the writer is merely making a request. He gave as respective examples: "May we have the pleasure of hearing from you soon" and "Would you please send us a duplicate copy of your invoice."

Fowler would stick question marks at the end of those two. So would I. They look incomplete, and a writer of each would want a response, though not a *yes* or *no* answer. *The Chicago Manual of Style* wants no question mark at the end of any "request courteously disguised as a question." But why give up the disguise—and the courtesy—prematurely?

D. *With other punctuation*

When a question mark does not end a sentence, may a comma follow? Most authorities think not. They approve of this form:

"Do you choose to run?" they asked.

A few others approve of this form:

"Do you choose to run?," they asked.

Some sentences may be followed either by question marks or by exclamation points, depending on the meaning to be conveyed. If an answer is sought: "How common is that mistake?" If the sentence is exclamatory or rhetorical: "How common is that mistake!"

The writer of a music textbook made a choice between the two marks, in describing Beethoven's attitude toward Napoleon:

A conqueror himself—did he not once declare, "I too am a king!"—he understood the Corsican.

The author chose the exclamation point. He attributed it to Beethoven, for it lies within the quotation marks. Thus the author's question is left without punctuation. It would have been preferable to omit the exclamation point and add a question mark:

. . . Did he not once declare, "I too am a king"? . . .

If the author knew that the exclamation point was part of the quotation and deemed it important, both marks could have appeared:

. . . Did he not once declare, "I too am a king!"? . . .

Note that the question mark follows the closing quotation mark when the question is that of the writer.

10. *Quotation marks*

Quotation marks are primarily used to quote what people say or write. "Well, I'm not a crook." / "Hail to thee, blithe Spirit!" The words enclosed in the marks are expected to reproduce the original words exactly; otherwise the marks should be omitted. Anything left out is replaced by an ellipsis (. . .). *See 5.* Anything inserted goes in brackets [ ], not parentheses ( ). *See 7.*

A magazine is interviewing a painter. Amid a long paragraph devoted entirely to a direct quotation of his, this sentence appears:

> She read me Malory's "Le Morte d'Arthur" and made it understandable.

The entire passage is enclosed, correctly, by double quotation marks (" "). Therefore the marks around *Le Morte d'Arthur* should be single quotation marks (' '). If the magazine were published in London, instead of New York, the procedure would need to be reversed: single *quotation marks* would go on the outside, double *quotation marks* on the inside. It is wrong to put double marks within double marks, or single marks within single marks.

Customarily the names of long literary, dramatic, or artistic works go in italics, also called italic type. *This is it.* When that type is unavailable or not desired for some reason, it is not wrong to put the names in quotation marks instead. (*See* Italic[s].)

In quoting someone who is quoting someone else, use double quotation marks for the main quotation and single quotation marks for the interior quotation. (In Britain reverse the procedure.) If the interior quotation marks are left out, the meaning may be unclear, as in the following press passage. "He" refers to the vice president.

> "He said Dave Keene called me a lap dog," said Mr. Dole, referring to one of his campaign aides.

A reader's first impression is that "me" refers to Mr. Dole. That interpretation would not fit the context, however. Interior quotation marks should have been inserted as follows:

> "He said 'Dave Keene called me a lap dog,' " said Mr. Dole. . . .

When a comma or period is needed at the end of a direct quotation, the conventional American practice is to put it inside the quotation marks. ("But," he said——) This is done for an aesthetic reason, whether or not the comma or period is part of the quotation. Some choose, on logical grounds, to put it outside the quotation marks unless it is part of the quotation. ("But", he said——) That practice is common in Britain. When a colon or semicolon is needed at the end of a direct quotation, placing it after the closing quotation mark is generally favored by both nations (". . . my land"; it is——), although a few publications have rules to the contrary.

A quotation that goes into more than one paragraph gets an opening quotation mark at the beginning of each paragraph; a closing quotation mark goes only at the end of the entire quotation. These are typical mistakes: On an editorial page, an isolated quotation is two paragraphs long and the second paragraph lacks an opening quotation mark. Elsewhere, an article begins by quoting three lines of a song in three paragraphs, of which the second and third lack opening quotation marks.

We do not add quotation marks to the examples that are set off typographically in this book and so are obviously quotations (often the longer ones). We do add the marks to quotations that run in the main text, to words and phrases taken from those quotations, and to typical sentences that illustrate usage. In addition, quotation marks go around certain words or phrases to indicate that the enclosures, though used, are nonstandard or questionable. Examples are the entry titles "AIN'T" and "LET'S DON'T."

Newspaper copy editors in the United States follow the British tradition in one respect: using single quotation marks for quotations in headlines.

(What Americans call *quotation marks,* the British call *inverted commas,* a term that is not precise. In a traditional type style, with curved quotation marks, only the opening mark of a pair of single quotation marks looks like an inverted comma [']. The closing mark looks like an apostrophe, which can be described as an elevated comma [']. Typewriters have straight, vertical quotation marks; in this respect, most computers are no improvement.)

See also **Quotation problems; QUOTE and QUOTATION; Tense,** *3;* **THAT,** *4.*

11. Semicolon

A. Weak period
Do not take the name literally. The *semicolon* (;) is not half of the colon (:), nor does it have anything to do with the colon. At different times, the semicolon acts as a weak period and a strong comma.

Just as a period does, the semicolon can end a complete thought. However, it links that complete thought—an *independent clause*—with another, closely related in meaning or form. "Three men went to bat; three men went down swinging." / "Money itself is not a root of evil; the love of money is." / "He came; he saw; he conquered."

In that way, the *semicolon* performs the linking function of a conjunction, like *and* or *but.* A writer might choose to use no semicolon and instead insert a conjunction ("He came, he saw, and he conquered") or to use neither and make each independent clause a separate sentence. ("He came. He saw. He conquered.")

B. Strong comma
Offering a stronger division than a comma, the *semicolon* is particularly useful in dividing a sentence into categories when the sentence already has commas.

Even when a conjunction connects independent clauses, a writer may choose to put a *semicolon* between them to show the division clearly. It is particularly desirable to do so when a clause contains a comma or is lengthy. This is a correct example from a book on world history:

> To many authorities it appeared at first incredible that a sub-man with a brain no larger than that of an ape could manufacture tools, crude indeed but made to a fairly standard and recognizable pattern; but the newest evidence leaves little room for doubt.

In that sentence, what follows the comma is parenthetical; what follows the semicolon is a main thought, and the semicolon so indicates.

Not only clauses benefit from the semicolon. It is needed to separate items in a series when any item is subdivided by a comma. "The club elected George Watkins, president; John Anthony, vice-president; and Theresa Jennings, secretary-treasurer."

The lack of semicolons jumbles the series below, from an autobiography. Readers could have trouble associating the names with the descriptions.

> John Major greeted me, my executive assistant, Colonel Dick Chilcoat, the British secretary of state for defense, Tom King, and my counterpart, British chief of defense staff, Marshal of the Royal Air Force Sir David Craig, in a sitting room at 10 Downing Street.

Replacing the first, third, and fifth commas with semicolons (and inserting *the* after the sixth) would have made the sentence more readily understandable.

C. Inconsistency

Newspapers are liable to be inconsistent in their use of semicolons in a series, and this is an example:

> Among the Americans at the Moscow forum were Norman Mailer, Gore Vidal and Bel Kaufman, the writers; John Kenneth Galbraith, the economist; Gregory Peck and Kris Kristofferson, the actors; several scientists, including Frank von Hippel, a Princeton physicist, and more than a dozen businessmen.

After the third semicolon, the system ends, permitting two chances for misunderstanding. Literally the message conveyed is that "several scientists" include all those mentioned thereafter. Dismissing businessmen from the scientific ranks, the reader could plausibly place "a Princeton physicist" in a separate category. If patient, the reader might succeed in deciphering the confused list, maybe even in diagnosing the problem: a missing semicolon after "physicist."

The writer is not to blame; an inexplicable rule of his newspaper (shared by various other papers) has instructed him to use a comma where the final semicolon belongs. But a comma does not perform the function of a semicolon. If the writer, economist, actor, and scientist categories need to be separated from one another by semicolons, does not the scientist category need to be separated from the businessman category by a semicolon?

12. Virgule

This / is a *virgule* (pronounced VUR-gyool). It is also known as a *slash* or *solidus* (SOL-uh-duss). Sometimes it is called a *slant, diagonal, bar,* or *shilling.*

The mark has specialized uses, particularly in technical, legal, and business writing. It is less suited to general prose than the marks of punctuation discussed in preceding sections.

The virgule is an alternative to a horizontal line in separating the two parts of a fraction, such as 13/16. It replaces *per* in such terms as *miles/hour* and *feet/second.* In science and medicine, *mg/km,* for instance, is an economical way to express milligrams of dosage per kilogram of body weight. When lines of poetry are written in regular text, the virgule indicates each new line: "On a battle-trumpet's blast / I fled hither, fast, fast, fast, / 'Mid the darkness upward cast." This book uses virgules to separate quotations when they are run successively in regular text.

The mark often represents *or,* notably in the term *and/or,* meaning either *and* or *or* as the case may be. Lawyers make use of it. A typical contract uses the term this way:

> Company and/or its insurer shall have the right to select counsel and to settle any claim upon the terms and conditions it and/or its insurer deems satisfactory.

A computer manual contains such headings as "Paper Size/Type" and "Short/Long Document Names," in which the virgule presumably means either *and* or *or.*

A computer program has an option called "Move/Rename File," in which the virgule substitutes for *or.* The program also has a table explaining that if the user presses "Up/Down Arrow" (meaning either the *up arrow* or the *down arrow*), the curser will move to "The top/bottom of the screen" (meaning the top or bottom of the screen respectively).

This \ is a *back slash,* or *backslash;* it is used for certain computer commands, and so is the regular *slash.*

In business, the mark in a combination like *vice president/labor relations* can replace *in charge of.* For the general public, the full term is more widely understandable.

Virgules have been increasingly used of late instead of traditional punctuation and even instead of words. The substitution may be no improvement: Take "secretary/treasurer" instead of *secretary-treasurer* or "bacon/tomato sandwich" instead of *bacon-tomato sandwich.* An original use of a virgule in lieu of a verbal description can even be ambiguous: Diners cannot be sure whether the virgule means *and* or *or* in a menu's "steak/lobster plate."

Some general writers seem to find the virgule stylish. One dispenses with commas and conjunctions to describe someone as a "writer/painter/photographer" and later writes, "She has this phobia/quirk/fatal flaw. . . ."

PUPIL and STUDENT.

An elementary-school child is a *pupil.* Anyone who takes personal instruction from a teacher also may be called a *pupil.* "Beethoven was Haydn's pupil."

One who attends an institution of learning above elementary school is a *student.* A *student* is also anyone who studies or investigates a particular subject, perhaps "a student of prehistory" or "a student of the drug problem."

A news story said:

The alleged victims [of abuse] were two boys, ages 3 and 4, both students at the S—— . . . Pre- & Elementary School. . . .

Three- and four-year-old "students"? It was not explained just what they would or could be studying. Elsewhere a photo depicted a cluster of diminutive moppets for whom the designation of "Students at the primary school in Portalesa, Brazil" hardly seemed fitting. And an article about an Indiana elementary school used the unsuitable noun a dozen times:

Students [range] from kindergartners to fifth graders. . . . The school . . . [encourages] students to think across subject lines. . . . Students play with board games and puzzles [and so on].

"Students" should have been *pupils* in each instance.

A child attending school used to be called a *scholar.* Now a scholar usually is an advanced academic specialist or a person who is learned in the humanities. Sometimes a school child is described as "a good scholar" or "a bad scholar." *Schoolboy* and *schoolgirl* are sometimes used, less often than they used to be.

PURPORT, PURPORTED. *1. An odd verb. 2. Other uses.*

1. An odd verb

Purport is a strange verb, for two reasons:

- Although it has the form of an active verb, it has the meaning of a passive verb. It means *is*—or *are* or *was* or *were*—*supposed* (to be) or *represented* (to be). The sense of *is* etc. is built into *purported,* and therefore *is* etc. should not be used with it. It is wrong to say, "The signature on the letter is purported to be genuine." Change "is purported" to *purports.*
- Its subject normally is not a person. A sentence like "He purported to tell investigators the whole story" is wrong. Changing "purported" to *professed,* or another appropriate verb, corrects the sentence. (One may say, "Miranda purports to protect a constitutional right." Although a subject may not be a person considered as such, the subject here really is a thing, a legal rule named after a person.)

The three excerpts below fall short on both scores. Each uses "is" or "was" with "purport" and makes a person the subject. The first two are from books.

> ... Jackson is purported to have said, "John Marshall has made his decision; now let him enforce it."

> Wellington is purported to have written to the British Foreign Office in London: "We have enumerated our saddles, bridles, tents and tent poles."

A replacement for each "purported" could be *supposed* or *believed*. In the sentence below, from a news story, "purported" could be changed to *professing* or *pretending*.

> Mr. Brucan said also that he had learned for the first time this afternoon that Mr. Munteanu was purporting to speak for the council on Monday mornings. . . .

2. Other uses

Purport is also a noun. It denotes the supposed significance or meaning of something: "the *purport* of his speech was that. . . ." *Purported* may be used as an adjective, meaning supposed.

Purport and *purported*—verb, noun, and adjective—do not confirm or deny the authenticity of anything (for example, a document or antique) but mildly question it. Without this element of modest doubt, *purport (ed)* is not the word to use.

Some people use "purport" (noun) instead of *purpose* or *purview*. They do so either mistakenly, thinking that the similarity of sound carries over to the meaning; or intentionally, seeking a fancy synonym. That some dictionaries support the confusion should be no surprise.

PURSUIT OF HAPPINESS. Millions listening on radio and television heard a prosecutor in a murder case tell the jury that he had read the Constitution the previous night and it said the two victims had the right to liberty and life and more: "It said they had a right to the pursuit of happiness." Not so.

Earlier, an anchor man wrongly stated on a television network: "The Constitution guarantees us life, liberty, and the pursuit of happiness." Had he substituted *property* for "the pursuit of happiness," he would have been right. The true word would have been irrelevant for the prosecutor.

The Fifth Amendment to the United States Constitution says that no person shall be deprived of "life, liberty, or property" without due process of law. The Fourteenth Amendment echoes that principle, prohibiting any state from depriving any person of "life, liberty, or property" without due process of law. The Constitution says nothing about happiness or its pursuit.

The document that does mention it is the Declaration of Independence, whose second sentence reads:

> We hold these Truths to be self-evident, that all Men are created equal, that they are endowed by their Creator with certain unalienable Rights, that among these are Life, Liberty, and the Pursuit of Happiness.

While of historical, philosophical, and literary interest, the Declaration of Independence has no legal significance.

PUSH. *See* ADVOCATE.

PUT. *See* INTO, *1*.

PUTSCH. *See* REVOLT and REVOLUTION.

Q

Q-TIPS. *See* VASELINE.

Quantities, measures. *See* AMOUNT and NUMBER; Collective nouns, *3;* FEWER and LESS; MANY and MUCH; Numbers; Verbs, *3.*

QUESTION. *See* Punctuation, *9B.*

Question mark. *See* Punctuation, *9.*

QUIP, QUIPPED. An impromptu, witty remark may be called a *quip* (noun). To make it is to *quip* (verb, intransitive).

It is probably rare that real wit or humor needs to be labeled as such, but the press seems to disagree. In typical fashion, a reporter added "he quipped" to a judge's remark, about how people mispronounced his name; and a columnist quoting a talk by a mayor explained that one remark was made "jokingly" and another was "quipped." None of the quotations displayed recognizable wit or humor, and the labels failed to rescue them. Crack(ed), gag(ged), jest(ed), and joke(d) are among the terms that have been so used.

QUITE. This adverb can be ambiguous: "He was quite truthful." Was he scrupulously truthful or just generally so? "The place is quite big." Is it immense or just sizable? Does "quite good" describe a superb show or a fairly enjoyable one?

Used strictly, *quite* means *completely, extremely,* or *really.* Used informally or casually, it means *somewhat, rather,* or *considerably.* In the casual vein, *quite* followed by *a* or *an* can suggest an indefinite number or amount ("quite a few") or something notable ("quite an array").

If *quite* is interpreted in the strict way, "quite complete" is redundant and "quite similar" is contradictory. Few critics insist on strictness under informal circumstances. In a more formal context, a vague *quite* can be deadwood.

A book uses it strictly at first:

The viola is not an outsize violin. Its proportions are quite different and its tone is quite distinctive.

Then casually. See whether "quite" makes any useful contribution here:

There are quite a number of fallacies regarding musical design which need to be exploded.

Quotation marks. *See* Punctuation, *10;* Quotation problems.

Quotation problems. *1. Accuracy and inaccuracy. 2. Inconsistency in person and tense. 3. Unnecessary quotation marks. 4. When is the quotation over?*

1. *Accuracy and inaccuracy*

Quotations, particularly direct quotations—those in quotation marks—are supposed to present what people have said or written. But not all writers and editors are scrupulous about quotations.

A linguistics professor in Arizona compared twenty-four newspaper articles with tape recordings of interviews, meetings, and speeches. Only 8 percent of 132 quoted sentences came out completely right. Most were compatible with the original, but some were dead wrong: "People from Spain" turned into "Mexicans" and "He has so impressed all five of us" became "He has so impressed us as interim county manager." Stories written by reporters who used tape recorders were not more accurate than those by reporters who just took notes. Few American journalists know shorthand.

Inaccurate quotations may represent unintentional error, inadequate skill or memory, lack of respect for quotation marks, doctoring of statements supposedly to improve them, or outright fabrication. The *Columbia Journalism Review* quoted three New York reporters who admitted making up quotations. Instead of interviewing parents whose children had died, "I made the quotes up," one said. Another put words in the mouth of a baseball manager. A third pretended to quote a bystander at a parade. Six others knew of imaginary quotations in newspapers and magazines.

A writer or editor is not obligated to quote anyone directly. A quotation that is important enough to use but improper, too long, poorly worded, or otherwise unsuitable as it is may be reworded, in whole or part, without quotation marks. Editors have been known to put such indirect quotations in quotation marks. It is a hazardous practice.

Deliberately altering a quotation can not only be unethical: the Supreme Court has said that it can be libelous—that is, false and defamatory—if it "results in a material change in the meaning conveyed by the statement" (1991).

For the misquoting of sayings, *see* **Clichés; THAT and WHICH, 4.** *See also* **LIBEL and SLANDER.**

2. *Inconsistency in person and tense*

Quotation marks are presumed to enclose the exact words that someone has used. The exact words quoted in this passage from a historical book are unlikely to have been uttered:

> A Senator . . . was so overwhelmed by the implications of the crisis that he "feels that the Executive has not gone so far as to justify" the attack on Pensacola.

Delivering a speech in the Senate, he probably did not say "I feels." He is more likely to have said "I feel." Even so, the sentence shifts awkwardly from past tense to present tense. The nonquoted and quoted parts need to fit together:

> [Example:] A Senator was so overwhelmed by the implications of the crisis that he said, "I feel that the Executive has not. . . ."

If the exact words of the speaker are uncertain (perhaps the author is quoting a contemporary account of the speech in the third person), it is best to omit the quotation marks:

> [Example:] A Senator was so overwhelmed by the implications of the crisis that he said he felt that the Executive had not. . . .

See also **Pronouns,** 7 (end); **Subjunctive,** 3 (teen-age lingo); **Tense,** 3; **THAT,** 4.

3. Unnecessary quotation marks

Quotation marks are often used unnecessarily. When nobody is being quoted, the marks can cast doubt upon a word or phrase. Four examples follow.

[Magazine:] First we'll separate the volunteers into two groups: a treatment group and a "control" group.

[Newsletter:] Our goal at any given time is to strive continually to be "the best".

[Notice at a bank:] . . . we will close our "teller counter service" at 5 p.m.

[Picture captions in an ad for a cosmetic surgeon:] "NOSE" BEFORE . . . "NOSE" AFTER

Control is a legitimate word, and *the best* is a legitimate phrase; neither needed quotation marks. The marks did not express confidence in the bank service. And there was no doubt that a woman pictured in the surgeon's ad had a *nose*. (The second example follows a closing quotation mark with a period, in British style, although the publication is American. *See* **Punctuation,** *10. See also* **CONTINUAL[LY]** and **CONTINUOUS[LY].**)

4. When is the quotation over?

A congressman made a speech in which he read a quotation. As heard on the radio, the quotation seemed to go on and on. Finally it became plain that he had finished his quoting but failed to say "end of quotation" or "so said ———" or "the words of ———" or even the dubious "unquote." (*See* **QUOTE and QUOTATION.**)

Whichever term is chosen, a speaker who quotes someone or something should indicate when the quotation has ended, unless it is well known and short. Otherwise listeners may not know when the speaker's own words have resumed, especially if they cannot see him. Even to a viewing audience, the transition may not be obvious if the speech is read from a paper or a prompting screen.

QUOTE and QUOTATION. *Quote* is properly a verb (transitive and intransitive). To *quote* is to repeat someone's words, usually acknowledging that they are another's words. You might *quote* a sentence, *quote* (a passage from) a book, *quote* (words of) Shakespeare or the pope, or *quote from* a magazine or a speech, saying "I quote."

Although it may pass in informal speech, using the verb as a noun is not appropriate in more formal media: "A frontispiece quote set the tone: 'All wholesome food is caught without a net or a trap.' " / "Drexel liked the quote so much that one of its investment bankers framed it." / "Reporters simply go out and lazily round up quotes to fit the poll results. . . ."

The newspaper, news service, and news magazine quoted above should have used the noun *quotation* or *quotations*. Use of "quote" to mean *quotation,* or "quotes" to mean *quotations* or *quotation marks,* is part of the jargon of editors, reporters, and writers.

The jargon includes "unquote," often used by speakers in lieu of *end of quotation.* It was created as an economical form in telegrams from news correspondents, not as a bona fide word.

A book publisher protested on national television that a magazine had published a derogatory "misquote" and that to do so was sloppy. A neater word is *misquotation.*

Occasionally a quotation is accompanied by an incomplete phrase, in this manner: " 'It's not true,' the Governor was quoted." It should be "was quoted *as saying.*"

See also **Punctuation,** *10;* **Quotation problems.**

R

RACE and NATIONALITY.
1. The difference. 2. Races of the U.S.A. 3. Who is colored?

1. The difference

Race (noun) has often been mixed up with other terms, including *nationality*. *Race* is a category of mankind distinguished by physical characteristics that are genetically transmitted, such as skin color, shape of head, type of hair, and facial features. *Nationality* concerns the nation one belongs to and is based on politics, geography, or culture. *Racial* and *national* (adjectives) mean pertaining to, or based on differences in, *race* or *nationality*. A newspaper confused the terms:

> All along the border the population is a strange mix of people and tongues: Polish, German, Czech, Hungarian, Romanian, Ukrainian and Russian—typical of the racial mix that Russia has throughout its far-flung country.

"Polish, German, Czech," etc. do refer to "people and tongues," that is, nationalities and languages. None of them are racial groups, so they are not "typical of the racial mix" in Russia, which extends to the Orient and does contain different races.

2. Races of the U.S.A.

Citizens of the United States share a common *nationality* while comprising many *national origins* and several *races*. Three leading racial divisions of the world are represented in this country: the *Caucasoid, Negroid,* and *Mongoloid*. Members of the first two groups are commonly known as *white* or *black*, respectively (nouns or adjectives), although nobody has skin that is really white or black. They are informal terms and need not be capitalized.

A somewhat more scientific alternative to *white* is *Caucasian*, though technically there are brown-skinned Caucasians. The corresponding term for *black* is *Negro*, which fell out of popularity in the late sixties but survives in the United Negro College Fund. (The word should always be capitalized and pronounced like KNEE-grow, even though *Webster's Third Dictionary* enters "negro" and condones the rather derogatory NIG-ruh. Eighteen of its entries use "nigger." Insulting terms of that sort appear with the qualification "usu. taken to be offensive.") *Black*, which had been considered derogatory, became the accepted word. In the eighties *African-American* caught on as a formal term. It has less utility, covering only Americans; it would not include, say, a black Congolese. Nor would it include a naturalized American who was one of the nearly 200 million nonblack natives of Africa.

Mongoloid or *Mongolian* to denote a racial division that includes Chinese, Japanese, Koreans, Mongolians, Tibetans, and others is usually restricted to scientific writing. *Yellow* used to be the popular adjective, even though no one is really yellow. It was supplanted by *Oriental.* Then *Asian* took over (its synonym, *Asiatic,* is offensive to some), even though the Indian subcontinent and the Middle East are part of the Asian continent and Japan is not.

Indian has long been used to refer to any aboriginal group of the Americas. Its use is said to date back to Columbus, who mistook San Salvador Island for India. Those in the United States are *American Indians.* In recent years that term has come to trouble some people (mainly non-Indians—many *American Indian* groups call themselves that), who foster "Native American" as a synonym. Users of that term exclude most native-born Americans and several indigenous peoples under the American flag: Aleuts, Eskimos, Hawaiians (*see* **Hawaii**), Samoans, and aboriginal inhabitants of other U.S. island possessions. American Indians used to be commonly considered the *red* race, although of brown skin, not red.

In summary, styles in racial designation come and go, and few of them make total sense. *See also 3.*

It suffices to use a term that many members of a group prefer. Not all members agree on any given term.

3. Who is colored?

The term "colored" is nearly obsolete, though it survives in the National Association for the Advancement of Colored People. It is odd that some who would consider it backward to call someone a "colored" person now have no qualms about calling him a person "of color." It can be a euphemism for *nonwhite* or for *black.* A large headline over a newspaper story about suburban minorities announced "Greener Pastures for People of Color." An article in another paper about a tribute to Jackie Robinson referred to the "obvious presence of such people of color. . . ." Users of that term should explain why they do not regard any tint of pinkish tan as a color.

Here is a paradox, brought up by a physics professor and later by the host of a radio talk show: From the standpoint of physics, black is colorless, being the absence of light, while white contains all frequencies of light. Therefore, if any people were literally black, they would be devoid of color; and if any people were literally white, they would be as colored as anyone could get.

RACK and WRACK. In writing that "the Palestinian uprising . . . had wracked the occupied lands since 1987," did a writer mean to say that it had ruined them? Probably the right word would have been *racked,* without the *w.*

To *rack* (verb, transitive) is literally to torture (someone) on the *rack;* more broadly to torture or torment with physical or mental pain, or to strain, especially by violence or oppression. The *rack* was a medieval instrument for torturing people by stretching their bodies. Two expressions are *racked with pain* (*or illness* etc.) and *rack one's brains* (*or memory* etc.).

To *wrack* (verb, transitive) is to destroy, ruin, or wreck (something). It is archaic and poetic. *Wrack* (noun) is violently caused damage or destruction, or wreckage of a ship cast ashore. The main use of the noun nowadays is in the expression (to bring to) *wrack and ruin.* Think of *wreck,* which also has a *w.*

Rack and *wrack* are pronounced the same. They come from separate Middle English words, which in turn may be traced to separate Middle Dutch words.

See also **WREAK and WRECK.**

RAGAMUFFIN. An obituary of a rather prosperous "bag lady" quoted an acquaintance: "She looked like a little rag muffin, like she didn't have a dime to her name."

Ragamuffin is the term, and it has nothing to do with muffins. It does have something to do with rags. The word comes from *Ragamoffyn,* the name of a demon in a fourteenth-century religious play, *Piers Plowman,* attributed to William Langland. Demons often were described as *ragged,* in the sense of shaggy.

At first *ragamuffin* referred to a man who was disreputable as well as ragged. It came to describe any poorly clothed and dirty person. Now it is usually reserved for an ill-clothed, unkempt, or dirty child.

RAIN, REIGN, and REIN. *See* **Homophones.**

RALLY. Was a TV panelist's use of *rallies* right? "When he sees one of his friends is in trouble, he rallies around that person."

The verb was right. The preposition was wrong. Make it "he rallies *to* that person." Two meanings of the verb *rally* (intransitive) were mixed up. It can mean to come to help, the meaning the panelist intended; or it can mean to get together for a common purpose, something one person cannot do: "Let's rally round the flag, boys."

The same verb can also mean to recover from a setback ("The patient rallied" or "Stocks rallied on Wall Street") or, in tennis, to exchange several strokes. *Rally* (transitive) means to call together for a common purpose ("He rallied his troops") or to bring back to activity ("She rallied her strength").

RAN and RUN. *See* **Tense,** *5A, B.*

R AND R. A U.S. Army general "said he was trying to arrange 'R and R,' rest and relaxation tours, inside and outside the kingdom." Reporting from Arabia, a newspaper got the expression *R and R* right but its meaning wrong. It is not "rest and relaxation." Neither is it "rest and recreation," a popular interpretation.

By U.S. Army regulations, it stands for *rest and recuperation.* That is the definition of *R & R* in all the U.S. armed services, the *Dictionary of Military Abbreviations* says.

Another general writes in an autobiography:

Soon after I joined the headquarters staff, I flew to Hong Kong for rest and recreation. For some GIs, R and R in this indulgent city meant wall-to-wall sex. For others, Hong Kong meant a shopping spree.

An enumeration of his purchases follows.

Range, true and false. *1. As a noun, numerical and other senses. 2. As a verb, numerical sense; RANGE or RANGING used. 3. RANGING implied. 4. Stale expression: "EVERYTHING FROM."*

1. As a noun: numerical and other senses

The numerical sense is what mainly concerns us first. In statistics a *range* is the difference between the highest and lowest in a set of figures. If the highest is 15 and the lowest is 5, the range is 10.

In ordinary use, it is the extent to which a series of numbers vary: "The price range is $10 to $20." / "The range in their ages is 13 to 17."

An appraiser said of an antique chair, "We would value it to be in the $3,000 range." As he used it, "range" had no meaning. No other figure was given. *Range* would be meaningful if he had placed the value, for instance, "in the

$2,000-to-$4,000 range." The value of a single figure can be expressed in many ways; for instance, "We would value it *at about* $3,000."

A *range* (noun) can also be an extent or scope of activity or existence ("the range of our weapons" / "the range of possibilities"), a region in which an animal or plant lives ("the range of this species"), an open area for livestock ("home on the range"), a place for the test firing or flying of weapons or rockets (a rifle range, a missile range); or the variation in pitch of a musical instrument or voice ("She has a range of three octaves").

2. As a verb, numerical sense; RANGE or RANGING used

In a numerical sense, the verb *range* (used intransitively) is strictly expressed in the following pair of examples:

Women's cycles also tend to be less expensive than men's, ranging from $1,000 to $4,000. . . .

The Communities' list of languages to foster ranges from Ladin, a neo-Latin spoken by about 30,000 mountain Italians, to Catalan, which has around 7 million speakers.

Used in that manner, to *range* means to vary within specified limits, or extremes. The limits may be, for example, prices of $1,000 and $4,000; about 30,000 and 7 million speakers; 147 and 160 pounds; first and sixth grades; Maine and Florida; adagio and vivace—or more subjective ones:

Chicken dishes range from satisfying—morsels sautéed with garlic and wine—to dreadful, such as the special chicken with sausage and peppers in a gelatinous sauce. . . .

The limits in that sentence are "satisfying" and "dreadful." There is a top and

a bottom. It is clear how they vary. But what is the nature of the limits in the example below, and in what way do items vary within them?

They [items auctioned] ranged from unpublished pinup-style photographs of Marilyn Monroe, taken in 1945, before she became a movie star, to a gold record awarded the Beatles in 1964 for the million-selling single "I Want to Hold Your Hand."

From the context, we cannot say that the items "ranged" in age or "ranged" in value between the photographs and the record. Then what was the essence of the limits and how did the items range within them? We can only guess.

To complicate the guessing game, writers will often add a third supposed limit, or more.

. . . For months the company had considered more than 200 new names, ranging from U.S.S.A. and Amcor to Maxus.

Do U.S.S.A. and Amcor together constitute some limit? Or is Amcor some notable landmark on the way to Maxus? If the names extended, say, from "Amcor to Zilch," the range would be clear. Now it is muddy.

Extra limits may appear on the "to" side:

These [problems] have ranged from high costs to traffic problems, a lack of police cooperation, antiquated equipment and a dearth of studio space.

Or the limits may be equally divided between the "from" and "to" sides:

The company began a program to teach workers English—a step also taken by many other employers ranging from nursing homes and resort hotels to insurance companies and manufacturers.

Or any extra one may get its own "to":

Taking part . . . are prominent church figures from many countries, ranging from top Vatican officers to evangelist Billy Graham to the Archbishop of Canterbury.

If things or people "range," ask *how?* The last five preceding examples, from press articles, leave us wondering. The monstrous sentence below, from a book, seems to give the reader five pairs of limits to puzzle over. What makes any of them a "range"?

As one examined the impressive range of Nixon's initiatives—from his appropriation of the war-making power to his interpretation of the appointing power, from his unilateral determination of social priorities to his unilateral abolition of statutory programs, from his attack on legislative privilege to his enlargement of executive privilege, from his theory of impoundment to his theory of the pocket veto, from his calculated disparagement of the cabinet and his calculated discrediting of the press to his carefully organized concentration of federal management in the White House—from all this a larger design ineluctably emerged.

What if one could not examine that "range," because its limits were hopelessly obscure? Then, I guess, the larger design would not ineluctably (inevitably) emerge.

If what follow "from" and "to" are arbitrary, if it is not obvious how things or people "range" within them, the device has no reason for being. Often it can easily be replaced by a term like *such as* or *including* or *among them* and a series of examples. Such usage would have suited the second sentence of the newspaper passage below.

Since East Germany's founding, advancing in the party hierarchy has meant access to a variety of privileges denied average citizens.

At this point, a phrase like *These have included* or *Among these have been* would be useful. Instead, the old "range from" device is trotted out (in the wrong tense and with other peculiarities).

These ranged from special housing, special stores where higher quality goods and foodstuffs were sold at lower prices to party members and Western goods could be ordered by mail, freedom to travel abroad, as well as use of Western luxury cars.

By the end of the sentence, the beginning of the sentence is forgotten. We are never told what anything ranges *to*.

3. RANGING implied

The word "range" or "ranging" often is left out but implied by "from . . . to . . . ," as in this sentence from a scholarly book:

The eighteenth century was an age of dictionaries—dictionaries of all kinds, from horsemanship to mathematics.

How do "all kinds" of dictionaries go "from horsemanship to mathematics"? Dictionaries normally go from *A* to *Z*.

He used references from Michael Jackson to the Sundance Kid. . . .

Why those two? Or does it mean that he (the president) quoted Michael Jackson referring to the Sundance Kid?

Vice Mayor Han Boping told a news conference that prices of 1,800 non-staple foods from canned goods to steamed dumplings will rise.

If any government decreed that "foods from canned goods to steamed dumplings shall rise in price," there would be chaos in the land.

Three variations follow.

> His commercial work . . . has appeared in reproduction in just about every graphic form imaginable, from billboards and calendars to album covers and playing cards.

> He [Aristotle] wrote on almost all subjects, from physics to literature, from politics to biology.

Would it make any less sense if the first said "billboards and album covers to calendars and playing cards" and the second said "from physics to politics, from literature to biology"?

> Almost all seeds of economic importance to man—from corn to cabbage to cowpeas—sit frozen in the National Seed Storage Laboratory's room-sized freezer vaults.

The function of the third "to" and whether only those seeds beginning with *c* are deemed of economic importance to man are among the questions raised by that journalistic aberration.

4. Stale expression: "EVERYTHING FROM"

Once upon a time, a writer wrote a sentence like this:

> They dined on everything from crudites to cream puffs.

It did not make sense—could you list "everything" between them?—but it was cute. "Everything from . . . to . . ." got to be a cliché, no longer cute and still senseless. A variation might appear; according to a dictionary of English usage, *jazz* "used attributively . . . may be applied to anything from language to stockings" (but not to words from *a* to *k* and *t* to *z*?).

Within a twelve-day period, six writers (three on one newspaper) wrote:

> . . . A long list of speakers criticized everything from the party leadership to the organization of the conference.

> . . . Correspondents prepare stories on everything from Soviet tank battalions to the roots of the Russian Orthodox church.

> They are factories producing everything from industrial ceramics to toys. . . .

> . . . Contracts . . . have been put on hold temporarily, as have purchases of everything from magazine and newspaper subscriptions to television sets, recreation equipment, lawn mowers and furniture.

> New age . . . [is] a catchall category encompassing everything from alternative life styles and alternative therapies to tarot cards and books about abductions by aliens in flying saucers.

> The special airlift aboard the C-5As also brought equipment and supplies—everything from photocopiers to desks, from crockery to light bulbs. . . .

Meanwhile a U.S. president said in an address:

> These microcomputers today aid the design of everything from houses to cars to spacecraft.

That should cover everything.

RAPE. *See* **Crimes**, *1*.

"RARELY EVER." *See* (-)EVER, *6*.

RASSLE, RASSLING. *See* WRES-
TLE, WRESTLING **and** RASSLE,
RASSLING.

RATHER. *See* KIND OF, 4; THAN,
2D.

RAVIOLI. *Ravioli* are stuffed, cooked
casings of noodle dough, usually square.
Upon consuming some for dessert (not
customarily the course in which they are
served), a restaurant reviewer wrote that
the "exquisite apricot raviolis and
poppy-seed ice cream invariably hook
you for a revisit." Drop the *s* in "raviolis." The noun *ravioli* already is plural. It
comes from an Italian dialect in which
ravioli is the plural of *raviolo*, meaning
little turnip.

Inasmuch as people do not commonly
buy, cook, or even eat just one of them,
the singular is not needed often. If it is
needed, *a piece of ravioli* is preferable to
"a ravioli." *Spaghetti*, a plural word,
should be treated similarly.

RAZE. *See* DEMOLISH.

REALLY. The adverb *really* deserves
respect. It has a real meaning: actually, in
fact, in reality, in truth. Instead, it was
treated as an empty locution in a Sunday
travel article about a place in Thailand.

> It's another world really—a misty,
> mountainous and mysterious land of
> hill tribes, rice paddies, superb arti-
> sans, opium, flowers and beautiful
> women even Thais find remote and
> enchanting.

Adding "really" to an obviously untrue
statement ruined what would have been
a passable metaphor. Another world
really is a quarter-million miles away at
the closest and not yet a topic for travel
writers. Besides, is any of the enumerated features too exotic for the world we
all know? (*See also* PADDY.)

Informally, *really* can substitute for *in-*
deed, serving as an intensive: "It has
really been a pleasure." Advertising
makes liberal use of it. A pants maker
has a farmer say: "They fit really good,
feel really comfortable, and work really
hard." It does not use *really* wrong, just
puffily. (What is bad is "good." *See*
GOOD and WELL.)

Those with modest vocabularies find
the word useful, sometimes in tandem.
In a radio program, a restaurant reviewer said about a cheese cake: "It's
really really light. It's really really good."

The phrase *not really* can be meaningful, contrasting reality with semblance:
"It's not really a lake that you see. It's a
mirage." It can also be misleading verbiage: Jack asks, "Has the package arrived?" Jill replies, "Not really." All she
may mean is *no*, but the response can
sound equivocal.

See also FACT, 4 (*reality, in reality*,
etc.).

REALTOR, REALTY. *Realtor* is
pronounced REE-ul-tur. *Realty* is pronounced REE-ul-tee. In the three quotations, from television and telephone,
those words are transcribed as heard:
"We lobbied the Board of REAL-a-
turs." / "Today REAL-a-tur Bill Adams
has more business than he can handle." /
"Hello, this is Carl ——— of ———
REAL-a-tee."

A *Realtor* is a particular type of real
estate broker, one who is an active member of a real estate board affiliated with
the National Association of Real Estate
Boards.

As a trademark, *Realtor* ought to be
capitalized, although some dictionaries
and newspapers give it in lower case. Often we do not know whether a writer or
speaker is using the designation the strict
way or loosely as a synonym for *real es-*
tate broker. The difference can be significant, inasmuch as an objective of the
association is the protection of the public
from dishonest practices.

Taken from the noun *realty,* meaning real estate, or landed property, *Realtor* was coined by C. D. Chadbourn, of Minneapolis, and adopted by the association in 1916.

REASON.   *1. Adding "BECAUSE." 2. Other redundancies. 3. "SIMPLE . . ."; "IT STANDS TO. . . . " 4. Superfluous "REASONS"?*

1. Adding "BECAUSE"

Because means *for the reason that.* "The reason is [or "was"] because . . ." says, in effect, "The reason is [or "was"] for the reason that. . . . " Four newspapers provide six examples.

The third reason for doubting reports of successes is because changes in the way cancers are recorded may be exaggerating the apparent gains in survival rates.

She said one reason that Sonrise wanted to list her as the general manager was because she is a woman.

In that pair, change each "because" to *that:* "The third reason . . . is *that* changes . . ." / ". . . One reason . . . was *that* she. . . . "

The reason she no longer smokes it, she said, is because as a lawyer in the public eye the penalties against her would be complicated by political considerations.

Either change "because" to *that* or leave out "the reason . . . is." The latter correction begins, "She no longer smokes it, she said, because. . . . "

. . . They have been taught: that the reason so few Germans intervened to stop the Holocaust is because the vast majority of Germany [sic] knew nothing about it.

Omitting "the reason . . . is" from that sentence (rather than inserting another *that*) is best. ". . . They have been taught that so few Germans intervened . . . because. . . . " (The colon is unnecessary.)

The reason the prominent land-use lawyer withdrew . . . was because of his potential conflict of interest.

Leave out either "because of" or "The reason . . . was." The latter correction begins, "The prominent land-use lawyer withdrew . . . because of. . . . "

The main reason the tabloids no longer deal with . . . disturbing subjects is because 90 percent of those buying the tabloids are women. . . .

"The main reason . . . is *that* . . ." or "The tabloids no longer deal with . . . disturbing subjects *mainly* because. . . . "
President Bush said during his campaign for reelection:

The reason we're going to win is because the American people have a clear choice. . . .

He was wrong—in the way he said it and also, as it turned out, in what he said.
See also **BECAUSE.**

2. Other redundancies

Why primarily means *for what reason* or *the reason for which.* Therefore a case can be made against pairing "reason" with *why.* It is like saying "the reason for the reason for which." An example comes from a television forum.

That's one of the reasons why Dole might have plateaued out a bit.

"Why" can be replaced with *that:* "That's one of the reasons *that* Dole. . . . "
Often there is a choice. If you prefer

to use *the reason,* it can be accompanied by *that.* "What is the reason *that* you sent me a new bill?" (not "the reason why"). / "Tell me the reason *that* she left so soon" (not "the reason why"). If you prefer to use *why,* "the reason" has no place: "Why did you send me a new bill?" / "Tell me why she left so soon."

Dictionaries differ on this point, and so do grammarians. While some consider "the reason why" redundant, some others call it an accepted colloquialism with a long history. But inasmuch as the phrase is not essential to the expression of any thought, it can easily be discarded (except in quoting those who have used it).

In his poem "The Charge of the Light Brigade," Alfred Lord Tennyson may have unwittingly encouraged the use of the phrase by writing: "Theirs not to make reply, / Theirs not to reason why, / Theirs but to do and die." Note that he used *reason* as a verb, meaning to think through logically; not in the questionable way, as a noun, meaning explanation or justification.

"The reason why . . . is because" compounds the redundancy. Example: "The reason why I can't go to work today is because of my back injury." Omit "The reason why" and "is."

Other redundant "reason" phrases are "the reason is due to" and "the reason is on account of." Examples: "The reason for the price increase is due to higher costs" (omit either "The reason for" or "due to") and "The reason that the game was called was on account of rain" (omit either "The reason that . . . was" or "on account of").

3. "SIMPLE . . ."; "IT STANDS TO . . . "

"For the simple reason that" is a questionable phrase. It may be unnecessary for those who find the reason obviously simple. Yet the "simple" can offend someone who did not know the reason, implying "You're a dope for not knowing this." A book on language says:

Nor can we read any Indo-European writings, for the simple reason that not a scrap exists.

Although the explanation is "simple" in its brevity, the fact presented may not be obvious to the reader. Later the book says:

English grammar is so complex and confusing for the one very simple reason that its rules and terminology are based on Latin—a language with which it has precious little in common.

This time the reason, though twice as long as the last one, is "very simple"; but the information is no more obvious.

Another dubious expression is "It stands to reason." With "that" added, it introduces the writer's or the speaker's opinion. It will sit well with the readers who agree with the opinion. To others, it can appear arrogant.

See also OF COURSE, 3.

4. Superfluous "REASONS"?

"I am resigning for personal reasons" is a satisfactory sentence.

"The staff is being reduced for economy reasons" is less satisfactory. Unlike *personal,* an adjective, *economy* is a noun; and although a noun can serve as an adjective if it has to, "for reasons of economy" would be a more normal expression. Moreover, *reasons* is not essential; the sentence makes sense without it.

A comparable example: "We are keeping this information confidential for national security reasons." Better: ". . . for reasons of national security." Still better: ". . . for national security." (Our concern here is only style, not substance.)

REBUT and REFUTE. To *rebut* is to oppose a statement or argument with contrary evidence or argument. "The chair will allow the lady five minutes to rebut the gentleman's statement." Using *rebut* (verb, transitive and intransitive; pronounced rih-BUT) does not imply a judgment of who is right or wrong.

To *refute* something is to prove it wrong or false. "The Ptolemaic theory of Earth as the stationary center of the universe was refuted by Copernicus and Galileo." Using *refute* (verb, transitive; pronounced rih-FYOOT) declares in effect that the original statement, belief, or allegation has been proven wrong or false. An almanac misused the word:

> The "character issue" stemmed from allegations of infidelity, which Clinton ultimately refuted in a television interview in which he and Hillary avowed their relationship was solid.

It may reasonably be said that he *rebutted* the allegations but not that he "refuted" them. In that interview, he denied a woman's statement that they had engaged in an affair. Six years later, in sworn testimony, he admitted having had an affair with the woman.

RECOMMIT. *See* COMMIT.

RECORD. "You're well on your way today to setting new records," a television quizmaster told three contestants, who had amassed substantial scores.

If *records* will be set, we can assume they will be "new" *records*. One might speak of a *new record* when comparing it with an *old record*.

"All-time record" is often redundant, although it might be apt in contrast with, say, "a modern-day record" or "a record for the century."

RE-CREATION and RECRE-ATION. *See* Punctuation, 4D.

REDUNDANCY, REDUNDANT. *See* Tautology.

Reflexive pronouns. *See* Pronouns, 3, 4, 5.

REFLEX, REFLEXIVELY. *See* INSTINCT.

RE-FORM and REFORM. *See* Punctuation, 4D.

REFUTE. *See* REBUT and REFUTE.

REGARDLESS. When we consider that generations of teachers have been instructing youngsters that *regardless* is correct and "irregardless" is incorrect, even illiterate, it is somewhat surprising to find an occasional educated person using the substandard word.

A physician said on a television news program, "We're obligated to do that biopsy irregardless of the physical findings." Of course *regardless* was the word to use.

A minister said on a radio talk show, about a sectarian movement in the news, "We have to voice our opinion, irregardless of some of the positive things that are going on." *Regardless.*

"Irregardless" should be shunned for good reason. It has two negatives. The prefix, "ir-," tends to cancel out the suffix, "-less." *See* Double negative.

Nowadays *regardless* is commonly used as an adverb. Often, with *of* following, it means *without regard for* or *in spite of.* This sentence is typical: "I will have it regardless of the high cost." It would not be wrong to end that sentence with *regardless* if the high cost was understood from the context.

Regardless as an adjective is found in old literature. It might mean showing no regard, heedless, or careless; for example, "With a book he was regardless of time" (*Pride and Prejudice* by Jane Austen). It might also mean paid no regard, that is, no notice or attention; or shown no regard in the sense of consideration or respect.

REGULATION, STATUTE, and LAW.

Although a governmental *regulation* and a *statute* both have the force of law, they should not be confused, as they were in an article:

> ... A Federal Communications Commission regulation ... says anyone in a region where an area code overlay exists is required to dial the area code for all local calls. ... It is not surprising that Nynex is itself seeking relief from an onerous statute.

If it is an FCC *regulation,* it is not a *statute.* The first is a rule issued by a public administrative agency. The second is a law enacted by Congress or a state legislature and approved by the president or a governor. A *statute* may present the basic principles of a law and leave the fine details—*regulations*—to a particular agency.

The Food and Drug Administration adopted a regulation (to be enforced by states) that required identification for tobacco purchasers looking younger than twenty-seven. A newspaper reported the news without telling of a new *regulation.* The text called it an FDA "crackdown." The headline said, "Teen Smokers Strike Out Under New Law." Neither was wrong in essence, but neither was precise.

To speak of a *law* is customarily to speak of a *statute,* rather than a *regulation.* There are both federal and state *laws;* a municipal law is called an *ordinance.*

Law or *the law* may be used in a general sense to mean the official rules that govern people. *The law* of the United States consists of the Constitution, acts of Congress, treaties, and court rulings. *The law* of each state is its constitution, legislative acts, and court rulings.

Regulation may be used in a general sense to mean governmental direction or control (e.g., "regulation of utilities").

RELATE.

To *relate,* as a transitive verb, is to tell ("She related an anecdote") or to bring into a reasonable association ("He related ancient history to current events").

As an intransitive verb meaning to have a connection or relationship (to something), *relate* goes back about four centuries. ("The critic eye ... examines bit by bit: How parts relate to parts, or they to whole"—Pope.) What is rather new, and questionable, is the popular adoption of a jargonistic use of the intransitive *relate.* To psychologists and social workers, it has meant to get along, interact, have similar ideas, and so on. ("Alice does not relate well with her classmates.")

A newspaper column described an erroneous change made in an author's work and commented, "Not pointing any fingers, but your columnist can relate." To end there, without indicating the relationship, is to be parsimonious with information.

REMAP.

To *map* an area, feature, or journey is to represent it or chart it on a map. To *remap* it is to map it again. It is a word that the general public has little need for. Headline writers need it as a synonym for *reapportion* or *reapportionment.*

It has slopped over into the bodies of articles. A political report said state senators of one party wanted "to keep the legislative primary in June, when the new remap plan would be ready" (rather than switch to March and run in old districts, favoring the other party).

Except for headlines, there is no excuse for *remap* instead of *reapportion(ment).* The two are not the same; as any cartographer knows, changing a map need have nothing to do with changing the distribution of legislative seats.

REMUNERATION and RENUMERATION.

During an investigation of political favoritism in a federal department, a congressman asked a former subordinate of the secretary of housing and urban development: "Are you saying or are you not saying that you think he received renumeration in any way, financial?" (Answer: not saying.) It was the wrong noun.

Remuneration, pronounced re-myoon-uh-RAY-shun, is compensation, reward, or pay for work, service, loss, etc. A related adjective, *remunerative,* means providing remuneration, profitable. Think of *money.*

Renumeration, re-new-muh-RAY-shun, a word that is seldom used except by mistake, means a new *numeration.* A *numeration* is a numbering, counting, or calculation, or a system of numbering. Think of *numbers.*

Repetition and its avoidance. *See* Ellipsis; FORMER; IS IS; LATTER; Numbers, *1;* ONE OF, *2;* Pronouns, *1;* SAID; Series errors, *1, 6;* Synonymic silliness; Tautology; THAT and WHICH, *3;* Twins, *2;* Verbs, *4, 5;* WHICH, *2;* WHO, *2;* WITH, *1.*

REPORT, REPORTED, REPORTEDLY. *See* ACCUSED, ALLEGED (etc.).

RESPECTABLE and RESPECTFUL. In a network telecast from New Hampshire, a news reporter said, "The Cuomo campaign has got to break into the double digits to be respectful." The last word should have been the adjective *respectable* meaning worthy of respect or having a good reputation.

The other adjective, *respectful,* means showing or characterized by respect or deference. "The boy was respectful to his elders."

RESPECTIVE, RESPECTIVELY. *Respectively* is useful in this sentence: "Mr. Graham and Miss Harrison teach boys and girls respectively." It tells us

that Mr. Graham teaches boys and Miss Harrison teaches girls. Without *respectively* one could suppose that each teacher teaches both boys and girls. *Respectively* indicates that each one in a series pertains, in the same order, to a particular one in another series.

In a column on presidential politics, two series that are supposed to jibe "respectively" do not:

> Earlier, senators Estes Kefauver and Eugene McCarthy and Robert Kennedy helped retire Harry Truman and Lyndon Johnson, respectively, with primary fights.

The first series contains three names. The second series contains only two. Those who are not versed in the appropriate political history cannot know how to match them. The sentence should have been reworded, without "respectively," perhaps like this:

> Earlier, Senator Estes Kefauver helped retire Harry Truman with a primary fight, and Senators Eugene McCarthy and Robert Kennedy did the same to Lyndon Johnson.

The sentence below would make sense without *respectively.* It makes no sense with it.

> The first quarter and third quarter respectively are the best seasons for television response, just as they are for print and mail.

What the author (of a book on marketing) meant to convey is obscure. The quarters seem to be equated.

Nor does *respective* serve any clear function in the next sentence, uttered by a mayor.

> This is a private-public partnership, benefits to flow to each one of the respective parties.

Writers sometimes use *respectively* (adverb) or *respective* (adjective) when the respectiveness is obvious: "Michael and Alice will play the parts of Romeo and Juliet respectively." / "The ambassadors from Britain and France returned to their respective countries."

Examples of more informative use: "Mr. and Mrs. Palmer serve as the chairman and treasurer respectively." / "The two defense attorneys are conferring with their respective clients" (not collectively).

RESTAURATEUR. A restaurant reviewer on the radio described two men as "a wonderful restauranteur" and "a legendary restauranteur"; a column and a news story each told of misfortune befalling a "restauranteur"; a national quiz show flashed a query about a "RESTAURANTEUR" on the video screen; and a radio announcer invited listeners to call in questions on "restaurants and restauranteers." All slipped.

A person who owns or manages a restaurant is not a "restauranteur" or "restauranteer" but a *restaurateur,* without *n.* Some dictionaries condone the first misspelling as a variant, but the style manuals of The Associated Press and *The New York Times* permit no *n.* *Restaurateur* comes unchanged from French. It originated in the Latin for *restore.*

Restrictive clause. *See* **THAT and WHICH.**

REVENGE and AVENGE. *See* **Confusing pairs.**

REVEREND. *Mister* is a title, a noun. *Reverend* is a description, an adjective meaning worthy of reverence. Of course, not all clerics are so worthy, but we traditionally give them the benefit of the doubt.

Reverend is comparable to the *Honorable* (or *Hon.*) that is often affixed to the names of public officials. Neither word is properly a noun. Just as a public official is not an "honorable," a clergyman is not a "reverend." (*See also* **HONORABLE, HONORARY, HONORED,** *1.*) A magazine and a newspaper were wrong:

The reverend spoke only for a moment. . . . But the reverend himself insists the young candidate . . . is now on his own.

The only person who offered him any help was a big-bellied reverend. . . . The New York Post ran a front-page photograph of the roly-poly reverend under a hair dryer.

Call him a *churchman,* a *clergyman,* a *cleric,* an *ecclesiastic,* a *minister,* a *pastor,* a *preacher,* a *priest* (if he is Catholic or Episcopal), or any of several other designations, depending on his faith, but do not call him a "reverend" if you want to be proper.

In referring to him, use *Reverend* or, better, *the Reverend,* only with a full name or title; for example, *the Reverend Joseph Cole,* not "the Reverend Cole." We would not speak of a senator as "the Honorable Adams," nor would we address him as "Honorable Adams." In writing, *the Rev.* may be used as an abbreviation.

After the first mention, it is correct to use *the Reverend* (or *the Rev.*) *Mr. Cole* or *the Reverend Dr. Jones* (if he is a doctor of divinity) or simply *Mr. Cole* or *Dr. Jones,* for instance. He may be addressed as *Mr.* or *Dr.* Some clergymen may be referred to and addressed as, e.g., *Father Williams* or *Pastor Robinson.*

It was improper to say that "the Reverend Jackson has been able to broaden his base" or to write that "he disputed the time frame recalled by the Reverend Sparks. . . . " Correction: "the Reverend Mr. Jackson" and "the Reverend Mr. Sparks." Another correct way is exemplified by a *New York Times* article that referred to "The Rev. Jesse Jackson" the first time and "Mr. Jackson" the next seven times.

The television interviewers and moderators addressing "Reverend Jackson" know not what they do. What is wrong with "*Mr.* Jackson"? The minister who tells us, "I'm Reverend Brown," instead of, "I'm Mr. Brown, the minister," or "I'm Pastor Brown," lacks both humility and (worse yet) verbal propriety.

It distressed a pastor's wife that people addressed him too informally in their correspondence. She wrote to a syndicated etiquette columnist, who advised using note cards printed with the heading "The Reverend and Mrs. William Smith." But that would be wrong, for *Mr.* Smith's title would then be left out. "The Reverend *Mr.* and Mrs. William Smith" or "*Pastor* and Mrs. William Smith" would suit a letterhead.

Being an adjective, *Reverend* properly has no plural, unlike the noun *Mister* or *Mr.,* whose plural is *Messrs.* Disregard "Revs. Brown and Smith."

Reversal of meaning. *1. Negatives. 2. Other examples. 3. Reasons.*

1. Negatives

Sometimes a writer, speaker, or editor does not say what he intended to say. He may say the very opposite.

Negatives—too many or too few—are among the sources of danger.

A news agency's dispatch from Cleveland, about an indictment of guardsmen in an infamous case, appeared this way in print:

> The grand jury charged the eight defendants willfully assaulted and intimidated the student demonstrators by firing weapons in their direction, violating their constitutional right to be deprived of liberty without due process of law.

The sentence affirms a "right to be deprived of liberty." To invoke the Fifth and Fourteenth Amendments, insert *not* before "to be deprived."

A court of appeals reversed a decision in a civil case, and then a newspaper reversed the appellate decision by leaving out one word:

> In finding that The Post did commit libel, the court rejected a number of arguments raised by Mr. Tavoulareas's lawyers.

"Did commit" should be "did *not* commit. . . . " (The mistake was not crucial, inasmuch as the headline and lead paragraph summarized the decision. *See also* **NOT,** *1F*.)

In a statement attributed to an Egyptian official, a positive form is mistaken for a negative form. He promotes population control, but some citizens are uneducated:

> "So what I propagate falls on deaf ears. . . . We have a problem with the literate and semi-literate."

The quotation has him saying in effect that those who read and write pose a problem. No doubt "literate" should be *illiterate.* The speaker may have had difficulty expressing himself in English. The reporter could well have paraphrased the statement and corrected it, unless the error escaped him too.

That a reporter quoted someone accurately is no excuse for the publication of a topsy-turvy statement. Regardless of origin, it reflects on both the quoter and the quoted.

If one is not careful, something and nothing can be confused. A radio physician said that anyone with back trouble should have a physician diagnose it before seeking "alternative" treatment, because infrequently the back reflects serious disease, like cancer. He asked rhetorically:

> Isn't that why you go to a doctor, to make sure that small chance that it's nothing awful?

The simplest correction would replace "small" with *large* or *good*. Better: ". . . to *exclude* that small chance that it's *something* awful?"

The next sentence was part of a stock market report on the radio:

> No one appeared panicky, predicting this is just a small glitch in a bull market.

No one is the subject of both *appeared* (verb) and *predicting* (present participle). The speaker literally reported "No one . . . predicting. . . . " Better: "No one appeared panicky. The prevailing view was that. . . . " (Aside from the problem of the negative subject, "predicting this is" is dubious. To *predict* is to foresee the future, not to describe the present.)

The final example in this section is a rhetorical blunder by Mayor Richard Daley of Chicago. After a riot near the Democratic national convention, he held a press conference to defend the police against allegations of brutality toward protesters.

> The confrontation was not created by the police. The confrontation was created by the people who charged the police. Gentlemen, get the thing straight, once and for all. The policeman isn't there to create disorder. The policeman is there to *preserve* disorder.

He probably wanted to say "preserve *order*." Instead he emphasized the wrong word and repeated the negative "dis-."

The possibility of reversing one's meaning inadvertently by using two or more negatives in a sentence is treated in **Double negative,** 2. These are some other hazards:

- "And" instead of *but* following a negative. *See* BUT, *1*.
- *As* with a negative. *See* AS, *4*.
- *But* with "that" or with a negative. *See* BUT, *2, 3*.
- *Not* with another negative, e.g., *not* or *un-*. *See* NOT, *1G*; PROOFREAD, PROOFREADING.
- *Which* used vaguely following a negative. *See* WHICH, *1*.

2. *Other examples*

A congressman is indirectly quoted here on the subject of drugs in public housing projects.

> However, Representative Charles B. Rangel . . . said many drug dealers were known to the tenants but were intimidated by them.

As published, the statement says the drug dealers were intimidated by the tenants. Changing the end of the sentence yields a more plausible message: ". . . but intimidated them" or ". . . but *the tenants* were intimidated by them."

A newspaper headline said, "Assembly barely defeats bill easing water pollution." In announcing that a majority of state assemblymen had declined to alleviate water pollution, the headline reversed the meaning of the news story underneath it. The defeated bill would have relaxed a statute against polluters of state waterways. "Assembly barely defeats bill *to ease pollution law*" would have been accurate (and fit the space available for the headline).

This sentence was part of a report from Jerusalem credited to a news agency:

> Arafat was also angered by Netanyahu's refusal so far to meet him

and to place Israeli troops in Hebron, the only West Bank Town still under occupation.

If the Israeli prime minister had refused to place troops in Hebron, would the Palestinian leader object? Following "and" with *decision* would make the statement true.

To write a headline saying "Cuomo Can Blame America's New Slavery On the Republicans' Neglect of the Poor," an editor probably had to be (1) ignorant of who William F. Buckley was and (2) unable to grasp irony and mockery. (Let us charitably discount the possibility of bias.) In answering a pro-Democratic speech delivered at Gettysburg, Buckley asked rhetorically in a column:

> Whose fault is the new slavery? You guessed it: It is the fault of the Republican Party. From which it follows, does it not, that if Abe Lincoln were alive today, he would be a Democrat?

After stating the neglect-of-the-poor charges, most of the column presented statistics meant to show the poor improving economically. Changing "Can" to *Can't* and putting quotation marks around "New Slavery" would have patched up the headline. But proper portrayal of the columnist's views required a rewrite, such as this: "Poor People Are Faring Better, Despite Cuomo's 'New Slavery' Talk."

Television showed a demonstration against Senator Dole during his presidential election campaign. A newscaster said the protesters objected to "Dole's backing of a ban on assault rifles." A factually correct version would have been "Dole's backing of a *bill to repeal the* ban on assault rifles."

3. Reasons

To offer a general explanation for such reversals would be guessing. Are they caused by absent-mindedness, care-lessness, haste, inattention, lack of thought, misunderstanding, or a mischievous goblin?

The first section deals with troublesome negatives. The second displays three patterns. First, a passive verb is confused with an active verb. Then a crucial noun is left out: *law* or *decision*. Last, ignorance of the views of a personage, Buckley or Dole, is displayed.

Some comparable sources of trouble and the titles of entries that deal with them are listed below.

- Expressions open to opposite interpretations. **Ellipsis; FORWARD and BACK (time); GO OFF and GO ON; GREAT; SCAN.**
- Pairs with opposite meanings. *See* **Confusing pairs** (*energize* and *enervate, hyper-* and *hypo-,* and *sanction* and *sanctions*); **DISINGENUOUS and INGENUOUS; EMIGRATE and IMMIGRATE; PRESCRIBE and PROSCRIBE.**
- Misunderstood terms. *See* **CREDITOR and DEBTOR; WILLY-NILLY; WITH PREJUDICE and WITHOUT PREJUDICE.**
- Misused tense. *See* **Tense,** *5E.*
- Special cases. *See* **Series errors,** 2 (end); **ZERO IN.**

Ambiguity and misunderstanding are treated in many other entries. Consult the cross-reference **Ambiguity.**

REVERSE. *See* **Verbs,** *1C.*

REVERT. This verb (intransitive) means to turn backward, figuratively. Its grandfather was the Latin *revertere,* a product of *re-,* back, and *vertere,* turn. *Back* is implied in *revert.* To *revert* to old ways, a former belief, a past situation, or a topic that came up before is to go back to it. In law, *revert* applies to property or money; it means to go back to a former owner.

In television programs, a member of a panel and an interviewer had these questions: "What's going to happen when Hong Kong reverts back to China?" And when youths go home to hostile lands after camping together, "Don't they simply revert back to who they were?" *Revert(s)* without "back" would have been enough each time.

REVOLT and REVOLUTION.

When Boris Yeltsin ordered the Russian parliament disbanded, some members and sympathizers rebelled and were crushed by forces loyal to Yeltsin. A newspaper's main headline read, "Bloody end to latest revolution in Russia."

"Revolution" was the wrong word. A *revolution* is an overthrow of a political system, or a forcible replacement of a ruler or ruling group, or the seizure of power by a militant group, in each case by forces within the country involved. (In a broader sense, any great social change may be called a *revolution;* for example, the *industrial revolution.*) The French Revolution, the American Revolution, the Russian Revolution (in 1917)—those were indeed *revolutions.* Power was seized; the old regimes were overthrown; new governments were set up.

In Russia in 1993, rebels failed in their attempt to overthrow Yelsin's rule, therefore no "revolution" took place. To be sure, there was a *revolt,* a *rebellion,* an *insurrection,* an *uprising.* Each noun denotes a violent attempt to overthrow a government. (Those terms, most commonly *revolt,* are used at times to describe nonviolent opposition movements. "California's Proposition 13 represented a revolt by taxpayers.") Of course, any such violent attempt at an overthrow may succeed; at that point the *revolt, rebellion,* etc. may be called a *revolution.*

Two related words are *coup d'état* (pronounced coo-day-TAH), a violent overthrow that is sudden, unexpected, and brought about by a small military group; and *putsch* (pronounced something like *push* but with a *t* in the middle), an attempted *coup d'état.*

RHETORICAL QUESTION. *See* Punctuation, 9.

RH FACTOR. *See* FACTOR.

RHINOCEROS. *See* Plurals and singulars, 1; Series errors, 5.

"RICE PADDY." *See* PADDY.

RIGHT confused with WRITE. *See* Homophones.

"RINGING OFF THE HOOK."

These press excerpts all raise the same question: ". . . His phone was ringing off the hook." / ". . . Bugakov's telephone was ringing off the hook with congratulations." / "Businesses have been ringing the phone off the hook to inquire. . . . " / "Her telephone was ringing off the hook yesterday with inquiries from journalists. . . . " / "And the phones rang off the hook at CBS."

How can a phone ring when it is off the hook?

RIVET. *See* Spelling, 1; UNIQUE.

ROBBERY. *See* Crimes, 3.

ROLE and ROLL. *See* Homophones.

ROMANCE LANGUAGE. The

host of a television program of interviews dealing with romantic encounters was talking about the French language. "It's a very romantic language, French, Spanish, and all those romantic languages," he said, confused. French and Spanish—along with Italian, Portuguese, Rumanian, and several regional tongues —are known as *Romance* languages.

Romance language has nothing to do with romance or any romantic quality of these languages. It has to do with their *Roman* origin. They all came mainly from Latin. English adopted its adjective *Romance* from the French *romance,* meaning the Roman language.

ROUND UP and ROUNDUP.

When cowboys *round up* cattle, they bring the animals together in a herd. *Round up* in two words is a verb.

The process or act of herding the cattle is a *roundup.* (In ranching, the herded cattle also are called a *roundup,* and so are the cowboys and horses used in the process.) *Roundup* in one word is a noun.

The terms are not limited to ranch activity. The police may *round up* suspects. Legislators may be *rounded up* for voting. Any act of rounding up animals or people could be called a *roundup.*

In writing a headline saying "Israelis flatten guerrilla base; roundup Shiite males in Tyre," a copy editor wrongly chose the noun, "roundup," instead of the verb, *round up.*

RUIN and RUINS.

Ruins can usually be seen. They are the remains of something that was built but now is destroyed or decayed. "They discovered the ruins of an ancient temple." / "The temple is in ruins."

The singular, *ruin,* may describe the same thing as ruins, that which is destroyed or decayed. "The town is now a ruin." / "The mansion has gone to ruin." Often, though, it is used in a more abstract sense. *Ruin* can refer to the cause ("Fire was its ruin") or to the action, condition, or process ("They witnessed the ruin of the economy").

The singular would have been more idiomatic in a column: ". . . Both [senators] had good reputations[,] now on the verge of ruins." Make it *ruin.* If the destruction were complete, "now *in ruins*"

would be an acceptable metaphor. An alternative to *ruin* in the more abstract sense is *ruination.*

Ruin is pronounced either ROO-in or ROO-n.

See also DEMOLISH.

RULE, RULING.

In a legal sense, to *rule* is to decide judicially, and a *ruling* is an official decision by a court or judge or an authorized body. The words are used inappropriately in the excerpts below. This is from a daily newspaper:

> The city attorney ruled that the council could not be bound in the future by its current intent to put charter reform on the . . . ballot.

A weekly in another city asked whether the city attorney there would

> receive a vote of confidence despite his recent high-handed . . . rulings?. . . . [He] has ruled in seemingly contradictory ways at various times. [And so on. "Ruled" or "ruling(s)" appears six more times.]

Unlike a judge, an attorney for either a public or private entity does not "rule" or make "rulings." He gives opinions. A court may *rule* otherwise.

Some commissions *rule* too, but their staffs do not. A dispatch by a news agency began loosely:

> The staff of the Federal Communications Commission ruled in favor of CBS yesterday on a complaint by five major Protestant churches. . . .

The next paragraph summarized what was fitly termed a "staff opinion."

Rule (verb, transitive and intransitive) can also mean to decree, govern, or dominate.

RUN and RAN. *See* Tense, 5A, B.

RUN and STAND. One who seeks to be elected to any governmental office in the United States *runs* for election. In the United Kingdom, one who seeks election to office *stands* for election. Yet a story in American newspapers said about Democrats in the Senate:

> . . . Several of their members who will stand for re-election next year were elected with the support of traditional black liberals.

It would suit a British paper. The American verb is *run*, not "stand." Unless the writer was new to the United States and unfamiliar with its idiom, her motivation for a usage so strange to American eyes and ears is obscure.

See also **Pronouns,** *3.*

RUN AWAY and RUNAWAY. A newspaper's TV guide listed, among scheduled programs, "Runaway With the Rich and Famous." If the program had dealt with a child fleeing from home, *runaway* (noun) might be right. However, inasmuch as the program urged watchers to *run away* (verb), the two words should have been kept separate.

RUN-OFF. *See* **MAJORITY,** *1.*

Run-on sentence. *1. Classical run-ons. 2. Comma faults.*

1. Classical run-ons

A computer company climaxed a magazine ad in this way: "They build more than computers they build relationships."

Signs throughout vehicles of a city's transit system say, "PLEASE HOLD ON SUDDEN STOPS NECESSARY."

Those are *run-on sentences.* A *run-on sentence* is like two (or more) sentences glued together, end to end. Each is an independent clause; that is, it has a subject and verb and could stand alone as an independent sentence. Right now the two are illegitimately paired, neither separate nor properly joined. They should be either granted full independence as two sovereign sentences or united by means of due punctuation. A semicolon (;) or a dash (—) would unite them properly.

Separated: "They build more than computers. They build relationships." / "PLEASE HOLD ON. SUDDEN STOPS NECESSARY." (Better: "SUDDEN STOPS *ARE* NECESSARY.")

Joined: "They build more than computers; they build relationships." Or "They build more than computers—they build relationships." A colon (:) could be used for punctuation instead. Any of those marks would fit the transit notice.

2. Comma faults

A common form of run-on (which some classify as a separate defect) is the *comma fault,* also known as the *comma splice.* It purports to make a comma the punctuation between two independent clauses. A comma cannot handle the job. It neither separates nor joins the two clauses adequately. The first example is from a main news story:

> In 1949 Gov. Alfred E. Driscoll, a Republican, offered him a seat on the New Jersey Superior Court, he gratefully accepted.

One way to correct the example is to change the third comma to a period and make the last three words a separate sentence. A second way is to change that comma to a semicolon. A third way is to substitute a conjunction, namely *and.*

Similarly, the comma is inadequate in this snippet from a magazine article:

> Catholics didn't sing, everyone knew that.

Split it into two three-word sentences or swap the comma for a semicolon or dash.

The failure to stop a sentence properly can produce ambiguity:

"I just can't stand the noise, from seven in the morning until quitting time it's driving me crazy," said Dee. . . .

Start a new sentence (or insert a semicolon or dash) either after "noise" or after "time." It depends on which meaning the speaker intended to express.

Anyone sensitive to English might object to being quoted faultily. A book editor had the mixed fortune to be helped in publicizing one of her books but to be saddled with two comma faults in one article.

. . . The news about astrology "is certainly the most titillating of this amazing account, that's what whetted the public appetite. . . . The Reagans are noted for their skill in handling the media, now their tactics are somehow being turned on them in the media."

A school principal could be displeased by the comma fault (and the omission of a second *in?*):

"I deal with kids in trouble, these kids were not trouble."

An extract from a book of essays is next. (Six other quotations are from a single, prominent newspaper.)

This time, though, it is not the single insect that is the Wonder, it is the collectivity.

Because the first thought leads into the second, a colon would be an additional option here. ". . . It is not the single insect that is the Wonder: it is the collectivity."

The following excerpt is abridged, but the full sentence has fifty-two words and five clauses, with four separable ideas. Why would the writer want to make it any more complex than it has to be?

. . . She could not comment on any specific cases, "but we have been working together for 14 months with the subcommittee, clearly we are concerned any time there is a allegation of serious wrongdoing. . . . "

It should be ". . . with the subcommittee. Clearly we are concerned" etc. (And "a allegation" should be "*an* allegation." But whose error was it? *See* **A and AN**.) The final quotation is a translation of a speech by a foreign leader:

So let us develop democracy and glastnost, let us be attentive to the needs of every nation and people, minorities included, let us find the ways of resolving their problems. . . .

Let us change the first and third commas to semicolons.

See also **FOREVER; Punctuation,** 2A, 3A, 11A.

S

SAFE-DEPOSIT BOX. Deposits in this box are safe. So it is a *safe-deposit* box, a metal box for storing valuables in a vault. These press excerpts are wrong:

> Barlow would keep the certificates in a safety deposit box and turn them over to the county for renewal. . . .

> Police accidentally discovered that safety deposit boxes in a Lithuanian bank were stuffed with four tons of radioactive material. . . .

Make it *safe-,* not "safety." *Safe* (adjective) describes the deposit, not the box. The writers may have been thinking of *safety pin* or *safety belt,* in which "safety" (a noun serving as an adjective) directly describes the hardware.

SAHARA. "When I awoke we were above the Sahara Desert," an author wrote. Another wrote, ". . . Imagine yourself engaged in an amateur archaeological dig somewhere in the Sahara Desert." That is the popular name that speakers of English give to the largest desert on earth, comprising 3.5 million square miles in northern Africa. It is not a serious lapse to use the phrase, though some find it redundant.

Sahara is not a typical geographical name, like Bering (Sea) or Falkland (Is-lands), imposed on a particular feature to distinguish it from others of its kind. It never had a special name. *Sahara* means *desert* in Arabic. (Arabs stress the *sa* or *ra,* depending on regional dialect. We stress the *ha.*)

Inasmuch as most of us English speakers consider it just a name and few of us know Arabic, "Sahara Desert" should not offend many ears or eyes. No one seems to object to "Gobi Desert," though *gobi* is a Mongolian term for a desert. But those who wish to be scrupulous in referring to the Sahara—or the Gobi—may omit "Desert." Similarly, "River" and "Mountains" may be omitted from mentions of the *Rio Grande* and the *Sierra Nevada* in recognition of the Spanish terms. (*Río:* river. *Sierra:* rocky mountain range.) And "Mount" need not preface *Fujiyama,* in Japan, though *Mount Fuji* will do.

Sometimes *sahara,* in lower case, means a desert in general: "If the soil is not cared for, fertile farm land can turn into a sahara." Used in that way, *sahara* is certainly enough.

See also **DESERT and DESSERT.**

SAID. As an adjective, meaning mentioned or named before ("said property" or "said witness"), it is legal jargon and should be restricted to legal or business documents. Synonyms are *aforementioned* and *aforesaid,* formal words that are a shade more usable in nonlegal contexts.

Nonlawyers use *said* as an adjective in the belief that they are being jocose. A columnist wrote, after quoting a literary passage: "This is a joke. However, said joke did not survive the ministrations of the proofreaders. . . . " The adjectival *said* had been classified as "WORN-OUT HUMOUR" by H. W. Fowler some seventy years earlier. It can usually be replaced by *the:* "However, *the* joke. . . . "

As a verb, *said,* or *say* or *says,* is normally a good, unbiased word, an indispensable tool of celebrated writers. Some writers, especially journalists, strive unnecessarily to avoid *he said* or *she said* or the like by substituting such verbs as *announce(d), assert(ed), aver(red), declare(d), disclose(d), maintain(ed), note(d), observe(d), report(ed),* and *state(d).* Each is a proper word when chosen to express its particular meaning, not arbitrarily as a synonym. Some substituted phrases may even suggest bias. *See* ACCORDING TO; FACT; POINT OUT.

SANCTION and SANCTIONS. *See* Confusing pairs.

SARCASM, SATIRE. *See* IRONY (etc.).

SAVING and SAVINGS. *See* Confusing pairs.

SAW and SEEN. *See* Tense, 5A.

SAY, SAYS. *See* SAID.

SCALD and SCOLD. In a television program on rescues, a policeman told of "a child who had been scolded by hot water." Sorry, Officer; you got it wrong. The child was *scalded.*

To *scald* (verb), rhyming with *called,* is to burn someone with hot water or steam (transitive) or to be burned by it (intransitive). To *scold* (verb, transitive and intransitive), rhyming with *told,* is to criticize adversely and angrily.

A *scald* (noun) is an injury caused by scalding. A *scold* (noun) is one who scolds often.

SCAN. Using and interpreting *scan* (verb, transitive) requires caution, for it has two contradictory meanings. Its strict meaning is to examine closely, carefully, and systematically; to scrutinize. This is correct:

> Astronomers scanning the sky through the Hubble Space Telescope have detected and photographed an object far beyond our solar system that appears to be a runaway giant planet. . . .

A modern, popular meaning of *scan* is to look at or read quickly and superficially: "I bought the paper, but I've only had time to scan the headlines." That is one meaning of *skim* (verb, transitive and intransitive). Perhaps whoever started using *scan* in that way was confusing the two words.

Trouble can arise when the context does not indicate which meaning of *scan* is intended: "Harris, scan this report and tell me what you think of it." Whether the boss wants his employee to *study* the report or *glance* at it is not clear.

The strict meaning of *scan* harmonizes with a technical sense: to beam electrons, light, or sound in a systematic pattern for transmission, reproduction, or reflection. *Scan* also means to analyze the meter and rhythm of verse. That is the oldest sense of the word; pertinent quotations in *The Oxford English Dictionary* begin with one from 1398 using *scanne.* (In those last two senses, the verb can be transitive or intransitive.)

The *Oxford* does not recognize the newer, popular use. *Webster's Third* does. Its two illustrations are "read several and scan the rest" / "scanned the film advertisements." But could one not scrutinize film advertisements?

SCARCELY. *See* **THAN,** 2E.

Scientific writing. *See* **Active voice and passive voice.**

SCRIP and SCRIPT. *See* **Confusing pairs.**

SEARCH AND SEIZURE. *See* **Warrant.**

SEASONABLE and SEASONAL. *See* **Confusing pairs.**

SECOND. A *second* of time is a 60th of a minute or a 3,600th part of an hour, strictly speaking. One learns not to take that noun literally all the time, perhaps after someone on the telephone has issued an order to "hold on a second."

Using the word for *a moment, a short while, minutes,* or *hours* can be absurd, particularly when a more exact unit of time is specified. In a TV discussion, this was said: "Apparently at the last second, hours before the [scheduled] announcement, the president changed his mind" (about giving needles to drug addicts). The panelist would have done well without "at the last second."

SEEING EYE. *Seeing Eye* is a trademark and therefore should be capitalized. Often it is not; a syndicated column refers vaguely to "an outfit that trained seeing-eye dogs. . . . "

The only outfit that has ever trained Seeing Eye dogs is The Seeing Eye, Inc., of Morristown, New Jersey. That institution is the best-known trainer of dogs to lead blind people.

If a dog has been trained elsewhere for the job or if you do not know whether such a dog is a Seeing Eye, then call it a *guide dog* or a *dog guide* or any doggone thing that describes it except "seeing-eye dog."

SEEN and SAW. *See* **Tense,** 5A.

"SELDOM EVER." *See* (-)**EVER,** 6.

SELECTION. *See* **Verbs,** 2.

SELF- prefix. Hundreds of hyphenated words are formed with *self-*, a combining form that has to do with the self, oneself, or itself. A few legitimate examples are the nouns *self-control, self-defense, self-government, self-preservation,* and *self-service;* and the adjectives *self-confident, self-conscious, self-employed, self-reliant,* and *self-taught.* When pertaining to inanimate objects, as in *self-cleaning, self-closing, self-locking, self-loading,* and *self-sealing,* the combining form means automatic or by itself.

Self- is sometimes superfluous, notwithstanding dictionary definitions. It contributes nothing to the meaning when a man is described as "a self-confessed war criminal." Omit "self-" and see if anything is lost in *self-collected, self-conceited, self-poise,* and many other combinations, some of them absurd: "His clan elders [in Somalia] . . . selected the same 33-year-old son . . . to become the new president of Mr. Aidid's self-proclaimed republic." If it was proclaimed by Mr. Aidid, it was not "self-proclaimed," i.e., proclaimed by itself.

-SELF, -SELVES endings. *See* **Pronouns,** 3, 4, 5.

SEMI- and BI- prefixes. *See* **BI- and SEMI- prefixes.**

Semicolon. *See* **Punctuation,** 11.

-S ending. *See* **Plurals and singulars,** 2A, K; **Punctuation,** 1G.

SENILE, SENILITY. A history book says of Samuel Adams, among the signers of the Declaration of Independence,

"He was fifty-four, an advanced age in this group, near senility." Whether the writing is cutely archaic or benightedly out of date is hard to say, but the use of "senility" calls for discussion.

Senior and *seniority* stem from the Latin *senex*, old. So do *senile* and *senility*, and in past centuries they merely meant aged and old age; moreover, they could be used approvingly: Writers referred to "senile Maturity of Judgement" (1661) and "vigorous senility" (1822).

In the mid-nineteenth century, diseases of lung, heart, and head began being prefixed with *senile:* for instance, *senile dementia*. Eventually *senile* (adjective) and *senility* (noun) took on a pejorative cast, pertaining to the infirmities thought to inevitably accompany old age, particularly mental incompetence.

Today it is known that different individuals age differently, that senility in the sense of mental deterioration is not an inevitable concomitant of aging, that some so-called senile behaviors are reversible, and that some younger people suffer symptoms associated with aging that some extremely aged individuals do not. George Bernard Shaw and P. G. Wodehouse were writing plays and novels respectively in their nineties. The comedian George Burns lived to 100 and was entertaining the country nearly to the end.

Sentence fragment. 1. *In writing*. 2. *Verbless newscasts*.

1. *In writing*

Isolated phrases can be effective at times, particularly in belles-lettres and drama. This is from *Romeo and Juliet:*

> O lamentable day! . . . O woful time! . . . Accursed, unhappy, wretched, hateful day! . . . O woe! O woful, woful, woful day!

Turning those phrases into complete sentences (e.g., "It is a lamentable day") would weaken, not strengthen, them. But most of Shakespeare's writings adhere to the norms of English sentence structure; and that is usually the best course for a writer, particularly in informative prose.

In general, nonfiction writers should strive to be clear, not to be literary. The information must flow smoothly from author to reader. An aborted sentence cuts off the flow.

Sometimes newspapers and more often newscasters use pieces of sentences, either through slovenliness or intentionally for some kind of effect. The effect usually is to hinder, not help, the reader or listener. This is from a daily:

> About a half-hour had passed when police finally noticed that the paddy wagon was empty. Except for a fifth guy who just sat there staring at the hole.

First we read that the wagon was empty—period. Then comes a sentence fragment telling us, in effect, that the previous message was untrue. The two pieces sorely need unification: ". . . the paddy wagon was empty, except for. . . . "

Normally a complete sentence has a subject (the doer of the action) and a predicate (what the subject does). But a subject and predicate may not be enough to make sense. A pair of authors wrote in an instruction manual for a computer program:

> Whereas the *Exactly as typed* option will save the word exactly as you input it. Selecting *Remove* takes the displayed word out of the dictionary.

Again two pieces cry for union. The opening fragment makes no sense alone; the conjunction "whereas" indicates that a more or less contrasting passage will follow later in the sentence. Change the first period to a comma and continue with "selecting. . . . "

A *sentence fragment* is also known as a *phrase* (particularly when it lacks a subject or a predicate), an *incomplete sentence,* and a *cut-short sentence.* It is roughly the opposite of a run-on sentence. Whereas the writer of the run-on does not know when to stop, it seems that the writer of the fragment does not know enough to go. (*See* **Run-on sentence.**)

2. *Verbless newscasts*
Each of these four excerpts from radio newscasts has the same fault: "On Wall Street the Dow Jones up. . . . " / "An unmanned rocket set to lift off at the Cape Canaveral Air Force station this evening." / "A Fairfield police officer clinging to life after five hours of surgery." / "A hostage situation continuing in the San Bernardino area."

Each lacks a verb, at least an auxiliary. (*See* **Verbs.**) The thoughts as broadcast are incomplete; listeners may be thrown off track, prepared for such completed sentences as these: "An unmanned rocket set to lift off at the Cape Canaveral Air Force station this evening *has burned up*"; or "A Fairfield police officer clinging to life after five hours of surgery *has lost his fight.*" Numerous additional examples of sloppy, verbless newscasting could be cited.

A simple *is* would rescue each of the four samples from fragmentation: ". . . The Dow Jones *is* up. . . . " / "An unmanned rocket *is* set. . . . " / "A Fairfield police officer *is* clinging. . . . " / "A hostage situation *is* continuing. . . . "

Other verbs could strengthen those sentences: "the Dow Jones *rose* . . ."; the "rocket *lifts* off . . ."; the "officer *clings* to life . . ."; the "hostage situation *continues.* . . . "

A newscaster announced on a radio network: "Jeffrey Dahmer, convicted of murder three years ago, murdered himself in a Wisconsin prison." The announcement was momentarily puzzling, raising the question of how someone could murder himself. The newscaster (or writer) had left out *was* or *has been* before "murdered"; it took over as an active verb, creating an absurdity.

See also **Punctuation,** 2C (colons and verbless writing).

SENTIMENT and SENTIMENTALITY. *See* **Confusing pairs.**

Sequence of events. *See* **Tense,** 5B.

Series errors. *1. AND shortage. 2. Confusion and distortion. 3. Inconsistency, unrelated to conjunctions. 4. Labeling. 5. Multiple paragraphs. 6. OR shortage. 7. Punctuation. 8. Repeated conjunctions. 9. Superfluous word.*

1. *AND shortage*

A. Illogical shift
What is out of place in this series? A, B, C, 4. Finding such a question on an intelligence test, most writers and editors would have no problem with it. Yet we constantly read or hear series just as illogical as that one. Take this sentence, from a syndicated column:

> She studied English, Yiddish, Hebrew, and married a man who had money.

That is typical. The writer enumerates a series of nouns (such as languages that someone studied) and then—without properly concluding the series—switches abruptly to a verb (an action of hers). Sometimes a series of adjectives shifts to a verb, or a series of verbs shifts to a clause, or a series is inconsistent in some other way.

Let us define a *series* as an enumeration, a list, or a set of grammatically equal words or phrases. (The plural form of the word is the same: many *series*.) Within a sentence, a conjunction, like *and*, commonly appears before the final item in a series. When we read or listen to an enumeration of items, *and* leads us to expect one more item.

Thus, the sample sentence is corrected in this way: "She studied English, Yiddish, *and* Hebrew and married. . . . " The added *and* ties the languages together. They make up a series of nouns. More precisely, the nouns may be considered a subseries; the main series consists of the verbs "studied" and "married," linked together by the second "and." (The marriage part remains irrelevant, but at least the sentence now is grammatical. The third comma becomes superfluous.)

This is a warning on cigarette packages:

Smoking Causes Lung Cancer, Heart Disease, Emphysema, And May Complicate Pregnancy.

The notice enumerates three maladies (nouns) that smoking causes. Seeing "And," we expect a fourth and last malady, e.g., "Complications of Pregnancy." Instead, the verb "May Complicate" appears. It can stay if we end the series of nouns right: ". . . Heart Disease, *And* Emphysema. . . . " (Why All The Capitals?)

This is from a prominent newspaper:

State court Judge Lawrence Weiss Friday sentenced Mr. B—— to 10 years in state prison, 18 months in county jail and fined him more than $46,000. . . .

The "and" leads us to expect that one more comparable item will follow: ". . . 10 years in state prison, 18 months in county jail, and *a fine of* more than $46,000. . . . " The writer started out

enumerating punishments (nouns), then switched to what a judge did (verb). To keep the final part of the original sentence, the series of nouns must be duly concluded: ". . . 10 years in state prison *and* 18 months in county jail. . . . " (*See also* ON, 1.)

The derailment of a series ranks high among the most common errors found in print. The main cause of it is the fear of repetition, even the repetition of so inoffensive a word as *and*. The little conjunction intimidates many writers. They seem to think they are rationed to one *and* per sentence. Just what cataclysmic events do they think would ensue if they transgressed that limit?

Repetition in the pursuit of clarity is no vice. The detriment from avoiding the *and* far outweighs any conceivable advantage. A disorderly series is as discomforting as an ill-fitting garment. What is worse: it can be confusing, as we will see in 2.

B. More shifts of nouns
Four more examples of a nouns-to-verb switch (from another prominent newspaper) follow below. The simplest way to repair the sentences is to replace each comma with *and*.

. . . He has brought shame to himself, scandal to his industry and shattered the legend of a man whose financial skills seemed invincible.

Mr. Itsuki . . . has sold 20 million singles, 4 million LP's and has a 15,000-member fan club. . . .

. . . One must do 20 pull-ups with the feet never touching the ground, 80 sit-ups in two minutes with the feet held down and run three miles in 18 minutes.

Below we have a shift from one category of nouns to another. "And" already appears twice. The thought of a third may be too much for an *and*-fearing writer.

> . . . The report was based on information from archives in the United States, Yugoslavia and "submissions and documents provided by Mr. Waldheim."

The main series consists of "information from archives . . . and 'submissions and documents. . . . ' " Neither "and" has anything to do with the *and* needed in the subseries ensuing from "archives in." The subseries is "the United States *and* Yugoslavia."

Amid the 1,550 largely impeccable pages of a general dictionary, under *past participle,* we find the sentence below, in which a series of nouns shifts to a prepositional phrase. The meaning is clear, but the lapse stands out in a dictionary that normally is strong in matters of grammar.

> It is used as a verbal adjective in phrases such as *finished work, baked beans,* and with auxiliaries to form the passive voice or perfect and pluperfect tenses in constructions such as *The work was finished* and *She had baked the beans.*

Replace the first comma with *and.* The second comma may then be deleted.

C. *Shift of adjectives to verb*

> He's capable, honest, intelligent, dull and tries too hard.

That press example and the four below display the same, incorrect form. There is a series of two verbs: an auxiliary verb ("is" or "was") and an active verb (e.g., "tries"). They are connected by "and." The first verb goes with a subseries of adjectives ("capable" etc.), which abruptly shifts to the second verb.

To correctly complete the enumeration of things that the subject is or was, insert *and* before "dull" in the example above; in the four below, replace each comma with *and.* The *and* needed to connect the adjectives has nothing to do with the existing "and" that connects the verbs.

> He was jobless, strapped for cash and owed $12,000 to friends and relatives.

> . . . Ameche is charming, gracious and still sports the pencil-thin moustache. . . .

> . . . It was modern, very well constructed and enjoyed a panoramic Bay view. . . .

> The weapon is six inches long, battery-powered and can deliver a charge of up to 40,000 volts.

D. *Skewed verb series*

One phrase is out of place in this sentence (from a New York newspaper):

> The House provisions would restrict American nuclear tests, weapons production, ban antisatellite tests in space and curb money for the President's 'Star Wars' research program. . . .

The three verbs, "restrict . . . ban . . . curb," all pertaining to "would," are inconsistent with the noun "weapons production." The noun hangs there senselessly, although it was meant to pertain to "restrict." Either insert a verb—e.g., "*hold back* weapons production"—or insert an *and* to complete the subseries "nuclear tests *and* weapons production." In addition, "American" is illogically applied to only one item; anyway it is unnecessary in a story about bills in the American Congress. (The quotation marks around "Star Wars" should be double. Single marks would be right in a British publication. *See* **Punctuation,** *10*.)

In each of the examples below (from the same newspaper and two books), an enumeration of verbs abruptly shifts to an independent clause (that is, a part of a sentence that could be a sentence itself). Place *and* in front of "pays" and "bank" and the first "put."

The job of mayor carries little in the way of patronage, pays only $5,000 a year and the incumbent . . . is always under political pressure.

To stay alive, you have to be able to hold out against equilibrium, maintain imbalance, bank against entropy, and you can only transact this business with membranes in our kind of world.

He [Johnson] read these [books], underlined words, put initials in the margins as cues, and his copyists put the words and the sentences in which they occurred on slips of papers.

Again, the single "and" is not enough. Its only function is to connect the independent clause (beginning "the incumbent is" or "you can only transact" or "and his copyists put") to the rest of the sentence. Another *and* is still needed to complete the series of things that "the job of mayor" does or that "you have to be able to" do or that Johnson did.

The next sentence begins enumerating verbs and suddenly shifts to nouns:

. . . The metal can damage the central nervous system, cause hearing loss, lowered intelligence, and irritability. . . .

The main series comprises "damage . . . *and* cause. . . . "

The final example in this section fails

to separate passive verbs from an active verb.

He will make "Biko" . . . about the controversial black leader (Steven Biko) who was arrested, imprisoned and subsequently died in jail.

"Was" applies only to "arrested *and* imprisoned." The *and* needed to join that subseries of two passive verbs has nothing to do with the "and" linking it to the active verb, "died."

Verbs, *5*, deals with a shortage of objects, which may be accompanied by a shortage of conjunctions, in a verb series.

2. *Confusion and distortion*

It [epinephrine] is employed therapeutically as a vasoconstrictor, cardiac stimulant, and to relax bronchioles.

If a lay reader of that excerpt from a medical dictionary concludes that two purposes for the drug have been enumerated, it is understandable. The writer should have replaced the first comma with *and,* omitting the second comma. Using a comma instead of a needed conjunction can make it appear that the second item is part of or explaining the first when it is really separate from the first.

In the next quotation, the lack of an *and* in the right place distorts the meaning. The phrases in question are all nouns.

Without mentioning Democratic presidential nominee Michael Dukakis by name, Bush attacked his opponent's lack of foreign policy experience, opposition to a missile defense program and U.S. aid for anti-communist insurgencies, such as the Nicaraguan Contras.

By logic and grammar, the sentence seems to be saying that Bush attacked

Dukakis's aid for insurgencies. One who had not been following the issues could have so concluded with good reason. After all, a conjunction heralds the end of a series, and here is an *and* just before the last of three grammatically equal items, all apparently coming under "his opponent's." Actually, there are only two main items: (1) "Lack of foreign policy experience" and (2) "opposition to a missile defense program and U.S. aid. . . . " Place *and* between those two main items to rescue the sentence. For extra clarity, you could elaborate: e.g., "*and Dukakis's* opposition *both* to a missile defense program and *to* U.S. aid. . . . "

The next example is inconsistent in more than one way. In attempting to avoid repetition at all costs, the writer became mired in confusion.

> Between 1983 and 1985, the town fined Ocean Spray $7,800, $6,600 in 1986 and will receive a a bill for $10,000 for 1987.

A correct sentence could say: "The town fined Ocean Spray $7,800 between 1983 and 1985 and $6,600 in 1986 and will give the company a bill of $10,000 for 1987." Presumably that is the meaning. The context provides no reason for the town's giving the company money. Furthermore, starting the sentence with the phrase "Between 1983 and 1985" leads one to expect that it will carry over to other parts of the sentence. "The town," the sentence's subject, is what ought to carry over to other parts, specifically to a series of two verbs: one telling what the town did—"fined"—and the other telling what it "will" do. Under "fined" comes a subseries: "7,800 . . . *and* $6,600."

3. Inconsistency, unrelated to conjunctions

In the example below from a quarterly journal, the trouble does not lie in a conjunction. An enumeration of nouns is marred by the introduction of an adjective.

Terminology may vary slightly, but the news dimensions/attributes are generally agreed to be timeliness, proximity, prominence, impact, conflict, magnitude, oddity and visual.

Following seven nouns, from *timeliness* to *oddity*, the adjective "visual" is out of place. Instead, a noun, such as *color* or *pictorialness* (or whatever the writer had in mind) would have been appropriate. *See also 5.*

4. Labeling

It should be unnecessary to point out that when a series is numbered (1, 2, 3, etc.) or lettered (A, B, C, etc.), the same system must be followed throughout. Yet here is what a TV network news man said on a radio talk show; he was stating his objections to Republican efforts in Congress to balance the federal budget:

> A, they're moving too fast; and *second*, they're meddling in social issues.

5. Multiple paragraphs

Sometimes the items in a series are listed in separate paragraphs. When they are, no conjunction is needed. A mark precedes each paragraph, unless a number or letter precedes it; the mark usually is a *bullet*, a black circle or square. The example below, from an article, is defective.

> The film features more than 12 minutes of computer effects from ILM . . . including:
>
> - A stampede of three-dimensional elephants, rhinos and zebras. . . .
> - A playful band of monkeys messing up the kitchen of a . . . mansion. . . .
> - The mansion is also invaded by a snarling lion and a thundering herd of rhinos.

The three bullets indicate three items in the series. As in any series, all of its items must be grammatically alike. The writer has set out to list various computer effects included in a film; the word "including" needs to fit each item. It does fit the first two items, which are noun phrases, but not the third item, which is a complete sentence. "Including" would fit the third too if it said, for instance: "*An invasion* by a snarling lion and a thundering herd of rhinos." To make the second item more compatible, begin it with a noun representing the action, comparable to "A stampede," for instance: "A messing of the kitchen of a . . . mansion by a playful band of monkeys."

6. OR *shortage*

What applies to the conjunction *and* in earlier discussions can apply to the conjunction *or.* This is from a book about the book business:

. . . Not all authors are promotable, well spoken, or have books that lend themselves to promotion.

After "promotable" insert *or.* (And omit the commas.) The "or" that joins the verbs, "are . . ." and "have . . . ," has nothing to do with the *or* needed to join the adjectives, "promotable" and "well spoken."

The following sentence is more complicated. It is from a government circular explaining that names, titles, and short phrases may not be copyrighted.

This is true even if the name, title, phrase, or expression is novel, distinctive, or lends itself to a play on words.

The sentence has three series. The first, consisting of four nouns, is perfectly proper. There is also a series of verbs, consisting of the second "is . . ." and "lends. . . . " Under the second "is," a subseries of two adjectives needs to be joined by a conjunction: "novel *or* distinctive."

7. *Punctuation*

In a series of two, the items are not ordinarily separated by a comma. In a longer series, you will find the last two items sometimes separated by a comma, sometimes not. It depends on what you are reading. *The Chicago Manual of Style,* used by book editors, favors the comma and so does this book. The style of nearly all newspapers is to leave out the comma, on the grounds that a conjunction takes its place. The book style goes "blood, toil, tears, and sweat." The newspaper style goes "blood, toil, tears and sweat."

The argument for omitting the comma is disputable, for both theoretical and practical reasons. A comma and a conjunction have different functions. A comma separates items; a conjunction joins them. If it is important to separate *blood* and *toil* and *tears* from one another, it should be just as important to separate *tears* and *sweat* from each other. The comma does so. The conjunction does not; it links all the four items into a series.

A related practice of many newspapers is odder yet: After using one or more semicolons to separate some items in a series, a writer turns to a comma to separate the last two items. Just as a comma does not have the function of a conjunction, it does not have the function of a semicolon.

Both practices can lead to confusion. Consistent punctuation is indispensable in a complicated series. It enables readers to mentally separate the different categories and place everything in the right category.

An article deals with "spies in the CIA, the NSA, the Navy's antisubmarine warfare program and Navy communications and Middle East intelligence operations." After "NSA" the boundaries get murky. To clarify them, follow "program" and "communications" with commas and delete the first "and" (assuming that five items are listed).

See also **Punctuation,** *3, 11.*

8. *Repeated conjunctions*

For emphasis or extra clarity, a conjunction may follow each item of a series. Excerpts from the Magna Carta (with emphasis added) will illustrate.

> No freeman shall be taken, *or* imprisoned, *or* disseized, *or* outlawed, *or* exiled, *or* in any way harmed . . . save by the lawful judgment of his peers or by the law of the land. . . .
> . . . For the sake of God, *and* for the bettering of our realm, *and* for the more ready healing of the discord which has arisen between us and our barons, we have made all these aforesaid concessions. . . .

9. *Superfluous word*

The problem with the sentence below, from a computer book, is not that it needs an extra conjunction but that it contains an extra article.

> Given the indicators in the status bar, you can tell the document number, page number, line number, and the position of the cursor.

The "the" just before "document number" covers all the four items enumerated. Omit the "the" just before "position of the cursor."

An unneeded pronoun, the second "she," appears in the next sentence, by a news agency. The first *she* is the subject for all the verbs.

> She stood alone in backing the 1986 U.S. bombing raid on Libya; followed Washington out of UNESCO in 1985; was the first to deploy U.S. cruise missiles in Europe in 1983; and last year, when the superpowers agreed to remove the missiles, she put aside her reservations and gave the deal a ringing endorsement.

See also IN A WORD; Numbers, 10B (end); Prepositions, 8. They contain examples of verbs and a preposition that are superfluous in series.

SERVE and SERVICE. *See* Confusing pairs.

SET and SIT. The sun, cement, and setters *set*. People, courts, and most objects *sit*.

"Set" in place of *sit* is dialectal and nonstandard—with some exceptions: clothing and setting hens *set* or *sit*. There is no exception in the sentence below, from an article:

> Are your mirrors secured to the wall, or are they setting on a bureau leaning against the wall ready to come down in a shower of glass?

Change "setting" to *sitting*. (And insert commas after "bureau" and "wall" to make it clear that the bureau is not leaning against the wall and the wall is not ready to come down.)

SET UP and SETUP. *Set up* is a verb (transitive) meaning to establish, begin, create, assemble, or place (something or someone) in a high or upright position. "He set up the business ten years ago." / "Can you set up the tent?" Informally it means to make (someone) appear guilty. "The police set him up."

Setup is a noun designating a plan, arrangement, or organization or the way in which something is set up. "The diagram describes the *setup* of our agency." Informally it denotes a supposed contest in which the outcome is known in advance. "This fight is a setup."

A note printed on software envelopes says, "You may setup your software on your new computer if you delete it from your old computer." Change "setup" to *set up*.

SEWAGE and SEWERAGE. *See* Confusing pairs.

SEX and GENDER. See GENDER and SEX.

SEXY. *Sexy* is a colloquial adjective that means arousing sexual desire or intended to arouse it. So when a network news program announced that the Democrats had found "an issue more sexy than deficits," many viewers must have been disappointed to learn that the issue was ethics and corruption. If the story had any sexual angle, it was not made clear.

The word has commercial value. Ads promoted "The Sexy European," not a human being but an automobile. Another car drew praise on the cover of an automotive magazine for being "Smooth, Strong, Silky, Sexy." The whys and hows of the supposed auto eroticism were not explained, nor was it specified whether the machines were male or female.

Shakespeare. *See* AS and LIKE, *1;* BORE, BORNE, and BORN; Clichés; DISCOMFIT and DISCOMFORT; HONORABLE, HONORARY, HONORED, *3;* KIND OF, *1, 3;* LITERALLY; Possessive problems, *1;* Prepositions, *3;* Pronouns, *2A;* Punctuation, *5A, 6;* Sentence fragment, *1;* SHAMBLES; THAT, *4;* THIS, *1;* VITAL; WEIRD; WHEREFORE and WHEREOF; WHO and WHOM, *2;* WILLY-NILLY.

SHALL. *See* Tense, *4.*

SHAMBLES. At one time a *shamble* was a table for the sale of meat. The Old English *scamel* had originated in the Latin *scamellum,* small bench.

The word took on the meaning of a slaughterhouse. Usually *s* would be added at the end, but the word might be construed as either singular or plural.

By extension, *shambles* became a scene of carnage or extensive bloodshed. In Shakespeare's *King Henry VI, Part III,* the king says: "Far be the thought of this from Henry's heart, / To make a shambles of the parliament-house!" It was probably a fresh metaphor in Elizabethan times.

The meaning of a literal slaughterhouse is obsolete. If you wish to use *shambles* in its purest extant form, you can still use it to describe a scene of widespread bloodshed. For instance, "Tribal enmity has made Rwanda a shambles." Whether you will be understood is uncertain, for casual use has watered down the word's common function to the point of triviality. The element of bloodshed is rarely present anymore. Sometimes the word is applied to extensive destruction. More often it is used to describe mere disarray or confusion, in the manner of the following examples.

[From a news agency:] The apartment was a shambles, with drawers open, clothes strewn around, "all the flatware on the floor, all the silverware out. . . ."

[A music review:] The second movement in "Jupiter" is outlandishly fast, while the finale is reduced to a manic shambles as the players audibly struggle to get in all the notes.

[A form letter:] . . . The Enforcement Division—perhaps EPA's most important arm—is a shambles.

[A headline:] His life a shambles, De Lorean faces a maze of legal troubles

There is no bloodshed, no destruction. Applied to those scenes, even *ruin* would be an extravagance. They might display *chaos, confusion, disarray,* or *disorder,* but is there "a shambles" anywhere?

To Sir Ernest Gowers, using "shambles" to describe a "mere muddle and disorder that is wholly bloodless is a SLIPSHOD EXTENSION emasculating the word." More grammatical authorities condone the looser uses than condemn them. But you may choose.

SHE and HER. *See* **Pronouns,** *10.*

SHEAR. *1. SHEAR and SHEER. 2. SHEAR OFF.*

1. SHEAR and SHEER

In reporting that a bank "has sheered its permanent employee roster by a chunky 11,000," a weekly paper showed that it was just as capable of mixing up words as a daily was. The verb that should have appeared was *sheared.*

To *shear* is to cut (something) with shears or as if with shears, to cut from, or to remove by cutting. To *sheer* is to swerve, to deviate, to turn away from a course ("The ship sheered off its course to rescue the survivors"), or to cause to swerve or deviate.

The two verbs (each transitive and intransitive) are pronounced the same; and *sheer* may have begun as a form of *shear,* which goes back to Old English. Nowadays, however, you do not *sheer* and *shear* alike.

See also **Homophones.**

2. SHEAR OFF

It is an aging cliché of the news business. A reporter is apt to choose "shear off" before *cut off, detach, sever, tear off, or fall off.* And it is seldom a sheep that is *sheared* or *shorn.*

A television reporter said, twice, that branches were "sheared off" in a Louisiana hurricane. Another reported that an aviation mishap in New York had "sheared off one of the aircraft's engines."

Using the verb in an odd, intransitive way, an article dealt with the inability of an airliner's pilots to know—until the plane landed, safely, in Florida—that one of the three engines "had sheared off and plummeted 35,000 feet." Evidence indicated that frozen water from a leaky lavatory might be the reason that the engine had *fallen off* or *severed.* But "shear off" can perhaps be misleading in a story about an air accident, suggesting *wind shear,* a sudden change in wind, as the cause.

SHIMMER and SHIMMY. To *shimmer* is to shine with a quivering or flickering light. It evolved from the Old English *scimrian* (spelling varied), which probably originated in Greek.

To *shimmy* is to wobble or shake abnormally or to do the *shimmy,* a dance popular in the 1920s. Also called the *shimmy shake,* the dance featured rapid shaking. *Shimmy* is a corruption of *chemise,* a woman's undergarment.

A travel writer, telling about a volcano, wrote: "Heat rays wavered, making the distant trees shimmy incandescently." The wavering heat rays and the adverb "incandescently" imply that she had seen the trees *shimmer,* not wobble or dance.

SHOULD HAVE and "SHOULDA." *See* **HAVE, HAS, HAD,** *2.*

Sibilant endings. *See* **Plurals and singulars,** *2A, K;* **Punctuation,** *1G.*

SIGHT confused with SITE. *See* **Homophones.**

SILICON and SILICONE. A scene in a situation comedy portrayed a steam bath and the thoughts of a female bather. Spying another who seemed to possess unnaturally gigantean breasts, the former thought, "Look who's here: Silicon Valley." The joke was on those who put on the program. Bodily implants have been made of *silicone,* not of *silicon.*

A talk show host made the opposite error when referring, seriously, to "Silicone Valley." It is *Silicon Valley,* which is not a real geographic name but a nickname given to a region at the southeastern end of San Francisco Bay, California, where many electronic and computer companies burgeoned in the 1970s and 1980s.

Silicon is the basic material in semiconductor devices used in computer circuits and various electronic products. Pronounced SILL-lick-con and symbolized by *Si,* it is an *element:* that is, a basic substance, not dividable into any other substance by normal means. It is the second most plentiful element on earth, although not found in pure form. The only element more plentiful is oxygen, which is combined with silicon as silica (SiO_2) in sand, rocks, and quartz.

A *silicone,* pronounced SILL-lick-cone, is a *compound:* that is, a substance composed of elements that are chemically combined and so lack individual identities. *Silicones* make up a large group of synthetic, polymeric compounds of silicon, oxygen, and hydrogen. (A polymer is a huge compound characterized by numerous duplicates of an ordinary compound, linked together.) They are used to manufacture adhesives, electrical insulators, liquids for hydraulic systems, lubricants, paints and varnishes, prostheses, and synthetic rubber. Forms of *silicone* that can be injected into the body have been used for breast augmentation.

SIMPLE and SIMPLISTIC. *See* **Confusing pairs.**

SIMPLE and SIMPLY. *See* **Adjectives and adverbs.**

Singulars and plurals. *See* **Plurals and singulars.**

SIRE. Promoting a forthcoming program about Queen Elizabeth II, a woman announced on television, "She sired children who have shaken the crown of England to its very core."

Put aside any doubts about the metaphor and the image it conjures of someone shaking the jewels and gilding off a royal crown. The main problem lies in the choice of the word "sired." Any of these would have been a better choice: *gave birth to, bore, bred, brought forth, produced.*

To *sire* is to father. It usually applies to four-legged animals. A stallion or bull is a *sire;* the opposite parent is a *dam;* and applying any such word to the queen of England is a dam shame.

See also **BEGET.**

SIT and SET. *See* **SET and SIT.**

SITE confused with SIGHT. *See* **Homophones.**

SITUATION. The noun *situation* is not always necessary when used in the sense of a state of affairs or a set of circumstances. For example, a booklet describes six crises:

> In this they were similar to numerous instances over the years in which Presidents have sent U.S. armed forces overseas without congressional authorization, in crisis situations.

The sentence could end *in crises.* It does not need "situations." Similarly, the use of "situation" (twice) seems superfluous in the excerpt below from a study in a quarterly journal.

> In this study of college student motivation, the author investigated the influence of a mastery goal situation versus a competitive goal situation.

See if the first four words are needed in this sentence from a book for prospective teachers:

> In a play situation, a student is manipulating various toys and objects in a room.

Consider "A student is *playing with* various toys. . . . "

Situation is more useful in this context: "What is the political situation in Iran these days?" The word can imply trouble or crisis: "The Cuban situation was grave." It can mean *location:* "The town's situation amid the peaks permitted spectacular views." It can also mean *job:* "I seek a promising situation in the computer industry."

SKIM. *See* SCAN.

SLANDER. *See* LIBEL and SLANDER.

SLASH. *See* Punctuation, *12.*

SLAY, SLAIN, SLEW. A book alludes to the shooting of a duck for dinner: "The shell was fetched, the duck slayed." To *slay*, meaning to kill, usually violently, is an acceptable verb in the context. No "slayed" exists, however. The past participle of *slay* is *slain:* ". . . the duck [was] slain."

The past tense of *slay* is *slew:* "Little David was a shepherd boy / Who slew Goliath and jumped for joy." The verb comes from Old English.

From Irish Gaelic we get *slew*, also *slue*, a colloquial noun meaning a large number or amount. *Slue*, also *slew*, means (verb, transitive and intransitive) to rotate and (noun) rotating. Its origin is uncertain; it has a nautical history. Both spellings are pronounced SLOO.

SLEW, SLUE. *See* SLAY, SLAIN, SLEW.

SMELL. *See* AROMA.

SNEAKED and "SNUCK." From TV accounts of an attempted coup in Moscow and rescues from the Polish ghetto: "Gorbachev and his son-in-law snuck into a closed room . . ." / "a friend snuck him in to see the children."

Sneaked should have been used in each instance. It is the proper past tense and past participle of *sneak* (verb, transitive and intransitive), meaning to move quietly and stealthily so as not to be observed, or to act in a secret or underhanded manner.

One dictionary describes "snuck" as chiefly dialectal, another as nonstandard. If chosen at all, it should be restricted to a frivolous context.

SOCIALIST, SOCIALISM. The president was quoted in support of economic reforms in noncapitalist countries:

"Even the Socialist world is beginning to see that Socialism isn't just another economic system—it's the death of economics. . . . "

Mr. Bush went further in his speech today, saying that reform efforts in the Soviet Union, China and other Socialist countries were part of "an exciting trend. . . . "

A capital *S* does not belong in "Socialist" or "Socialism" unless it is part of the name of a party or movement (e.g., the *Socialist* Party) or is in a title. The capitalized term needs to be distinguished from general references to an economy or a political idea: *socialist* or *socialism*, with a lower-case *s* (a *socialist* economy).

The Soviet Union was run by Communists, with a capital *C*, who considered their economic system to be *socialism* or a *socialist system*. It is a system in which the means of production and distribution are owned and controlled by the state. In their theory (and it was theory in the most hypothetical sense) socialism would ultimately develop into *communism* (adjective *communist*), an ideal system of economic equality in which the state became unnecessary.

Under any theory, the regime could be described as *Communist*, with a capital

C, in the sense that it was led by Communists: members of the Communist Party. The type of regime actually in effect under Communists could be called *Communism*, with a capital *C*.

SO FAR AS. *See* FAR.

SOFT-BOILED. *See* BOIL.

SOLE and SOUL. *See* Homophones.

SOME. *1. Before a number. 2. SOME PLACE and SOMEPLACE. 3. SOME TIME and SOMETIME.*

1. Before a number

Some in front of a round number means approximately or about. Thus "some 5,000 people" implies a rough count, above or below the exact total. "Some" does not go with a number that is or appears precise, as in this sentence:

> . . . The company, in a newspaper advertisement, promoted a supposed $149 fare to London from New York in type size some 136 times larger than the note, which indicated that the fare was "each way" of a required round-trip purchase.

Omit "some." A phrase like "some 100 times" would be a normal place for it. But the number 136 is or appears to be exact.

Odd is a similar term, when connected to a round number, except that it indicates only an excess, never a shortage. "I estimate that 500-odd people were present." Remember the hyphen, unless you are describing "odd people."

Some and *-odd* should not go together ("some 40-odd executives"). Neither is necessary if a figure is described in some other way as an approximation or an estimate. Finally, *some* or *-odd* goes with a sizable number, not with a small digit.

2. *SOME PLACE and SOMEPLACE*

Someplace (adverb) means at, in, or to some place. It is more informal than *somewhere*, which has the same meaning. Some critics scorn *someplace* in writing even when it is used correctly. An editor used it incorrectly:

> Is it possible for someplace peaceful and nice and affordable . . . to be preserved from greed and speculation . . . ?

Correction: "for *some place that is* peaceful and nice and affordable" or "for *some* peaceful and nice and affordable *place*."

If *someplace* is acceptable at all, it is interchangeable with *somewhere*, as in "Let's go out someplace." *Somewhere* is no substitute for "someplace" in the press quotation.

The American Heritage Dictionary termed *someplace* informal, and 83 percent of its usage panel rejected as a writing sample "an unspecified target someplace between Inchon and Seoul."

3. *SOME TIME and SOMETIME*

Distinguishing *some time,* an adjective and noun, from *sometime,* an adverb, can be confusing.

- *Some time* usually means an indefinite period of time: "They plan to spend some time in Nepal."
- *Sometime* means at an indefinite point in time: "Come up and see me sometime." / "He lived sometime during the Tang Dynasty."

However, *some time* can have the second meaning when next to certain words: "I'll come back *at some time* in the future." / "The troupe appeared here *some time ago.*"

As a test, omit *some time* or *sometime:* If the sentence makes no sense, use the phrase. If it still makes sense, use the single word (or a synonym, such as *at some time or other*).

As an adjective, meaning occasional, *sometime* or *sometimes* is uncommon and disparaged by a number of critics: "his sometime[s] occupation."

Sometimes means occasionally or now and then. "Sometimes I'm happy." It may modify an adjective: "this sometimes deadly ailment."

SOMEBODY. *See* Pronouns, 2C.

SOME ONE and SOMEONE. *See* ONE as pronoun, 3; Pronouns, 2C.

SOME PLACE and SOMEPLACE. *See* SOME, 2.

SOMETHING OF. *See* KIND OF, 3.

SOME TIME, SOMETIME, and SOMETIMES. *See* SOME, 3.

SOMEWHAT. *See* KIND OF, 4; IDENTICAL.

SOONER. *See* THAN, 2E.

SORT OF. *See* KIND OF; TYPE.

SOUR GRAPES. After spending $28 million of his own money in an unsuccessful campaign for a Senate seat, a candidate futilely tried to undo the election on grounds of electoral fraud and irregularities. A newspaper editorial attacked his claims as "an expensive case of sour grapes."

Something that a person would like to have but pretends to dislike because he cannot have it is *sour grapes*. The term can also apply to the disparagement of the prize. Inasmuch as the losing candidate had nothing ill to say about the office of senator, "sour grapes" was not relevant. A rewrite: "the last resort of a sore loser."

The Aesop fable of the fox and the grapes gave rise to the expression. A fox desired some high-hanging grapes but failed to reach them in several leaps. He walked away, remarking, "They are sour!" Translations from ancient Greek disagree on whether the fox spoke in jest or in seriousness, and they disagree on what the moral was.

SPANISH AMERICA and LATIN AMERICA. *See* LATIN(-)AMERICAN.

SPAT and SPATE. "A spat of wet weather is causing problems. . . . " It was said on a TV news program.

The noun *spat* has several meanings: a minor quarrel, a partial shoe covering, a sound like that made by rain, and an immature oyster. None fits the quotation. *Spate* is the noun that was needed. It is a sudden, heavy rain; or an unusually large rush or outpouring of something; or, in Britain, a flash flood.

Conceivably a couple frustrated by inability to play golf or tend a garden could engage in "a spat of wet weather," but that was not the televised story.

SPEAK, SPOKE, and SPOKEN. *See* Tense, 5A.

SPEAK TO, TALK TO. To "speak to" a motion, meaning to comment on it, is part of the jargon of parliamentary procedure.

To adapt it to general use introduces an element of ambiguity to the language. It makes a good deal of difference whether "The president will speak *about* Congress" or "*to* Congress." Besides, the little preposition *to* is overworked enough as it is.

Nevertheless, an anchor man said, "House members stayed open all night to speak to this issue," the flag. A counterpart of his found a presidential debate "talking to issues the people wanted to hear about." A flowery newspaper story about a tribute to a late baseball player said, "And Ralph Branca and Joe Black could speak to the vulnerable yet unbending man who lived a career so compelling" (etc.). Could they really "speak to" him? He was dead.

Generally, you speak or talk *to* a person or *to* a group. You speak or talk *about* issues or matters, sometimes *of* or *on* them: "The House members spoke about flag burning." / "We talked about the weather." / "Speak of the devil." / " 'The time has come,' the Walrus said, 'to talk of many things. . . . ' " / "The professor will speak on the importance of good English."

SPECIE and SPECIES. *See* Confusing pairs.

Spelling. *1. Errors. 2. Irregularity and tradition. 3. Principles.*

1. Errors

Vice President J. Danforth Quayle was responsible for the most prominent misspelling of an English word in recent history when he miscorrected a school child's spelling of *potato* by placing an "e" at the end. The plural, *potatoes,* has the *e,* not the singular. Similarly a *tomato* becomes *tomatoes* in the plural.

Spelling in English is hazardous. Errors appear in books, periodicals, and the best newspapers.

One newspaper in that category happened to misspell *expel* in its main story on the front page: "Keep the foreigner away from your holy shrines so we will all stand as one to expell the darkness. . . . " (Saddam Hussein of Iraq was being quoted. Americans have often considered him a villain, but making him out a bad speller as well may be going too far.)

The same paper has also printed misspellings of such words as *advisory* (misspelling it "advisery"), *interference* ("interferance"), *minuscule* ("minis-

cule"), *mobile* ("mobil"), *prerogative* ("perogatives"—several times), and *warrant* ("warrentless").

Headlines in several other newspapers have contained these misspellings: *achieve* ("acheives"), *catastrophic* ("catastropic"), *indecisiveness* ("indeciciveness"), *minuscule* ("miniscule" again), *optometrist* ("optomitrists"), *psychiatric* ("psyciatric"), *scrapping* ("scraping"), and *sufferers* ("suffers"). A banner reads "Protestors want officers fired," using an old "-or" variant instead of the customary *protester(s). See* WHOSE, 2, for a worse mistake.

Apologize ("apoligize"), *delegate* ("delagate"), *ingenious* ("ingenius"), and *prosthesis* ("prothesis") have been misspelled in books dealing with the music industry, famous people, English usage, and medicine, respectively. A cookbook misspells four words: *cayenne* ("cayene"), *coarsely* ("coarsley"), *foreword* ("foreward"), and *pomegranate* ("pomegranite"). *See also* FOREWORD and FORWARD. A book instructing would-be book publishers misspells four other words: *afraid* ("affraid"), *bulge* ("buldge" twice), *rivet* ("rivit"), and *simplest* ("simplist"); and it disconnects a fifth: *whatever* ("what ever"). It also confuses *lose* with "loose."

A lexicographer misspells *resistible* ("resistable") in a book dealing with the English language. Some copies of two general dictionaries misspell *millennium* ("millenium") and *vichyssoise* ("vichysoisse").

Webster's Third Dictionary gives several misspellings as variants, thereby tending to encourage the errors. It condones spelling *harebrained* as "hairbrained," *marshal* as "marshall," *nickel* as "nickle," *prophecy* and *prophesy* as each other, *restaurateur* as "restauranteur," and *therefore* as "therefor."

Writers are not always responsible for the misspellings that appear under their names. Editing and typographical misspellings occur, especially the latter. Typographical misspelling may reflect the pressing of wrong keys or the transposition or omission of letters. Some outlandish combinations are obviously errors and the easiest to notice before publication. (At first I typed "thekr" instead of *their* in the first sentence of this paragraph.) Mistakes by writers or editors tend to be more plausible; often the misspelling can be pronounced the same as the correct word. Someone simply spelled it wrong.

On many occasions, words that I spelled correctly in my copy turned up in print misspelled, usually by a typesetter, sometimes by an editor. For instance, *framers* (of the Constitution) came out "farmers" and *pastime* was changed to "pasttime." *See also* **OCULIST** (etc.).

Here is an alphabetical list of other words that I have found to be publicly misspelled, mostly in newspapers but also on the television screen and in corporate and governmental printings. The style of the examples above is repeated; first the correct spelling appears, then in parentheses the misspelling:

academy ("accademy")
accommodations ("acomodations")
acquiescent ("acquiscent")
alley ("alee")
bawdy ("baudy")
benefiting ("benefitting")
cabaret ("caberet")
commitment ("committment")
competitive ("competative")
deceit ("deceipt")
depositor(s) ("depositers")
entirety ("entirity")
ideology ("idealogy")
irreverent ("irreverant")
nonsense ("nonsence")
observer(s) ("observors")
phonetically ("phoneticly")
repetition ("repitition")
stretched ("streched")
supersede(s) ("supercedes")

transmogrify ("transmorgrify")
vegetarian ("vegeterian")
wait ("wate")
weird ("wierd")

In the collection for this book, the most common spelling mistakes are the substitution of letters (e.g., an "i" for the first *u* in *minuscule*) and the omission of letters (a *c* and an *m* in *accommodation*). Less common mistakes are the addition of letters (a "t" in *pastime*) and the transposition of letters (the *e* and *l* in *coarsely*). Those four kinds of error are further illustrated respectively in the entries **SHEAR; LEAP, LEAPED, LEAPT; MARSHAL; NICKEL.**

Misunderstanding of words and use of deviant forms come up in the entries **ALL RIGHT; BEGET; COMPLAINANT; DETERIORATE; DUM-DUM BULLET; GRIEVOUS, GRIEVOUSLY; HAREBRAINED; IMMEMORIAL; KUDOS; MISCHIEVOUS, MISCHIEVOUSNESS; RAGAMUFFIN; RESTAURATEUR.**

The main problem in the pairs of words listed in **Confusing pairs,** such as *adverse* and *averse,* is not misspelling as such but the mixing up of words, which can amount to misspelling.

Likeness of sound in a pair such as *right* and *write* or *accept* and *except* accounts for some lapses. *See* **Homophones.**

A few contractions are confused with possessives and vice versa. *See* **ITS and IT'S; WHOSE,** 2 (confused with *who's*); **YOUR and YOU'RE.** *See* **TILL and "'TIL"** for a word that is mistaken for a contraction.

A is wrongly attached to a few words. *See* **A WHILE and AWHILE; HOLD; LOT,** 2.

The tendency to unite phrases and hyphenated terms is considered in **Joining of words.** *See* **(-)EVER,** *1,* for an example of the breaking up of words, a rarer phenomenon.

See also FLAMMABLE (etc.); -IZE, 2; PAY; Plurals and singulars; -Y ending.

2. Irregularity and tradition

Critics of English spelling complain about its irregularity, its many ways of representing a sound. For instance, the *a* sound in *day* appears also in *aim, cabaret, exposé, gauge, great, lake, mating, nee, obey, veil,* and *weigh.* The *sh* sound in *ash* is also in *appreciate, crescendo, machine, motion, ocean, passion, schnauzer,* and *sure.*

Approaching it from a language like Spanish, with almost entirely regular, phonetic spelling and one basic sound per vowel, English may seem totally chaotic. But compared with written Chinese, which has no alphabet and thousands of characters to learn, written English is tolerably phonetic. Its twenty-six letters do represent sounds, at least in combination. It has its rules for spelling, and most spellings follow regular patterns. Unfortunately, the rules all have exceptions, and many of the irregular words are frequently used. Good spellers keenly sense how words sound and (to handle irregularity) how they look.

Spelling in English reflects a multicultural history and includes patterns of Old English, French, Greek, Latin, and other languages, mainly the Romance. To begin with, English had fewer characters than sounds, requiring combinations of letters to represent many sounds. The written language failed to keep up with sound changes, such as the silencing of the *k* and *e* in *knave.* Significant episodes included respelling by French scribes after the Norman conquest; changes by early printers, many of them foreign, who often justified (evened) lines by adding or subtracting letters; and a sixteenth-century fashion of imitating Latin and Greek forms—even, for instance, putting the *s* in *i(s)land,* a word of Old English origin, in the misbelief that it came from the Latin *insula.* English in North America reflects to some extent the aboriginal, immigrant, and Latin-American traditions.

Since the nineteenth century, movements have arisen to reform spelling and thereby make learning easier for children and improve the spelling of the general public. They won the support of such luminaries as Charles Darwin and Alfred Tennyson. Andrew Carnegie financed a simplified-spelling board, which faded away. George Bernard Shaw's will created a new alphabet, of forty letters, which never caught on. *The Chicago Tribune* once attempted innovations like "telegraf" and "frate" but then returned to customary spellings. Readers may have thought the phonetic spellings were mistakes.

"Words should be spelled as they sound," many people have said, unaware of hazards. A rapid and radical change to a wholly phonetic system might quickly render obsolete centuries of literature and considerable knowledge. Some books would be revised, but the mean techniques of much modern book manufacturing might not permit them to endure. It could be confusing if, say, the homophones *sew* and *sow* were spelled the same as *so.* And if speech determined spelling, speakers of English from different places might have trouble reading one another's writings.

In England, a request of mine for directions to Bath was met with a stare until I thought to pronounce it BAHTH. Much earlier, an old record on which a baritone sang of a place where flying fishes PLY and the dawn comes up like thunder out of China 'cross the BY gave me my first lesson in Australian English. American pronunciations too vary by region. Take the word *court,* which a New Yorker or Bostonian is apt to pronounce CAUT and a Southerner COAT while many to the west say CORT.

Minor reforms are feasible. Americans accepted those by the lexicographer

Noah Webster (1758–1843), who changed the British -*our* and -*re* endings (as in *honour* and *centre*) to -*or* and -*er* (*honor* and *center*).

3. Principles

A. The best rule

The rules of spelling and their exceptions are so extensive that we can only hint at them here.

Many spellings have to be learned, one by one. Rules will not help in distinguishing the words ending in -*able* such as *peaceable* from those ending in -*ible* such as *feasible*. Nor will rules help in segregating -*ant* words (*defendant*) from -*ent* words (*dependent*); -*or* words (*inspector*) from -*er* words (*invader*); or words with -*seed* sounds from one another (*precede, proceed, supersede*).

When in doubt, look it up. That is the best rule.

B. Doubling; suffixes; prefixes

The last letter of a word is often doubled when a suffix is added: for example, *fit* becomes *fitting* and *begin* becomes *beginner*. (A suffix is a word part affixed to the end of a basic word to alter the meaning.) At the end of a one-syllable word or a word accented on the last syllable, a single consonant is apt to be doubled before a suffix starting with a vowel. In the two examples above, the suffixes added are -*ing* and -*er*. Other examples are *bag, baggage / deter, deterrent / remit, remittance / ship, shipped*.

The last letter of the basic word, or root word, is not doubled if adding the suffix shifts the accent to a previous syllable: *con-FER, CON-fer-ence* and *pre-FER, PREF-er-ence* (but *con-FERRED, pre-FER-ring*, etc.).

At the end of a word accented on a syllable besides the last, a single consonant is usually not doubled before a suffix starting with a vowel. Examples are *develop, developing* and *happen, hap-*

pening, but an exception is *handicap, handicapped, handicapping*.

A final *l* is retained before a suffix beginning with *l*: *cruel, cruelly / formal, formally / national, nationally*. Otherwise, suffixes do not usually double *l* endings in America (*dial* becomes *dialed, dialing* and *marvel* becomes *marveled, marveling*) but do in Britain (*dialled, dialling* and *marvelled, marvelling*). Almost conversely, -*ll* endings stay double in America when prefixes are added (*roll, enroll*) but are made single in Britain (*enrol*). And double letters in *combat(t)ing, worship(p)ing*, and other words are more common in Britain.

In America, affixing a prefix does not usually vary the spelling of the parts, even when the last letter of the prefix and the first letter of the root word are the same: *Mis-* plus *state* gives *misstate*. *Over-* plus *run* gives *overrun*. (A prefix is a word part affixed to the beginning of a basic word to alter the meaning.)

A word ending in *c* requires the addition of *k* before an *e, i,* or *y* suffix if a hard pronunciation of *c* remains: *mimic, mimicked / panic, panicky / traffic, trafficking*. In *music, musician* and *toxic, toxicity* the pronunciation of *c* becomes soft.

C. I before E?

The misspeller of *achieve* seems to have forgotten the old pedagogic mnemonic, or memory aid, "*I* before *E, /* Except after *C.*" Unfortunately, the misspeller of *weird* seems to have remembered it.

Scores of words use *ei*, including *caffeine, counterfeit, either, foreign, forfeit, height, heir, leisure, neither, plebeian, protein, seize, stein,* and *veil*; various -*ing* words like *being* and *seeing*; and words with the prefix *re-*, like *reinstate* and *reiterate*. Even the exception in the rhyme has exceptions: *Conscience, financier, omniscient, prescient, science,* and *species* are all *cie* words.

Some have been taught an extra verse to the mnemonic, "Or when sounded like *a* / As in *neighbor* or *weigh*," which may be more useful than the main verse.

D. Silent E

The silent *e* generally makes a short vowel sound long; for example, turning *can* into *cane*, *rot* into *rote*, and *sit* into *site*.

The silent *e* is usually omitted before a suffix starting with a vowel: *adore, adoring; debate, debatable; mate, mating; quote, quotation; write, writing.* Among the exceptions are some words that would be transformed if the *e* were removed: *dye, dyeing* / *hoe, hoeing* / *shoe, shoeing* / *singe, singeing.* Many words that end in *-ce* or *-ge* are exceptions too when the *e* preserves the soft sound: *change, changeable* / *encourage, encouragement* / *grace, graceful;* but *i* suffixes are an exception to the exception and do drop the *e: changing, encouraging.*

The *e* is usually retained before a suffix starting with a consonant: *careless, lately, statement.* But some words ending in *-le* do drop the *e* before the suffix *-ly* (*gentle, gently* and *simple, simply*).

E. Spelling checkers

Most word-processing programs for computers have features to help users verify and correct the spelling of words in their documents. They are called *spelling checkers, spell checkers, spellers,* or the like. Useful devices, they often save the users from mistakes in spelling or slips of the keyboard by highlighting words considered wrong and suggesting alternatives.

They will not rescue slips in grammar or word selection as long as every word typed is a recognized word. They will find nothing wrong if you type *bake* instead of *brake, complement* instead of *compliment, loathe* instead of *loath, phrase* instead of *phase,* or *them* instead of *theme* (a mistake I made). And having

been devised by human beings, they are not infallible even within their province. One popular program disapproved of *ads, em, exposé,* and *wracked;* approved of *checkouts* but not *checkout* and *coworkers* but not *coworker;* and suggested that *afterword* be "afterward," *temblor* be "tumbler," *backdoor* be "bookstore," and *obvious* be "obi" (a Japanese sash or a type of sorcery).

SPINSTER. *See* BACHELOR and SPINSTER.

Split infinitive. *See* Infinitive, 4.

SPOKE and SPOKEN. *See* Tense, 5A.

SPOKESMAN. 1. *"-PERSON."* 2. *"-WOMAN."*

1. "-PERSON"

Those who are squeamish are well advised to avert their eyes. We are about to quote the *s*-word.

In the course of a day's work, a columnist for a metropolitan newspaper tapped out the following sentences on his computer keyboard:

A spokesperson for the Dallas Police Department acknowledged that the matter is "under investigation." . . .

A spokesperson for Cruise told Page 2 that the idea of Spielberg directing "Rainman" was always presented to Tom as a possibility. . . .

According to a Jovan spokesperson, the fragrance company was put "through a hoop" over Lyne's work.

"They cut out a shot of a lady in a wet slip and toned down a shower scene," said the spokesperson. . . .

"They cropped that to an above-the-waist shot," said the spokesperson.

Although most writers do not display such voracity for bad language, that clumsy barbarism, "s——," is polluting the English tongue.

A radical weekly uses it regularly along with a grotesque plural version:

> Spokespeople for most of the groups he attacks agree that his factual research is often . . . accurate.

The correct word, of course, is *spokesman,* plural: *spokesmen.* A *spokesman,* i.e., one who speaks for another or others, may be either male or female. *See* -MAN-, MAN.

The three sample sentences below all use the correct word. The first (referring to Mrs. Clinton) is from a television forum on PBS. The other two are from *The New York Times.*

> She's no longer a national spokesman for him [President Clinton].

> Kathy Pherson, a spokesman for the C.I.A., refused in a telephone interview to confirm or deny the C.I.A.'s involvement in training or advising the Honduran police and army.

> Justice Brennan, 82 years old, hit his head and received stitches to close the wound, said Kathy Arberg, a spokesman for the court.

The *Times* and Associated Press style manuals instruct staff members not to use "spokesperson."

The two passages below, from other papers, are embodiments of illogic:

> At its Tuesday/22 general meeting, the club will host White Panther spokesman Tom —— and a spokesperson for the mayor.

> . . . Only $400,000 worth of that advertising was aired before the end of the reporting period on Sept. 30, said Steven M. ——, spokesman for the Committee to Conserve the Courts. . . .

> But Janet ——, spokesperson for Crime Victims for Court Reform and Californians to Defeat Rose Bird, said momentum is on the side of the anti-Bird campaign.

One of each pair is a "-man" and the other is a "-person"? Nonsense. Each is a *spokesman.*

2. "-WOMAN"

Some journalists and broadcasters who cannot abide the gracelessness and ignorance represented by that illegitimate word are drawn to another three-syllable word:

> In Washington, the State Department's spokeswoman, Margaret Tutwiler, said Kohl was "responding to the deepest aspirations of his people for German unity."

> "The Sandinistas . . . realize their brand of communism is bankrupt and obsolete," said the State Department spokeswoman, Margaret Tutwiler.

If you consider it necessary to describe the Brontë sisters as "authoresses" and "poetesses," you will probably want to use "spokeswoman."

Modified in the manner of the final example however, it could be misleading:

> . . . Some outsiders have also said that as the chief spokeswoman, she reinforced the image of the White House as a preserve of the young and inexperienced.

"Chief spokeswoman" could suggest that she was the chief only of the White House's female spokesmen. The intended meaning probably was that she served as the *chief spokesman* for the White House; that is, the person in charge of speaking for the president.

The Associated Press manual condones "spokeswoman." The *Times* manual says to use *spokesman* for both men and women.

STAFF. A recording tells callers to a city library, "All of our staff are helping others." It is not wrong, though it has a British flavor. *Staff is* would be the more customary way in the United States.

Staff is a collective noun meaning the employees, assistants, or officers who carry out the work of a particular enterprise or organization. The plural in that sense is *staffs*.

A *staff* is also a flagpole, walking stick, or rod; or the set of five parallel lines that music is written on. In those senses, the plural is either *staffs* or *staves*. A musical *staff* is sometimes called a *stave*.

An informal term for a member of a staff is a *staffer*. Regarding that word, *The New York Times* tells its own staff, "Do not use for *staff member(s)* or *member(s) of the staff*."

See also Collective nouns, *1;* WHO and WHOM, *1.*

STAND and RUN. *See* RUN and STAND; Pronouns, *3.*

STANDARD. *See* CLASSIC.

STANDARD-BEARER. *See* Joining of words.

STAR and SUN. The discovery of a distant galaxy prompted a news agency to issue this dubious statement: "The core apparently contains at least 30,000 closely packed suns. ... "

No more precision characterizes a discussion of galaxy clusters in a book of popular astronomy: "But not even our galaxy, with its 100 billion suns, is independent and self-sufficient. ... "

In both instances, *stars* would be preferable to "suns." A *star* is a celestial body that emits its own light. A *sun* is a star that is the center of a system of planets, the way the *Sun,* the star closest to us, heads our solar system. (The *Sun* is often spelled with a lower-case *s:* "The sun suddenly emerged from the clouds." In an astronomical context, a capital *S* may be appropriate.)

A *planet* is a large celestial body that is illuminated by reflected light from a star and revolves around it.

STATEMENT. *See* FACT.

STATIONARY and STATIONERY. *See* Homophones.

Statistics. *See* Comparison, *1;* FRACTION; LIFE EXPECTANCY and LIFE SPAN; MEAN (noun); Numbers; Range, true and false, *1, 2.*

STATUTE, LAW, and REGULATION. *See* REGULATION, STATUTE, and LAW.

STATUTE MILE. *See* KNOT.

STAVE(S). *See* STAFF.

Stealing. *See* CRIME, MISDEMEANOR, and FELONY; Crimes, *3.*

STEREOTYPE. *See* Clichés.

STICK UP, STICKUP, STICK-UP. *See* Crimes, *3.*

STEVEDORE and LONGSHOREMAN. The awkwardness of the sentence to be quoted here, from a book on language, is not the main point. One word particularly interests us.

Clipped forms [such as *ad* and *gym*] ... have much common use, from stevedores to executives, in our spoken language and informal written language.

The intended meaning is that those forms are often used by people of all classes, including laborers and executives. That is not the literal meaning. A *stevedore* is a type of executive. Many people, lexicographers among them, misconceive him to be a laborer who loads and unloads ships. That is not the way a *stevedore* is likely to use the word. He sees himself as a contractor who arranges the loading and unloading of ships. He does not do the actual laboring; he hires men to do it. The workingmen call themselves *longshoremen*.

Note the difference between the names of the companies, such as Stevedoring Service of America and Metropolitan California Stevedore Co., and the names of the labor unions: the International Longshoremen's Association (in the East) and the International Longshoremen's and Warehousemen's Union (in the West).

STINT. "Quayle says he's healthy now despite two recent stints in the hospital," a newscaster announced over a radio network. The former vice president did not become a hospital worker; he was a hospital patient. The broadcaster wrongly used "stints" when *stays* would have been a better choice of words.

A *stint* (noun) is usually an allotment of work or piece of work. For instance, "He finished his daily stint at the factory." A *stint* can be also a limitation, often an undue limitation.

To *stint* can mean to limit or restrict one (verb, transitive) or to limit or restrict oneself, to get along on a trifling allowance (verb, intransitive).

STOMACH. The host of a radio talk show spoke of a woman's "carrying that baby in her stomach." And a movie reviewer wrote that a character resented that he had to "share his woman with that baby in her stomach."

The *stomach* is an organ of digestion. Unless each woman had been emulating the dining behavior of a mythological monster, the anatomical reference in each instance was misplaced. If neither the radio man nor the movie reviewer had the stomach for *womb* or *uterus*, each could have got by with *abdomen, belly,* or *middle.* Of those three nouns, *abdomen,* the part of the trunk between the chest and the pelvis, is the most scientific; *middle* is the vaguest. *Belly* is a standard word, but much of the public feels that it is unrefined. *Tummy* is baby talk for *stomach.*

As a synonym for the abdomen, "stomach" is suitable only for casual conversation, if that. It is best to avoid using one organ as a synonym for another organ, particularly when talking to one's physician.

An old saw has it that "the way to a man's heart is through his stomach." If you believe it, don't think of being a surgeon.

STRAIGHTFORWARD. *See* **Adjectives and adverbs.**

STUDENT. *See* **PUPIL and STUDENT.**

Subject. *See* **Clauses; Complement; Nouns,** *4;* **Pronouns,** *4, 6, 10;* **Sentence fragment,** *1;* **Verbs,** *1A, 3.*

Subjective case. *See* **Pronouns,** *10;* **Pronouns' classification.**

Subject(ive) complement. *See* **Complement; Verbs,** *1F.*

Subject-verb agreement. *See* **Verbs,** *3.*

Subjunctive. *1. Among the moods. 2. Forms of the subjunctive. 3. Mistakes.*

1. Among the moods

Of the three moods, the *subjunctive* mood is used least frequently. For generations, writers on language have been declaring the *subjunctive* "moribund" / "almost disappeared" / "just about dead." As long ago as 1860, a writer found "good reason to suppose that it will soon become obsolete altogether." While the *subjunctive* has declined over the centuries, it stubbornly refuses to expire.

Most English-speakers handle the subjunctive at some time or other. Everyone does who has scrawled "Wish you were here" on a postcard; sung "If I Were a Rich Man" or used a variety of other sentences containing *if*; uttered or understood such idioms as *be that as it may, come what may, heaven forbid,* and *perish the thought*; or attended formal meetings, which commonly make use of expressions like "I move that members be notified. . . . "

Whereas the *indicative* mood deals with facts or supposed facts and the *imperative* mood directly commands a second person, the *subjunctive* mood essentially concerns ideas. It presents an action or state of being as a mental conception, not as a fact. More specifically, it expresses contingencies, desires, exhortations, hypotheses, impossibilities, orders (indirectly), prospects, requests, suppositions, and wishes.

The *subjunctive* (from the Late Latin *subjunctivus*) was so named because it was considered suitable for *subjoined* clauses; that is, subordinate clauses. To *subjoin* is literally to append.

See also **Mood.**

2. Forms of the subjunctive

The *subjunctive* mood may be complicated in some respects, but its conjugation of verbs is simple: A verb does not change with the person, whether first, second, or third, singular or plural. Verbs have three forms in the *subjunc-*

tive. (They resemble and therefore are named after tenses in the *indicative* mood, but the term *tense* would be misleading in the *subjunctive,* which lacks clear time distinctions.) We list the three verb forms (A, B, and C) followed by a number of common auxiliary verbs that also express the *subjunctive* mood (D).

A. The so-called *present subjunctive* uses the root, or basic version, of a verb.

It appears in clauses following the verbs *advise, ask, beg, demand, insist, order, recommend, request, require, suggest, urge, warn,* and so on. Often such a clause contains the word *that.* "The boss ordered that she *work* late tomorrow." / "The committee recommended that the bill *pass.*" / "Is it necessary that the office *be* closed?" / "We request that the audience *remain* standing." / "I suggest he *think* twice about it."

Clauses containing *lest* use that form. "We must strengthen the levee, lest the river *flood* us again."

The same form is found in many Biblical passages, like the following. (Subjunctive verbs are emphasized.) ". . . I fear him, lest he *come* and *slay* us all. . . ." / "For there is hope for a tree, if it *be* cut down, that it will sprout again. . . . Though its root *grow* old in the earth, and its stump *die* in the ground, yet at the scent of water it will bud. . . . "

B. The so-called *past subjunctive* uses what in the *indicative* mood would be the past tense. But the verb *be* takes *were* for all persons. Often *would* appears in the sentence.

The *past subjunctive* appears in clauses that follow the verb *wish.* "I wish I *had* a million dollars." / "She wishes she *lived* in Paris." It is also found in poetic sentences expressing the meaning of *wish* in other ways: "Would God I *were* the tender apple blossom." / "O, that I *were* a glove upon that hand. . . . "

It appears also in many conditional sentences: those sentences in which one action depends on another. Such sentences may contain *if* and *would*. The *if*-clause may be contrary to fact, hypothetical, impossible, or unlikely: "If George Washington *returned* today, he would be shocked." / "I wouldn't do that if I *were* you."

A conditional sentence in which the *if*-clause expresses a possibility may use that pattern (although it does not have to): "If an emergency *arose* tomorrow, we would be ready." / "Would you keep it confidential if I *told* you a secret?" As an option, such a sentence may be cast in the simple future tense of the *indicative* mood. "If an emergency *arises* tomorrow, we *will* be ready." / "*Will* you keep it confidential if I *tell* you a secret?"

C. The *past perfect subjunctive* is the only one of the three forms to pertain to time. The time is the past. Resembling the past perfect tense of the *indicative* mood, it uses *had* and a past participle.

Its use implies that what is said about a past action or condition is contrary to fact. "If he *had run* just a bit faster, he would have escaped." / "I wish that Wintergreen *had won* the election." / "*Had* we *bought* the land then, we would be rich today."

D. Various *auxiliary verbs* can also express the *subjunctive mood*. Among them are *could, ought, may, might, must, should,* and *would*.

The action or condition that one of those auxiliary verbs pertain to may be either contrary to fact or possible. "I *could* have danced all night." / "She *ought* to have said no." / "The dog *may* be a biter." / "It seemed for a while as though the argument *might* get violent." / "You *must* have been a beautiful baby." / "If you *should* get lost, give me a call." / "We *would* need to pay more."

See also MAY and MIGHT; WAS and WERE.

3. Mistakes

The Stephen Foster song "Dixie" and the folk song "Cindy"—which say "I wish I was in Dixie" and "I wish I was an apple"—demonstrate a common deviation from *subjunctive* form. We will not try to revise those famous old songs. Just be aware that to say "I wish it *was* better news" or "I wish I *was* in his position"—instead of "it *were*" and "I *were*"—may be judged at best colloquial and at worst illiterate.

Furthermore, the meaning can hinge on the choice of mood. The consequence of choosing the wrong one can be misunderstanding. Let us illustrate through two similar sentences.

A. "She suggested that he *attend* meetings regularly." Using the *subjunctive*, the sentence means that she suggested (proposed) his presence at the meetings.

B. "She suggested that he *attends* meetings regularly." Using the *indicative*, the sentence implies that he goes to the meetings already, a fact disclosed by her suggestion (hint).

The following two examples come from a book of travel reminiscences. (They are taken out of context deliberately to demonstrate the grammatical errors in both.) Both use the *past tense* when they should use the *present subjunctive*.

I suggested we flew along. . . .

But he had insisted they tried again. . . .

Each sentence seems to say that the subject made a factual statement about something that had already happened: that we had flown along and that they had tried again. The context shows the meaning that was intended; in each case the subject was making a proposal for future action: "I suggested [proposed that] we *fly* along. . . . " / "But he insisted [urged that] they *try* again. . . . " (The "had" was unwarranted.)

The sentence below, from an autobiography, contains a similar error in the choice of verb form, although the meaning is not compromised.

> . . . I got a call from Senator Sam Nunn's secretary telling me to make sure that on the next afternoon I watched C-Span, the cable TV channel. . . .

It should be "to make sure that . . . I *watch* C-Span. . . . " The secretary was recommending future action, not bringing up past action.

Each of the following three sample sentences, from news reports, seems to be part *subjunctive* and part *indicative*. Such switching of moods within a thought will not do.

> OTS Director Ryan imposed mild restrictions that would apply to Bush if he again becomes a director of a bank or savings and loan.

> President Clinton made his opposition clear and the measure would face almost certain veto if it passes the Senate in its present form.

> Newly elected Prime Minister Sosuke Uno said today that he was deeply concerned that China could be isolated internationally if it does not move to end the violence.

In the first sentence, change "becomes" to *became*. In the second sentence, change "passes" to *passed*. (As an alternative, make each sentence wholly *indicative*: "restrictions that *will* apply to Bush if he again becomes . . ." and "the measure *will* face almost certain veto if it passes. . . . ") In the third sentence, change "does" to *did*.

The following sentence contains essentially the same error: disagreement in mood. The fact that part of it is a quotation makes no difference.

If an adult picks up their lingo, "teenagers would consider it contaminated and stop using it," Chapman says.

Change "picks" to *picked*. (An alternative is to change "would" to *will* but exclude it from the direct quotation: "If an adult picks up their lingo, teen-agers will 'consider it contaminated. . . . ' ") The appended attribution, "Chapman says," does not affect the main thought.

The error in the following example is a superfluous word.

> It's recommended that the elderly and those having trouble should stay indoors.

Omit "should." Alternatively, keep "should" but omit "It's recommended that."

Using the *subjunctive* in place of the *indicative* is a relatively uncommon error, one that is found in a book on word usage.

> It's in the very nature of oral communication between human beings that much of it be tentative, inexact, finding its way.

The statement is presented as a fact. It has none of the elements that call for the *subjunctive*. Change "be" to *is*, thereby recasting the sentence in the *indicative* mood.

After the auxiliary verb *could, may, might, must, should,* or *would*, sometimes the *have* is erroneously replaced by "of." *See* HAVE, HAS, HAD, 2.

See also Tense, 4C.

SUBSEQUENT TO. *See* AFTER.

Substantive. *See* Nouns, *1* (end).

SUCCESSOR. *See* PREDECESSOR and SUCCESSOR.

SUCH.

1. *Adjective, adverb; SUCH A.*
2. *Pronoun; AS SUCH.* 3. *SUCH AS.*

1. Adjective, adverb; SUCH A

This sentence is correct: "There is no such thing as a ghost." After *no such*, the article "a" or "an" is not needed.

Such is usually an adjective, as in the preceding example. It has acquired an adverbial use too. "I never before saw *such* tall peaks" and "saw peaks *so* tall" are now equally idiomatic.

Some people use *such* adverbially in sentences like this one, which to others may seem incomplete: "I had such a good meal at that restaurant." It becomes complete when we add, for instance, "that I intend to go there again tomorrow."

2. Pronoun; AS SUCH

The use of *such* as a pronoun is resisted by grammarians, though it goes back centuries. Among Biblical uses: "and *of such* [livestock] shall be my hire [wages]" and "Now Moses in the law commanded us, that *such* [any adulteress] should be stoned. . . . "

The critics are vague in scorning "*Such* is life" or "They serve pizza, spaghetti, ravioli, and *such*." One finds it too casual, another too formal. The strongest objection is to *such* in place of ordinary pronouns, particularly personal pronouns. Accordingly in "I have allspice and often use *such* in cooking," change "such" to *it*. In "We have a cat and a dog and love *such*," change "such" to *them*, or perhaps just add *animals*, depending on meaning.

This is one of two uses of *as such*: "The situation is a hot potato and we should treat it *as such*." Some critics would replace "as such" with *one* or *that*. Others would accept it as idiomatic. *As such* is unquestionably an idiomatic phrase when it means *in itself*, as in "He craves power *as such*."

3. SUCH AS

The phrase *such as* precedes an example. It is superfluous to add "for example" / "for instance" / "and the like" / "and so on." A book says, "The power bases in the music business aren't concentrated in any one group (such as, for example, the major agencies . . .)." Delete "for example" and the two commas.

Such as normally introduces a noun, not a preposition: "They have performed in leading cities of Europe, such as in Paris and Rome." Delete the second *in*.

Another faulty use goes this way: "I brought only such tools that I needed for the job." Make it *such . . . as* or change "such" to *the*. Modern idiom rejects the pairing of *such* with "that" (or "which" or "who" or "where") in that type of construction. But *such that* is proper here: "The rigors were such that most contestants failed to finish." In the first instance, *such* precedes the noun; in the second, *such* follows the noun and a linking verb.

SUFFER.

That which lacks feeling cannot suffer. Only a living person or creature can suffer. Despite that truism, we hear on the news:

> A nuclear submarine has suffered some kind of accident in the Norwegian Sea.

A vessel, even when moving and called "she," is not animate. Find a substitute for "suffered" (such as *been in* or *had*) or restructure the sentence. ("Some kind of accident has happened to . . ." or "has befallen. . . . ")

From the North Atlantic theater, we move to northern California, where a victim of earth movement "showed city engineers the damage his house has suffered" and a temblor struck two playhouses:

. . . [The] Geary Theater suffered earthquake damage when plaster fell from its proscenium and a lighting grid collapsed. . . . The Golden Gate Theatre suffered damage to a stairwell.

Proper wording (". . . the damage to his house" and "The earthquake damaged . . .") would not require us to suspend our disbelief in the suffering of inanimate objects.

See also SUSTAIN.

Suffix. *See* **Adjectives and adverbs** (-ly); **Gerund** (-ing); **-IZE ending**; **Participle**; **PEOPLE as a suffix**; **Plurals and singulars**; **Pronouns,** *3, 4, 5* (-self, -selves); **Punctuation,** *4D* (hyphenated forms); **Spelling,** *1, 3*; **UP,** *3*; **-WISE ending**; **-Y ending.**

SULTRY. Oppressively hot, sweltering weather, days, or air may be described as *sultry,* particularly if humid. *Sultry* is applied also to figurative heat, such as feverish passion or temper. That adjective serves loosely in other ways, such as a euphemism for *sexy.* A movie reviewer so used it: "Jessica . . . looks and sounds so sultry . . . that Roger and Eddie find her equally alluring."

A restaurant reviewer turned to it for help in expressing her fervor for an Italian appetizer: "The sultry eggplant was especially good with the fresh sourdough bread dipped into the marinade." A flowery writer might metaphorically picture some Mexican or Asian foods as *sultry,* but the bland eggplant?

SUN. *See* STAR and SUN.

SUP. *See* DINE.

Superlative. *See* BETTER and BEST (etc.); **Comparative and superlative degrees**; MORE and MOST; MOST with superlative; **Numbers,** *10D.*

SUPPORTIVE. *Supportive* has been an established adjective. It means providing support or help; e.g., a *supportive* group. Now we hear the faddish phrase "supportive of."

A mayor of New York wrote, "I have always felt very supportive of civil rights." Before such a circumlocution became a popular habit, he might have written simply, "I have always supported civil rights."

The phrase is wishy-washy at best and grammatically dubious. It is like "Lord, be helpful of us" instead of "Lord, help us." More illustrations follow.

John A—— . . . called the book "a pioneering effort. I'm very supportive of the book."

John should have ended with "supportive" and left out the rest.

McCarthy . . . was supportive of this proposal.

. . . The rest of the board of directors . . . has been supportive of Mr. A——.

. . . The editor of the Hindustan Times, a paper generally supportive of the Government, said. . . .

Tightened versions would say, "McCarthy *supported* this proposal" / ". . . The rest of the board of directors . . . has *supported* Mr. A——" / "a paper generally *supporting* the Government."

Possibly using "supportive of" as a model, some writers have brought forth the abnormity below.

In Baku . . . one historian who took part in a meeting with Dr. Sakharov was dismissive of the physicist and Nobel Peace Prize winner.

Weinberger's antagonist, George Shultz, was dismissive of Cap's approach.

Change "was dismissive of" to *dismissed*.

SUPREMACY, SUPREMACIST.
A community had prohibited a demonstration by a racist group and a comedian was proposing a compromise: "Any white supremist who wants to enter the square should first be able to spell the word 'supremist.' " The trouble with his joke was that no such word existed. He needed the word *supremacist*.

A *supremacist* is one who believes in the *supremacy* of one race or social group or either of the sexes. A common example is that of the *white supremacist*, a believer in *white supremacy*; that is, the leading role of the so-called white race.

Changing one letter in *supremacist* gives us *suprematist*, an adherent of *suprematism*, an artistic movement emphasizing abstract, geometric forms. The Russian painter Kazimir Malevich started it in 1913. He was best known for his painting "Suprematist Composition," consisting of a white square on a white background. Except for the coincidental emphasis on whiteness, *supremacists* have nothing to do with *suprematists*.

SURE.
Being *sure* (adjective) means having no doubt that something is true or will come about. Thus it was a contradiction for a national TV reporter to say (about the possibility of lawsuits that claim discrimination based on looks), "I hope we don't have these lawsuits, but I'm sure we will." If he was sure that something would happen, how could he reasonably hope that it would not?

A woman called a radio doctor to express fear about possible thyroid cancer. Recommending an examination, he re-

marked, "I'm sure it's not gonna turn out to be anything, but you always want to be sure." His "sure" was not so *sure* as hers would be. If he was really *sure* of her symptom's benignity, there need not have been any "but."

Uttered by loose lips, "sure" can amount to little more than *guessing*. Whether it is used strictly or frivolously may not be apparent, so enfeebled has the word become from misuse. To emphasize certainty, a more reliable adjective may be *certain*, which implies that one's conviction is based on evidence or experience. If it is based on faith, consider using *confident*.

Sure and *secure* both originate in the Latin *securus*, free from care, safe.

SURNAME. See LAST NAME and SURNAME.

SUSPECTED. See ACCUSED, ALLEGED etc.

SUSTAIN.
To *sustain* a loss or injury is to endure it or experience it. An inanimate object does not endure or experience anything. Therefore "sustained" does not suit this sentence:

Hundreds of San Francisco buildings may have sustained hidden damage in Tuesday's temblor. . . . "

Better: ". . . may have *received*" or "*Hidden damage may have been done to* hundreds. . . . "

Some authorities shun *sustain*, even for people, in the sense of suffering a specific injury. "He sustained a broken arm" is a modern, journalistic locution. They would reserve *sustain* for a special, traditional meaning: to bear up under, to stand against without yielding; e.g., "An explorer had to sustain hardship." / "His troops sustained the siege for a month." Accordingly, to "sustain" an injury is contradictory when it is fatal.

Sustain (verb, transitive) has other senses: to maintain, prolong, support, or uphold as valid; e.g., "She sustains my faith in humanity." / "I had no desire to sustain the conversation." / "He sustains himself by odd jobs." / "Objection sustained."

See also SUFFER.

SWAMPED. *See* INUNDATE, INUNDATED.

SYMPATHY. *See* MERCY and PITY.

Synonymic silliness. 1. *"Elegant variation."* 2. *How it causes confusion.*

1. *"Elegant variation"*

H. W. Fowler called it "elegant variation," probably in sarcasm. Usually more silly than elegant, it is a conspicuous introduction of synonyms, stemming from the misbelief that repetition per se is undesirable and repeating a word in a sentence or paragraph (or other unit) is an evil. It is characteristic of journalists but not restricted to them. Six newspapers, a magazine, and a book supplied the examples in this section.

> Fifth-seeded Todd Martin beat 10th-seeded Mark Philippoussis 6–3, 7–5. . . . Sixth-seeded Michael Stich overwhelmed Andrei Medvedev 6–4, 6–1. . . . Defending champion Jana Novotna ousted Anke Huber 6–4, 6–4.

In the absence of any clear-cut distinctions among the beating, the overwhelming, and the ousting, we must conclude that the three tennis victories were functionally equal.

> As concert halls became bigger, and audiences larger, music became gradually more and more difficult to understand at first hearing.

Similarly, "bigger" does not appear to differ substantially from "larger" in that excerpt, from a magazine article.

> On the East Coast, cocaine supplies are dwindling and prices are jumping. On the West Coast, the white powder is readily available but prices have rocketed.

In a story about precipitation in the winter, "the white powder" may be snow. In the excerpt above, it is probably cocaine. The writer just could not bear to repeat the word. Note too that on the East Coast prices jump, while on the West Coast they rocket.

> Hernandez said all ivory revenue must go toward the conservation of elephants and development programs for communities whose crops, homes and lives are threatened by the world's largest land mammal.

The writer's substitute for *elephant(s)* was "the world's largest land mammal," but he could have used *them*. (Some writers' favorite *elephant* substitute is "pachyderm," a term that includes the hippopotamus, the rhinoceros, and other thick-skinned beasts.)

The paragraph below is the fifth in a news story about Suffolk County, New York.

> At a news conference here, Mr. Halpin said that the bill would cost the county on eastern Long Island businesses millions of dollars for additional worker benefits—principally for eye care—and that it had already discouraged many new companies from settling in Suffolk and made several existing ones consider relocating.

The writer had used the name "Suffolk" three times. He wanted to refer to *Suffolk businesses* but felt that he simply had to find a substitute for *Suffolk*. So he found it, a phrase of six words, and heedlessly stuck it into a sentence that would be long and complex even without it. "Suffolk" appears later in the sentence anyway. If the writer had inserted his six-word synonym there, it might be tolerable. As it is, the readers read that "the bill would cost the county on eastern Long Island businesses," and they soon have to retrace their steps.

> Rabies caused the death of a 13-year-old boy, the first human in San Francisco to die of the rare disease in nearly half a century, health officials have reported.
>
> The victim . . . died Dec. 15 but was not diagnosed as having the rare disease until several days later. . . .

The writer wanted to avoid repeating "rabies" but seemed to have no qualms about repeating "the rare disease," which is more conspicuous than the name of the disease and probably unnecessary, given the frequency.

Similarly, in the passage below, "AIDS" conspicuously becomes "the deadly disease" twice and then "the fatal disease."

> CHICAGO—Companies must educate employees about AIDS to prevent "groundless hysteria" when a co-worker contracts the deadly disease, the U.S. surgeon general said Tuesday. . . .
>
> Koop said company education program should tell employees how the deadly disease is spread.
>
> The fatal disease has no cure.

A book of popular science asks, in referring to the change in weight of a radioactive object, "Would not its surface dust off a little, or corrode that much?" The (two) authors appear to have introduced "that much" to avoid repeating

"a little." The phrases are almost opposites.

In broadcasts, Hawaii has repeatedly become "paradise"; the John F. Kennedy household, "Camelot"; Mars, "the red planet"; Microsoft, "the software giant"; the New York Stock Exchange, "the big board"; Elvis Presley, "the king"; and the U.S. Supreme Court, "the high court."

2. How it causes confusion

The drive to avoid repetition and find a synonym at all costs can result in more than just ungainly expression. The danger of confusing the reader or listener is far more serious than the danger of boring him.

In telling what is new, if the writer varies not only that which changes but also that which remains constant, the readers may have trouble grasping what is new. Three press examples follow:

> Shorter work shifts for young doctors replaced the customary 36-hour shifts for medical interns and residents.

Did hospitals replace "medical interns and residents" with "young doctors" when reducing the work shifts? Probably not; one phrase is probably the writer's synonym for the other. But if the staff members did not change, why change what we call them? It was not even necessary to use nouns twice. A pronoun would have worked: "Shorter work shifts for medical interns and residents replaced *their* customary 36-hour shifts."

When a topic is unfamiliar or exotic, readers (or listeners) may not realize that two terms are supposed to mean the same thing. A news story about the discovery of an enzyme in the stomach contains this sentence:

> People have higher blood levels of alcohol when the substance is injected

into the blood than they have when they drink the same amount of alcohol.

It is reasonable for readers to think at first that "the substance" is the enzyme. But the context indicates it is *alcohol*. The writer was just synonymizing and never thought to use the pronoun *it*.

This is about an election in Japan:

It also is the first time since the Liberal Democratic Party came into existence in 1955 that the ruling conservatives face a parliamentary election as the underdogs.

The story never explains outright that the Liberal Democratic Party is the "ruling conservatives." American readers who are uninitiated to Japanese politics and unaccustomed to finding liberals described as conservatives may be excused if they mistake them for two different parties.

SYSTEMATIC and SYSTEMIC. *See* **Confusing pairs.**

T

TABLE as verb. *See* CHAIR, 2.

TAKE and BRING. *See* BRING and TAKE.

TAKEN and TOOK. *See* Tense, 5A.

TAKE PLACE. *See* HAPPEN, OC-CUR, and TAKE PLACE.

TALK TO. *See* SPEAK TO, TALK TO.

Tautology. The country had heard many tributes to the late Justice Thurgood Marshall but nothing else quite like a statement by the moderator of a television forum: "His funeral this week marked the end of his life."

It was a type of *tautology,* a statement that is undeniable but uninformative and usually characterized by the repetition in essence of a thought. It may contain contradictory elements, as in a sentence from a well-known book: "This uncertain change toward warmth may go on or it may not."

An American general exhibited tautological mastery. As secretary of state, he addressed the Organization of American States and imparted this intelligence about the Falkland Islands: "It is quite clear that the crisis has reached a critical point." Later, in a so-called presidential debate, he said, "There are finite limits

to what Europe can do," as though distinguishing them from *infinite* limits.

That last quotation illustrates another meaning of *tautology:* the unnecessary repetition of a word, phrase, or sentence, or its meaning; or an example of such repetition. A synonym is *redundancy* (noun). That which is unnecessarily repetitious is *redundant* (adjective). A term with similar meaning is *pleonasm,* the use of more words than are necessary to express an intended meaning; or an example thereof. (The words are pronounced taut-TOL-uh-gee, re-DUN-dense-see, re-DUN-dent, and PLEA-uh-nazm.)

Repetition per se is not wrong; it can be beneficial when it aids clarity. More confusion results from efforts to *avoid* repetition than from repetition.

Here, however, we consider *unnecessary* repetition. It may be obvious: "This evening ABC will have a special *Prime Time* special." Usually it is somewhat more subtle.

When a participant in a televised talk show called a detective in a murder case racially prejudiced, the host jumped in, informing all, "It's an alleged allegation." No one asked him, "What other kind of allegation is there?"

Interviewed on television about a kidnaping, a policeman said, "We've had a canine dog in the area, trying to locate the suspects." The interviewer failed to ask him, "What other kind of dog is there?"

An anchor woman announced in a national news program, "Washington has been expecting Russia to expel an American diplomat, but so far that hasn't happened yet." The sentence did not need both "so far" and "yet."

In a report on a straw poll at a convention in Florida, a TV man said, "Each one of those votes cost him [Senator Dole] about $1,800 apiece." Either "Each one of" or "apiece" could have been discarded.

This is from a newspaper: "The legal defense group's report said women in particular are being singled out for harassment" (in the military). They "in particular" are being picked on if they are being "singled out."

Another newspaper said the "Party of the Democratic Revolution . . . will likely choose . . . its two-time presidential also-ran in 1988 and 1994" to run for mayor of Mexico City. The paper could have left it to the readers to add one and one.

Still another paper said a man was convicted of making a "false misrepresentation in the sale of a security"—as distinguished from a true misrepresentation?

Three hosts of talk shows on a radio station uttered these remarks: (In support of car travel rather than public transit to save time:) "Forty-five minutes is forty-five minutes." (On commitments made by news media:) "Off the record is off the record." (Of the president and his aides:) "To the extent that they should be held accountable, they should be held accountable."

Most of us, authors included, are occasional tautologists. A book about books tells us, "Every book is a book yet each one is an individual combination of author, content, publisher, timing" (etc.). It is indisputable that a book is a book, a rose is a rose, boys will be boys, business is business, a deal is a deal, and that's that.

See also **Twins; Verbosity;** and the cross-reference **Repetition and its avoidance.**

TEAM OF. *See* **Collective nouns.**

TEAR, TORE, TORN. A hurricane in Florida was being described for a national radio audience: "There were roofs completely tore up."

"Tore" was wrong. It is standard English only as the past tense of the verb *tear:* "He *tore* the book." The past participle of *tear* is *torn,* which should have been used: "There were roofs completely *torn* up" (or, better, "Roofs were completely . . ."). Other examples: "He has *torn* the book" and "The book is *torn.*"

TEMBLOR and TREMBLER. A *temblor* is an earthquake. A *trembler* is someone or something that trembles. To tremble is to shiver or quake, so the words are close enough to be easily confused.

In commenting on a terrorist attack on U.S. servicemen in Saudi Arabia, a panelist on a television forum sought a picturesque metaphor. U.S. forces were "in a deep fault between the twentieth century and the eleventh century," he said. "This was a trembler." He meant it was a *temblor.*

Both words seem to have originated in the Latin *tremulus,* trembling. But *temblor* came via Spanish, in which it means a tremor or shiver; while *tremble(r)* came via French, in which *trembler* means to tremble.

Tense. *1. Definitions. 2. Don't swap tenses in the middle of a sentence. 3. Fit quoted and nonquoted parts together. 4. Look to the future grammatically. 5. Perfect your perfect tenses. 6. Tell the story in the past or present, not both.*

1. Definitions

Tense is a form of a verb that indicates the *time* of an action: past, present, or future. It usually says something also about the *completion* or *continuation* of the action.

Mistakes in tense are rife in print, let alone speech. We will turn to illustrations in later sections, headed by suggestions for the orderly use of tenses. Here we list the main tenses and some typical uses.

A. The *past* tense (also called the *preterit* or *preterite*). It indicates that an action occurred in the past ("She went home an hour ago") or that a state or condition existed in the past ("It was the best of times").

B. The *present* tense. It indicates that an action occurs now ("The earth revolves around the sun" / "He is here") or occurs customarily ("I go to work daily") or that something exists now ("The house still stands").

C. The *future* tense. It indicates that an action is going to take place. ("A courier will deliver the letter." / "I'll be there.")

D. The *perfect* tenses. *Perfect* in grammar indicates when an action was, is, or will be completed. Three are as follows:

- The *past perfect* tense (or *pluperfect*)—the action was completed before a given time in the past or before a certain other occurrence. ("They had fled Germany by the time the war started.")
- The *present perfect* tense—the action is completed now. This tense links the past with the present. It may refer to an action or actions that began in the past, continuing or recurring until the present. ("Business has been good." / "Man has hunted since prehistoric times.") Or it may refer to a past action that affects the present. ("They have given the police clues.")
- The *future perfect* tense—the action will be completed in the future,

whether or not it has already started. ("The staff will have totaled all the receipts by tomorrow noon.")

E. The *progressive* tenses (or *progressive forms*). They indicate that an action was, is, or will be continuing. ("I was running." / "The Lees are visiting us." / "He will be singing."

Some general principles, quotations, and commentary follow. The discussions here concern the *indicative* mood; that is, the ordinary verb form for communicating information. For other forms, consult **Mood; Subjunctive.** The basic form of a verb is discussed under **Infinitive,** which includes 3, the *perfect infinitive. See also* **Verbs.**

2. Don't swap tenses in the middle of a sentence

It seems that the writer of the following sentence, a columnist, could not decide whether to tell his story in the *past* tense or the *present* tense, so he used both.

He then took off at breakneck speed and as I zoomed down the road at 60 mph this guy pulls alongside and points at the laundry.

The passage is fairly clear but untidy. It is as though the writer wore one black shoe and one white. He should have chosen one tense or the other and stuck to it, at least for the duration of the sentence. (A comma after "60 mph" would have helped also.)

The quotation below should have been entirely in the *past* tense. It is not plausible the way it stands.

. . . William Lowe, president of I.B.M.'s entry systems division, said earlier this year that the company is investing as much in future RISC-based products as it has put into its PS/2 personal computer line.

"Earlier this year," when he talked about then current spending, he "said . . . that the company *was* investing" as much in the future products "as it *had* put into" the personal computer line. We do not know what the company "is investing" now or has invested since "earlier this year."

Such shifting from *past* to *present* or to *future* is common in the popular press, and it is not always a product of ignorance. On one newspaper, the city editor told us staff members that it was considered ungrammatical to write that way, but he instructed us to do it anyhow.

In a normal sentence, if the main verb is in the *past,* the verb of a dependent clause also goes in the *past.* "He *said* [main verb] that he *did* [dependent verb]." In the *present,* "He *says* that he *does*" is correct. "He *said* that he *does*" is incorrect and illogical.

A book mixes the *past* and the *present:*

> Supper of desert survival rations, dehydrated stew and rice, was delicious when you're hungry.

"Was" clashes with the contracted *are* in "you're." Make it either "*is* delicious when you're hungry" or "was delicious when you *were* hungry."

The following passage adds an awkward mixture of plural and singular to its shift from *past* to *present.*

> But all five books became best sellers. And while the chain stores eventually jumped aboard the sales bandwagon, it was independent bookstores that are responsible for their success.

Better: ". . . it was *the* independent *bookstore* that *was* responsible . . ." or "independent bookstores *were* responsible. . . . " (And change "their" to *the*

books' so that no one thinks "their" refers to "the chain store.")

Here an adverb pertaining to the *present* purports to modify a verb in the *past:*

> Currently, 30 people on Death Row nationwide committed murder when they were under 18.

Opening the sentence with "currently" sets the scene in the *present* for the whole sentence. Therefore the main verb cannot be "committed" or any other verb in the *past.* Place "currently" after "people," or else revise the rest of the sentence. One possible revision adds two words: "Currently, 30 people *who* committed murder when they were under 18 *are* on Death Row nationwide."

An attribution, like *he said* or *she said,* parenthetically inserted in a sentence, usually does not affect the other verbs. This excerpt is acceptable: "Toward that end, she explained, DHS is working with . . . universities. . . . "

While generally favoring consistency in tense, most authorities would make an exception for supposed timeless truths: "He said that the universe is finite," rather than "*was* finite." / "It showed that crime does not pay," rather than "*did* not pay." Some, more conservative, would not make that exception. You may decide for yourself.

See also 6; **Anachronism,** 2.

3. Fit quoted and nonquoted parts together

Parts of a sentence must fit together grammatically, whether or not some of it is a quotation.

In the second sentence below, the quoted part does not match the nonquoted part. The passage is from a history book.

> No one, Tory or Whig, could design a British victory out of what had hap-

pened at Lexington and Concord. Nor had the peasants "ran for their lives."

The two halves of the second sentence do not jibe. It starts out in one tense (pluperfect) and finishes in another (preterit). You may not say the peasants "had . . . ran. . . . " A change like this would put the whole sentence in one tense, yet keep the quotation intact:

> Nor was it true that the peasants "ran for their lives."

An alternative would be to keep the first half of the sentence but change the quotation, making it indirect:

> Nor had the peasants run for their lives.

The quotation marks must be removed because the quotation no longer is exact. (Anyway, the book fails to indicate who is being quoted.)

4. Look to the future grammatically

A. WILL and SHALL

The modern use of the *future* tense is fairly easy. *Will* with an infinitive usually does the job. "When will they ever learn?" / "I will be there with bells on." / "You will do fine." In colloquial speech only half of *will* may be needed: "I'll be seeing you." The *present* can indicate the future in some constructions: "He performs here tomorrow." So can a *progressive* tense: "He will be performing here" or "He is going to perform here" (which becomes, in loose colloquial speech, "He's gonna perform . . .").

Shall usually implies determination or legal requirement. "We shall overcome." / "It shall be unlawful to. . . . " Now and then *shall* is otherwise needed: "Shall we dance?" / "Shall I draw up the papers?" (The formal use of the two words, now obsolete in the United States and even disappearing in England, prescribed *shall* for the simple future in the first person and for determination, obligation, inevitability, etc. in the second or third person. *Will* was used the other way: for the simple future in the second or third person and for determination etc. in the first person.)

B. Dependent clauses

Two types of recurrent mistakes concern a dependent, or subordinate, clause:

- Repeating *will* in a dependent clause instead of using the *present* tense. "The administration of Mayor Harris will end at noon tomorrow when John Bradley will take office as mayor." The second "will" is superfluous. Change "will take" to *takes*.
- Using *will* in a dependent clause when the main verb is in the *past* tense. "Edison predicted that he will perfect the incandescent lamp." Inasmuch as *predicted* is in the *past* tense, *will* has to go in the *past* tense too; its *past* tense is *would*. "Edison predicted that he *would*. . . . " It is the future from his standpoint, years ago. "Will"—the future from our standpoint—makes no sense. Similarly, ". . . Smythe . . . was told that he will be sent back to . . . Maze Prison" needs correction: "was told that he *would* be sent back."

The same principle holds when the future is suggested in other ways: "K—— said he plans to present the case to the district attorney." / "M—— said she plans to fight the denial in court if necessary." Change "plans" to *planned*. We know their plans at the time they were interviewed, but their plans may have changed by now. *Expect, forecast, intend, look forward to,* and *predict* are among other verbs that suggest the future.

C. Conditional sentences

Another problem concerns the conditional sentence: a sentence in which a future action depends on something else happening. The problem takes two forms:

- Mixing "will" and some verb in the *past subjunctive,* which are incompatible:

  > But the assistance will be suspended late in November if any of the major Congressional committees dealing with the money objected to its continuation.

Either change "objected" to *objects* or change "will" to *would.* The latter gives us the subjunctive mood. (*See* **Mood; Subjunctive.**) Such use of *would* should not be confused with *would* as the *past* tense of *will* in the indicative mood, the ordinary verb form.

- Mixing the subjunctive "would" and some verb in the *indicative,* which are incompatible:

  > The government estimates that Hong Kong . . . would lose as many as 20,000 jobs if Bush doesn't extend the trading agreement.

This time, "would" should be *will.* An alternative is to change "doesn't" to *didn't* or *did not.*

D. Distortion of meaning

More than grammatical tidiness may be involved. Confusion of tenses made the two excerpts opaque and misleading.

> The directors of the Nicaraguan Resistance, the Contra alliance, said at Sapoa they will present the government with a list of prisoners that they had wanted liberated yesterday.

To be compatible with "said," which is in the past tense, "will" should go in the past tense: *would.* "Will" says something is going to happen. In actuality, the presentation of the list may be completed already. A further correction (this foreshadows section *5*) is to omit "had." It wrongly implies that the directors' desire for a liberation preceded the Sapoa event, five days ago, and then ended.

The tenses below are so badly confounded that the time of the main action is not apparent.

> Upon completion of that term, [Judge] Jackson put him on supervised probation for a year, meaning that he must report regularly to a probation officer and be subject to periodic drug tests.

It seems to be saying that two events occurred in the past; that after the convict finished serving his term, the judge put him on probation. That is not the intended meaning. The phrase "Upon completion of that term" should have been followed by a clause like this, in the *future* tense: "he will be on supervised probation." Instead, the phrase is followed by the irrelevant clause "Jackson put him . . . ," which falsely unites with it.

5. Perfect your perfect tenses

A. Be sure of the participle and use it with an H-word

The *past perfect* tense uses (1) *had* and (2) the past participle of a verb. ("They *had eaten,* so they were not hungry.")

The *present perfect* tense uses (1) *have* or *has* and (2) the past participle of a verb. ("I *have worn* this suit for years." / "She *has shown* courage.")

H. L. Mencken listed over 100 past participles (or "perfect participles") that he found misused in "common" or "vulgar" American speech. Often they were used in place of the past tense; for instance, "I been" and "I done" instead of *I was* and *I did*. He said such misuse was an old practice, common in other English dialects but particularly well marked in the American dialect.

The opposite, the use of the past tense in place of the past participle, is another old practice. At one time, Mencken wrote, "even the best writers were apparently unconscious of its inelegance": Shakespeare's plays contain such forms as "I have *wrote*" / "I am *mistook*" / and "he has *rode*." (*Written, mistaken,* and *ridden* are now standard.)

Such lapses are rare in published material nowadays but not in oral speech. In broadcasts a Washington state legislator and a Washington, D.C., correspondent for a newspaper muffed *has run* and *have run* respectively: "The fact that the child has ran away could be for any number of reasons." / "He [Gingrich] would never have ran for president."

The sentences below were uttered by members of the general public and heard on the air. (Correct forms are in brackets.)

"I must have ate [eaten] lunch with fifteen MPD patients." / "It shouldn't have broke [broken] like that." / "Maybe they should have gave [given] him some treatment program." / "She had just took [taken] her car to the car wash." Each speaker wrongly used a past tense in place of a past participle. Another erred the opposite way: "I looked over to the left and I seen [saw] a tornado."

Sometimes an incorrect participle gets into print:

Egypt's chief religious official has also spoke on behalf of Abu Zeid, saying he could not be ordered to divorce. . . .

Although "spoke" was accepted as the past participle of *speak* from the fourteenth to eighteenth centuries, now it is *spoken. Spoke* is the past tense.

A travel book leaves out the participle altogether:

but it is quite possible thousands of F-M listeners have or will hear it from this exact spot.

"Have" does not go with "hear." A correction: "have *heard* or will hear. . . . " (A hyphen in *FM* is unnecessary.)

See also **Participles.**

B. Do not confuse the sequence of events

A sequence of events is subject to confusion in the press. When a writer fails to make it clear which events came first, second, and third, the problem may amount to shortcomings in the use of the *perfect* tenses.

An account of a shooting rampage contains this passage:

Bobby S——, 20, was in fair condition at Denver General Hospital. He escaped from the restaurant and ran to nearby apartments to call police.

The escape and the run took place *before* his stay in the hospital. Therefore the *past perfect* (not the *past*) is the tense to use: "He *had* escaped from the restaurant and *run*. . . . " (Following that sentence, if a still earlier event was described, the *past perfect* tense would be used again; for instance, "He had been cleaning the kitchen when the shooting began.")

Conversely, the next sentence uses the *past perfect* tense unnecessarily in lieu of a simple *past tense*.

His client and the two cops were yelling and cursing when the lieutenant on duty showed up. Incredibly, less than a minute later, the lieutenant had hauled off and punched W—— in the face.

The punching followed the yelling and cursing. Therefore it is most clearly described in the *past* tense. For example: "Incredibly, within a minute, the lieutenant hauled off. . . . "

Next, the sequence of two events is mistakenly reversed by the use of the *present perfect* instead of the *past perfect*:

The Mohajir group called the strike to demand the release of more than 100 of its workers it says have been kidnaped by members of the Pakistan Students Federation. . . .

The alleged kidnaping came first; then the Mohajir group called the strike and talked. So change "have been kidnaped" to "*had* been kidnaped." (Still better: ". . . 100 of its workers *who,* it *said, had* been kidnaped"—adding the relative pronoun and placing the talking with the striking.)

C. *Mind your P's and H's*

The press often shows misunderstanding of the *perfect* tenses and their relation to the *past* and *present.* Sometimes the problem is the intrusion of a certain word or phrase.

F.B.I. officials have previously acknowledged that the agency recruited an informer . . . to join Cispes.

The *present perfect* tense is functionally equivalent to the *present* tense. Its *have* or *has* does not mix with "previously" or "in the past." Here are three alternative ways to repair the sample sentence:

1. Omit "previously," using the *present perfect* correctly: "F.B.I. officials have acknowledged. . . . " (They made the acknowledgment at an indefinite time before this moment.)

2. Omit "have" and insert *had* before "recruited": "F.B.I. officials previously acknowledged [they did so in the *past*] that the agency *had* recruited an informer. . . . " (The phrase *had recruited* is in the *past perfect.* The agency had done the recruiting *before* the officials did the acknowledging.)

3. Change "have" to *had* and insert *had* before "recruited," using the *past perfect* twice: "F.B.I. officials *had* previously acknowledged that the agency *had* recruited. . . . " (Again the recruiting preceded the acknowledging. The officials had done the acknowledging before something else happened: viz. the latest news was made public.) "Previously" is unnecessary with the *past perfect* but may be used for extra clarity.

To combine *have* or *has* with "previously" or "in the past" creates a monstrous nontense. (Dare we dub it the *highly imperfect?*) A favorite of writers of scientific papers, it has stumbled its way into the popular press as well.

Contra spokesmen have previously stated they use Claymore mines. . . .

Omit "previously." As an alternative, omit "have" and put "use" in the past tense: "Contra spokesmen previously stated they used. . . . "

The private meeting, which hasn't been disclosed previously, could create additional political and legal problems for the embattled attorney general. . . .

In the past, Mr. Meese has maintained he had an "extremely limited" role with the pipeline. . . .

In the upper sentence, "previously" could well be changed to *until now.* In the lower, leave out "In the past."

Mr. Dukakis, displaying more humor and emotion than he has in the
past, poked fun at the criticism of his
lack of charisma.

The sentence is doubly wrong. The auxiliary verb "has" should be changed to
had. Even so, it is not enough. What
verb links up with it? Not "displaying."
Make it "... than he *had displayed.* ..."

D. *Stay in the right time frame*
The three press sentences below make
essentially the same mistake: shifting
back in time from the *present perfect*
tense. It is functionally equivalent to the
present tense.

The chorus of critical statements
about Colonel North, largely from
Administration officials, has reached
such a crescendo that Elliott Abrams,
the Assistant Secretary of State for In-
ter-American affairs, was moved to
offer a spirited defense.

Change "was moved" to "*has been*
moved." The action started in the past,
but it has continued until approximately
the present, and the present cannot affect
the past. (*See also* CRESCENDO.)

MGM-UA has produced few films
lately while its controlling shareholder ... sought a buyer.

Make it "*has* sought. ... " The two actions have gone on at about the same
time.

... The group tried to restore order
after a demonstration on Saturday
night got out of control, and had later
provided safe escort for endangered
Americans.

Scrap "had." The escort was provided
later, not earlier; so the *past perfect* is unwarranted.
The *present perfect* tense in the first

clause of the second sentence below does
not belong there. The *past* tense is used
elsewhere throughout the passage, from
a newspaper story.

For a while it appeared that the parties would simply be canceled. ... But
as the Emperor's blood pressure has
risen and fallen in twice-daily readings, a consensus slowly emerged.
Parties were all right, as long as no
one had too much fun.

The consensus "emerged" in the past
"as"—at the same time that—the Emperor's blood pressure *rose and fell* in the
past. There is no reason here to link the
action of the past to the present, which is
what the *present perfect* tense does.
Similarly, the *present perfect* is unwarranted in this sentence, from a book of
essays:

... Nearly all the linguistic tendencies
of the present day have been displayed
in earlier centuries. ...

Change "have been" to *were,* in the *past*
tense. "Earlier centuries" are history.

E. *Watch out for a change in meaning*
In the sample below, an excerpt from
a newspaper story about an election in
Haiti, the use of a wrong tense reverses
the meaning intended to be conveyed.

"The election process was great,"
Carter said, playing down the technical glitches as not surprising in a
country that has never had a totally
free election.

"... Has never had" indicates that the
country never had a totally free election
up to the time that the sentence was
written. It was written on the day after
an election was held. Therefore one
could logically conclude from the excerpt that the election was not totally
free. But the context suggests the oppo-

site. A correction is in order. Omit "has," so that the action is in the past tense; and, to leave no doubt as to the meaning, put in a qualifying word or phrase: ". . . a country that never *before* had a totally free election" or ". . . a country that never had a totally free election *until yesterday.*"

A television reporter's sloppy use of tense risked creating misunderstanding in an inflammable international atmosphere. He spoke of a recently negotiated agreement to provide access to all sites in Iraq for weapons inspection, "something Iraq has refused to do." Using "has"—the *present perfect*—incorrectly implied a current refusal by Iraq, contrary to its agreement. Using *had*—the *past perfect*—would have correctly indicated Iraq's refusal before the agreement was reached.

6. Tell the story in the past or present, not both

Even when individual sentences are grammatical, a passage may be stylistically flawed when tenses shift from sentence to sentence. Three books provide examples. (Emphasis is added.)

The paragraph below vacillates from *past* to *present*, from *present* to *past*, as though the author could not make up his mind.

During the first period of the renaissance madrigal . . . the principal leaders *were* the Flemish musicians who had settled in Italy. The composer's chief concern at this stage *is* to give pleasure to the performers. . . . In its middle phase . . . the renaissance madrigal *becomes* a conscious art form. . . . Both Lassus and Palestrina . . . *enriched* the literature of the form during these years. [*See also* THESE and THOSE.]

The *historical present*—that is, the *present tense* used to tell of past events—is an established rhetorical device. It

suits not only historical accounts but also descriptions of books and summaries of dramatic and literary plots. If chosen, it is generally best to continue it till the story is over.

Another author shifts from *future* to *present* (acceptable) to *past* (unacceptable) in one sentence.

The course we *will* follow *begins* just before World War I; it *was* the recognition of the discontinuous behavior of the atom, the quantum theory.

Change "was" to *is*.
Either *present* or *past*—but not both—would be appropriate in the final example.

Wagner in "The Ring" *employs* six harps; and Berlioz, of course, *made* liberal use of the instrument. [*See also* OF COURSE, 2.]

Change either "employs" to *employed* or "made" to *makes*.

TESTAMENT and TESTIMONY.

A *testament* is a will. In modern use it is relegated to the legal phrase *last will and testament*, which is redundant but well established.

Testimony is evidence, particularly a statement made by a witness under oath in a court. It can be used figuratively: "This gift bears testimony of my love."

The two words have significance in Biblical theology. *Testament*: a covenant, a promise by God to man; hence the Old Testament and New Testament. *Testimony*: the decalogue or other precepts of God.

Both originating in the Latin *testis*, a witness, they have been differentiated over the centuries but sometimes confused in contemporary times. Occasionally "testament" is used when *testimony* is meant, and some dictionaries condone the mix-up.

On network television a reporter described the scene of a ship accident at New Orleans.

> For now it is wedged between a pedestrian playland and a busy commercial route. There it sits, a glaring testament that a river offers the best of both worlds and shows no mercy when those worlds collide.

Her use of "testament," in lieu of *testimony,* was either a lapse or an instance of poetic license.

THAN. 1. *Confused with THEN.* 2. *With various words.*

1. *Confused with THEN*

The mistake in both of these published sentences would not have been considered a mistake a few centuries ago: ". . . Women have smaller brains then men by an average of 10 percent." / "Time and his genius for bureaucracy taught him . . . to be a monarch rather then a representative." The writers (of articles condemning an anthropology professor and an FBI director respectively) probably know better; inadvertence or typographical error could be to blame.

Than has been spelled differently from *then* since about 1700. Here are other differences between the words:

- *Than* is a conjunction, a connecting word, in a sentence expressing comparison ("John is faster than Fred"), preference ("I would rather be right than president"), or difference or exception ("He said nothing, other than his name, rank, and serial number").
- *Then* can be a noun, meaning a particular time ("Until then, let's keep in touch"). *Then* can be also an adverb, meaning at a certain time in the past ("She was thinner then"), next ("Then he drew his sword"), in that case ("Then why should I go?"),

or moreover ("These shoes fit well, and then they're comfortable").

In careful speech, they are pronounced differently, *than* rhyming with *can;* and *then* rhyming with *pen.* Speaking hastily, people often pronounce both like *then.*

2. *With various words*

A. *"AS"*

A comparison using *as* and a comparison using *than* do not mix. The idioms are confused in these grim statistical items from television news: "The rate of crib deaths is twice as high for black infants than for whites." / ". . . A child is fourteen times as likely to die of gunshot wounds in this country than in Northern Ireland." Each "than" should be *as:* "as high . . . as" / "as likely . . . as."

Than would be right in a construction like this: "Ford grew richer than Croesus." Or this: "It's more popular than any other novel in print." *Than* commonly follows (1) an adjective with the suffix *-er* or (2) the adverb *more* or *less* plus an adjective.

See also **AS,** *3.*

B. *"DIFFERENT"*

Phrases like *brighter than* and *louder than* are proper, containing comparatives. It is incorrect to say, "Donkeys are different than mules." *Different from* is the accepted idiom. *Different* is not a comparative. *See also* **DIFFERENT,** *1.*

C. *Personal pronouns*

A common puzzle is the choice between *than I* and *than me,* between *than we* and *than us,* and so on. The choice of pronoun depends on its function in the *than* clause.

In "Myrtle plays better than he does" no one disputes the *he;* it is the subject of the verb *does.* Now what if that verb is dropped? Though unexpressed, it is understood. The sentence "Myrtle plays better than he" (that is, than he *does*) construes *he* as the subject of that unexpressed verb.

In "The company rewarded nobody more than him" (that is, than *the company rewarded* him), *him* is construed as an object of an unexpressed subject and verb. *See also* **Pronouns**, *10,* especially E.

D. RATHER; "PREFER"

"Rather" sometimes is superfluous before *than*: "I'm more concerned with affirming a principle rather than settling the case." Being a comparative, *more* goes with *than*. "Rather," a comparative adverb, becomes redundant.

At times *rather than* is correct but a verb form that follows is questionable: "We will depend on our own staff, rather than turning [?] to the national office." Change "turning" to *turn*. As a conjunction, *than* ordinarily links parallel elements: "Johnny is playing rather than studying." / "He runs rather than walks." / "I slept rather than worked." / "They chose to call rather than write [or "to write"]. There is a trend, however, toward treating *rather than* as a preposition, in the manner of this book excerpt: "James delivered the address himself, rather than falling [fell?] back on inexperienced theological students." Some grammarians accept the *-ing* form as idiomatic, especially at the start of a sentence: "Rather than getting fired, I quit my job."

Prefer should not be followed by *than* or *rather than*. Normally you prefer one thing *to* another: "I prefer chocolate to vanilla."

E. SOONER; "HARDLY" or "SCARCELY"

Than often follows a comparative adjective or adverb: "He looks *bigger than* you." / "It goes *faster than* any other car." *Sooner* is a comparative adverb, often followed by *than*. Here the earliness

of two actions are being compared, correctly: "No *sooner* had we arrived *than* the show started." To substitute "when" is an error. Confusion with *hardly* or *scarcely,* neither of which is a comparative, appears to be at the root.

This is correct: "Hardly [or "scarcely"] had we arrived *when* the show started." To substitute "than" is an error.

THAN ANY. *See* ANY, *1.*

THANK, THANKS. The president of Bolivia was quoted (although in which language and under what circumstances he spoke was not stated):

> Bolivia's unemployment rate stands at 23 percent, thanks to the currency devaluation and other "brutal" economic reforms imposed on the country by the World Bank to reduce the country's roughly $4 billion foreign debt, Zamora says.

No one is likely to offer thanks for an unemployment rate of 23 percent, unless one's intention is bitter sarcasm or the hiring of cheap labor. Neither accounts for the statement, judging from the context and the word "brutal" (rather than, say, "kindly").

You would not expect anyone to offer thanks for the collapse of a road either. A television announcer said in a preview of the news, "Highway number 101 collapses near Salinas, thanks to the floods of '97."

At least three dictionaries define *thanks to* as "thanks be given to." For a secondary definition, they offer such phrases as "on account of," "owing to," and "as a result of." But plainly it is not always appropriate to replace them with *thanks to.*

Thanks (noun, plural) is an expression of gratitude. To tell someone *thanks* (interjection) is to say *thank you* informally.

To *thank* (verb, transitive) is to express gratitude (to someone or something). Occasionally it can mean to blame, when used in a sarcastic sense: "We have ourselves to thank for the defeat." One dictionary's alternative definition of *thank* as "blame"—with no mention of its special, sarcastic meaning—can be misleading.

THAT.
1. *Anti-THAT prejudice; unidiomatic sentences.* 2. *Errors of omission: wrong road, ambiguity.* 3. *Need for a pair; AND THAT, BUT THAT.* 4. *Unnecessary THATs.*

1. Anti-THAT prejudice; unidiomatic sentences

Some publications and press services harbor an irrational prejudice. They are *that*-haters. They consider *that* (as a conjunction or relative pronoun, introducing a clause) to be usually unnecessary. In their style books, they instruct their writers to do without it whenever possible.

Sometimes it may indeed be possible to omit *that*; for instance, after *said* and a few other verbs: "She said the money was safe." / "He thinks the car is defective." Some clauses of other construction may hold together idiomatically without *that*: "This is the school I attended." On the other hand, unless one has orders to the contrary, it usually cannot hurt to put it in: "This is the house that Jack built."

Often the mass media print or broadcast sentences that are unidiomatic without *that*. Although the meaning is understood in the following four sentences, the clauses in each do not hold together gracefully. An asterisk indicates the spot where one would normally connect them with *that*.

[A movie criticism on television:] He is jealous * she has made a new male friend.

[A television report:] For those who died [on the U.S.S. *Iowa*], the thought * it was not an accident only deepened the tragedy.

[A newspaper item:] ... She arrived at court for a jury trial on charges * she slapped a Beverly Hills motorcycle cop.

[A newspaper column:] ... Their [Democrats'] lone window of opportunity is the voters' sense * they're being left out.

See also THAT and WHICH; WHO, THAT, and WHICH.

2. Errors of omission: wrong road, ambiguity

The absence of *that* is more serious in certain sentences in which a verb, such as *believes* or *reported,* has a clause as its direct object. Omitting *that* after the verb can make a fragment of the clause falsely appear to be the direct object. The reader may be sent down the wrong road and have to start the sentence again.

The first two of three press examples are from a newspaper that is not one of the *that*-haters and cautions its staff members against just this sort of thing.

At the same time, he said, he believes the people he has met since coming to the United States last week have been surprised at "our openness, our friendliness and our desire to bring peace to the entire world."

The company reported 47 percent of those who had taken the test had failed because of admitted transgressions or attitudes.

Although acknowledging New Mexico, like most states, offers a "fair reporting privilege" shield from libel lawsuits, the judge said the privilege did not apply because the Journal was reporting on a statement it itself had made.

In the first example, "believes" seems at first to have "the people" as its object. "He believes the people he has met since coming to the United States last week" forms a false thought—one that is plausible until "have been surprised" comes along. Following "believes" with *that* would have prevented the problem.

In the next two examples, "The company reported 47 percent of those who had taken the test" and "Although acknowledging New Mexico" also form false thoughts. "Reported" and "acknowledging" should each be followed by *that*.

Omitting *that* can render a sentence ambiguous when time is an element: "The Governor said on June 30 the state's debt stood at $57 million." If (a) he was telling what the size of the debt was on that day, follow "said" with *that*. But if (b) that was the day when he said it, follow "30" with *that*. (Another way to correct the sentence is to to put "on June 30" [a] at the end or [b] at the beginning.)

See also ASSURE (etc.), 2.

3. *Need for a pair; AND THAT, BUT THAT*

A single *that* may not be enough in a sentence containing a series of comparable clauses.

Doctors say that some home remedies help but others may be harmful.

Who is saying "others may be harmful"? If it is the doctors, follow "but" with *that*. If it is the person speaking, make that fact clear; e.g., "But evidence shows that others. . . . "

When the phrase *but that* or *and that* does begin a clause, normally the *that* parallels a *that* in the previous clause. Each of these two sample sentences omits the first *that:*

Mr. Bush said "no specific mission" was under discussion, but that Mr. Reagan was being kept informed.

. . . He said the imagery of the Palestinian uprising in the occupied West Bank and Gaza Strip had inspired some Jordanians and that other pressures were at work.

". . . Said *that*" would balance each sentence better. Although the meaning may be understandable without *that,* a tidier sentence could be easier to read. This is particularly true for sentences that are longer and more complicated:

Mr. Bush said the arrangement, which follows months of delicate negotiations with Japan, would safeguard sensitive computer software and that American companies would be guaranteed roughly 40 percent of the production work on the new jet fighter.

Some readers probably glanced back to see what "and that" referred to. "Mr. Bush said *that*" would have helped them. How could it have hurt?

A book on relativity fails to put elements of a sentence in proper relation. Two hypothetical space ships reach relative speeds of light.

. . . Observers on each ship would think the other ship had shrunk to zero in length, acquired an infinite mass, and that time on the other ship had slowed to a full stop!

To follow "think" with *that* would begin to improve the sentence. (It contains a defective series. Replace the first comma with *and. See* Series errors.)

The same principle of parallelism applies to *and which* and *and who*. *See* WHICH, 3; WHO, 2.

After *no doubt* or *no question*, "but that" is not strictly legitimate. *See* BUT, 2.

4. Unnecessary THATs

That is usually unnecessary before a direct quotation that is complete or starts at the beginning:

Shakespeare wrote, "Neither a borrower nor a lender be; For loan oft loses both itself and friend, And borrowing dulls the edge of husbandry."

Before a fragment of a direct quotation, *that* may be desirable:

Shakespeare wrote that "borrowing dulls the edge of husbandry."

Take care, however, that the *that* is not inside the quotation marks. This is wrong:

Shakespeare wrote "that borrowing dulls the edge of husbandry."

Sometimes a second "that" is erroneously inserted in a sentence when its function is already performed by the first *that*:

The party contends that as long as the present government remains in power that the nation will not mend its shattered economy.

". . . Contends that" includes everything that follows, because all of it is one thought. A second *that* is superfluous.

See also THAT, ALL THAT.

THAT, ALL THAT.

This is a British import of recent decades, an illogical colloquialism that should dispel any notion that the best English must come from England. It is the slovenly use of "that"—often preceded by a meaningless "all"—usually after a negative.

When used properly as an adverb, *that* means to the extent or degree stated or indicated. For instance, "The paper says 5,000 people attended, but I don't think *that* many were there."

A columnist told of people's fears during a gale and added, "There weren't that many people using umbrellas." How many people are "that many"? The preceding paragraphs did not state or indicate any number, so "that" did not refer to anything. It should have been discarded.

A book of popular science says, ". . . The actual telescopic effect is not *that* difficult to discover" and "Our daily understanding of our actions is not that far from a scientific account." Nothing was said about difficulty of discovery. Nothing was said about distance from science. "That" could have been omitted both times without sacrificing any meaning.

No standards of coldness, difference, time, or harm had come up when a network newscaster said illogically, "It wasn't warm, but it wasn't that cold"; a columnist wrote, "In my opinion, men and women are really not that different"; and an article said:

. . . It didn't take that long [for a presidential candidate to use a slanderous rumor]. . . . The last week's events may not have been that harmful.

Where were the editors to ask: How harmful? How long? How different? How cold? How far? How difficult? Some of them were putting vague *that*'s of their own into headlines: "For Corn Belt Farmers, Oat Bran Isn't That Chic."

Placing "all" before a misused "that" just adds another superfluous word, one that can sometimes be misleading. The two words were paired legitimately in a question asked by a television reporter, "Why would he want to give Democrats all that money?" *All* (adverb), meaning the entire amount (of), modified *that* (adjective), referring to a sum previously mentioned. The two words together modified *money* (noun).

But "all that" was superfluous in an editorial: "Voters do not always take elections for the European Parliament all that seriously. . . . " And an autobiography could have omitted the phrase five times; examples: ". . . The old man had not done all that badly. . . . I was not all that distressed. . . . "

"All that" contradicted a previous statement in each of three articles. One reported layoffs and declining profits at a television network and then added:

And according to . . . a media consulting firm, . . . the outlook is not all that bright.

If the writer had painted a bright picture but wanted to introduce some ominous fact, he could reasonably say "the outlook is not all that bright."

These are contradictory excerpts from a movie review and a record review:

. . . Dodge is a fairly boring guy and his co-workers aren't all that interesting either.

Sales have slumped in recent times, owing partly to poor-quality sound. Most of his recordings did not sound all that good when newly made in NBC's drably dry Studio 8H.

The expression introduces another opportunity for misunderstanding to the language. A headline dispensed a vague message:

Air bags not all
that safe, studies say.

If "not all," are some? And how safe is "that safe"? A review of a television series compared it with other series and said, "These guys aren't all that much fun." Are some of them? And this is from a news story:

A 69-year-old enthusiast of more rapid liberalization, Mr. Zhao had not been all that popular recently. . . .

The story did not say anything earlier about popularity; thus it provided no standard for gauging what "all that" meant. Had Mr. Zhao not been *very* popular? Had he not been popular at all? Was his popularity down to 35 percent? We have to guess. (We have to guess also what his age or liberalization policy has to do with his popularity. *See* **Modifiers,** 2.)

What has become popular is the substitution of "that" or "all that" for factual information. People holding a casual conversation or even the writer of a subjective column on some trivial subject may get away with it. It stands out sorely in a sober presentation of news or other facts.

The newspaper last quoted has run a periodic column by a maven in word usage, who should be expected to set us straight. This is an excerpt: "What, then, do you do when *strong* becomes pejorative and *weak* is not all that bad?"

A book by a self-styled word wizard uses an empty "that" term six times. In the example, a study on frequently used words is discussed:

The front-runners, whatever their order, should not be all that different today or any day. Our English, written or spoken, doesn't change all that much.

The author is evidently unaware of at least one change: the spread of a faddish expression that he uses twice in one paragraph.

Its insidious effects are manifested

four times in a compilation by a writer known for his sophisticated vocabulary: ". . . Really, the figure was not all that surprising. . . . There wasn't all that much to choose from. . . . " And so on.

Both "that" and "all that" appear in one sentence of an article. ". . . The jokes in the book are not in the main that great, not all that creative." How the terms differ and just what they mean are anyone's guess.

In a book for writers and editors, the problem is somewhat different; a standard for comparison is given: "Compared to a number of other professions, editing hasn't really been around all that long." Drop "all that." The opening phrase makes another comparative modifier redundant. (*See also* COMPARED TO and COMPARED WITH, *1*; REALLY.)

The final quotation is from a magazine essay by a professor of English, protesting the lowering of standards of behavior: ". . . Common decency has not been all that common for long stretches of human history." May one also protest the lowering of standards of English usage and all that fuzziness?

THAT and WHICH. *1. The difference. 2. Indiscriminate WHICH; mix-up of THAT and WHICH. 3. "THAT" in place of WHICH. 4. Versions of a famous phrase.*

1. The difference

Two book titles, *The Light That Failed* and *The Mouse That Roared*, help to illustrate the distinction between *that* and *which* (used as relative pronouns). *That* seemed to the authors to be the natural word to use. The books were not called *The Light* Which *Failed* and *The Mouse* Which *Roared*. The titles would have appeared stilted had they contained "Which." Furthermore, to many readers *That* firmly ties *Light* to *Failed,* and *Mouse* to *Roared.*

"Which" would suit a sentence like this: "The light, which failed only once, has long been a reliable beacon for seafarers." The clause within the commas is not essential to the main thought, so it starts with *which*. In contrast, take this sentence: "We need to replace the light that failed, but the other lights serve us well." *That failed* is an essential clause, hence *that*.

The *that* clause is called a *restrictive clause* (or, in Britain, a *defining clause*). No comma precedes it. The *which* clause is called a *nonrestrictive clause* (or, in Britain, a *nondefining clause*). Commas set it apart.

Sometimes the meaning of a sentence depends on the proper choice between the two pronouns. It makes a difference whether the boss tells his new employee (1) "Get the widget, *which* we always use for this type of work" or (2) "Get the widget *that* we always use for this type of work." Just what the new employee is to get depends on a single pronoun. If we assume that the boss knows his grammar, the first sentence implies that he has only one widget; the second sentence implies that he has more than one widget and insists on a particular one and that the newcomer had better find out which one.

Writers began consciously making the distinction between those two pronouns in the relatively recent past. In the book *The King's English*, first published in 1906, brothers H. W. and F. G. Fowler took a notable step toward increased clarity when they wrote:

. . . *That,* when possible, is the appropriate relative for defining and *which* for non-defining clauses. . . . It would contribute much to clearness of style if writers would always make up their minds whether they intend a definition or a comment and would invariably use no commas with a defining clause and two commas with a nondefining. [But the call for an invariable use of *two* commas was a mistake. The "non-defining" clause, or nonrestrictive clause, may come at the end of a sentence and need only one comma to set it apart.]

Practices in earlier centuries were chaotic. Literature suggests that some writers sensed differences between the two pronouns while others did not; often *which* was forced to serve both functions. The principle enunciated by the Fowlers had a good deal of influence in both Britain and the United States. By no means was there rapid or even general conformity. Numerous writers continued to favor a restrictive *which*. Emphasis is added in this 1920 passage from a work by H. G. Wells (and in the examples that follow):

. . . These nine main language groups . . . are the latest languages, the survivors, *which* have ousted their more primitive predecessors. There may have been other . . . ineffective centres of speech *which* were afterwards overrun by the speakers of still surviving tongues, and of elementary languages *which* faded out. We find strange little patches of speech still in the world *which* do not seem to be connected with any other language about them.

The first *which* seems to be nonrestrictive; the other three seem to be restrictive and, under the Fowler principle, replaceable by *that*. We cannot be positive of an author's intent when he uses *which* in both ways; at least he should precede each nonrestrictive *which* with a comma. Wells apparently has done so. Seven pages later, the word appears four times in one sentence.

The alternation of settlement, nomadic conquest, refinement, fresh conquest, refinement, *which* is characteristic of this phase of human history, is particularly to be noted in the region of the Euphrates and Tigris, *which* lay open in every direction to great areas *which* are not arid enough to be complete deserts, but *which* were not fertile enough to support civilized populations.

The first *which* and the second seem to be nonrestrictive; the latter two seem to be restrictive. Again, a comma correctly precedes what appears to be each nonrestrictive use. Still, we cannot be positive of the meaning of *which* when it is used in both ways. Such usage persists to the current day among many writers, although many others do observe the distinctions between *that* and *which*.

2. Indiscriminate WHICH; mix-up of THAT and WHICH

Some writers who use "which" in restrictive clauses at least set off nonrestrictive clauses with commas. Others seem totally baffled by the grammar and the punctuation and either (a) use "which" without the comma for both types of clause or (b) use "that" and "which" interchangeably. Trying to determine exactly what a writer intended can be an insoluble puzzle for a reader. There are writers who think *that* is more "colloquial" and *which* is more "literary." Nonsense. Each word has a clear function.

In the following passage, a newspaper writer uses "which" restrictively in his first sentence; in his second, he correctly chooses *which* for a nonrestrictive clause but fails to precede it with a comma.

. . . Increasing civil suit judgments against city, county and state governments are being caused by several factors, including . . . a court ruling *which* allows governments to be sued. . . .

The legislature in 1976 passed the Tort Claims Act *which* allows citizens to sue the government. . . .

In the first sentence, "which" should be *that*. In the second, a comma belongs after "Act" to make it clear that what comes after the comma is explanatory and not an integral part of what comes before.

A card listing postal rules contains two restrictive clauses using "which." Both are wrongly separated from the main sentence by commas.

Mail, which is properly addressed to a post office box or caller service number, will be delivered through that post office box or caller service. . . . Any information on the application, which changes or becomes obsolete, must be corrected by promptly updating the Form 1093 on file. . . .

Not all mail will be delivered; not all information must be corrected. Each "which" clause is essential to the main idea of the sentence. Thus all the commas should be deleted and each "which" should be *that*.

The sample sentence that follows, from a book criticizing American education, contains both *that* and *which* with no comma, used in a roughly parallel way. The precise intent of the author is uncertain.

But there is one dangerous new trend *that* threatens to wreak havoc upon our educational system—a new thrust *which* can kill America's traditional enthusiasm for constantly improving the nation's schools and colleges. . . .

See also **PREVENT.**

3. *"THAT" in place of WHICH*
"That" appears to be used nonrestrictively, and therefore erroneously, in both of the following examples.

Maximus is in the early stages of the program *that*, when it hits full stride, could be processing 100,000 recipients [of welfare payments].

TV Guide is the nation's largest selling weekly magazine, with a circulation of more than 17 million, *that* earned an estimated $75 million profit last year.

In both of the examples, "that" appears to be used nonrestrictively. In the former example, "that" ought to be *which* and preceded by a comma. The clause *"which . . . could be processing 100,000 recipients"* is a nonrestrictive clause; the information it adds could be tossed out without damage to the first part of the sentence. The article talks of only one program. If there were another program, "that" might properly be used restrictively, distinguishing the program *"that could be processing 100,000 recipients"* from another program.

In the latter example too, "that" introduces a nonrestrictive clause, so it ought to be *which*. The clause *"which earned"* etc. merely gives supplementary information.

An exception to the restrictive-*that* principle is customarily made to avoid a double *that*, as in "That that I see I believe." Rather than follow *that* (demonstrative pronoun) with another *that* (relative pronoun), you can make the second word *which*: "That which I see. . . . " But technically the double *that* is not wrong.

4. *Versions of a famous phrase*
The final passage is out of the ordinary. A columnist erred by inadvertently improving the grammar of a historic personage. (The emphasis is the columnist's.)

President Franklin D. Roosevelt did not say that Dec. 7, 1941, was "a day that will live in infamy." He said it was "a *date* that will live in infamy."

Not exactly. The item was headed "You Could Look It Up." It was a good idea. Three books of quotations did match the columnist's version in toto. But three others gave "a date *which* will live in infamy," a quotation confirmed by reprints of the speech in three more books and, conclusively, by a sound recording of the speech. A booklet accompanying the recording was the least accurate: "Franklin D. Roosevelt declared it a 'day that will live in infamy'. . . . "

The popularity of the "that" version, which paradoxically is the more grammatical, should at least hearten adherents to the Fowler principle.

THAT, WHO, and WHICH. *See* **WHO, THAT, and WHICH.**

THE. *1. Generalities. 2. Intrusion. 3. Omission. 4. Pronunciation.*

1. Generalities

The definite article, *the,* is the most common word in English. It usually introduces a particular thing or individual or group, one that was mentioned before or whose existence is known or presumed to be known. (*See* **A and AN** for a discussion of the indefinite article.)

Typically, something or someone that is preceded by *a* or *an* when first mentioned is later preceded by *the* (if not replaced by a pronoun): "One of the people I met there was *a* professor from St. Louis. . . . *The* professor said. . . . "

The may precede a noun on first mention if the noun is specific and known. "*The* country is behind him," but "He was a man without *a* country." / "*The* hats [specific ones] look good on you," but "Hats [in general] look good on you."

We may speak of "Thomas Edison,

the inventor" because of his fame but "Joe Doaks, *a* store clerk."

In addition, idiom calls for the definite article in various expressions and constructions. It must go in a superlative ("It's the biggest") but not often in a comparative ("This one is bigger"). "She is in *the* hospital." (In England one is simply "in hospital.") "I took *the* bus," but "I went by bus." / "They read *the* papers," but "They read books." / "*The* evening is my favorite time of day," but "Evenings are for relaxation."

A single *the* can serve for multiple nouns when the nouns pertain to one person or idea: "the lord and master" / "the vice president and general manager" / "the pain, pleasures, and satisfactions of life." More than one person or idea gets a separate *the:* "the chairman and the president" / *The Prince and the Pauper* / "the star and the planet." *The* may occasionally be repeated for emphasis when not essential to the meaning: "Here she is: the one, the only. . . . "

Besides serving as an article, *the* can be an adverb, used with a comparative adjective and meaning *to that extent* or *by that.* "The more the merrier." / "They are none the wiser."

See also **A and AN.**

2. Intrusion

A. Of THE
Too many journalists have the habits of omitting the article *the* where it belongs (*see* 3) and sticking it in where no article belongs or where *a* or *an* would be more appropriate.

In the following excerpts from three press stories, each intrusive "the" is emphasized; it does not apply to anything that was mentioned before or that any reader would already know about.

When *the* headaches began, Gabel took aspirin and kept working. When he suffered a seizure and lost consciousness, doctors found *the* malignant brain tumor.

Nothing was said before about headaches or a brain tumor. Nor could readers have expected them to be mentioned. Delete the first "the." Replace the second "the" with *a*.

> According to authorities the [fraudulent investment] scheme operated from 1979 to 1987. The two salesmen were Hank . . . and Nate. . . .

The second "the" sends a reader back to look—in vain—for any mention of salesmen.

> *The* video cameras are barely noticeable around *the* perimeter of *the* beige building, noiselessly filming pictures of *the* empty sidewalk, *the* fenced-in lot and *the* vacant entrance lobby.

That sentence was the first in a news story. Omit the opening "The." Keep the next *the* (every building has a perimeter) but change every succeeding one to *a*, except for "*an* empty sidewalk."

Sometimes the unwarranted use of *the* can cloud the meaning of a sentence. A news story tells of a mother in Illinois who was charged with manslaughter for allegedly causing her newborn baby's death by using cocaine during pregnancy. Midway in the story it says:

> Cocaine use by the mother has been linked to health problems in the baby. . . .

Was it talking about that Illinois mother and her baby or about mothers and babies in general? If the latter, as the context suggests, make it, "Cocaine use by mothers has been linked to health problems in their babies. . . . "

A book relates an experience of "the Scottish physician, Alexander Hamilton. . . . " The indefinite article, *a*, would be more appropriate. In the United States he is not famous enough for *the*; the American statesman with the same name is. One could well say "*the* statesman Alexander Hamilton" but "*a* Scottish physician, Alexander Hamilton. . . . " (Note that the comma does not belong in the *the* phrase. *See* **Punctuation,** *3D*.)

B. Of noun; of editorial opinion

A front-page story in a Nevada newspaper shows that (1) the intruder can be the noun that follows *the* and (2) *the* can intrude a point of view in a supposedly unbiased piece.

> Houston Police Chief Lee Brown . . . wants Bush to set up a national crime commission. The panel would examine the root causes of crime and drug abuse—including urban joblessness and poor education.

The first sentence mentions "a . . . commission." The second mentions "the panel." We can guess that they are the same, but why should we have to? If "a . . . commission" is correct, the second reference should be to *The commission* or simply *It*. *See also* **Pronouns,** *6B*; **Synonymic silliness.**

The second "the" poses another problem. It implies that "the" root causes of crime and drug abuse have been determined and are commonly known. If that was the chief's opinion, it should have been made clear. Otherwise a more objective phrase than "the root causes" was needed; examples: *alleged causes / some possible causes / social ills that some say cause.*

C. Of modifier

Often the noun following *the* does not change but new information is sandwiched between them. This passage is from a book of travel reminiscences:

> On the way we stopped to pick up a lone white figure walking along the road. . . .
> The tall, bearded figure got in the car. . . .

Were there two figures? Probably not, inasmuch as the latter sentence is the first to introduce a "tall, bearded figure." Therefore to precede the entire phrase with "The" is unwarranted. Normally *the* applies only to something that has been stated or is well known, not to new information. The only thing in common between "lone white figure" and "tall, bearded figure" is *figure*. Thus the second sentence can properly speak of *The figure* and the adjectives should be placed elsewhere; for instance: "The figure, tall and bearded, got in the car. . . . " (A comma after "lone" in the former sentence is desirable too.)

These in essence are the first two sentences of a news story:

> . . . A city-financed apartment building . . . will officially open tomorrow in Queens.
> The 14-story building in Flushing includes a medical center, social services, emergency alarms . . . and closed-circuit television. . . .

The opening sentence says nothing about a 14-story building. It mentions only "a city-financed apartment building." The second sentence would be tidier by kicking out the "14-story" intruder and uniting the natural couple, "The" and "building." Among various possible rewordings: "The building has 14 stories and includes a medical center, social services. . . . " (In the first sentence *Flushing, Queens* would help those unfamiliar with the geography of New York City.)

Another news story mentions "the appointment of a commission of inquiry" in Israel. The next sentence says, "The three-man commission ruled yesterday that. . . . " Readers can assume that just one commission is involved, but a neater story would put *The* together with *commission*. Either mention the three men in the first sentence or reword the second to put the modifying phrase elsewhere, e.g., "The commission, made up of three men, ruled yesterday that. . . . "

Still another news story mentions the governor of Louisiana by name and title in the lead sentence. Below, the article refers to "the one-time cotton farmer and Harvard Business School graduate" (with no identification), and later it quotes "the 45-year-old conservative Democrat" (with no identification). Unless different people are being described, connect those descriptive phrases to the governor (by name or title or both) and change each "the" to *a*. (*See also* **Modifiers, 2.**)

There is more justification for a reporter's designations of Andrei Sakharov, a world-famed Russian, as "the physicist" (twice), "the physicist and human rights campaigner," and "the longtime human rights campaigner." (That last one may be on the borderline.)

3. *Omission*

A peculiarity of more than a few journalists when writing is to omit a word that they would not think of omitting when speaking: the definite article, *the*. They will not leave it out every time, only sometimes: at the beginning of a sentence, for instance. A newspaper column tells of a parade in Massachusetts:

> Focus was dedication of the restored home of Katharine Lee Bates, the lady who wrote "America the Beautiful."

Would the columnist *speak* like that: "Focus was . . . "? Certainly not. If he used *focus* at all, he would precede it with *the*. He would probably even put another *the* before "dedication." Notice that the sample sentence uses *the* three times. If it were consistent, it would say "dedication of restored home of Katharine Lee Bates, lady who wrote 'America Beautiful.' " (Such a sentence is not recommended either, of course.)

This is from a caption for a picture of a well-known bridge:

Spanning San Francisco Bay, the landmark was world's longest until 1961.

The logic that permits one definite article (before "landmark") but omits another, just as desirable (before "world's"), is obscure.

What accounts for those odd omissions? Is it rationing of definite articles by the newspapers; or is it an idiosyncratic newsroom rule of yore, perpetuated and varied by generations of journalists imitating the mannerisms of other journalists? A newspaper editor of mine forbade staff members to start any story with an article, definite or indefinite. "It's weak," he explained. If the writings gained anything, it was circuity, not strength.

A newscaster said a kidnaping victim "made her escape and was able to call police." A press service reported that a gunman's victim "ran to nearby apartments to call police." Observe that journalists "call police." Most others "call *the* police"; this is idiomatic when *police* is construed as singular (a department), which is commonly the case, rather than plural (policemen).

4. Pronunciation

Before vowel sounds, *the* is usually pronounced THEE. Examples: *the apple, the ooze, the M-1.*

Before consonants, *the* is pronounced THUH, voiced, with almost no vowel: *the car, the watermelon, the yellow.* In a dialectal variation, some pronounce *the* that way before vowels as well.

The is pronounced either way before the long *e* sound, as in *the easel.*

THEE, THOU, and YE. *See* Pronouns, *10A.*

THEFT. *See* CRIME, MISDEMEANOR, and FELONY; Crimes, *3.*

THEIR. *See* Homophones; Possessive problems, *4;* Pronouns, *2.*

"THEIRSELF" or "THEIRSELVES." *See* Pronouns, *5.*

THEM and THEY. *See* Pronouns, *10;* Pronouns' classification.

THEM and THOSE. Let the grizzled prospector of story exclaim, "There's gold in them hills!" Were his English corrected, it would not ring true. It behooves the rest of us to speak of *those* hills, *those* fruits, or *those* days.

Those and *them* are pronouns (noun substitutes). *Those* is also an adjective (a modifier of a noun). *Them* is not.

You can either "forgive *those* who sin" or "forgive *them* who sin" (or not forgive at all). But a radio host who said that many suicides in Iran "are due to them kind of laws" was dead wrong. "Those kind" would not be right either, combining a plural adjective and a singular noun. Any of these work: *those kinds of law* or *that kind of law* or *laws of that kind.*

See also KIND OF, *1;* Pronouns, *2* (misuse of *them*); THESE and THOSE.

THEMSELVES and "THEMSELF." *See* Pronouns, *5.*

THEN. *See* FORMER; THAN.

THEORY. *See* HYPOTHESIS and THEORY.

THERE, anticipatory. *See* **Expletives.**

THERE confused with THEIR. *See* **Homophones.**

THERE in contractions. *See* **Contractions,** *1*.

THEREFORE and THEREFOR. Although they look similar and are both adverbs, the three-*e* word and the two-*e* word have different accents and meanings. The first syllable is emphasized in THERE-fore, the second syllable in there-FOR. *Therefore* means *as a result, consequently, for that reason, hence.* "I think; therefore I am." / "Now, therefore, be it resolved. . . . "

Therefor means *for it, for that, for them, for this:* "Lessee shall be provided with said machines and the supplies needed therefor." / "The fine therefor shall be not more than one hundred dollars." Like *therefrom, thereof, thereto, therewith,* etc., it is used mainly in legal documents, occasionally elsewhere for a formal or archaic effect.

Under *therefor, Webster's Third Dictionary* presents "THEREFORE" as a second meaning, in effect sanctioning the misspelling of the latter.

THERMONUCLEAR. *See* **NUCLEAR.**

THERMOS. *Thermos* is a trademark for a portable container that keeps liquid or food hot or cold by means of a partial vacuum between the outer and inner walls. A problem is exemplified by a statement in a theater review that "actors balance thermoses in the sand" and by suggestions for take-out meals in a cookbook:

> Put one of the sauces . . . in a small, wide-mouthed thermos and use as a dip. . . . Put your favorite soup in a thermos. . . . Take [instant soup] in thermos.

If it is a *Thermos,* it gets a capital *T;* if an imitation, it may be called a vacuum bottle, vacuum jar, or the like.

THESE and THOSE. *These* is the plural of *this. Those* is the plural of *that.*

A book says, about the renaissance madrigal, "Both Lassus and Palestrina . . . enriched the literature of the form during these years." *Those* years— about 1550 to 1580.

"It's hard to make ends meet *these* days," but "*Those* were the days!" *See* **THIS,** *1*.

THEY and THEM. *See* **Pronouns,** *10*; **Pronouns' classification.**

THEY misused. *See* **Pronouns,** *2*.

THINK, past participle. The past tense of *think* is *thought:* "I thought so." The past participle also is *thought:* "I have thought about it." It is not "thunk."

A participant in a news forum said: "Who would have thunk that the Russo-American summit would have a frisky Russian president and an American president in a wheelchair?" The rhetorical questioner, known as an English-language maven, probably knew better. What was he thinking?

THIS. *1.* THIS *and* THAT. *2. Vague* THIS.

1. THIS and THAT
Let us talk of *this* and *that.* Each has several functions.

- As an adjective: *this* woman; *that* mountain.
- As a demonstrative pronoun: *this* tastes sweet; *that* was historic.

• As an adverb: the fish was *this* big; was it *that* bad?

Both words refer to the thing or person mentioned or understood. Whether the thing or person is here or there determines which word to choose. When referring to something near, in space or time (or, sometimes, thought), use *this;* to something relatively far, use *that.* The words may be used in comparing two things, one close and the other more distant: "Isn't *this* melon bigger than *that* one?" *See also* **THESE and THOSE.**

When something is about to be stated, *this* is suitable. ("This poem expresses my sentiment:" / "This above all: to thine ownself be true"). Often *that* is clearer in referring to what was already stated. ("Our review validates the current National Security Council System. . . . That system is properly the president's creature. . . . Having said that. . . . ")

For a few decades, *this* has tended to encroach upon the province of *that.* A modern book says, "This year Boswell went again to London, once more beset by the anxiety of departure." Customarily *this year* refers to the year we are now in. The author is referring to 1773, mentioned six sentences back in the previous paragraph. *"That* year" would have been preferable.

At the same time, *this* has tended to usurp the functions of nouns and other pronouns, including *it, he,* and *she,* and its use has swelled. The excerpt that follows is from a government memorandum. It uses *this,* the pronoun, in three consecutive sentences. Alternative suggestions are offered in brackets. (Emphasis is added. In an omitted passage after the first sentence, the speaker praises Iran for its supposed cooperation. Our concern here is solely verbal.)

"Regarding the commitment of the U.S. to turn a page, *this* [it?] is ex-pressed by my presence on behalf of the President. . . . *This* [That?] spirit, if it had been present in our first encounter, would have made clear we could reach some agreement. Unfortunately, we have reached *this* point after a year and three efforts, where we thought we have an agreement. *This* [The delay, frustration?] has affected the President's view of our ability to reach an agreement. . . . *This* [It?] affected his faith in our ability to work together."

The next section contains several additional examples of the overuse of *this,* emphasizing the serious matter of comprehension.

2. *Vague THIS*

A companion to the excessive dependence on *this* is the absence of any clear antecedent. An antecedent is the noun that a pronoun represents. It is hazy or nonexistent in the excerpts to come.

. . . Quayle is among 51 senators who signed a letter urging Mr. Shultz not to issue a visa for Mr. Arafat.

This would make it even more difficult for a Bush Administration to relax American conditions for dialogue with the P.L.O. . . .

What is the antecedent of "this"? The letter? Something else? Something not explicitly mentioned, such as Mr. Shultz's nonissuance of a visa? We must guess.

I rejoice when European countries throw off tyranny through the will of the people, and I wonder whether this could have prevented the Nazi scourge.

What is "this"? The will of the people? The will of the German people, had it been different? The collective will of European people to intervene during the thirties? A vague "this" is no replacement for adequate thought.

In the book excerpt that follows, "this" appears three times in five sentences. The first time, the antecedent may be *phenomenon.* The second time, the pronoun *it* might have been a better choice. The third is more conjectural; replacing "This" with a noun would have made the meaning clearer. (Emphases and parentheses are in the book. Brackets are added.)

"And this occurs in the case of opaque surfaces"; the hues depend on the nature of the reflecting body. Here Leonardo deals with the point or sheet of light that is reflected on smooth and polished surface. This [It?] is one aspect of what is called *riverberazione* in Manuscript A. Properly speaking, *lustro* is separate from reflection (*riflesso*) in which a specular image is produced. This [?] is important insofar as it involves the transfer of a neighboring color on the local tint of a given object.

Initially, the last "This" seems to stand for "reflection," the phenomenon mentioned last. But the context suggests that *lustro,* or luster, is a better guess. A little later, the following passage appears.

It was the moment of *sfumato*—of grace, of ambiguity—that for Leonardo tended more and more to become integrated in the finality of the painting. This [?] was all the more faithful to its vocation since it was capable of impressing upon the conscience the strangeness of the real that it had to explore.

"Ambiguity" (not "grace") sums it up.

THOSE and THEM. *See* **THEM and THOSE.**

THOSE and THESE. *See* **THESE and THOSE.**

THOU, THEE, and YE. *See* **Pronouns,** *10A.*

"THUNK." *See* **THINK, past participle.**

THUS. *Thus,* meaning *accordingly, therefore,* or *in this* (or *that*) *way,* is an adverb. To append "-ly," as these extracts do, adds nothing to the meaning and an inane cuteness to the style.

Democratic pollster Peter Hart yesterday described the problems facing Dukakis and Jackson thusly: "We have one candidate who . . ." [etc.].

Salisbury's reasoning—advanced in vivid detail in his book—goes thusly:
The American Establishment, as it evolved . . . [etc.].

"Thusly" fits no serious discussion, if anything. It should have been stripped of its suffix and turned into *thus,* or replaced by a synonym such as *in this way* or *as follows.*

TILL and "'TIL." A caption for a locally televised news report (on damaged freeways) read "CLOSED 'TIL SPRING." Soon after, an episode in a national television series was titled "'Til Death Do Us Part" (concerning the killing of husbands). Later a motion picture titled *'Til There Was You* came to theaters.

Till, with two *l*'s, is the word that was needed. It takes no apostrophe, because it is not a contraction. Meaning *until,* it is a bona fide word and may be used in all writing, formal and informal, although *until* is more common as the first word of a sentence. As a preposition, each means either *up to the time of* ("I worked *till* [or *until*] midnight") or, with a negative, *before* ("The game doesn't start *till* [or *until*] 8"). As a conjunction, each means *up to the point that* or *up to the time of* ("He stayed *till* [or *until*] the job was done"). "Up till" or "up until" is redundant.

There is a word *til*, with no apostrophe, which comes from Hindi and denotes the sesame plant, particularly as used in India, for food and oil. Other meanings of *till* are (noun) a money container, glacial drift, and (verb, transitive) to prepare land for farming.

Time. *See* A.M., P.M. (etc); Anachronism; Any, *5;* "AT THIS POINT IN TIME"; A WHILE and AWHILE; BIG TIME; FORWARD and BACK; Tense; THAT, *2;* WHEN, WHERE in definitions.

TIME-HONORED. *See* HONORABLE, HONORARY, HONORED, *4.*

Titles. *1. Imitation titles. 2. Social titles. 3. Titles of office.*

1. Imitation titles

It is a journalistic peculiarity to stuff a description or job title in front of someone's name as though it were a formal title of respect. The beginning of this quotation will illustrate:

> Outgoing Deputy Chief of Staff for Public Affairs Selma ———— said in a news release Friday that [Governor] Carruthers was informed of her resignation and those of Mike ———— and Bruce ———— a week ago.

Imagine calling up a governor's staff assistant and asking, "Is this 'Outgoing Deputy Chief of Staff for Public Affairs Smith?'" That mouthful (without the "Outgoing" and the name) might constitute her formal job title, but it is not a title that normally precedes a name, in the

manner of a social title or a title of office. If it followed the name, it would be just as informative and not nearly so cumbersome: "Selma ————, deputy chief of staff for public affairs." (All those capital letters are unnecessary. So is "Outgoing." If the woman has submitted her resignation, of course she is going out.)

To suspend a name pending a long description is usually too awkward for broadcasting but habitual in the press. Some short, bona fide titles, such as *Senator,* may precede names. *(See 2 and 3.)* And "the actress Jane Roe" and "a plumber, John Doe" are idiomatic forms. What smacks of journalese is "Actress Jane Roe" or "Plumber John Doe." In its style book, The Associated Press condones "astronaut John Glenn, movie star John Wayne, peanut farmer Jimmy Carter."

It gets worse when a long job title is piled up in front of a name. Further examples follow below. Perhaps the writers thought they were being terse. The first saves no words from the piling-up; each of the others saves two small words. (Smoother wordings are in parentheses.)

"Supervisor of Correctional Education Bill Lane" (Bill Lane, supervisor of correctional education); "California Energy Commission Chairman Charles Imbrecht" (Charles Imbrecht, chairman of the California Energy Commission); "Youth Guidance Center chief probation officer Fred Jordan" (Fred Jordan, chief probation officer of the Youth Guidance Center); and "former deputy staff chief and now Transportation Secretary Andrew Card" (Andrew Card, former deputy chief of staff and now secretary of transportation). Note that there is no "staff chief" or "Transportation Secretary"; the terms are *chief of staff* and *secretary of transportation.*

The practice is not new. A monstrous specimen was attributed to a dispatch received in a newspaper office from a wire service, probably in 1939:

VICE-PRESIDENT-IN-CHARGE-OF-EVAPORATED-CONDENSED-AND MALTED MILK-CHEESE-MINCE MEAT-AND-CARAMELS ARTHUR W. RAMSDELL AND VICE-PRESIDENT-IN-CHARGE-OF-CASEIN-ADHESIVES-AND-PRESCRIPTION-PRODUCTS WILLIAM CALLAN WERE ELECTED TO THOSE OFFICES TODAY BY THE BOARD OF DIRECTORS OF THE BORDEN COMPANY.

The habit extends to fictional people and includes the creating of descriptions. A movie review said, "Carrey plays slick Los Angeles lawyer Fletcher Reede." A more natural phrasing might be "Carrey plays a slick lawyer of Los Angeles, Fletcher Reede."

The idea, or at least popularizing, of imitation titles has been ascribed to *Time* in its early years. The magazine still displays phrases like "Asian-American fund raiser John Huang" and "GOP virtuecrat William Bennett." (The latter used to be called "drug czar William Bennett.")

Even figures from the past may get such treatment in the press. A caption recalled the appointment of "Presbyterian elder and Warren G. Harding campaign manager Will Hays" in 1922 as president of an organization to protect Hollywood's reputation.

Fortunately, historical authors are not ready to write of "Italian Navigator and Discoverer of the New World Christopher Columbus," or of "Commander of the Continental Army in the American Revolution and Father of His Country George Washington."

See also **Modifiers**, 4.

2. *Social titles*

During the Reagan administration a newspaper item said:

Reagan will address the grandparent-volunteer group at . . . Epcot Center [on a drug topic]. . . . Reagan plans to return to Washington on Wednesday afternoon.

To most Americans, the subject of each sentence could be only one person, President Ronald Reagan. It was not. The story was about Nancy Reagan.

Nobody meeting her would address her as "Reagan." She would be "Mrs. Reagan" even to her worst enemy. But the particular newspaper had a style rule that everyone must be called by his or her last name on the second reference, with no title. So the staff followed it, regardless of the resulting absurdity.

Two administrations later, a controversy arose over a newspaper's publication of private comments by Hillary Clinton. An article about the matter appeared in a magazine (for the newspaper industry). The first sentence apparently suggests that President Clinton had stuck up for his wife:

Clinton was said to be furious her remarks were publicized. . . .
This was the second time Clinton dined with women feature writers at the White House. . . .
One man who was once asked to the White House for a tête-à-tête with Clinton is . . . [etc.].

The person repeatedly called "Clinton" was not President William J. Clinton but *Mrs.* Clinton. The practice of omitting the social titles of women had become widespread, and the magazine was following it too.

It can be confusing, as we see. It does not reflect the norm of civil behavior—would *you* call her "Clinton"?—though the press professes to mirror society. And it can be considered degrading to deprive women of their titles. To deprive men of their "Mr." has long been commonplace among American newspapers.

Even children get the icy, surname-only treatment. A story about a malpractice suit said:

> Hospital staff failed to electronically monitor Chan's fetal heart tone . . . [while] her mother was in labor. . . . As a result, Chan suffers from cerebral edema and seizures [etc.].

Who, outside the press, would refer to a fetus and a girl of five that way?

Some publications grant social titles only to the subjects of obituaries. Others will not have them even then. This is typical of more than one daily: "Howard died June 10, days before her 80th birthday." Broadcasting has picked up that rude style. An anchor woman repeatedly referred to the late actress Audrey Meadows as "Meadows." Though called "*Miss* Meadows" in life, in death she was not afforded the respect of a title.

The Associated Press (AP) will not refer to a man as *Mr.* unless it is combined with *Mrs.,* as in *Mr. and Mrs. John Smith.* AP does use social titles (it calls them courtesy titles) for women. It prefers a woman's own full name and no title on the first reference: *Mary Smith;* on the second reference, the form is *Mrs.* or *Miss* or—if she prefers—*Ms. Smith* or just *Smith.*

Allowing both sexes social titles is getting rare in the press. In second and later references, *The New York Times* will usually put *Mr.,* or another bona fide title, before a man's surname. Its general policy has long been to use the full name and no social title for a woman on the first reference in a news story, thereafter to use the title *Miss* or *Mrs.* with the surname.

In 1986, the newspaper amended its policy: It would use *Ms.* when the woman preferred it or when her marital status was not known. Earlier, *Ms.* "had not passed sufficiently into the language to be accepted as common usage. The *Times* now believes that 'Ms.' has become a part of the language. . . . " In practice, it seems to be the paper's female title of first resort.

Ms. may be traced at least to the 1950s. A leaflet on letter writing by an association of office managers suggested its use to solve a problem: how to address women of uncertain marital status. And a manual for secretaries recommended: "If in doubt about 'Miss' or 'Mrs,' use 'Miss' or 'Ms' (meaning either 'Miss' or 'Mrs.')."

Promoted by feminists and assigned the pronunciation MIZ, *Ms.* became common in the seventies. The traditional *Miss* and *Mrs.* were said to be discriminatory—although polls suggested that most women favored them and disliked *Ms.* For instance, betrothed maidens objected to the society pages' raising doubt about their marital status.

Business has accepted *Ms.* An executive says, "I myself find it very useful, often having occasion to address letters to women whose marital status is unknown to me and not easily discovered."

News people have cause to like it, just as they like leaving out titles altogether. By using "Ms. Smith," they need not take the trouble to find out if a woman is *Miss* Smith or *Mrs.* Smith. And if they can say just "Smith," they may not even have to find out if a person is a woman or a man. (Some first names, including Dale, Lee, Leslie, Marion, Robin, and Toby, are of dual gender, and foreign names may be puzzling.)

Mr. and *Mrs.* are abbreviations of *mister* and *mistress,* which for centuries has usually been pronounced MISS-iz when referring to a married woman. Unlike them, *Ms.* is an artificial entity that represents no single word and has no plural. (*See* **Plurals and singulars,** 2H.) Nor does it have a distinctive pronunciation; it borrows from musty, regional dialect, in which *Mrs.* is pronounced MIZ. At least one clerk of a law court, announcing names of jury panelists, regularly pronounced it "EM ESS," like the abbreviation of master of science, multiple sclerosis, millisecond, manuscript, missile system, or Mississippi in postal code.

Miss is still used, with a surname, in addressing or referring to a girl; or a woman who has not married; or a woman by her professional name, even if she is married and has a different personal name. (In a news story, Elizabeth Taylor was called just "Taylor" twice and then, in a flash of civility, "Miss Taylor.") *Miss* or *madam* is used without a surname to address a female stranger. ("Miss, you dropped your purse.")

Traditional etiquette decrees that when *Mrs.* precedes a full name, it shall not be the woman's own name ("Mrs. Agnes Cooper") but her husband's ("Mrs. *John* Cooper").

To say "I am Mr. Doaks," instead of "I am Joseph Doaks," is considered immodest, unless one is addressing schoolchildren. And this is a matter of word usage rather than etiquette, but it is not correct to say "His name is Mr. Edwards"; rather, "*He* is Mr. Edwards" and "His *name* is George L. Edwards." *See also* REVEREND.

Mr. and *Mrs.* with a name are always abbreviated. It is never "Mister Doaks." But they are never abbreviated when used as words: "Hey, mister, do you have a match?" / "I have to call the missis" (or "missus").

Publications that use social titles have exceptions. The *Times* omits them from sports stories and from references to famous people who are no longer living. An eastern newspaper that I worked for excluded *Mr.* from the names of arrested men. When I asked why, the city editor replied, "Any son of a bitch that gets himself arrested doesn't *deserve* to be called mister."

3. *Titles of office*

Some job titles may precede names, and they are short: *President, Governor, Senator, Representative* (or *Rep.* for short), *General, Colonel, Dean, Profes-*

sor, etc. A title that precedes a name begins with a capital. That goes only for an official title, not a pseudo title like "Drug Czar" or "Rock 'n' Roll King" or "Cherry Blossom Queen." (For citizens of a republic, we seem remarkably fond of royal appellations.)

Dr. is another title that may precede a name, when the doctorate is earned and not just honorary. It is superfluous when the degree follows a name. Frank A. Robinson, M.D., or George B. Sanders, Ph.D., is enough.

No other title should precede *Dr.* "Superintendent of Schools Dr. Ambrose Walker" goes too far. Better: Dr. Ambrose Walker, superintendent of schools. Nor should any other pair of titles be combined, as in "County Supervisor Mrs. Frederick J. Van Buren." The office can go after the name.

An official position or office mentioned in a general sense does not merit an initial capital: "He has decided to run for governor." When the word identifies a particular holder of the office, it may reasonably be capitalized: "The Governor has signed. . . . " Another reasonable style is that of The Associated Press. It calls for all titles to be in lower case when not affixed to a name: "The pope gave his blessing" but "Pope John Paul gave. . . . " An article, attributed to AP, was inconsistent:

> . . . He . . . became the first Virginia mayor to lose his seat in an election on recalling him from office. . . . The City Council can pick a member to serve as Mayor, go outside . . . for a Mayor, or do nothing.

In each instance, *mayor* is used in a general sense; it does not refer to a particular person, so no capital *M* is warranted.

An official title of modest length is customarily capitalized before the name: "Attorney General Janet Reno said. . . . " But it needs no capitals after the name: "Janet Reno, the attorney general, said. . . . " Sometimes a lawyer in no official position is called, for instance, "Attorney Roger U. Nelson." There is no title of "attorney," hence no compelling reason to put it in front of a name, particularly with a capital *A*. (*See also* **ATTORNEY and LAWYER**.)

When the name of a person is introduced in any writing or talk, an identifying title or description normally is necessary, unless the person is famous enough to need none—Jefferson and Lincoln come to mind. A book about travels in Africa tells an anecdote in which "Bokassa" is mentioned three times with no title. The fourth time, he is "Emperor Bokassa" (the ruler of the Central African "Empire"—now Republic—until 1979). The first mention would be a better place for the title, in case the name of that tyrant is unfamiliar to any reader.

In a long piece with a sizable cast of characters, one identification per person may not be enough. Reading "O'Brien said . . . ," readers may strain to remember him if he was identified twenty paragraphs back and other names have since been introduced. Let memories be refreshed: "Dr. O'Brien, the director, said. . . . " Then no one need search, guess, or give up.

Once a person has left a public office in which he held a prominent title, such as *President, Senator, Judge,* or *Ambassador,* continuing to attach that title to his name is no longer necessary, if it makes any sense at all. Yet there is an American tradition of doing just that. People will persist in addressing a one-time *Senator* Scott that way, even though he has legally been *Mr.* Scott for many years. The *Honorable* honorific has staying power too. *See* **HONORABLE** (etc.).

For titles of books, etc., *see* **Capitalization; Italics; Punctuation,** *10*.

TO. *1. Missing. 2. Overworked.*

1. Missing

In light of the many functions of *to*, its appearance more than once in a sentence should disconcert nobody. Yet sometimes a single *to* is left to handle a double load.

A notice offering a reward for information about the perpetrators of a crime said:

IN CASE OF A DUPLICATION OF INFORMATION OR DISPUTE, THE BOARD OF DIRECTORS . . . WILL BE THE SOLE JUDGE AS TO WHOM THE REWARD SHALL BE PAID OR AS TO THE MANNER IN WHICH THE REWARD MAY BE DIVIDED.

The first "TO" is part of the phrase "AS TO." But the writer evidently expected the same "TO" to perform double duty in the phrase "TO WHOM," something it could not do.

Another *TO* could be slipped in next to the first one, but "AS TO TO WHOM" looks strange. A better way is to follow "SHALL BE PAID" with the additional *TO*. A further improvement is to replace each "AS TO" with a sharper preposition: ". . . THE SOLE JUDGE *OF* WHOM THE REWARD SHALL BE PAID *TO* OR *OF* THE MANNER IN WHICH THE REWARD MAY BE DIVIDED."

In another statement, "as to" and "to which" get only one *to* between them:

As to which additional commodities the guaranteed price should be applied, Mr. Gaitskell said. . . .

". . . Applied *to*. . . . "
See also **Prepositions,** *4*.

2. Overworked

Each of two dictionaries enumerates twenty-seven meanings of *to,* mostly as a preposition.

A frequent function is to indicate the infinitive of verbs (to go, to eat). In that capacity *to* has no meaning itself and does not fulfill the normal function of a preposition, though classified as one.

To can also indicate accompaniment ("dance to the music"), addition ("adding insult to injury"), agreement ("to my liking"), benefit ("It goes to a good cause"), contact ("a blow to the jaw"), direction ("I'm going to town"), extent or result ("It's burned to ashes"), limit ("We stayed to the end"), possession ("It belongs to us"), purpose ("I work to support my family), ratio ("The odds are two to one"), and many other things.

To occasionally is an adverb meaning toward something implied or understood ("They kept the ship to" [the wind]) or to a point of contact ("She soon came to" [consciousness]).

This two-letter word is overworked as it is. It ought not to be loaded with still more tasks: "The best present for the person on your list who has everything is . . . a gift membership to the . . . Institute." In that sentence, from a newsletter, the idiomatic preposition would be *in*.

The star of a situation comedy was directed to say, "One night I came home to find my ex-husband having sex with three hookers in my lingerie." Perhaps nobody in the audience would seriously remark, "There must be a better reason to go home," but that construction does mimic *to* used in the sense of *purpose*. Better: "I came home *and found*. . . . "

Similarly: "ABC put two of its better dramas . . . on Saturday nights only to see them squashed" and "Students . . . demonstrated in support of the protesting workers, only to feel let down when the strikes did not spread. . . . " Probably few if anyone would take such sentences literally and think that the network or the students showed masochistic tendencies; nevertheless "only to" is a peculiar form. The same points would be made concisely with "*and saw* them squashed" and "*and felt* let down. . . . "

An established use of *to* is to indicate a compulsion to perform an action:

"You are to report for work tomorrow morning at 8." Headline writers have converted that to a simple future: "State to appeal judge's ruling," meaning that the state *will* appeal. Except in headlines, a construction like "The rainy season is to begin soon" is no substitute for the simple future: "*will* begin soon."

To has so many meanings that it can easily be misinterpreted when used carelessly, conveying a distorted message. For instance: "George Fox . . . defied Oliver Cromwell to found the Society of Friends in the seventeenth century." A reader who thinks "to found" serves there as an infinitive can interpret the sentence as saying that Fox dared Cromwell to found the society—which is historically wrong. Either *by founding* or *in order to found* would eliminate the ambiguity. Although several critics condemn the phrase *in order to* as a usually excessive replacement for *to* alone, it need not be avoided when, occasionally, it makes the meaning clear.

See also COMPARED TO and COMPARED WITH; Gerund, *3*; HAVE, HAS, HAD, *4*; Infinitive; Prepositions, *1, 7*; SPEAK TO, TALK TO; TO, TOO, and TWO.

TOGETHER WITH. *See* WITH, *2*.

TOO.   *1. Meanings. 2. Omission of O.*

1. Meanings

Two meanings of *too* (adverb) that are suitable for both formal and informal purposes are (1) *also, in addition* ("They pay well and give benefits too"), and (2) *excessively, overly* ("These shoes are too big for my feet"). Used in the first sense, *too* should not start a sentence, but *then too* may.

Too has several colloquial uses. Sometimes it is merely an intensive, used in contradicting someone. "He is too the best player." *So* could be used instead.

At times *too* preceded by a negative

substitutes for *not sufficiently* or *not at all*. Such use is sometimes unnecessary, illogical, or, worse yet, ambiguous.

A book says that (1) "Not too much light can be shed" on the origin of certain words and (2) "Addison wasn't too appreciative of" word games. A newcomer to colloquial English might be puzzled. Why would we want "too much" light instead of just enough light? And why should Addison have been "too appreciative" as long as he was appreciative enough? The contexts indicate that the "too" is unnecessary in each case. In the first sentence, "Not much light . . ." would have communicated the message. The second sentence might be justified as a touch of irony, although "Addison did not appreciate . . ." would be more straightforward.

In those excerpts, "too" is just an illogical colloquialism. It can be downright ambiguous: "Your dress is not too good for the party." Literally someone is being told that she is not overdressed. According to the colloquial sense, however, she can get the message that she is wrongly dressed. Another example of ambiguity: "I can't regard this book too highly." The speaker may consider the book to be the ultimate in brilliance or not good enough to merit much regard.

With some modifiers—*all too, but too,* and *only too*—it can mean regrettably or unfortunately. "The rumors are all too true." / "They're only too eager to take your money." In modern use, *only too* is often a mere intensive, equivalent to *very* (a use deplored by Sir Ernest Gowers). "We're only too pleased to be of service."

Too can be part of a hyphenated adjective, such as "a *too-familiar* complaint" or "the *too-trusting* visitor."

See also **NONE**, 2.

2. *Omission of O*

Not infrequently those who do not work with written words leave out the second *o* in *too,* producing the preposition "to." Occasionally professional writers or typesetters err in that way, as someone did in an article in a computer magazine:

If program files get out of order, which happens all to often for me, First Aid comes to the rescue.

". . . All *too* often. . . . " No computer program yet invented will guard against a mistake of that sort.

See also **TO, TOO, and TWO.**

TOO GOOD TO BE TRUE. *See* **Ellipsis** (near end).

TOOK and TAKEN. *See* **Tense**, 5A.

TORE, TORN. *See* **TEAR, TORE, TORN.**

TORTUOUS and TORTUROUS. The adjectives *tortuous* and *torturous* share a Latin root and are often confused, yet they have different meanings in English.

Torturous, as it suggests, pertains to torture or great pain ("a torturous inquisition"). It is pronounced TORE-chur-us.

Tortuous means twisting, not straightforward, or very complex ("the tortuous trails"). It is pronounced TORE-chew-us.

A lawyer said his client's plea of guilty to an assault charge was made under a "very torturous set of circumstances." He probably meant *tortuous.*

Webster's Third Dictionary gives *tortuous* as one of the meanings of *torturous,* thereby encouraging the confusion.

Both adjectives, and the related adverbs *tortuously* and *torturously,* trace to the Latin *torquere,* to twist. So do the verbs *torture* and *torment,* the noun *tort* (injury in a legal sense), and the adjective *tortious* (TORE-shus, pertaining to a tort).

TO SAY NOTHING OF. Discussing lexicographical tradition, two authors write:

> Inevitably, Webster and Richardson, to say nothing of Webster and Worcester, disliked one another.

If the authors intended to say nothing of Webster and Worcester, why did they say anything of them?

"To say nothing of" is one of several peculiarly contradictory expressions and words. *See* **NOT TO MENTION; Verbal unmentionables.**

See also **INEVITABLE.**

TOTAL. *1. "A TOTAL OF." 2. Singular vs. plural verb.*

1. "A TOTAL OF"

In an enumeration such as "two owls and a hen, four larks and a wren—a total of eight birds," *a total of* is a useful phrase; it denotes *a sum of* the items.

The phrase "a total of" frequently starts sentences like these in the press:

> A total of 60 police and protesters were injured in the scuffles. . . .

> A total of 402 Iowans who said they would definitely or probably attend the state's precinct caucuses . . . were interviewed. . . .

> A total of 143 nations . . . joined in approving two resolutions challenging the closing of the observer mission. . . .

What is the need for "a total of" when only one figure is mentioned? Obviously someone has counted the injured people, the Iowans, or the nations and come up with a *total*.

The usual purpose is to get around a journalistic and literary taboo on starting a sentence with a figure. "143 nations," or the like, is never supposed to be written. When, as a young reporter, I asked an editor why, he said only, "It would look strange." Maybe so at first, because the rule has precluded initial figures, at least in texts. Headlines may start with figures.

Even if we accept the rule, "A total of" is usually a superfluous beginning. "Sixty police" is easy to write and read. "One hundred two Iowans" is not too hard. "One hundred forty-three nations" is just a little harder.

An article contained the pair of sentences below. The latter is particularly awkward.

> A total of 167 delegates will be selected from the state's 34 assembly districts. . . .

> A total of 2,081 of the 4,161 delegates will be needed to win the nomination.

Is the 4,161 not the *total?* Better: "Of the 4,161 delegates, 2,081 will be needed. . . . "

See also **Numbers,** 11.

2. Singular vs. plural verb

A subject starting with "*the* total of" ordinarily takes a singular verb. "*The* total of 1.7 million votes *was* the highest ever recorded in the state." But a subject starting with "*a* total of" often takes a plural verb. "*A* total of 1.7 million votes *were* cast in the state." The first example emphasizes the total as a statistic. The second emphasizes the votes that were cast.

Some writers fix on *total* and make every verb singular, however unidiomatic: votes "was" cast.

See also **Collective nouns,** 2.

TO, TOO, and TWO. Pronounced the same, the three words are confused by writers from time to time, perhaps

out of absent-mindedness or carelessness. It is hard to believe that a writer does not know the differences among *two* or 2, the number between 1 and 3; *too,* the adverb meaning excessively and also; and *to,* the two-letter workhorse indicating direction, extent, purpose, infinitive (with a verb), and many other things.

A manual suggests a reason for the failure of a computer printer: "The page is to complex for the printer's memory capacity. . . . " Change "to" to *too.* And this is from a restaurant review: "Children will probably enjoy two the fried taro patty. . . . " Change "two" to *too.*

See also **TO; TOO,** 2.

Trademarks. A *trademark,* also spelled *trade-mark,* is a distinctive name, design, picture, symbol, or other device on goods offered for sale. It distinguishes the goods of a particular manufacturer or seller from similar goods produced or sold by others.

Technically, a brand name, such as Pepsi-Cola or Sunkist, is a *trademark;* while a distinctive name of a business such as Kmart Stores or Bank of America, is a *trade name* (usually two words). Often, especially in popular usage, *trade name* is applied to the product too.

Registration of either at the U.S. Patent and Trademark Office or a corresponding state office is not essential, but it affords legal protection in case of infringement. In preventing unauthorized use of a mark or name, the law not only protects ownership but also helps to protect the public from deception.

The name of a product that is a trademark should always begin with a capital letter. It is accurate usage; besides, it helps keep the name from going into the public domain, losing its precise meaning, and penalizing the owner for its success. Aspirin, escalator, and yo-yo are among former trademarks.

Manufacturers advertise and take other steps to encourage capitalization of such trademarks as the Coca-Cola nickname *Coke,* which contrasts with *coke,* a coal product and slang for cocaine. After *Webster's Third Dictionary* came out, G. & C. Merriam Co. had to revise some 300 entries when owners of trademarks like Kleenex and Frigidaire threatened suit over the lack of initial capitals.

Every product has a generic name—soda pop, facial tissues, refrigerators, and so on—that can be used in lieu of a brand name. Some publications take pains to avoid mentioning the commercial names of products except in advertisements. "But if a trade name [trademark] is pertinent to a story, use it," *The New York Times* tells staff members. Its example: "The robbers escaped in a white Cadillac sedan."

See also **BAND-AID; JELL-O; KODAK; SEEING EYE; THERMOS; VASELINE; XEROX.**

TRADITION. *See* **HONORABLE, HONORARY, HONORED.**

TRAGEDY. *Tragedy* signifies a serious play with a very sad ending, or a play of that sort as a genre. It is a drama depicting a character's struggle with an overpowering adversary through a series of solemn, pathetic, or shocking events, ending in calamity. Typically the protagonist's passion or character flaw leads to his undoing.

When it does not pertain to drama, *tragedy* (noun) suggests an event or series of events characterized by or ending in calamity or great suffering and usually death. *Tragic* (adjective) means pertaining to or having the character of either a dramatic tragedy or a general tragedy; it can mean calamitous or disastrous.

Tragedy or *tragic* is frivolously invoked at times to describe a state of affairs that is merely disagreeable or undesirable but involves no calamity or great suffering. A book speculates on the loss to English literature if Joyce, Shaw, Swift, and other literary masters of Ireland had written in Gaelic:

> Their works would be as little known to us as those of the poets of Iceland or Norway, and that would be a tragedy indeed.

That might be unfortunate (if "that" refers to unfamiliarity with the works of the Irishmen), but why would it be a "tragedy"? How would our ignorance of a literature cause us—much less the readers of that literature—calamity or great suffering? (The analogy is imperfect. The Irish literati included non-poets; and our ignorance of Norwegian does not preclude our familiarity with the dramas of Ibsen. An Icelander and three Norwegians, including the poet Bjørnson, won the Nobel Prize for literature.)

In another book, the *absence* of a tragedy is perversely labeled a "tragedy."

> For a man with Theodore Roosevelt's need for personal fulfillment, it was a sort of tragedy that he had no war—not even a Whiskey Rebellion.

The author seems to imply that war, with its killing and suffering, is of no moment if it brings a president "personal fulfillment."

See also DISASTER.

Transitive and intransitive verbs. *See* Verbs, *1*.

TRANSPIRE.
To use "transpire" instead of *happen* or *occur* or *take place* is loose and pompous. The pomposity of "transpired" clashes with the informal styles of the movie review and book that are quoted here. See if anything would be lost by replacing "transpired" with, say, *happened*.

His speech . . . is intended to be taken straight—I guess. In light of everything that's transpired, however . . . the speech is a hoot, and the screening audience was snickering disrespectfully. . . .

"You took this receipt to Follope. He said to you, 'Thank you,' but now, several days pass, nothing has changed."
This was precisely what had transpired.

The loose use tends to devaluate a valuable word. To *transpire* (verb, transitive or intransitive) is literally to give off vapor, moisture, odor, etc. through a body, plant, or other surface. Used figuratively about information, to *transpire* (verb, intransitive) is to leak out, to become known, or to come to light. For example, "The committee made its decision three months ago, but the facts did not transpire until yesterday." No other single word expresses that meaning.

TRAVESTY.
A *travesty* is a type of burlesque or satire. It is a piece of literature or drama that (1) ridicules its genre or (2) treats a serious work or lofty theme absurdly, grotesquely, or ironically.

Travesty is used figuratively, usually with *justice,* to suggest a grotesque or distorted imitation. The phrase "travesty of justice," describing an unfair law or legal decision, has become a cliché since Edith Wharton used it in 1923 in *A Son at the Front:* ". . . It's an iniquitous law, a travesty of justice" (that permits France to conscript an American).

If a figurative meaning is intended, "travesty" alone is apt to make no sense: A newspaper article reported that Israeli leaders opposed blanket compensation for Palestinians claiming damages from

Israeli army actions during the intifada, or uprising.

But Leah Tesemel, an Israeli lawyer who represents several Arab claimants, said travesties had been committed against Palestinians, beyond what courts would consider as legal armed response. . . .

You can no more "commit" a travesty than you can "commit" a comedy or a satire.

An article in another paper dealt with a school board's approval of educational materials on the Sino-Japanese conflict.

However, some who worked on the original curriculum proposal say that the administrators' revision of the materials omits the context and images necessary to convey the travesty's impact.

Was it a mistyping of *tragedy* or a display of ignorance? To call the killing of millions a "travesty" is bizarre.

Travesty entered England in 1648, as a French verb, in the title of *Le Virgile Travesty en Vers Burlesque,* Virgil travestied in burlesque verses, by Paul Scarron. Meaning to disguise, *travestir* was an adaptation of the Italian *travestire,* from the Latin *trans-,* across, and *vestire,* to clothe.

TREAD.   The past tense of *tread* (verb, transitive and intransitive) is *trod.* "We took our packs and trod the path for three hours." To use *trod* in a present sense is an error. *Webster's Third Dictionary* tends to sanction the error, uncritically quoting, "The eccentric is forced to *trod* a lonely way." Make it *tread.*

The past participle is *trodden* or *trod.* "The boy has trodden [or "trod"] this road often." The other forms are regular: *treading, treads.* In archaic times the past tense was *trode.*

Among the meanings of *tread* are to walk, step, or dance on or along; to trample; to oppress; and to pump the feet (in water).

TREASON.   *See* **Crimes, 5.**

TREMBLER and TEMBLOR.   *See* **TEMBLOR and TREMBLER.**

TRILLION.   *See* **BILLION.**

TRIO.   A *trio* is a group of three singers or musicians, or a musical composition for three voices or instruments. In a more general sense, a *trio* can be a group of three people who are connected in some joint action or at least closely associated. The Three Stooges might qualify, but not three strangers who happen to be in an elevator at the same time. It is a journalistic cliché to use the word for any three people.

An article concerning the Salvadorian civil war says, "The trio was cooking spaghetti and beans when a knock at the door came at 10:45 p.m." The three people were not three musicians or three cooks at a restaurant but a woman and two friends of hers who came, separately, seeking refuge. To call them a "trio" stretches the word thin. Better: "The *three were* cooking. . . . " Having linked them into a unit ("The trio was cooking"), the writer evades the grammatical snare ("when *it heard* a knock") and never again mentions the group in the remaining thirteen paragraphs.

TRIUMPHAL and TRIUMPHANT.   The difference between these adjectives is subtle. *Triumphant* means victorious, also elated over victory. "The army is triumphant." / "Their triumphant feeling was short-lived." Using the word to mean *triumphal* is obsolete. *Triumphal* goes with something commemorating or honoring a triumph: "We walked under the Triumphal

Arch." / "The band played Verdi's Triumphal March." *Webster's Third Dictionary* promotes confusion of the two words by giving "TRIUMPHANT" as a meaning of *triumphal.*

The related adverbs are *triumphantly* and *triumphally. Triumph* (noun) is victory, conquest, or distinguished achievement. To *triumph* (verb, intransitive) is to be victorious.

TROOPER and TROUPER. *See* Homophones.

TROOP, TROOPS, and TROUPE.
Paraphrasing a bill in the U.S. Senate, a television panelist said it would put the president on notice that "you're going to require prior congressional approval before you send one troop into Haiti."

"One troop" sounded odd. The speaker may have meant one *serviceman* or one *soldier.* The singular, *troop,* denotes a unit of Boy Scouts or Girl Scouts and, sometimes, a nondescript group of people or animals. In the military sense, a *troop* technically is a subdivision of a cavalry regiment; otherwise the plural, *troops,* is nearly always used, meaning armed forces collectively or any body of soldiers prepared to fight: "Troops have been shipped to Haiti."

A number may precede *troops* when the idea is to refer, impersonally, to a group; but not when the idea is to refer to individuals. Thus, "They have some 300 troops at the border" but not "The five troops described their experiences."

Troop is not to be confused with *troupe,* pronounced the same, meaning a group of entertainers.

"TRUE" or "FALSE" FACTS. *See* FACT, 3.

TRUSTEE and TRUSTY. *See* Confusing pairs.

TRUTH. *See* FACT, 4; Twins, 1.

TRY AND and TRY TO. A television panelist said of a presidential candidate, "He wants to try and get out as many Republicans as he can." Was "try and" correct or should it have been *try to?*

It passed muster. The consensus of authorities is that *try and* is a colloquial idiom that need not be avoided when it seems natural in speech, although some find it too casual for careful writing or even for the heights of oral eloquence. None impugn the good standing of *try to.*

The two phrases are not identical in meaning. "Let's try to stop them" and "Try to remember where you put the keys" literally call for attempts. On the other hand, "Try and stop me" is not a literal instruction but an expression of determination, and "Let's try and win" offers encouragement. "We will try to reach our goal next month" implies resolution, while "We'll try and repair it soon" implies "Don't count on it."

TUMMY. *See* STOMACH.

TURBID and TURGID. *See* Confusing pairs.

'TWAS (it was). *See* Expletives.

Twins. *1. Legal. 2. Nonlegal.*

1. Legal
A candidate for city treasurer who promised, in a written statement, "I will scrutinize each and every receipt" was using legal language. Doubling and sometimes tripling of ideas in more or less redundant phrases has been characteristic of lawyers for ages. By augmenting *each* with *every,* or *null* with *void,* they presumably have sought to add rhetorical weight and insure understanding.

Some are just ritual phrases, such as the triplet *the truth, the whole truth, and nothing but the truth,* which is directed at laymen. Two other triplets, *ready, willing, and able* and *way, shape, or form* have been adopted by the lay public. So have *any and all, fit and proper, part and parcel, peace and quiet, separate and distinct,* and *various and sundry.* The Constitution uses *aid and comfort* and *full faith and credit.* Other common legal twins include *aid and abet, cease and desist, free and clear, save and except, sole and exclusive, terms and conditions,* and *true and correct.*

Many combinations have set meanings established by court decisions. Less familiar ones may risk unexpected interpretations, so the legal drafter should make sure that each word is necessary. Two words are not necessarily better than one. *See also* **TESTAMENT and TESTIMONY; UNLESS AND UNTIL.**

2. Nonlegal

Many nonlegal twins exist as clichés. They include *alas and alack, betwixt and between, bits and pieces, bow and scrape, fair and square, fast and furious, fear and trembling, first and foremost, free and easy, hale and hearty, hem and haw, hook or crook, hue and cry, kith and kin, leaps and bounds, lo and behold, might and main, nerve and fiber, nook and cranny, pillar to post, pomp and circumstance, pure and simple, rack and ruin, rags and tatters, rant and rave, really and truly, right and proper, safe and sound, so on and so forth, thick and fast, to and fro, trials and tribulations, ways and means,* and *well and good.*

Some twins, like *flotsam and jetsam, jot or tittle,* and *spick and span,* are inseparable. Anyone using an isolated *alack, betwixt, fro,* or *main* (noun) is not likely to be understood nowadays but might have been in past eras.

One of the words may provide an additional shade of meaning or it may be just an empty synonym in legal style. *Cranny* does supplement *nook,* as *kith*

does *kin.* Yet such pairs are hackneyed expressions. Whether a particular phrase will best convey one's message is worth a thought.

The pairs listed above are just fraternal twins. There is also a class of identical twins, including *boy oh boy, by and by, day by day, eye to eye, ha ha, man to man, more and more, neck and neck, on and on, out(-)and(-)out, over and over, so(-)so, (call) a spade a spade, through and through, time after time, up and up, (if) worst comes to worst, (what's) done is done,* and the British *hear, hear* and *ta ta.*

See also **Clichés; Tautology.**

TYPE. 1. *Noun: followed by* OF. 2. *TYPE and KIND; other meanings.*

1. Noun: followed by OF

As a noun, *type* usually means either (a) a category or class or (b) a person, creature, or thing with the features of the category or class. "What type of animal is it?" / "A baboon is a type of monkey." / "The guiro is an instrument of the percussion type."

When *type* is followed by the name of the category or class, *of* should intervene.

As recorded in an autobiography, a father wrote to his son that as a teenager "you will establish definitely the type person you will be. . . . " And in a magazine, a witness to a plane crash was quoted as saying, "I won't tell you it's a seven-twenty-seven, but it's that type aircraft."

Idiomatic English calls for "type *of* person" and "type *of* aircraft." We do not say, "I wonder what species flower it is" or "I like this variety apple."

Commercial appropriations of the word—e.g., "silk-type material"—are understandable, if sometimes shady. Imitation of the commercial pattern, in an attempt to be droll, may account for slangy phrases like "reading-type material" in lieu of *type of reading material.*

2. TYPE and KIND; other meanings

Used strictly, *type* fits a clearly defined group ("Citrine is a type of quartz") while *kind* or *sort* has more general application. ("That is the kind of weather I like." / "She is the sort of person who gets along with everyone.") Strict users appear to be in the minority.

The noun *type* can also denote printed characters ("The manuscript has been set up in type") or the metallic blocks producing them in traditional printing. *Type* can serve as an adjective when it pertains to printing, as in *type style* and *type faces,* or when it is united with a technical term, as in *Type AB blood.* As a verb, *type* (present participle *typing*) can mean to operate a typewriter or computer keyboard ("She types eighty words a minute") or to classify ("They typed him as a vagrant").

See also **KIND OF.**

U

ULTIMATUM. An *ultimatum* is not just any demand. This noun, along with the adjective *ultimate,* stems from the Medieval Latin *ultimatus,* meaning final. An *ultimatum* is the ultimate demand or proposition or statement of terms presented by the government of one country to the government of another country before launching war or using force. The threat of hostilities is expressed or implied in the statement. *Ultimatum* is too important a word to be treated in the casual way it often is.

"Iran issued an ultimatum to Britain," a newscaster announced on television. Iran's demand, that Britain ban a book, was backed by the threat of severed relations but not hostilities. Therefore calling it an "ultimatum" is not a precise use of the word. At least the demand had an element of finality. Not so in the next instance, reported in a newspaper article:

> When city officials discovered that [an unauthorized street clock] last month, they issued an ultimatum to the restaurant's owners. If you want permission to erect the clock . . . you must first remove it.

There "ultimatum" is evidently supposed to be humorous, so its irrelevance to international relations does not alone preclude its use. However, the officials' proposition carried no threat of forceful action and was not final. The next sentence says, "But discussions that began last week produced a less severe solution yesterday." So no "ultimatum" was issued, even stretching the word to the bursting point.

The South Korean government issued a statement asking the United States to clarify news reports of official spying on the Korean president. A story about the statement starts out with a contradiction: "The State Department yesterday rejected another South Korean ultimatum, the second in two days." Aside from the Koreans' obvious reluctance to wage war on the United States, the fact is that they made two successive demands, so the first cannot be truly recorded as an "ultimatum."

A front-page headline: "Vatican Issues an Ultimatum. . . . " According to the story, the Vatican's envoy to Panama "delivered an ultimatum" to General Manual Noriega, the Panamanian leader, during the U.S. invasion: His sanctuary at the embassy would expire. What the envoy delivered was more like an eviction notice. The idea of the smallest state in the world threatening military violence is ludicrous.

UNDESCRIBABLE. *See* INDESCRIBABLE, UNDESCRIBABLE.

UNEMPLOYED, UNEMPLOY-MENT. *See* JOBLESS.

UNEXPRESSIBLE. *See* **Verbal unmentionables.**

UNINTERESTED. *See* DISINTERESTED and UNINTERESTED.

UNIQUE. "It is absolutely the most unique place in the world," a secretary of the interior said about the Grand Canyon. A scientist said about mammoths, "They were very unique animals." An orchestral manager was quoted as saying, "Ojai is something so unique among festivals."

Unique (adjective), from the Latin *unicus,* only or single, means being the only one of its kind or without an equal. The Sun, as a star, is *unique* in the solar system but not in the universe.

To call something or someone "the most unique" is as meaningless as calling it "the most only one." Uniqueness cannot vary in degree. So adverbial qualifiers like "most" / "very" / "so" / "rather" / "more" / "somewhat" cannot apply to *unique.* Some of them may apply to weaker adjectives such as *exceptional, extraordinary, outstanding, rare, remarkable,* or *unusual.* A *very rare* bird has a few specimens; only the final specimen will be *unique.* It is possible to qualify *unique* with adverbs like *truly, really, nearly, most nearly,* or *more nearly,* which do not purport to change the degree of *unique.*

But the speakers quoted above are not in the word business. Those in the mass media should know better, should they not?

On television a newscaster said, "The budget bill was rather unique," and an announcer described "America's most unique travel adventures." A magazine said that "the most unique mail order items" were not the most expensive. And the word appeared twice in a news story about a tribute to a baseball player:

> [Jackie Robinson] lived a career so compelling and unique its retelling once again riveted. . . . The obvious presence of such people of color underscored the unique relationship baseball has had with minorities since 1947. . . .

Robinson's career was *unique*—not "so" *unique,* though *so unusual, so extraordinary,* etc. would be correct. The second sentence is grammatically sound, though the aptness of "unique" may be debated. Minorities are in other sports. Journalism need not ape the advertising industry, which tries to persuade us that every product is "unique." (Another error in the first sentence is the intransitive use of "riveted." *Rivet* is a transitive verb: "its retelling riveted *the audience.*" *See also* **RACE and NATIONALITY,** *3.*)

Surely an educator should be expected to know the proper usage of words. A high school supervisor in the Southeast told a television interviewer that not everyone was capable of teaching. "It takes a very unique individual. . . . " (One who speaks properly?)

UNLESS AND UNTIL. The phrase "unless and until" befits a legal document. Separately, *unless* and *until* have different meanings. Together, they are usually excessive in normal prose.

The conjunction *unless* means if not, or except when. The conjunction *until* means up to the point that, or up to the time of. When combined in "unless and until," they add up to an overblown phrase. Usually one word or the other, depending on the context, can be scrapped with no loss of meaning. This sentence, from a book, illustrates the two words in combination:

> Those laws [governing matter under very extreme conditions] are im-

portant for understanding how the universe began, but they do not affect the future evolution of the universe, unless and until the universe recollapses to a high-density state.

Unless is enough. The universe will continue to evolve, if it does not recollapse. To use "until" alone might suggest that recollapsing is a sure thing. The addition of "and until" is unnecessary and more legalistic than scientific.

Sometimes "or" replaces "and," yielding the phrase "unless or until." The result is the same.

A comparable phrase is "if and when." *If* means in the event that. *When* means at the time that. Here too one word or the other, depending on context, usually can stand alone. A variation of the phrase is "when and if." Such phrases can be left to lawyers.

See also **Twins.**

UNLIKE. *1. Clarity. 2. Comparability.*

1. Clarity

Unlike can be clearer than *not . . . like:* "Campbell is not a college graduate, like his predecessor, Morgan." Was Morgan graduated from college or not? If he was, a better way to begin is "*Unlike* his predecessor. . . . " But if he was not, a better way is "Like his predecessor. . . . " *See also* **LIKE,** *1;* **NOT,** *1E.*

Users of *unlike* must make it clear just what they are contrasting. The contrasted elements need to be isolated and not obscured by modifiers. In this sentence from a newsletter, nine modifying words precede the noun "lift":

> Unlike other GGT buses, the new Flxible buses features an Americans with Disabilities ACT (ADA) approved front door wheelchair lift which allows for a 45-seat bus capacity.

The extent of the difference between the buses is blurred by the pile-up of modi-

fiers and the ambiguous "which." *See* **Modifiers,** *4;* **THAT and WHICH.** (Another mistake is a noun-verb disagreement in number: It should be "buses *feature.*" *Flxible* is a brand, not a mistake.)

2. Comparability

The prepositions *unlike* and *like* are opposite in meaning but alike grammatically. Whereas *like* likens one thing to another, *unlike* contrasts one thing with another. Either way, the things need to be comparable to make complete sense. In the use of *unlike,* we encounter the same problem of false comparison that was shown in the use of *like.*

This remark was made on a national telecast: "Unlike thirty years ago, we now have sunscreens to shield us from daily exposure." A time in the past and what we now have belong to different categories. "Unlike *what we had* thirty years ago . . . " is a correction.

Unlike occasionally serves as an adjective: "the unlike duckling."

See also **LIKE,** 2.

UNMENTIONABLE. *See* **Verbal unmentionables.**

UNQUALIFIED. *See* **DISQUALIFIED and UNQUALIFIED.**

"UNQUOTE." *See* **QUOTE and QUOTATION.**

UNSPEAKABLE. *See* **Verbal unmentionables.**

UNTHINKABLE. Two dictionaries offer the identical opening definition of *unthinkable:* "Not thinkable; inconceivable." Such a definition is paradoxical. Anything you can think is thinkable. Anything you can conceive is conceivable. Just to mention something, albeit to condemn it as wrong or impossible, is to think of it.

This discourse is to reject, not the word, but the definition and inappropriate use of the word. When all four panelists in a television discussion agreed that U.S. withdrawal from Saudi Arabia was "unthinkable" (a word suggested by the moderator), they all thought of it. The proposition might have been called *unacceptable, undesirable, unfeasible,* or *unreasonable* (or *a good idea,* had panelists been selected who did not all think alike), but was it really "unthinkable"?

The same two dictionaries offer an identical second definition: "Not to be thought of or considered." That one is more tenable. There may be certain concepts that, though they can be thought, *should not* be thought. In that sense, dictators regard democracy as *unthinkable;* and, in promoting their product, cigarette companies regard the danger to health as *unthinkable.* Normally you can think what you want in our society. Our laws restrict only what you *do;* thought-control is generally unacceptable.

It is verbal profligacy to use "unthinkable" just to express disagreement with a proposition, unless it is horrible or evil beyond contemplation. To use it to describe something that actually exists or has already been done ("the administration's unthinkable actions in Latin America") is preposterous.

See also **Verbal unmentionables.**

UNTIL. *See* **TILL and "'TIL"; UNLESS AND UNTIL; UP,** 2 (end).

UNUTTERABLE. *See* **Verbal unmentionables.**

UP. *1. As a verb. 2. In phrases. 3. Prefix and suffix.*

1. As a verb

As a verb, *up* is more or less colloquial and not for all occasions.

Using it in the (transitive) sense of raise or increase—to "up prices" or "prices were upped"—is scorned by some critics, one of whom calls it "journalese." At least one expression of that sort has become established: to *up the ante,* meaning to increase the stakes, particularly in a poker game.

To *up* (intransitive) is also to rise or get up, or to act unexpectedly or suddenly: "She upped and walloped him on the jaw."

2. In phrases

When added to a number of verbs, *up* (adverb) forms distinctive phrases, in which *up* does not bear its literal meaning: *higher* or the opposite of *down.*

Make up, for instance, can mean to put together, form, arrange, complete, compensate for, become friendly again, or put on (cosmetics). We *bring up* (children or topics), *get up* (in the morning), *keep up* (an activity or appearance), *look up* (information in a reference book), and *turn up* (something lacking).

Up may intensify verbs, adding an element of completeness or thoroughness. Treasure-hunters *dig,* hoping to *dig up* riches. To *dress* is less formal than to *dress up.* To *tear* a book damages it; to *tear up* the book destroys it. *Clean up* and *tie up* are somewhat intensified versions of *clean* and *tie* in literal senses, and they have respectively the additional meanings of make a lot of money (colloquial) and delay or immobilize.

Nevertheless, *up* goes unnecessarily with some other verbs, making no difference in their meanings. Two professors wrote that "some of the resources freed up by pruning military outlays should permit Democrats to advance the 'pocketbook issues'. . . . " No one is likely to miss "up" if it is removed from a sentence like that or phrases like these: "end up" (the meeting), "light up" (a cigar), "finish up" (the job), "head up" (a committee), "make up" (the beds), "match up" (cloths), "open up" (the gate), "pay up" (the money), "write up" (an article).

The "up" in "hurry up" / "join up" / "wait up" adds nothing to *hurry, join, wait.*

Instead of telling someone just to *listen,* it is fashionable (at this writing) to tack on the appendage "up." On a radio news network, the remark "Listen up, Steven Spielberg" prefaced a broadcast of a computer-generated portrayal of a dinosaur cry.

Up is the first word in sundry phrases. Among useful ones are *up against,* meaning confronted with; *up for,* presented for (election, trial, etc.); *up to,* occupied in, capable of, or equal to; and *up to date,* current. ("These accounts are *up to date*" or "These are the *up-to-date* accounts.") The "up" is redundant in "up until" or "up till," inasmuch as *until* or *till* means *up* to a point or time.

See also CAUGHT and CAUGHT UP.

3. Prefix and suffix

Up- is joined as a prefix in many words. Some of them, accenting the *up-,* are *upbeat, upbraid, upgrade, upkeep, upright, uprising, uproar, upshot, upstart,* and *upward.* Others, such as *upheaval, uphold, upholster,* and *uproot,* accent the second syllable. Still others give about equal stress to both syllables: *upside* (*down*), *upstairs, upstream,* and *uptown.* The stress may vary, as in *upset:* the noun is UP-set, the verb up-SET; the adjective goes either way. Dictionaries disagree on the pronunciation of some other *up-* words.

Up is hyphenated in the adjectives *up-and-coming,* meaning advancing toward success; and *up-and-down,* meaning fluctuating in direction or vertical.

As a suffix, *-up* may or may not be joined by a hyphen. Examples are the nouns *breakup, buildup, holdup, setup, windup, close-up, make-up,* and *shake-up* (all accenting the first syllable). As verbs, each of the root words would be separate from *up.* Dictionaries do not agree what to hyphenate, and several dictionaries show no pattern behind their choices. For instance, one book runs *wind-up, shakeup,* and a choice between *make-up* and *makeup.* Another spells them *windup, shake-up,* and *makeup.*

A usable rule of thumb for words with *up* suffixes (suggested by Roy H. Copperud) is to follow the root word with a hyphen if it ends in a vowel.

See also UPCOMING; PICK UP and PICKUP; ROUND UP and ROUNDUP; SET UP and SETUP.

UPCOMING. *Upcoming* dates back to the fourteenth century. For about 500 years it was solely a noun, meaning the action of coming up; for instance, "From the hill, we watched their upcoming." Then it began to be used also as an adjective, in a similar sense, e.g., "the upcoming travelers."

Its adjectival use as a synonym for *anticipated, approaching, coming,* or *forthcoming,* as in "the upcoming election," began still later. *The Oxford English Dictionary* can trace that "chiefly U.S." application only as far back as 1959.

In its newest sense, *upcoming* has not won general acceptance. Use it if you have to, but never as a replacement for *coming up,* the way a telecast of entertainment news misused it: "With the new season upcoming, optimism is high." The flavor is German, not English. Change "upcoming" to *coming up* or just *coming.*

A predecessor of the original *upcoming,* by about three centuries, was *upcome,* a rare verb meaning to come up.

See also **Backward writing,** *3.*

US and WE. *See* **Pronouns,** *10.*

USE. *See* UTILIZE, UTILIZATION.

USE TO and USED TO. Each of the samples below displays a wrong tense of the verb *use*. Past should be present and present should be past.

" 'What did your name used to be?' this reporter couldn't resist asking." Change "used" to *use*: " 'What did your name *use* to be?' "

"I use to like people for what I could get out of them." Change "use" to *used*: "I *used* to like people. . . . "

Used to, indicating a former state or a former activity, often is correct. But when *did* goes with a verb, it takes over the job of casting the verb's action in the past. In that way, *use* is no different from other verbs. We say, "When *did* she *leave?*" (not "left") or "I *did* not *sleep*" (not "slept").

The fact that *used to* and *use to* sound so similar can account for the confusion.

In the negative, two constructions are possible. One may say either "He did not *use* to drink much" or He *used* not to drink much." The first is more common, especially in speech. The meaning of *use to* may be expressed in other ways: "He did not drink much in the past" or "in past years" or "in those days."

Used to can mean accustomed to. "I am used to hard work." / "We were used to walking barefoot." That sense employs only *used,* the past participle, and only in the passive.

UTILIZE, UTILIZATION. *Utilize,* often conscripted as a high-flown synonym for *use* (verb, transitive), has its niche. It implies putting to practical use something that has not been practical so far, or making something more productive or profitable by finding a new use for it.

These are appropriate examples: "Many companies would like to utilize the natural resources of the Antarctic." /

"Silicon was utilized in the computer revolution." In the examples below (from a book and a newspaper), "utilize" is used loosely.

> You should be able to boost your usual weekly or monthly sales figures from time to time by utilizing one of the more popular promotional techniques.

If the techniques are already in popular use, *using* will do in place of "utilizing."

> To avoid becoming a rape victim, there are several precautions to follow as well as a variety of defenses to utilize if assaulted.

Again, *use* is enough. *Utilize* would be the right word in speaking, for instance, of "a variety of common objects to utilize as defenses." (*See also* **Crimes,** *1.*)

A related noun is *utilization,* which at times is forced to serve as a pretentious synonym for the noun *use.* In a dictionary article, a linguist describes a million-word sample of American writing containing 61,805 word forms.

> As already suggested in our discussion of the frequency of words of different length, word utilization in actual use varies enormously.

The sentence would be improved by changing "word utilization in" to *their.*

Another synonym for *use* is *employ* (verb, transitive), which has its own nuance: to apply or devote to an activity. "She employed her time and energy in helping the poor." Of course *employ* also means to hire or to use the services of an employee.

V

VASELINE. *Vaseline* is a brand of petroleum jelly, used for medicinal purposes. As a trademark, it should be capitalized.

A book of language instruction for newcomers prints the commercial names of several products in lower case. In sample dialogue, a customer tells a pharmacist, "I'll need some vaseline, too." Another commercial product that the book incorrectly mentions in lower case is Q-Tips. *See also* **BAND-AID.**

H. L. Mencken, who refused to capitalize *Vaseline* and many other trademarks, wrote that it had entered German and French dictionaries and, as *fan-shih-ling*, was among four "Americanisms" borrowed by the Chinese. (The others were *p'u-k'e*, poker; *tel-lu-feng*, telephone; and *ch'ueh-ssu-teng*, charleston, the dance.) He described its origin: Robert A. Chesebrough coined it in 1870 or so, drawing from the German *wasser*, water, and the Greek *elaion*, oil, for he believed that the decomposition of water gave rise to petroleum.

VENAL and VENIAL. *See* **Confusing pairs.**

VENUE. *Venue* is a legal term. It is the locality in which a crime is committed or the cause for a civil suit occurs. It is also the political division from which a jury is called and in which a trial is held. When a lawyer requests a "change of venue," he wants the trial moved elsewhere.

Lately it has been used as a highfalutin synonym for a variety of simple words, which would generally be quite adequate and often be more specific. It has been particularly common in show business, but some in other fields too are forcing it into service. This is from a book about marketing (emphasis added):

> Still, consider if this [a newsletter] is a good *venue* for you. . . .
>
> But particularly for consultants whose strong suit is not the written word, it [use of a newsletter service] is a plausible *venue*.

Before "venue" began circulating pretentiously outside the legal community, the writer might have used *medium* (first sentence) and *course* (second sentence).

A weekly newspaper chose to use "screening venue" rather than *movie theater*. A restaurant reviewer preferred "lunch venue" to *lunchroom*. A radio commercial for language instruction used "venues" in place of *schools*. And a notice posted at a legitimate theater announced "EVENTS AT OUR OTHER VENUS" (sic).

VERBAL. *1. Oral and verbal. 2. Popular definition. 3. Technical meanings.*

1. Oral and verbal

A lawyer did not write this sentence, which is looser than it may seem.

A written, detailed contract has the virtue of specifically spelling out terms and mutual obligations, but it also binds a lot tighter than a verbal agreement.

The opposite of a *written* contract is an *oral* contract; that is, one that is spoken rather than written. All contracts or agreements are *verbal*, because they have to do with words, whether or not the words are written down.

Verbal (adjective) pertains to words. It can have any of these senses:

A. In words or through the use of words. Songs communicate in both musical and *verbal* ways.
B. Emphasizing words as such, without regard to the ideas or facts that they convey. This is purely *verbal* criticism, not substantive.
C. Word for word. A *verbal* translation is literal, rather than literary.

Verbal and *oral* both come from Latin, in which *verbum* means word and *oris* means mouth.

Oral has other mouth-related meanings. An *oral* vaccine is one that is swallowed. *Oral* hygiene is health care for the mouth.

The adverbs related to *verbal* and *oral* are *verbally* and *orally*.

2. Popular definition

"Verbal" often serves in popular speech as an antonym for *written*. General dictionaries offer that loose use among their definitions. But why choose a fuzzy word when using a precise one is so easy?

The Random House Dictionary adds a note defending the use of "verbal" to mean spoken: The practice dates from the sixteenth century; it rarely produces confusion; one can tell the meaning from the context.

Contrarily, *The American Heritage Dictionary* (first edition) cautioned against the application of *verbal* to terms such as *agreement, promise, commitment,* and *understanding;* it can mean what is written, while *oral* cannot. *Verbal* (says the third edition) "may sometimes invite confusion," as in this example: Does "modern technology for verbal communication" refer to devices like radio and telephone or those like telegraph and fax?

Webster's second edition said, in the main text under *verbal,* that "by confusion" it was taken to mean spoken. *Webster's Third* drops that qualification.

3. Technical meanings

In grammar, *verbal* has some technical meanings. *Verbal* (adjective) means pertaining to a verb, or having the function of a verb, or used to form verbs (such as the *verbal* suffix *-ize*). A *verbal* (noun) is a word or phrase formed from a verb that is used as a noun or adjective. Gerunds and at times infinitives and participles may be called *verbals*.

Verbal unmentionables. *Unmentionables* is a euphemism for underwear, little used now, except in an attempt to be humorous. It was once applied to trousers. We are assigning the designation of *verbal unmentionables* to a category of paradoxical expressions or words. What distinguishes each is that it seems to discourage any reference to the very thing it is used to refer to. If taken literally, it might not be used at all.

Expressions include *it* (or *that*) *goes without saying, needless to say, not to mention, not to say, to say nothing of,* and *words cannot describe.* Single words include *inconceivable, indescribable, ineffable, inexpressible, unimaginable, unmentionable, unsayable, unspeakable, unthinkable,* and *unutterable.*

This quirk in our language is far from new. In *Eureka,* an essay on the universe, published in 1848, Edgar Allan Poe wrote that "a certain *inexpressibly* great yet limited number of *unimaginably* yet not infinitely minute atoms" had radiated from a primordial particle; that traveling from the star 61 Cygni, even at an "*inconceivable* rate, light occupies more than ten years"; and that stars give "birth and death to *unspeakably* numerous and complex variations" of life. (Emphases are added.)

To hint at or mention something while feigning an unwillingness to mention it is a rhetorical device known as *apophasis* (a-POF-a-sis), adopted from the Greek word for denial. A guest on the air who says "I won't plug my restaurant, Joe's Eatery" is using it.

See also INDESCRIBABLE, UNDESCRIBABLE; OF COURSE, *3;* NOT TO MENTION; TO SAY NOTHING OF; UNTHINKABLE.

Verbosity. Using many words or too many words, either in writing or in speaking, is *verbosity* or *wordiness*. Usually it means using more words than are necessary to communicate one's meaning. *Verbosity* (pronounced vur-BOS-ih-tee) can in addition imply an instance of speech or writing that is obscure, pompous, or tedious; or a tendency toward such speech or writing.

A noun with similar meaning is *prolixity* (pronounced pro-LIX-ih-tee), the quality of or tendency toward such excessive length or elaboration in speech or writing as to be tiresome.

The related adjectives are *verbose* (vur-BOAS), *wordy,* and *prolix* (PRO-lix or pro-LIX).

Nouns pertaining to unnecessary repetition are *pleonasm, redundancy,* and *tautology. See* **Tautology.**

The prose of government, academia, art, science, business, and other fields can be verbose, jargonal, or just windy. An official in southern California reported that an earthquake was mild by saying, "We have not activated the disaster mode." To announce that an epidemic was going away, the director of a federal health agency said, "There is a downslope on the curve of occurrence." A Tennessee school board considering curricula decided that "pre-assessment, post-assessment, learning alternatives and remediation will be an integral part of instructional modules within the framework of program development." A collegiate dean in Wisconsin said she had worked at "conceptualizing new thrusts in programming."

An artist wrote this of her abstract paintings: "A strong frontal progressive image of light through the layers declares the present, which is, life existing in the now." (*See* **Punctuation,** *3D.*) A plaque in an art gallery said of another abstract artist, "Through the use of layering, her paintings invoke a sense of continuum, a present tense portrayal that reveals a connection to our past as well as preparing ground for the future." (*See* **EVOKE and INVOKE.**)

The beginning of a study by two professors in a scientific journal is quoted below. The study deals with pigeons. Had it dealt with people, it might have been complicated.

In general, research on concurrent choice has concentrated on steady-state relations between the allocation of behavior and independent variables that are associated with reinforcement or aspects of responding. The development of quantitative models describing stable-state choice has been successful, and is exemplified by the generalized matching law (see Davison & McCarthy, 1988, for a review), which provides a description of the relation between behavior-output ratios and reinforcer-input ratios when two variable-interval (VI) schedules are concurrently available.

Now some bedtime reading for stockholders, excerpts from a corporation's annual report:

The portion of sales hedged is based on assessments of cost-benefit profiles that consider natural offsetting exposures, revenue and exchange rate volatilities and correlations, and the cost of hedging instruments. . . . For foreign currency denominated borrowing and investing transactions, cross-currency interest rate swap contracts are used, which, in addition to exchanging cash flows derived from rates, exchange currencies at both inception and termination of the contracts. . . . Because monetary assets and liabilities are marked to spot and recorded in earnings, forward contracts designated as hedges of the monetary assets and liabilities are also marked to spot with the resulting gains and losses similarly recognized in earnings.

Popular language has deadwood too. "In spite of the fact that" can often boil down to *although;* "was in attendance at" to *attended;* "for the reason that" to *because;* "of a friendly (or cheerful etc.) character" to *friendly* (or *cheerful* etc.); "is in possession of" to *has;* and so on. Recent decades have brought many roundabout expressions, such as "I am supportive of him" instead of *I support him;* "at this point in time" instead of *now;* "in terms of" and "all that" used unnecessarily; "for" *free* and *listen* "up"; and "person" and "people" as suffixes.

Even a short piece can be too long if it has unnecessary components. A long work is not necessarily too long if it is tightly composed. That means being concise and to the point; preferring active verbs to passive verbs and fresh expressions to clichés; avoiding highfalutin, obscure, or superfluous words and phrases; not being too abstract; illustrating generalities with specific examples; favoring simple sentences over complicated ones; using long sentences sparingly and with clear, consistent structure; and using grammar, sentence structure, and vocabulary carefully.

Verbosity should not be confused with *verbiage,* an instance of (not a tendency toward) an overabundance of words. *Verbiage* can also denote a style of using words, such as *legal verbiage* in a court document.

Among pertinent entries are **Active voice and passive voice; ADVOCATE; "AT THIS POINT IN TIME"; A WHILE and AWHILE; BOTH; BUCOLIC; CAUGHT and CAUGHT UP; CHARACTER; Clichés; CONSENSUS; DEMOLISH; Expletives; FRACTION; FREE; IDYLLIC; IN ATTENDANCE; IN TERMS OF; IS IS; KNOT; LIKE, *3;* MEAN (adjective); OFF and "OFF OF"; ON, *2;* PEOPLE as a suffix; PERSON; PERSONAL; PRESENTLY; REVERT; SITUATION; SUPPORTIVE; THAT, ALL THAT; Twins; UP, *2;* WITH.**

Verbs. *1. Basic facts. 2. Creation from nouns. 3. Mistakes in number. 4. Problems in using auxiliaries. 5. Shortage of objects.*

1. Basic facts

A. What is a verb?

A verb is typically a word of action. It tells what someone or something does. "The boy *works.*" / "This monkey *howls.*" / "Paris *fell* on that day."

The person, creature, thing, or abstraction—that is, the *subject*—need not act overtly. The subject may just exist in some way, or something may happen to the subject. The verb tells us that. "I *am* the captain." / "They *live* in Detroit." / "The city *was besieged* for two years."

B. Verb phrase

A verb may consist of more than one word, usually termed a *verb phrase.* "The dog *has eaten* my manuscript." /

"The kettle *is whistling*." / "I *will return*." In each example, *has* or *is* or *will* serves as an *auxiliary verb* (also called a *helping verb* or just an *auxiliary*). It combines with the *main verb* (the word that expresses the main action), e.g., the participle *eaten* or *whistling* or the infinitive *return*, in a *verb phrase*.

Many (*composite* or *phrasal*) verbs have adverbial tails: *burn down, check in, hold up,* and so on.

C. Transitive and intransitive verbs

Verbs fall into two main categories: *transitive* and *intransitive*.

* A *transitive* verb needs an object to complete the meaning. An object is that which (or one who) receives the action or is affected by it. In "He makes money," *makes* is the verb; *money* is its object. In "Jenny plays the harp," *plays* is the verb; *the harp* is its object.
* An *intransitive verb* completes its meaning without needing an object. "Jesse *ran*." / "I *hope*." / "*Stop!*" (The subject, *you,* is implied.)

A given verb may fit both categories or just one of them. In most general dictionaries, an abbreviation like *v.t.* (verb, transitive) or *v.i.* (verb, intransitive) indicates whether or not a verb's particular meaning needs an object to complete it.

(Some verbs that are commonly transitive [requiring objects] are used intransitively [without objects] in legal writing. A book on law says, "The owners . . . defended on the ground that . . ."; and later, "The Supreme Court affirmed." That is, the owners *defended themselves* against an accusation; and the Supreme Court *affirmed the judgment* of the lower court. Another book says, "The Court of Appeals, after a careful review of the record, reversed." Inasmuch as the latter book is for laymen, *reversed the judgment,* a transitive use of the verb,

would be more idiomatic. *Reverse* has also a general intransitive sense: "The machine reversed.")

Confusion between the two categories comes up in **ADVOCATE; CLINCH; COMMIT, COMMITTED; CULMINATE; LAY and LIE; LIVE,** 2; **OBSESS** (etc.).

D. Predicate

Another important term is the *predicate*, the part of a sentence (or clause) that tells about the subject. It consists of the verb and any object, modifier, or complement it may have. In the sentence "Yankee Doodle went to town, riding on a pony," everything after "Yankee Doodle" is the *predicate*.

E. Objects, direct and indirect

An object like *dams* in "He built dams" is a *direct* object. It tells what or who receives the action. A transitive verb may have an *indirect* object too. It tells to whom (or what) or for whom (or what) the action is done. In "I gave my love a cherry," *my love* is the indirect object; *a cherry* is the direct object.

F. Linking verb

A special type of intransitive verb is a *linking* verb (also known as a *copula* or a *copulative verb*). It links the subject with a word that identifies or qualifies it: "Tubby *is* a *cat*." / "We *became fat*." / "She *seems happy*." Is links *Tubby* with *cat*. Became links *we* with *fat*. Seems links *she* with *happy*. Note that it is not "happily." The linking verb is not modified. (The *subjective complement,* the word linked to the subject, may be a noun, adjective, or pronoun.) *See also* **BAD and BADLY; FEEL; GOOD and WELL; Pronouns,** 10D.

G. More

Hundreds of word entries deal with verbs, from **ABIDE and ABIDE BY** to **ZERO IN.** So do some topic entries besides this one, including **Active voice and passive voice; Complement; Infinitive; Mood; Sentence fragment; Subjunctive; Tense.**

2. Creation from nouns

A group that declares its opposition to pollution says in a brochure, "Our staff attorneys and scientists . . . watchdog government and corporate actions. . . ." The staff members may *watch* those actions, but *watchdog* is a noun. They can no more "watchdog" actions than singers can "songbird" melodies.

The Weather Service announced on the telephone, "Please selection the expanded menu for weather information." *Selection* is a noun. Just as we cannot "adoption" or "perception," neither can we "selection." We can *adopt, perceive,* or *select.*

This is not to say that a verb should never come from a noun, but those supposed verbs are longer than the regular verbs, fill no need, and just repeat the nouns.

Some verbs formed from nouns have gained full acceptance. Among them are *diagnose* from *diagnosis; donate* from *donation; edit* from *editor;* and *scavenge* from *scavenger.* Not everyone is comfortable with *burgle* from *burglar, emote* from *emotion,* and *enthuse* from *enthusiasm.* Most accept *orate,* from *oration,* in a contemptuous sense. *Surveil,* from *surveillance,* is fairly new to dictionaries.

A verb like those is called a *back-formation,* a word that seems to be the parent of another word but really developed from the latter.

Escalate, a back-formation from *escalator,* came out of the Vietnam era. Meaning to heighten (the war), the verb served a purpose. It has a shortcoming that limits its value, however. Escalators go down as well as up.

Similarly, when a television reporter said, describing a traffic accident, "The car was accordioned," how promising was that makeshift verb? An accordion may be either pulled out or squeezed in.

During telecasts of the Olympic games, commentators like to say, for instance, "I think she has great chances here to medal"—instead of *win a medal.* They may find such a verb useful, but its general use should be discouraged. Sounding just like *meddle,* it has an inherent potential for misunderstanding.

A reporter spoke of the need "to inert fuel tanks" in airplanes. Did *insert* mislead her? Or is a national telecast an occasion for experimenting with verbs that have not entered the dictionaries?

A columnist wrote, "If he doesn't income average, Mr. Lucky's federal income tax alone will be $456,400." We will probably not see much of that purported verb again, fortunately, for income averaging has since been abolished.

3. Mistakes in number

It is an elementary rule that a singular subject takes a singular verb; a plural subject takes a plural verb. Sometimes people find it tricky to interpret or just slip up.

The essential noun of the subject controls the number of the verb. Do not be distracted by any intervening words. That noun and its associated auxiliary verb are emphasized in these correct examples: "The *information* about the arrests *was* released yesterday." / "This *book* of new poems *has* just been published." In the next example, also correct, the essential noun is plural and it follows a qualifying phrase that fools some writers: "A total of 1.3 million *votes were* cast for both candidates." *See* **TOTAL.**

A cooking columnist and a news reporter should have known better but may have been distracted by irrelevant, singular nouns:

I like to serve it [a French fish dish] with croutons on top that is flavored with olive oil and crushed black pepper.

The layoffs, which trimmed the party's paid staff to 35, was just the latest indication of tough times for California Democrats.

The "croutons . . . *are* flavored. . . . "
The "layoffs . . . *were* just the latest. . . . "
This was reported in a radio newscast:

Senator Patrick Leahy, Democrat of Vermont, is among senators who is opposed to calling witnesses.

Yes, he "is among senators," but those senators "*are* opposed." *See* ONE OF, 3.
Usually a subject made up of two or more nouns or pronouns (or both) that are connected by *and* demands a plural verb. "Frankie and Johnny *were* lovers." An exception is made when the nouns or pronouns express just one idea or identify just one person: "The hue and cry over this issue *surprises* me." / "Our vice-president and general manager *is* here." The two examples that follow call for no exception.
A university president wrote that college applicants need, not prestigious institutions, but "the firm knowledge that their education and growth as human beings depends on themselves alone." Change "depends" to *depend*. Education and growth are two ideas.
Another president—of the United States this time—said, "Democracy and freedom is what the concept of the new order is about." Make it "Democracy and freedom are. . . . " They are two ideas. *See* DEMOCRACY, FREEDOM, and INDEPENDENCE.
Contractions do not excuse errors in number. "Here's the pitching probables for the three-game series against the Pirates . . . ," a sports item said. "Here's," a contraction of "Here is," should be *Here are. See* Contractions, 1.
Traditionally a phrase or clause introduced by the expression *along with, as well as, in addition to, together with*, or just *with* does not affect the number of the verb. By that view, the expression either is not a part of the subject or is a subordinate part. (Grammarians give varying explanations.) For instance, "The farm, as well as the house, *is* up for sale." A few critics allow a plural verb if the items are supposed to get equal emphasis or if a plural feeling prevails.
Nouns with exotic endings account for many errors. A common error is to mistake a plural, like *media* or *phenomena*, for a singular. *See* Plurals and singulars, which lists many pertinent entries.
At times a group may be either singular or plural, but a sentence should not treat it in both ways. *See* Collective nouns.
The functions of many common words and phrases are often misunderstood. They include *each, every, either, neither, or,* and *nor* and words and phrases with (-)one. These examples (like all those following in this section) are correct: "Each of the athletes *is* vying . . ." / "Neither he nor I *was* chosen." / "Everyone in these parts *knows* everyone else." / "He's one of the few people who *live* here." *See* Number (grammatical) for a list of many pertinent entries.
Placing the verb before the subject does not change the need for agreement: "In this square *stand* the county's first residence and the original courthouse."
When a fraction is followed by a prepositional phrase, the latter determines the number: "One-fourth of our taxes *go* to support government waste." / "Two-thirds of the county *lies* under water."

4. Problems in using auxiliaries
Sometimes it works: letting two auxiliary verbs (helping verbs) help one main verb. "We can and must win," for instance, avoids repeating "win."
But sometimes this locution turns into

a trap: "The fair shows what our county can and is accomplishing." To say "can . . . accomplishing" is wrong, even with the two words in between. A simple correction presents the main verb twice, in the two forms needed: ". . . can accomplish and is accomplishing."

A similar example: "This department may—and occasionally has—looked outside for its leadership." To say "may . . . looked" is wrong. A correction finishes one idea before turning to the second: ". . . may look outside for its leadership, something it has occasionally chosen to do."

Several decades ago there arose a false doctrine that declared a verb phrase to be an indivisible unit; no auxiliary verb might be separated from a main verb; any adverb must go outside that unit.

By that rule, instead of saying "The facts have *long* been known" (correct), one had to say "The facts *long* have been known" (questionable). And not "The vehicle is *slowly* gaining speed" (correct) but "The vehicle *slowly* is gaining speed" (questionable). The second sentence of each pair is less idiomatic than the first, though clear.

It may not be as clear if instead of saying "He appears to have *partly* recovered" (correct), one says "He appears *partly* to have recovered" (incorrect). Which verb the adverb belongs to may not be immediately apparent.

Even conservative grammarians have no sympathy for that doctrine, which seems to have developed from the fear of splitting infinitives. It is not only permissible to split verb phrases but desirable when idiom and meaning so demand. Splitting infinitives is not necessarily wrong either. *See* **Infinitive**, *4.*

See also **WHO**, *3*, concerning the person of a verb following *I who* or *you who.*

5. Shortage of objects
Multiple verbs in a sentence may have the same object: "She buys, cooks, and

serves food." *Buys, cooks,* and *serves* share one object: *food.*

If another word or phrase follows the object, the verbs may or may not share the object. Here the verbs do: "We invited and welcomed Ben in." Both *invited* and *welcomed* fit both *Ben* (the object) and *in.*

This faulty sentence is another story: "He insulted and threw the people out." Only the second verb accepts the object (*the people*), because only that verb accepts the tail word (*out*). *Threw* and *out* go together; *the people* is locked up between them, unavailable to *insulted.* The defect may be fixed by relocating the noun and inserting a pronoun: "He insulted *the people* and threw *them* out."

A defective sentence in a biography presents four verbs that are supposed to be transitive. Only the last has an object (*them*).

> For the younger ones, Emma was their mother-figure, who fed, dressed, bathed, and put them to bed.

The verb *put* goes with *to bed.* The object, *them,* is locked up in between. It is unavailable to the other three verbs, which do not go with *to bed.* A correction is to insert another *and* and another *them:* "who fed, dressed, *and* bathed *them* and put them to bed."

VERTEBRA and VERTEBRAE.
A *vertebra* is any one of the thirty-three bones of the spine. It is pronounced VUR-tuh-bruh.

Vertebrae is plural, using a Latin form. It is pronounced either VUR-tuh-bree or VUR-tuh-bray. An alternative plural is *vertebras,* VUR-tuh-bruz.

Said on a television news program: "She has a broken vertebrae" (-bray). Correction: "She has a broken *vertebra,*" designating one of the bones, not more than one.

The *spine* is known also as the *backbone, spinal column,* or *vertebral column.*

VERY. 1. *Limitations.* 2. *Overuse.*

1. *Limitations*

Very is a very common word and a legitimate one, classified as both an adverb and an adjective. Its use as an adverb is limited and the subject of divided opinion.

Bearing the sense of extremely or truly, *very* easily modifies words that are solely adjectives: *large, strong, brightest.*

Hardly anyone would try to say, "The medicine very helps him" or "The speakers very praised her." *Very* does not modify verbs, even though modifying verbs is a normal activity of adverbs. But may we say, "He is very helped by the medicine" or "She was very praised by the speakers"? In other words, may we use *very* before a past participle, which is a verb used as an adjective?

Those with easy-going ears and eyes would say *yes.* Those who are more particular would probably give a qualified *no* and disapprove of those examples. Such critics have included seven-eighths of *The American Heritage Dictionary*'s usage panel, which rated "She was very disliked by her students" unacceptable in writing but approved "He seemed very worried." The difference is that *disliked*—like *helped* and *praised*—is not in common use as an adjective. People do not usually speak of "the disliked teacher" any more than "the helped patient" or "the praised woman." But *worried,* as in "the worried parents," is considered to be a full-fledged adjective as well as a past participle.

When in doubt, a writer should reword the thought. A participle may be properly intensified in several ways, with or without *very.* "He is *very much* helped" or "*greatly* helped." / "She was *very highly* praised" or "*profusely* praised."

When *very* serves as an adjective, *the* often precedes it, but not invariably. The adjective can mean actual (his *very* words), identical (this *very* spot), mere

(the *very* thought), necessary (the *very* solution), precise (the *very* center), or utter (the *very* bottom).

2. *Overuse*

An episode in an old comedy series on television depicted an intellectually deficient anchor man straining to write a thoughtful essay. He could get no further than "Freedom of the press is very, very good and very, very important."

Inexperienced writers indeed tend to resort to *very* too freely. Speakers too, both amateur and professional, are known to overdo it. A restaurant critic on the radio described a county's restaurants, "some of them very, very small but all of them very, very good." A TV reporter said, at the scene of a search for a missing person, "The bushes get very, very thick. It would be very, very easy to lose someone out here."

A second *very* says nothing that the first does not say. And if one *very* is inadequate, perhaps what is needed is an alternative adverb—or a stronger adjective and no adverb. For instance, an alternative to "very, very small," is *extremely small* or *tiny.*

VIABLE. *Viable* (adjective) means capable of living. A human fetus or a newborn is *viable* when it has developed to the stage at which it can survive outside the womb. Usually at twenty-eight weeks it reaches the stage of *viability* (noun), the capacity to live and grow.

A *viable* seed is one that is capable of taking root and growing.

The adjective or noun may be used figuratively for something that does not possess life or its potential, just as *born* and *live* may be so used: "Many doubted that the new country could survive, but it proved its viability."

The essential idea is the capability of existing and surviving. Where is that sense in the passage below, from an encyclopedia?

The invention of the semi-conductor device known as the transistor in 1947 . . . ushered in what many have called the second industrial revolution. After a decade of further developmental work, the transistor became a viable alternative to the electron tube. . . .

If the device could exist for a decade after its invention and 1947 was the year of its invention, 1947 was when it became *viable*. It seemed to be *viable* enough then to start a revolution. If *commercial, durable, effective, feasible, practical, practicable,* or *usable* was meant, the writer should have used it.

A retired appellate judge, who used to be expected to use words judiciously, said of the jury system, "I'm beginning to wonder about its viability." How can one doubt the *viability* of a system that has existed for centuries? If the speaker meant *advantage, benefit, usefulness, value, workability,* or *worth,* he should have said so.

Whether the age of a president mattered to voters was a question on a television panel. A panelist quoted Richard M. Nixon:

> He said he thought that the baby boomers, having seen Clinton in there, would decide that was no longer viable to have somebody [like] that.

In "viable," the panelist seems to have meant nothing more than *desirable*.

For the four following uses, one could substitute *feasible, practical, promising,* or a comparable adjective. Television: "For an engineer, the standard is whether it works or whether it's commercially viable." / An editorial: "The voters . . . instructed our city officials to develop a viable plan for the waterfront." / An article: ". . . Switching to computer programming is not a viable option." / A headline: "Private fire dept. may not be viable."

Feasibility, practicality, or a comparable noun could have replaced "viability" in an article: ". . . Giving the [Internet] system a new purpose has unearthed fundamental problems that could well put off commercial viability for years."

The English language adopted the French *viable,* likely to live, derived from *vie,* life, which came from the Latin *vita,* life.

See also **VITAL.**

VICE and VISE. *See* **Homophones.**

VICIOUS and VISCOUS. *See* Confusing pairs.

VIRGULE. *See* Punctuation, *12.*

VIRTUAL, VIRTUALLY. *Virtual* (adjective) means being so-and-so in effect or in essence, though not in actual fact or name. This is a strict use:

> Gorbachev . . . has calmly accepted the dissolution of what had been a virtual Soviet empire of Communist satellites in Eastern Europe. . . .

While it was never officially called anything like the "Soviet Empire," it amounted to that.

Often "virtual" or "virtually" (adverb) becomes just a fancy way of saying *near* or *almost*. *Almost* would be preferable to "virtually" as loosely used twice in this passage:

> . . . Samuels has major expenses and virtually no income. . . . "Virtually everybody who knows about this has called to volunteer". . . .

An editorial about a candidate for the U.S. Senate illustrates confusion about *virtual:*

First, the notion that he is a "virtual candidate" under the direction of his wife . . . is absurd and, frankly, misogynist.

Let us postulate, for argument's sake, that the man's wife was the politically ambitious one, was telling him what to do, and was doing things that a candidate would do. Then *she* would be the *virtual* candidate. The husband would be the official candidate, perhaps a puppet candidate, but not a "virtual" candidate.

In computer applications, the adjective is used for *simulated:* "virtual reality."

See also VIRTUE.

VIRTUE.

Virtue usually denotes either good moral quality (in a person) or merit (in a thing). It can also mean efficacy, effective force, especially the power to strengthen or heal: a drug's *virtue.*

A speaker was technically correct but risked being misunderstood: "The great virtue of using that stuff is that it's ubiquitous. It's available everywhere." He was talking about the "virtue" of using the particular explosive that blasted the World Trade Center in New York. Better: "To the terrorists, the benefit of that stuff is. . . . "

An obsolete meaning of *virtue* is that of manly merit, courage, or strength. Those are meanings of the Latin *virtus,* the source of *virtual* and *virtuoso* as well as *virtue. Virtus* stems from *vir,* a man or male, the source of *virile.* Yet *virtue* and *virtuous,* with the meanings of chastity and chaste, have often been applied just to women.

VISCOUS and VICIOUS. *See* Confusing pairs.

VISE and VICE. *See* Homophones.

VISITING FIREMAN. *See* -MAN-, MAN.

VITAL.

Vital (adjective), stemming from the Latin *vitalis,* of life, has essentially the same meaning in English: relating to life, characteristic of life, essential to life, imparting or renewing life, or living. We speak of *vital* statistics, *vital* energy, the *vital* organs, *vital* fluid. "When I have pluck'd the rose, I cannot give it vital growth again" (Shakespeare). In creation "the Spirit of God . . . vital virtue infused and vital warmth Throughout the fluid mass" (Milton).

By figurative extension, *vital* is used to mean essential or indispensable to the life or existence of something. "Water is vital to agriculture." But the word is degraded when it replaces *needed, wanted, important, significant,* or less substantial adjectives.

Those in the news business, enamored of short and exciting words, have long overused and trivialized *vital.* A copy editor will choose it for a headline over *needed,* if not *important,* as a matter of course. One TV reporter called Egypt "a vital American ally" and another said, "Helicopters are vital to modern military operations"—meaning that the U.S. could not survive without Egypt or fight without helicopters?

The following samples, from a headline and two articles, may illustrate the ultimate degradation of that word of life: its application to devices for the mass destruction of life.

"How a Vital Nuclear Material Came to Be in Short Supply" / "The shortage of tritium, a vital material for nuclear weapons, arrived right on schedule." / "The Savannah River Plant, near Aiken, is the nation's only source of tritium, a perishable gas vital to thermonuclear warheads."

All the blame cannot be placed on the news business. Prime Minister Margaret Thatcher of the United Kingdom declared that "Short-range nuclear missiles are absolutely vital" (not just "vital" but "absolutely vital"). The chairman of the

Joint Chiefs of Staff proposed "a reduced but still vital nuclear force to deter nuclear adversaries."

In the seventeenth to nineteenth centuries, *vital* could be legitimately used to mean destructive to life. A *vital wound* would be a *fatal wound* today. When news people or public officials speak of a diabolic weapon as "vital," let us think of the word in that archaic sense.

See also **VIABLE.**

VIZ. (namely). *See* **Punctuation,** *2A*.

Voice. *See* **Active voice and passive voice.**

VULGARITY. *See* OBSCENE, OBSCENITY.

W

WAITER, WAITRESS. *See* **PEO-PLE as a suffix; PERSON,** *1* (end); **WAIT FOR and WAIT ON.**

WAIT FOR and WAIT ON. You *wait for* a bus. A waiter *waits on* patrons. To *wait for* something or someone or some event is to remain inactive or in anticipation until it or the person arrives or the event takes place. To *wait on* someone is to serve the person.

Wait on is dialect or slang when used in place of *wait for* as a newscaster used it in speaking of a budget bill "that everyone is waiting on" and as a magazine did: "You don't boot up your juicer or even your video. So who wants to wait on their PC?" (The plural "their" disagrees with the singulars *wants* and *PC*. *See* **Pronouns,** *2*.)

Among several obsolete or rare meanings of *wait on* is to pay a formal visit to someone considered a superior. "He waited on the king in his palace."

See also **ON,** *2* (end).

WAKE, AWAKE, AWAKEN, WAKEN. *1. First choice: WAKE (UP). 2. The other verbs. 3. Past tense; participle; other forms.*

1. First choice: WAKE (UP)

When the alarm clock rings in the morning, do you wake, wake up, awake, awaken, waken, or go back to sleep?

The *(a)wake(n)* verbs, Old English descendants, all mean to arouse from sleep or a state like sleep, or to come out of that state. The distinctions in usage are complicated. In general, *wake* is the utility tool, good for most everyday use. The other words are substituted in figurative or poetic use, in the passive voice, or for the sake of formality or meter.

Wake is the only one that goes with *up.* The *up* does not affect the meaning. You cannot go wrong with it. Tagging it onto *wake* is common and idiomatic when *wake* is used as an intransitive verb, especially so in the imperative and the present tense: "Wake up!" / "We wake up at 7 a.m." In the past tense, *up* is optional: Either "I woke up at dawn" or "I woke at dawn" is acceptable.

When *wake* is used as a transitive verb, it is just about as common and idiomatic with the *up* as without it: "We should wake him" or "We should wake him up." / "Don't wake the baby" or "Don't wake up the baby."

Unlike the other three words, *wake* has the additional sense of be or remain awake. It is commonly expressed in the phrase *waking hours.*

2. The other verbs

In figurative and poetic senses, the verbs starting with *a—awake* and *awaken*—are favored: "They awakened to the danger." / "The country has awaked." / "Awake! for morning in the Bowl of Night Has flung the Stone that puts the Stars to Flight." Sometimes, however, the other words are so used: "Wake up, America!"

In the passive voice, the words ending in *n*—*awaken* and *waken*—are often chosen: "The world was awakened by the event." / "They were wakened by the bell."

Although each of those verbs has been used both transitively and intransitively, usually *awake* is intransitive—"She finally awoke to the problem"—and *awaken* and *waken* are transitive: "Revere awakened the town." / "The rooster wakens us each morning."

3. Past tense; participle; other forms

The past tense of *wake* is *woke,* and the past tense of *awake* is *awoke.* For the past participle of *wake* or *awake,* simply add *d:* "She had waked [or "waked up"] at 5 a.m." / "The world has awaked."

For either the past tense or the past participle of *awaken* or *waken,* just add *-ed: awakened, wakened.*

When a political party spokesman said on American television that "the country has woken up," he used a participle that would have been more acceptable in Britain. In the U.S. it is *has* (or *had*) *waked.*

In saying that "Africa . . . has awoken to life a second time," the translator of a book used an obsolete participle. *Has* (or *had*) *awaked* is the modern style.

A policeman said (about the victim of an intruder), "She wasn't positive how she became awoken." Make it "how she became *awake*" (adjective) or "how she was *wakened*" (past participle).

The gerund of *wake*—"WAKING"— is the title of Chapter XI of Lewis Carroll's *Through the Looking Glass.* The title could have been "AWAKENING," but then it would not have rhymed with the title of Chapter X, "SHAKING."

WANT and WISH. *See* WISH.

WARRANT. A *warrant* is a written authorization. A *warrant of arrest,* or *arrest warrant,* is a court order, usually to a law enforcement officer, to arrest someone for a particular reason and bring him before the court.

When a television newscaster announced, "The FBI has issued arrest warrants for two young white men," he was confused and inaccurate. The Federal Bureau of Investigation makes arrests. It does not issue "warrants" for those arrests. Only a judge or magistrate may issue an *arrest warrant* or a *search warrant.*

A *search warrant* directs a law enforcement officer to search a person, place, or thing for property or evidence needed for a criminal prosecution and bring it before the judge or magistrate.

WAS and WERE. An article said that Congress was cutting the Pentagon's budget requests for a defense program. It commented:

> But even if the "Star Wars" program was not running into budgetary problems, there would be other doubts about [it]. . . .

"Was" should be *were.* The *were* form (the past subjunctive of the verb *be*) is used in clauses describing situations that are purely hypothetical or plainly contrary to fact. More examples are "I wish that I *were* rich" and "He acted as though he *were* king."

When the situation is not hypothetical or contrary to fact but merely uncertain or conditional, *was* is the form to use (for the verb *be* in the third person): "She looked out to see whether it *was* raining." / "He promised to cut spending if he *was* elected." / "If that nugget we saw *was* real gold, the man struck it rich."

See also **Mood; Subjunctive.**

WATCH and WATCHDOG. *See* Verbs, 2.

WAY and "A WAYS." An editor of a California weekly wrote: "Zap [North Dakota] seems like such a long ways from home." A network anchor man addressed this comment to women politicians: "You've come a long way. There's still a ways to go." And a reporter on the same news series said about the Los Angeles Police Department: "The commission's chairman believes LAPD still has a ways to go."

"A ways" is regional and colloquial. Combining singular and plural words, it is not acceptable in strict usage. *A* and *way* are both singular and may be combined ("such *a* long *way* from home") or a synonym may be preferable ("still *a distance* [or "*some distance*"] to go").

WE and US. *See* Pronouns, *10.*

WEATHER and WHETHER. *See* Homophones.

WEIRD. *Weird* means eerie, mysterious, occult, supernatural, unearthly, uncanny. This adjective has been watered down in popular speech, particularly that of juveniles, to describe what is merely different from the norm, out of the ordinary, unconventional, or unusual. In a TV cartoon, a husband says, "Your guitar teacher looks pretty interesting, and by 'interesting' I mean weird." (No, he means *unconventional.*) The wife replies, "Well, she *is* weird."

The word's ancestor was the Old English noun *wyrd,* meaning fate or destiny. It became *werd* or *wird* in Middle English; its related adjective was *werde* or *wirde,* concerning or having the power to deal with fate or the Fates. In Shakespeare's *Macbeth,* the three witches call themselves "the weird sisters."

WELL. *See* AS, *5;* GOOD and WELL.

WENCH and WINCH. "Were you alone on the boat or was there a crew milling about with wenches and jibs and such?" The host of a television show probably was not trying to be funny when he asked that question.

A *wench* is an archaic term for a young woman. It could refer particularly to a country girl, a maidservant, or a prostitute. Today it is used, if at all, in a humorous or facetious way.

The word intended by the host was probably *winch,* a machine for hoisting. It has either a motor or a hand crank that winds a rope or a chain around a drum as a load is lifted.

WEND and WIND. Seeing the highway blocked by earthquake damage, Los Angeles motorists proceeded to "wind their way" either northward or southward. So said a newscaster on television, possibly aiming for *wend* but missing. To *wend* is to direct (one's way) or to go. Still, if the road was a winding one, "wind" (long *i,* as in *find*) could be acceptable.

A similar use was questionable in a radio report on "the Chinese New Year's parade, which is continuing to wind its way down San Francisco streets." *Wend its way* (*his way, her way,* etc.) is the expression. The route did not wind. Some of the participants, however, carrying along stylized Chinese dragons, did proceed in a twisting or curving manner, so perhaps they were *winding* their way.

WENT. *See* GONE and WENT.

WERE. *See* WAS and WERE; Subjunctive.

WHAT EVER and WHATEVER. *See* (-)EVER.

WHEN AND IF. *See* UNLESS AND UNTIL.

WHENCE and **"FROM WHENCE."** A senator said, "These young people [cadets] are a reflection of the society from whence they came." A critic wrote, "No one is seriously urging the novelist to return to the verse epic, from whence he sprang." And this was in a travel article: "Thus, people returned to Brussels from whence they had wandered."

Whence means from where or from which place. *From* is part of the meaning. ". . . The society whence they came" / ". . . the verse epic, whence he sprang" / ". . . to Brussels whence they had wandered" are enough.

WHEN EVER and WHENEVER. *See* (-)EVER.

WHEN, WHERE in definitions. Teacher: "What is the real meaning of *dumb?*" Johnny: "That's when you can't talk." The teacher would probably accept the boy's answer. He lacks the verbal facility to say "inability to speak." Children explain things that way—and so, alas, do some adults: "A perfect game is where no batter of the losing team reaches first base." Better: "A perfect game is a baseball game in which. . . . "

Using *when* or *where* to connect a word or phrase with a definition or explanation is not necessarily forbidden. It is acceptable, at least informally, if the definition or explanation deals with time, after the *when;* or place, after the *where:* "Dusk is when it starts getting dark." / "The range is where the buffalo roam." For more completeness, insert a noun between the *is* and the *w* adverb: "the time" or "the place." General dictionaries favor noun phrases, without *when* or *where,* such as "the start of darkness in the evening" and "a large, open area suitable for animals to wander and graze."

An author tells of lessons in flying a small airplane. "The only thing" that fazed her "was when David [the instructor] demonstrated" a certain maneuver. A clause beginning with the adverb *when* is not a thing, a noun. Better: "was David's demonstration of. . . . "

WHEREAS. *See* **Sentence fragment,** *1.*

WHERE EVER and WHEREVER. *See* (-)EVER.

WHEREFORE and WHEREOF. A radio host recommended a far-off restaurant. Having been there, "I know wherefore I speak," he said. If he meant "I know what I'm talking about" and was intent on making his point through archaic language, the word to use was *whereof* (adverb). It can mean of which, of whom, or whence. What he said in effect was "I know why I'm talking."

Wherefore (adverb) means for what, for which, or why. Shakespeare's Juliet asks, "O Romeo, Romeo! wherefore art thou Romeo?" *Wherefore* is not just an elegant synonym for "where," contrary to the belief of some. The moderator of a television forum titled a sequence, about shortcomings in the economy, "Wherefore Art Thou, Rosy Scenario?"

Wherefore can also be a noun meaning cause or reason, as in "Never Mind the Why and Wherefore" (from Gilbert and Sullivan's *H.M.S. Pinafore*). Both *whereof* and *wherefore* have been used as conjunctions too.

WHERE in definitions. *See* **WHEN, WHERE in definitions.**

WHETHER. Something is missing from a sentence in an article for consumers:

New York's new law . . . also requires that every automobile-insurance policy . . . provide consumers with collision coverage for cars they rent—whether they buy collision coverage for their own cars and whether they rent more expensive cars than they own.

Each *whether* demands *or not,* either immediately ("... whether *or not* ... and whether *or not* ...") or later ("... whether they buy collision coverage for their own cars *or not* and whether they rent more expensive cars than they own *or not*").

Most of us probably would stick in the *or not* automatically, whether or not English grammar figured in our occupations. Perhaps the writer of the quoted sentence gave a vague thought to the matter: Somewhere in his past, some editor had instructed him that "whether" alone was enough, that "or not" was superfluous.

At times, it is true, *whether* alone is enough. That is so when *whether,* introducing an indirect question, can be replaced by *if.* For example: "I asked whether [or *if*] he had bought collision coverage for his car." In such a sentence, *or not* is unessential, though it cannot hurt.

Otherwise, *whether* introduces a set of possibilities or alternatives, connected by *or.* The gist is often that something takes place or exists regardless of other events or conditions. "We will meet whether it rains or not." / "We will meet whether it rains or shines." / "I'll quit after this hand, whether I win or lose." / "The problem will persist whether one candidate or the other is elected." In such sentences *whether* (conjunction) means essentially *in either event.* It can mean just *either:* "He intends to get what he wants, whether honestly or otherwise." / "The cabinet was considering whether to enter the war or to remain neutral."

Or may be followed by another *whether:* "Whether we win or whether we lose, we've put up a good fight." The extra "whether we" is unnecessary but acceptable. There may be more than two possibilities: "Whether we win, lose, or draw...."

Each example below (from a syndicated advice column and an authoritative law book) contains a redundant pair of words and lacks two needed words.

DEAR DAD AND MOM: You are under no obligation to foot the bill for your daughter's wedding regardless of whether she and her fiancé lived together prior to their marriage.

Thus ... a novel completed in 1980 ... would enjoy Federal statutory protection at fixation in manuscript or other form, which protection would continue for the life of the author plus fifty years, regardless of whether published.

In each example, omit "regardless of" and insert *or not* after "whether" or after the final word of the sentence.

An occasional expression is *whether or no,* meaning *in any case.* "The delegation flies home tomorrow, whether or no."

WHICH. *1. Ambiguity. 2. Overuse. 3. Parallels; people; possessives.*

1. Ambiguity

Everything is clear here: "Come and see the show, which opened last week." *Which* (as a relative pronoun) represents the *show* (a noun) and introduces a clause giving further information about it.

Too often, *which* is meant to represent something other than the normal noun or noun phrase that a pronoun is supposed to represent (its *antecedent*). For instance: "My neighbors were celebrating boisterously, which kept me up till 2 a.m." The thing that "kept me up" may be inferred, but a sharper sentence would specify it. *Which* might be changed to *and the noise.*

Can *which* ever stand for the entire idea of a preceding statement? Maybe. It depends on one's tolerance for disorder and whether or not the material is ambiguous. "Which" has been applied to amorphous ideas so often that when a noun does precede it, it may not be clear what "which" is meant to stand for. "The job requires her to walk dogs, which she dislikes." Does she dislike the task or dogs? Changing "which" to either *a task* or *animals* would answer the question.

Carelessness about antecedents sometimes results in sentences that say the opposite of what the writers intended. A sentence in an autobiography refers to a general:

Norm Schwarzkopf did not suffer fools gladly, which you can get away with in the absolute command environment of the battlefield.

"Which" has no literal antecedent. To "suffer fools gladly" seems to be it, and the "which" clause seems to say that you can do so in the environment of the battlefield. The context suggests the reverse meaning: You can refuse to do so in the environment of the battlefield.

This sentence from an article (in a weekly paper) deals with a presidential election campaign:

Nor does he [Jerry Brown] have the money to buy TV time, which is the kiss of death in a state like Texas, with its 23 media markets.

It says that "TV time . . . is the kiss of death in . . . Texas." From the context, it appears that the writer meant roughly the opposite: The lack of television exposure is ruinous in Texas. ("Kiss of death" describes something that is supposedly

helpful though actually harmful. In the quotation, the expression is misleading. Where is the "kiss"?)

Which is more liable to cling to the closest preceding noun or noun phrase than to some vague idea in a writer's mind.

See **THAT and WHICH** for a discussion of restrictive and nonrestrictive clauses and how a failure to discriminate between them can cause confusion.

2. Overuse

Journalists, with their aversion to repetition, are fond of the pronoun *which.* It permits a writer to avoid repeating a noun after the first mention. The sample below (from a picture caption) illustrates overdependence on the word.

There were no injuries in the blaze, which ruined the third floor of the building, which was being remodeled.

Presumably the two *whiches* were invoked to prevent repetition of "blaze" and "building," although the writer did not seem to mind the repetition of *which.* But it was not necessary to repeat both nouns when a personal pronoun could replace one of them. Nor did everything need to be stowed into one, graceless sentence. This is a possible rephrasing: "There were no injuries in the blaze. It ruined the third floor of the building, which was being remodeled."

3. Parallels; people; possessives

A clause starting with *and which* normally needs to follow a parallel *which* clause. The same principle applies to *but which. See also* **THAT,** *3;* **WHO,** *2.*

"And" serves no purpose here; either replace it with a comma or insert *which is* after the first comma: "Acme Corp., the city's largest employer and which recently announced an expansion, has been bought by a Japanese company." If *which is* is inserted, the second *which* becomes optional: "Acme Corp., which is the city's largest employer and [which] recently announced" etc.

The clauses usually need to be truly parallel, if "and" is to make sense. This example mixes a *that* (restrictive) clause and a *which* (nonrestrictive) clause: "Buses that run during rush hours and which most passengers take will soon cost more to ride." Delete "and" and enclose "which most passengers take" in commas. *See* **THAT and WHICH,** *1*.

Which refers to things, not to people. Two relative pronouns refer to people: *who* and *that*. *See* **WHO, THAT, and WHICH.**

Which has two possessive forms: *of which* and *whose*. *Whose* applies both to people and to things. *See* **WHOSE,** *1*.

WHICH and THAT. *See* THAT and WHICH.

WHICH and WHO. *See* WHO, THAT, and WHICH.

WHO. *1. Ambiguity. 2. Journalistic stand-by. 3. Verb: person, number.*

1. Ambiguity

Which name does the "who" represent in this item by a news agency?

> Bobbie Arnstein, executive secretary of Playboy magazine magnate Hugh Hefner, who was appealing a 15-year drug sentence, was found dead today in a hotel room, an apparent suicide victim.

The relative pronoun *who* tends to affix itself to the nearest preceding name or designation. In this instance it is "Hefner." Three paragraphs later, the story makes it clear that Miss Arnstein, not Mr. Hefner, had been the convict. The clause "who was appealing a 15-year drug sentence" should have been re-moved and turned into a separate sentence, with *She* in place of "who."

2. Journalistic stand-by

This deals mainly with the overuse of *who* clauses. (*See also* **WHO and WHOM; WHO, THAT, and WHICH.**)

When a journalistic writer wants to present a fact about a person but cannot think of any logical place for it, he is liable to put it in a clause beginning with *who* that he stuffs into some sentence, whether relevant or irrelevant. (*See* **Modifiers,** *2*, for other tricks.)

These two sentences lead off two consecutive paragraphs in a news story about a criminal trial:

> The attacker, who became known as "the South Shore rapist," was said to have stalked his victims for days, confronted them in their bedrooms as they slept and put a screwdriver to their throats. . . .
> The defendant, who was ashen faced and expressionless during the announcement of the verdict, faces a maximum of life in prison.

A case could be made for the *who* clause the first time. In the second sentence, it is irrelevant. The defendant's facial appearance has nothing to do with the penalty. Later in the same story, we find these three sentences, two of them consecutive:

> Mr. C———, who spent most of his time in court taking notes, did not take the stand in his own defense. . . .
> Mr. C———, who was a suspect in a string of similar crimes in Florida, fell under suspicion in the Long Island attacks in November 1986 and was placed under surveillance.
> Mr. C———, who had served time in jail for stealing a car, was surreptitiously taped talking with his parole officer about his broken foot, an Alco-

holics Anonymous meeting and other subjects.

Individually the three sentences are passable. Each *who* clause pertains to the rest of the sentence. But the sum of those "Mr. C———, who" sentences does not amount to admirable style. In the last one, it seems plain that the writer repeated the name just to follow it with "who had served" etc. The normal means of referring to the subject would be the pronoun *he*. "He had served time ... and was ..." or "Having served time ..., he was. ... "

In THAT, *3*, and WHICH, *3*, the point is made that a clause starting with *and that* or *and which* normally follows a comparable *that* or *which* clause. The principle holds for *and who* (and *but who*): In "Adams, a candidate for mayor and who has served on the City Council for four years, said ... ," the "and" serves no function and ought to be deleted. It can stand if "who is" is inserted after the first comma; if it is, the second *who* becomes optional: "Adams, *who is* a candidate for mayor and [who] has served" etc.

3. Verb: person, number

In the sentence "He who hesitates is lost," obviously *who* represents *he* (that is, *he* is the antecedent of *who*). Therefore, the verb *hesitates* is right, agreeing with the subject, the pronoun *he*. Both words are in the third person, singular.

Confusion can enter in the first or second person, singular. In an English translation of a German comic opera, a man says, "It is I who are honored." Correction: "It is I who *am* honored." *Who* does not change normal conjugations. The verb agrees with what *who* represents; above, it represents *I*, which does not go with "are" or "is." Similarly, "Is it you who *have* [not "has"] made the decision?"

In the sentence "It is people like her

who restore my faith in humanity," *restore* is the right form of the verb. The question to be asked is what *who* represents. Here it represents certain *people*. It is the same when *that* substitutes for *who*.

See also ONE OF, *3*.

WHO and THAT, WHO and WHICH. *See* WHO, THAT, and WHICH.

WHO and WHOM. *1. The basics. 2. The critics. 3. WHOEVER and WHOMEVER.*

1. The basics

All speakers of the English language know the meaning of *who* or *whom*: what person(s) or which person(s). What many of us do not know is when to use each. It could be the foremost grammatical puzzle we face. So difficult can it be, it is no wonder that professional writers, editors, and public speakers mix up the two pronouns perpetually.

In brief, *who* is in the subjective (or nominative) case; *whom* is in the objective (or accusative) case. Thus the sentences "*Who* stole my heart away?" and "I saw *who* slew the dragon" are correct. *Who* is the subject of the former sentence; in the latter sentence, it is the subject of the clause "who slew the dragon." And the sentences "I know *whom* she kissed" and "Never send to know for *whom* the bell tolls" are also correct. In the former sentence, *whom* is the object of the verb *kissed;* in the latter sentence, *whom* is the object of the preposition *for.*

Often the puzzle gets more complicated: "The jurors disagreed on *who* [or *whom?*] they felt had the stronger case." *Who* is right; it is the subject of the clause "who ... had the stronger case"; and the whole clause is the object of the preposition *on.*

A four-column headline in a leading

newspaper said: "Who Do They Thank When the Staff Get a Raise?" Probably it did not look bad to most readers, although technically the first word should have been *Whom,* the object of the verb *Thank.* (More likely, some noticed the British-style "Staff *Get*" instead of "Staff *Gets.*" *See* **STAFF.**)

An advertiser in the personal ads was

ABANDONED

By her boyfriend whom has found other interests of which she is not one of anymore.

"Whom" should have been *who,* the subject of the verb *has found,* and preceded by a comma. (Among the ad's faults, "of . . . of" is redundant and "anymore" is not pertinent. Could it be that he scorned her English?)

A network anchor man made a similar mistake in the choice between *who* and *whom:*

You'll meet the man whom, some say, bears at least some of the blame.

". . . The man who. . . . " *Who* is the subject of the verb *bears;* the phrase "some say" amounts to only a parenthetical explanation. (Whether the copy that was read really had commas or not is not known, but it does not matter.)

Often you can test the choice by reducing the sentence or clause to its bare bones and changing the *w*-pronoun (relative pronoun) into an *h*-pronoun (personal pronoun). The newspaper sample becomes "They thank *him.*" *Him* is objective; therefore use *whom,* also objective. The television sample becomes "*He* bears blame." *He* is subjective; therefore use *who,* also subjective.

Some may be asking, Must we solve a puzzle every time we intend to open our mouths or put pen to paper? *Whom* appears headed the way of *shall,* to be reserved for special occasions but no longer of regular utility. Meanwhile, as a rule of thumb, use *whom* only when you are confident that it is right. When in doubt, use *who.*

2. *The critics*

The use of "who" in place of a proper *whom,* at least in popular speech, is met with tolerance by many language authorities. They are less tolerant of the use of "whom" in place of a proper *who.* Writers and speakers so use "whom" not infrequently in the belief that it is the object of the following verb, the grammarian George O. Curme wrote (in the thirties).

This incorrect usage was very common in Shakespeare's time: "Arthur, *whom* they say is kill'd tonight On your suggestion" (*King John, I, ii, 165*).

Curme could understand the popularity of *who,* especially at the beginning of sentences: "*Who* did they meet?" is not unnatural.

A contemporary of his, H. L. Mencken, wrote:

The schoolmarm . . . continues the heroic task of trying to make her young charges grasp the difference. . . . Here, alas, the speechways of the American people seem to be . . . against her. The two forms of the pronouns are confused magnificently in the debates in Congress, and in most newspaper writing, and in ordinary discourse the great majority of Americans avoid *whom* diligently, as a word full of snares. When they employ it, it is often incorrectly, as in "*Whom* is your father?" and "*Whom* spoke to me?"

In 1783, Mencken noted, Noah Webster denounced *whom* as usually useless and argued that common sense sided with "*Who* did he marry?"

Theodore M. Bernstein found it understandable that spontaneous speakers, lacking time for the grammatical analysis required, would occasionally err. However, he wrote (1965), "The transgressions of the writer, however, are not so easily overlooked." Within ten years, though, Bernstein was advocating the doom of *whom*, its banishment from the English language, except in one context. His sole exception was "when it follows immediately after a preposition and 'sounds natural' even to the masses." Examples: "To *whom* it may concern" / "He married the girl for *whom* he had risked his life." He called *whom* "useless and senseless . . . a complicated nuisance." Of twenty-five "experts in English," fifteen agreed with him; six disagreed; four were in between.

On the conservative side, Wilson Follett mocked "some liberal grammarians" who opposed *whom* in its orthodox uses but who condoned its misuse in such sentences as these:

"I know perfectly well whom you are." [The misuser thinks "whom" is the object of *know*. The correct pronoun is *who*, the subject of *are*.]

"He resists a reconciliation with his sweet wife, whom he insists is a social butterfly." [*Who* is right; "he insists" is parenthetical, as though within commas.]

He suggested that the writers used "whom" wrongly for fear of sounding ignorant and that, in contrast, a historian wrongly used "who" for fear of sounding superior:

"M. departed eight days later in humiliation as the man who, more than anyone else, the President had repudiated."

The "radical grammarian" approves, Follett said, even though

who makes you anticipate a clause of which it is the subject and leaves you jolted when you find that this clause is never coming.

On the liberal side, Roy H. Copperud found "*Who* are you going with?" and "*Who* did you invite?" not only correct but preferable to *whom*. As for the use of "whom" instead of *who*, he accompanied the Shakespearean quotation of Curme's and other classic lines with this comment:

. . . When the critics of such errors must indict the translators of the Bible, together with Keats and Shakespeare, as having known no better, their preachments take on a hollow ring. . . .

A century earlier, the grammar in two Biblical passages, *Matthew 16:15* and *Luke 9:18,* had been found wanting. In the King James Version (1611) they said, respectively:

He saith unto them, But whom say ye that I am?

[H]e asked them, saying, Whom say the people that I am?

The English Revised Version (1881) changed each "whom" to *who;* and *who* remained in the Revised Standard Version (1946), amid modernized syntax ("who do you say . . ." / "Who do the people say . . .").

The Oxford English Dictionary finds *whom* "used ungrammatically for the nominative WHO" by such writers as Shakespeare and Dickens:

Tel me in sadnes whome she is you loue. [*Romeo and Juliet,* I, i, 205. The *Oxford* prefers original spellings.]

A strange unearthly figure, whom Gabriel felt at once, was no being of this world. [*The Pickwick Papers*.]

The *Oxford* says *whom* is "no longer current in natural colloquial speech."

3. WHOEVER and WHOMEVER

The principles that apply to *who* and *whom* apply to *whoever* and *whomever,* which mean anyone that or no matter who. A network anchor man said:

Whomever does buy the yacht will not be allowed to sail her.

Whoever is the subject. A person normally would say, "I wonder *who* will buy the yacht," not "whom."

On a television forum, a journalist said (about a political caucus in Iowa):

There are going to be stories about it, depending on whomever wins.

Change "whomever" to *whoever;* it is the subject of the verb *wins.* Omit "depending on," which is superfluous.

WHODUNIT.   *See* DO, DID, DONE.

WHO EVER and WHOEVER.
See (-)EVER.

WHOEVER and WHOMEVER.
See WHO and WHOM, 3.

WHOM.   *See* WHO and WHOM.

WHOSE.   1. *For people and things.* 2. *WHOSE and WHO'S.*

1. For people and things

Whose is the possessive form of both *who* and *which.* Thus *whose,* unlike *who,* applies not only to people but also to things. An alternative possessive form of *which* is *of which,* though applying this phrase sometimes yields an awkward product. *Whose* is proper here:

To the last fibre of the loftiest tree
Whose thin leaves trembled in the
    frozen air. . . .

The poet (Shelley) could have written ". . . the loftiest tree / The thin leaves of which trembled. . . ." Fortunately he did not.

2. WHOSE and WHO'S

Whose, the possessive pronoun, as in "Whose broad stripes and bright stars," should not be confused with *who's,* the contraction of *who is,* as in "Who's afraid of the big, bad wolf?"

A newspaper's main story dealt with the closing of a thoroughfare (called the Great Highway) because of sand blown onto it. The headline, nearly across the front page, read: "Great Sandway - who's fault?" The editor had erroneously written "who's" instead of *whose.* (He had also used a hyphen instead of a dash. *See* **Punctuation,** 4.) Later, two magazines similarly confused those words, which are both pronounced HOOZ:

He's an astronaut and an older American who's sixth sense a few years back, led him to search for the places NASA's work might overlap. . . . [The comma is not needed. *See* **Punctuation,** 3*D*.]

The security deposit may not be used for . . . repairing defects that existed prior to occupancy by the tenant who's deposit is in question. . . .

The opposite mistake was made by a candidate for a metropolitan school board in a statement sent to voters, opposing a proposed new election system:

They've tried this in Cambridge, Massachusetts and they're still trying to figure out whose their mayor.

Who is or *who's*, not "whose," would have been right. (A comma is needed after "Massachusetts." *See* **Punctuation, *3A*.**)

See also **Punctuation, *1B*.**

WHO, THAT, and WHICH. *1. Animals and things. 2. Choice in referring to people.*

1. Animals and things

Animals (excluding humans) and inanimate objects are not entitled to the relative pronoun "who." Use *that* or *which* for them. When to use each is discussed in **THAT and WHICH.**

Who suits only people. *That* also is acceptable for people. **See 2.**

"Who" does not belong in any of the following six excerpts. *That* should replace it in the first three examples, *which* in the next three. (In the former group, each has a restrictive or defining clause; in the latter, a nonrestrictive or nondefining clause.)

The first example is a headline in a supermarket tabloid: "Goat who ate dynamite is walking bomb." A goat gets *that,* not "who." (Another, typical headline in that issue: "DOG DRIVES TO HOSPITAL AFTER OWNER HAS HEART ATTACK IN CAR." Would that word usage were the only problem.)

Although organized entities, such as companies, unions, associations, and institutions, are made up of people, they are not people. Change each "who" to *that* in the pair below, from a book and a newspaper.

> AT&T, a communications giant who never knew true competition until deregulation, now embraces the customer loyalty program concept.

> Unions who represent civil service employees argue that . . . the basic work skills needed are essentially the same. . . .

A literal fish story, from a magazine, is quoted next. Sea creatures and birds, like beasts, have no claim to "who."

> Unlike birds (and some solitary or pair-forming fish species), who feed or shelter their young, and mammals, who suckle them, schooling fishes abandon eggs and larvae to float away on the currents.

"Unlike birds . . . , *which* feed or shelter their young, and mammals, *which* suckle them. . . ."

Likewise, each "who" should be *which* in the pair of press sentences below. Countries, governmental bodies, and other geographical and political entities are not people, although people belong to them.

> It was unclear whether Angola and Cuba, who are eager to sign the protocol, would adapt so readily to South Africa's schedule.

> His veto forces a showdown with the 18-member County Legislature, who will vote on Tuesday on whether to override it and enact the bill.

See also **WHOSE, *1*.**

2. Choice in referring to people

Just as *who* should not represent lower creatures and things, *which* should not represent people. A network anchor man was out of line in telling of "an American couple which went to London" to look for a nanny. Either *who* or *that* would have been suitable in place of "which."

Both *who* and *that* are used as relative pronouns to refer to people. It is a matter of personal preference.

That, if chosen, should introduce only a restrictive (essential or defining) clause. "He was the best pitcher *that* ever joined our team." / "The architects *that* designed those structures display great imagination." *Who* may be substituted in each instance. Further examples of the restrictive use of *who* have traditionally come up at political party conventions: ". . . a man who achieved . . ." / ". . . a man who represents . . ." and so on.

Who (sometimes *whom*)—never "that" or "which"—begins a nonrestrictive (unessential or nondefining) clause referring to a person or persons. "Do you know Helen Johnson, *who* used to work here?" / "The Millers, *who* live next door to us, came to the office today." Notice that a comma precedes *who* in a nonrestrictive clause. A pair of commas is needed when the nonrestrictive clause does not end the sentence.

H. W. Fowler, the grammarian, not only condoned the application of *that* to people: he proposed "the establishment of *that* as the universal defining relative, with *which* & *who(m)* as the nondefining for things & persons respectively." If politeness stood in the way, Fowler had a subtle compromise: At least save *who* for particular persons ("You who are a walking dictionary") and *that* for generic persons ("He is a man that is never at a loss").

There has been little movement toward applying *that* to people. Fowler was more successful in getting *that* accepted as a restrictive (defining) relative pronoun for nonhuman subjects. Conceding that his proposal might not win out, he added a caveat that remains important:

> Failing the use of *that* as the only defining relative, it is particularly important to see that *who* defining [restrictive] shall not, & *who* nondefining [nonrestrictive] shall, have a comma before it.

See also **THAT and WHICH; WHO; WHO and WHOM.**

WHY. *See* (-)EVER; REASON, 2.

WILL and WOULD. *See* **Double negative,** *1;* **Subjunctive,** 2, 3; **Tense,** 4.

Will (legal). *See* **TESTAMENT and TESTIMONY.**

WILLY-NILLY. *Willy-nilly* (adverb) essentially means without choice, under compulsion. "The soldiers were sent willy-nilly into a perilous land."

It is the remnant of an aged expression: *will he, nill he,* meaning whether he will it or not will it; that is, whether he is willing or unwilling. Any other personal pronoun could be substituted. Shakespeare used the expression in *The Taming of the Shrew:* ". . . Your father hath consented / That you shall be my wife; your dowry 'greed on; / And, will you, nill you, I will marry you." To *will,* or to desire, is still used. To *nill* (descended from the Old English *nyllan*) is an obsolete verb, meaning not to will, not to desire. Do not confuse *nill* with the noun *nil,* nothing (from the Latin *nihil*).

Willy-nilly (adjective) means being or occurring whether one wishes it or not: "a willy-nilly experience." Sometimes the word is used loosely as a synonym for *indecisive* (adjective), (possibly under the influence of *shilly-shallying*). Some users wholly misunderstand *willy-nilly,* projecting sundry meanings into it.

The host of a radio talk show said financial considerations had to moderate expenditures for highway safety: "We can't just go out and willy-nilly do whatever we think is going to be helpful." Any of a number of adverbs would have fit better: *at will, exorbitantly, extravagantly, freely, limitlessly, unlimitedly, unrestrainedly.* Each suggests that the action would be performed willingly. The speaker chose a word with the opposite sense.

The chairman of a Senate committee that was conducting an investigation said, when asked if the president would be subpoenaed, "You don't send off subpoenas willy-nilly." Certainly you don't send off subpoenas unwillingly; the recipient is the one who must act *willy-nilly*. The senator may have meant *carelessly, hastily, thoughtlessly,* or one of the previously mentioned adverbs.

WINCH. *See* **WENCH and WINCH.**

WIND SHEAR. *See* **SHEAR,** 2.

-WISE ending. They must think that adding a *-wise* to the word is efficient:

- A radio reporter asked a heart-attack specialist, "Where does the future lie technology-wise?" The reporter probably believed she was using language sharply and economically by tacking "-wise" onto the noun instead of having to say "as far as technology is concerned." But a crisper question would be, "What technology lies ahead?" or "What inventions are needed?"
- A lawyer used similarly roundabout language in commenting on a defendant's performance in court: "Demeanor-wise he's coming off fine. Testimony-wise he couldn't be worse." The lawyer could have said, in a more straightforward way, "His demeanor is fine. His testimony couldn't be worse."

Although *-wise* has long been scorned as a suffix taking the place of *concerning, with reference to,* or *with respect to,* it does have legitimate functions in two other senses. It signifies (1) direction or manner, as in *clockwise* and *otherwise,* and (2) knowledge or wisdom, as in *penny-wise* and *worldly-wise.*

In those two functions it roughly parallels the word *wise,* meaning (noun) manner, method, or way and (adjective)

possessing wisdom, shrewdness, prudence, or erudition. The noun is used mainly in the phrases *in any wise, in no wise,* and *in this wise.*

WISH. A supermarket posted a sign saying, "If you wish for canned SALMON please ask checker at checkstand for it." To *wish for* something is to possess or express a longing or deep, heartfelt desire for it. The phrase can additionally mean to seek to acquire or achieve the thing by supernatural means, through the medium of a genie, fairy, shooting star, wishing well, birthday cake, or chicken bone.

"If you wish canned salmon," omitting the "for," would have been an improvement, although a number of critics consider the verb *wish* followed by a simple object to be a genteelism, an excessive refinement. *Want* is the verb to use in that grammatical context, particularly when the desire is so prosaic or transitory.

To *wish* blends well with an indirect object ("I wish you luck"), a clause ("I wish I had a nickel"), or an infinitive ("Do you wish to file a complaint?"). With an infinitive, *want* works as well or better.

Wit. *See* **QUIP, QUIPPED.**

WITH. *1. Common misuse. 2. Function; meanings; number.*

1. Common misuse

It is an amateurish practice to fasten an extra thought to a sentence by the use of a nearly meaningless "with." Yet the practice is habitual in the popular press, even among the best newspapers. A front-page story in a leading daily provides three illustrations. (Emphasis is added.)

Complexity has become a significant bottleneck in computing, *with* designers finding that their machines are encrusted with powerful computational routines that are rarely used. . . .

The competitive pressures have led to a "benchmark war" between makers of different microprocessors *with* each manufacturer issuing impressive reports on performance. . . .

The competition to gain "design wins," the semiconductor industry's phrase for having their product accepted by computer makers, has created some bitter feelings, *with* companies rancorously challenging the performance claims made by others.

Each paragraph could easily be made simpler and clearer by separating the thoughts. Omit "with" and start a new sentence, putting the verb in the present tense.

Complexity has become a significant bottleneck in computing. Designers *find* that. . . .

The competitive pressures have led to a "benchmark war" between makers of different microprocessors. Each manufacturer *issues* impressive reports. . . .

The competition to gain "design wins" . . . has created some bitter feelings. Companies rancorously *challenge* the performance claims. . . .

An alternative to two separate sentences is two independent clauses, separated by a semicolon:

Complexity has become a significant bottleneck in computing; designers find that. . . .

(In the third paragraph of the excerpt, "having their product" is questionable. Better: "having *its* product" or "having *products*.")

Another typical example, from the front page of a mainly financial newspaper, concerns a South African election:

But the trend was unmistakable, with the ANC capturing more than 60% of the vote.

The sentence is shorter and plainer than the previous samples, but "with" is just as inane. Take it out and see if the sentence needs it. Or follow "unmistakable" with a colon, semicolon, or dash and "the ANC *captured* more than 60% of the vote." Or follow the comma with "*and* the ANC *captured*" etc.

In the following sentence, "with" is not just wishy-washy; it can send readers down the wrong track.

Luaus are still popular on Oahu with everyone eventually succumbing to their lure.

"Luaus are still popular on Oahu with everyone" forms a complete thought, but not the writer's thought. Any of these could replace "with": a comma; a semicolon and the clause "everyone eventually *succumbs* to their lure"; a comma and *where* or *and* followed by that clause; a period and a new sentence worded like that clause.

Journalists often treat repetition like the plague, but the writer of the following sentence did not seem to mind the "with . . . with."

At the same time, Syria rejected the P.L.O.'s discussion with the United States, with official newspapers declaring that peace in the Middle East "should be taken by force."

When repeating a word helps to make a sentence clear, one need not shun repetition, particularly when the meaning of the word is the same. In the excerpt, however, the first *with* indicates interaction; the second has negligible meaning and can mislead readers. After "United States," a new sentence is desirable: "Official newspapers declare that. . . . " (The double "with" in the opening example is less conspicuous.)

The "with" form is not restricted to newspapers. A scholarly book uses it six times; for example:

And *Griswold v. Connecticut* (1965) created a new constitutional right to privacy, with the opinions in the case basing this right on several provisions of the Constitution.

Omitting "with the opinions in the case" would sharpen the sentence.

Before attaching an extra thought to a sentence, a writer needs to consider how the extra thought relates to the first thought; and whether or not it must be attached; and, if it must, whether or not the connecting word, phrase, or punctuation shows the relation.

2. *Function; meanings; number*

Unlike *and, with* is not a connecting word, or conjunction, the way it is most often misused. It is a preposition, like *of, by,* and *for.* (*See* **Prepositions,** *1.*)

Its dozens of senses include the following: accompanying ("The Smiths are with their children"), agency ("Clean it with soap and water"), association ("Dessert comes with the dinner"), causation ("They wept with joy"), closeness ("She's sitting with that soldier"), contrast ("The Earth is tiny compared with Jupiter"), entrusting ("Leave it with the receptionist"), manner ("She sang with feeling"), membership ("Are you with us?"), opinion ("It's all right with me"), opposition ("He argued with the umpire"), possession ("Who is the boy with the drum?"), presence ("It's filled with helium"), and relationship ("He's friendly with people").

When *with* has the sense of accompa-

nying, does a singular verb remain singular? "The computer with the printer costs [or "cost"?] $1,900." What of *along with* or *together with*? "Mr. Farrell, *along with* his son, is [or "are"?] arriving this evening."

The established view is that the verbs remain singular: *costs, is,* etc., inasmuch as *with* is a preposition and not a conjunction. But some grammarians allow a plural verb if the items or individuals get equal emphasis.

Despite the many meanings of *with*, it is sometimes chosen over more appropriate prepositions. An ad announced a lecture entitled "The Rules" by two authors (of a book by that name): "Proven Secrets for dating and marrying Mr. Right with ELLEN FEIN and SHERRIE SCHNEIDER. . . . " Would that make him a bigamist? Maybe no one really thought so, but *by* would have been better than "with."

WITHER and WRITHE. "That person you can see withering in pain . . ."—it should be *writhing* in pain. An anchor man made the mistake on a national telecast. He confused two verbs (intransitive) that look somewhat similar but have different meanings, pronunciations, and Old English origins.

To *wither* is to dry up, lose freshness, or shrivel. To *writhe* is to squirm, twist, or contort the body. Each verb has a transitive sense, meaning to cause (something or someone) to have the particular effect. The first word is pronounced WITH-er, the second RYTH (each *th* voiced as in THE).

WITH PREJUDICE and WITHOUT PREJUDICE. The defense in the O. J. Simpson murder trial made a motion. A radio newscaster said the motion was "that charges against Simpson be dismissed without prejudice, meaning he could not be tried again." She got it backward.

When a legal action is dismissed *without prejudice,* it is as though the case were never brought to court. It means (in a criminal case) that the prosecuting side may try the defendant again on the same charges, or (in a civil case) that the plaintiff may bring a new suit on the same claim.

Conversely, the dismissal of a legal action *with prejudice* amounts to a final judgment on the merits of the case. It bars any new prosecution on the same charge or any new suit on the same claim. A defense attorney in any legal case wants the court to dismiss the case *with prejudice,* for then the defense has won. That was the motion of the Simpson defense.

Those legal uses of *prejudice* (noun) have little to do with its common use to signify bias. However, witnesses and occasionally jurors or judges may be said to harbor common *prejudice,* either antagonism or favoritism.

Prejudicial (adjective) is often used in legal contexts to mean harmful to the rights of a party, whether because of bias, emotion, or error.

Literally *prejudice* means prejudgment. It originates in the Latin *praejudicium,* same meaning, from *prae,* before, and *judicium,* judgment.

WOMAN. *See* -MAN-, MAN.

WOOD and WOODEN. A fire was caused by children who put paper towels close to what a radio newscaster called "a wooden stove." He must have meant a *wood* stove or *wood-burning* stove. Obviously you could not have a stove made of wood.

Wood is a perfectly good adjective; it means containing, used on, or related to wood, or existing in a wood or forest. Moreover, *wood* is an alternative to *wooden,* meaning made of wood; for instance, both a *wooden* bowl and a *wood* bowl are right.

WORDINESS, WORDY. *See* Verbosity.

Words that sound alike. *See* Homophones.

"WORLD'S OLDEST PROFESSION." *See* "OLDEST PROFESSION."

WORSE and WORST. *See* BETTER and BEST, WORSE and WORST.

WOULD and WILL. *See* Double negative, *1;* Subjunctive, *2, 3;* Tense, *4.*

WOULD HAVE, WOULD'VE, and "WOULD OF." *See* HAVE, HAS, HAD, *2.*

WRACK. *See* RACK and WRACK.

WREAK and WRECK. A television reporter predicted that the traffic pattern on a main thoroughfare during a forthcoming municipal event would "wreck some havoc." Whether she mistook "wreck" for *wreak* or simply did not know that the latter should be pronounced REEK is not clear.

Hurricanes and tornadoes *wreak,* that is, inflict, havoc. It is not possible to "wreck" havoc, because to *wreck* is to destroy and *havoc* is destruction. As for the TV prediction, to *wreak havoc* would be an overstatement—the traffic pattern would more likely cause confusion or something of the sort—unless the reporter foresaw some destructive accidents.

See also RACK and WRACK.

WREST and WRESTLE. "... The guerrillas slowly wrestled victory from black Africa's biggest army," a front-page newspaper story said.

The right verb is not "wrestled" but *wrested.* When you *wrest* something from someone or something, you obtain it or usurp it by forceful pulling and twisting, persistent effort, violent action, or underhanded method. (It is a transitive verb.)

To *wrestle* (transitive or intransitive verb) is to grapple with someone, especially in a contest. Followed by *with* or *against,* it can mean to struggle.

For a passage about gorillas that really wrestle, see the next entry.

WRESTLE, WRESTLING and RASSLE, RASSLING. A sign at a zoo's gorilla enclosure said, in part: "Through games of chasing and rassling, the bonds of trust and friendship are formed."

The standard noun is *wrestling,* the standard verb *wrestle.* "Rassling" or "rassle" is dialectic or very informal, not on the same plane as a fancy phrase like "the bonds of trust and friendship."

Other deviant spellings are *rassel, rastle, wrassle,* and *wrastle.*

WRITE confused with RIGHT. *See* Homophones.

WRITHE. *See* WITHER and WRITHE.

X Y Z

XEROX. The only criticism to be leveled at an absorbing book about an incident of modern history is that it treats a proper noun as a common noun:

> . . . Bosbin had yet another set of conditions to impose: that the *Globe* promise to defy any court injunction and that it provide the services of its xerox machine. . . . The investigation had been aided by . . . the Los Angeles advertising woman who made a xerox machine available to Ellsberg. . . . The advertising woman who lent Ellsberg her xerox machine . . . testified again. . . .

Either use a capital *X,* if it is indeed the *Xerox* brand, or call the device a copier, copying machine, photocopier, or the like. *Xerox* is a trademark. Capitalize it, just as you would capitalize the name of any similar machine labeled Canon, Kodak, Konica, Minolta, Mita, Panasonic, Ricoh, Royal, Savin, Sharp, or Toshiba.

The dry photographic process that the various copiers use is *xerography,* from the Greek *xeros,* meaning dry, and *graphein,* to write.

To make a *photocopy* of a document is to *photocopy* it or, if the context makes it clear, simply to *copy* it. "Xerox" as a verb is questionable. The pronunciation is ZEER-ox.

-Y ending. *1. Conjugation. 2. Suffixes.*

1. Conjugation

A national advice columnist advised mothers of young children to quiz them on the details of any trips taken with family friends or relatives. The headline, in at least one newspaper, was "Be Happy She Prys."

"Prys" was a misspelling. *Pries* is right. She or he *pries.* I, we, you, or they *pry.* The past tense and past participle of *pry* is *pried,* for all persons.

The conjugation of a verb ending in *y* may depend on whether a consonant or a vowel precedes the *y.*

A. Preceded by a consonant. In the present tense, the *y* is replaced by *-ies* for the third person, singular (e.g., he or she). In the past and perfect tenses, the *y* is usually replaced by *-ied* for all persons. Otherwise the verb is not changed.

Thus he, she, or the baby *cries* (not "crys"). I, we, you, they, he, or she *cried,* had *cried,* and have *cried.* I, we, you, or they *cry.* Everyone is *crying,* will *cry,* and would *cry.*

The forms are similar for the other *-ry* verbs (*dry, fry, try*); the *-fy* verbs (*amplify, beautify, clarify, classify, defy, electrify, qualify,* and so on); the *-ply* verbs (*apply, comply, imply, multiply, ply, reply, supply,* etc.); and miscellaneous other *y-ending* verbs (*ally, deny, prophesy, spy*).

Fly has its own irregularity in the past tense: You, I, he, or any other person *flew*. (He *flied* is right only in baseball.) It is like the other *-ry* verbs in the present tense: I *fly*, he *flies*, and so on.

B. Preceded by a vowel. Usually a verb in which the final *y* follows a vowel is conjugated normally. He or she *prays* or *employs*. I, we, you, and they *pray* or *employ*. All persons *prayed* or *employed*. And so on.

For some exceptions, *see* LAY and LIE; MAY and MIGHT; PAY; SLAY, SLAIN, SLEW.

2. Suffixes

There are general rules for adding a suffix to a basic word ending in *y*. They depend on whether a consonant or a vowel precedes the *y*. The rules have many exceptions.

A. Preceded by a consonant. If a consonant precedes the *y*, usually the *y* changes to *i*—unless the suffix begins with *i*.

Some examples are the change of *beauty* to *beautiful* and *beautify; happy* to *happily* and *happiness;* and *holy* to *holier* and *holiest*. While *cry* becomes *crier* and *defy* becomes *defiant*, both retain the *y* when *-ing* is added: *crying, defying*—the suffix begins with *i*.

Among exceptions are *dryness, babyhood,* and *ladylike*. The change of *accompany* to *accompanist* and the changes of *military* to *militarism* and *militarize* are exceptions to the *i*-suffix exception.

To make a common noun like *army, lady,* or *sky* plural, *-ies* is added: *armies, ladies, skies*. When a proper noun is made plural, the *y* remains: *Germanys, Marys*.

The *y* remains when a possessive *'s* is added: *anybody's, everybody's, Harry's, Mary's.*

B. Preceded by a vowel. If a vowel precedes the *y*, usually the *y* remains. Examples are *enjoyment, joyous, obeyer, payable,* and *playful.*

Among exceptions, *day* changes to *daily;* and *gluey* changes to *gluier* and *gluiest*. Adjectives that end in *-wy*, like *chewy, dewy, showy,* and *snowy*, change the *y* to *i: dewier, showiness,* etc.

To make a noun like *day, key,* or *toy* plural, add *s*. But the plural of *colloquy* is *colloquies.*

As suggested in **Spelling,** *3:* when in doubt, look it up.

"YES, VIRGINIA."

If Francis P. Church, the editor of *The Sun* in New York, had known what his poetic editorial was starting, he might have responded differently to the eight-year-old girl who wrote in 1897 to ask, "Is there a Santa Claus?" (Perhaps, "No. Sorry, Virginia, but that's the way it is.") Seven words—"Yes, Virginia, there is a Santa Claus"—have become hackneyed. Imitators, who may never have read the whole editorial, appropriate from two to five words for conversion to a variety of uses.

(An ad for a general store:) "Yes, Virginia, There is an After Christmas SALE." (A subtitle of a network TV forum:) "Yes, Virginia, there are four candidates [for governor of Virginia]." (A local TV newscast:) "Yes, Virginia, it can snow in San Francisco." (A column:) "Yes, Virginia, computers make mistakes." (An editorial:) "No, Virginia, there is no incumbent-protection plan." The writer of the last sentence did not even keep the "Yes." It is puzzling why he had to drag Virginia into it at all.

YET.

See BUT, *5;* TAUTOLOGY.

YIDDISH.

Two Jewish languages exist: *Hebrew,* an ancient Semitic tongue, akin to Arabic but with its own alphabet; and *Yiddish,* a medieval tongue based on High German, incorporating words from Hebrew and Slavic languages and written in most of the Hebrew characters. Millions of Jews speak neither; they speak the languages of the countries in which they live.

A general's autobiography tells of Jamaican family friends

> so close they were considered relatives. "Mammale and Pappale" we called them. Don't ask me why the Jewish diminutives.

The precise modifier would have been *Yiddish,* pertaining to the language. *Jewish* is not a language and not a synonym for *Yiddish,* although using it that way is a common mistake, rather than a blunder. That apparently occurred in Israel. Later in the same book we read:

> In Jerusalem my counterpart . . . , the Israeli chief of staff, threw a party for me, at which I surprised the guests with some Bronx-acquired Yiddish.

Did the general think that Yiddish was the official language of Israel? It is *Hebrew.*

See also **JEW, JEWISH.**

YOU and ONE in the same sentence. *See* **ONE as pronoun,** *1*.

YOUR and YOU'RE. *Your* and *you're,* pronounced alike, should not be confused in writing. *Your,* as in "To your health," is the possessive form of the pronoun *you. You're,* as in "You're next," is the contraction of *you are.*

A writer did confuse them when he quoted a sitcom character saying, "Who do you thank when you're whole body is feeling so good inside?" It should be "*your* whole body."

See also **Punctuation,** *1B;* **WHO and WHOM,** *1*.

YOURSELF, YOURSELVES. *See* **Pronouns,** *3, 4*.

YOU WHO. *See* **WHO,** *3*.

"YOU WON'T BELIEVE." A television play was promoted with the line "A true story with an ending you won't believe." I passed it by, thinking "If a play is not believable, why see it?"

"You won't believe" how overused that fad phrase is. Or maybe you will.

Z. The twenty-sixth and last letter of the English alphabet is pronounced in two ways. The American way is ZEE. The British way is ZED.

The pronunciation of *z* comes up in a book by a scientist. A passage describes a modern theory in physics (unifying the electromagnetic force and the weak nuclear force):

> . . . In addition to the photon, there were three other spin-1 particles, known collectively as massive vector bosons, that carried the weak force. These were called W^+ (pronounced W plus), W^- (pronounced W minus), and Z° (pronounced Z naught). . . .

The author has told us how to pronounce the *o*—as *naught* (NAUT)—but not how to pronounce the Z. He is British. The theory was propounded by two academics, one in the United States and one in Britain. The book was published simultaneously in the United States and in Canada, where ZED is preferred.

See also **ZERO and O.**

ZERO and O. The figure *o* is a *zero* or *cipher* or *naught* (also spelled *nought*), the arithmetical symbol for nothing or the absence of any quantity. It is the zero mark on a thermometer and the point where the graduation of a scale begins. The word *zero,* like *cipher,* originates in the Arabic *sifr,* zero. The plural is *zeros* or *zeroes.*

An announcer has pronounced the

ZERO IN

numbers in the television series "Beverly Hills, 90210" as "nine oh two one oh." That is how the figure *o* (zero) is often pronounced in informal speech—like the letter O. But they are not the same and usually do not look the same when printed. In most common type styles, the figure is narrower; the letter is rounder.

See also **Z; ZERO IN.**

ZERO IN. The district attorney who was supervising the O. J. Simpson murder case had just been interviewed by Barbara Walters on the matter of domestic violence in general. He said, "I'm glad you zeroed in on not just talking about this one case." In using the phrase *zero in* to refer to the avoidance of something, he reversed its meaning.

In a general sense, to *zero in* is to move near, close in, converge. For example, "The police are zeroing in on the suspect." *Zeroed in* is the past tense and past participle, *zeroing in* the present participle.

In military terminology, to *zero* or *zero in* is to adjust the sights of a rifle so that the target aimed at is hit. To *zero in on* a target is to take precise aim at it.

See also **ZERO and O.**

REFERENCE WORKS

Many of the reference works consulted in the preparation of this book are listed below. They are arranged alphabetically by title, except for several authors mentioned in the text. Names of authors, editors, or directors are listed for most of the works.

Acronyms, Initialisms & Abbreviations Dictionary, Julie E. Towell and Helen E. Sheppard, Detroit: Gale Research Co., 1988.

The American Heritage Dictionary of the English Language, 1st ed., William Morris, Boston: Houghton Mifflin, 1970; 3rd ed., Anne H. Soukhanov, 1992.

The American Heritage Dictionary, 2nd college ed., Margery S. Berube, Boston: Houghton Mifflin, 1991.

American Rhetoric from Roosevelt to Reagan: A Collection of Speeches and Critical Essays, Halford Ross Ryan, Prospect Heights, Ill.: Waveland Press, 1987.

The Associated Press Stylebook and Libel Manual, Norm Goldstein, ed., Reading, Mass.: Addison-Wesley Publishing Co., 1996.

Ballentine's Law Dictionary, 3rd ed., James A. Ballentine (William S. Anderson, ed.), Rochester, N.Y.: The Lawyers Cooperative Publishing Co., 1969.

Bartlett's Familiar Quotations, 16th ed., Justin Kaplan, Boston: Little Brown, 1992.

Theodore M. Bernstein, *Watch Your Language: A Lively, Informal Guide to Better Writing, Emanating From the News Room of The New York Times,* Great Neck, N.Y.: Channel Press, 1958.

———, *The Careful Writer: A Modern Guide to English Usage,* New York: Atheneum, 1965.

———, *Miss Thistlebottom's Hobgoblins: The Careful Writer's Guide to the Taboos, Bugbears and Outmoded Rules of English Usage,* New York: Farrar, Straus and Giroux, 1971.

———, *Dos, Don'ts & Maybes of English Usage,* New York: Times Books, 1977.

Black's Law Dictionary, 6th ed., Henry Campbell Black, Joseph R. Nolan, and Jacqueline M. Nolan-Haley, St. Paul, Minn.: West Publishing Co., 1990.

Britannica Book of English Usage, Christine Timmons and Frank Gibney, Garden City, N.Y.: Doubleday and Britannica Books, 1980.

Byrne's Standard Book of Pool and Billiards, Robert Byrne, San Diego: Harcourt, Brace, Jovanovich, 1987.

The Cambridge Encyclopedia of Language, David Crystal, Cambridge, England: Cambridge University Press, 1987.

Cassell's Latin Dictionary, D. P. Simpson, New York: Macmillan Publishing Co., 1968.

The Chicago Manual of Style, Chicago: The University of Chicago Press, 1982.

The College Standard Dictionary of the

English Language, New York: Funk & Wagnalls, 1941.

The Collins-Robert French Dictionary, Glasgow: Collins Publishers, 1987.

The Columbia Guide to Standard American English, Kenneth G. Wilson, New York: Columbia University Press, 1993.

The Columbia-Viking Desk Encyclopedia, 2nd ed., William Bridgwater, New York: Viking Press, 1960.

Common Errors in English: And How to Avoid Them, Alexander M. Witherspoon, Philadelphia: Blakiston Co., 1943.

Commonsense Grammar and Style, Robert E. Morsberger, New York: Thomas Y. Crowell Co., 1972.

The Compact Edition of the Oxford English Dictionary, 2 vol., Oxford, England: Oxford University Press, 1971.

The Concise Oxford Dictionary of Current English, 6th ed., J. B. Sykes, Oxford, England: Clarendon Press, 1976.

Roy H. Copperud, *Webster's Dictionary of Usage and Style,* New York: Avenel Books, copyright 1964, 1982 ed.

———, *American Usage: The Consensus,* New York: Van Nostrand Reinhold, 1970.

———, *American Usage and Style: The Consensus,* idem, 1980.

Copyediting: A Practical Guide, 2nd ed., Karen Judd, Los Altos, Calif.: Crisp Publications, 1990.

Crown's Book of Political Quotations, Michael Jackman, New York: Crown Publishers, 1982.

George O. Curme, *A Grammar of the English Language,* 2 vol., Essex, Conn.: Verbatim, copyright 1931–1935 (1978 printing).

Dictionary of American Underworld Lingo, Hyman E. Goldin, New York: Twayne Publishers, 1950.

A Dictionary of Euphemisms & Other Doubletalk: Being a Compilation of Linguistic Fig Leaves and Verbal Flourishes for Artful Users of the English Language, Hugh Rawson, New York: Crown Publishers, 1981.

Dictionary of Military Abbreviations, Norman Polmar, Mark Warren, Eric Werthem, Annapolis, Md.: Naval Institute Press, 1994.

A Dictionary of Modern Legal Usage, Bryan A. Garner, New York, Oxford, England: Oxford University Press, 1987.

Dictionary of Quotations, Bergen Evans, New York: Delacorte Press, 1968.

The Elements of Grammar, Margaret Shertzer, New York: Macmillan, 1986.

The Elements of Style, 2nd ed., William Strunk, Jr., E. B. White, New York: Macmillan, 1972.

The Encyclopedia Americana, 29 vol., Lawrence T. Lorimer, Danbury, Conn.: Grolier Inc., 1995.

Encyclopedia of Banking & Finance, 10th ed., Charles J. Woelfel, Chicago: Probus Publishing Co., 1994.

The Encyclopedia of Mammals, David W. Macdonald, New York: Facts On File, 1984.

The Encyclopedia of Phobias, Fears, and Anxieties, Ronald M. Doctor and Ada P. Kahn, New York: Facts On File, 1989.

The Encyclopedia of Textiles, Judith Jerde, New York: Facts On File, 1992.

Facts About the Supreme Court of the United States, Lisa Paddock, New York: H. W. Wilson and New England Publishing Associates, 1996.

Family Legal Guide: A Complete Encyclopedia of Law for the Layman, Inge N. Dobelis, Pleasantville, N.Y.: Reader's Digest, 1981.

Wilson Follett (Jacques Barzun, ed.), *Modern American Usage: A Guide,* New York: Hill & Wang, 1966.

H. W. Fowler and F. G. Fowler, *The King's English,* Oxford, England: Oxford University Press, 1906; 3rd ed., 1931.

H. W. Fowler, *A Dictionary of Modern English Usage,* London: Oxford University Press, 1st ed., 1926 (1952 printing).

———— (Ernest Gowers, reviser), idem, 2nd ed., New York: Oxford University Press, 1965.

Funk & Wagnalls New College Standard Dictionary, New York: Funk & Wagnalls, 1947.

Funk & Wagnalls New "Standard" Dictionary of the English Language, Isaac K. Funk, New York: Funk & Wagnalls, 1949.

Karen Elizabeth Gordon, *The Transitive Vampire: A Handbook of Grammar for the Innocent, the Eager, and the Doomed,* New York: Times Books, 1984.

————, *The New Well-Tempered Sentence: A Punctuation Handbook for the Innocent, the Eager, and the Doomed,* New York: Ticknor & Fields, 1993.

Ernest Gowers, *Plain Words: A Guide to the Use of English,* London: His Majesty's Stationery Office, 1948.

Great Speeches of the 20th Century (audio-cassettes and booklet), Gordon Skene, Santa Monica, Calif.: Rhino Records, 1991.

The Guide to American Law: Everyone's Legal Encyclopedia, 12 vol., St. Paul, Minn.: West Publishing Co., 1984.

The Guinness Book of World Records, Stamford, Conn.: Guinness Publishing Ltd., 1997.

The Handbook of Good English, Edward D. Johnson, New York: Facts On File, 1991.

Harper Dictionary of Contemporary Usage, 1st ed., William and Mary Morris, New York: Harper & Row, 1975; 2nd ed., 1985.

Harrap's Standard French and English Dictionary, J. E. Mansion, London: Harrap, 1967.

The Home Book of American Quotations, Bruce Bohle, New York: Dodd, Mead, 1967.

The Home Book of Quotations, Burton Stevenson, New York: Dodd, Mead, 1967.

Information Please Almanac, Otto Johnson, Boston: Houghton Mifflin, 1997.

Kind Words: A Thesaurus of Euphemisms, Judith S. Neaman and Carole G. Silver, New York: Facts On File, 1990.

Lend Me Your Ears: Great Speeches in History, William Safire, New York: W. W. Norton, 1992.

The Macmillan Dictionary of Political Quotations, Lewis D. Eigen and Jonathan P. Siegel, New York: Macmillan, 1993.

Macmillan Dictionary of Psychology, Stuart Sutherland, London: Macmillan, 1989.

H. L. Mencken, *The American Language: An Inquiry Into the Development of English in the United States,* New York: Alfred A. Knopf, 4th ed., 1936; *Supplement I,* 1945.

The New American Roget's College Thesaurus in Dictionary Form, Albert H. Morehead, New York: World, 1962.

The New Century Dictionary of the English Language, 2 vol., H. G. Emery and K. G. Brewster, New York: Appleton-Century-Crofts, 1952.

The New Encyclopaedia Britannica, 15th ed., 32 vol., Chicago: Encyclopaedia Britannica, Inc., 1995.

The New Roget's Thesaurus of the English Language in Dictionary Form, Norman Lewis, New York: G. P. Putnam's Sons, 1964.

The New Shorter Oxford English Dictionary: On Historical Principles, 2 vol., Lesley Brown, Oxford, England: Clarendon Press, 1993.

The New York Public Library Writer's Guide to Style and Usage, Andrea J. Sutcliffe, New York: HarperCollins, 1994.

The New York Times Manual of Style and Usage: A Desk Book of Guidelines for Writers and Editors, Lewis Jordan, New York: Times Books, 1976.

Patricia T. O'Conner, *Woe Is I: The Grammarphobe's Guide to Better English in Plain English,* New York: G. P. Putnam's Sons, 1996.

The Oxford Dictionary of English Grammar, Sylvia Chalker and Edmund Weiner, Oxford, England: Clarendon Press, 1994.

The Oxford Dictionary of Modern Slang, John Ayto and John Simpson, Oxford and New York: Oxford University Press, 1992.

The Oxford Dictionary of Quotations, Angela Partington, Oxford, England: Oxford University Press, 1992.

The Oxford English Dictionary, 2nd ed., 20 vol., J. A. Simpson and E. S. C. Weiner, Oxford, England: Clarendon Press, 1989.

Eric Partridge, *A Dictionary of Slang and Unconventional English: Colloquialisms and Catch-phrases, Solecisms and Catachreses, Nicknames and Vulgarities,* 8th ed. (Paul Beale, ed.), New York: Macmillan, 1984.

———, *Usage and Abusage: A Guide to Good English,* New York: Harper & Brothers, 1942; 4th ed., London: Hamish Hamilton, 1948; American ed. (Janet Whitcut, ed.), New York: W. W. Norton & Co., 1995.

The Public Speaker's Treasure Chest: A Compendium of Source Material to Make Your Speech Sparkle, Herbert V. Prochnow and Herbert V. Prochnow, Jr., New York: Harper & Row, 1977.

Questions of English, Jeremy Marshall and Fred McDonald, Oxford, England: Oxford University Press, 1994.

The Random House Dictionary of the English Language, 1st ed., Jess Stein, New York: Random House, 1979; 2nd ed., Stuart Berg Flexner, 1993.

Respectfully Quoted, Suzy Platt, Washington, D.C.: Library of Congress, 1989.

Scarne's New Complete Guide to Gambling, John Scarne, New York: Simon & Schuster, 1974.

Slang and Euphemism: A dictionary of oaths, curses, insults, sexual slang and metaphor, racial slurs, drug talk, homosexual lingo and related matters, Richard A. Spears, Middle Village, N.Y.: Jonathan David Publishers, 1981.

Standard Handbook for Secretaries, Lois Irene Hutchinson, New York: McGraw-Hill, 1956 (1964 printing).

Taber's Cyclopedic Medical Dictionary, Clayton L. Thomas, Philadelphia: F. A. Davis, Co., 1973.

Thorndike-Barnhardt Comprehensive Desk Dictionary, Garden City, N.Y.: Doubleday, 1962.

A Treasury for Word Lovers, Morton S. Freeman, Philadelphia: ISI Press, 1983.

A Treasury of the World's Great Speeches, Houston Peterson, New York: Simon & Schuster, 1985.

Urdang Dictionary of Current Medical Terms for Health Science Professionals, Laurence Urdang Associates, New York: John Wiley & Sons, 1981.

Video Hound's Golden Movie Retriever, Martin Connors, James Craddock, et al., Detroit: Visible Ink Press, 1997.

Webster's Collegiate Dictionary, 4th ed., Springfield, Mass.: G. & C. Merriam, 1934; 5th ed., 1944.

Webster's Dictionary of English Usage, E. Ward Gilman, Springfield, Mass.: Merriam-Webster, 1989.

Webster's New Illustrated Dictionary, Edward N. Teall and C. Ralph Taylor, New York: Books, Inc., 1968.

Webster's New International Dictionary of the English Language, 2nd ed., unabridged, Springfield, Mass.: G. & C. Merriam, 1957.

Webster's New World Dictionary of the American Language (College Ed.), Cleveland: World, 1960.

Webster's Seventh New Collegiate Dictionary, Philip B. Gove, Springfield, Mass.: G. & C. Merriam, 1965.

Webster's Third New International Dictionary of the English Language Unabridged, Philip B. Gove, Springfield, Mass.: G. & C. Merriam, 1976; Merriam-Webster, 1993.

The Weather Almanac: A Reference Guide to Weather, Climate, and Air Quality in the United States and Its Key Cities, Comprising Statistics, Principles, and Terminology, Frank E. Bair, Detroit: Gale Research Inc., 1992.

Wicked Words: A Treasury of Curses, Insults, Put-Downs, and Other Formerly Unprintable Terms from Anglo-Saxon Times to the Present, Hugh Rawson, New York: Crown, 1989.

Words: The New Dictionary, Charles P. Chadsey, William Morris, and Harold Wentworth, New York: Grosset & Dunlap, 1949.

The World Almanac and Book of Facts, 1995–1998 eds., Robert Famighetti, Mahwah, NJ: K-III Reference Corp., 1998.

The World Book Encyclopedia, 22 vol., Dale W. Jacobs, Chicago: World Book, Inc., 1996.

FOR THE BEST IN PAPERBACKS, LOOK FOR THE

In every corner of the world, on every subject under the sun, Penguin represents quality and variety—the very best in publishing today.

For complete information about books available from Penguin—including Puffins, Penguin Classics, and Compass—and how to order them, write to us at the appropriate address below. Please note that for copyright reasons the selection of books varies from country to country.

In the United Kingdom: Please write to *Dept. EP, Penguin Books Ltd, Bath Road, Harmondsworth, West Drayton, Middlesex UB7 0DA.*

In the United States: Please write to *Penguin Putnam Inc., P.O. Box 12289 Dept. B, Newark, New Jersey 07101-5289* or call 1-800-788-6262.

In Canada: Please write to *Penguin Books Canada Ltd, 10 Alcorn Avenue, Suite 300, Toronto, Ontario M4V 3B2.*

In Australia: Please write to *Penguin Books Australia Ltd, P.O. Box 257, Ringwood, Victoria 3134.*

In New Zealand: Please write to *Penguin Books (NZ) Ltd, Private Bag 102902, North Shore Mail Centre, Auckland 10.*

In India: Please write to *Penguin Books India Pvt Ltd, 11 Panchsheel Shopping Centre, Panchsheel Park, New Delhi 110 017.*

In the Netherlands: Please write to *Penguin Books Netherlands bv, Postbus 3507, NL-1001 AH Amsterdam.*

In Germany: Please write to *Penguin Books Deutschland GmbH, Metzlerstrasse 26, 60594 Frankfurt am Main.*

In Spain: Please write to *Penguin Books S. A., Bravo Murillo 19, 1° B, 28015 Madrid.*

In Italy: Please write to *Penguin Italia s.r.l., Via Benedetto Croce 2, 20094 Corsico, Milano.*

In France: Please write to *Penguin France, Le Carré Wilson, 62 rue Benjamin Baillaud, 31500 Toulouse.*

In Japan: Please write to *Penguin Books Japan Ltd, Kaneko Building, 2-3-25 Koraku, Bunkyo-Ku, Tokyo 112.*

In South Africa: Please write to *Penguin Books South Africa (Pty) Ltd, Private Bag X14, Parkview, 2122 Johannesburg.*